T29944/SN 10/8/79

£30

mv

West Yorkshire Architects and Architecture

Derek Linstrum

West Yorkshire

Architects
and
Architecture

Lund Humphries · London

First edition 1978
Published by
Lund Humphries Publishers Ltd
26 Litchfield Street London wc2

SBN 85331 410 1

Designed by Herbert Spencer
Made and printed in Great Britain
Typeset by Keyspools Ltd, Golborne, Lancashire
Printed by Lund Humphries, Bradford, Yorkshire
Bound by Dorstel Press, Harlow, Essex

Frontispiece:
Leeds, Grand Theatre (G. Corson 1876–8);
a detail of the elaborate *carton-pierre* and
plaster decoration of the auditorium.

FOR MY MOTHER, AND IN MEMORY OF MY FATHER,
WHO BROUGHT ME UP TO KNOW AND LOVE OUR NATIVE COUNTY

Acknowledgements

This study is based on a lifetime's experience and increasing knowledge of West Yorkshire architecture, and I cannot adequately thank all the people who, over the years, have given me information and welcomed me to their houses and churches. However, I wish to acknowledge the help I have received from Dr Andor Gomme, who suggested I should undertake this book, and from Professor Maurice Beresford, Mr Howard Colvin (who has also helped to amplify the biographical information in the list of architects), Dr Terry Friedman, Mr John Roberts (who also gave me valuable information about Bradford buildings), and Dr Jeremy Taylor, who have read parts or the whole of the manuscript and given me useful comments and facts. I would also like to thank Mr John Ayers, Mr Jon Booth, Mr Peter Brears, Dr David Chappell, Mr Ian Dewhirst, Mr Colin Dews, Dr Joan Kerr, Mr and Mrs Brian Payne, Mr Cyril Pearce, Mr Kenneth Powell and Mr Christopher Webster for their help in various ways. Mr John Taylor and Miss Charlotte Burri, of Lund Humphries Publishers, have sympathetically and uncomplainingly watched the text grow in size during its writing, and Dr Herbert Spencer has expertly integrated it with the illustrations in his design for the book. The librarians and archivists in the public offices in Bradford, Halifax, Huddersfield, Leeds and Sheffield, the Yorkshire Archaeological Society, and the Thoresby Society, have been unfailingly helpful and allowed me to quote from material in their collections; but I would like to thank especially Mrs Anne Heap of the Leeds Reference Library for cheerfully bringing hundreds of books for me to refer to.

Owners of private houses generously allowed me to photograph them, and I wish to record my gratitude to the Earl of Harewood (5,42), Lord St Oswald and the National Trust (36,43), Mr George Lane Fox (32–34), Mr and Mrs Muir Oddie (39,40), the Misses Sugden (14,23) and Mr Granville Wheler (20) for their help. Paintings, drawings and photographs are reproduced by kind permission of the Earl of Harewood (41), Mr John Holmes (18), Mr N.K. Howarth (221), Mr Alex G. Jackson (13,15,16, 54,63,65,66,115,127,131,136,139,149,224,232, 249,250,270,272), Mr Granville Wheler (21,31), Mr David Wrightson (98,113), Richard Green Galleries, London (296), British Library Board (28), Bradford Art Galleries and Museums (50), Halifax Antiquarian Society (61), Kirklees Libraries and Museums Service (30,227), Leeds City Libraries (25,53,119,129,169,172,178,179, 180,190,195,251,252), Leeds Polytechnic (222,244), National Monuments Record (57,58), Pontefract and District Archaeological Society (59), Wakefield City Art Gallery (17), Yorkshire Archaeological Society (48,274), Yorkshire Post (69,183). Mr David Whiteley and Mr Christopher Hutchinson have kindly assisted by copying many of these items, and others from my own collection.

The majority of the illustrations have been photographed specially for this book by Mr Keith Gibson, who has been a patient collaborator with whom it has been a pleasure to travel around the region searching for the perfect view under ideal conditions. The result needs no commendation from the grateful author (1–12,14,19,20,22,23,27,32–40,42,43, 45,47,51,52,60,62,64,67,68,70–97,99–112,114, 116,117,120–126,130,132,133,135,138,140–148, 150–168,170,171,174–177,181,182,184–189, 191–194,196–216,218–220,223,226,228–230, 233–241,243,245,247,248,256–,263,265,267, 268,271,273,275–277,280–295,297).

DEREK LINSTRUM
The King's Manor, York
Wedgewood Grove, Roundhay, Leeds

Contents

	Map	page 8
	Abbreviations	10
	Prologue	11
1	The architectural profession	25
2	Great estates and country houses	47
3	Comfort, opulence and respectability: housing the middle classes	93
4	Working-class housing and municipal enterprise	125
5	Medieval churches and monasteries	151
6	Georgian churches, chapels and meeting houses	185
7	Beautiful copies: the revival of the pointed arch	209
8	Building for education	237
9	Theatres and music halls	269
10	The clothing trade . . . in all its glory: cloth halls, mills, warehouses and exchanges	281
11	Markets and market halls	311
12	Municipal grandeur	329
	Epilogue	363
	A select biographical list of Yorkshire architects (1550–1900) who worked in West Yorkshire	369
	Index of persons	387
	Index of places	392

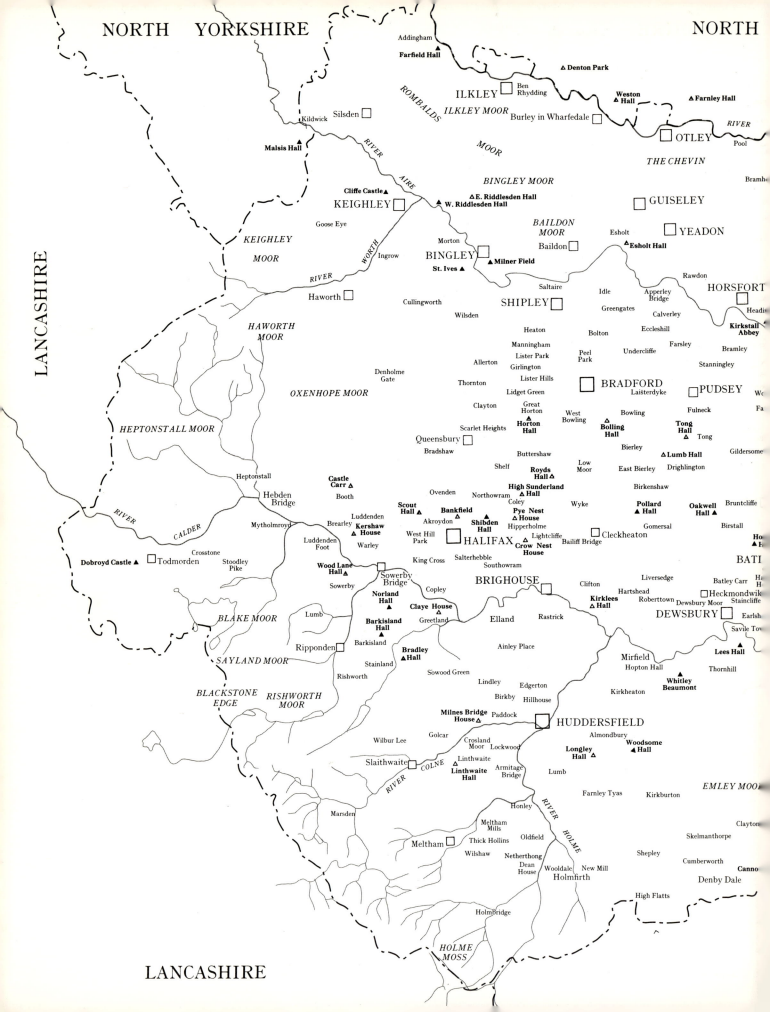

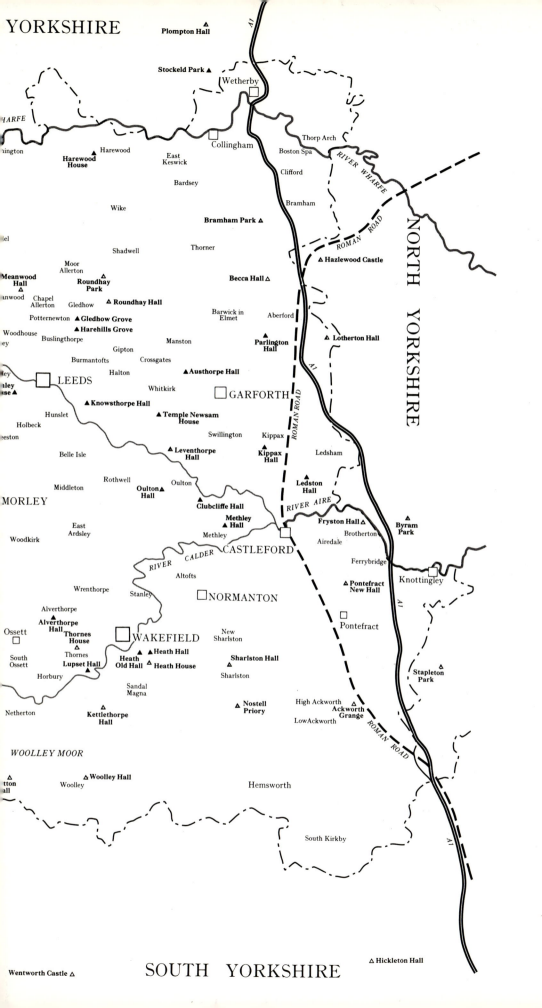

YORKSHIRE

Plompton Hall ▲

Stockeld Park ▲

Wetherby

WHARFE

Thorp Arch

Collingham

Boston Spa

Harewood

Clifford

East
Keswick

Bramham

Harewood
House ▲

Bardsey

RIVER WHARFE

ROMAN ROAD

NORTH YORKSHIRE

Wike

Bramham Park △

Shadwell

Thorner

Moor
Allerton

▲ Hazlewood Castle

Meanwood
Hall △

Becca Hall △

Roundhay
Park ▲

anwood △

Chapel
Allerton

Gledhow

▲ Roundhay Hall

Barwick in
Elmet

Aberford

Potternewton

▲ Gledhow Grove

Woodhouse

▲ Harehills Grove

Parlington
Hall ▲

▲ Lotherton Hall

ey

Buslingthorpe

Gipton

Manston

Burmantofts

Crossgates

A1

Halton

▲ Austhorpe Hall

ley

□ LEEDS

Whitkirk

□ GARFORTH

ROMAN ROAD

ley
se ▲

▲ Knowsthorpe Hall

Hunslet

▲ Temple Newsam
House

Holbeck

Swillington

Kippax

eeston

Belle Isle

▲ Leventhorpe
Hall

Kippax
Hall ▲

Ledsham

MORLEY

Middleton

Rothwell

Oulton

Oulton △
Hall

Ledston
Hall ▲

RIVER AIRE

▲ Clubcliffe Hall

Fryston Hall △

Byram
Park △

East
Ardsley

Methley
Hall ▲

Woodkirk

Methley

RIVER CALDER

CASTLEFORD □

Brotherton

Airedale

Ferrybridge

Knottingley □

Woodkirk

Wrenthorpe

Stanley

Altofts

□ NORMANTON

A1

Alverthorpe

Alverthorpe
Hall ▲

New
Sharlston

▲ Pontefract
New Hall

Stapleton
Park △

Ossett

Thornes
House □

□ WAKEFIELD

□ Pontefract

South
Ossett □

Thornes

▲ Heath Hall

Sharlston Hall ▲

Lupset Hall ▲

Heath
Old Hall ▲

△ Heath House

Horbury

Sharlston

Sandal
Magna

Netherton

Kettlethorpe
Hall △

▲ Nostell
Priory

High Ackworth

Ackworth
Grange

ROMAN ROAD

Low Ackworth

WOOLLEY MOOR

△ Woolley Hall

Woolley

Hemsworth

tton
all △

South Kirkby

A1

△ Hickleton Hall

Wentworth Castle △

SOUTH YORKSHIRE

Abbreviations

A	*Architect* 1869–
AJ	*Architect's Journal,* 1919–
AR	*Architectural Review,* 1896–
Ayers	Ayers,J.H., *Architecture in Bradford,* Bradford 1972
B	*Builder,* 1843–
BA	*British Architect,* 1874–1919
Baines	Baines,E., *History, directory and gazetteer of the county of York,* Leeds 1822
BN	*Building News* (later *Architect & Building News*), 1856–1926
BO	*Bradford Observer* 1834–1901
Colvin	Colvin,H., *A biographical dictionary of English architects 1660–1840,* London 1954
CB	*The West Riding of Yorkshire: contemporary biographies,* Brighton 1902
CL	*Country Life,* 1897–
Crabtree	Crabtree,J., *A concise history of the parish and vicarage of Halifax,* Halifax 1836
E	*Ecclesiologist,* 1841–68
HAS	*Transactions of the Halifax Antiquarian Society,* 1901–
HC	*Halifax Courier,* 1853–1921
HG	*Halifax Guardian,* 1832–1921
James	James,J., *The history of Bradford and its parish,* London 1866 (first pub. 1841)
James C	James,J., *Continuation & additions to the history of Bradford and its parish,* London 1866
LAC	*Leeds Arts Calendar,* 1947–
LI	*Leeds Intelligencer,* 1754–1866
Linstrum	Linstrum,D., *Historic architecture of Leeds,* Newcastle-upon-Tyne 1969
LM	*Leeds Mercury,* 1718–1939
Parsons	Parsons,E., *The civil, ecclesiastical, literary, commercial and miscellaneous history of Leeds, Halifax, Huddersfield, Bradford, Wakefield, Dewsbury, Otley and the manufacturing district of Yorkshire,* Leeds 1834
Thoresby	Thoresby,R., *Ducatus Leodiensis,* Leeds 1816 (ed. Whitaker, T.D.)
TS	*Publications of the Thoresby Society,* 1889–
Walker	Walker,J.W., *Wakefield, its history and people,* Wakefield 1939
Watson	Watson,J., *The history and antiquities of the parish of Halifax,* London 1775
Whitaker	Whitaker,T.D., *Loidis and Elmete,* Leeds 1816
YAS	*Journal of the Yorkshire Archaeological Society,* 1870–
YP	*Yorkshire Post,* 1866–

Prologue

With time and labour, the crag took human shape, and there it stands, colossal, dark and frowning, half statue, half rock, in the former sense, terrible and goblin-like; in the latter, almost beautiful, for its colouring is of mellow grey, and moorland moss clothes it, and heath, with its blooming bells and balmy fragrance, grows faithfully close to the giant's foot.

Preface to Emily Brontë's *Wuthering Heights*, 1848

The West Riding was created as an administrative convenience more than a thousand years ago, when the land between the Humber and the Tees was subdivided into three thirdings or thridings, distinguished as north, east and west. It survived as the largest and most varied of English counties until 1974, when Local Government reorganisation, another administrative convenience, removed the historic boundaries from the map of Yorkshire. The Dales, the ruined abbeys of Fountains and Bolton, the cathedral city of Ripon, the spa town of Harrogate, the market towns of Selby, Skipton, Grassington and Pateley Bridge, were merged in North Yorkshire. Sheffield, Rotherham, Barnsley and Doncaster became the nucleus of South Yorkshire, and with them went Conisbrough Castle, Wentworth Woodhouse and Wentworth Castle, and such places as Cawthorne, Tickhill, Bawtry and Penistone. Goole, Rawcliffe and Snaith went into Humberside, and what remained became the prosaically named West Yorkshire. It is a remarkable testimony to the architectural wealth and quality of the former West Riding that the much reduced county still possesses an overwhelming quantity of buildings of note within the conurbation of Leeds, Bradford, Halifax, Huddersfield, Wakefield and their satellite towns.

However strongly sentiment, old allegiances and a sense of history might regret the change, the new grouping is not irrational. There was little in common between the activities and interests of the farmers in Dentdale and the cutlers in Sheffield except a violent nationalism and a participation in the propagation of the Yorkshire mystique which are not likely to be removed by the alteration of lines on a map; this mystique insidiously affects all who come within its influence, as when Sir John Vanbrugh wrote from York in 1721 that he had found 'many more Valuable and Agreeable things and Places to be Seen, than in the Tame Sneaking South of England'.[1]

The redistribution, whatever its faults, has attempted to rationalise the county as it exists in the twentieth century, taking into account the changes since a bleak, vast territory was partitioned in the tenth century; and by isolating the West Yorkshire conurbation from the

1 Webb,G.(ed), *The works of Sir John Vanbrugh*, London 1928,iv,138.

1. Pennine landscape and vernacular architecture in the Calder valley. In the foreground is a limewashed farmhouse with a stone-slated roof and a simplified stepped-headed window in the gable. To the right, Heptonstall illustrates the compact form of a Pennine hilltop community. The monument in the distance on the extreme left is Stoodley Pike, first built in 1814–15 to commemorate the surrender of Paris to the Allied Armies.

2. The industrialisation of the Pennine landscape; the Calder valley, looking across towards Skircoat Moor on the fringe of Halifax from Copley, the village built in the 1840s and 50s to serve Copley Mill. Immediately behind the row of model dwellings is the 23-arched viaduct (1852) connecting Halifax with the Lancashire and Yorkshire Railway. On the skyline in the centre is the monumental Wainhouse Tower (I.Booth and R.S.Dugdale 1871–5), 253 feet high, built as a chimney connected with J.E.Wainhouse's dye works.

other parts of the old West Riding, it has demonstrated that a region's human and architectural identity is conditioned by natural resources, climate and the changing patterns of social life; it is 'the expression of national life and character', as John Ruskin told his 'good Yorkshire friends' in Bradford in 1863.[2] No region, however strong its identity, can be separated entirely from its neighbours; but it is believed that in this study of West Yorkshire architects and architecture, a clearly defined character emerges as a result of confining it within the revised boundaries except for an occasional brief trespass over them when it becomes necessary.

Bounded to the north by the Wharfe, to the east by the Great North Road, to the west by the almost inviolable line between the territories of the white and red roses, and to the south by a less neatly identifiable natural or historic feature, the new county consists of the redefined and enlarged administrative areas of Leeds, Bradford, Wakefield, Kirklees and Calderdale; for the sake of clarity, the more familiar names of pre-1974 boroughs (e.g. Halifax, Huddersfield, Dewsbury, Pontefract) have been used throughout this study. Physically, the conurbation has strongly marked architectural differences which persist, within general regional characteristics in even the smallest townships, and the group of industrial towns is surrounded by an outer ring of varied landscapes; Pennine moorland and river valleys; farmland and woodland; villages as different as Boston Spa and Sowerby, Ackworth and Woolley; the 'improved' scenery of eighteenth-century landscape-gardeners, and the dramatic natural contrasts of rocky escarpments overlooking valleys matched in scale by the viaducts crossing them and by the intervening mills and chimneys.

The sense of drama is seldom absent, and a tour of the county reveals one great panorama after another in which Nature and Architecture have occasionally collaborated or, too often, conflicted as industrial exploitation has stretched out from the original small market towns to coalesce in a wasteful, squalid erosion of the landscape; yet the uncompromising contours of the terrain and the bleakness of the hilltop sites have to some extent preserved the form and character of the landscape. There is an Apocalyptic quality in the sudden revelation of Halifax from Beacon Hill, or of Bradford from Bowling or Scarlet Heights, or of the view from Whitley Beaumont towards Huddersfield in which Castle Hill appears silhouetted in the middle distance against the remoter dark line of the Pennines. No less dramatic are the visions of the wide Calder valley at Copley as seen from the road to Sowerby Bridge or from the railway line which, on either trans-Pennine route, still offers views as exciting as when they were put on stone by nineteenth-century lithographers.[3]

The view from Armley towards 'the busy town of Leeds, softened by its misty vapour, and the bold rising ground beyond it' has changed since Humphry Repton saw it in 1810,[4] but the Kirkstall cooling towers have added an additional powerful symbolism to the industrial landscape. Less altered is the prospect from the steep road up to Heptonstall, looking back on the crowded cluster of Hebden Bridge,

2 Ruskin's lecture delivered in Bradford in 1863, reprinted in *The crown of wild olive*, London 1866 under the title of 'Traffic'; see 306ff.

3 See e.g. Butterworth,E., *Views on the Manchester and Leeds railway*, London 1845.

4 Quoted from Humphry Repton's *Red Book* for Armley House, in the collection of Mr and Mrs Paul Mellon.

13

3. Halifax, as seen from Beacon Hill;
illustrating the dramatic quality of the
stone-built town in its setting of steep
hillsides in a confined valley.

the town which developed from it in the valley below; and higher still
is the unchanging, deep wooded glen of Hardcastle Crags. In a
different, more humanised category is the upward sweep of the
parkland and woods of Bretton framed by the trees along the
precipitous Woolley Edge, or the gentler undulations of 'Capability'
Brown's landscape at Harewood, in which the microcosmic mansion,
lake and woods are extended apparently to embrace the rocky climax
of Almscliff Crag and the whole of Wharfedale as far as it can be seen
up and down the winding valley.

These are the West Yorkshire landscapes, beloved and recorded by
generations of romantic watercolourists, the frames and foundations of
its architecture; they are contained, geographically, within the east
flank of the Pennines, composed of austere, lateral, blunt spurs of hills
which slowly subside until they merge with softer hills and wide
prospects, ending in a level plain which extends beyond the eastern

4. Many areas of Pennine landscape, even close to the large towns, retain a sense of lonely, empty grandeur. The romantic silhouette of the Victoria Tower (1897) adds a man-made element to the distant view towards Castle Hill, Huddersfield from the ruined belvedere at Whitley Beaumont (J.Paine c.1752–4).

boundary of the region as the Plain of York. On their summit are the sources of the three rivers which cross the region, the Wharfe, the Aire and the Calder. The most northerly, which forms the upper boundary, rises in the Wharfe Gap at the foot of Dodd Fell, passing through the carboniferous limestone hills with what Ruskin called 'a peculiar *sweeping* power ... like a black Damascus blade', through the Strid at Bolton Abbey in the valley where Ilkley, Otley, Wetherby and Boston Spa grew up, until it joins the Ouse at Nun Monkton. The Aire rises in the romantic limestone landscape of Malhamdale, painted by artists from James Ward to John Piper,[5] on the moors Ruskin wrote of as 'exposed to drift of rain under violent, nearly constant, wind. They break into wide fields of loose blocks, and rugged slopes of shale; and are mixed with sands and clay from the millstone grit'.[6] Water oozes out everywhere, and the Aire disappears underground to emerge again from the foot of the dark-streaked, bare white rocky face of Malham Cove, flowing on sluggishly through Gargrave and Skipton, Bingley, Shipley and Leeds, ever more polluted until it reaches Castleford, where it joins the Calder. Rising in the Calder Gap, the third major river was described by Defoe as being augmented by 'all the Rills or Brooks of Water which we cross'd; following those little Brooks with new Eye, we could observe, that at some distance to the Left there appeared a larger Valley than the rest [in which] was a considerable River ... which, having received all those little Brooks, was risen to a little Flood; and at the next Village we pass'd it over a stately Stone Bridge of several great Arches'.[7] This was Sowerby Bridge, from which point the Calder flows on through Brighouse, Mirfield, Dewsbury and Wakefield until it joins the Aire, receiving on the way the little Spen

5 See Piper, J., *Buildings and prospects*, London 1948, 133ff.

6 Ruskin, J., *Praeterita*, Orpington 1886, ix, 290.

7 Defoe, D., *A journey through Great Britain*, London 1927 (reprint), ii, 603.

15

5. The natural qualities of the dramatic Wharfedale landscape were humanised and 'improved' by Lancelot 'Capability' Brown in his design for Harewood, where he was directing the construction of the lake and the planting in 1772.

from the north and the larger Colne and Holme from the southwest.

The industries which provided the source of the prosperity of West Yorkshire developed in the valleys of these rivers, stimulated by the construction of canals in the eighteenth century, and railways in the nineteenth; and with that self-sufficiency traditionally regarded as an element in the regional human character, the quantity and quality of the local stone has been primarily responsible for the architectural character of the buildings erected to serve the needs of the industrial communities. North of the Aire Gap, carboniferous limestone predominates; but apart from a broad belt of magnesian limestone along the eastern boundary of West Yorkshire on the line of the Great North Road, practically the entire region is situated on or close to the millstone grit which extends from the Gap southwards, with strata running down eastwards to the Yorkshire coalfield. At times, as in the southern part of the parish of Bradford, it lies at a great depth; but in other parts it appears on the surface, as at Shipley where it forms the summits of the purple moorlands around Haworth. This is the millstone grit landscape which still appears as it did to Elizabeth Gaskell in the 1850s when she travelled from Keighley to Haworth:

The soil in the valley . . . is rich; but, as the road begins to ascend, the vegetation becomes poorer; it does not flourish, it merely exists; and, instead of trees, there are only bushes and shrubs about the dwellings. Stone dykes are everywhere used in place of bridges; and what crops there are, on the patches of arable land, consist of pale, hungry-looking, grey-green oats . . . Haworth village . . . is situated on the side of a pretty steep hill, with a background of dun and purple moors, rising and sweeping away yet higher than the church, which is built at the very summit of the long narrow street. All round the horizon there is this same line of sinuous wave-like hills; the scoops into which they fall only revealing other hills beyond, of similar colour and shape, crowned with wild, bleak moors – grand, from the ideas of solitude and loneliness which they suggest, or oppressive from the feeling which they give of being pent-up by some monotonous and illimitable barrier, according to the mood of mind in which the spectator may be.[8]

6 'Grey stone abounds', noted Mrs Gaskell, 'and the rows of houses built of it have a kind of solid grandeur connected with their uniform and enduring lines. The framework of the doors, and the lintels of the windows, even in the smallest of dwellings, are made of blocks of stone'. The generic name, York stone, covers a variety of quarries around Leeds and Bradford, of which Bramley Fall was the best known, supported by innumerable others such as Howley Park, Bolton Wood, Cliffe Wood, Spinkwell, Park Spring and Pool Bank; or there are those in the Halifax–Huddersfield area such as Crosland Moor, Hipperholme and Elland Edge. There are many local variations of colour and texture; there are the smoother, finer-grained carboniferous sandstones from the upper coal measures beds, but more common are those from the underlying beds of millstone grit, so called because it was the material from which the millstones in the Pennine corn-mills were traditionally made. They are well known for the large blocks in which they can be obtained, and it has been noted that, 'especially when it is the dark millstone grit, [the massiveness of the masonry] seems to endow the buildings with a positively Cyclopean character which . . . helps to produce the impression of a rugged and purposeful

8 Gaskell, E., *The life of Charlotte Brontë*, London 1947 (reprint), 16f.

6. Main Street, Haworth typifies the universal use of stone in Pennine towns, which produces a distinctive homogeneity.

7. Claye House, Greetland (c.1650). The intractable nature of millstone grit is reflected in the bold, simplified detailing of this door lintel and its massive, curved hood.

8. Bradford, Currer Street; the huge lintel, weighing approximately four and a half tons, illustrates the tough architectural character engendered by millstone grit.

architecture'.[9] This inherent character was in perfect sympathy with the austere spirit of the Cistercians who built Kirkstall Abbey, and the blackened, ruined walls of Bramley Fall stone stand as a testimony to the durability of the material and its resistance to weather and pollution.

From the late eighteenth century, new quarries were opened to supply the increased demand, and advertisements such as this began to appear in the *Leeds Intelligencer*:

This is to inform the Public, that John Prince has opened the Stone-Quarry at Meanwood, belonging to Jeremiah Dixon, Esq., where all Persons may be served with Blocks of a most excellent and very durable Grit Stone of any dimensions for Columns, Pedestals, Pilasters, Troughs, Cisterns, Ashler for Mills, Dams, Arches, or any other Work, scapled at the Quarry.[10]

Yet carboniferous sandstones are not materials which lend themselves to intricately carved decoration, and the *Builder* warned its mid nineteenth-century readers of the excessive amount of time required if carvings were to be well executed 'on account of the nature of the material, which is so destructive to edge-tools'. It pointed out the obvious fact that 'the only material for sharpening edge-tools is sandstone [and] the same kind of stone which is experimentally found to sharpen tools most expeditiously will also be the readiest to destroy their cutting edge ... instead of the chisels cutting the stone, the stone cuts the chisels'.[11] As a consequence, the bold, relatively simple treatment of the masonry of seventeenth-century houses, with massive door heads cut into various patterns of broad curves and scallops, or vigorously, often crudely, carved simplified Classical doorways with ungrammatical columns and entablatures, derived largely from the quality of the stone itself.

Similarly, nineteenth-century architects evolved a manner of detailing this tough, coarse material in which the large quartz grains glitter subtly when caught by the light. On the purple-brown moorland, the varied browns, buffs and greys harmonise with the muted landscape from which the stone came; but when used in

7

9 Clifton-Taylor,A., *The pattern of English building*, London 1972,133f.

10 *LI*, 25 June 1776.

11 *B* (1856),xiv,306f.

9. Leeds, the Town Hall (1853–8), a part of the east façade. In his detailing of monumental Neo-classical architecture, Cuthbert Brodrick exploited fully the quality of millstone grit in the simplified, bold modelling and the surface tooling.

industrial towns in the pre-Clean Air Act days, millstone grit possessed the unique distinction of turning completely, solidly black as if it were a velvety form of basalt or unpolished jet. For that reason, as well as because of the material's intractable nature, it was essential to perfect a form of broadly formalised decoration with sharp arrises, exaggeratedly simple modelling, and large-scale surface tooling. The use of battered, buttressed plinths, deep horizontal rustication, finely jointed ashlar, and a minimum of carved decoration produces an effect of monumental strength that seems to have been transferred from the quarries themselves to the West Yorkshire streets.[12]

The traditional visual homogeneity of the Pennine towns, and their identification with their natural setting, is due to the total use of stone, for paving and roofing as well as for the walls. 'The neighbourhood abounds in stone', commented the *Builder* in a reference to Bradford. 'The pavement of half London came from the little village of Idle, near Apperley, hard by.'[13] Less true today than in 1859, that statement is nevertheless a remarkable confirmation of the strength and durability of York stone, once the universal paving material in mills and churches, as well as for pavements. The quarries around Elland, in which the stone is highly laminated, is another source, and the name of Elland flagstone has been given to the products from an extensive area around Halifax, including Southowram, Northowram, Queensbury, Hipperholme and Lightcliffe. Many of these stones were found suitable for roofing, and after the best in the outcrop became worked out galleries were driven inwards or, in the second half of the nineteenth century, shafts were sunk to allow underground galleries to be formed. The 'thakstones' were usually at least an inch thick, fixed with oak

12 The nobility of the nineteenth-century Italianate warehouses and commercial buildings was in harmony with the quality of the stone. The style also offered an opportunity for subtle variations in colour and texture by the use of stones from different quarries in one façade. Two are commonly combined, but W.B.Gingell's Leeds and West Yorkshire Assurance Company's office in Leeds (1852–5) was built of three; Bramley Fall for the heavily vermiculated plinth, Pool Bank for the finely rusticated ground floor and Venetian windows, and Rawdon Hill for the two upper storeys, columns, entablature and pedimented window heads.

13 *B* (1859),xvii,755.

20

10. Boston Spa, High Street; the
magnesian limestone which is the
traditional material in the villages
along the eastern boundary of the region
has given a different, gentler character
to the architecture.

14 The names given to the various sizes by
the Pennine slaters included such mysterious
ones as 'farewell' (the smallest and last
course), 'short skirtchens', 'long skirtchens',
'short becks', 'long becks', 'bachelors',
'wippetts', 'twelves' and 'thirteens', all of
which were marked on the strips of wood
used as slaters' rules. See Walton, J., 'The
English stone-slater's craft', *Folk Life*
(1975), xiii, 38ff; Walsh, J.F., 'Elland
flagstone and millstone grit', *HAS* (1948),
117ff.

15 The proven disastrous result of using
sandstone and limestone together on a
façade has helped to keep the two within
quite strictly defined areas, although George
Gilbert Scott misguidedly imported a
magnesian limestone of dubious quality from
Steeton in Derbyshire and used it for
dressings on All Souls', Halifax, the church
he believed 'on the whole, my best'. The
wallstones were from a local Halifax quarry,
and there is no sadder or more salutary
example to be seen in the county of the
interaction of the two stones than on this
once proud building.

pegs and laid in diminishing courses from the eaves to the ridge of the
shallow-pitched roofs which are characteristic of traditional Pennine
buildings.[14]

Although the carboniferous sandstones were by far the commoner
stones used in West Yorkshire, the belt of magnesian limestone along
the eastern boundary resulted in a different architectural character in
that relatively confined area. Country houses such as Ledston Hall and
Hazlewood Castle, the churches and cottages in Aberford, Ledsham,
Bramham and Boston Spa, are built of the softer, creamy-white
stone generally associated with buildings in York and the surrounding
plain north-east of the city.[15] The magnesian limestone area was also
the one in which brick began to supplant the traditional stone as a
building material. It was a rare, fashionable material when used in the
first build of Temple Newsam in the early sixteenth century, and it
was still rare when the house was practically rebuilt in a greatly
enlarged form a century later. The bricks were made on the site, and
the owner supplied the materials necessary for the making and
burning.

It was such an unusual material in the early seventeenth century
that the Red Hall, built in Leeds in 1628, was given that name because
of its strange appearance among the stone buildings; but, partly
because of its non-combustible quality, partly because its use in
London had set a fashion, but principally because of its relative
cheapness as a material and in the labour costs of walling, the use of
brick increased rapidly during the eighteenth century. The Revd. John
Watson, writing in 1775, noted that although stone was durable and
handsome in appearance, 'where much pains are taken about it, it is

attended with great expence; a circumstance which, amongst other reasons, has of late years brought up the custom of making bricks . . . which is likely to continue' in Halifax,[16] where some houses and the prominent Square Chapel had already been built of the new material. Their red walls gave rise to the local rhyme

Halifax is built of wax,
Heptonstall o' stooan:

although the following couplet appears to be a *non sequitur* to the effect that

I' Halifax ther's bonny lasses,
I' Heptonstall ther's nooan.

Nevertheless, despite the occasional use of brick, Halifax, Huddersfield and Bradford continued to be built largely of stone, even for the rows of nineteenth-century working-class houses; but Leeds and Wakefield, which were close to deposits of suitable clay in the Castleford and Normanton area, as well as in their own outlying districts, largely abandoned stone except for churches and public buildings.

By the 1860s, the *Builder* was reporting, not entirely accurately, that the experience of the industrial towns 'seems to be adverse to stone, and in favour of brick, both on account of the softening of the stone and the loss of the effect of any enrichment by carving'.[17] The virtual rebuilding in stone of the centres of Bradford, Halifax and Huddersfield in the middle decades of the nineteenth century hardly confirms this general statement, but the writer confidently asserted 'Good hard brick does not lose its colour, but rather improves'. The tax on bricks had been abolished in the 1850s, and the introduction of mechanisation in their manufacture had made them even cheaper. Greater popularity brought innovations, and the *Builder* jubilantly referred to the 'red, blue and black bricks' which could be obtained, and the 'encaustic tiles and string-courses, in bright colours [which] will relieve the heaviness of the sombre tone of the whole'. It enthusiastically recommended the use of terra-cotta instead of carved stone, which represented a great saving in cost, and it was confident that all these new materials would not only stand up to the industrial climate, but offer 'a field for design, both in form and colour, that will give our architects opportunities for exercising every artistic faculty they possess'.

Although these materials were relatively rarely used in the stone-built towns nearer the Pennines, Leeds became a multi-coloured town. Dull orange-red bricks were used in combination with millstone grit dressings, beautifully subdued in tone and not inharmonious among the stone façades; but gradually, brighter colours were introduced in terra-cotta dressings and coloured glazed tiles, until by the beginning of the present century, the Leeds streets had realised the enthusiastic vision of Halsey Ricardo. 'Think of whole streets vibrating with colour', he exclaimed;[18] and in Park Row he would have found orange and red brickwork, faience ranging in colour from hard, dead white through various shades of cream and stone, and a leaven of millstone grit to add a note of traditional sobriety. The extensive new

16 Watson, 9.

17 *B* (1862), xx, 623.

18 *RIBA Jnl* (1896), iii (3rd series), 365ff. Examples of extensive use of terra-cotta facing in Leeds are the *Yorkshire Post* offices (1886–7, now demolished), the Liberal Club (1890), and the Metropole Hotel (1897–9), all by Chorley and Connon. It was used by Alfred Waterhouse, not only predictably for the offices of the Prudential Assurance Company in other towns as well as in Leeds, but also on the bank for William Williams, Brown and Co. (now Lloyd's, 1898) and the Yorkshire College (now the University of Leeds, 1877 onwards).

11

11. Leeds, King Edward Street; Burmantofts faience, the last of the indigenous West Yorkshire building materials, had a great vogue at the end of the nineteenth century. This detail illustrates the way in which the façades (F.Matcham 1900–04) were divided into units for moulding and baking.

11 development in Queen Victoria and King Edward Streets was faced with vibrant, hot reds and oranges, varied by glittering patches of mosaic; Albion Place had been partly rebuilt as uniform creamy stone-coloured façades with green colonettes on the attic storey, and Duncan Street offered white glazed façades moulded into projecting bays, gables and domed cupolas to contrast with the blackened Corn Exchange at the east end.

This transformation, and the virtual abandonment of stone facing for commercial buildings was due largely to the development of faience on an estate of 150 acres at Burmantofts. A single shaft, sixty-six yards deep, led to a system of galleries, from which was extracted buff and red clay as well as coal; the one was used to bake the other, and the whole process was undertaken with the minimum of handling. The faience was not an immediate success, as Cosmo Monkhouse wrote in 1885. 'Materials which seek to supersede other materials to the qualities of which we have become accustomed must always be at a great disadvantage, and faience has a hard battle to fight before it conquers our domestic prejudices . . . It has one grand quality – versatility; it can serve many masters, it can imitate many substances. There is scarcely any design which an artist can conceive, whether he be painter, sculptor or architect, which cannot be realised in baked clay'.[19] The possibilities were unlimited, and the Burmantofts factory supplied façades for British colonies throughout the Empire. 'Windows and doorcases, sometimes whole façades, of houses are made of pottery, and the blocks of which they are composed penetrate deeply into the body of the building. Sometimes the architect supplies drawings which are complete, even in the detail of the ornament;

19 Monkhouse,C., 'Burmantofts faience', *Magazine of art* (1885),viii,471ff. As evidence of this facility, Maurice B.Adams made a design for remodelling the offices of Wilcock and Co. in Burmantofts (*BN* (1880),xxxviii, 628). In the same issue, Adams's designs for two interiors decorated with Burmantofts faience were illustrated.

23

sometimes the decoration of the ornament is left a good deal to the potter . . . The designs have to be divided into bits, each of which has to be moulded and baked in one piece'. Finally they appeared in the glazed greens, buffs, blues and browns distinctive of Burmantofts ware.[20] It is the last of the indigenous West Yorkshire building materials, but one of the most characteristic in central Leeds, where 'the hard texture and glazed surface . . . give a practical guarantee that the impurity of the air . . . can affect it only in such a way as could easily be reversed by washing'.[21]

These are the natural settings for West Yorkshire architecture, and the raw materials from which the 'terrible and goblin-like' giant conurbation has grown. The following pages discuss the men who designed the buildings, and the motives which stimulated their patrons and clients, private and corporate, to erect them. The buildings themselves have been grouped thematically, in an attempt to interpret rather than to catalogue; inevitably it has not been possible to include every worthwhile example in this tightly packed built-up area, nor to deal fully with the more recent work which is likely to remain in existence for a long time, but it is believed that those selected represent the traditional architectural character of the region – the crag which took human shape. Like the pervasive haunting genius of *Wuthering Heights*, at times this character appears dark and frowning, at times almost beautiful; and even when most urban, there is a line of hills on the horizon and a sense of being close to the moorland and heath. 'The two most frightful things I have ever yet seen in my life', wrote Ruskin, 'are the south-eastern suburb of Bradford (six miles long), and the scene from Wakefield Bridge by the chapel';[22] that is one face of the West Yorkshire image, common to all industrial regions, and certainly not improved since Ruskin's time; but the view from the other side can reveal a different scene.

20 Their brown-gold internal facings can be seen in the staircase to the Great Hall in Waterhouse's Yorkshire College (University of Leeds) buildings, and very similar decorations are still in the banking hall in Waterhouse's William Williams, Brown and Co.'s bank, (now Lloyd's) in Park Row, under the later remodelling. Photographs of this interior were used in some of the Burmantofts catalogues. The octagonal entrance-hall in the School of Medicine (W.H.Thorp 1894) is completely faced with faience which includes unusual blue-green shades, and incorporates several Latin mottoes alluding to healing. The dining-room in the old Queens Hotel (decorated by C.Trubshaw in the 1890s) was decorated with ivory and gold faience wall coverings in a rococo style.

21 *BN*, (1880),xxviii,628.

22 Ruskin,J., *Fors clavigera*, Orpington 1875,v,46.

1   The architectural profession

I like him very well – he agreed to all I proposed.
Miss Anne Lister of Shibden Hall on her architect, 1835

'An architect ... is a man who is capable of envisaging a building, complete and in detail, before one stone is laid upon another and is also capable of so conveying his vision to the actual builders that they are able to translate it into actual reality.'[1] It is difficult to better that definition, since it includes all those in history, whatever they were called, who have been responsible for the buildings in which Man has lived, worked and worshipped. The foundation of the Institute of British Architects in 1834, and the subsequent Royal charters it received, set a professional stamp on architecture in this country and gave a code to its practitioners; but designers of buildings were not invented in 1834. In the Middle Ages the responsibility was usually that of a master mason, sometimes from a family of good standing, who had served his apprenticeship, learnt his craft, worked as a journeyman (i.e. as a hired man for a daily rate of pay), and then become a master with his own shop. He was normally a freeman, a member of a guild, probably of a lodge of masons; and those who were the designers of important buildings had learnt the traditional rules of proportion and the methods of setting out by means of geometry.

    Inevitably, York was the centre of the crafts in medieval Yorkshire; not only was a regular force required for the construction of the Minster, but there were also around forty parish churches on which to work, as well as secular buildings. Nevertheless, there must have been master masons in other parts of the county, working on churches and castles. Philip of Gamston, and Robert Gamston, for example, are two names associated with Pontefract Castle in the early fifteenth century when 'a new tower outside the castle to the north' was erected, and there was more new work 'in the castle called the Constabulary' in 1405–12. In 1441, two masons from Pontefract were consulted about a proposed new tower at Tutbury,[2] but these are only names. By the late sixteenth century, clearer figures emerge, such as the Akroyd family of Halifax, who designed and built Heath Grammar School and were probably responsible for Bradley Hall, Methley Hall and Howley Hall. As a result of their employment by the Savile family, the Akroyds and Bentleys of Halifax were induced to go to Oxford where they were employed to build the new quadrangle of Merton College, the Bodleian Library and the Schools Quadrangle.[3] John Bentley was described as a most skilful architect (*Johannes Bentleius Eboracensis ... architectus*

1 Salzman,L.F., *Building in England down to 1540 – a documentary history*, London 1952,4f. See also Harvey,J., *The mediaeval architect*, London 1972.

2 Colvin,H.(ed), *The history of the King's Works*, London 1963,ii,781ff,1060.

3 Hanson,T.W., *Halifax builders in Oxford*, Halifax 1928; Crump,W.B., 'Methley Hall and its builders', *T S* (1945),xxxvii,313ff. The successive 'architects' of the Schools Quadrangle were all Yorkshiremen; John Akroyd (d.1613), John Bentley (d.1613), Michael Bentley (d.1618) and Thomas Holt (d.1624).

4 Hanson, op.cit.,274. Holt was buried in Holywell churchyard.

5 Girouard,M., *Robert Smythson and the architecture of the Elizabethan era*, London 1966,109ff; see 52.

6 Leeds Archives Department. There are contracts between Sir Arthur Ingram and various craftsmen, e.g. with Nicholas Booth, plasterer, 'to frett the gallery, architrave freeze and cornice to be a yeard deep . . . to wainscot the gallery with fir deals' (13/71/1), with Francis Gunby, joiner 'to make and set up where Sir Arthur shall appoint 400 yards of wanscott or seiling' (13/71/2), and with various brick manufacturers (13/71/3,5). Ingram had to provide at his own cost on the site 'straw wood or coles found needful and necessary for the making and burning'. See also Gilbert,C.G., 'Light on Sir Arthur Ingram's reconstruction of Temple Newsam', *L A C* (1963),no.51,6ff.

7 See 55ff. for a discussion of the Halifax–Bradford houses.

8 Sheffield Ref Lib; Copley MSS, C3/63518/K.

9 Leeds Archives Dept. Minute book of Leeds Pious Uses Committee 1664–1788, Part I, 151,153,154. (DB 197/1). See 330.

peritissimus) on his monument, and Thomas Holt, another Yorkshireman who found work in Oxford, was commemorated as *Thomae Holt Eborac. Scholarum publicarum architecti*.[4] Facts such as these confirm that designs were not necessarily made by master masons in their native regions only; Robert Smythson from the Midlands is believed to have designed New Hall, near Pontefract for Edward Talbot in the 1590s,[5] and may have been consulted about other West Yorkshire houses. He certainly provided a design for Burton Agnes Hall, near Bridlington in c.1601. Typical of the organisation of a building in the early seventeenth century is Sir Arthur Ingram's reconstruction of Temple Newsam under the direction of a supervisor who received directions from the building owner himself. He was responsible for supplying materials, paying workmen and ensuring the owner's instructions were carried out.[6] The supervisor or agent negotiated rates with the craftsmen; but it was the master mason or master carpenter who was regarded as the major figure in the building operations and was often responsible for the design, wholly or in part, even if he was not commonly referred to as an architect. It was out of this tradition that the architectural profession evolved.

Although Halifax had families of masons whose influence can be seen in the design of many sixteenth and seventeenth-century houses in the Halifax–Bradford area, York remained the natural centre of the building crafts in the county, as it had been for centuries.[7] The Etty family, for example, was employed on many major Yorkshire buildings from the late seventeenth century onwards, as master carpenters or, when necessary, as designers. John Etty died in 1708/9 and was described on his monument in All Saints' church, York as one who had 'acquired great knowledge of Mathematicks, especially Geometry and Architecture in all its parts far beyond any of his Co-temporares in this City'.

His art was great, his industry no less,
What one projected, the other brought to pass.

He was employed as carpenter and, in some cases, as architect, by several Yorkshire landowners; in 1701, Sir Godfrey Copley of Sprotbrough Hall near Doncaster received a request from Etty, who was laid up with a broken leg, for the loan of Jean Marot's volume of engravings, *L'Architecture Française*, to study during his inactivity.[8] Etty rebuilt part of the west wing of Temple Newsam in 1674, and his son, William, laid out part of the landscape around the house for the 4th Viscount in 1712. Two years earlier, in June 1710, the Leeds Pious Uses Committee 'agreed . . . with Mr. William Etty of York Architect for the repairs of the Moothall in Leeds . . . performing the same Exactly according to the Draught by him made and given in'. Three months later the Committee agreed 'to take down and rebuild the Remainder of the Moothall',[9] according to Etty's design, after which the new Baroque front was ready to receive Andrew Carpenter's statue of Queen Anne. Etty was well known beyond the immediate surroundings of York, and in 1717 Admiral Delaval, the Northumbrian landowner, wrote of intending 'to persuade Sir John

Vanbrugh to see Seaton Delaval if possible and to give me a plan of a house . . . and if he cannot come, he'll recommend a man at York who understands these matters'.[10] Vanbrugh obliged with a design, but Etty was employed to supervise the work from 1719, and then from 1721 to act as clerk of the works (or, in effect, executant architect) at Castle Howard by Vanbrugh, and later by Hawksmoor. In 1723 Etty was providing another design for an important building in Leeds; Ralph Thoresby, the Leeds historian, received in that year 'a draught, the south front of our new church [Holy Trinity]; it was drawn by Mr. Etty of York, who has also made us a wooden modell for our workmen to go by'.[11] Probably he also made the design for Sheepscar Hall, the ashlar-faced house in Leeds built for Nathaniel Denison, as well as being employed by various landowners; he visited London to observe the new buildings, and he subscribed to such valuable books as James Gibbs's *A Book of Architecture*; and when he died in 1734, Hawksmoor wrote that 'as [Etty] was a usefull man to the World they will almost certainly miss him'.

Another York craftsman whose name is associated with several buildings in the county was William Thornton, described on his monument in St Olave's church in York as

Joyner and Architect, by the ablest judges of the former kind of work, he was look'd upon as the best artist in England, and for architecture, his reparation of Beverley Minster ought to give him a lasting memorial.

As well as executing the skilful structural restoration at Beverley, following Hawksmoor's report and recommendations in 1713, Thornton is now credited with the design (probably with the collaboration of the owner) of John Bourchier's Beningbrough Hall; on the strength of that, it is reasonable to suggest he was responsible for Robert Denison's house in Leeds,[12] work at Ledston Hall for Lady Elizabeth Hastings (with whom Thornton was in London in January 1719/20)[13] and no doubt other as yet unidentified buildings in West Yorkshire. A more obscure figure is Thomas Mann of York, a stonemason who erected the Market Cross in Pavement in 1672. Apparently he executed additions to Londesborough Hall, North Yorkshire, for Richard, 1st Earl of Burlington, c.1676, following a design provided by Robert Hooke; and in 1680 he sent Richard Beaumont a plan of a proposed new wing at Whitley Beaumont.[14]

The architectural achievement of master masons and joiners ('Workmen advanc'd to the degree of Architects', as Hawksmoor referred to them with the slightly patronising air of one who had been trained by Sir Christopher Wren), is obscured at times by the contributions of the gentlemen who made designs for their own houses or those of their friends. Occasionally a name emerges, such as that of Lancelot Freson of Leeds, who told the Court of Arches in 1665 that 'for the space of these twenty years last past' he had been 'employed about and undertaken the Building and reparacons of manye houses and structures for divers gentlemen and persons of quality within the County of York';[15] that suggests a degree of professionalism, but so far Freson has not been identified as the author of any building, and he remains an obscure figure. A little more is known about Theophilus

10 Webb,G.(ed)., *The complete works of Sir John Vanbrugh*, London 1928,iv,xxxi.

11 Yorkshire Archaeological Society, MS 10; letter dated 15 May 1723 from William Cookson to Ralph Thoresby (reprinted in *T S* (1912),xxi,258f.). See 186.

12 See 96.

13 See 61.

14 Kirklees Library and Museum Service, Whitley Beaumont Papers WBM/5.

15 Lambeth Palace Library, Court of Arches records Bbb 69. (Information from Mr Howard Colvin).

16 The inscription on Tong Hall reads:
HANC ANTIQUAM FAMILIAE
SEDEM/BIENNIUM INTRA/DE NOVO
EREXIT, PERFECITQUE/GEORGIUS
TEMPEST BARONETTUS/AUSPICANS AB
ANNO SALUTIS/MDCCII/DOMINI
THEOPHILI SHELTONI DE
HEATH/INGENIO PRUDENTIAQUE VERE
ARCHITECTONICA.

17 Kirklees Library and Museum Service,
Whitley Beaumont Papers WBM/8a-c.

18 Holmes,R.(ed)., *The book of entries of the
Pontefract corporation 1653–1726*, Pontefract
n.d.,283.

19 Collick,T.R., 'The patronage of Robert
Benson: 1675–1731', *A R* (1965),cxxxviii,
429f.

20 Lady Wentworth to her son, Lord Raby,
in 1709, 'Your brother Wentworth tels me
Mr. Benson is to loock affter your buildin in
Yorkshire'. Cartwright,J.J., *The Wentworth
papers 1705–39*, London 1883,84.

21 Collick, op.cit.

22 Cartwright, op.cit.

23 I am indebted to Mr Granville Wheler for
showing me this drawing, which is inscribed
'Lord Bingley's design for Ledstone'; it is
possible the drawing was made by a
draughtsman under Bingley's direction,
maybe John Wood.

24 Collick, op.cit.,430. Whitehall Palace was
burnt down in 1698, and over the following
years there were various proposals for
rebuilding it, including making use of Inigo
Jones's designs of 1639; but the death of
Queen Anne in 1714 brought the idea to an
end.

Shelton, Registrar of Deeds in the West Riding from 1704 to 1717, described as DOMINI THEOPHILI SHELTONI DE HEATH INGENIO PRUDENTIAQUE VERE ARCHITECTONICA on a tablet on the south front of Tong Hall.[16] The house was built for Sir George Tempest in 1702, and it can be assumed Shelton was responsible for the design of his own house, Eshald House (later known as Heath Hall), which was built shortly after 1694 when he acquired the property. He can also be given the credit for Lupset Hall, built by his brother-in-law Richard Witton in 1716, and probably Alverthorpe Hall, built by Daniel Maude in the first decade of the eighteenth century. In 1699 he gave Richard Beaumont a design for a handsome garden house to be built at Whitley, telling the landowner that 'with the help of a pair of compasses you may very easily find all the Dimensions & how every thing is placed in it'.[17] How Shelton gained a knowledge of architecture which enabled him to make such an accomplished design as Tong is as yet unknown, but evidently his reputation was not confined to his family circle and friends; he made the design for the Market Cross at Beverley (1714), and almost certainly for that in Wakefield (1707). In 1710, the Corporation of Pontefract decided to erect a cupola on the tower of St Giles's, according to 'a modell . . . Theophilus Shelton, Esq., shall draw for that purpose',[18] but nothing was done.

A more influential West Yorkshire landowner who enjoyed a reputation as an authority on architectural taste was Robert Benson, who became 1st Lord Bingley in 1713. He travelled to Italy during the last years of the seventeenth century and was known as one who 'lived very handsomely in the country without being a drinker though very gallant concerning the ladies'.[19] He returned to Yorkshire and entered public life in 1700, a career which took him to the Treasury within a decade. Meanwhile Benson was building Bramham Park, his new Yorkshire house, for which it was only natural he should act as architect. Lord Raby persuaded Benson to advise on the design and execution of his new wing at Stainborough in 1709,[20] and the 2nd Earl of Bute wrote to Raby (or 1st Earl of Strafford of the second creation as he had become) in 1713 and referred to 'the consummated [architectural] experience of Bingley'.[21] One of Benson's sensible opinions has survived in a letter dated 1711 from Peter Wentworth to Lord Raby: 'When I was at the Duke of Shrewsbury's my Lord Scarborough was there and he was talking of his building, and they did agree there was no building without a Surveyor, even when they agreed by the great, Wch agrees with the advice Mr Benson is always desiring to send you word, you must be at the expense wch in the main will be mony saved, for a blunder in building is not to be repaired without a great expense and loss of time and labour.'[22] A recently discovered design made for Lady Elizabeth Hastings to demonstrate how Ledston Hall could be remodelled as a Palladian house shows that Bingley provided his friends with neat drawings embellished with a decorative cartouche.[23] An astonishing letter dated 1713 refers to 'Lord Bingley's skill in architecture, for the Dutch Gazettes say he is to have the care of seeing Whitehall rebuilt';[24] unfortunately nothing

25 The Duke of Chandos wrote to Lord Bingley in 1719, praising the latter's 'judgement . . . I have the greatest opinion of, and to whose good taste I shall always readily submit my own'.

26 Wood,J., *Essay towards a description of Bath*, London 1765,232.

27 Sir William Robinson was on very friendly terms with William Wakefield, and obtained a design from the latter for Rokeby, his Yorkshire house; but when it was built in 1725–30, it was according to Robinson's own ideas. Wakefield prepared plans for the York Assembly Rooms, and although they were passed over in favour of Burlington's, Robinson thought they would have been 'full as convenient as my Lord's and [would have] saved a great deal of money'.

28 Verney,M., and Abercrombie,P., 'Letters of an eighteenth century architect', *A R* (1926),lx,51.

29 Gwynn,J., *London and Westminster improved*, London 1766,47; Lees-Milne,J., *Earls of creation*, London 1962,103ff.; Wittkower,R., *Palladio and English Palladianism*, London 1974,115ff,135ff. Burlington's influence probably helped the appointment of a fellow Yorkshire landowner, the Hon. Richard Arundell of Allerton Mauleyer (now Allerton Park) as Surveyor-General of the King's Works (1726–37); yet another Yorkshire landowner, Thomas Worsley of Hovingham, held this office from 1760–78.

30 Linstrum,D., 'Two Wentworth houses', *L A C* (1971),no.68,5ff; see 65ff.

more is known of this important project, but his advice was sought in 1719 by the Duke of Chandos who was rebuilding his great palace of Cannons in Middlesex.[25] Bingley employed a surveyor named John Wood for about five years at Bramham Park from 1722 to 1727, and it was probably among the avenues and cascades of the West Yorkshire estate that the first ideas for the layout of the city of Bath were being considered; Wood 'procured a Plan of the Town, which was sent me into *Yorkshire*, in the Summer of the Year 1725, where I, at my leisure Hours, formed [a] Design'.[26]

Another well-known gentleman architect was William Wakefield of Huby Hall, near Easingwold; 'examine all Mr. Wakefield's designs and the many alterations he has made in the old houses of his friends', wrote Sir Thomas Robinson to the Earl of Carlisle in 1730, 'we shall always find state conveniency with good economy inseparable companions'.[27] Robinson himself, a colourful figure in society, was another Yorkshire landowner and amateur architect. He designed his own house at Rokeby (1725–30), and he condemned the professional William Kent (a Yorkshireman whose studies in Italy were undertaken at the expense of a number of gentlemen including Sir William Wentworth of Bretton) for incurring extra cost to his patrons by often giving 'his orders when he was full of Claret, and as he did not perhaps see the works for several months after, he had indeed a pretty concise, tho' arbitrary, manner to sett all right, for he would order without consulting his employers, 3 or 4 hundred pounds of work, or more, to be directly pull'd down, and then correct the plan to what it ought to have been at first'. Robinson, whose chief architectural achievement was the west wing of Castle Howard, self-righteously wrote 'Your present architect drinks little Claret and never frames an opinion, with regard to Architecture witht. much thought and study – afterwards never makes any alteration'.[28]

Robinson was a member of the circle that revolved around the august figure of the 'Apollo of the Arts', Richard Boyle, 3rd Earl of Burlington and 4th Earl of Cork, Vice-admiral of the county of York (1715–33), Lord Lieutenant of the West Riding (1715–33) and East Riding (1715–21), and designer of the York Assembly Rooms, one of the county's most remarkable buildings. It was only his social position that prevented Burlington, who 'merited as a man of science the greatest honour' from being 'classed as an architect by profession'.[29] Following his youthful visits to Italy and his discovery of the genius of Andrea Palladio and the talents of William Kent, Burlington settled down to a life in London, Middlesex and Yorkshire which combined patronage of the arts, the building of his villa at Chiswick, and the management of his Londesborough estates. His official duties in the county inevitably drew into his company a number of landowners who were contemplating building, and Burlington was available to advise them. Sir William Wentworth of Bretton[30] designed his new house with the assistance of Colonel James Moyser, who was a valued member of Burlington's Yorkshire circle and principally responsible also for the design of Nostell Priory for Sir Rowland Winn. Burlington himself designed Colonel Gee's house at Bishop Burton and Kirby Hall for Stephen Thompson,[31] and probably assisted his friend John Aislabie of Studley Royal with the design of some of the buildings in his spectacular landscape;[32] but there were undoubtedly several other houses of which it could be said, as of Wentworth Woodhouse, that 'the whole finishing will be entirely submitted to Lord Burlington'. His presence in the county encouraged the fashion for Palladian architecture, a style that lent itself to long, relaxed discussions in country house libraries about the niceties of proportion and Classical details; but after all the references had been made to the precious folios of Vitruvius, Alberti, Palladio and Colen Campbell's *Vitruvius Britannicus*, the designs had to be executed.

Burlington himself employed draughtsmen, who profited from their experience and became architects. One was Henry Flitcroft, 'Burlington's Harry', who had previously been apprenticed to a London joiner; it is said he was brought to Burlington's attention by falling off a scaffold and hurting his leg while working on the Earl's house in Piccadilly. When Flitcroft was recovering from his injury, he was seen drawing by Burlington who, 'noticing his more than ordinary talent', took him into his service.[33] Daniel Garrett was another of Burlington's protégés, who acted as his personal clerk of the works and draughtsman. According to Sir Thomas Robinson, 'My L^dp Burlington has a much better opinion of Mr Garrets knowledge and judgment than of Mr Flitcrofts, or any Person whatever, except Mr Kent, he ... has had care and conduct of ... all my L^ds designs he ever gave'.[34] Both Flitcroft and Garrett rose to what has been called 'the dignity of a semi-independent practice' as an architect; the former provided the design for the east wing of Wentworth Woodhouse, and the latter worked at Temple Newsam and Kippax. Yet the execution of many buildings was largely in the hands of the Ettys and their fellow masons and joiners, who often made the drawings and decided on the decorative details with the help of published builders' pattern books. An unusual example of this is St Peter's church, Sowerby, built in 1763–6 by John Wilson, a local master mason who used as the source of his design the published plate of William Etty's Holy Trinity, Leeds, by then almost forty years old.[35]

The two most important eighteenth-century Yorkshire architects owed their introduction to practice to some extent to Burlington's circle. In about 1737 James Paine, still in his teens, came to Nostell Priory to supervise the construction of the house designed by Colonel Moyser, Burlington's friend, for Sir Rowland Winn.[36] This was his chief occupation for the next decade, but the erection of the Doncaster Mansion House to Paine's design in 1745–8 advertised his talents to the gentry who attended the town's famous race meetings, and he subsequently worked on at least ten estates in Yorkshire. Paine provided a mid eighteenth-century definition of architectural knowledge as being based on geometry, 'this very essential requisite', and 'the art of design, or drawing ... in a degree beyond the mere mechanical part of drawing geometrical lines; an architect should be able, at least, to sketch the human figure; be well skilled in drawing ornaments of every kind, and have a good taste for landscape; ... to

31 Burlington's design for Bishop's Burton is in the RIBA Drawings Collection (VI/I); Woolfe, J., and Gandon, J., *Vitruvius Britannicus*, London 1771, v, pls. 70–1 give *E. of Burlington and R. Morris* as the architects of Kirby Hall.

32 I am grateful to Mr W.T.C.Walker for this information.

33 Colvin, 206ff.

34 Webb, G., 'Letters and drawings by Hawksmoor for the Castle Howard mausoleum', *Walpole Society* (1931), xix, 160. Another letter from Robinson notes 'all those who I have recommended Mr Garret to have thanked me for doing it' (ibid., 161).

35 Leeds Archives Department, Sowerby parish records 17 (on deposit); see 187.

36 See 67f.

these necessary qualifications may be added, a competent knowledge of mechanick powers and hydraulics'.[37] He should know 'the quality and value of every material employed in the construction and decoration of a building, and also . . . the value of the labour of the several artificers'. Paine believed 'an architect should be *bred an architect*', and brought up his only son James, who was baptised in St Giles's, Pontefract in 1745, to follow his own profession; the two were painted by Sir Joshua Reynolds in a portrait now in the Ashmolean Museum. The elder Paine gave up his residence in Yorkshire some time in the 1740s, building up a large country house practice all over the country; but his move from the county left the field clear for John Carr, whose career epitomised the changing status of an architect during the second half of the eighteenth century.

Like many architects, Carr came from a building background.[38] His father, Robert, was a quarry owner and master mason in Horbury, who was referred to as an architect and also held an appointment as one of the two Surveyors of Bridges to the West Riding; the young man assisted his father, and between 1752 and 1753 he made a meticulously drawn record of the existing bridges in the county on Robert Carr's behalf.[39] There are a few references to John Carr's building activities; in 1748 Stephen Thompson of Kirby Hall wrote 'I have got a clever young fellow of a mason at the head of my works', and in the following year Carr was building alterations and additions to Askham Richard Hall. His introduction to Edwin Lascelles, at least as early as 1748, was probably as a builder who could also make plans, and the new stables at Gawthorp (later Harewood) were designed by John Carr and built by him and his father. When admitted as a Freeman of York at the age of thirty-four in 1757, Carr was still described as a stonecutter; that, added to the known existence of 'a Raff Yard, Garth, and a Kiln' at the rear of the house he bought in Skeldergate, York in 1751,[40] confirms Carr continued to act as contractor for many years after he had started to provide his patrons with designs for their houses.

The building of Kirby Hall, designed by Burlington and Roger Morris, must have brought Carr to some extent within the Earl's circle. The young mason was responsible for the design of the internal finishings of this Palladian house which is contemporary with another of his earliest known houses, Huthwaite Hall, near Penistone, and also with his proposal for Lascelles's stables; evidently Carr was making rapid progress. Like Paine, it was his association with a public building (the grandstand on the Knavesmire at York in 1754–6) that introduced him to many of the numerous gentry who were to become his patrons. There are at least eighty country houses in Yorkshire which were designed or altered or added to by Carr, or about which he was consulted.[41] His practice extended into other parts of England, even to Portugal, and when he died in 1807 he left behind his portraits in oils by Sir William Beechey and in marble by Joseph Nollekens, a fortune of £150,000, and a reputation for reliability, conscientiousness and professionalism. His neat drawings, whether annotated sketch elevations and plans, presentation designs, or working details, all

37 Paine, J., *Plans, elevations and sections of noblemen and gentlemen's houses*, London 1767, i, iif.

38 Colvin, 122ff; Wragg, B., 'John Carr of York', *West Yorkshire Society of Architects Journal* (1957–8), xvii, Dec 8ff, Mar 11ff.

39 Booth, A., 'Carr of York and the book of the bridges', *YAS* (1955), xxxviii, 367ff. There are two copies, one in the County Bridges Section, Wakefield, the other in the Leeds Archives Dept. John Carr was also Surveyor to the Justices of the North Riding 1772–1803 at a fee of £100 per annum. His survey of North Riding bridges is in the North Yorks C.R.O.

40 Harvey, J., *York*, London 1975, 155. The house cost £150. Raff is foreign timber, usually in the form of deals.

41 *The works in architecture of John Carr*, York 1973; a list published by York Georgian Society.

signed with his decorative, swirling signature, indicate the attention he paid to each stage of a building. It was appropriate that when the London Architects' Club was founded in 1791, Carr was one of the four from outside the capital invited to become Honorary Members. Among the fifteen original London members was Robert Adam, with whom Carr had worked at Harewood House, and from whom he had derived a Neo-classical taste in decoration which can be seen throughout the country in Carr's houses, and in the Horbury church which he built in 1791–3 and presented to the town as his architectural monument.[42]

Adam was the first important London architect to work in West Yorkshire. He brought with him the sophistication and polish acquired during four years on the continent and an acquaintance with such distinguished artists as Giovanni Battista Piranesi and Charles-Louis Clérisseau, and most of the English Grand Tourists in Rome;[43] and he confidently 'tickled up' Carr's drawings for Harewood 'so as to dazzle the eyes of the squire'. But it is noticeable that Edwin Lascelles, who had obtained designs from William Chambers, and probably from other architects, had confidence in the Yorkshire Carr, whom he had tried out as architect and builder on the new stables before deciding to employ him to design the house; in an unusual compromise, the completed building was externally Carr's, internally Adam's.[44] Landowners were in the habit of obtaining a selection of designs from different architects and then using them for their own purposes to adapt or alter as they chose. At Temple Newsam, drawings for rebuilding the south wing were supplied by Carr in 1765, 'Capability' Brown in 1766, and Adam in 1778, but the work was not executed until 1796 when it was undertaken by Thomas Johnson, who was probably working to a design made by his father, William, who was Lord Irwin's agent; in his obituary, the elder Johnson was described as 'architect'.[45] Sir Thomas Gascoigne had designs from Carr, Thomas Atkinson and Thomas Leverton between 1772 and 1781 for rebuilding Parlington Park; and his heir, Sir Richard Gascoigne, obtained a further series from William Pilkington, and from Watson and Pritchett, between 1810 and 1818. But nothing was done.[46] Beilby Thompson of Wetherby Grange had a plan from 'the great Mr. Wyatt' and then handed it over to Carr for amendments to suit his own ideas.[47] At Sledmere, Sir Christopher Sykes designed his own house after obtaining plans from Carr and Samuel Wyatt;[48] and at Harewood, Humphry Repton's 1801 design for the entrance arch and lodges was altered by Carr's mason, John Muschamp, so much that Repton felt humiliated and said so.[49]

By the end of the eighteenth century, a number of local architects had begun to emerge. Some, like William Lindley of Doncaster, had been trained professionally; in 1774 he offered his services in the *York Courant* and referred to having been 'an Assistant to Mr. Carr of York upwards of 20 years'. Others seem to have made designs for buildings as well as holding an official position, like John Moxson, who was Surveyor of the Highways in Leeds, Thomas Bradley of Halifax, who was Engineer to the Calder and Hebble Navigation, or Bernard Hartley of Pontefract who was the first of three generations of the

42 See 189ff.

43 Fleming, J., *Robert Adam and his circle in Edinburgh and Rome*, London 1962.

44 See 73ff.

45 *LI*, 1 June 1795.

46 Friedman, T.F., 'Romanticism and neo-classicism for Parlington', *LAC* (1970), no.66, 2ff. The one building which resulted from all these designs is the triumphal arch dated 1782 and built from a design by Leverton. It commemorates American independence and is traditionally believed to have affronted the Prince Regent on one of his visits to Yorkshire.

47 Leeds Archives Dept. Wetherby Grange MSS. Letter from Beilby Thompson to Carr, 9 Feb 1784 (LF 118/18).

48 The designs are in Sir Richard Sykes's collection at Sledmere.

49 Stroud, D., *Humphry Repton*, London 1962, 111.

same name to hold the office of Surveyor of Bridges to the West Riding.[50] Some, like John Sutcliffe of Halifax, were millwrights who specialised in setting up industrial buildings and machinery,[51] but regarded themselves as equivalent in status to an architect; in 1791 he was asked to make a design and estimate for Benjamin Gott's mill in Leeds, and spent 'near 7 weeks in drawing the plans'. In his claim for payment of £162.13s.0d. Sutcliffe asserted there were 'few Engineers perhaps none but myself in the same situation but what would have charged from £30 to £40 for the design of the plans, over and above the time spent in drawing them. This Mr. Wyate of London and Mr. Car of York have always done'.[52] Gott objected and suggested asking Carr to arbitrate, but finally it was John Rennie who reported 'As to the drawings I can with truth say they are much beyond what I would have charged on what I conceive to be their true value'.[53] Sutcliffe resigned and poured out his scorn in exceptionally unprofessional terms on his ex-employer, 'You have acted the part of Dark Desynting Hypocrite and have shown yourself to be a man in whose narrow shrivl'd contracted Bosom there is no Room for the admirable virtues of truth Charity Honour and integrity to dwell in'.[54]

Some eighteenth-century architects, like Thomas Johnson of Leeds, were involved in the sale of building plots, and their names appear as agent[55] in newspaper advertisements which also often reveal the way in which an architect acquired his knowledge and experience; William Belwood, for example, who designed the stables at Newby Hall,[56] had acted as superintendent of the works at Harewood House. He advertised to that effect in the *Leeds Mercury*, 'respectfully to acquaint his Friends and Public, That he is now settled in Lendall YORK, and proposes making DESIGNS FOR BUILDINGS from the plainest to the most elegant and in the different tastes; also designs Temples; and Ornamental Buildings, Green Howses, Bridges, etc. with Estimates, likewise measures and values the different Articles'.[57] Another advertisement illustrates a common background of many who became architects; in 1807 William Lawrance of Leeds informed 'his numerous Friends that he has declined the Business of Joiner and Carpenter ... [and] begs Permission to offer his Services to the Public as an ARCHITECT, SURVEYOR, and VALUER OF BUILDINGS; and to inform them, that he intends carrying on the Business of a RAFF-MERCHANT on his premises in Simpson's Fold, and shall be happy to receive a Share of their Commands'.[58] The combination of architecture, contracting and dealing in timber was not uncommon in more exalted places than Simpson's Fold. Several of the Wyatts, for example, including James, the Surveyor to the King's Works, contracted for buildings which they had designed, and there were timber yards behind the London houses of Samuel Wyatt and his nephew, Jeffry. The latter was supplying building materials from London for the new wing at Bretton Hall built in 1811–14 to his design; in 1813 Wyatt informed the agent, 'I have written this day to Mrs. Beaumont requesting a thousand pounds as I shall have about 500£ to pay for the glass and the moment the money arrives the Glass shall be sent'.[59] John Nash told a Royal Commission he saw no reason

50 See 369ff. for biographical information.

51 Tann, J., *The development of the factory*, London 1970, 101.

52 Cusworth Hall MSS., J.Sutcliffe charges 22 Dec 1792.

53 loc.cit., J.Rennie to Wormald, Fountaine and Gott 2 Mar 1793.

54 loc.cit., J.Sutcliffe to B.Gott 13 Aug 1792.

55 *LI*, 31 Aug 1795. It was customary for architects to act as estate agents; in *LI* 28 June 1827 there is an advertisement of the lease of a dwelling house, outbuildings and three warehouses, for which applications had to be made to 'Mr.Chantrell, architect'.

56 These stables have been attributed at different times to Adam and to Carr, but Belwood's design is in the Pennington–Ramsden MSS, Cumbria C.R.O.

57 *LM*, 11 July 1775.

58 ibid., 17 Jan 1807.

59 Allendale: BEA/C2/B40/22; Linstrum, D., *Catalogue of the drawings collection of the Royal Institute of British Architects: the Wyatt family*, Farnborough 1973, 7ff.

60 Soane, J., *Plans, elevations and sections of buildings*, London 1788,7.

61 *LI*, 16 June 1817.

62 A Leeds builder who acted as architect at times was G. Nettleton, whose book of drawings and alterations is in the Leeds Archives Dept. (Nettleton Papers, acc.1339). Other papers in the same deposit have identified the architects responsible for several buildings for which Nettleton was the contractor.

63 Colvin, 136f.

64 Beckwith, F., *Thomas Taylor, Regency architect*, Leeds 1949.

65 *LI*, 9 Sept 1811. In 1822 Taylor sent a 'View of the Pantheon at Paris' to the exhibition of the Northern Society for the Encouragement of the Fine Arts, which might be taken as evidence of his acquaintance with French architecture.

66 *Building Chronicle*, May 1857.

67 See 369ff. for biographical information and works.

68 See 369ff. for biographical information and works.

69 See 369ff. for biographical information and works.

70 See 369ff. for biographical information and works.

71 See 369ff. for biographical information and works.

why one man should not act as architect, speculator, builder and supplier; but there was a growing feeling, expressed in John Soane's Royal Academy lectures in the 1780s and exemplified by the formation of the Architects' Club in 1791, that a separation between architecture and the other building skills was desirable. The architect, said Soane, 'is the intermediate agent between the employer, whose honour and interest he is to study, and the mechanic, whose rights he is to defend ... If these are the duties of an Architect, with what propriety can his situation, and that of the builder or the contractor, be united?'[60]

It is doubtful if such scruples greatly disturbed West Yorkshire, where the early nineteenth-century urban expansion was creating a need for public buildings, factories, churches and villas. This encouraged a number of architects to set up in practice, and in 1822 there were five in Leeds, five in Wakefield, two each in Bradford, Halifax and Huddersfield, and one in Pontefract. Some, like Joseph Cusworth of Leeds, had been trained locally; he advertised in 1817 that he had previously worked with Thomas Johnson.[61] Some, like Joseph Kaye of Huddersfield (described as 'a funny old man [who] has been known to say after taking a Contract for a Church, that he had forgotten the Estimate for the Tower'), were primarily builders;[62] but three in Leeds were outsiders who had been attracted by the prospect of work to set up practice in the growing town. Robert Dennis Chantrell had trained in John Soane's office from 1807–14 (at a premium of 100 guineas) and arrived in Leeds in 1819.[63] Thomas Taylor,[64] who was already well established by that time, first worked for a London builder and then in James Wyatt's office, where 'he was in the Habit of making Plans, Elevations, and Sections, for executing some of the most distinguished Buildings in the Kingdom'. That was how he advertised his qualifications, soliciting 'the Commands of those who may have Occasion for his Professional Services', promising satisfaction, and drawing attention specially to his 'careful Studies of all the superior French Buildings, [by which] he is enabled to arrange Architectural Decorations in a superior Style'.[65] John Clark had arrived in Leeds from Edinburgh in the 1820s, and the success of his design in the competition for the Leeds Commercial Buildings in 1825 persuaded him to set up in practice permanently in the town.[66]

Taylor, Chantrell and Clark became, in effect, local West Yorkshire architects, although they brought with them experience gained in London and Edinburgh; and it is noticeable how seldom during the 20s, 30s and 40s there was recourse to an architect outside the area. For example, out of the sixteen churches built in the West Riding between 1821 and 1829 with the aid of the first Parliamentary Grant, all but one were the work of Yorkshire architects – Taylor, Chantrell, John Oates of Halifax[67] and Peter Atkinson of York.[68] The much longer list of West Riding churches built with the aid of the second Parliamentary Grant shows the same characteristics; out of eighty-three, almost all were designed by local architects. Chantrell, Oates and Atkinson appeared again; then there were Woodhead and Hurst of Doncaster,[69] Charles Child (who had been Oates's clerk of the works),[70] James Mallinson and Thomas Healey of Bradford,[71] Charles

72 See 369ff. for biographical information and works.

73 See 369ff. for biographical information and works.

74 See 369ff. for biographical information and works.

75 Calderdale Archives Dept. MS diary of Anne Lister, SH:7/ML/E,1834. She made notes of likely sources for her new buildings at Shibden Hall during her travels. In Warwick she thought 'the drop-style' of St Mary's church 'very pretty – nice *model*', and she was tempted to build her new lodge as a replica of Micklegate Bar, York.

76 See 369ff. for biographical information and works.

77 Chantrell's practice was continued by his son, John, at 5 East Parade, Leeds.

78 See 369ff. for biographical information and works.

79 He had moved from 1 Kirkgate to 1 Cross Bank Street.

80 Isaac Hordern recalled 'I remember hearing that the Directors [of Huddersfield railway station, which Kaye built] were very much afraid of the expense & after the station had been about half completed, they sent for Mr. Joe Kaye & told him they were not prepared to carry out the plans as arranged, & the answer he gave the Directors was that, in that case he should be measured off & they would find they would have as much to pay as if he had completed his contract which had been taken so low that he should be glad to be paid off by measurement'. *Isaac Hordern's notes relating to the Ramsden estate and Huddersfield.* Yorkshire Archaeological Society, MS 491; see 369ff. for biographical information and works.

81 See 369ff. for biographical information and works.

Watson and James Pritchett of York,[72] William Perkin and Elisha Backhouse of Leeds,[73] John Dobson,[74] C.W. Burleigh and Philip Boyce of Leeds, and a few others who made single appearances.

The owners of the villa-mansions outside the towns were equally faithful to the local architects; Benjamin Gott's employment of Robert Smirke at Armley House was exceptional. There is an interesting personal account of how an architect was selected in the 1830s by Miss Anne Lister of Shibden Hall, who was intent on enlarging and medievalising her house.[75] Although she was impressed by Chantrell's 'very neat modern Gothic Church, quite new, at Morley', she first tried a local man and consulted William Bradley of Halifax who 'came to take the ground plan of the house, [and] asked for a month to make his plan of castellated additions'. However, subsequent inquiries led Miss Lister to believe Bradley was '*not a man to be depended on – very idle* – never right in his estimates – not fit to be an architect, except in a soft stone country – not fit for stone like ours'. She was then recommended to consider Bernard Hartley II of Pontefract, who was 'employed in the county, *one of the most honest men* to be had – *he might be trusted implicitly*'. Thomas Lees, an architect from over the Pennines, was thought of, but although 'a *very* clever man . . . not quite to be taken at his word'. Miss Lister then went over to York to look at the work of John Harper,[76] who had trained in the London office of Benjamin Dean Wyatt. She met the young man, who had been described to her as 'a rising man', and tried out his abilities by asking him to make plans for the conversion of Northgate House, Halifax into an hotel and casino; the result was judged 'well arranged – handsome elevation – in good taste', and Harper was appointed as her architect for the conversion and also for the much larger commission at Shibden Hall. 'I like him very well – he agreed to all I proposed', she noted in her diary with the satisfaction of a client who has found an obedient architect.

By 1853 the number of architectural practices in West Yorkshire had increased considerably. There were three in Wakefield, ten each in Halifax and Huddersfield, thirteen in Bradford and twenty-three in Leeds, and individual architects in several towns. A few of those in the 1822 Directory had passed on to a younger generation, such as Chantrell's in Leeds[77] and John Billington's in Wakefield;[78] Benjamin Jackson in Leeds[79] and Joseph Kaye in Huddersfield[80] appear to have been active still, and in Pontefract the third generation Bernard Hartley was carrying on the family practice as well as being Surveyor of Bridges to the West Riding; but the majority were newly established though often from a local building background. Two of the most important practices in the region were relatively new in 1853, and each had come from Hull on the strength of a single outstanding commission. Henry Francis Lockwood was born in Doncaster, and set up practice in Hull in 1834 after training in London; in 1849 a company of shareholders was formed in Bradford to promote a new hall (later known as St George's), and Lockwood was appointed as architect with his new partner, William Mawson.[81] Their Bradford practice, started in 43 Kirkgate, dominated the town's architecture for the next twenty-five years. Almost all the important municipal buildings, many commercial ones, as well as the famous town of Saltaire, came their way; and they were well known in London for their entries in national competitions as well as for such executed work as the City Temple, Holborn (1873–4) and the Civil Service Stores in the Strand (1876–7). The other migrant from Hull was the young Cuthbert Brodrick, a pupil and assistant of Lockwood, who won the competition for Leeds Town Hall in 1853 and opened an office at 30 Park Row. His handful of public buildings includes the town's finest examples of Victorian municipal enterprise, and he too was well known outside West Yorkshire. His entries in national competitions, such as the Government Offices in Whitehall (1857), brought favourable notices, and in 1866 Brodrick was selected as one of six architects to submit a scheme in limited competition for remodelling the National Gallery. He prepared an abortive design for a Customs House in Bombay, but his most important executed buildings were in his native county, in Leeds, Hull, Scarborough and Ilkley; all were built between 1853 and 1869, the year in which he went to live near Paris and abandoned the profession in which he had seemed destined to rise to the top.[82]

Apart from these two practices, the other mid nineteenth-century ones in West Yorkshire were probably little known outside the region (or, in many cases, outside the town where they had their office), but they and their successors largely shaped the local architecture for the rest of the century by training articled pupils and later taking them into partnership so that several firms maintained a sense of continuity for a number of generations. There was a tendency for a practice to be closely identified with one town, outside which it rarely worked; Leeds had Brodrick, William Reid Corson and his younger brother George,[83] Perkin and Backhouse, Adams and Kelly,[84] Thomas Ambler,[85] etc; Bradford had Lockwood and Mawson, Samuel Jackson,[86] Milnes and France, Andrews and Delaunay (later and Pepper);[87] Huddersfield had John Kirk and Sons;[88] and Halifax had the Horsfalls, Roger Ives, and John Hogg.[89] But the local men were sometimes set aside in favour of one of the leading architects from London, the first of whom was George Gilbert Scott.

Scott's first appearance in Leeds was as early as 1843 when, in partnership with William Bonython Moffatt, he designed St Andrew's, Cavendish Street; then, in 1847, he built another church in the town, St John the Evangelist, Little Holbeck, and he was working in Wakefield on the restoration of the medieval chantry chapel and the building of St Andrew's, Peterson Road. In 1853 Scott met Edmund Beckett Denison, a member of a notable family of Leeds bankers, who is better known in architectural history under his later title of Lord Grimthorpe.[90] Denison's opinion of architects was low, and his belief in his own omniscience led him to preach it was folly to employ a professional unless he was prepared to be instructed by one who knew better than anyone else what was required. Although the law was Denison's profession, he saw himself as the instructor of architects. He lectured the members of the RIBA on their incompetence in their own

82 Brodrick opened an office in London in 1863. See Linstrum, D., 'Cuthbert Brodrick: an interpretation of a Victorian architect', *Journal of the Royal Society of Arts* (1971), cxix, 72ff.

83 See 369ff. for biographical information and works.

84 See 369ff. for biographical information and works.

85 See 369ff. for biographical information and works.

86 See 369ff. for biographical information and works.

87 See 369ff. for biographical information and works.

88 See 369ff. for biographical information and works.

89 See 369ff. for biographical information and works.

90 Ferriday, P., *Lord Grimthorpe*, London 1957.

91 'Have the public any security whatever that any man who calls himself an architect does understand his business practically even as much as the builders whom he professes to instruct, or that he will exercise any efficient superintendence'. (Lord Grimthorpe to the members of the RIBA, December 1874). As Mr Ferriday comments (ibid.80), 'it was not much fun for the architects because so much of what he said was true'.

92 The Becketts had been bankers in Leeds since the second half of the eighteenth century. By marriage Sir Edmund Beckett, 4th Baronet, (1787–1874), inherited a fortune from Sir Thomas Denison (one line of the Denisons, a Leeds family, became Earls of Londesborough, and Elizabeth Denison (d.1861) became Marchioness Conyngham, one of the hated 'mistresses' of the ageing George IV). Sir Edmund took the name of Denison in addition to his own. He became a railway king in the 1840s and beat George Hudson in the battle for the Great Northern railway, the building of which made him praised as 'the greatest benefactor to Doncaster that the town has ever known'. It was his eldest son, Edmund Beckett Denison II (1816–1905) who became 1st Baron Grimthorpe in 1886 and concerned himself with architecture and clock-making as well as his chosen profession, the law.

93 Demolished in 1964, the greatest single loss in Leeds. A (1870),iv,315 called it 'next in importance to the Town Hall ... one of [Scott's] happiest efforts'.

94 See 227f.

95 See 136ff,344ff.

96 E (1845),iv,203f.

headquarters,[91] and bullied everyone who came within reach of his scorn. He bullied and bought his way to the Chancellorship of the Diocese of York, and then he bullied the unfortunate architects who were working within its boundaries. But the Beckett Denisons had great influence in the West Riding,[92] and Scott knew how to humour the lawyer, who pompously announced he had found Scott 'quite above the professional vanity of refusing to listen to the suggestions of an amateur'. In 1857 the foundation stone was laid in Doncaster of St James's church, nominally designed by Denison but executed by Scott, who consented to be architectural whipping-boy; and shortly afterwards Scott was employed to design a Gothic *palazzo* in Leeds for Beckett's Bank, the family business.[93] By that time he had met Edward Akroyd, and was building All Souls' church, Haley Hill, Halifax, complacently referred to as 'on the whole, my best';[94] he was preparing a design for Halifax Town Hall, being consulted about the layout of Akroydon,[95] building St Thomas's church, Huddersfield, and restoring the parish church in Wakefield.

Scott had broken into the West Yorkshire architectural world with his accustomed forcefulness, no doubt to the resentment of some of the local practitioners. It is interesting to note that the *Ecclesiologist* discussed whether or not it was better to employ a local architect, and the opinion was not entirely in favour of the London man.

It is true that London architects are perhaps generally among the most eminent, and ... really the best. But it is also undeniable that the nature of their practice is the most unfavourable that can be conceived for attaining a real appreciation of ecclesiastical design and its true principles, especially as adapted to the wants of country parishes. A London architect in full practice has so much on his hands ... that he has no time either to think, or study, or make the researches necessary for the furtherance of his art, and the improvement of his acquired ideas.

The *Ecclesiologist* wrote of the 'repetition of the same bad idea in a dozen new churches', which resulted from such overwork, and contrasted those country architects who, 'though under the present system they are little likely to become as well known as their merits may deserve, should if competent, be patronized, encouraged, instructed, and brought forward on every occasion of work having to be done in their district'. The writer referred to the knowledge of local materials and character which were better known to the local man, but also pointed out that a bad local architect, 'who obtains much and general promiscuous practice, is one of the greatest evils which a district can possess ...'

We now often hear of regrets that such and such a party was employed ... and that the employers did not know better than to entrust the work to such incompetent hands. But party interests, or private favour, will sometimes prevail over every precaution in choosing an architect. Perhaps the only safe way in conducting any large work is to refer if possible the nomination of the architect, or at least the design and drawings when completed, to an architectural society, or some really competent judges.[96]

Such a solution would no doubt have suited the future Lord Grimthorpe, especially if he were invited to be one of the 'really competent judges'. Certainly, the competition system which had been the foundation of many successful careers, was coming under sharp criticism. In 1860 the *Builder* noted that plans for a Corn Exchange in Leeds were to be advertised for. A month later a letter signed 'scru' was published, in which the anonymous writer complained that not only designs were being asked for, but also complete working drawings, specifications, and details 'sufficient to enable contractors to tender from'. He suspected 'the lucky author of the first prize will ... have his hundred pounds handed over to him, and "no further questions asked", as the custom is with fortunate finders of gentlemen's pocket-books, or ladies' pet-dogs'. He also looked with some suspicion at the condition that if the cost of the selected plan, when contracted for, exceeded the architect's estimate, he was to forfeit his claim to the premium.[97] The Borough Engineer immediately reassured the competitors that the Council intended to instruct the successful architect to execute the design as well as paying him the premium,[98] and in August it was announced that the locally familiar names of Cuthbert Brodrick, William Hill,[99] and Lockwood and Mawson had been awarded first, second and third places.

Only four months after Brodrick's design for the Corn Exchange had been accepted, the competition entries for yet another Leeds building, the Mechanics' Institute, were on view. The *Builder* suavely wrote that 'those who were interested in the cause of architectural beauty looked forward to a display of originality at least, and probably of some genius ... it was certain that good men were working hard in this competition'.[100] The writer complimented Leeds on the high standard it demanded from its new architecture; but then his tone changed.

It has been stated that three plans out of the whole were selected for ultimate comparison and choice, and that the authors of these three were Mr. Brodrick, Messrs. Perkins and Backhouse, and Mr. Shaw;[101] all, oddly enough, Leeds architects. It is, moreover, no secret as to who are the authors of the majority of the designs; and, whilst examining the plans for this criticism, we invariably heard the spectators speak of the designs as Mr. So-and-so's, and not by the motto attached to them.

The critic disagreed with the committee's choice, and he was suspicious of their behaviour, obviously believing that Brodrick's reputation had swayed the decision. 'It is right and just', he concluded, 'that others beside local men should have a fair choice. Competitional morality on the part of committees is not high. We should be glad to hear a satisfactory explanation of this instance of competitional injustice'. The following week, W.H. Crossland's letter was published, in which he asked if it was true the designs had been sent to Scott for his opinion; if so, the writer, who had sent in a Gothic design favourably noticed by the *Builder*, would no longer feel himself an injured competitor, but nevertheless he protested at the 'underhand manner in which the committee ... had acted throughout the whole proceedings, but especially at the conclusion of this competition'.[102] A week later Henry Garling wrote sensibly that 'had the gentlemen of Leeds intended to have given the commission to their fellow-townsman, no one would have complained ... But we have a right to complain that, with this foregone conclusion, they invite architects to lose money, and time more valuable than money, in a hopeless combat'.[103] The secretary of the Mechanics' Institute

97 *B* (1860),xviii,355.

98 ibid.,370.

99 ibid.,515; see 369ff. for biographical information and works.

100 ibid.,831.

101 See 369ff. for biographical information and works.

102 *B* (1861),xix,14.

103 ibid.,29. Henry Garling was not a Yorkshire architect, but his prize-winning Second Empire design for the War Office in the Whitehall competition (in which Brodrick's had been placed fifth) had been set aside in favour of Scott's. Obviously he, like Brodrick, was on the side of Classicism versus Scott's Gothic.

attempted to explain away the criticisms and accusations, but agreed that for some inexplicable reason Scott had not even seen the designs and Brodrick's had been selected 'without any professional assistance whatever', an admission quite properly criticised by the *Builder*. The fact that Brodrick's Institute is one of the best buildings in Leeds only adds weight to Garling's common sense.

In 1864, it was Bradford's turn to cause trouble with a competition, this time for the new Exchange. Ten names were submitted, including Brodrick, Lockwood and Mawson, and Milnes and France; but there were also some bright young Gothicists, including William Burges, Norman Shaw, Philip Webb and George Edmund Street. The last failed to submit, as did Brodrick, but Alfred Waterhouse's unofficial assessment (there were no professional advisers) commended the designs by Burges and Shaw, believing the latter's possessed 'the maximum of accommodation with the minimum of expense'. Lockwood and Mawson's entry was the costliest as well as standing 'highest in unproductive area', and all the committee members save one voted solidly for it. In spite of the usual mottoes attached to the designs, it was well known that *Experientia* meant Lockwood and Mawson who, seeing the wind was blowing towards the Gothic, abandoned their expected Italianate design and confounded the supporters of their opponents. Once again there was a bitter correspondence in the local newspaper. There were accusations of deliberately low estimates and unprofessional behaviour; but one suggestion that 'if any other than [Burges or Shaw] were to be selected', the entries submitted should be referred to a committee composed of Scott, Street, Butterfield, Waterhouse, Bodley, Ruskin, Beresford Hope, Denison, J.H. Parker, and Sir Henry Acland, was not accepted. The prospect was daunting, but Lockwood and Mawson remained the victors.[104]

In 1861 the *Builder* announced that Lockwood and Mawson had been awarded the first prize in a competition for a new General Infirmary at Leeds, but there was a change of site, and then the Building Committee thought again about the procedure and considered how best to resolve the appointment of an architect for this important building. William Beckett Denison, youngest brother of Edmund (who was probably the *éminence grise*), wrote to three London architects to ask their opinion, and the replies provide some evidence about the current attitudes to competitions among the leading men, and their thoughts about collaboration between London and provincial practitioners.[105]

George Edmund Street[106] firmly declined to take part in an open competition – 'I never compete in this way save in the case of great national works in which the credit to be secured by success is so great as to justify me in making the venture'. Nor was he enthusiastic about even a limited competition, believing architects 'ought not to be asked to spend their time & give all their artistic energy to a scheme the event of which is to be judged of finally by a committee appointed in the ordinary fashion'. He concluded, 'the most honest advice to give you is to go at once to some good architect who has already erected

104 Saint,A., *Richard Norman Shaw*, New Haven 1976,54ff.

105 This correspondence is in the Brotherton Library, University of Leeds (Gott papers, 6/3–10,17–18). William Beckett Denison (1826–90), who conducted the correspondence, was a younger brother of Lord Grimthorpe, and a great philanthropist in Leeds (see 145). He lived at Nun Appleton Hall, a late seventeenth-century house commemorated by Andrew Marvell, and greatly increased in size in 1863 by E.B.Lamb.

106 George Edmund Street (1824–81) is not well represented in West Yorkshire. He added a nave and aisles to St Michael's, Thornhill in 1877, and designed the reredos in Leeds parish church in 1872.

some similar work which satisfies you . . . & entrust the work to him without competition'. Scott's opinion tallied with Street's, and he too had strong reservations about the methods by which some contests had been settled.

I once entered upon a select competition precisely similar to yours & under circumstances the most favourable as regards the character of the Committee. Yet it was found one of the physicians of the Hospital had allied himself with a competitor, had actually worked hard with him in the whole arrangement & when the designs were exhibited was daily in the room pointing out to influential persons there the merits of the design he himself had been concerned in making & the faults real or attributed of others.

Benjamin Ferrey,[107] an architect of an earlier generation, replied that he never engaged in open competition but would consider one limited to say eight 'honorable men' who would be paid for their work; but he too recommended, 'select your architect at once, put him in communication with your medical staff & he will build you a better hospital than you will probably obtain by any competition'.

The Building Committee pondered these replies and wrote to ask William Tite's[108] opinion, which was also against a competition; and an eminent medical man who was consulted had no doubt that 'if Gilbert Scott will undertake the plan he will do it well . . . Make a push for Scott . . . Scott's work will hand him down to posterity. He is now undoubtedly the first, & such an important building as yours should be associated with a public name'. It was; and it was Scott's. But there was still the question of the supervision of a contract two hundred miles away from London. Should there be a collaboration with a local architect? There was discussion about this in the preliminary correspondence, and Scott had strong feelings, replying that he had 'on several occasions joined with local architects' but had invariably repented of it. 'It has always turned out a prolific source of annoyance & vexation & as to saving trouble it increases it two fold'. Then he thought better and substituted 'ten' for 'two'. It was true he had agreed to collaborate with William Perkin of Leeds on Beckett's new bank in Park Row; that had been done 'to avoid clashing with your architects, but with a conviction that I should have double trouble for half the remuneration with a less satisfactory result . . . If the local authorities desire a local architect I would strongly recommend them to employ one at once & so trust to him for the result'. The Building Committee bowed to Scott's argument and he, in turn, agreed to consider appointing 'an assistant who would devote his time exclusively to this work, whether in Leeds or elsewhere'.

This was an unusually amicable way of appointing an architect, in contrast to the competition system which continued in spite of the growing discontent. Brodrick was one of the ten architects in a limited competition of 1866–7 for a remodelling and extension of the National Gallery; his submission was 'great in pillars . . . and when we have said this, we have said nearly all that can be said of the design',[109] sneered the critic in the *Building News*, but he found little to praise in any of the entries. Nor did the First Commissioner of Works, who chose not to make an award at all, to the fury of the competitors who accused him

107 Benjamin Ferrey (1810–80) seems not to have been employed at all in West Yorkshire and was a curious contestant to consider.

108 Sir William Tite (1798–1873) had won the competition for the Royal Exchange, London in 1841. He had been associated with Huddersfield in the 1850s when he was employed by the Ramsden estate.

109 *BN* (1867),xiv,17. 'Everyone who knows Mr Brodrick's works at Leeds and elsewhere need scarcely be told that the composition is severe to a fault. Its great mistake is the monotony which results from an excess of Corinthian pillars'.

of a 'breach of faith' that would 'confer a lasting injury upon every one' of them.

In 1869, Bradford announced its intention to build a Town Hall, but the unsatisfactory competition conditions caused so many questions to be asked that the competitors were virtually told they might do as they liked, and the selection of the winning entry was suspected of being nothing but a formality. Four hundred applied for the conditions, but only thirty submitted designs; few were from Yorkshire, as it was widely believed the choice had already been made. On the closing day, one of the competitors observed a procession through the streets of Bradford of a set of large drawings by a local architect, completely uncovered and open to view. 'There was a very pretty bit of innocent by-play at the opening of the sealed envelopes',[110] but there was little surprise that the selected entry submitted under the motto *Let Bradford Flourish* was the work of the town's favourite architects, Lockwood and Mawson. Then came a charge of plagiarism in the newly launched journal, the *Architect*. Edward Godwin wrote to ask why William Burges's name had not been attached to the winning design, since he presumed from certain features in it that Burges 'had acted as consulting architect'.[111] The following week Burges replied that he had not been consulted, 'although I confess there are many points in it that I recognise'.[112] Lockwood and Mawson defended their design by quoting from their report that 'the central clock-tower is based upon that of the celebrated campanile of the Palazzo Vecchio at Florence, the arrangement of the upper windows upon the Galerie des Rois and the Galerie Intermédiaire of Amiens Cathedral'. The sources were impeccable, and the affronted architects were 'prepared to apologise in the most frank manner if these tolerably well-known examples should prove to be the exclusive copyright of Mr. Burges'.[113] Godwin had the last word by silkily observing that his belief 'Mr. Burges was connected with the design ... was founded upon the similarity which exists between a bay of Mr. Burges' design for the Law Courts and a bay of the design for the Town Hall'; nor could he discover any likeness between the Bradford design and Amiens cathedral, but he begged to apologise 'to all the architects concerned, including the gentleman who designed "the Galerie des Rois and the Galerie Intermédiaire"'.[114]

Week after week the professional journals printed angry letters and accusations about the competition system. One of the architects who sent in a design for the Halifax Building Society's headquarters in 1869 wrote to the *Builder*:

Sir, The particulars of this competition were advertised in your journal *last year*, the building to cost only £5,000. The drawings have been sent in nearly seven months! No notice has yet been sent to the competitors that anything has been done. A poet has written something about learning 'to labour and to wait'. Alas! the common lot of architects; but surely it is time the Halifax Building Society's directors were up and doing. In any case, the competitors will do well to have their 'hearts prepared for any fate'. A VICTIM.[115]

The Halifax Infirmary competition caused more trouble, and one disheartened competitor concluded, 'I can only hope that the day may

110 *B* (1869),xxvii,840.

111 *A* (1869),ii,266.

112 ibid.,279.

113 ibid.,290.

114 ibid.,302.

115 *B* (1870),xxviii,671.

be not far off when every respectable architect will decline to send in competitive designs'.[116]

The RIBA appointed a committee to investigate the competition system in 1871, and in the following year a code of regulations was drawn up; but the complaints went on. One of the aims in founding the Institute in 1834 'for establishing an uniformity and respectability of practice in the profession' was not easily achievable. 'A RESIDENT' of Leeds wrote to the *Architect* in 1870 to complain about certain members of the architectural profession in that town. 'Professional etiquette . . . can hardly be said to exist . . . One gentleman advertises in a local newspaper his readiness to make special arrangements when required; another announces his willingness to allow a reduction in terms on work designed for a charitable or religious object . . . The large practice of one gentleman is notoriously sustained by heavy commissions to estate agents and others for introducing business, and even the levying blackmail from contractors is by no means unknown. Under such conditions as these, how is it likely that architecture can flourish?'[117]

In the face of such irregularities, professional consolidation was essential, and provincial societies were established. In 1874 the Bradford Society of Architects and Surveyors was founded at a meeting in the Victoria Hotel, one of the many buildings in the town designed by Lockwood and Mawson. Henry Lockwood was the obvious choice as the first President of the Society which intended to promote personal acquaintance and good feeling between members, to afford mutual assistance by advice and mediation, to obtain and consider information affecting either profession. The Society, which is still in existence, laid down the rule that its membership should consist 'only of gentlemen who at the time of their election are . . . in practice on their own account as architects or surveyors: or the sons of members of the society who have been duly articled or educated as architects and surveyors'. Two years after the foundation of the Bradford Society, a meeting was held in Leeds to discuss the formation of the Leeds Architectural Association; once again, there was an obvious choice of President, and the first meeting was in January 1877 when George Corson assumed the leadership of a group of eighty architects. The Association has continued until the present day, under different names; in 1883 it became the Leeds and Yorkshire Architectural Society, in 1914 the Leeds and West Yorkshire Architectural Society, in 1928 the West Yorkshire Society of Architects, and in 1968 it became a part of the Yorkshire Region of the Royal Institute of British Architects.

By the end of the century, the number of architects had increased dramatically. According to the 1891 Directory, there were 239 in West Yorkshire, ranging from 59 in Leeds, 57 in Bradford, 19 each in Halifax and Huddersfield, 14 in Wakefield, down to single representatives in such towns as Otley, Ilkley, Hebden Bridge and Honley. Yet these figures need to be treated cautiously, as they appear to have included surveyors and estate agents, as well as men in official positions in local authority offices who had not been trained as

116 *A* (1871),vi,83.

117 ibid.(1870),iv,337.

architects. Corson took up the office of President of the Leeds and Yorkshire Architectural Society again in 1897, and in his address at the opening of the 22nd session he drew attention to the increasing frequency with which architectural work, 'in former days ... confined to members of their profession ... of late years ... had drifted into the hands of the City Engineer, who was certainly not an architect'.[118] Corson was voicing a common complaint that only trained or suitably experienced men should be entitled to use the name of architect; it was a long-fought issue, to some extent settled by the Architects' (Registration) Act of 1931 'to protect the public from persons who are unqualified to exercise the profession', and the subsequent Act of 1938 which restricted the use of the title *architect* to those whose names were on the Register. For the first time in history, it was possible to define an architect; builders, engineers and talented amateurs who had played their part in the past were excluded from the profession, as Soane had argued they should be a century and a half earlier.

The reputation of a profession depends upon its training and its standards of competence, two constant topics of discussion since the formation of the Institute of British Architects in 1834. Joseph Hansom, the Yorkshire architect who founded the *Builder* in 1842, wrote in the first number of that influential journal about 'bringing together ... a number of youths and their associate teachers, probably from all quarters of the world ...; the contact of various minds, influenced by various national peculiarities, but all bent upon one comprehensive enterprise of attainment; the working together in the various practical development of progress, under practical instructors, and for practical and intelligible ends – these and a number of other circumstances of a favouring character, must conduce to a rapid progress and an extensive and sound proficiency'.[119] Hansom was an interested party in this wordy injunction, as he was in fact advertising classes he had set up, but full-time training was a long way away. The traditional system of training by pupilage, regarded as an essential element of an architectural education, was only gradually complemented and then supplanted by attendance at an evening or day school, and finally by a full-time course.[120] The obituary of Thomas Ambler, who died at the age of 82 in 1920, shows how this change had begun by the 1860s; his father, intending him to be brought up to the building trade, articled him to a well-known builder, 'but young Ambler aspired to something higher', and entered the office of George Smith, where 'he had an oppprtunity of learning about architecture, and the knowledge he gained was supplemented by attendance at classes at the old School of Art. Ultimately, while still in Mr Smith's service, he had devoted himself entirely to the designing of buildings and the drawing of plans'. In his twenty-third year Ambler set up practice in Leeds.[121]

Ambler's obituary records a typical career of a successful nineteenth-century architect; but was it the way in which to create a respected profession? 'A RESIDENT' of Leeds, in his letter to the *Architect* in 1870 about the state of the profession in that town, thought not.

118 Wilson,T.B., *Two Leeds architects*, Leeds 1937,75.

119 B (1842),i,6. 'Mr.Hansom, Architect of the Birmingham Town Hall, &c.&c., has associated with his practice an Institution to give enlarged facilities to students in Architecture and Architectural Engineering; and to form a superior class of Architectural Sculptors, carvers, Modellers, &c. to be engaged in his own office and works until competent to practise a liberal and lucrative profession ... The terms are moderate'.

120 The effect this training was having on the pupilage system can be inferred from a speech by Charles E.Milnes, President of the Bradford Society of Architects and Surveyors in 1907, in which he 'alluded to the growing competition amongst architects largely owing to the training obtainable by youths in technical colleges – and strongly advocated [limiting] the number of pupils in ... offices as one way of checking the overcrowding (BN (1907),xcii,162).

121 YP, 14 Jan 1920.

The town possesses nearly fifty architects ... The majority have received no liberal education or professional training of any sort, but have been brought up, in the first instance, to some building trade, or have assumed the title of architect solely on the strength of a smattering obtained at one of the local schools of science and art. Few of them ever travel beyond the confines of their own borough, sketching is almost entirely neglected, and for literature the professional weekly journals usually suffice. Into the hands of these gentlemen most of the work drifts, partly from the inability of the public to distinguish between false and genuine art, and in a great measure owing to the unscrupulous lengths to which many resort for the purpose of gaining practice.[122]

There could be no adequate reply to 'A RESIDENT' except an affirmation; but what form of training was available in West Yorkshire? The Leeds School of Art had held classes in building construction and architectural design ever since it was established in 1846 as a Government School of Design in which John Ruskin showed interest.[123] It had branches in Wakefield, Halifax and Ackworth, and later in Keighley, Bradford and Huddersfield. There was a modelling class for carvers and architectural students, and it was possible to attend a 'Mechanical or Architectural Class' for two evenings a week for a fee of four shillings a quarter. The completion of Brodrick's new Institute in 1865 enabled the classes to be extended, and the 1885 Annual Report noted that 'in the matter of Architectural Drawing there are always a few good students who, with infinite pains and application, produce work reflecting credit on themselves and the School'. In 1899 there were thirty-three pupils as students, and their syllabus included three main subjects: *Architecture*, the classical orders, historic styles and terms in use, with the warning that 'candidates cannot be too strongly impressed that architecture consists of buildings, not of representations of them'; *Architectural design*, including planning, proportion and 'skill in the putting together of the parts of a design'; *Building construction and drawing*, materials, construction, mechanics and draughtsmanship. In 1902 the Leeds and Yorkshire Architectural Society (then negotiating with the proposed University of Leeds for the establishment of a Chair of Architecture) agreed to collaborate in these part-time classes, and the President assured his colleagues that when Bedford and Kitson's new School of Art was opened, 'there will exist in the city of Leeds a School of Architecture which should justify its title'.[124] In 1915 the courses and examinations were recognised by the Royal Institute of British Architects for exemption from its Intermediate examination, and fourteen years later from its Final; but the establishment of a University Chair proved elusive and tantalising until it was finally dispelled in 1968 when the School became a department in the new Polytechnic. For many years the Bradford College of Art organised a part-time course, which came to an end in the late 1960s during the national reorganisation of Higher Education. On the other hand, the course which was inaugurated at Huddersfield School of Art in 1921 became a part of the Huddersfield Polytechnic when it was founded in 1970; five years later it was recognised for exemption from the RIBA Part I examination.

122 A (1870),lv,337.

123 A class in drawing and design was begun at the Huddersfield Mechanics' Institution in 1842, to which were shortly added classes in mechanical drawing, architectural drawing and modelling. One lecturer defined his aim of furnishing 'elevations and ground plans such as are used in this neighbourhood, in preference to those engraved designs in brick, of houses and buildings around London, which are at present in use'; modest though that seems, it is worth noting that three-quarters of the class members were in the cabinet and joinery business. In Bradford, a drawing class started in 1841 also developed into a school of design, and by 1850 there were 31 members of the mechanical and architectural drawing class; but on the whole, such classes were not intended to train to a professional standard. It could hardly be expected that from them could 'spring a James Watt or a Christopher Wren, a Simpson or a Davy, yet from them come supervisors of railway works, foremen of foundries and machine-makers' establishments, and "clerks of the works" at the erection of great public buildings'. (*Chambers's papers for the people* (1850),iii,20).

124 *Yorkshire Daily Observer*, 7 Nov 1902; see Linstrum,D., 'The phantom chair', *YP*, 5 Mar 1968.

Corson's Presidential address in 1897 had also drawn attention to the unsatisfactory position of architects who worked in a public office, usually under an engineer. The battle for recognition of the independent status of the official architect was long, and it was not accomplished without opposition from private practitioners. Bradford Corporation appointed a City Architect in 1901, and five years later there was a statement 'intended to show that a considerable saving had been effected by the establishment . . . of the City Architect's Department, and the consequent carrying out of much architectural work by him instead of by architects in private practice'. There were objections to this by local architects, who held a meeting under the chairmanship of T.C. Hope; they had a beautiful art gallery in the Cartwright Memorial Hall, he said, but with a great deal of bare wall to cover. 'Was there any man in the Town Hall who would dare to suggest that we should create a picture department, and engage a municipalised painter who, with his assistants, should cover these bare walls with paintings?'[125] The *Builder* supported the private architects, upholding standards of design and thinking: 'If we are to regard architecture as an art and not a mere ratepayers' business, the parallel is perfectly logical'. Nor was the official architect's cause served by such an opinion as Sir Raymond Unwin's that 'where there is scope for fresh ideas of design leading to an advance in architectural planning, the outside architect is more likely to be successful and to contribute than one who is cumbered about with much serving'.[126] The status of the municipal architect remained an anomaly until after the Second World War when the other West Yorkshire county boroughs and the West Riding County Council[127] set up separate architects' departments as Bradford had done in 1901.

According to the 1977 issue of the *RIBA Directory* there are 109 practices in West Yorkshire. This appears low when compared with the figures in nineteenth-century town directories, but it emphasises the tendency for practices to be composed of relatively large groups of partners and associates, as well as illustrating how much work is executed today by architects in the public service. A general disillusionment with the environment of the 70s, frequently shared by architects themselves, has resulted in public criticism of the profession and self-searching within the headquarters of the Royal Institute of British Architects. Possibly a future historian will see the present decades as a period of transition from an admirable nineteenth-century ideal of professionalism to a different role that has yet to be defined. When Ernest William Beckett MP opened the new School of Art in Leeds in 1903, he reminded his audience that his 'distinguished relative'[128] had 'impressed upon him as one of the maxims of life, "Don't put your faith in architects"'; but, maybe wiser than his uncle, Lord Grimthorpe, he recognised 'we could not all be our own architects, and we must put our faith – a guarded faith, perhaps – in somebody'. So far, no better candidate has been proposed.

125 *B* (1906),xci,366.

126 *RIBA Journal* (1935),xliii,862.

127 The West Riding County Architect's Department disappeared in 1974 as a result of Local Government reorganisation; see 'Requiem for an office', *AJ* (1974),clix,1235ff.

128 *YP*, 9 Oct 1903; Ernest William Beckett was the nephew of the 1st Lord Grimthorpe (his 'distinguished relative') and succeeded him in 1905 as 2nd Baron. Less well known for his architectural interests, he did nevertheless build a curious pastiche at Ravello early in this century with the assistance (so it is said) of a waiter called Nicolo Mansi who offered his services as amateur architect. He named it Villa Cimbrone, and constructed it mostly out of old fragments; the lower storey overlooking the Bay of Salerno is a small crypt traditionally said to have been based on the *cellarium* of Fountains Abbey. The 2nd Baron, who died in 1917, is reputed to have been buried in the pseudo-classical temple of Bacchus on one of the terraces of his Mediterranean villa.

2　Great estates and country houses

Of all the great things that the English have invented and made a part of the credit of the national character, the most perfect, the most characteristic, the one they have mastered most completely in all its details . . . is the well-appointed, well-administered, well-filled country house. The grateful stranger makes these reflections . . . as he wanders about in the beautiful library of such a dwelling, of an inclement winter afternoon, just at the hour when six o'clock tea is impending.

Henry James in 1879 on Fryston Hall, Lord Houghton's Yorkshire seat.

'If you builde a new house remember that I tell you itt is a matter wherein you may shew a great deale and a great want of discretion, itt being nothing soe easy a thing to builde well as men take it to bee that know it not, and therefore at your perill look well about you'.[1] The advice of Thomas Wentworth, 1st Earl of Strafford, to his kinsman Michael Wentworth of Woolley, was timely considering the number of houses being built during the late sixteenth and early seventeenth centuries. Fortunes were being made, state appointments were bringing their titular rewards, estates were changing hands, and as always the standing of the owners was reflected in their houses. 'Considering that your houses, in my judgement, are not suitable to your quality, nor yet your plate and furniture', wrote the great Earl to his nephew Sir George Savile of Thornhill, 'I conceive your expence ought to be reduced to two thirds of your estate, and the rest saved to the accommodating of you in that kind'.[2]

Strafford himself had set an example in Yorkshire by building additions on the King's Manor, his official York residence as Lord President of the Council in the North,[3] and by making alterations and improvements to Wentworth Woodhouse, his ancestral estate, and Gawthorp Hall, the old home of the Gascoignes which he had acquired through marriage. From the latter he wrote in 1624 of the content he found in country-house life, 'Our harvest is all in; a most fine season to make fishponds; our plums all gone and past; peaches, quinces, and grapes almost fully ripe . . . These only we countrymen muse of, hoping in such harmless retirements for a just defence from the higher powers . . . possessing ourselves in contentment'.[4] At Gawthorp he made new apartments 'all wainscotted . . . and collored like wallnut tree', but his major work in West Yorkshire was the extension of Ledston Hall, which he bought from William Witham in 1629. Strafford was building too in Ireland, where he held the appointment of Lord Deputy; but while his plans were being executed in Dublin, Cosha and Naas, where he was erecting a magnificent house that was intended to exceed in size

1 Wentworth,G.E., *MS history of the Wentworths of Woolley, compiled from papers and letters found at Woolley.* Brotherton Library, University of Leeds, Wentworth-Woolley Hall papers, BV 36/1.15.

2 Knowler,W.(ed), *The Earl of Strafford's letters and despatches*, London 1739,i,170.

3 R.C.H.M., *City of York*, London 1975, iv, 170.

4 Whitaker, 165. Sir Thomas Wentworth to Sir George Calvert, 31 Aug 1624.

47

the Cecils' Hatfield House,[5] his fellow landowners were working on their architectural aggrandisements in West Yorkshire. The Wentworths and the Saviles, two families with ramifications which spread all over the West Riding and entwined in most of the county family trees, were in the forefront.

The Wentworths were great builders. Their architectural ambition was to reach its height in South Yorkshire in the early eighteenth century when rival branches strove to outdo one another at Wentworth Woodhouse and Stainborough (Wentworth Castle), but it was liable to break out at any time in any one of the numerous branches. Strafford's daughter complained that the workmen engaged on the extension of the King's Manor did not pay any attention to their work unless she was superintending them, although she was only four years old.[6] A century earlier, Sir Thomas Wentworth of West Bretton had commemorated his marriage to Isabell, daughter of Thomas Wentworth of Elmsall, in the 1530s by furnishing one of the rooms of his house with an oak bed and cupboard of outstandingly fine workmanship which incorporated an impressive display of armorial pride.[7] There is no record of the appearance of this house, although an inventory of Sir Thomas's household effects taken after his death in 1542 suggests it was not large; possibly it was comparable with Lees Hall, Thornhill, or Shibden Hall, two fifteenth-century timber-framed houses with a central hall, screens passage, and cross-wings containing a kitchen and parlour. In 1599, Michael Wentworth bought the Manor of Woolley from Francis Woodrove; with it he acquired the 'House . . . with gardens orchards and courtes', which was rebuilt in the 1630s, probably as an H-shaped plan with a near-central entrance to the screens passage. It was constructed of stone, with a roughly regular arrangement of mullioned and transomed windows, and the cross wings and entrance bay were crowned with Flemish gables.[8] There are some similarities to Strafford's rebuilding of Ledston, and in 1635 Michael Wentworth wrote to his famous kinsman, who had cautioned him to 'look well about' before starting to build, hoping to see him at 'our newe house att Woolley . . . before I dye'.[9]

In the great building period which started at the end of the sixteenth century, the genealogically complicated Savile family played an important role. They possessed great estates; for example, when Sir Henry Savile died in 1558 his properties consisted of '300 messuages, 300 tofts, 10 water-mills, and 22,080 acres, in which were not included the extensive wastes and commons, which in the parish of Halifax alone amounted perhaps to as much more'.[10] Sir John Savile, of another branch of the family, rebuilt Bradley Hall, Stainland in 1577–1604, employing the masons John and Abraham Akroyd; the house was largely destroyed by fire in 1629, but it is known that the masons incorporated in the stone façade a large wheel window made up of six circles revolving around a seventh in the centre. This might have been the first example of what was to become a unique feature of seventeenth-century houses in the Halifax–Bradford area. Although Robert Smythson made designs for similar geometric patterns which express an Elizabethan delight in formal shapes and intricate

5 Wedgwood,C.V., *Thomas Wentworth, first Earl of Strafford 1593–1641: a revaluation*, London 1961,225f.; see Craig,M., 'New light on Jigginstown', *Ulster journal of archaeology* (1970),xxxiii,107ff.

6 Knowler, op.cit.,i,55.

7 These furnishings are now at Temple Newsam, Leeds. See Linstrum,D., 'Two Wentworth houses', *LAC* (1971),no.68,5ff.

8 I am grateful to Mr Geoffrey Markham, who showed me his draft article on the history of Woolley Hall. The gables were remodelled or restored c.1814 by George Woodhead, but it is believed they were very similar in design in the seventeenth century.

9 Letter of 13 May 1635 from Thomas Wentworth, Earl of Strafford to Michael Wentworth, Sheffield City Libraries, W.W.M. (Wentworth Woodhouse Muniments) Str.P.15(68), quoted by permission of Earl Fitzwilliam and his Trustees.

10 Whitaker, 312.

12

13

12. Shibden Hall; constructed as a timber-framed H-plan house in the early fifteenth century, its present-day appearance is due principally to the alterations and restorations of the 1830s (J.Harper).

13. Woolley Hall; rebuilt in the 1630s, the house was altered in the late eighteenth and early nineteenth centuries. In this drawing (G.Woodhead 1814) the original house is in the centre, and the later alterations can be seen clearly.

14. Wood Lane Hall, Sowerby (1649) has preserved the elaborate finials on the gables and battlements, and the wheel window over the porch entrance, which is identical to one at New Hall, Elland.

15. Methley Hall; the sixteenth-century house was partly remodelled in 1778 (J.Carr), and again in 1830–6 (A.Salvin), when Carr's façade was replaced by the turreted design seen in this photograph of the 1880s.

16. Howley Hall; built c.1590, and demolished c.1730. This late eighteenth-century engraving was made from a painting (present provenance unknown), of which the author is suggested to have been John Settrington.

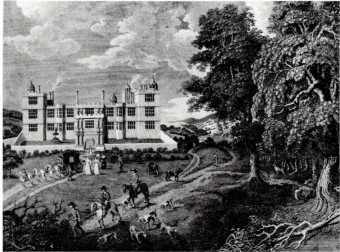

11 RIBA Drawings Collection *Catalogue*, vol.S/94.29,30. Repd. Girouard,M., *Robert Smythson and the architecture of the Elizabethan era*, London 1966, pls.4,90.

12 Ambler,L., *The old halls and manor houses of Yorkshire*, London 1913,25.

13 Hansom,T.W., 'Halifax builders in Oxford', *H A S* (1920),253ff.

14 Camden,W., *Britannia . . . enlarged by the latest discoveries by Richard Gough*, London 1789,iii,41. The castellated character suggests a comparison with two Smythson designs, Bolsover (started 1613, probably to John Smythson's plans) and Slingsby (built c.1630 to John's design although Robert had made designs c.1599).

15 See Crump,W.B., 'Methley Hall and its builders', *T S* (1945),xxxvii,313ff. Detached banqueting houses have rarely survived, but a fine late sixteenth-century example may be seen at Weston Hall, near Otley. This is three-storeyed, with a projecting bay and armorial panels. It was built by Sir Mauger le Vavasour.

16 Atkinson,D.H., *Ralph Thoresby the topographer: his town and times*, Leeds 1887,ii,146f. The screen was dismantled when the house was being demolished, and it is stored at Temple Newsam.

17 Whitaker, pl.opp.238; Scatcherd,N., *The history of Morley*, Morley 1874,115ff. Howley Hall's end was extraordinary; in 1730 'by the false representations of a designing agent . . . to the Earl of Cardigan, then its owner, an order was given for its demolition; that mad mandate was carried into effect. The colossal masses which composed the angles were blown up with gunpowder, immense quantities of its wrought stone were dispersed through Morley, Birstall, Batley and the neighbouring hamlets; many rooms at Wakefield were adorned with the wainscotting, and the Presbyterian meeting house at Bradford was fitted up with the same material' (Parsons, i,348).

18 Parsons,D., *The diary of Sir Henry Slingsby, Bart.*, London 1836,52. 'Let a man propose to himself never so great matters', wrote Slingsby, 'yet shall another come yt may exceed him & go beyond him; if he build his house like Nebuchodonoser yt he may say, is not this great Babell yt I have built, if another yt shall exceed him come, he shall think yt all vain wch he hath done or made' (op.cit.,45). 'I shall ever disuade my son from affecting building, unless it be wth great moderation . . . I have observ'd how it hath done so ill wth many: some after having laiden ye foundation of an house, have faint'd under it, & so left it; others having build'd it, selleth it, as he who selleth his horse to defray ye charges of it; others, conciet'd of their invention, are not at rest till they vent it' (op.cit.,45). This diary

'ingenious devices',[11] it seems to have been only in the Pennine area of West Yorkshire that they were used as windows. It is very likely that many of these houses were the work of one family or closely related group of masons, and certainly one design for a wheel window is repeated on three different houses, and another on two.[12] As the Akroyds have been shown to have worked at Bradley (and at Heath School where there is yet another of these windows)[13] they are obvious contenders. One of the identical pair can be found at Wood Lane Hall, Sowerby; the other is at New Hall, Elland, a Savile property since the fifteenth century, and the Akroyds are believed to have been employed on yet another of the family possessions which showed many of the Halifax characteristics.

This was Methley Hall, which Sir John Savile bought from the Watertons after he had started work at Bradley. He largely rebuilt the fifteenth-century house from 1588 onwards, leaving his son Sir Henry to complete it in 1612, by which time it appeared like 'a castle round a square court. In the front were three towers, that in the middle through which the grand staircase was, and another tower at each end of the front'.[14] There was a walled forecourt with an entrance gateway, and a drawbridge which survived until the eighteenth century, but this semi-fortified character was not in evidence on the west front which was more in the Halifax domestic tradition, nor in the small banqueting or summer house which was built immediately outside the enclosure.[15] Methley's principal rooms were a Great Hall, in which was a notable carved screen of two superimposed orders, and a Long Gallery in which the painted glass in four ten-light windows was filled with a rich display of Yorkshire armorial splendour, 'the nobility and gentry . . . marshalled according to the Wapenstakes in the several Ridings'.[16]

Methley became the chief seat of the main branch of the family, but another Sir John Savile (later Baron Savile of Pontefract and first Mayor of Leeds), Strafford's implacable enemy at Court, was the head of an illegitimate branch. His principal seat was at Howley, where he was building at exactly the same time as his relative at Methley, but on a bigger scale. The date 1590 is said to have been seen in several places in the long-demolished house which was built in a semi-fortified style around an open courtyard sixty yards square. There were square corner towers, three storeys high, and in the centre of the main front was an entrance porch framed with superimposed coupled orders. Like Methley, Howley had a walled forecourt, entered through a gateway which repeated the design of the porch.[17] It was an ambitious design, intended to impress, and no doubt other Yorkshire landowners were watching its progress critically or enviously. Sir Henry Slingsby of Redhouse wrote, 'We see an emulation in ye structure of our houses, if we behold yt at Tibbalds, and yt of my Ld of Suffolk's at Audley End: So, in this country my Ld Everie's at Maulton; my Ld Savil's at Howley: Sr Arthur Ingram's at Temple Newson'.[18]

A few miles away from Methley, a smaller house was being built c.1585 on a hilltop south of Wakefield by John Kaye, Deputy Steward

17. **Heath Old Hall; J.C. Buckler's watercolour shows the c.1585 house as it was in 1813.**

18. **Pontefract New Hall; built c.1591, but in a ruinous condition in 1885 when this photograph was taken.**

17

18

includes a rare description of early seventeenth-century decoration: 'Edward Horseley a Painter in York is now painting ye lodging chamber above ye new Parlour, in colours suitable to those hangings I have bought to hang it wth all. Y^e hangings I bought of Peter Pope in Bednall Greene, as also those y^t are in ye with-drawing Roome to ye new Parlour, wherein ye 9 Muses are. Those in ye Lodgin chamber are calfe skins silver'd, & wrought upon wth a large flower in blew worstett; they come short of ye ground having ye breath of a pannell of wainscot below y^m & a frieze & cornish above y^m. The chimney peice is paint'd answerable in blew & sylver' (op.cit.,5).

19 Girouard, op.cit.,109ff; Green, Lady, *The old hall at Heath, 1568–1888*, Wakefield 1889.

20 Girouard, op.cit.,137f; Tew,T.W., *Miscellaneous papers*, Pontefract 1892,136ff. The latter reference suggests that old material from St John's Priory was used in the building of the house. Tew also believed there was an entrance hall 'of noble proportions' on the ground floor, state apartments on the first, and a gallery ninety feet long on the second.

of the Honour of Pontefract under Sir Henry Savile of Thornhill.[19] This was Heath (Old) Hall, and once again there was a family connection; Sir Henry's daughter was Kaye's mistress and bore him seven children before their union was legalised. The similarity of Heath to Barlborough Hall, the Derbyshire house attributed to Robert Smythson, has inevitably caused his name to be suggested as the designer of the Yorkshire house. Its battlemented square form with a projecting central entrance bay and two octagonal turret-bays rising high above the balustraded parapet stood proudly on its open site overlooking Wakefield; the Long Gallery was placed along the entrance front over the Hall, and the Great Chamber was at right angles to the former on the first floor. A similar house was Kippax Hall, built by Sir Thomas Bland *c.*1589, but extensively remodelled in the seventeenth and eighteenth centuries; this too seems to have been square in plan with projecting square and canted bays, and it fitted into what can be seen as a distinctive group of West Yorkshire houses which might have been influenced by Robert Smythson. Certainly, they were all within a short distance of Pontefract New Hall, built by Edward Talbot, later 8th Earl of Shrewsbury, around 1591. This important, though largely forgotten, Yorkshire house is believed to have been built from a Smythson design, a likely event since Talbot's stepmother was the indefatigable Bess of Hardwick.[20] Like the latter's superb house in Derbyshire, Pontefract was a building with square towers rising above the parapet, and large mullioned windows; but the arrangement of bays and recesses, of windows and walls, betrayed a nervous tension absent in the serenely shifting modelling of Hardwick's towers and glittering façades.

This was a notable West Yorkshire group; but Howley was demolished in 1730, Methley in 1950, Heath in 1960, Kippax in 1965 and Pontefract in 1961. Temple Newsam and Ledston alone remain to recall the quality of these Elizabethan-Jacobean houses, and both are more interesting today because of their later additions and remodellings. Temple Newsam must always have stood supremely overlooking the Aire valley. The historic property of the Knights Templar came into the possession of Lord Darcy of Temple Hurst in

21 Gilbert,C.G., 'Light on Sir Arthur Ingram's reconstruction of Temple Newsam 1622–38', *LAC* (1963),no.51,6ff; Fawcett,R., 'The early Tudor house in the light of recent excavations', ibid.(1972),no.70,5ff.

22 Darcy was executed as a result of the part he played in the Pilgrimage of Grace; his estates were confiscated by the Crown, and in 1554 Henry VIII gave Temple Newsam to Matthew, Earl of Lennox, husband of his niece Margaret Tudor. Their son, Henry Stuart, Lord Darnley, who married Mary Queen of Scots in 1565, was born and educated in the house. After the imprisonment of the Countess of Lennox by Elizabeth I, Temple Newsam was once again confiscated by the Crown. James I gave it to Ludovick, Duke of Lennox, who sold it to Sir Arthur Ingram for £12,000.

23 These figures were still in position in 1808 when Lady Wharncliffe visited Lady Hertford and noted that 'on each side of the porch one goes in at, stand two statues of Knights Templars'. She 'was delighted with [the] old house, the shape of a half H', and especially with 'the balustrade round the top, composed of a *quotation* from Scripture, the letters of iron, each a yard high, and appearing no more than a foot from below'. Grosvenor,C., and Beilby,C.(ed), *The first Lady Wharncliffe and her family (1779–1856)*, London 1927,i,152. However, the inscription is not from Holy Writ, but reads: ALL GLORY AND PRAISE BE GIVEN TO GOD THE FATHER THE SON AND HOLY GHOST ON HIGH PEACE ON EARTH GOOD WILL TOWARDS MEN HONOUR AND TRUE ALLEGIANCE TO OUR GRACIOUS KING LOVING AFFECTION AMONGST HIS SUBJECTS HEALTH AND PLENTY BE WITHIN THIS HOUSE. These letters were originally carved out of stone; they were replaced by iron copies in 1788.

1488, and between that date and his execution in 1537 he built a house which appears to have been designed around a large, central courtyard entered through a gateway in the north wing and facing the Great Hall in the middle of the south wing.[21] To the west were the private apartments, in the wing which seems to have been least altered when the house was remodelled after 1622. In that year the estate was bought by Sir Arthur Ingram, a business man of dubious honesty but great wealth, with whom Strafford was politically allied at Court in opposition to Sir John Savile of Howley. Ingram's rebuilding was so extensive that little evidence is left of Darcy's work; nor is it certain how much of the latter's grand design had been achieved before his execution, nor what, if anything, the Earl of Lennox built during the time he owned Temple Newsam.[22] Yet it is worth noting that the central section of the west wing, obviously different in date from the rest of the fabric of the present house, would correspond in many ways to the turreted, square form of Heath, Kippax, and Ledston in its pre-Strafford form.

Ingram demolished the east wing of Temple Newsam and largely rebuilt the north and south wings, incorporating the Great Hall and Chapel in his own structure, which is to all appearance a Jacobean house, crowned with a loyal and pious sentiment in giant letters in the balustrade. A direct reference to the antiquity of the site, which the new owner probably assumed he had acquired with the property, was made by placing two large figures of Knights Templars as supporters to the pediment over the main entrance.[23] A series of projecting bays creates an effect of ordered variety in the external aspect, but the sense of tension and drama in the great Elizabethan houses is lacking; there

19. Temple Newsam; the south-west corner of the courtyard, as rebuilt after 1622. The central section on the right probably incorporates fabric of the earlier (1488–1537) house; the Classical cupola was added in 1796.

is a feeling that this is the close of a tradition, as indeed it was in the 1620s. Looking at the stone mullioned bays and brick walls with stone quoins, it is necessary to be reminded that Inigo Jones's Banqueting House in Whitehall was completed in the year Ingram bought the Temple Newsam estate. The only part of his rebuilding which appears to have been influenced by the new Italian fashion was a two-storeyed Banqueting House south-west of the house, shown in a Knyff-Kip view but demolished long ago.[24]

Ingram's ambitious pile overshadowed all other West Yorkshire houses, but it is possible to see Strafford's projected remodelling of Ledston as a rival. Between 1629 and the day in November 1641 when he set off for London 'with more danger beset, I believe, than ever man went with out of Yorkshire', the Lord President of the Council in the North had been extending the square Elizabethan house which incorporated a thirteenth-century chapel.[25] The first addition was a wing to the south with a symmetrical elevation and central first-floor entrance; then a larger one to the north which probably included some earlier service buildings. The final result (although when it was achieved is not known for certain) was a house built around three sides of a courtyard and with an entrance into a Great Hall in the centre of the east front; it has some obvious and not surprising similarities to Strafford's ancestral home, Wentworth Woodhouse, as it was at that time. There is a tradition that the workmen engaged on the building threw down their tools and left when they heard of Strafford's arrest, and the top floor of the north-west wing to this day suggests a partly finished Long Gallery, leading one to suppose Wentworth probably completed building much of the shell of the house before his death. The scrolled and pedimented gables,[26] which are a prominent feature of the

20

21

24 Wild,D.G., and Gilbert,C.G., 'Excavation of garden banqueting house', *L A C* (1967),no.60,4ff. The building accounts show that the house was richly decorated with ornamental plasterwork and paintings. It was probably demolished by 'Capability' Brown in the 1760s.

25 Oswald,A., 'Ledston Hall', *C L* (1938), lxxxiv,556ff,580ff.

26 This form of gable first appeared in England in the houses of Sir Fulke Greville and Lady Coke in Holborn, both recorded by John Smythson on his London visit in 1618–9; Girouard, op.cit.,185; Faulkner,P.A., *Bolsover Castle*, London 1972,23. On the whole, the evidence at Ledston supports the theory that Strafford built at least some of these gables, if not all; maybe Lewis added the rest for the sake of symmetry.

20. Ledston Hall from the south east, showing the corner towers and scrolled, pedimented gables of the seventeenth-century building, from which time the entrance gateway dates. The diagonally placed lodges were added c.1720, probably at the time the mullioned, transomed windows were replaced by sashes.

21. Ledston Hall; the Elizabethan house, the central part of the building, is slightly to the left of centre of the west front shown in this painting by John Settrington (1728). To the left, at the end of the terrace, is the garden-house c.1720.

27 Ambler, op.cit.; this is still the best history of these houses, as it includes some which have disappeared since 1913, as well as many valuable measured drawings and carefully recorded details. The following articles should also be referred to: Stell,C.F., 'Pennine houses: an introduction', *Folk Life* (1965),iii,5ff; Atkinson,F., and McDowall,R.W., 'Aisled houses in the Halifax area', *Antiquaries Journal* (1967), xlvii,77ff.

28 Wood Lane Hall, Sowerby (owned by John Dearden 1649), Norland Hall (John Taylor 1672), Horton Hall (Thomas Sharp 1676) and West Riddlesden Hall (Thomas Leach 1687) were given as examples, to which can be added New Hall, Elland (John Foxcroft 1640), Shibden Hall (built by the O(a)tes family in the fifteenth century), and several others. The demolition of Elland Old Hall in 1976 revealed that much of the original fourteenth-century framing existed behind the rebuilt façades.

29 Typical examples are Oakwell Hall (owned by John Batt 1583); Shibden Hall; Linthwaite Hall (built by the Linthwaite family c.1600 and added to by the Lockwoods after 1615); Woodsome Hall (sixteenth century, enlarged in 1600 and 1644); Royds Hall (begun 1548, rebuilt by William Rookes 1640), and Pollard Hall, Gomersal (Tempest Pollard 1659).

exterior, are similar to those at Bolsover Castle which date from about the time Strafford bought the Ledston estate; possibly he consulted John or Huntingdon Smythson, who were working at Bolsover as well as at Welbeck where there were similar gables on the Riding School. But it is not possible to establish with any certainty what the house looked like in 1653 when it was sold to Sir John Lewis, who had made a fortune during his nine years as factor for the East India Company.

Yet, in spite of its size and the fashionable gables which set Ledston apart from other West Yorkshire country houses, it is immediately recognisable as being closely related to the group built in the Pennine area between 1600 and the Civil War, or even until the end of the century. These were not quite country houses, but manor houses and the residences of clothiers who had made a moderate fortune from their part in the domestic industry and combined their activities with farming. Many of these houses had been built of timber in the fifteenth or sixteenth century, either as aisled halls or as a central hall with solar, cross-passage and service rooms. When Louis Ambler was writing his classic work on these buildings[27] more than sixty years ago, he noted several stone houses in which remains of timber framing could be seen, or which were obviously recasings.[28]

The most common form of these Pennine houses is one with a large central hall, often open to the roof and having a screened cross-passage at one end, and a gabled wing at each side. This produced a generally long, low house built of millstone grit with stone slates on a low-pitched roof, and a characteristic elevation of low, wide gables and a large central window of three, four or even seven lights.[29] Some houses had projecting entrance bays, and some had doorways with widely spaced flanking columns and entablatures which are vigorously ungrammatical according to the Classical rules but closely related, nevertheless, to those on grander houses, such as Burton Agnes, in other parts of Yorkshire. There are the wheel windows already referred

23

22

55

22. Woodsome Hall (c.1582–1600), a relatively unaltered house in which the entrance front opens on to a paved, balustraded terrace.

23. Wood Lane Hall, Sowerby; the window to the left of the doorway (pl.14) lights the single-storey hall, which has preserved its mid-seventeenth-century appearance.

30 Wheel windows can be found on Barkisland Hall (owned by John Gledhill 1632); New Hall, Elland; East Riddlesden Hall (James Murgatroyd 1642); Wood Lane Hall, Sowerby; Kershaw House, Luddenden (either Midgley or Murgatroyd 1650); Lumb Hall, Drighlington (Brookes family, mid seventeenth century), and Horton Hall.

7

24

to,[30] and other local features such as stepped mullion windows, elliptical windows, and Gothic survivals with ogee tops; and there is an inexhaustible variety of door heads in which contrasting curves appear in every conceivable combination in the shaping of the soffits of the lintels, which more often than not conveniently incorporate the initials of the owner and the date of building.

This vigorous Pennine tradition continued throughout the seventeenth century, with occasional surprises like the long, flat, battlemented façade of Abraham Sunderland's demolished High Sunderland (1629) which stood like a theatre backcloth on the moors near Halifax, its large mullioned windows reflecting the light, and its

26. Scout Hall (1680); the arrangement of five windows on each side of a central doorway suggests a knowledge of Caroline houses elsewhere, although the symmetry was broken by the elliptical windows. (Horner, J., *Buildings in the town and parish of Halifax*, 1835)

31 Omnipotent faxet, stirps Sunderlandia sedes/Incolet has placide, & tueatur jura parentum,/Lite vacans, donec fluctus formica marinos/Ebibat & totum Testudo perambulet orbem!
High Sunderland was demolished in 1950; part of the decorative stonework, including the gateway, is in the possession of the Halifax Museum.

Opposite:

24. High Sunderland (1629); unlike the majority of West Yorkshire houses of this date, which are gabled, the main front was topped by a balustraded parapet and crocketed pinnacles corbelled out on human masks. (Horner, J., *Buildings in the town and parish of Halifax*, 1835)

25. Knowsthorpe (or Knostrop) Hall; the pilastered porch of this late seventeenth-century house was unusually on the central axis of the hall, facing the fireplace, and this formality was emphasised by the approach between gate-posts surmounted by diagonally set obelisks and flanked by ornamental seats. (Watercolour by J. Greig, 1857)

intricately arabesqued Classical gateway at an angle to the main front like a proscenium entrance through which a procession of actors was about to enter. Everything connected with this isolated building was dramatic, from the gigantic figures over the entrance and on the Banqueting House attached to the main building, to the Latin inscription on the south front which supplicated the Almighty, with vivid imagery, to allow the race of Sunderland to 'quietly inhabit this seat . . . until an ant drink up the waters of the sea, and a tortoise walk round the whole world'.[31]

Towards the close of the century a more disciplined design was emerging. The partly demolished west wing of East Riddlesden Hall, built by Edmund Starkie in 1692, has pediments over regularly spaced four-light windows with moulded architraves, which light the 'piano nobile'; at Knowsthorpe Hall, the porch of the Baynes's demolished late seventeenth-century house was built in the centre of the Hall façade (instead of in the traditional position at one end) so that the elevation could be axially balanced; and Scout Hall, built for John Mitchell in 1680, is at first glance (even in its ruinous state) a rectangular house with a symmetrical three-storeyed façade and a hipped roof. There are no gables, no porches, no multi-light windows, although a closer look reveals that there are still many Pennine features and that the symmetry is illusory; but Scout Hall represents the closing of a tough regional tradition which had been consistent throughout the range of houses from small manors to great mansions.

The new fashion which reached West Yorkshire at the end of the seventeenth century can be seen in such a design as Austhorpe Hall (1694), a rectangular brick house with a regular pattern of

57

27. Austhorpe Hall (1694) represents a break with the West Yorkshire tradition in the use of brick, and the adoption of a symmetrical plan with a central hall.

28. Eshald House, Heath (1694–1703); the view in the Warburton Sketchbook (1718/19 attrib. Samuel Buck) shows the tall, square design with turret-like corner chimneys, and a domed cupola rising behind the roof balustrades. The garden-house on the right, like the house itself, was presumably designed by the owner.

29. Tong Hall (T.Shelton 1702) was altered c.1780 when an additional storey was built. This engraving by Jan Kip of a drawing by Leonard Knyff (*Britannia Illustrata*, 1707–15) usefully recorded the garden design.

30. Whitley Beaumont; the north façade, a Baroque design probably executed or designed by Thomas Mann after 1680.

31. Ledston Hall; C.Bridgeman's design for elaborating the formal garden east of the house.

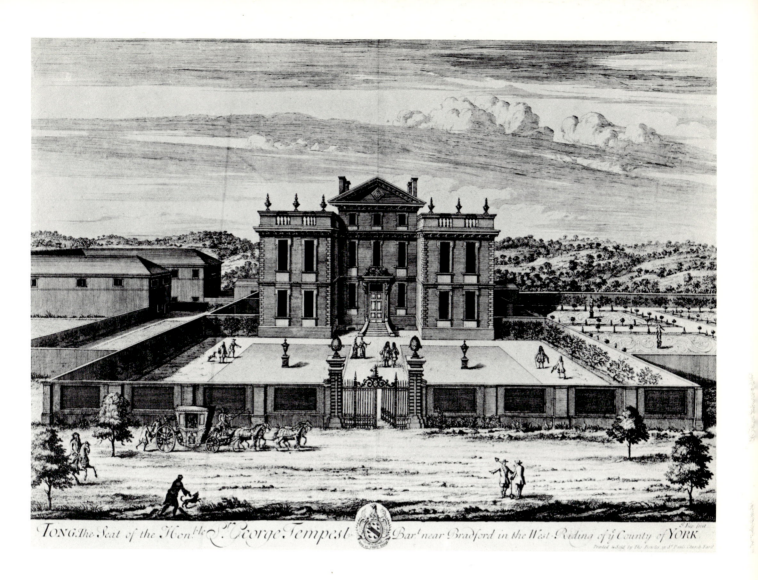

TONG, the Seat of the Hon.ble S.r George Tempest Bar.t near Bradford in the West Riding of y.e County of YORK

fenestration, stone quoins and dressings, and a pedimented doorway. There are several houses of this character in the Leeds–Bradford–Wakefield area, of which the finest is Sir George Tempest's Tong Hall, built in 1702 after the earlier timber-framed house had been burnt down in 1700. An inscribed stone tablet on the south front records that Theophilus Shelton, Registrar of Deeds in the West Riding, was its designer, and it can be assumed he also designed his own house on the estate he bought at Heath in 1694. Eshald House, as he called his property, was a square house crowned with a balustraded parapet and a domed cupola;[32] like Tong, it incorporated windows linked vertically by panels, and the same characteristic appears on Esholt Hall, built in 1706–09 for Walter Calverley,[33] Austhorpe Hall, and other houses in the area. There is no evidence that Shelton spent his time designing houses for his friends, but it is very likely that he provided his brother-in-law, Richard Witton, with the plans for Lupset Hall, near Wakefield;[34] built in 1716, the house is similar to Tong, with the exception of the latter's central pediment and the addition of an ashlar centrepiece. Maybe he also made the design for a building with a cupola (referred to as an observatory) at Clubcliff (or Clumpcliffe) Hall, Methley for John Savile, and for Daniel Maude's Alverthorpe Hall, near Wakefield,[35] a house in which a tablet inserted in the wall philosophically expresses the confidence of a man who has built for posterity:

NUNC MEA, MOX HUJUS, SED POSTEA, NESCIO CUJUS (Now mine, then thine, but afterwards I know not whose).

Tong Hall, a house in which there was an early use of sash windows (probably in imitation of those specified in 1697/8 for the Duke of Leeds's house, Kiveton Park), is a sophisticated design for its date in West Yorkshire. The strong vertical emphasis and the relatively narrow central section flanked by projecting lower wings produced a tensely balanced façade. There is no explanation of how Shelton acquired a knowledge of architecture; possibly he had visited the Low Countries or possessed engravings of Dutch houses. Architectural books from Holland and France were frequently quoted sources, and reference has already been made to John Etty's request to borrow Sir Godfrey Copley's copy of Jean Marot's *L'Architecture Française*. Robert Hooke, Wren's colleague in the Royal Society and in the rebuilding of the City churches, bought such books for his own valuable library, and the design he made for additions to the 1st Earl of Burlington's Yorkshire house, Londesborough, was apparently influenced by Dutch examples. Hooke probably never visited the county, and his plan was executed by Thomas Mann of York, who also made architectural designs. In 1680 he sent Richard Beaumont a drawing of proposed additions to Whitley Beaumont, a house which had been remodelled at the end of the sixteenth century and had a Great Hall in the middle of the south front, flanked by wings to east and west of a courtyard. Mann's plan appears to be the original of the 'new and magnificent front' which incorporated a centrepiece with giant pilasters and a segmental pediment. On the inner face, there was 'an arcade of stone connecting the different apartments'.[36]

28

29

30

32 British Museum, Warburton Sketchbook Landsdowne MS 914, 97V. Others in this group of late seventeenth-century houses are the demolished Horsforth Hall, built for John Stanhope c.1694, and Castley Hall, Bramhope, built for Robert Dyneley c.1699.

33 William Pape was employed as mason, but there is no record of a designer's name.

34 Walker, 649.

35 ibid.,656.

36 Whitaker, 31. A letter in the Whitley Beaumont papers (Kirklees Library and Museum Service WBM/5) from Thomas Mann of York, dated 25 May 1680, refers to proposed additions. Little is known of Mann, although he appears to have been responsible for executing additions to Londesborough Hall in the mid-1670s for Richard, 1st Earl of Burlington. Whitley Beaumont was sold in 1917, when it was stripped of much of its decoration (some panelling is said to be in a modern house in Roehampton); it was demolished in 1952, and the only relic is a ruinous belvedere (octagonal and domed within a square) designed by James Paine on the highest point on the estate, overlooking Huddersfield and the surrounding country.

60

37 loc.cit., WBM/8. A letter dated 1 Sept 1699 to Beaumont, enclosing designs. The signature is missing, but the letter was written from Heath, where Shelton lived, and the neat style is unmistakeable.

38 I am indebted to Mr Granville Wheler for the information that Thornton's name appears in payments for work at Ledston. A drawing in his collection of Ledston papers is inscribed 'The Late Wm Thorntons Plan for a House for J.Stables'; the owner or tenant was probably a member of a Pontefract family of that name.

39 See Beard, G., *Georgian craftsmen and their work*, London 1966, 48ff. for a discussion of Thornton's work. The buffet is illustrated in Hill, O., and Cornforth, J., *English country houses – Caroline*, London 1966, 235.

40 Leeds Archives Dept., Ledston coll. LXVI 971–13, 41/42, 45/46. Bridgeman was paid three times in 1731, according to the ledgers of C. Hoare and Co; 27 March, £5 19s 6d; 5 April, £21 0s 0d; 23 October £7 10s 6d (information from Dr Peter Willis). However, as Thomas Coke died in 1727, it seems that the design of the garden must have been contemplated for several years. A series of four paintings made by John Settrington (in the collection of Mr Granville Wheler) show Ledston as it was (or, more probably, as it was intended to be) in 1728; they illustrate a formal east garden with statues, similar to that in Bridgeman's design. To the west (pl.21) are parterres below the terrace and garden-house built for Lady Elizabeth (probably by William Thornton). Coke was well known as a connoisseur, and Vanbrugh referred to him in 1708 as 'a great Lover of Musique And promoter of Operas'; he devoted many years to laying out his formal garden at Melbourne, with some assistance from Henry Wise (Hussey, C., *English gardens and landscapes 1799–1750*, London 1967, 57ff). William Kent was at Ledston in 1739, but there is no evidence that he did any work there (Wheler, G.H. ed., *Hastings-Wheler family letters*, 1693–1739, Wakefield 1935, ii, 173).

41 Mr Granville Wheler has kindly shown me a plan for improving Ledston, which is inscribed in an eighteenth-century hand, 'Lord Bingley's plan for finishing Ledstone'.

42 Walker, 665f; Robert Benson the elder had risen from being an attorney's clerk to an appointment as clerk of assize to the Northern Circuit, and by some means (said not to be above suspicion) he prospered. During the Commonwealth he bought an estate at Wrenthorpe, close to his native Wakefield, and after the Restoration he came under the patronage of Sir Thomas Osborne, later 1st Duke of Leeds and the builder of Kiveton Park. Benson died in 1676, and his son was brought up by his widow and her second husband, Sir Henry Belasyse (later of Brancepeth, Northumberland and related to the owner of Newburgh Priory).

Coincidentally, Shelton also made a contribution to Whitley Beaumont, providing the owner in 1699 with a design for a square, brick garden house with stone quoins, crowned with a pyramidal roof and an ornamental cupola.[37]

Lady Elizabeth Hastings, who inherited Ledston in 1701, was another landowner who attempted to conform to new fashions and improved her old house. She employed William Thornton of York,[38] who probably inserted a Baroque doorway in the centre of the east front, built a brick garden pavilion with a Venetian window at the end of the newly constructed west terrace, and remodelled several of the main rooms in the house; the Dining Room has fine quality woodwork, including a buffet in a niche, painted to match the Derbyshire marble linings of the lower part. There are no records of when the work was executed, but Thornton travelled to London with Lady Elizabeth in 1719/20, presumably on business connected with Ledston.[39] At the same time as she was improving her house, Lady Elizabeth was at work on her garden. Charles Bridgeman, Royal Gardener to George II, made a design for laying out the ground on the east side with a 'Lawn or parterr ... encompassed with a double Terras, & enclos'd ... wᵗʰ an Espalier of Dutch Elms ... cut fanwise'. The axial layout, which seems to have been made more or less according to Bridgeman's design, continued on the higher level as a long avenue or 'Grand Walk'; half way along, on each side, was an 'open Grove ... planted ... with standard English Elms' and forming places 'both Airey & shadey ... for walking & are very agreeable among close wood quarters'. The woods on each side were cut into by diagonal walks leading to statues, and serpentine paths connecting variously shaped clearings; one was a 'little parterr ... of Grass & evergreen [which] will be very entertaining'.[40] Thomas Coke of Melbourne, Derbyshire, was asked for an opinion on the design, to which he added 'a little of my own'. It would be surprising if Lady Elizabeth had not also consulted her neighbour Robert Benson, 1st Lord Bingley, about her garden. She certainly turned to him for architectural advice, and in return she received a plan for pulling down part of the Elizabethan fabric of Ledston and regularising the west front.[41] Bingley proposed building a large portico leading to a Saloon, which was to be linked to a remodelled Great Hall, moving the entrance from the east front to the west; but a great deal of demolition would have been necessary, and Lady Elizabeth evidently prudently preferred the less costly improvements she evolved with Thornton's help.

Bingley had a great reputation as an architectural connoisseur. He had travelled in Italy during the last years of the seventeenth century, and returned to Yorkshire in time to be chosen as Deputy Lieutenant for the West Riding in 1700. Elected MP in 1702, he became a Commissioner of the Treasury in 1710, Chancellor of the Exchequer in 1711, and Ambassador to Madrid in 1713. Yet in this political life he found time to become knowledgeable about architecture, enlarging on the studies he had made in Italy, and advising his fellow landowners about their houses. From his father, who had died in 1676, Bingley inherited a house at Wrenthorpe,[42] near Wakefield, and an estate at

32. Bramham Park; the layout of canals, cascades and avenues on the south-west side of the house. On the left, the Ionic Temple (now Chapel) by J.Paine (c.1760), on the right, the Gothic Octagon.

33. Bramham Park, presumably designed by the owner, 1st Lord Bingley (c.1703–10), was partly gutted by fire in 1828 and rebuilt 1906–14 (D.Blow) when the central doorway was inserted.

43 The building of Burley-on-the-Hill, Rutland began in 1696 to a design by an unknown architect. The owner was Daniel Finch, 2nd Earl of Nottingham.

Bramham granted by the Crown for his public services. It was at Bramham that he began to build a house, possibly in 1703 when he allied himself with another landowner who was engaged in building by marrying Elizabeth Finch, niece of the owner of Burley-on-the-Hill, Rutland.[43]

According to Colen Campbell, the work at Bramham was finished by 1710, but there are no known documents to confirm its beginning or end; nor is the name of its architect recorded. The old and often repeated reference to 'an Italian' can be discounted, and suggestions that Giacomo Leoni or Thomas Archer might have been responsible, are not convincing. A stronger case might be made on stylistic grounds in favour of James Gibbs, whom Bingley certainly knew professionally through the Commission for Building Fifty New Churches in London in 1713 (by which time the house itself was probably complete); yet the most likely designer was the owner himself, who was consulted by

44 Yorkshire Archaeological Society, MS 328. Unpublished ms 'Account of my journey begun 6 Augt 1724', probably written by Wyndham Knatchbull of Mersham-le-Hatch. See Friedman,T.F., and Linstrum,D., 'Country houses through Georgian eyes', 'A tour of architectural splendour', *C L* (1973),cliii,268ff,334ff. for a discussion of this manuscript.

45 Oswald,A., 'Bramham Park', *C L* (1958),cxxiii,350ff,400ff; Lees-Milne,J., *English country houses – Baroque*, London 1970,201ff; Hussey,C., *English gardens and landscapes 1700–1750*, London 1967,7off.

46 Neale,J.P., *Views of seats*, London 1822,v. Gibbons's name is also attached to the interiors of Tong Hall and Whitley Beaumont (where the chapel was described as 'fitted up with excellently carved oak, and in the taste formed by Gibbons, if not executed by him'). Although Gibbons was in Yorkshire at the beginning of his career in the late 1660s, and probably introduced the taste for naturalistic carving in the Dutch tradition, it can be assumed that this work in Yorkshire houses was executed by York carvers (such as John Etty) who had taken advantage of the opportunities offered at Castle Howard to perfect their technique and train apprentices to work in the new manner.

34. Bramham Park; the Stone Hall, a cube of thirty feet, survived the fire in 1828 although the ceiling was destroyed.

many Yorkshire gentry about their building operations, and who almost certainly laid out the gardens surrounding the house. A visitor in 1724 wrote of riding 'wth Ld Bingley thro' his 3 noble woods, all cut out into most beautiful Stars & Avenues, but all of underwood. The Wilderness next the House was high, & full of Stars, & in the main Avenue there is a cascade wch falls 30 Steps & 28 feet in Height, Tho' there are to be two others, the greatest a fall of 40 feet, & both on each side of an Obelisk 26 feet high'.[44] This remarkable woodland garden, formal yet following irregularities in the site rather than eliminating them in the French manner, is the first of the creations of Art and Nature for which Yorkshire was to become famous as the eighteenth century advanced. Obelisks and temples, Classical and Gothic, were to be added to the Bramham landscape, but at first there were no buildings apart from 'Lord Bingleys new Stone House'.

Bramham is a remarkably plain, serene design. The long horizontal lines of the parapet, cornice and string courses on the garden front are broken only by the slightly projecting end bays; and the entrance front exaggerates the horizontality by continuing it at each side in lower flanking wings interrupted by open colonnades.[45] The precise, regular appearance of the house is a reflection of the almost perfectly symmetrical plan, with a group of rooms and a staircase on each side of a square hall; thirty feet high as well as on plan, the last is completely faced with ashlar and ornamented with Corinthian giant pilasters and entablature. Much of the interior of the house was destroyed in a fire in 1828, but Neale described the 'rich and tasteful carvings of Grinlin[g] Gibbons . . . [in] the truly elegant apartments'.[46] The surviving woodwork is delicately and elaborately carved in the manner of the naturalistic decorations at Castle Howard and Beningbrough, and it is recognisable as the work of craftsmen employed in the great houses which were influencing the design of relatively small ones; this can be seen, for example, in the five-bay façade of Kettlethorpe Hall (1727), which incorporates Baroque pediments over the ground-floor windows, or in the more ambitious giant Corinthian pilasters and carved pediment on the seven-bay façade of Farfield Hall (1728).[47]

In a well-known quotation from one of Vanbrugh's letters from Castle Howard, the architect wrote in 1721, 'Here are Several Gentlemen in the[se] Parts of the World, that are possess'd w[ith] the Spirit of Building';[48] and many were devising their own designs. Not only was Lord Burlington frequently in Yorkshire and willing to advise, but by the late 1720s there were several publications to assist landowners ambitious to build; in particular there were the three volumes of Campbell's *Vitruvius Britannicus* (1715, 1717, 1725) and Gibbs's *A Book of Architecture* (1728). It is worth noting that among the subscribers to the last were seventeen Yorkshire landowners, of whom at least nine were building in the 1720s and 30s. Many had also seen the wonders of Italy for themselves, and the list of visitors to the University of Padua,[49] a recognised institution to visit on the way to Venice, includes well over thirty Yorkshire landowners during the years between the inscription of William Wentworth, later 2nd Earl of Strafford, in 1646 and that of Edwin Lascelles in 1738. The stimulus given to Lord Bingley, who was in Padua in 1694, by his travels, has already been discussed, and other West Yorkshire gentlemen shared his enthusiasm.

Sir Edward Gascoigne of Parlington Park made the Grand Tour in 1724–6, recording his visit to Padua in 1725, and while in Rome he undertook a course of instruction with 'ye Architect master';[50] in Florence he met Alessandro Galilei, the Grand-Ducal architect, and commissioned from him a design for a house, a monument to his father (which was erected in 1729 in All Saints, Barwick-in-Elmet but was later destroyed), and marble chimneypieces and table tops for his Yorkshire home.[51] In the 1730s, Parlington was being Italianised by Giovanni and Giuseppe Artari, Francesco Vassalli and Martino Quadri with plaster figures from Classical mythology in the Hall and Drawing Room, and angels and a Transfiguration in the Chapel.[52] Sir Rowland Winn of Nostell Priory acquired the customary knowledge of architecture during his travels in Italy; after his return he took a professional look at English houses and commissioned a series of views of selected examples for his collection. Sir William Wentworth of Bretton spent three years on the Grand Tour from 1709 to 1712, visiting Padua in 1710. His cousin, Thomas Wentworth, Lord Raby (who signed himself in Padua as 'Raby the true not the counterfit that is at Venice' in 1705), took the opportunity of his diplomatic appointment to Berlin to obtain a design for his new wing at Stainborough from Jean Bodt, Frederick the Great's architect; in supervising the erection of his building, Raby invoked the experienced assistance of Lord Bingley, and he commissioned Sir William Wentworth to buy works of art in Rome to decorate his new apartments. On his own account, however, Wentworth refrained. 'I

47 Downes,K., *English baroque architecture*, London 1966,94.

48 Webb,G.,(ed.)., *The complete works of Sir John Vanbrugh*, London 1928,iv,138.

49 Brown,H.F., *Inglesi e Scozzesi all'università di Padova dall'anno 1618 sino al 1765*, Venezia 1921.

50 Done,E., 'Sir Edward Gascoigne, Grand Tourist', *LAC* (1975),no.77,9. Pietro Paolo Coccetti is suggested as the possible instructor.

51 Kieven, E., 'The Gascoigne monument by Alessandro Galilei', ibid.,13ff.

52 Done, op.cit.,10. Parlington was demolished after the Second World War, sadly without being recorded.

35. Bretton Hall (c.1720); as seen from the Deer Park, the house is substantially as designed by the owner, Sir William Wentworth, and Col. James Moyser. The Doric portico and the segmental bow on the left were added by Jeffry Wyatt (1811–14).

53 Quoted in Oswald,A., 'Bretton Park', *C L* (1938),lxxxiii,352; nevertheless, Wentworth probably brought back with him some of the Roman fragments surviving in the grounds of the house.

54 Information based on an annotated copy of *The builder's dictionary*, 1734, in the Metropolitan Museum.

55 It was Wentworth who had agreed to continue making an allowance to Kent after his first supply of money had been spent, and he subscribed to Kent's *The designs of Inigo Jones* in 1727. (Walpole,H., *Anecdotes of painting in England* (1862 edn),iii,777).

shall be very well content with the walls of Bretton just as they are', he wrote, 'so that I have but a good glass of Ale and Bear to make my friends welcome with when they honour me with his company'.[53] Marriage in about 1720 with Diana, daughter of Sir William Blackett of Newby Hall (and eventually his co-heiress), changed this contented bachelor view of the old house and Wentworth began to build.

The design of the new house at Bretton, a rectangular building not unlike Bramham but larger and more stark in lacking attached wings or pavilions, was made by Wentworth himself with the help of Col. James Moyser.[54] This amateur architect was an acquaintance of Burlington, who presumably recommended his friendly services to Wentworth, who was one of the group of gentry who had sponsored William Kent, Burlington's favourite protégé, in his studies in Rome.[55] Wentworth thought of employing Kent (who had not yet turned to architecture) to decorate his new house, but there is no evidence he did, although a design made by the exiled Earl of Mar for giving Bretton 'the Beauty of wch it is capable wth a small additional expence' refers to improvements to the 'salonn' which would make it

35

56 See Linstrum, 'Two Wentworth houses', op.cit.,10,pl.2. Mar's drawings are in the Register House, Edinburgh (Mar-Kellie MSS, RHP nos.48–9).

57 Wentworth, op.cit.,40,220.

58 Hussey,C., *English country houses – early Georgian*, London 1955,187ff. The genesis of the house is obscure. The similarity of Campbell's design (RIBA Drawings Collection, *Catalogue*, Campbell/40) is too close to be accidental, yet he died in 1729, four years before the assumed commencement of building. Possibly Moyser had access to Campbell's designs, maybe through a connection formed when Campbell designed Sir Charles Hotham's house in Beverley. However, there is also an estate plan dated 1731 and signed by Joseph Perfect, a member of the Pontefract family who were nurserymen from the early eighteenth century until 1811 (see Brockwell,M., *Catalogue of the works of art at Nostell Priory*, 1915). This plan shows a rectangular house with four corner pavilions; and another plan, made by Stephen Switzer *c.*1733–5 to illustrate his proposals for the gardens, incorporates a similar house plan but with quadrant connecting corridors as in the final design.

59 Brockwell, op.cit. There are several drawings in the collection which show alternative proposals for the east front and the pedimented central section.

60 Woolfe,J., and Gandon,J., *Vitruvius Britannicus*, London 1767,i,9.

61 Paine,J., *Plans, elevations and sections of noblemen and gentlemen's houses*, London 1767,i,i.

'proper to be decorated by Mr Kent'.[56] Nor is it possible to find a connection between the landscaping of Bretton and Kent, tempting though it is to think he might have designed the octagonal Gothic tea-house on the island in the Upper Lake. Nothing is known about the genesis of the two lakes and the planting, except that they were formed by 1777 when a paragraph in a letter refers to some of the joys of country-house life: 'We have now such fine weather, that we go upon the Lake and we are rigging out a Fete and preparing Illuminations & Fireworks to be exhibited upon the Island of Venus'. Possibly the landscape was largely the creation of Sir William Wentworth and his son Sir Thomas; or perhaps James Brindley, the famous canal-builder who was constructing a dam at Woolley, the neighbouring estate owned by Godfrey Wentworth, in 1766[57] was employed to advise on the damming of the little river Dearne to form the large irregular sheets of water at Bretton.

Moyser's name is also associated with the design of Nostell Priory, which shares many common characteristics with Bretton. After the Dissolution, the Priory estate had passed through several owners' hands until it was bought by Sir George Winn in 1654. His descendant, Rowland, succeeded in 1721, and after marrying Susannah Henshaw, the daughter of a London merchant, in 1729, he decided to rebuild. Once again Moyser was recommended, probably by Burlington, but it seems likely that a design for a large country house made by Campbell[58] was taken as a model for the Moyser-Winn house. An additional interest attached to Nostell is that it introduced the talented, nineteen-year-old James Paine to Yorkshire in about 1737, not as designer of the house at first but as supervisor of the building operations. His duties would have included the detailing of the building, and although Nostell does not appear in the published volumes of his designs, there is little doubt he was effectively its architect and responsible for the design of the interior.

Nostell is a larger house than Bretton, but the plan form of a symmetrical group of rooms and corresponding staircases on each side of a central hall, which was used for both, derives from the same Palladian model. The main rooms at Nostell, unlike those at Bretton, are placed on the *piano nobile*, with access from ground level through a colonnaded, central hall (as in the monumental east wing of Wentworth Woodhouse, that epitome of Palladianism). Externally, Nostell resembles Bretton in the regular pattern of windows and the pedimented surrounds to those lighting the main rooms, but Winn's house has the additional dignity of pilastered, pedimented centrepieces standing on rusticated basements. The design of the east front went through a series of amendments,[59] and is less successful than the west; the pavilions too were subject to changes of mind, and only two were built. The building operations were unusually protracted, but Paine rightly praised the quality of workmanship, and it was claimed 'no expense has been spared in the best of all kinds of materials'.[60] He also believed that in the execution of the house he had 'acquitted himself so much to the satisfaction of his employer, that he had reason to flatter himself he should not be disappointed in the pursuit of his studies'.[61]

36

36. Nostell Priory; the east front lacks the curved colonnades and pavilions which were intended to flank it, according to the design made by the owner, Sir Rowland Winn, and Col.Moyser c.1729.

37. Heath House (J.Paine 1744), a pure exercise in Palladianism.

Nor was he, but he does not appear to have been employed on other work until the 1740s.

Paine's principal achievements in his large country-house practice lie outside the topographical scope of this study, but during the years he was working at Nostell his local reputation was growing. His first **37** West Yorkshire house was a relatively small one at Heath, on the north-west side of the common and between the Elizabethan Heath Hall and the late seventeenth-century Eshald House. Begun in 1744, Paine's work was an enlargement of an existing house for Robert Hopkinson, a Wakefield attorney. Although only sixty-eight feet wide, the house has a palatial façade in which Paine skilfully incorporated most of the elements of Burlingtonian Palladianism while avoiding an impression of overcrowding.[62] The rusticated basement is surmounted by a three-bay central section with Ionic attached columns and a pediment, and the wide bays terminate with coupled pilasters of the same giant order.[63] It is, one might say, the work of a young man who wanted to demonstrate he knew all the rules.

Paine was obviously an obedient Palladian at the time he designed Heath House, and it is possible he was the architect of Milnes Bridge House, William Radcliffe's new mansion (c.1750) near Huddersfield, which incorporates the characteristic Palladian idea of two interlocking temple fronts in the main façade. He remained a Palladian, but over the following years he reached those conclusions he set down in the introduction to his published designs; '. . . we have received some real advantage from Palladio, and other Venetian masters, whose works were studied with great application by our countryman Inigo Jones; yet experience daily convinces us, that the houses built by that great master, are very ill adapted to our climate, still worse to our present mode of living, and consequently are not proper models for our imitation'.[64] Two near-contemporary houses, Stockeld Park (1758–63), North Yorkshire, for William Middleton,[65] and St Ives (1759) for Benjamin Ferrand,[66] illustrate this rational view of Palladianism. They have much in common. Both are planned as a compact group of rooms around a spacious central staircase-hall; both demonstrate Paine's love of the apsidal form in planning; and both are designed as high pedimented central blocks with lower side wings, although the surface treatment differs considerably in elaboration.

The façades of Stockeld reveal Paine as a skilled manipulator of the Palladian vocabulary; in such a combination as the canted bays and the giant arches rising into the broken pediments on the side wings can be seen an assured mastery which justifies his bold words about disregarding the Palladian rules. Paine's liking for a giant recessed arch form is revealed on other West Yorkshire buildings attributed to him, notably New Grange, Kirkstall[67] and a house in Pontefract market place; but the façades of St Ives were startlingly austere. In the engraved designs, the effective height of the central block is reduced by the continuation across the façade of the dentilated cornice of the side wings, and by the insertion of a continuous string-course in the attic storey. There is no ornament, except for a modest doorcase

62 The coupled pilasters as terminations probably derive from Jones's Banqueting House, and the whole design is reminiscent of one published by Kent in *The designs of Inigo Jones*, ii,pl.6.

63 Paine, op.cit.,pls.lxi–lxii.

64 ibid.,i,ii.

65 ibid.,i,pls.xli–xlvi. The proposed pavilions were not built, and the house was enlarged by Detmar Blow at the end of the nineteenth century.

66 ibid.,i,pls.lxiii–lxvi. The house has been demolished. A design for the entrance gateway, signed 'J.Vilett 1763', is in the Ferrand collection in the Yorkshire Archaeological Society, MD290,Box 9.

67 Now a part of Leeds College of Education, New Grange was built by Benjamin Wade in 1626, when its front was inscribed: 'Except the Lord build the house, thy labour in vain that keeps it; it is the Lord that keeps thee going out and in. B.W.1626'. It was enlarged by Walter Wade, and during the nineteenth century it was occupied by John Marshall, then by Thomas Benyon, and then the Beckett family.

38. Temple Newsam; the suite of rococo apartments in the north wing (1738–45) ends in a richly decorated small Library, which was adapted as a chapel in 1877 by G.F.Bodley, who inserted the organ.

68 Illustrated in the catalogue, *The destruction of the country house*, London 1974,pl.273.

69 Now demolished. Stapleton was sold to Edward, Daniel and Edwin Lascelles in 1762. Edward Lascelles held it for 17 years, leaving it shortly before succeeding to the Harewood estate.

70 Leach,P., 'Designs from a practical man', 'A pioneer of rococo decoration', 'In the Gothick vein'. *CL* (1974),clvi,694ff, 766ff,834ff.

71 Simon,J., 'The Long Gallery ceiling at Temple Newsam', *LAC* (1974), no.74,5ff; Friedman,T.F., 'The Georgian library', ibid.(1975),no.76,10ff. The plasterwork was executed by Thomas Perritt and Joseph Rose, and the woodwork was carved by Richard Fisher. The main decorative elements, the chimneypieces and overmantels, were taken from Isaac Ware's *Designs of Inigo Jones and others*, London 1735. Those in the Long Gallery are based on a design by Kent (pl.36), and that originally in the library was made up from two, the chimneypiece by Jones (pl.5) and the overmantel by Kent (pl.34). Richard Doe, a mason, is recorded as working in the Long Gallery in 1740, presumably on the chimneypieces.

72 The design for the temple is in the RIBA Drawings Collection (see *Catalogue* vol. G-K/12.1); Harris,J., 'The Dundas empire', *Apollo* (1967),lxxxvi,170.

73 Was it perhaps a confusion between Gothic and Elizabethan? If so, maybe Garrett added the stone bays at Temple Newsam which have recessed panels with trefoil heads carved in the corner mullions. It is difficult to be certain when these additions were made. The south wing was rebuilt in 1796 by William Johnson, after designs had been obtained from Robert Adam and 'Capability' Brown; but the other eighteenth-century work might have been by Garrett.

38

with a bracketted entablature, and the whole effect is one of geometric severity. Internally, Stockeld possesses an elliptical staircase hall that is a brilliant exercise in spatial design, worthy of comparison with Kent's better-known design in 44 Berkeley Square. The same curved balusters as at Stockeld are found in the more modest New Grange, Kirkstall, which was remodelled in the 1750s for Walter Wade. The plasterwork in New Grange is rococo, as was the decoration in the remodelled Great Hall at Whitley Beaumont, executed by Paine in the 1750s for Richard Beaumont.[68]

Apart from some garden buildings and extensions to the stable at Bramham, and a new staircase and hall at Stapleton Park[69] for Edward Lascelles (later 1st Earl of Harewood), the rest of Paine's career as a country-house architect lies outside the West Yorkshire region. Although he was indebted to the Burlington circle for his introduction to architectural practice at Nostell Priory, he quickly became independent; his contemporary, Daniel Garrett, on the other hand has been overshadowed by the figure of Burlington, who employed him as a draughtsman. It is only recently that he has begun to emerge as a figure of some importance in country-house architecture in the North.[70] He is a convincing candidate as the designer of the stables at Temple Newsam, where he was certainly employed to design ceilings in the house, which were executed by Thomas Perritt of York. On the strength of that knowledge, it is reasonable to attribute to him the rococo ceilings in the Library and the Drawing Rooms designed *en suite* with the remodelled Long Gallery, in which George I's portrait is surrounded by those of George II and his family in a series of thirteen medallions arranged within a geometric pattern on the vast ceiling made for Henry, 7th Viscount Irwin between 1738 and 1745.[71]

Garrett's largest architectural design in West Yorkshire was the remodelling of the Elizabethan Kippax Hall for Sir John Bland *c.*1750 or, more likely, for Thomas Davison Bland after he inherited the estate in 1756. The compact square house, which had been added to in the 1660s, was extended in a conventional Palladian manner by screen walls and large, balancing service wings with pediments and cupolas. The walls of the new rooms were panelled in a geometric pattern of circles, squares and octagons below an elaborate but conventional cornice. What was not conventional is the extraordinary mixture of Palladian and Gothick detailing. It is now thought that Garrett was responsible for the building of the Gothic Temple at Aske Hall in North Yorkshire;[72] if so, the experience must have influenced his work at Kippax, in which the screen walls between the house and the service wings were decorated with ogee-headed niches and quatrefoil windows. Stranger still was the addition of two large canted bays with ogee roofs and ogee window heads on the otherwise plain extensions to the house, and an equally charming but incongruous Gothick refacing of the central bay of the original Elizabethan house.[73] The remodelling of Kippax in this manner obviously influenced the eighteenth-century alterations to another Elizabethan house, Methley, two or three miles away. The equally strange Gothick bays added to the east front have hitherto been accepted as part of John Carr's remodelling of

39. Heath Hall; Eshald House (pl.28) was enlarged c.1754 (J.Carr) when wings and service buildings were added to make it the most important house in the unique village of mansions. On the right is Dower House, built c.1740 for 'Mr Roebuck'.

74 Woolfe and Gandon, op.cit.,v,pls.70–1. It is possible that another early Carr work (perhaps undertaken by father and son) was the pedimented, arcaded stable at Newland Hall, dated 1745, and built for John Smith.

1778, but perhaps Garrett had been there earlier. However, the introduction of Carr into the West Yorkshire country-house world coincided with the beginning of renewed building activity.

Carr's public career as an architect began with the erection of the grandstand on the York Knavesmire in 1754. His design had been selected in preference to that by James Paine, yet so far as is known Carr's only house designs up to that time had been for Huthwaite Hall (1748) and Arncliffe Hall (1753–4). He had also made his contribution to Kirby Hall,[74] the house designed by Burlington and Roger Morris, and before his introduction to the niceties of Palladian architecture he had been well trained by his father, Robert, a quarry owner and mason from Horbury; with such a combination, it is not surprising Carr was so quickly successful. His first known important country house was local, in the sense that it was only a few miles from his native Horbury. The site was the remarkable village of Heath, where by this time there

75 The painting is in the collection of the Society of Dilettanti, London. See the catalogue of the exhibition, *The age of Neo-classicism*, London 1972,911f.

76 Oswald,A., 'Heath Hall', *CL* (1968), cxliv,692ff,756ff,816ff; Hall,I. and E., *Heath: an architectural description*, Heath 1975. It is interesting to compare the growing sophistication of Carr's work, as illustrated by Heath, with the Palladian designs of other mason-architects; e.g. Hope Hall, Halifax, built in 1765 for Christopher Rawson (possibly by Thomas Bradley or James Green), incorporates a large Venetian window in a typical pattern book assemblage of a pedimented house with side wings and pavilions.

77 Mauchline,M., *Harewood House*, Newton Abbot 1974,37.

78 Sir John Cutler, a friend and relative of Sir John Lewis (who bought the other Strafford estate at Ledston), acquired Gawthorp from Strafford's son, 'a careless extravagant spendthrift [who] soon squandered away his property'. Cutler's meanness became a legend, referred to by Alexander Pope in *Moral essays*, iii, 'Of the use of riches'. After his death, Gawthorp passed to Elizabeth, Countess of Radnor and to John Boulter before being purchased by Henry Lascelles in 1739 (Whitaker,167). Parsons, i,259, gives 1721 as the date of purchase, but Carr made an estate valuation in 1739 of £63,827 (Mauchline, op.cit.,173).

were three houses, the Elizabethan Heath Hall, Theophilus Shelton's Eshald House and James Paine's Heath House. Eshald seems to have been bought in 1709 from Shelton (who died in Nottingham in 1717) by John Smyth, whose possessions eventually passed in 1731 to his grandson of the same name. There is no accurate record of the year in which Carr was employed to enlarge the house, but 1754 has been accepted as a likely date for the beginning of work which probably extended over a long period and was completed by Smyth's son, yet another John, who succeeded to the estate in 1771 and made a brilliant marriage five years later to the eldest daughter of the Duke of Grafton. He made the Grand Tour, became a member of the Society of Dilettanti, and appeared in one of Sir Joshua Reynolds's paintings of a convivial group of reunited Tourists drinking the health of Sir William Hamilton.[75] It is a predominantly Yorkshire group, which also includes two other patrons of Carr, Walter Spencer-Stanhope of Horsforth and Cannon Hall, and Richard Thompson of Escrick Park.

The remodelling of Eshald House, which was renamed Heath Hall (the earlier one becoming Heath Old Hall), incorporated Shelton's work but overlaid it on the entrance front with Ionic three-quarter columns and a pediment. At each side Carr added a wing with canted bays on both entrance and garden fronts; the south contains a Dining Room and a circular Study, and the north a Drawing Room. Between the two a long vista was contrived across the whole length of the enlarged house. Additional dignity was created by extending the house on each side with a detached pavilion, pedimented and crowned by a cupola, which was to become an almost obligatory feature of Carr's many service buildings in Yorkshire houses. Smyth's house was even further extended on the south by a stable set back from the pavilion and forming a group of buildings around a courtyard.[76] Internally, Carr's decorations immediately set a standard from which he never departed during his long career. The plasterwork and woodwork are of a high quality throughout (as is the almost exactly contemporary work in Arncliffe Hall), but the Drawing Room occupying the whole north wing is quite simply among the finest in the county. Seemingly based on a published but unexecuted design by William Kent for Houghton Hall, Norfolk, the architectural framework of three Venetian arches on each of the long walls is complemented by rococo plasterwork by a yet unidentified craftsman, possibly Joseph Rose. It was an auspicious beginning to a remarkable career, but long before Heath was finished Carr was occupied with another commission, one which was to prove as influential on Yorkshire country houses in the second half of the eighteenth century as Castle Howard had been in the first.

In 1754 Edwin Lascelles received a written assurance that 'Mr. Carr presents his services and when Ever yo've occasion for him upon the least notice he'll be ready to wait upon you'.[77] Lascelles had inherited the estates of Gawthorp and Harewood in the previous year, including Gawthorp Hall, which had been the property of Thomas Wentworth, Earl of Strafford, in the seventeenth century;[78] he improved the old house by adding a portico and remodelling and redecorating the interior, but already he had resolved to rebuild 'on a spot rather elevated above that of old Gawthorp . . . which commanded a rich home view over fields and woods'.[79] Some years earlier he had obtained a design for a stable, which was built by John Carr and his father, Robert. There is no evidence for the long-held belief that William Chambers was the designer of this heavy quadrangular building with an internal colonnade of coupled Tuscan columns; it is the work of the younger Carr, designed in 1748 before Edwin Lascelles inherited the estate but when he was acting for his father,[80] and it explains the letter Carr wrote in 1754. It is a building which possesses the sturdy conservatism of a mason who has relatively recently taken to designing. Nevertheless, Chambers was consulted about the house in 1755–6, shortly after his return from six years in Paris and Rome. His ambitious design was a scholarly essay which might have been favourably commented on in the French Academy in Rome, but it was not calculated to please either the Yorkshire landowner or the Earl of Leicester, to whose Palladian judgement it was referred.[81] Chambers was discomfited, and Lascelles, who had probably obtained designs from other architects as well, turned to the local man who was building his new stables and working nearby at Plompton (and later at Goldsborough Hall) for his brother Daniel,[82] who evidently had no taste for grandeur and wished 'Mr Carr would have shown his more humble style of Architecture . . . or would Exercise these sublime parts of ye Art upon a Noble Subject'. Edwin Lascelles provided one.

Carr's plans slowly took shape; they were submitted to Lord Leicester for a connoisseur's opinion in March 1758, but within a few months Lascelles was discussing his new house with Robert Adam, who had just returned from Italy. 'I have made some Alterations on it', wrote Adam to his brother James, 'But as the plan did not admitt of a great many that has prevented the fronts from being much Changed likewise'. Yet he casually added concerning the plan, 'I have thrown in Large Semicircular Back Courts with columns betwixt the House & Wings', to give an increased sense of monumental grandeur to the plan.[83] Lascelles took his time to come to a decision, finally compromising by instructing Carr to amend the plan to one which was not strictly symmetrical and incorporated a semicircular courtyard as suggested by Adam, but in the west wing only. Ironically, this feature was built but removed in 1762, and the completed house was virtually entirely Carr's design. Palladian in its planning, it consists of a pedimented central section of geometrically proportioned rooms grouped around a large Entrance Hall; this is linked to end pavilions by connecting wings which are, in fact, apartments in a planned circuit. It is a design that owes much to the third version of Colen Campbell's Wanstead Park, Essex, but it can also be related to the Anglo–Palladian villa form, on account of the convenient, compact planning and the reduction of the traditional Palladian basement on the north front.[84] From the south, the house is more conventionally elevated so that the main rooms overlooking Brown's landscape are on the *piano nobile*. As in all Carr's buildings, the masonry of Harewood was meticulously detailed and executed; there is an almost mechanical

79 Whitaker, 168.

80 Whitaker appears to have been the first historian to make this attribution to Chambers, probably based on oral misinformation. An engraving, 'A perspective view of the stables at Gawthorp. Built by Edwin Lascelles Esqʳ. 1748', signed 'J.Carr', which was engraved from a drawing by William Lindley, Carr's pupil (Wakefield Art Gallery and Museums, *Drawings and engravings illustrative of the county of York*,x,pl.7), seems to settle this long-confused point, although according to Miss Mauchline the stables were built in 1755 (op.cit.23ff).

81 Harris,J., *Sir William Chambers: Knight of the Polar Star*, London 1970,40,pls.43–5. Chambers made use of the design for one of the pavilions in the Casino for the 1st Earl of Charlemont at Marino, Dublin.

82 Mauchline, op.cit.,24,31.

83 ibid.,39.

84 The basement was reduced even more in height by Sir Charles Barry in the 1840s when he made extensive alterations and additions to turn the house into an Italian *palazzo*. Externally, the greatest loss was the portico on the south front.

41

40. Heath Hall; the rococo plasterwork
in the Drawing Room is unsurpassed in
the many houses Carr built.

41. Harewood House (J.Carr 1759–71);
T.Malton's watercolour view (1778) from
the north east shows the house before it
was turned into an Italian *palazzo*
(C.Barry 1843).

perfection in the pattern of the chamfering of the rustication, and in
the practically invisible joints in the ashlar of the superstructure. 'Let
us do everything properly & well, mais pas trop', urged Lascelles; and
his architect obeyed.

One might speculate if Carr, left to his own devices, would have
designed the decoration in a combination of rococo and Palladianism
such as he had used at Heath; but it was in the interior that Adam was
the leader, even though he was working within the restrictions of
Carr's plan which denied to him the apses, half-domes and colonnaded
screens which added another dimension to rooms elsewhere in which
his imagination was able to expand. Nevertheless, in the rooms at
Harewood Adam introduced his Neo-classical decoration to Yorkshire,
as well as his favourite executants, Joseph Rose II the plasterer,
Antonio Zucchi and Angelica Kauffmann the decorative painters, and
the Otley-born Thomas Chippendale the cabinet-maker. Skilled

42

43. Nostell Priory, the Saloon as decorated by R.Adam, who retained the original shell of the room but added the apse on the right. The plasterwork, including the central medallion representing Evening and Dawn, was by J.Rose, and A.Zucchi painted the large Classical landscapes 1766.

Yorkshire craftsmen, Maurice Tobin the ironsmith and Daniel Shillito the woodcarver, as well as Carr himself, gained a knowledge at Harewood of the new taste in decoration which they subsequently incorporated in other houses in the county. The *Leeds Mercury* (9 Oct 1770) published effusive verses in praise of the new house:

Hail, Glorious Structure, Noblest of our Isle,
Finish'd by Artists bred on every Soil;
What Gold can furnish, or what Taste can shew,
Beyond conception strike the astonished View.'

Many of the same craftsmen were employed at Nostell Priory, where Adam was consulted in 1765 by the 5th baronet, another Sir Rowland Winn, immediately after his inheritance of the estate and the partly completed house.[85] The original design, with quadrants linking four pavilions to the house, had been abandoned. The west and east pavilions had been built, but neither of the others had been started.

85 Hussey,C., *English country houses – mid-Georgian*, London 1955,187ff.

86 See Croft-Murray,E., *Decorative painting in England 1537–1837*, London 1970,ii,296ff, for details of Zucchi's work at Harewood and Nostell. The latter contains examples of plasterwork by two generations of craftsmen, the earlier attributed to Joseph Rose I and Thomas Perritt, and the later to Joseph Rose II who had visited Italy and was so conversant with Neo-classical decorative design and details that he was able to act as designer as well as executant at Sledmere in the 1780s. See Beard,G., *Georgian craftsmen and their work*, London 1966,70ff. and *Decorative plasterwork in Great Britain*, London 1975,73ff.

87 Stroud,D., *Capability Brown*, London 1975,105ff; Mauchline,op.cit.,108ff. According to Jewell,J., *The history and antiquities of Harewood*, Leeds 1819,31, the gardens and pleasure grounds 'were partly laid out by Mr.Brown . . . and a part of them by Mr.Sparrow, a part by Mr.White, and very great additions have been made of late years by Mr.James Webb, who has lived at Harewood House upwards of forty years, and was one of Mr.Brown's pupils'.

88 Whitaker, 169.

89 Stroud, op.cit.,115ff.

Nor had all the rooms been decorated. Adam designed a pair of north wings *c*.1779, continuing the planes of the main face of the house but breaking out on the west in a large segmental window. He proposed to build a balancing wing on the south, but once again only a part of the whole was executed; the north-east wing was built, though left unfinished inside until 1875, and the result is an unbalanced composition from almost every angle. Internally, Nostell Priory demonstrates the change from Paine's rococo decoration of the 40s to the new Classical spirit of Adam and his colleagues twenty years later. The two styles are combined in some rooms, as in the Dining Room in which Zucchi's painted arabesques within severely rectangular panels were interpolated between rococo overmantels and overdoors; yet the panels between the earlier scrolled and garlanded plaster frames are the work of Zucchi, who painted large Classical landscapes for the Saloon, as he did for the Music Room at Harewood.[86]

Landscaping was not confined to the painted walls. Lancelot 'Capability' Brown was called to Harewood in 1758, but it was not until 1772 that he was there directing the construction of the lake and the planting of the valley on the south side of the house[87] to produce 'one of the most beautiful domains in the Kingdom . . . Great planters have usually been blessed with long lives to enjoy the workmanship of their own hands, but few have seen their labours prosper like the planter of Harewood', thought Whitaker, who wrote enthusiastically of the 'widely extended view of Wharfedale [which] may, within the compass of a short walk, be contrasted with the soft and beautiful home scene which opens around the house'.[88] During the years between 1758 and 1772 Brown had been constantly at work on most of the major estates in the country, including Temple Newsam where he created a magnificent scene for Charles Ingram, later 9th Viscount Irwin. His first visit was probably in 1761, and plans were sent off after some delay 'by the Leeds Machine which sets out from the Swan and Two Necks, Lad-Lane'.[89] Although the whole design was not executed, and the proposed lake was never made, Temple Newsam was considered one of Brown's finest landscapes. In 1767 an anonymous poem was published on the subject of *The Rise and Progress of the Present Taste in Planting Parks, Pleasure Grounds, Gardens, etc . . .*; it was dedicated to the owner of Temple Newsam, where Brown had created

The charms of Nature gracefully combin'd,
Sweet waving hills, with wood and verdure crown'd,
And winding vales, where murmuring streams resound:
Slopes fring'd with Oaks which gradual die away,
And all around romantic scenes display.

The poem, with its references throughout to Brown's work, is a tribute to his genius:

Born to grace Nature, and her works complete
With all that's beautiful, sublime and great!
For him each muse enwreathes the Laurel Crown,
And consecrates to Fame immortal Brown.

Other Yorkshire landowners, though not contemplating improvements on as large a scale as Ingram's, took advantage of

90 See Stillman, D., *The decorative work of Robert Adam*, London 1966, 77ff. Designs for the Drawing Room are in Sir John Soane's Museum, vol.50, no.70 and vol.23, no.151. The house was demolished following a sale in 1922.

91 The east wing was remodelled to contain the two new rooms. Bolling Hall has been a Bradford Corporation museum since 1915.

92 Allendale, BEA/C2/B40/35; these papers are from Bywell Abbey, temporarily desposited at Bretton Hall. Carr's design for the pilasters in the Dining Room, dated Oct 1793, suggests 'The Capitals will be best done in Cast work by Mr Waterworth Carver in Doncaster'. The painted medallions are very similar to those by Theodore de Bruyn (1730–1804) which were provided in 1789 for Carr's Dining Room at Farnley Hall. Bruyn trained in Antwerp, probably arriving in England c.1760, and becoming a student at the Royal Academy at the age of 43. Other known work in Yorkshire includes the decorations in the C18 chapel at Carlton Towers for Thomas Stapleton c.1777. Carr also designed at least two buildings in the grounds of Bretton; the large Gothic 'Bella Vista' and a composite 'Temples of Virtue and Honour' (Allendale, BEA/C2/MPD 17/15, 20/17a, 17b).

93 Oswald, A., 'Hazlewood Castle', *CL* (1957), cxxii, 138off, 1426ff. By 1800 the old fortified manor house had acquired a Georgian appearance, although battlements were retained on the south front. The finest of the interiors attributed to Carr is the remodelled Great Hall, with a Doric order and a deep coved ceiling. There is good plasterwork in the Adam/Carr manner.

94 Friedman, T.F., 'Romanticism and classicism for Parlington', *LAC* (1970), no.66, 16ff. Carr supplied designs in 1772 for a new house, but so did other architects over the next forty years. Thomas Leverton was the only one who had a design built, but it was not for the house; it was a triumphal arch commemorating 'LIBERTY IN N. AMERICA TRIUMPHANT MDCCLXXXIII' as the frieze proclaims.

95 Neale, op.cit., v, describes the rooms Carr decorated and considers the house 'much better finished, in respect to the decoration of the interior; than most of its size in the kingdom'. There was an 'elegant drawing-room, thirty-seven feet by twenty-five, its ceiling in ornamental compartments, green, gold and white, and the walls hung with crimson damask, with gilt mouldings, etc.; the chimney-piece is a handsome entablature, supported by Ionic columns of Sienna marble', and so on.

Brown's visits to consult him about their estates; in 1779 he was at Whitley Beaumont, the elevated site with vast open views across to the Pennines and over the Calder valley, and in 1782 he was at Stapleton Park, a property owned by Edward Lascelles (later 1st Earl of Harewood) which was leased to Charles Philip Stourton (later 17th Baron Stourton) and was known as Stourton at that time. During this latter journey to Yorkshire, Brown was consulted by Sir John Ramsden of Byram Park to prepare a plan for the estate where Thoresby had been shown 'very curious gardens' seventy years previously, but Ramsden was intent on bringing everything up to date to conform with the latest taste.

Byram was another of the West Riding houses to which Adam's 'regiment of artificers' moved on in the 1780s to decorate the main rooms. No doubt he had been recommended by William Weddell, the owner of Newby Hall (where Adam worked in 1767–80) and Ramsden's uncle by marriage. The Drawing Room at Byram was transformed in the Etruscan style, and there were painted Classical landscapes in the overdoors. The Library was subdivided by colonnaded screens, and the compartmented ceiling and deep cove were decorated with the familiar Adam motifs;[90] yet by this time they had become equally familiar to Carr and his craftsmen, who were employed by owners of older houses to provide up-to-date interiors, as by Charles Wood at Bolling Hall in 1779–80[91] and Colonel Thomas Richard Beaumont at Bretton in 1793. The West Bretton Wentworth line ceased in 1792, and the estate passed to the last Sir Thomas's illegitimate daughter Diana, Mrs Beaumont; improvements began almost immediately and ceased only with the death of this wealthy, capricious lady who was known in Yorkshire and London as 'Madame' Beaumont, renowned for her ostentatious manner of living and her assertive manner. Carr remodelled the Library and Dining Room at Bretton with Adamesque plasterwork, fireplaces and doorcases, and in the latter room he introduced *grisaille* painted medallions in the wall decoration.[92] At about the same time he remodelled some of the interiors at Woolley for Godfrey Wentworth, and he was back at Cannon Hall over the hill from Bretton, where he had been working on and off for John Spencer since 1764.

Carr was a conservative architect. Until the end of his career he continued using the formula evolved at Harewood of Neo-classical interiors within a Palladian plan and exterior. One of the reasons for this adherence to a proven precedent probably lies in the landowners for whom he was mainly working. He was employed by the old county families, such as the Vavasours of Hazlewood Castle,[93] the Gascoignes of Parlington Park,[94] the Saviles of Methley Hall,[95] and those already referred to; but many of his patrons belonged to the group of Leeds and Wakefield merchants whose wealth, acquired in the seventeenth and eighteenth centuries, enabled them 'to vie with the nobility in their magnificence'. Whereas the early eighteenth-century ideal had been a town house, the next generation looked to the country. As early as 1709 William Milner of Leeds bought the Fairfax property of Nun Appleton House; and eight years later James Ibbetson bought another

96 See Wilson,R.G., 'The Denisons and Milneses; eighteenth-century merchant landowners', *Land and industry* (ed.Ward,J.T., and Wilson,R.G.), Newton Abbot 1971,145ff.

97 Now demolished. See *H A S* (1925),20ff.

98 Now demolished. See Richardson,G., *The new Vitruvius Britannicus*, London 1802,i,pls.lxiv–lxvi. Titus Salt bought this house in 1867 (he had previously leased it from 1844–58), and it was the scene of the great entertainments he gave for the workpeople from Saltaire (see Balgarnie,R., *Sir Titus Salt, Baronet*, London 1877,237ff). Between 1858 and 1867, Salt leased Methley Hall, which Henry Lockwood improved for him, adding hothouses and conservatories.

99 Richardson, op.cit.,pls.liv–lvi.

100 ibid.,pls.li–liii. The house was burnt down in 1951.

101 Hussey,C., *English country houses · late Georgian*, London 1956,214ff.

Fairfax property at Denton, where Carr was to design a house in 1770 for the Leeds merchant's nephew. The Denisons of Leeds invested heavily in landed estates, but they moved outside Yorkshire.[96] Jeremiah Dixon, another Leeds merchant, bought the Gledhow estate and built or enlarged his house, probably in 1764, with the help of Carr, who built Leventhorpe Hall in 1774 for Richard Green, who then sold it to Thomas Ikin of Leeds.

In 1779 James Milnes, a Wakefield merchant, commissioned Carr to design a house on the estate he had bought outside the town, and in 1786 his brother Robert acquired the Fryston estate and immediately remodelled the house; five years later the latter was awarded a Gold Medal by the Society for the Encouragement of Arts, Manufactures and Commerce for having planted 384,300 trees on his land. John Blayds, a Leeds banker and merchant, bought Oulton Hall in the 1790s, and Benjamin Gott Armley Park in 1803; Thomas Nicholson, a London banker with connections by marriage with Leeds merchants, bought the Roundhay estate in 1797. The late eighteenth-century West Yorkshire merchant landowner required a particular type of country house; one that was convenient and not ruinously expensive to build or maintain; one that was not unlike those of the established county families; and one that was unpretentiously conformist. Carr, a fellow Yorkshireman who had succeeded in his profession and had been Lord Mayor of York, was exactly the man to provide what was required. Perhaps more than those of any other eighteenth-century architect, his houses measured up to that ideal of Inigo Jones, 'solid, proportionable according to the rules, masculine and unaffected', which might have been devised especially for the merchant landowners.

Carr remained faithful, when the occasion demanded, to the full Palladian plan of a house with quadrants and pavilions. Pye Nest, built *c*.1775 for John Edwards, a Halifax merchant,[97] was such a design (which Thomas Bradley practically reproduced in 1778 when he built Crow Nest for William Walker);[98] and Denton Hall in Wharfedale (now over the border in North Yorkshire), built in 1778 for Sir James Ibbetson, is a simpler and more domestic version of the familiar precedent.[99] Externally, Denton might be regarded as a small edition of the central section of Harewood; internally, the sequence of rooms is skilfully varied on the longer axis, moving in turn from octagon to domed circular staircase, behind a colonnaded screen, and through a lobby into a Breakfast Room with apsidal ends. Thornes House, built in 1779 for James Milnes on an elevated site with 'a charming view of the town of Wakefield, and its two handsome churches', was planned in a compact manner derived but scaled down from Harewood.[100] Externally, it had more a character of a town house with its flat façade ornamented with a pediment and fluted Ionic pilasters. Behind these reticent stone fronts Carr devised delicately detailed Adamesque interiors, which at times attained a formal splendour, as in the Dining Room at Farnley Hall, North Yorkshire.[101] In this house, built for Walter Fawkes in 1786–90, the conservative Palladian most closely approached those severe, Neo-classical, geometric houses associated with the Wyatts and criticised by S.P. Cockerell for resembling 'blocks of stone';[102] but the rooms are precisely decorated with the exquisite repertory of Neo-classical ornament, and the 'imperial' staircase gives an impression of a much grander scale than Walter Fawkes's house possesses.

These are country houses on large estates, but their compact form was the model for the residences which began to be developed by merchants on suburban estates at the end of the eighteenth century. 'Utility, convenience and beauty' were the most desirable qualities of houses for what was called 'the middling and higher class of mankind ... This class possessing or having cultivated a taste for beauty, ornament is added to their apartments, either by elegance in the architectural finishing, or by introducing fine furniture, pictures, &c. and generally in both ways'.[103] It was in answer to these requirements that designs were made on estates close to the town but so placed that industry seemed remote. 'Whether it be the Villa of the Prime Minister, or the Merchant, its character supposes seclusion from intruders, with a command of view, rather than of territory', thought Humphry Repton; 'because, the vicinity of a populous neighbourhood, and consequent excessive value of land, will hardly ever allow of a large extent of demesne attached to it'. This useful definition of a special category of house, which might be referred to as a villa-mansion, appeared in the *Red Book* Repton produced in 1810 for Benjamin Gott, who had bought an estate at Armley in 1803.[104]

Repton neatly captured the atmosphere of a manufacturer's villa-mansion in noting that 'instead of the adjoining landed property being appropriated to the feeding of a few sheep or cattle, almost every acre suggests hundreds of human beings, whose labour and ingenuity are usefully directed to the aggrandisement of the country; while it increases the happiness, by increasing the employment of each individual'. Gott's estate was nicely balanced between a view of the ruined Kirkstall Abbey which Thomas Girtin and J.M.W. Turner sensitively painted about the time Armley changed hands, and a distant sight of the Leeds mills. The distance was, as Repton realised, 'very precarious' and likely to become 'less, and less, as the increasing prosperity of the town daily increases its dimensions, and brings it nearer, and nearer'. He referred to 'the change so recently produced on Mr. Blayd's house in Park-lane, which was lately in the Country though it is now surrounded by streets and other houses'. Repton was also consulted in 1810 by John Blayds, who had bought a house and estate at Oulton,[105] but in architectural and scenic terms Armley was by far the more important.

The house Gott had acquired with his estate had been built *c.*1781 by Thomas Woolrich, a Leeds merchant, in the Carr manner with a canted bay projecting on the east front.[106] Repton's critical judgment was that 'the general outline was good so far as it relates to proportion, but ... it looks like the work of an ignorant country builder, after the design of the more experienced Architect: and may be compared to a good story told in ungrammatical language'. Yet its situation is dramatic, overlooking the whole of the Aire valley in the direction of

102 Farington, J., Typescript of journal in the Royal Library, Windsor, 1352, 10 Nov 1798.

103 Loudon, J.C., *A treatise on forming, improving and managing country residences*, London 1806, i, 70.

104 Repton's *Red Book* for Armley House is in the collection of Mr and Mrs Paul Mellon. See Harris, J., *A catalogue of British drawings ... in American collections*, New Jersey 1971, 172, pls. 121–3.

105 Repton's *Red Book* for Oulton Hall (collection of Dr A.H. Calverley) is on deposit in Leeds City Archives. There were several additions to Oulton; in 1837 John Clark built a stable; in 1839 Sydney Smirke made alterations and additions, including a conservatory; in 1851 and 1874 Perkin and Backhouse added to the house, and in 1851 W.A. Nesfield built new lodges and gates.

106 It seems to have been very similar, e.g. to Crow Nest House.

107 The attribution to Smirke seems to be based solely on Neale, op.cit.,v; but there is no reason to doubt it in spite of a lack of any evidence. The date of remodelling and the building of the portico is not known for certain. The side wings have been removed, reducing the impressiveness of the house, and the view of the Aire valley from the house is less beautiful today than in Repton's watercolour.

108 See Friedman,T.F., 'Aspects of nineteenth-century sculpture in Leeds', *L A C* (1972),no.70,18ff; Friedman,T.F., and Stevens,T., *Joseph Gott, sculptor,* catalogue of exhibition 1972.

109 Schinkel,K.F., *Aus Schinkel's Nachlass,* Berlin 1862–3,iii,86f. 'Die innere Einrichtung kann man königlich nennen, schöne Bilder finden sich überall . . .'

110 See Linstrum, 30. Roundhay Park was bought by Leeds Corporation in 1871, and the house is now the Mansion Hotel. The large estate was landscaped slightly before the house was built (see 120ff.).

111 ibid.,30. Now Chapel Allerton hospital.

112 ibid.,32. Now the Hospital for Women, Roundhay Hall was the home of Edward Allen, 1st Lord Brotherton and of the library which became the nucleus of the Brotherton Library in the University of Leeds (see *Roundhay Hall; the library of Col. Sir Edward Allen Brotherton, Bart.,* Leeds 1926).

113 ibid.,30. Now Meanwood Park hospital.

114 Now known as Potternewton Mansion, an annexe of Park Lane College of Further Education.

115 Now demolished. Photographs are in the Leeds Reference Library.

44

Leeds (including Gott's mills at Armley, Burley and Bean Ing) in what Repton called 'a Panorama stare' in his proposals for improving the landscape and house. Although the landscape was partly executed according to his recommendations, the house itself was remodelled by Robert Smirke,[107] who had returned from Greece in 1805. The design followed Repton's proposals in general, but differed in the character given to the house by its severe detailing and the incorporation of a tetrastyle Ionic temple portico, into which projects the canted bay of the earlier building.

It is a sophisticated design, in accordance with Repton's belief that 'the great world of London must be copied at the distance of two hundred miles . . . Organs, pianofortes, and harps, and tables of every kind . . . cabinets, and sophas, and footstalls, and music stands, and workboxes, and flower pots, and clocks, and bronzes, and cut glass, and China, and Library-tables; covered with books, and pamphlets, and reviews, and newspapers; which contribute to the elegant and rational enjoyment of modern life'. Such was the ideal interior in 1810, and inside Armley Gott placed his Neo-classical sculptures by Joseph Gott and Francis Chantrey, portraits by Thomas Lawrence as well as a collection of paintings by older masters.[108] Important visitors to Gott's mills were invited to Armley, and Karl Friedrich Schinkel, who was there in 1826, was greatly impressed by the gardens, the cultivated taste evident in the contents of the house, and the great Ionic portico which lent to the hill overlooking Leeds something of the character of an Acropolis.[109]

Armley was the first Greek Revival mansion in West Yorkshire, and it gave a lead to other manufacturers who were following Gott's example and building on their suburban estates. The Leeds area provides the most numerous examples, especially around the villages of Gledhow, Moortown, Roundhay and Chapeltown. The Roundhay estate of some 1,300 acres north of Leeds was large by any standard, but the house designed by John Clark for Thomas Nicholson c.1826 was modest and convenient behind the dignified Ionic portico.[110] The

44. Armley House; the garden front was remodelled by Robert Smirke with a Greek Ionic portico after 1810. The wings he added (seen in this old photograph) have been removed.

116 William Lindley made a design for new offices (Allendale BEA/C2/B40/17) and a few sketches for garden buildings; William Atkinson exhibited a design at the Royal Academy in 1807 for what is presumably the entrance known as Archway Lodge, a triumphal arch with lodges. Atkinson seems to have built several garden buildings at Bretton, and might have been responsible for the layout of the new gardens north of the house. His enthusiasm for collecting rare botanical specimens and minerals would have recommended him to the owner; he also made some proposals for redecorating the Drawing Room (Allendale BEA/C2/B40/59).

117 Linstrum,D., *Sir Jeffry Wyatville: architect to the king*, Oxford 1972,109ff; 'Two Wentworth houses', op.cit.,5ff; Oswald,A., 'Bretton Park', *CL* (1938),lxxxiii,530ff,554ff. Bretton is also notable for Wyatt's camellia house, George Basevi's monumental stables (1842–52), and the glass dome, sixty feet in diameter and forty-five feet high, erected in 1827 at an estimated cost of £15,000; the last was taken down in 1832 after the materials had been sold for about £560 (see Loudon,J.C., *An encyclopaedia of cottage, farm and villa architecture*, London 1839,980,pl.1732; possibly he was the designer). 'The Drawings convey but a slight idea of the truly fairy-like REPERTORIUM OF FLOWERS', commented the sale catalogue, which also lists the complete fitting-up of the grotto, Mrs Beaumont's museum, and the so-called 'Magna Charta Window' fifteen feet high and thirteen feet wide which included 'the armorial bearings of the barons assembled at Runnymede' on painted glass. Thomas Wentworth Beaumont (1792–1848) was a patron of the arts, who sent Patrick Macdowell (1799–1870) to Italy to study sculpture; he bought several of the sculptor's subsequent works, including the nine-feet high group of 'Virginius and his Daughter' which was exhibited at the Great Exhibition in 1851 and now stands at the end of the terrace in the Italian Garden at Bretton (which is now a College of Education).

118 In 1772 Godfrey Wentworth is reputed to have 'added a great deal' to Woolley, but it is not clear what he did before his death in 1789. There are decorations that can be attributed to Carr c.1796, after Godfrey Wentworth Wentworth became the owner. There was a fire in that year which burnt 'the hall . . . & the Organ in it, & I suppose the Staircase, as the Architect said, he could now build a better one'. There were several alterations and additions made by George Woodhead (who remodelled the south and east fronts c.1814), Charles Watson (who designed a new organ-case in 1807 and a lodge and gateway in 1814), and Jeffry Wyatt (who made the design for the main entrance from the Wakefield–Barnsley road in 1820 and an unexecuted one for a large conservatory across the south front which could be converted into an open loggia in Summer by removing the sashes). The

same architect was employed by John Hives to design the similarly Ionic Gledhow Grove[111] in the wooded, hilly countryside where a visitor in 1805 thought 'cultivation appears to have reached its zenith'. There was also Roundhay Hall,[112] built in the 1820s for John Goodman, probably by Clark, who remodelled Thomas Denison's c.1780 Meanwood Hall[113] for Christopher Beckett in an Italianate style c.1834. There was Harehills Grove,[114] a neat, Neo-classical house with a segmental Ionic porch, built for James Brown; and south of the town in the still beautiful Aire valley, Abraham Rhodes built an elegant Wyatt-like domed villa on his estate at Knowsthorpe,[115] and John Blayds improved his house and landscape at Oulton, even if he failed to execute all Repton's suggestions.

Some of these villa-mansions, especially those designed by Clark, are richly decorated; but the finest early nineteenth-century interiors are those designed by Jeffry Wyatt at Bretton. Carr's initial improvements of 1793 had been followed by additions designed by William Lindley and William Atkinson,[116] and then Wyatt was brought in to add a large new wing which was built in 1811–14.[117] New gardens were laid out on the hill above the house, and conservatories were built to house rare exotics collected by 'Madame' Beaumont, who also amassed 'specimens of all that is most rare and precious in the mineral kingdom', and commissioned 'a very splendid and highly decorated painted glass window . . . representing the armorial bearings of the barons assembled at Runnymede'. The 2,000 minerals and the painted glass (which were all sold after her death in 1832) were fitted in to the new rooms Wyatt provided and decorated in an appropriately grand manner for his patroness. The Music Room has pilasters decorated with gilded arabesques and a shallow barrel-vaulted ceiling painted in *trompe l'œil* with trophies of musical instruments; in an apse stood a chamber-organ in a carved mahogany case, and above it a line of panels of ruby, green and blue engraved glass allowed a colourful light to glow on the gilt and mirrors; but the most spectacular effect is where the early eighteenth-century staircase was opened up at the half-landing to create a dramatic view to a large new vestibule beyond. The effect of the interpenetrating spaces and *chiaroscuro* is heightened by vast painted wall-panels of Roman ruins and architectural fragments, probably the work of Agostino Aglio, who was employed at the nearby Woolley from 1814.[118] He decorated the Drawing Room there with Italian landscapes within an architectural framework, and he recorded his work in a publication[119] which includes a view of the temporary pavilion erected and decorated for the coming-of-age of Godfrey Wentworth.[120] Aglio continued to be employed at Woolley until 1847, by which time his style of decoration had become richer and more Italianate.

It would not have been out of place in Bankfield, the mansion close to Halifax which was enlarged for Edward Akroyd in 1867.[121] The original house was a plain stone villa, but it was transformed by the Atkinson brothers of York into a Barry-like Italian *palazzo*. The *piano nobile* is reached by a grand staircase entered from a deep *porte-cochère*, and the main rooms were all decorated with paintings from Classical

drawings (with the exception of Woodhead's) are in the Wentworth-Woolley Hall papers in the Brotherton Library, University of Leeds (no accession nos.). Woolley Hall is now a College of Education.

119 Aglio,A., *Sketches of the interior & temporary decorations in Woolley-hall*, London 1821. These decorations were destroyed c.1900. See Linstrum,D., 'Last of the classical decorators', *C L* (1966),cxlii,444f.

120 'The Ball Room was formed by a splendid temporary erection about 70 feet long & the interior was embellished in a most superb manner by the exquisite pencil of Aglio, a celebrated Italian Artist. A succession of landscapes surrounded the room, divided by square pillars of transparent substance decorated with flowers, & lighted within so as to produce a most charming effect. The ceiling was a beautifully painted blue Sky: & from it were suspended a profusion of lights in Chandeliers shedding over the room mid day brilliancy. The roof was supported by two rows of pillars, over which were thrown folds of white Cambric arranged in such a manner as to resemble fluted marble which gently undulated with the motion of the Dance'.

121 Now Bankfield Museum.

122 See Mauchline, op.cit.,124ff.

123 See Ward,J.T., 'Landowners and mining', op.cit.,63ff.

124 In Charles Kingsley's *The water babies*, (1863), the owner of the old, stylistically mixed Harthover Place thought 'it was only an upstart fellow who did not know who his own grandfather was, who would change it for some spick and span new Gothic or Elizabethan thing, which looked as if it had been all spawned in a night, as mushrooms are'.

125 See 114ff. for examples of villas in the Gothic or Elizabethan style.

126 Girouard, op.cit.,179; *B* (1869),xxvii, 945ff.

127 Castle Carr Estate sale particulars, 4 Aug 1874.

128 *A series of picturesque views of castles and country houses in Yorkshire*, Bradford 1885,61; *B* (1873),xxxi,204ff. Now demolished, Milner Field was built of cavity wall construction. It was famous for its conservatories, of which 'Mr. Salt has been his own architect and builder'. Some of the furniture designed by Charles Bevan in a Gothic style and made by Marsh and Jones for Titus Salt has survived. It was described in *BN* (1867),xiv,260 as having a 'groundwork . . . of satinwood; the inlays of amboyna, purple heart, orange wood, black and harewood etc. are cut by Mr. Vert. The mouldings round the panels are relieved with

mythology or, in the Library, with references to the great literary figures whose works formed the basis of an English gentleman's education and collection of books. Barry's remodelling of Harewood in the 1840s had some effect in introducing a vogue for the Italianate style,[122] but by the 60s there were other styles from which to choose.

It is perhaps surprising there were not more Gothic, castellated and Tudor mansions built in the essentially picturesque West Yorkshire landscape; but the hereditary nineteenth-century landowners already possessed houses. They were ready to improve, helped by the increased wealth brought to many by the exploitation of coalmining on their estates;[123] but to build a new house would have invited comparison with the *nouveaux riches*,[124] some of whom did build in an 'old English' style.[125] When John Fielden built his mansion in 1869 on the Dobroyd heights overlooking the Halifax, Rochdale and Burnley valleys, John Gibson designed it as a castle.[126] The rooms are grouped around a central Saloon in which columns of Devonshire marble are crowned by capitals carved to represent English national sports. Panels over the doors recall various stages of the cotton manufacture on which the fortune which paid for Dobroyd Castle was based. Even the central ceiling decoration over the gas lights in the Billiard Room is symbolic; its figures represent Energy. The rooms were finished with expensively inlaid woods and variegated marble fireplaces, but in spite of its corner towers and battlements, the exterior lacks the air of fantasy such a castle needs.

Dobroyd Castle looks best at a distance, and so did Castle Carr, an unloveably grim 'stately pile of buildings in the Norman and Elizabethan styles of architecture', approached through a fortified gatehouse 'and presenting a bold and broken outline' as it faced the heights of Midgley Moor. It was designed for Joseph Priestley Edwards by Thomas Risling c.1850 and completed for Priestley's son by John Hogg; but it was for sale in 1874 when it was described as 'peculiarly adapted for the formation of a Hydropathic Establishment'. Planned around three sides of a large enclosed courtyard, it contained a sequence of interiors as forbidding as its external clothing of battlements and towers suggested; from the 'Grand Entrance . . . up a handsome Flight of Stone Steps, past two figures of Crusaders . . . through a Carved Stone Screen . . . to the Ante Hall which has an elaborate Oak Ceiling . . . on the Right Hand side is the Grand Banqueting Hall or Ball Room . . . the ceiling is Oak-framed on Corbels . . . The Fireplace is of massive Stone on Marble Pillars with Carved Stone Capitals . . . The Mantel is surmounted by Marble Pillars with Carved Stone Capitals supporting a Norman Arch . . . adjoining is the Picture Gallery . . . with Norman Arches . . . and leading therefrom is the Grand Hall . . . paved with Stone . . . and herein is the Principal Staircase which is of Stone . . . the Newel being capped with a Carved Figure of a Talbot Hound, couchant . . . Communicating with the Grand Hall is the Drawing Room . . . The Library is approached by descending a few steps . . . adjoining is the Billiard Room . . . the Fireplace projects, and is of Massive Stone, with a figure of a Talbot Hound on either side . . . over the Mantel is a handsome Bronze,

45. Bretton Hall; the Wentworth–Moyser house was enlarged by Jeffry Wyatt (c.1811–14), who created this theatrical effect at the point where the new wing joined the earlier staircase-hall. The ruin-paintings are attributed to A.Aglio.

49

46. Woolley Hall, the Drawing Room as redecorated by A.Aglio c.1814 and recorded by him in a series of published lithographs (1821).

gold'. See Hutchinson,C., 'Furniture by Marsh and Jones of Leeds 1864–1872', *LAC* (1977),no.88,11ff.

129 Linstrum, 78; see also 116.

130 *A series of picturesque views*, op.cit.,45f. The battlements have been removed from what was described as 'undoubtedly one of the finest residences which have been constructed in Yorkshire, or even the whole Kingdom, during the last decade'. The prevalence of French Second Empire taste was due to Mrs Butterfield, a niece of Judge Roosevelt of New York, who had been 'received into the English and French Courts, and was one of the favourites of the Empress Eugenie'. Cliffe Castle is now a museum.

representing a Stag Hunt . . . The passages and corridors are all Paved with Stone, with Norman Arches over openings.'[127]

Milner Field, built in 1871–3 for Titus Salt junior to a design by Thomas Harris,[128] was far more romantic than Castle Carr in a Burges manner with massive towers, machicolations and monumental chimney stacks. It was raised on a terrace with a steeply battered wall and a circular corner tower with a conical roof. The lower service wing stretched away on one side, and in the background was an octagonal Glastonbury-like kitchen, such as E.W. Pugin had built at Carr House, Meanwood in 1867.[129] Indeed, there were several of the younger Pugin's mannerisms in Milner Field; but it is of Godwin and Burges one is most reminded by this now demolished, compelling design in which the interiors were decorated with Thomas Nicholls's carvings, glass by Saunders and Company, and paintings by Fred Weeks.

Cliffe Castle, near Keighley, built for Henry Isaac Butterfield in 1875–8 by George Smith (whose portrait is carved in the stonework in the Entrance Hall) was called 'a castle in every sense of the word . . . a modernised Tudor castle which, while it maintains faithfully the external architectural characteristics of the Elizabethan period, should also present the elegance and delicacy of treatment of the modern architect'.[130] Two of the towers rise to a height of about eighty feet, and a later addition by Wilson Bailey in the 80s provided an equally gigantic dome, sixty-five feet in diameter, in the Winter Gardens attached to the Ballroom. The Entrance Hall leads into the staircase through an arcade of polished alabaster columns with gilded Caen stone capitals, and 'every one of the rooms has its distinctive colouring and arrangement, and the furnishings and ornamentations are in each case en suite'. There were glittering candelabra hanging from the ceilings painted by M. Leroux, who was brought from Paris, and the walls were

50

Above:
48. Castle Carr (T.Risling c.1850, completed J. Hogg) was built around a stone paved courtyard entered through 'a fine Norman Arch, with Portcullis, Enclosed by a Pair of massive Oak Doors, Studded and Ornamented with Iron'. (1874 sale particulars)

49. Milner Field (T.Harris 1871–3), built for Titus Salt junior close to Saltaire as a romantic Wagnerian pile elevated on a semi-fortified terrace (*Builder*, 15 March 1873).

Opposite:
47. Dobroyd Castle (J.Gibson 1869); despite the castellated external appearance, the plan consists of rooms grouped formally around an octagonal Saloon, beyond which rises an 'Imperial' staircase in a well to which mirrors give an illusion of an infinity of colonnades.

50. Cliffe Castle (G.Smith 1875–8); the suite of five drawing-rooms along the east front (illustrated in this c.1890 photograph) communicated 'one with the other by sliding doors formed of large bevelled-edged mirrors'. The owner's ambition was to procure 'interior arrangements which for efficiency and splendour should not be surpassed'.

panelled with silk and satin. Carpets were woven in France, and an ormulu-mounted malachite fireplace was installed in the Grand Saloon. Even the books in the Library were French. Candelabra previously owned by Byron, and others that had lighted the rooms of Napoleon (whose family was represented by busts on marble pedestals on the staircase landing), furniture that had belonged to the Duc de Mornay, were among the vast collection of furnishings and *objets d'art* inside Cliffe Castle; and the owner's bed was the one on which Rossini had 'passed away to his rest'. Powell Brothers of Leeds provided the coloured glass, including one window which shows 'all the present and past members of the Butterfield family, including those related by marriage, also the steward of the estate . . . the late Emperor of France and the Empress Eugénie, whilst the Madonna and Child are figured at the top. All the figures (except, of course the Madonna and Child) are represented as being in Elizabethan dress'.

The overstuffed, uncomfortably opulent interiors of many of these new country houses contrast tellingly with those of the old county families, still securely established in their mellowing houses despite the changes which were taking place beyond the boundaries of their estates. When Henry James was staying at Fryston in 1878, as the guest of Lord Houghton, he drove over to Bretton on a sledge through the snow to visit Lady Margaret Beaumont, 'a drawling, lisping fine lady enclosed in her great wintry park and her immense, dusky, pictured, luxurious house – with her tea-table at one elbow and a table-full of novels at the other'.[131] Another glimpse of Late Victorian country-house life in West Yorkshire was caught by Augustus Hare, who arrived at Temple Newsam, where 'In an immense gallery, hung with red and covered with pictures . . . I found Mrs. Meynell Ingram and Freddie Wood sitting . . . the light from the fire and the lamps gleamed on a little tea-table and a few chairs round it, all beyond was lost in dark immensity . . . It was like arriving at a bivouac in the desert'.[132]

It was at Temple Newsam, the great house so vividly recorded in Hare's few lines, rather than in one of the new mansions, that the most convincing work in an older style was executed. In an attempt to restore some of the original character, which had disappeared in successive Georgian alterations, the Hon. Mrs Meynell Ingram replaced the sash windows with leaded lights and renewed some of the stone mullions; and in 1894 she authorised the construction of a new staircase designed by Charles Eamer Kempe.[133] Better known as a designer of stained glass, Kempe was a knowledgeable antiquary who modelled the staircase on one previously in Slaugham Place, Sussex; plaster casts were taken and sent to Temple Newsam to ensure the carvings corresponded accurately to the original. The elaborate plasterwork in the stairwell was based on examples well known to Kempe, who also re-styled the Dining Room in a similar manner; fragments of genuine old plasterwork in the house were used as models for the new work, and a fireplace copied from one at Hardwick Hall was crowned with an overmantel which heraldically commemorates the connection of Lord Darnley, father of James I, with Temple Newsam.[134]

Whatever might be thought about the ethics of these improvements, Kempe's staircase is a magnificent tribute from the Late Victorian Age to the Tudor–Jacobean; but its designer is reported to have protested to his patron on one occasion, 'You can't play about with old houses like this'. The introduction in new work of architectural details taken from other houses was not uncommon. In the 1830s John Harper had been a pioneer when he designed unusually convincing alterations and additions to Shibden Hall for Miss Anne Lister by studying decorative lintels, fireplaces and balusters in seventeenth-century buildings in the Halifax area, and then incorporating copies of them in the new work. At the end of the century Walter Henry Brierley was the leading Yorkshire exponent of this traditional designing by imitation;[135] but Sir Edwin Lutyens refused to work in this way when commissioned by Ernest Hemingway, a Bradford merchant, to build a house on an

131 Edel,L., *The conquest of London*, London 1962,318.

132 Hare,A.J.C., *The story of my life*, London 1900,iv,283.

133 Mrs Meynell Ingram's brother, Charles Wood, 2nd Viscount Halifax, embarked on a large-scale rebuilding in baronial style of Garrowby Hall in 1892. His architect was Walter Tower, partner of C.E.Kempe (see Hussey,C., 'Garrowby Hall', *CL* (1949),cvi, 394ff,466ff).

134 Gilbert,C.G., 'C.E.Kempe's staircase and interiors at Temple Newsam', *LAC* (1969),no.65,7ff.

135 See unpublished thesis by Carus, C., *Walter Henry Brierley 1862–1926: York architect*, University of York 1973. Brierley's mastery of traditional design can be seen at its most convincing in the house built for the headmaster of the School for the Blind when that institution occupied the King's Manor, York; it is dated 1900.

51

136 Hussey,C., *The life of Sir Edwin Lutyens*, London 1953,133ff; Weaver,L., *Lutyens' houses and gardens*, London 1921,105ff; Butler,A.S.G., *The architecture of Sir Edwin Lutyens*, London 1950,i,32ff.

137 Hussey, op.cit.,557.

unpromising site in a suburb of Ilkley.[136] Yet, though only four acres in extent, it appeared to continue uninterruptedly over the moors towards the south until it reached the horizon. It was, wrote Lutyens, **88** 'an ultra suburban locality over which villas of dreadful kind and many colours wantonly distribute themselves ... The material was York stone – a stone without a soul to call its own, as sober as a teetotaller'. He recalled how he had 'been scolded for not being Yorkshire in Yorkshire. The other villas have a window from this, a door from that etc – a pot-pourri of Yorkeological details'. Instead of following tradition in that second-hand way, Lutyens was faithful to his own definition that it 'consists in our inherited sense of structural fitness, the evolution of rhythmic forms by a synthesis of needs and materials, and the avoidance of arbitrary faults by the exercise of common sense coupled with sensibility ... The best old work was composed'.[137]

89

52. Heathcote, Ilkley; the garden front of
Ernest Hemingway's house (E.Lutyens
1906), in which every detail was left to
his architect by a client who 'had the
judgement to value the policy of the free
hand'.

In designing Heathcote, or Sanmichele as Lutyens privately called it, he took up again that Classical grammar on which so many of the great country houses had been based; but unlike the Palladians, he went back beyond the Vicentine master's rules to the Doric Order as used by Sanmichele in Verona earlier in the sixteenth century. 'That time-worn doric order – a lovely thing', he called it. 'You can't copy it. To be right you have to take it and design it'. That was how Lutyens produced this remarkable house, an intellectual exercise as subtle and satisfying as any undertaken by his predecessors. The high central section flanked by projecting lower wings or pavilions echoes Paine at Stockeld and St Ives; the sculptural form of the façades recalls Vanbrugh and Hawksmoor at Castle Howard; the precision of the ashlar can be compared with Carr's at Harewood; the unity of design achieved by the patron's wish that the architect should design every piece of furniture and choose every hanging and carpet can be found only perhaps in Adam's work at Nostell; and like the early nineteenth-century merchants' villa-mansions, Heathcote's plan is practical and workable.

When Heathcote was being built in 1906, in the long Edwardian summer, the country house tradition was coming to an end. Soon the last game of croquet would be played on the sunlit lawn, and the last rubber-tyred brougham would drive away to the station on a Monday morning. By a strange chance of Fate the great tradition in Yorkshire was finally epitomised in an Ilkley suburb; coincidentally, Lutyens, in describing the genesis of Heathcote, called it 'no mean game, nor [one] you can play lightheartedly', echoing those wise words of the Earl of Strafford three hundred years earlier, that it was 'nothing so easy a thing to builde well as men take it to bee that know it not'.

3 Comfort, opulence and respectability: housing the middle classes

Ah, yet, e'er I descend to th'grave
May I a small house, and large garden have.
Abraham Cowley, *The Mistress*, 1647

53. Leeds, the Drawing Room in the house built by John Thoresby in Kirkgate in the early seventeenth century. The brick chimney-stack on the right-hand side of the drawing (W.A.Holton 1878) was built by Ralph Thoresby in 1678 as a precaution against fire.

In the early eighteenth century, Leeds was 'very large, [with] abundance of wealthy Merchants in it', and Ralph Thoresby, son and grandson of merchants, is a reliable witness to the quality of their residences at that time. His grandfather, John Thoresby, had built a **53** timber-framed house in Kirkgate in the early seventeenth century, inside which was a room with a plastered, vaulted ceiling in a Late Tudor manner, a survival of an earlier building tradition which can be compared with the relatively late use of a Gothic style for St John's church, Leeds in 1632. When John Thoresby's house was built, timber-framed houses lined the streets and market places in the West Yorkshire towns; in 1628 the houses in Briggate, Leeds were described as 'verie thicke and close compacted together, being ancient meane and lowe built; and generallie all of tymber; though they have stone quarries frequent in the town, and about it; only some few of the richer sort of the inhabitants have theire houses more large and capacious, yett all lowe and straightened on their backsides'.[1]

There are few useful contemporary descriptions of pre seventeenth-century houses in the towns, although a lease dated 1432 refers to a house built for William Greenwood in the Holdsworth Ing, Ovenden, Halifax. It was eight bays long ('*de octo laquearibus contiguis . . . Anglicé, viij crukkes*') and was to be covered '*cum tegulis . . . Anglicé, sclatestones*'; the interstices between the timber crucks were probably filled with stone slates and the whole was then rendered with clay and straw. The interiors of fifteenth-century houses were generally distempered over the plaster and wainscot, often with a repetitive pattern representing tapestry. Robert Savile, who acquired Shibden Hall in 1504, lined the walls and ceiling of his hall with oak, and painted the latter sky-blue, the beams dark brown with crimson lining to the edges, and the bosses silver. An inventory of 1536 indicates that the walls of the vicarage in Halifax, then occupied by an unusually wealthy incumbent, were covered with 'fine *say*', a type of worsted tapestry, which was striped and fringed; some of the beds had testers and hangings, and there were carpets for the tables and cushions for the chairs,[2] but this must have been an exceptional interior in Halifax or any of the other West Yorkshire towns.

Thoresby referred to the old house of the Rockley family in Lowerhead Row, Leeds (which was bought by John Harrison about

1 Corporation of London MSS R.C.E. No.60; see *Northern History* (1975),x,126f.

2 Roth,H.L., *The Yorkshire coiners 1767–1783*, Halifax 1906,154ff.

54. Wakefield, the timber-framed house in Kirkgate (1566) known as 'Six Chimneys'. (Kilby, T., *Views in Wakefield*, 1853)

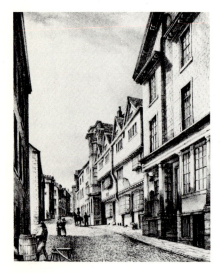

55. Halifax, the Wool-Shops in the 1830s, showing a double-jettied timber-framed house flanked by eighteenth-century buildings; all were demolished in the 1830s. (Horner, J., *Buildings in the town and parish of Halifax*, 1835)

3 Walker, 592ff. 'Six Chimneys' was demolished in 1941.

4 This house has been re-erected in Leeds Road and is now known as 'Daisy Bank'. See Roth, op.cit., 175ff.

5 ibid., 215; this is a quotation from the *Halifax Courier* 1887, and should not be taken too literally.

6 *HAS* (1955), 62. Quoted from a MS, probably written by Thomas Sutcliffe of Ovenden Hall.

7 Whitaker, 79f.

the beginning of the seventeenth century) as 'a Timber-Building, and of the most Antique Form of any I have seen; Instead of Deals or Boards for the Floors, were Oak-Planks of so considerable a Thickness, that Joysts were made of them for part of the new Bricke-Building'. Whitaker added a note in his edition of Thoresby's history, that he had seen a drawing of this house made by the historian, and that it 'consisted of a Centre and two Wings, with a pointed Door Way at the lower End of the central Part, all of Timber'; in fact, he was describing a cross-passage house with wings, such as could probably have been found in most West Yorkshire towns. There were fine timber-framed houses in Wakefield, such as 'Six Chimneys', built in Kirkgate in 1566 with a double jettied front, and surviving until relatively recently; or a house in Northgate in which was a richly decorated ceiling modelled with the Royal arms and heraldic figures, and dated 1596; or others in Westgate which had elaborately carved barge-boards and moulded finials.[3] 'The House at the Maypole', a re-erected (and heavily restored) house which stood at the corner of Crown Street and Corn Market in Halifax is a valuable survival of a framed building with vertical and diagonal struts, and three corbelled bays;[4] this obviously decorative arrangement of the structural timbers and struts, which seems to have been common in many merchants' houses in West Yorkshire, appears to confirm that in at least some cases the frames were intended to be left exposed and not plastered over. Yet one would hesitate before subscribing entirely to a nineteenth-century view that the façades in Halifax ever appeared as one romantic writer imagined they were in 1778 when the Piece Hall was opened: 'The timbers of the ancient overhanging houses in the streets had been newly painted in colours of black, brown and maroon, the interstices in each case being white, and the buildings presented a new and gay appearance'.[5] It is perhaps more valuable to have a description of what Halifax was really like in 1778 by a writer who recalled 'the old Houses [which] had clumsy Ugly Balconies, or the projection of the upper Stories supported upon Pillars that left a kind of covered way . . . stone Spouts to convey the Water from the tops of the Houses that in Rain came pouring down into the Street, and Signs to Inns, &c. hung out as supporters almost into the middle of the street'.[6] John Horner's early nineteenth-century lithographs of Halifax tally exactly with this description.

Whitaker's dismissal of 'all the timber buildings which I have seen' as 'wretchedly dark and comfortless within' was an opinion already reached by some seventeenth-century merchants. Nor did the early nineteenth-century historian think the stone buildings of the sixteenth century much of an improvement; their 'high narrow windows, . . . diamond "quarrels", . . . stone floors (I am now speaking of the best houses in the town), together with the absence of shutters and curtains, afford but a melancholy picture of the dwellings of thriving manufacturers down to the reign of Charles I'.[7] Nor is he likely to have thought very highly of the dark interior of the Old Hall (later known as Wade Hall) in Leeds, in which the walls of the principal room were 'covered with wainscot, and the chimney piece is richly ornamented . . .

The staircase is of massive construction . . . the turned balusters, the broad handrail, and the massive stocks, surmounted with carved standards, are all of polished oak . . . At the head of the staircase a little square lobby of panelled oak leads into another fine old room, with its wainscot unpainted, and ornamented with a deep frieze very richly carved in foliage and grotesque heads. The chimney piece is handsomely decorated'. Like much woodwork of this time, it was based on strangely bastardised versions of Italian Mannerist decoration and was strongly architectural with columns dividing the sections of wall panelling, framing the fireplace, and even appearing as little Classical temple fronts in the carved panels in the overmantel. The quality of craftsmanship can be assessed from that in the nearby St John's church, with which the interior of the Old Hall must have been contemporary, and there is no lack of evidence of the richness of decoration in merchants' houses in other towns. The plasterwork in Halifax houses, or the fireplace in Todmorden Old Hall, are well known examples.[8]

The introduction of brick, believed Whitaker, was 'a very material step towards modern comfort', and as coarse strong clay could be found in West Yorkshire, brick was commonly used in Leeds and Wakefield from the late seventeenth century; it partly superseded stone even in the region around Halifax and Bradford where the material was so plentiful. In Leeds, there was the Red Hall in Upperhead Row (traditionally so called because when this three-gabled house was erected in 1628 by Thomas Metcalf, it was the first brick building in the town), and others could be found in the area around St John's known as Town End, including the old timber-framed parsonage which Thoresby noted had been 'new cased with brick'.[9] Safety, as well as fashion, was responsible for much rebuilding; in 1678 the antiquary was busy in his Kirkgate house 'taking down the pictures, beds, &c., in order to the workmen's pulling down the chimneys, to build them more safely, conveniently, &c., of brick'.[10] The use of this material was evidently still worthy of note in the 1730s; several advertisements in the newspapers drew attention to it, as the one in the *Leeds Mercury* in 1737 which offered 'a large and convenient Dwelling House . . . all new cased with good Brick, and several new brick Chimneys carried up from the Rooms . . . and a fashionable new Stone Fire Stead'. The other feature that receives particular mention in the notices of houses for sale or (more frequently) to let, at this time, is the provision of sash windows. The *Leeds Mercury* for 3 November, 1730, for example, offers 'A good new fashionable House, Sash Windows, five Rooms on a Floor, four Stories high . . . situate in Northgate in Wakefield'.

It is to Thoresby that we owe descriptions of early eighteenth-century Leeds which indicate the grandeur of merchants' houses which disappeared long ago. He referred to Kirkgate and Boar Lane, where were 'several Gentlemen's houses therein', but more particularly he wrote of a scene that is difficult to visualise when confronted by the squalor of present-day Call Lane. He described a footpath which went from 'the Church to the Bridge . . . thro' the Fields by certain *Gardens*

8 The description of the interior of the Old Hall is quoted in Stocks,J.E., 'The church of St John the Evangelist', *T S* (1919),xxiv,194. For plasterwork of the seventeenth century in Halifax, see *Y A S* (1922),xxvi,144ff.

9 The facing of timber-framed houses with brick or stone was common practice, and several apparently eighteenth-century buildings still conceal an earlier structure behind their façades. The 1707 'Act for the better preventing mischiefs that may happen by fire' laid down regulations about the use of brick; it was not applicable outside London, but the enforced use of brick in the metropolis helped to set a fashion and a standard of safety for the provinces.

10 See Atkinson,D.H., *Ralph Thoresby, the topographer: his town and times*, Leeds 1885,i,62. Possibly Thoresby's rebuilding of his chimneys was suggested by the 1667 'Act for the re-building of the city of London'.

11 Thoresby, 76. Jacques Parmentier (1658–1730) moved from London to Yorkshire *c.*1700. He was introduced to Thoresby by Henry Gyles, the glass painter, in a letter dated 26 Jan 1702/3, in which he was described as 'a most excell[t] Artist, either in painting noble hystory or faces after the life, as many of his peices both here and at Hull do testifie. What favours you can do him in acquainting him with gentlemen of your acquaintance I shall take it as done to my selfe'. (*TS* (1912),xxi,128). Parmentier painted the portrait of Thoresby which is in the possession of the Society of Antiquaries of London, and he was employed at Castle Howard (1707), Holy Trinity, Hull (1712), John Moyser's house in Beverley, Bradford Manor House, St Peter's, Leeds, Richard Wilson's house in Mill Hill, Leeds, as well as John Atkinson's house in The Calls. See Walpole,H., *Anecdotes of painting*, London 1862 edn.,ii,631, and Croft-Murray,E., *Decorative painting in England 1537–1837*, London 1957–70,i,256f,ii,320f.

12 The doorway is taken from pl.51, *Porta del Giardino del Sigr. Prencipe di Pelestrina alle Quattro fontane*, and the window from pl.89, *Altra Finestra contigua a l'antecedente, nella facciata dell'Oratorio*. Thus, both Pietro da Cortona and Francesco Borromini acted, at second hand, as designers of the Leeds house.

13 Bourchier was in Italy in 1704, and it is quite likely that he brought back Rossi's book, borrowing from it when the design of his own house was being made, and making it available to his builder as a source of details for other houses.

14 James, 296; Ayers, 2. The doorway was incorporated in a design made by Lockwood and Mawson in 1870 for a drinking-fountain in Peel Park, Bradford.

15 The house was demolished in 1968.

16 Micklegate House was a plain, five-bay house, three storeys high, which might have been designed by John Carr or John Watson. Single-storey wings, three bays wide, were added on each side, and that on the west contained the ceiling illustrated in pl.59. It is very likely that Giuseppe Cortese was the craftsman responsible; he was working in Yorkshire from *c.*1725, and he died at York in 1778, his executors being the Wakefield cabinet-maker Edward Elwick and the York plasterer James Henderson. Cortese worked at several of the great houses in the county, such as Newburgh Priory (1739–67), Studley Royal (1745–52), Gilling Castle (*c.*1750) and Burton Constable (1769); but he also executed decorative plasterwork in the Beverley Guildhall (1762), St Peter's, Sowerby (1766), and John Royds's house in Halifax (1766). (See Beard,G., *Decorative plasterwork in Great Britain*, London 1975,213).

(particularly Alderman *Cookson's* who has lately erected here a very pleasant seat, with Terras Walks &c)'; and in 'the adjoining Orchard ... *John Atkinson* Esq, ... is now building a delicate House, that for the exquisite Workmanship of the Stone-work, especially the Dome, and for a painted Stair-Case, excellently performed by Monsieur *Permentier* &c, exceeds all in Town'.[11] John Cossins's famous plan of Leeds, dated 1725, shows a small elevation of Atkinson's house, five bays wide, three storeys high, with a central segmental pediment and a domed cupola over the staircase. Cookson's is similar in size and disposition of elements, but has a balustraded gallery in the centre of the roof. There are five grand houses illustrated on the plan itself, and fifteen larger-scale façades in the margins; on the whole, they appear superior to those on Cossins's slightly later plan of York, but not a single example survives and architectural documentation of them is virtually non-existent.

Almost all these merchants' houses were constructed of brick, with stone quoins and cornices, string courses and keystones. Some incorporated entrances to passages leading to warehouses at the rear, but none of Cossins's examples illustrates this. One house is decorated with giant pilasters, but the most common design is of a five-bay, three-storey façade with a central emphasis. An old photograph of 10 Town End, built for Robert Denison and subsequently owned by the Sheepshanks family, is an example which probably indicates the quality of decorative detailing on the other, unrecorded houses. An especially interesting feature of Denison's house is that its designer or builder owned, or had access to, a copy of Domenico de Rossi's *Studio d'Architettura Civile*, published in Rome in 1702. The entrance doorway and the central first-floor window are copied directly from plates in Rossi's book,[12] which must have been a remarkably scarce item in early eighteenth-century West Yorkshire; yet it was known to the builder of John Bourchier's house at Beningbrough, north of York, which was begun in 1716.[13] As it is now believed that William Thornton, the York joiner, was largely responsible for that distinguished building, he is the likely author of Denison's house (and possibly of similar designs for other Leeds merchants).

Denison's house is not unlike the Manor House, Bradford, rebuilt in 1705 for William Rawson and, like Atkinson's in Leeds, decorated by Parmentier; Andromeda and Perseus, Bacchus and Ariadne, occupied the walls of the staircase, and the ceiling above represented the Four Seasons. The available illustrations of the exterior of this demolished building are not sufficiently clear to enable the source of the central decoration to be identified, but it was richly Baroque.[14] Another Leeds house, built for Nathaniel Denison as Sheepscar Hall (later known as Bischoff House), can probably be related to William Etty's design for Holy Trinity church and the craftsmen who built it. Unusual in Leeds because of its ashlar facing, it had quoins, 'Gibbs' surrounds to the lower windows, and triangular pediments over those on the first floor. The staircase in this last survivor of the Leeds merchants' houses testified to the fine quality of their interior fittings,[15] as did the plasterwork and fireplaces in Micklegate House, Pontefract;[16] this was

56. Leeds, 10 Town End; Robert Denison's house (pre-1725) represents the new fashion for brick buildings with stone dressings, and it illustrates the use of details from plates of Roman buildings. It is shown here in a photograph c.1880.

57. Leeds, Sheepscar Hall (or Bischoff House), built for Nathaniel Denison (pre-1725) possibly by W.Etty.

one of several fine houses in what the actor-manager Tate Wilkinson called 'that little Montpellier' of Yorkshire in 1776. An advertisement in the *Leeds Mercury* for 30 December 1729/30 suggests how pleasant life was in the town:

To be Lett or Sold A Handsome well built new House, neatly finish'd . . . situate in Pontefract, in a Healthfull Air, with large and beautiful Prospects, together with very pleasant Gardens, planted with Evergreens for Ornament, and Fruit Trees of the best kind both Standards and against the Walls. There is also a Wilderness adjoining to the Gardens very handsomely disposed into Walks and Yew Hedges intermixed with flowering Shrubs and Fruit Trees and also a commodious cold Bath.

This is a relatively rare description of a garden surrounding a West Yorkshire town house, and it probably reflects the influence in the Pontefract area of the well-known family of Perfects, nurserymen who supplied trees and plants to several of the great houses in the county. Paul Jollage's map of the town, published in 1742, shows the large gardens attached to several of the Pontefract houses, some of which can be seen in Thomas Malton's 1777 view of the Market Place. Two of the buildings which survive from that time in the Market Place are of unusually fine quality. The present Barclay's Bank, once successively a private house and the *Black Bull*, can probably be attributed to James Paine who was supervising the erection of Nostell Priory; the giant recessed arch and broken pediment distinguish this façade immediately, but perhaps less obvious is Robert Adam's responsibility for the remodelling of the *Red Lion* on the opposite side of the street in 1776, when he too was working at Nostell.

No designers' names can be confidently attached to other houses, such as Northgate House, Halifax, built in 1735–42 for Richard Clapham,[17] or Meanwood Hall, Leeds, built c.1760 for Thomas Denison,[18] or Denison Hall, Leeds, built c.1786 for John Denison following an advertisement for sixty or eighty stonemasons to execute the work, or for many others which survive only in brief descriptions or photographs. The knowledge that John Carr designed merchants'

17 Wilson, J., 'Northgate House', *HAS* (1959), 1ff.

18 Lumb, G.D., 'The family of Denison of Great Woodhouse, and their residences in Leeds', *TS* (1909), xv, 251ff.

60

97

58. Leeds, Sheepscar Hall (or Bischoff House); the main staircase, possibly executed by John de Goulons, carver at Holy Trinity church, Leeds.

59. Pontefract, Micklegate House; the central figure of Justice in the ceiling of one of the rooms, possibly the work of Giuseppe Cortese.

60. Leeds, Denison Hall, Hanover Square; built c.1786 for John Denison in a Neo-classical manner with semicircular side bays flanking a pedimented centre; internally, the best feature is a domed, elliptical staircase-hall.

61. Halifax, John Royds's house (or Somerset House), George Street; an impressive group of a central house flanked by warehouses (J.Carr 1766), of which only a part remains.

houses in Wakefield and Halifax suggests he might have been more frequently consulted than is generally recognised. It is very likely that he rebuilt the old Leeds residence of Sir William Lowther for Jeremiah Dixon 'very handsomely' with a stone front in the 1750s;[19] and he has been credited with a number of houses in the Halifax group known as 'The Square', built for John Caygill close to the Piece Hall (to which he had been one of the most generous subscribers) in the late 50s. These houses (unusually built of brick in the predominantly stone town) were designed around a communal garden, and were approached through an entrance gate which provided greater security and privacy. Their principal rooms were said to have 'handsome fireplaces and decorated ceilings and cornices',[20] but they are unlikely to have been comparable internally with the magnificent house Carr designed in Halifax for John Royds in 1766, facing on to 'pleasure grounds tastefully

19 According to Thoresby, there were several houses in Boar Lane, Leeds which were owned by Sir William Lowther in 1715; they were sold to Sir William Rooke in 1732, and one was subsequently sold to Richard Wilson, then to John Dixon, who died in 1749. His son, Jeremiah, 'Pulled down the old House and rebuilt it very handsomely, the Stone for the Front being brought from Huddleston Quarry' (Thoresby,5). This is interesting for showing that millstone grit was not used exclusively in Leeds, and that the magnesian limestone associated with York Minster was used in special circumstances in the eighteenth century outside the limestone area. It must have been very expensive and regarded as a great luxury, which is presumably why Thoresby particularly mentions Dixon's use of it on the façade of his new town house.

20 *HAS* (1961),72.

21 Crabtree, 359.

22 The building has been badly mutilated, but the Saloon retains Cortese's decorative plasterwork.

23 Walker, 463ff. Pemberton Milnes had a passion for building and brickmaking; the brick kilns were on the Wakefield–Ossett road, and were afterwards converted into ornamental fishponds as part of a layout including planting and 'a little Grecian summerhouse'. Milnes's interest was referred to in a verse of Lord Effingham's coalition song, quoted in Walker, op.cit.;
Oh, Pemberton Milnes,
Not all thy brick-kilns
Can consistency give to thy clay,
First to sign the requisition,
Then to join the coalition
And make a Milnes his engagement betray.

24 In 1864, a compulsory purchase order was authorised by Act of Parliament to enable the West Riding and Grimsby Railway Company to build a station on land surrounding Pemberton Milnes's house, which was then put to various uses. It was the subject of a Public Inquiry in 1975, which resulted in refusal to allow demolition; but it is only a relic of what it was.

25 Wilson,R.G., 'The Denisons and Milneses; eighteenth-century merchant landowners' *Land and industry* (ed.Ward,J.T., and Wilson,R.G.), Newton Abbot 1971,162ff; Clarkson,R., *Memories of merry Wakefield*, Wakefield 1889,46ff; Walker, 463f; Taylor,K., *Wakefield District heritage*, Wakefield 1976,74ff.

26 This orangery was given to Westgate Chapel by Daniel Gaskell, and it is still in use as a social centre; an insignificant fragment remains of John Milnes's house.

27 Richardson,G., *New Vitruvius Britannicus*, London 1802, pls 51–3. Thornes House was converted into a Local Authority school and burned down in the 1950s.

arranged, and secluded from observation by a high wall'.[21] This was a composite building; the central section was a residence and bank, and on each side were warehouses. The whole design was seventeen bays long, subdivided into seven sections which were varied at roof level by the inclusion of pediments on two, and a central solid parapet decorated with Neo-classical reliefs. The exterior of the whole building is in the combination of West Yorkshire vernacular and Palladian proportion that Carr developed so successfully. The walls are built of coursed Elland Flags wallstones with dressed quoins and window-surrounds; only the large windows in the central section have moulded architraves, pediments and blind balustrades, and the doorways are the simple, pedimented type with Tuscan half-columns which Carr used so often on his town houses in York and elsewhere.[22] Internally, Royds's house was on an unusually lavish scale; Giuseppe Cortese was employed to decorate the Saloon with rococo plasterwork incorporating scenes from Aesop's fables inside fantastic cartouches, and great set-pieces which traditionally represent Royds as Neptune surrounded by four of his daughters as naiads on the ceiling, while his wife takes the part of Britannia in a swaggering patriotic group, dated 1766, over the fireplace. The splendour of Royds's house was such that he was able to act as host to the Danish king, Christian VII, during his tour of England.

The Milnes brothers, who were merchants in Wakefield and owners of one of the largest export houses in the whole Yorkshire cloth trade, all employed Carr as their architect in Westgate. They made their own bricks and imported their timber from Russia, the source of much of their wealth because of the virtual monopoly they enjoyed of trading in cloth with that country.[23] An older, gabled house on the north side of the street was altered for Robert Milnes in the 1750s, and it was behind this that the firm of Milnes, Heywood and Co. had its counting houses. At about the same time, Carr designed a house on the opposite side of Westgate for James Milnes; and in 1752 it was the turn of Pemberton Milnes, who chose a site close to his brother Robert's house. Pemberton's was said to have been 'rather smaller than the rest … [and] rich in carving and plasterwork'.[24] The finest of the four was John Milnes's, built as a rectangular house in 1773 and then extended in the 1790s when quadrant wings were added; behind the west façade was formed a suite of a Library, a Drawing-room with a typical projected bay with canted sides, and a magnificent Ballroom 'most beautifully finished – the ceilings were painted by Italian artists'.[25] There were extensive gardens behind this house, but unfortunately all were close to where the railway company chose to build a station, and the only recognisable survival of all this mercantile splendour of the Milnes brothers is a colonnaded orangery built for Pemberton.[26]

The later history of the Milnes family explains some of the changes which occurred in merchants' houses in the last decades of the eighteenth century. In 1779–81 Carr built Thornes House outside the town for James Milnes,[27] whose brother Pemberton had recently bought an estate at Bawtry and subsequently gained the reputation of having 'drunk more port wine than any gentleman in Yorkshire'.

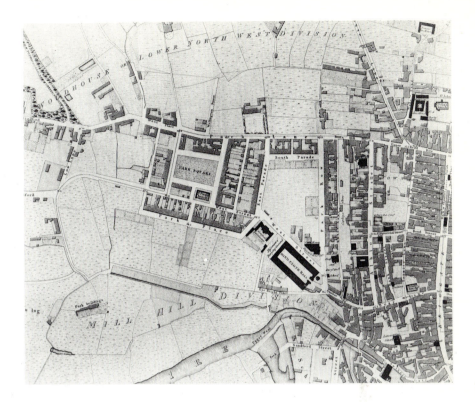

62. Halifax, John Royds's house (or Somerset House); Giuseppe Cortese executed the plasterwork in the Saloon, of which this detail illustrates Britannia, triumphing over weapons of war and offering Peace. Dated 1766, it is probably a reference to the Peace of Paris (1763), which can be said to have established Britain as an Imperial Power.

63. Leeds, the Parks estate; begun in the 1760s, the pattern of terraces and squares developed around the Mixed or Coloured Cloth Hall, the source of the wealth of most of the residents.

Robert Milnes bought the Fryston estate in 1786, and this move into landed society of the wealthy merchant families coincided with the breakdown of the monopoly many of them had enjoyed; the competition of the manufacturers forced them out of business in the end, but not before many had become established landowners and married into county families. At the transitional stage, in the last quarter of the eighteenth century, the merchants lived in two worlds. In Leeds, for example, William Denison had a house in Kirkgate furnished with books and Italian paintings, but looking on to a yard in which were his counting house, dressing and packing shops, stables and a dung hill. Away from his work, Denison lived on his estate at Ossington, was painted by Gainsborough, and after his death was commemorated by Nollekens in a church on his own land designed by Carr.[28]

Towns were growing, gardens were being built on, and the middle classes moved. The wealthiest left the towns altogether for their country estates; the less wealthy bought houses in the new squares and terraces. The first of these urban expansions began in Leeds in the 1760s on an estate known as the Parks, 140 acres of green fields west of the town. A grid layout was made of parallel streets, first of Park Row and East Parade running north to south, connected by South Parade which ran east to west to form a square; this was then extended further west by the parallel Park Place and Park Lane, with Park Square between them as the potentially most fashionable part, farthest from the Mixed or Coloured Cloth Hall and the Infirmary, which lay on the south side of the first square. However, they were not exclusively residential. A 1792 notice of sale reveals that Thomas

63

28 Wilson, op.cit.,161f. Nollekens's monument to Robert Denison is illustrated in Penny,N., *Church monuments in romantic England*, New Haven 1977,pl.44.

64. Leeds, Park Square; the houses, of which those illustrated are on the north side, were built to individual designs rather than in accordance with a uniform façade.

Lloyd's 'capital Mansion-House' in South Parade had as neighbours smaller houses 'and large and commodious Cloth Stuff and Wool Warehouses, with good Press Shops, Dressing Shops and other conveniences'; there were also tenter-frames in some gardens. Building was slow; by 1780 there were only a dozen houses in Park Row and South Parade, but by 1793 sixty-four houses had been finished.

Other sites in Leeds were being offered for development; Robert Denison's house in Town End was for sale in 1791, and its estate was described as 'capable of being converted into one or more Rows of elegant Buildings . . . or otherwise of forming a handsome Street', which was 'now making' in 1792. In 1795, Thomas Johnson, who had already laid out Albion Street, advertised for sale plots of building land in Woodhouse Lane which commanded 'a most beautiful, picturesque, and extensive prospect';[29] it was developed later as relatively small houses known as Blenheim Terrace. Unlike similar developments in London and Edinburgh, these terraces and squares

29 *LI*, 31 Aug 1795.

65. Wakefield, South Parade; begun in the 1790s (W.Lindley). The design for West Parade, on the right (C.Watson 1804) was not executed. (Aquatint by J.Cawthorne 1804)

30 See Wilson, R.G., *Gentlemen merchants: the merchant community in Leeds 1700–1830*, Manchester 1971, 198ff. The most extensive survivals of this eighteenth-century development are in Park Square, but there is much in Park Place (n. side), and a few houses in East Parade (w. side).

31 A characteristic of late eighteenth-century houses in Wakefield is the giant semicircular-headed blank arch in the centre of the façade. It appears on houses in Northgate and Westgate, in Barstow Square, and on Silcoates House, built for John Lumb *c.*1748, but remodelled later. Perhaps it was a feature introduced by William Lindley, who also made use of it in Doncaster, e.g., the Dispensary (1793).

32 Eight acres were bought in 1751 by William Charnock, a merchant, whose children developed the land as South Parade.

33 Parsons, i, 312.

64 were not designed with uniform façades to which the builder had to conform; but as they were all plain brick houses with more or less standard sash windows and pedimented doorcases, the effect was harmonious and domestic rather than grand. The houses varied in size; one in Park Lane had a drawing-room and dining-room, six bedrooms and servants' quarters. Another, in South Parade, had in addition a library and breakfast-room, and there were eleven bedrooms and spacious quarters for eight horses.[30] One occupied by Samuel Buck had 'Six Rooms on a Floor, fitted up with neat Paper, Marble Hearths and Chimnies decorated, Grates, etc. and below Stairs are all Kinds of Fixtures, and Two Stables, Coach and Cowhouses'. This last description illustrates how the erection of new town houses stimulated craftsmanship, so that Robert Rhodes could advertise in the *Leeds Mercury* (21 Nov 1769) that 'he hath lately furnished himself with a good assortment of the Finest Marble from Italy &c . . . for Chimney Pieces, Side board Tables, Monuments, Mortars, or any article in the Marble Way'; Thomas Sunderland, in the same newspaper (25 Dec 1770), referred to his employment at Harewood House as a painter and offered to execute 'House Painting . . . Pencil-Work, Coach, Chaise and Sign-painting, History Pieces, Landscapes &c.' The refinements of life were all becoming available.

The development of late eighteenth-century housing in Wakefield followed a pattern of changing requirements and taste from an enclosed group such as Barstow Square off Westgate,[31] to the first attempt to 65 build a fashionable terrace in the 1790s when South Parade was started, to a design by William Lindley,[32] on a sloping site overlooking the open country and the Milnes' estate at Thornes; and then to a more ambitious scheme around St John's church, north of the town. The St John's development was controlled by John Lee, a Wakefield solicitor who bought the site and was largely responsible for obtaining an Act of Parliament to build the church designed by Lindley and Watson which forms the nucleus of the layout; 'for beauty of situation, elevation of buildings, regulation of plan, and tasteful arrangement of ground', it was thought 'equal, if not superior to anything of the kind in the county of York'.[33] The architects, who designed the whole layout, set the church in the middle of St John's 66 Square, around which brick terraces were built on the north and west

66. Wakefield, St John's Square and Street; designed as a formal layout around the church (1791–5) with uniform façades. (Aquatint by J. Cawthorne 1804)

sides. Lee speculated in building some houses at his own expense, and in other instances he leased the ground to builders or to the Union Society, established in 1790 to raise a fund 'by a Society of Artificers or other persons, in and for the purchasing of Plots or Parcels of Ground . . . and building thereon Messuages, Dwellinghouses and other Edifices',[34] For his own occupation, Lee built St John's House, at the south end of the west terrace, overlooking open country; it is the largest in the whole layout, with a seven-bay façade, pedimented central section and tripartite first-floor window with a fan lunette. The other house elevations to the square are uniform, although minor variations appear to have been permitted in the doorcases. The overall elevational design continues the axial layout towards the east as St John's North (originally Street), a long formal terrace with a pedimented central house of five bays, flanked by others of three. This design 'for uniformity towards the Southerly front [with] good sashed windows, Stone Door Cases and Stone Window Sills' was made by John Thompson; the later buildings are not conceived in the formal manner of the layout, which concludes (rather weakly) with a neat three-bay house in Leeds Road which responds to the east end of the church.

There is nothing remarkable about the standard late eighteenth-century architecture of these Leeds and Wakefield layouts, except that they were planned, rational and orderly. They provided an exclusive little social world, mainly for merchants, but also for those who lived by the law, medicine and the church; the fortunate residents in houses on the Parks estate also enjoyed exclusive pew and interment rights in St Paul's church, Park Square. The Wakefield development contributed much towards making it 'by far the most agreeable town in this district', in the opinion of Edward Parsons. 'There is a more general diffusion of comfort . . . and both the appearance of the town and the manners of the inhabitants are indubitably superior to those of the places which are exclusively peopled by clothiers'.[35] St John's retained its exclusiveness, and is still a pleasant residential area, but the Parks estate in Leeds was doomed by a lack of control over the neighbouring developments, and especially by the sale to Benjamin Gott of a site to the west on which to build his great factory. Smoke from Bean Ing, and even from the distant Kirkstall Forge, 'emitting its volumes of smoke by day, and its pillars of flame by night', as well as other unwelcome forms of pollution from the dye-houses in the vicinity, made the houses both undesirable and unhealthy. In 1810 Humphry Repton had noted that 'Mr. Blayd's house in Park Lane, which was lately in the Country . . . is now surrounded by streets and other houses';[36] but in 1834 Parsons wrote that whereas previously 'only a few houses in Park Lane could be seen between [Spring Gardens] and Park Square, the scene is now completely changed. Large dyehouses and manufactories line the northern side of the river; streets of cottages open from the great western road', and the avenue 'which conducts the traveller to St. Paul's Church and Park Square is now one of the meanest, the most irregular, and the most unpleasant in the whole circumference of Leeds'.[37] How different it was from the

34 The last five houses at the east end of St John's Street were built by the Union Society.

35 Parsons, i, 315.

36 Repton, H., *Red Book* for Armley House, 1810. Collection of Mr and Mrs Paul Mellon. The house owned by John Blayds, referred to in this extract, was on the site of Leeds Town Hall.

37 Parsons, i, 171.

104

38 ibid.,i,153. *LI* 9 Oct 1828 refers to 'plans of layout and elevations of streets, villas and fancy cottages' which could be seen at the offices of the architects, Watson and Pritchett, York.

39 Thoresby Society, Box A; two plans, s. *Watson and Pritchett*, d. *September, December 1823*.

40 loc.cit,; plan s. *Henry Teal, Surveyor*, d. *1824*; plans s. *J.P.Pritchett*, d. *1836*, and *George Smith*. Joshua Major (*1787–1866*), landscape gardener, lived at Knostrop, near Leeds. He was the author of *A treatise on insects most prevalent on fruit trees* (1829), *The theory and practice of landscape gardening* (1852), and *The ladies' assistant in the formation of their flower gardens* (1861). He was also a frequent contributor to the *Gardeners' magazine* edited by J.C.Loudon. As well as laying out Hanover Square, Major was responsible for the landscaping around Wells House, Ilkley (1856) and 'The People's Pleasure Grounds' at Meltham Mills (see 143). His design for Woodhouse Cemetery, Leeds (1833), submitted jointly with William Perkin, was awarded second prize.

41 Hanover Square was, in a sense, completed later, but not according to the original intention. The later houses are small and nondescript, and a former chapel and its schoolrooms occupy part of the south side.

42 The two houses in Woodhouse Square, now known as Waverley House, cost £1,931 14s 9½d. Clark's commission was £56 5s 3d. (Information from Mr and Mrs Payne).

43 Belmont was built *c*.1786 for Joseph Oates, Claremont *c*.1790 for Samuel Elam, Belle Vue House *c*.1793 for Michael Wainhouse, and Springfield House *c*.1797 for Thomas Livesey. All have survived, although not always in their original condition.

quiet little area of plain stone-faced houses that had been built in Halifax around Holy Trinity church, or the formal groups that were being laid out, probably by Joseph Kaye, in Huddersfield in the 1820s. Clearly it was no place for the wealthy Leeds merchants and professional men, who were rapidly retreating up the hill to the north.

There was 'a magnificent plan . . . of erecting some spacious and elegant streets, squares, &c. [at Buslingthorpe] upon the whole of which the name of the New Town of Leeds was to be imposed';[38] but in spite of some expensive preparatory site work, the scheme foundered. The owners of estates in Little Woodhouse, immediately to the north of Park Lane, were anxious to develop their land; George Rawson, for example, who owned Denison Hall (then known as Hanover Place and divided into two residences), obtained plans in 1823 from Watson and Pritchett for laying out the southern portion of his estate as a square.[39] Presumably the success of the Wakefield layout had recommended the York architects as suitable designers for a similar idea. They made alternative proposals, one for a conventional square with terraces on the east, west and south sides, leaving the existing mansion in a reduced garden to form the north; the other was for a triangular layout in which the mansion was at the north corner or apex, with terraces along the three sides. The first alternative was selected, and work began on a few plots in the east and west terraces; houses were erected with uniform brick façades in which the only decorative elements were stone doorcases with a corbelled cornice, and a stone panel below the ground-floor windows. The central garden was landscaped with winding paths, flower beds and shrubberies by Joshua Major, a landscape gardener, in 1824;[40] but there were few other takers for the sites. Parsons deplored, in 1834, the incomplete state of Hanover Square. 'Were [it] completed in a style corresponding with the buildings which have already been erected, it would be the greatest ornament of the town'; but in spite of an attempt in 1836 to interest purchasers in the south terrace, for which Pritchett made a design of seven-bay houses, and George Smith an alternative proposal of three-bay houses, the square was never completed.[41] Nor was the nearby Woodhouse Square, which was laid out in the 30s; a pair of houses on the west side was erected for the Atkinson family to John Clark's design in 1840,[42] and a terrace on the south was built in the late 40s and early 50s, but that was all. It was too late; the industrial smoke defeated the developers' intentions, and there had been a change of taste away from houses in terraces and squares in favour of villas.

In 1816, Whitaker had commented on 'the Erection of many Villas in a Style of Elegance [in the] healthy and pleasant Hamlet' of Little Woodhouse on the higher ground north of the ill-fated Parks area. These were plain brick houses, normally five bays wide, with pedimented central sections and pilastered, pedimented doorcases. They were built in the 1790s and given such names as Belmont, Mount Pleasant, Claremont and Belle Vue;[43] very similar to villas of the same size in the St John's area in Wakefield, they might have been designed by Watson. Most still survive, although their gardens were partly built

67. Leeds, Woodhouse Square; laid out
in the 1830s, but slow to develop, the
south side was built in the late 40s and
early 50s (R.W.Moore).

68. Leeds, Woodsley House, Clarendon
Road; a monumental villa
incorporating a spacious pillared
staircase-hall (J.Clark attrib.1840–1).

44 Thoresby Society; Martin,S.D., and
Fox,J., *Plan of an estate at Little Woodhouse
... as laid out in lots for sale, 1847*. This
illustrates the layout of Clarendon Road and
the division of the Atkinson estate as
building plots. John Clark designed two
houses in Hyde Terrace which were built
*c.*1840 and must have been among the
earliest in the new development. In Preston
Place, Blundell Place and Lyddon Terrace,
most of the houses were designed by John
Samuel Morrish.

45 Woodsley House is now the Albert
Mansbridge College, University of Leeds.

46 Jones's design for one of the floors is in
the V. and A.

over later in the nineteenth century. By the 30s, Little Woodhouse was
'rapidly losing its character as a beautiful village, although it is still
one of the most pleasant and airy situations around Leeds'; and by the
40s it was being laid out with new roads. Terraces of Late Georgian
brick houses, such as Lyddon Terrace and Springfield Place, had been
built on the north and east fringes of the village from the early 30s, and
a few large detached or semi-detached villas with moderately sized
gardens were appearing.[44] Yet it was still a green hillside in 1858 when
Queen Victoria visited Leeds to open the Town Hall and was the guest
of the Mayor, Sir Peter Fairbairn, in his handsome Italianate villa,
68 Woodsley House, in Clarendon Road. Built in 1840–1, probably from a
design by Clark, this is a brick house with stone dressings and attached
giant columns; inside, there is an imposing 'Imperial' staircase and
Greek decoration.[45] Farther down the road, John Atkinson's
Woodhouse House (the original residence in the village) was being
slowly encroached on; in 1791 it had been described as surrounded by
thirteen acres 'of rich Pasture Land with the Plantations therein ...
command[ing] a most extensive and beautiful Prospect, which cannot
be interrupted by any Buildings or Plantations'. That had proved an
optimistic belief by the 1840s, but Atkinson added a new Italianate
wing (probably designed by Clark) to the plain vernacular Georgian
house, and in 1847 he employed William Reid Corson and Edward la
Trobe Bateman (two young architects who had recently set up
practice in Leeds) to add a garden room and redecorate the interior of
the house. They had both been pupils of Owen Jones, and it was to
69 their master they turned for a design for the paved floor in the
handsome domed staircase-hall and the garden room. Blues, browns
and yellows are glowingly composed in a geometrical mosaic pavement
incorporating a gigantic eight-pointed star in the middle of concentric
circles and panels of Greek motifs.[46] Atkinson wrote to the Leeds-born
Charles Cope R A (whose large painting 'All nations looking unto
Christ' hangs above the altar in Clark's nearby St George's church) for

69. Leeds, Woodhouse House,
Clarendon Road; the circular staircase-
hall decorated by W.R.Corson and E.la
Trobe Bateman (1847) with assistance
from Owen Jones and the young
J.E.Millais.

a recommendation of a student from the Royal Academy who could
decorate six lunettes in the same staircase-hall, and as a consequence
the young John Everett Millais spent a summer vacation in Atkinson's
house painting allegorical figures on canvas panels to fill the blank
spaces.[47]

The establishment of the Northern Society for the Encouragement
of Fine Arts in 1808,[48] and its subsequent exhibitions, had helped to
encourage patronage of living artists, some of whose work could be
found in the 'numerous mansions and elegant villas built by those
whose commercial enterprise or manufacturing industry have elevated
their families [and in the] immense number of excellent houses,
sometimes beautifully situated . . . all of them indicating the comfort,
opulence and respectability of their owners'.[49] Some of these were the
large villa-mansions discussed elsewhere in this study, but the fashion
set by them was followed on a smaller scale in the villas which began to
surround them. Headingley Hill became the favoured residential area
in Leeds from the 30s onwards, when building plots south of the old
village and on the high ridge between the Aire and Meanwood valleys
began to change hands. The east side of Headingley Lane was
gradually developed principally as detached villas, designed in various
styles; the single exception to this type of housing was Headingley

70 Terrace, a formal composition of five three-bay houses, with
colonnaded porches, set back from the road behind a private garden.

Headingley Hill House was erected for William or James Hargreave
71 c.1836 as a symmetrical Greek villa in the manner of Francis
Goodwin's published designs:[50] all the details of planning and
decoration are worked out with precision, and it is obvious an architect
was in control. Chantrell, Clark (or even Goodwin who entered a
competitive design for Commercial Buildings, Leeds in 1826 when he
was supervising the erection of the Central Market) are obvious

72 contenders. The Priory in Cumberland Road was occupied by John
Child, the architect of St Anne's RC church, and it is likely he was

47 *Magazine of Art* (1896–7), 280ff. The
painted lunettes are in the collection of the
Leeds City Art Galleries; the subjects are
'Childhood', 'Youth', 'Manhood', 'Age',
'Music' and 'Art'.

48 Fawcett,T., *The rise of English provincial
art*, Oxford 1974,21ff.

49 Parsons, i,191,235.

50 Design no.8, 'Villa in the Grecian Style',
in Goodwin,F., *Domestic architecture . . . a
series of designs . . . in the Grecian, Italian and
Old English styles*, London 1833–4.

70. **Leeds, Headingley Terrace; a formal terrace of five villas and a private garden (1840s). In the background is Headingley Hill Congregational Church (C.Brodrick 1864–6).**

71. **Leeds, Headingley Hill House; built c.1836, probably from a published design by F.Goodwin.**

73

74

51 Now used by the North Regional Association for the Blind.

52 The major part of the extensive Cardigan estate was sold in 1888; see the estate plans in Leeds Reference Library.

53 *A series of picturesque views of castles and country houses in Yorkshire*, Bradford 1885,68

54 ibid.

responsible for the design of his own charming little Tudor-Gothic villa; possibly he also designed Ashwood for Joseph Austin, a prominent member of the Roman Catholic community. This is a refined Tudor house, betraying the influence of 'Commissioners' Gothic' in its thin detailing. There are others in a similar style, including the large Headingley Castle with a tower and *porte-cochère*;[51] but the most individual design in the first group of these Headingley villas is North Hill House, built in 1846 for William Walker. Symmetrical in plan and elevation, the main façade is elaborately detailed with traceried windows and a slightly projecting doorway framed by panelled, pinnacled buttresses, all suggesting the designer had been referring to the plates of St George's Chapel, Windsor and Henry VII's Chapel, Westminster in A.C.Pugin's *Specimens of Gothic Architecture* – an adaptation that would have caused the younger Pugin to add a scathing footnote to his *True Principles of Christian Architecture*. Yet, maybe more important than the individual houses, was the gradual growth of the area as a place with its own character and a sense of order and unity that had not been deliberately planned; it was (and is still in parts) a place of high stone walls, narrow ginnels, overhanging trees leaning out from private gardens – and silence.

At the same time as the village of Headingley was becoming the favoured middle-class residential area in Leeds (developing as smaller villas and terraces on the Earl of Cardigan's estate west of Headingley Lane, and then out to Far Headingley later in the century),[52] Bradford was growing out towards Manningham, 'a little isolated collection of houses clustered together in the neighbourhood of the park and the old manor house'.[53] In the early 40s, it was separated from Bradford by 'green fields traversed by pleasant pathways, and shadowed thickly in some places by fine-grown timber; . . . in the distance lay the vista of the valley of the Aire, whilst behind beyond the vale . . . would be seen the heights of Bolton'.[54] It was across these green fields that Manningham Lane was bringing the middle classes to live, first in such developments as the elegant Eldon Place, designed in 1845 by James Richardby as three-bay, three-storey terrace houses, or the smaller terraces of two-bay houses built by the Hallfield Building Club in 1848–52 from plans by Thomas Dixon. Then came the less sophisticated Hanover Square, an odd attempt to build a formal layout with quadrant corners and central pediments, but executed in a vernacular style with vaguely Tudor windows. Immediately to the north, however, after Manningham Lane passed from the old township of Bradford to that of Manningham, the standard of layout and design changes dramatically.

Mornington Villas was developed strictly according to a plan between 1852 and 1874 at right angles to the road and on sloping ground, with a small number of large semi-detached villas, some designed by Lockwood and Mawson and some by T.C.Hope after a start had been made by Dixon; at the top of the rise and along the ridge, Apsley Villas continues as a long, curved terrace of two-storey houses with plain ashlar facings and Italianate doorways, completed **75** *c.*1855. Back in Manningham Lane, Blenheim Terrace was built with a private roadway in 1865 to Samuel Jackson's design: this is the finest of the Manningham terraces, incorporating ten houses of only moderate size in a well-balanced composition of bay windows and restrained Italianate doorcases, and an alternating rhythm of

72. Leeds, The Priory, Cumberland Road; presumably designed in the 1830s by J.Child, the first occupant.

73. Leeds, Ashwood, Headingley Lane; built for Joseph Austin (J.Child attrib.c.1836), the father of Alfred, poet-laureate in 1896.

windows, triple-arched and coupled. This is mid-Victorian terrace housing at its best, precisely detailed and skilfully executed, and superior to the impressive but restless Lindum Terrace (1873) and St **76** Paul's Terrace (1874) which Hope designed farther along Manningham Lane.[55] The sight of Mallinson and Healey's large church at the end of St Paul's Road suggests a greater degree of formal, large-scale layout of Manningham than there was, but unusually the result is visually and environmentally successful.

The opposite side of Manningham Lane was developed principally with detached and semi-detached villas built in the grounds of earlier houses. The group known as Clifton Villas was built from 1865 onwards by different architects; all the houses are Italianate-Classical, whereas Rose Mount,[56] originally the only one on the site, was built for John Douglas in 1849–51 by Andrews and Delaunay in a gaunt, institutional Tudor style with Dutch gables. The firm's contemporary railway station at Keighley appears to have been influential. Further along Manningham Lane, in about 1840, J.G.Horsfall had moved into Bolton Royd, an elegant Greek villa for 'a gentleman wearied during the day with the incessant clack of the loom';[57] the site was thirty-five acres in extent, but most of it was sold and developed in 1866–71 as the Oak Estate, for which Hope planned a layout of detached, semi-detached and terrace housing. The most striking of the individual houses is Oakwell, designed in 1868 by Andrews and Pepper in a plain style, and enlarged twenty years later by James Ledingham in a characteristically idiosyncratic manner with a tall, hipped tower and a lower addition with a half-timbered upper storey. Because of the original pattern of ownership, and the way in which the sites were developed, each of the estates on this side of Manningham Lane appears to be a private, secluded enclosure; the most picturesque is **77** Mount Royd, an isolated enclave screened by trees from the road, and containing four pairs of semi-detached villas designed by Lockwood and Mawson in 1863–4. Alternating from mildly Gothic to quietly

55 I am greatly indebted to Mr John S.Roberts for the information about these developments in Manningham.

56 Now Bradford Education Committee's Teachers' Centre.

57 *A series of picturesque views . . .*, op.cit.,68. Now used by Bradford Education Committee for adult classes.

74. Leeds, North Hill House; built for William Walker (1846) by an unidentified architect who had a great enthusiasm for the Perpendicular style.

75. Bradford, Blenheim Terrace, Manningham; the finest of the Bradford terraces (S.Jackson 1865).

76. Bradford, St Paul's Terrace, Manningham (T.C.Hope 1874); a terrace which had to accommodate itself to the sloping site leading to St Paul's church (Mallinson and Healey 1847–8).

58 Leeds Archives Dept., *A plan of houses . . . showing what may be built at a cost of £403.0.0 each at St. John's Hill, the property of D.& J.Eastwood*. The popularity of this type of three-bedroomed terrace house can be demonstrated in every town, but it is interesting to see that an identical plan (in this case with a small ground-floor kitchen and a first-floor bathroom) was repeated fifty-nine times on the south side of Harehills Avenue, Leeds when it was developed *c*.1899.

59 Leeds Reference Library. Boyne,W., Extra-illustrated copy of *Loidis and Elmete*, v,ii. J.Fallowfield Masser was the promoter.

Italianate in their details, these houses overlook open sloping lawns to a private wooded glen beyond a stone, rustic Gothic balustrade, in an ideal *rus in urbe* situation.

Such delectable, secluded groups were not the general rule; nor were there many advantageous building sites like those in Park Road, Halifax on which six pairs of dignified, ashlar-faced Italianate houses with double fronts could be erected in 1856 to John Hogg's designs facing the open space of People's Park that would remain green and shady in perpetuity, thanks to Crossley benevolence. Such villas were for the well-to-do middle classes. Far more typical are the terraces of houses that can be found in every West Yorkshire town, of which a group in St John's Hill, Leeds is representative. The land, in the township of Headingley-cum-Burley, was owned by D. and J. Eastwood, who obtained a design for a terrace of six houses from local architects, Wilson and Bailey in 1864. A coloured lithograph was issued, showing a group of brick-built houses, each with a bay window and a Dutch gable, and of a type that was to remain standard for another forty years.[58] In the basement were a breakfast-room and kitchen, on the ground floor a drawing-room (15′ 10 by 14′ 6) and dining-room (14′ 0 by 14′ 6) and a staircase passage 6′ 4 wide, on the first floor two double bedrooms and a single, and two attics at the top. Each house sold for £340, plus £63 for 315 square yards, totalling £403. A similar terrace of houses had been offered for disposal in a different way in the 50s, when an advertisement drew attention to a lottery of 'A splendid range of first-class buildings . . . Seven Spacious Dwelling-Houses . . . with Gardens, Coach House, and Stables connected . . . They are four stories high, with pressed brick fronts, stone doorways, cleansed Ashlar up to the ground floor, with moulded string courses, and double-faced quoins at each angle'.[59] 4,800 subscribers were invited to buy a ticket costing one guinea; but the Government acted and prosecuted the promoters of such schemes, including the originator of this, who was found guilty and imprisoned behind the

77. Bradford, Mount Royd, Manningham; a picturesque group of four pairs of semi-detached villas (Lockwood and Mawson 1863–4) overlooking what is now a wooded private glen.

78. Leeds, 7 Alma Road, Headingley; a distinguished villa (C.Brodrick 1859) exhibiting the same understanding of bold architectural forms and the nature of millstone grit as do his public designs.

79. Huddersfield, 82–82A New North Road; a pair of Classical villas (W.Wallen attrib.) in a stylistically mixed development of 'residences of the "merchant princes" of Huddersfield'.

80. Huddersfield, Ebor Mount, New North Road; a group of Tudor villas (J.Kirk 1873).

battlemented towers of the newly built Borough Gaol at Armley.[60]

The *Builder* was critical of the new middle-class housing of the 60s in Leeds, referring to such residences as the proposed terrace in St John's Hill as 'only fit for grooms and railway porters', which were being produced by 'a brick-and-mortar crusade which is defiling every green spot near the town'.[61] The writer continued to attack 'the most brainless new buildings . . . that can be conceived [which] have been set up. Expensive houses are being erected in every direction, – perfect abortions . . . One fine example of Domestic architecture, in or very near to Leeds, would revolutionize the house-building of the town'. The article concluded by claiming (as many critics have repeated since the 1860s) that 'architects regard the designing of houses as beneath them, except in a few special instances'. Yet the drawings for most speculative developments were signed by architects, even if they were not always the best in the town. Cuthbert Brodrick, the leading architect in Leeds, designed a terrace of three brick-built houses with stone dressings in Moorland Terrace in 1859; and in the same year he

78 was responsible for a detached house, 7 Alma Road, Headingley, which might have been adopted by the *Builder* as its 'one fine example of Domestic architecture'. The ashlar façade has a boldly treated gable with overhanging eaves and large, positive brackets that are a Brodrick hallmark; the twin bay windows curve out from the house in a manner anticipating the porticoes of the 1861 Corn Exchange, and the stonework is as precisely detailed as in his civic buildings.[62] It is a noble house, but the *Builder* chose to praise instead the residences in the New North Road in Huddersfield. 'In this street', thought the critic, 'there is great variety in point of style in the different houses; both the Gothic and Classic examples are to be seen, frequently juxtaposed, and with an effect which is eminently satisfactory'.[63] These houses form a part of the mid nineteenth-century residential area built on the hill behind the railway station, stretching out through Edgerton towards the north-west into the country where the large detached houses on miniature estates were to be built at Lindley. There are plain terraces of two-bay houses with neat Classical doorways in Wentworth Street, and a handsome pedimented terrace of five large houses in Trinity Road with Taylor's Holy Trinity (1816–19) in its leafy churchyard in the background, and Greenhead Park across the road. As an entity, this is one of the most successful middle-class areas in the region; but the correspondent in the *Builder* rightly drew attention to the quality of New North Road. 'No two houses are alike except where they are quite detached; and this is productive of a charm which, as far as my own experience goes, is without exception in

79 England'. Such published designs as Francis Goodwin's or, more
80 particularly, those in S.H.Brooks's *Designs for Cottage and Villa Architecture* (c.1840) seem to have provided models for the detached, semi-detached, or small groups of terraced villas which, although varied in style, are uniformly constructed of the local stone; it is a material which looks equally well in a pedimented Greek design or one with gables, crockets and other romantic ornaments. 'In regard to the different styles of architecture which are displayed in this book', wrote

60 Perkin and Backhouse 1847. See Linstrum, 64.

61 *B* (1862),xx,623, The criticism applied principally to the development of the Cardigan Estate, which was then in the very early stages. Yet, according to the deposit plans, over 80% of the houses built in this area during the next 40 years were designed by architects. (Information from Mr Frank Trowell).

62 Headingley houses are badly documented, but Brodrick designed Moorland Terrace (1859), and probably 9 Alma Road, and 'Ashfield', Grove Road. These all incorporate recognisable Brodrick detailing, but it is known he designed plain stone houses without any decoration except for an Italianate doorway (e.g. the Rectory, Thorpe Bassett, North Yorkshire, 1857); such houses are difficult to identify, but there are many in Headingley.

63 *B* (1862),xx,623.

Brooks in his preface,' much must be necessarily left to the taste of the projector; as one may prefer a mixed style of architecture, while another gives the preference to the pure Grecian, Italian, Tudor, or Elizabethan, and in this respect the fashion of the day possesses no little influence'.

There was no lack of individuality in the larger houses built for the wealthier manufacturers, for whom the villas in Manningham, Headingley and New North Road were not sufficiently prestigious or private. They preferred instead to live in such houses as **81** J.T.Fairbank's Heaton Mount, built in 1864 for Robert Kell on a nine-acre site farther away from Bradford. The house is 90 feet wide, and its main front has two large Italianate bays, a colonnaded porch, and a high ornamental parapet decorated with urns. Inside, there is a central **82** hall with a double staircase, heavily carved oak, painted windows 'from one of the best ateliers in Birmingham', brightly painted ceilings, cut-glass chandeliers and central heating.[64] Fairbank also designed Bowling Park House in an Italianate style for Abraham Mitchell in 1865; although the site was extensive, the house itself was not unusually large, but Mitchell's collection of paintings grew so large that a new gallery was added, 'in place of the ordinary conservatory arrangement'.[65] Another Italianate house on the fringe of Bradford is Grove House, Bolton, designed by Samuel Jackson for Atkinson Jowett in 1860, as a symmetrical composition with two broken-pedimented gabled wings with quoins, canted bays and coupled windows under a segmental pediment; between them is a loggia in the form of a Venetian window.[66] The Louis Quinze style was preferred for Sir Frank Crossley's mansion, Belle Vue, Halifax; George Henry Stokes designed it in 1856–7 with a quietly restrained façade screening a rich interior containing a staircase more appropriate for a town hall **83** than for a house.[67]

Yet the style of residence favoured most by the wealthier middle class was one with allusions to an Elizabethan or Gothic past, such as

64 *A series of picturesque views . . .*, op.cit.,71f. Now the Management Centre, University of Bradford.

65 ibid.,57f. Now an office of Bradford Corporation Welfare Department.

66 ibid.,113f.

67 ibid.,85f. The staircase is described as it was seen originally: 'The support of the railings is of red marble, the pillars being of turned white marble streaked with red, and the balustrade of massive polished and moulded slabs of the same valuable stone of a beautiful rich green hue'. The library was 'filled with walnut bookcases and furniture, and with a very elaborately carved and painted roof'. The drawing-room's panelled walls were tinted 'a cool greyish-green', and it was furnished with 'carved walnut, inlaid with coloured woods, and with ormulu attachments'. The doors in the main rooms are 'about twelve feet in height and of solid walnut and mahogany, enriched in some cases with fine carvings'. Belle Vue is now Halifax Public Library.

81. Bradford, Heaton Mount; designed (J.T.Fairbank 1864) with large bays 'almost forming in fact small rooms in themselves'.

82. Bradford, Heaton Mount; the oak
newels are carved with foxgloves and
surmounted by bronze figures bearing
lights, and the electro-bronzed iron
balustrades continue the same theme.
The central figure in the painted glass
'from one of the best ateliers in
Birmingham ... is a representation of
Phoebus with the Hours of the Sun'.

83. Halifax, Belle Vue; Sir Frank
Crossley's Louis XV mansion
(G.H.Stokes 1856–7) stands on a
restricted site between the People's
Park and the public cemetery.
Nevertheless, 'outside the
disadvantages of the situation Belle Vue
possesses every requisite which could
be desired' including a monumental
staircase.

68 *B* (1863),xxi,206f. Manor Heath was
demolished in the late 40s.

69 Now empty; the grounds are used as a
public park.

70 *A series of picturesque views ...*, op.cit.,
122f. Demolished; in 1899 it was said to have
been untenanted for many years.

John Crossley's Manor Heath, Halifax, designed by Parnell and Smith
in 1852–3,[68] or West Royd, Farsley, which John Butler built in 1866 in
a Tudor style but with a French Gothic tower from plans by Andrews
and Delaunay;[69] or there was Woodlands, erected in 1866 in Toller
Lane for Angus Holden. Milnes and France were the architects of this
many-gabled house with tall chimney stacks and a large, battlemented
central tower; the ground floor of the tower, 'vaulted with stone and
paved with encaustic tiles of elegant design, having emblazoned in the
centre the coat of arms of the proprietor', led into a huge central hall,
open to the roof, 'from which ... a softened light was shed through
the stained glass with which the dome was filled, upon the walls
wainscotted in oak and coloured woods'. The staircase balustrade, the
door plates and hinges, were made by Francis Skidmore; and the light
to the Music-room filtered through glass by Burne-Jones.[70] The Pre-
Raphaelites were supplying glass for other houses in the district; in
1861 Aldam Heaton commissioned three panels from Rossetti for
Woodbank, his house in Bingley, and in the following year his
neighbour, Walter Dunlop, bought panels illustrating the story of
Tristram and Iseude (now in Bradford City Art Gallery) for Harden
Grange from Morris and Company. Another house in the Bingley area,
Oakwood, was designed in a plain Tudor manner by Knowles and
Wilcox in 1864 for Thomas Garnett, who commissioned glass for the

84

71 Taylor, N., and Symondson, A., 'Burges and Morris at Bingley', *AR* (1968), cxliv, 34ff. Some of Burges's designs for Oakwood (which is now a country club) are in the RIBA Drawing Collection (see *Catalogue*, B/118).

72 See Linstrum, 79. Spenfield is now an office of the Yorkshire Water Authority.

73 'The art of Christopher Dresser', *The Studio* (1898), xv, 104f. Dresser was a prodigious worker, and among all the designs he turned out were 142 carpet designs for Crossley's, and 158 sketches for silk damasks for Ward's of Halifax (Pevsner, N., 'Christopher Dresser, industrial designer', *AR* (1937), lxxxi, 184).

74 *A series of picturesque views* ..., op.cit., 96f.

75 Now Moorlands School.

76 Now demolished, St. Ives was built as a girls' school and residence.

77 *BA* (1884), xxi, 16. Ten years earlier, the same journal (1874) ii, 378, published a long description of Dunearn (which has been demolished). In it, the house was described as 'apparently aimed to show ... to what purpose an unfettered architect may work ... The walls are of Weetwood stone, pitch faced. Red granite coupled pillars are used in the open porch, and coupled pillars, with Caen stone caps and bases in the arcades, in the morning room. The caps are of concave form, and the carving recessed from the face, the pillars being arranged in pairs of serpentine, Devonshire, and Irish green marble'.

78 ibid. (1874), ii, 378. The chimneys, which the writer thought 'conflict to some degree with the pretensions of the tower', were taken down *c*.1970.

staircase window over the entrance from the Morris firm in 1865; it includes designs by Morris himself as well as by Burne-Jones. William Burges was also designing furnishings for two of Garnett's rooms, from which survives the Dining-room fireplace with a gabled overmantel and a carving by Thomas Nicholls of a mythical imp-like figure.[71]

The relatively plain exteriors of such houses as Oakwood often contradict their internal opulence. George Corson's design of 1875 for Spenfield, James Walter Oxley's house in Far Headingley, Leeds suggests nothing externally of the magnificent entrance hall with marble shafted columns and carved stone capitals, or the exquisitely decorated Drawing-room furnished by John Faulkner Armitage in 1888 with carved woodwork, stained glass and rich metalwork.[72] Thomas Shaw's house, Allangate, on the fringe of Halifax, was partly redecorated by Christopher Dresser, 'perhaps the greatest of commercial designers' and 'a household word to people who are interested in design';[73] in the Library, 'the dado is of a delicate chocolate shade charged with a gold floral pattern, treated according to conventional Greek art, the upper portion of the walls being of a cool green tone', and Dresser regarded the ceiling as 'his own veritable masterpiece'. The Drawing-room had a double ceiling, the lower 'of open trellis work of oak decorated in blue and black ... with gold bosses at each of the intersections. The spaces or panels of the upper ceiling visible through this trellis work are painted with floral patterns. The dado is of crimson with floral stencil-work in gold and black. The cornice is an artistic combination in blue, black and gold, and the upper walls are tinted a cool buff relieved by designs in chocolate and gold'. The windows were partly filled with stained glass, and between them were fixed 'medallions of stained glass, surrounded by ebonized and gilded framework', which were lit by natural light during the day, and by 'powerful gas jets' at night; the effect was 'extremely novel and charming'.[74]

A late romanticism was at its height in the 60s, when George Corson was designing large houses in Headingley, such as Fox Hill (for Francis William Tetley 1862) which rises out of the trees on its hilltop height above Meanwood Woods with Wagnerian splendour,[75] or the strangely forbidding St Ives, built in 1869 on a similarly commanding site;[76] hammer-dressed stone and towering gables created an impression of unwelcoming impregnability, slightly softened in Corson's own house, Dunearn, built in 1871. In this design, he introduced half-timbering, tile-hanging, and tourelles flanking an open entrance porch, producing 'a certain massiveness which, like much of the late Mr. Burges' work, borders very closely on mediaeval coarseness'.[77] Such excesses were soon looked upon in a colder light, as when E. W. Pugin's 'use of gargoyles' was thought 'such as few but those imbued with mediaeval ardour would now be led to indulge in'.[78] The criticism was of Carr House (later Meanwood Towers), designed in 1867 for Thomas Stewart Kennedy as a riotous combination of bays, gables, pierced parapets, enormous chimney-stacks, and the offending gargoyles. The owner indulged himself in building an organ inside this extravaganza for his own enjoyment, as did Louis John Crossley in

84. Bingley, Oakwood; Thomas Garnett's house (Knowles and Wilcox 1864) contains a staircase window from the Morris firm.

85. Bingley, Oakwood; Thomas Garnett also commissioned designs from W. Burges for furnishing two of his rooms, including this fireplace carved by T. Nicholls.

86. Leeds, Spenfield, Far Headingley; James Walter Oxley's house (G. Corson 1875) contains richly decorated rooms, stained glass, brasswork and inlaid woods.

87. Huddersfield, Banney Royd, Lindley; Edgar Wood designed W. H. Armitage's house (1890) using traditional Yorkshire elements but incorporating English *art nouveau* details.

79 *A series of picturesque views . . .* op.cit., 100f.

80 *B A* (1889),xxxi,445. Two designs are illustrated, one for W.B.Gordon in Parsons Road, and a pair of villas in Park Drive for J.Whittingham. The issue of 1894,xli,87, illustrates a country cottage at Oakworth, built of local stone with brown tiles and a doorway with a carved lintel in the West Yorkshire tradition.

81 Ambler,L., *The old halls and manor houses of Yorkshire*, London 1913. This is still the great reference book on the subject, and Ambler had the assistance of Yorkshire architects in assembling the measured drawings which are so valuable; many were subscribers.

Moorside, a restless-looking design of gables and chimney-stacks built in Huddersfield Road, Halifax, to a design by H.J.Paull. The Billiard-room contained 'a very complete case of sections of the different submarine cables in the world'; the Drawing-room was 'furnished throughout in ebonised wood and gold', and an organ in a carved case was set in the central opening of a carved alabaster screen. In 1882 an electrical laboratory and workshop were added to the house, and an electric tramway ran through part of the garden.[79]

In the 80s and 90s, James Ledingham was designing in a stylistically mixed but idiosyncratically effective manner in Bradford on the Rosse estate where he was using jettied gables, half-timbering and 'Queen Anne' details.[80] By the 90s, picturesque qualities were being discovered in those sixteenth-century stone houses in West Yorkshire which Whitaker had thought 'melancholy', but which Louis Ambler was beginning to record for publication.[81] William and Arthur Sugden were providing designs for houses in the Keighley area, such as Currerwood at Steeton (1895) which was described as possessing 'a nice robust character'; it was built of local stone, with mullioned windows, gables, kneelers, and the roofs were 'covered with stone or grey slate as was customary in the sixteenth and seventeenth century work of this district'.[82] These details (described by Lutyens as 'Yorkeological'[83]) became more widely used, and were incorporated in the houses Edgar Wood designed in Lindley, Huddersfield. His first Yorkshire house was Briarcourt, built in 1894–5 for his brother-in-law, Herbert Sykes, and decorated internally with Jacobean style woodwork and plaster.[84] In 1890, he began to build Banney Royd for William Henry Armitage, with gables, kneelers and mullioned windows, but this time the decorations were in Wood's own 'modern' style which incorporated many elements of the English *art nouveau*.[85]

The middle-class mansions, villas and terraces so far discussed were all within a short distance of the mills and factories, warehouses, banks and offices which provided the means for their upkeep; but the development of the railways offered an alternative way of living. Laisterdyke and Thornbury, for example, grew as a new commuter suburb east of Bradford in the late 50s on the Great Northern Railway Company's Bradford–Leeds line; it was developed, principally in the form of terraces, by building clubs which bought land from the Calverley estate. The alternative Midland Company's line between Bradford and Leeds, completed along the Aire valley in 1846, made accessible such villages as Rawdon, Calverley and Apperley, and it was 'only natural that it should be specially sought after by gentlemen in either of the two towns whose commercial ventures have been attended with . . . a measure of success . . . The valley on each side of the line is dotted with fine buildings standing in well-wooded grounds, which, when viewed by the traveller from his swiftly rolling seat, afford an ever-varying panorama . . . and at the same time testifying more eloquently than words to the wealth and enterprise of the mercantile community'.[86] Older houses, such as Rawdon Hall (built by George Rawdon c.1600)[87] or the newer Calverley House (built by Thomas Thornhill in 1806),[88] often found different owners after the railway had been built; but many new houses were built in the wooded valley.

Lockwood and Mawson designed Ferncliffe at Calverley c.1855 for Briggs Priestley as a pedimented, Italianate villa,[89] and in 1869 they provided Moses Bottomley with 'a very good specimen of the ornamented Elizabethan order' at Woodleigh Hall, Rawdon; with its central square belvedere tower, its gables and oriels, it was thought 'an agreeable change from the many Italian and Franco–Italian erections which abound in the locality'.[90] Architects took full advantage of the surrounding scenery, and when Milnes and France designed Knottfield House, Calverley for Hermann Averdieck in 1874 they incorporated a large octangular tower as well as a more conventional Italianate belvedere from which could be seen the delectable panorama of 'hill and vale, woodland and meadow, private houses embowered in trees, and villages clustering round their picturesque old churches which lie stretched around on all sides'.[91] The hinterland villages in the valley were also swollen in size after the railway had made them easily

82 *BA* (1895),xliv,291.

83 Hussey,C., *The life of Sir Edwin Lutyens*, London 1950,134. The reference is from a letter to Sir Herbert Baker about Heathcote Ilkley; see 88ff.

84 Archer,J., *Partnership in style*, Manchester 1975 (exhibition catalogue), 29; *BA* (1895), xliv,133.

85 Archer, ibid.,47. Banney Royd is now an office of the West Yorkshire Fire Service. Wood also designed an interior for Birkby Lodge, Huddersfield (1901), reproduced in *Academy Architecture* (1902),xxii,119, and a clock tower at Lindley (1900–02) which bears the inscription 'This tower was erected by James Nield Sykes, Esq.,J.P. of Field Head, Lindley, for the benefit of his native village in 1902'. The sculpture and copper top were the work of T.Stirling Lee.

86 *A series of picturesque views . . .*, op.cit.,13.

87 ibid.,26.

88 ibid.,54.

89 ibid.,52.

90 ibid.,42. Demolished.

91 ibid.,13; *BA* (1874),ii,322. Knottfield had painted glass by Clayton and Bell in the lantern, tiles in the hall and conservatory by Oppenheimer, and carved oak chimneypieces by Gillows of Lancaster. Demolished; its site is now occupied by Airedale Crematorium.

87

accessible, but the development of Ilkley was the largest single gain to middle-class commuters.

In 1837 Ilkley was a township with 691 inhabitants, a place 'much frequented in the summer, for the benefit of a cold bath, which is supplied from a spring issuing out of a neighbouring hill'.[92] The health-giving properties of its waters was the basis of Ilkley's early nineteenth-century popularity, stimulated by the building of the Ben Rhydding Hydropathic Establishment in 1843–4 in the Scottish baronial style which became much favoured in the town,[93] and by Cuthbert Brodrick's Wells House, an enormous hotel-baths which stood on the edge of the moor like a miniature Blenheim, surrounded by gardens laid out by Joshua Major, when it was opened in 1858.[94] Nine years later the railway, passing through Guiseley, Menston and Burley-in-Wharfedale (which were all affected by its coming), reached Ilkley's little Palladian station (J.H.Sanders 1864), and the population began to increase; 1,043 in 1861, 2,511 in 1871, 4,013 in 1875, and 7,455 in 1901. The first extensive land sales were in 1867, and 'from the years 1870 to 1880 there was an increasing building mania, which by the latter date was found to have been by far too vigorous, and altogether in excess of demand . . . In the year 1880, building speculation had been carried on to the extent that about 150 houses of one description or another were wanting tenants'.[95] Green Lane, a quiet place of cottages and gardens, became The Grove, the new shopping street parallel to Church Street in the old village; and at the east end, facing the station, William Bakewell built a pleasant little Town Hall in 1906–08.

West View, south of the old village and close to the station, became the nucleus of a residential area stretching up towards Rombalds **88** Moor, east towards Ben Rhydding, and finally west as an extension of The Grove. It was a mixed development, catering for 'the wealthy tradesmen, merchants and manufacturers' who had to 'seek further afield for the quiet and picturesque nooks in which their own residences could be placed',[96] and for those who worked for them in Bradford and Leeds.[97] Various architectural styles were employed for the large houses built in Queens Drive and the surrounding area on the moorland south of the town. Richard Norman Shaw designed St Johns in 1878–9 for John William Atkinson in a Tudor style with mullioned windows and tall, diagonally set chimney-stacks;[98] but the gaunt, spiky stone house, Woodbank, which Thomas Ambler designed for Thomas Parkinson Muff in a 'modified style of domestic Gothic architecture' is more typical of the Ilkley style of the 70s.[99] Westwood **89** Lodge (George Smith 1875), on the fringe of the moor, and the neighbouring Shandon (1875), which once overlooked Woodbank's three acres of garden laid out 'in a succession of turf-clad terraces', are two of many examples of this type of house; humanised though they have been by the prolific growth of trees and shrubs, they still form a curious background to the groups of moorland sheep which graze on the patches of common land around which the Leeds and Bradford businessmen built their residences.

There are Scottish baronial skylines in Cowpasture Road, palatial

92 Lewis,S., *A topographical dictionary of England*, London 1837,ii.

93 Ben Rhydding Hydropathic Establishment 'formerly consisted of a central building, with a turreted tower over the main entrance, and wings extending forward on either side'; it was 'continously being enlarged, altered or embellished'. Craiglands, another hydropathic establishment (now an hotel), is also Scottish baronial in style, as is Ilkley Hospital (1862) in The Grove.

94 Wells House was designed in the form of a solid square building with corner towers and cupolas (later removed), planned around a large central hall. It is a beautifully detailed building, similar in many respects to 7 Alma Road, Headingley. It is now Ilkley College of Education.

95 Shuttleworth, *Guide-book to Ilkley*, nd,43; Collyer,R., and Turner,J.H., *Ilkley: ancient and modern*, Otley 1885,253.

96 *A series of picturesque views . . .*, op.cit.,27.

97 The middle classes from both Bradford and Leeds were attracted to Ilkley, but it was more closely associated with the former; Harrogate was perhaps more congenial or convenient for those in Leeds.

98 Saint,A., *Richard Norman Shaw*, New Haven 1976,282.

99 *A series of picturesque views . . .*, op.cit.,27.

Italianate villas such as Arden Lea in Queens Drive, and the neighbouring Arden Croft (T.C.Hope 1897) which stands out vividly against the dark conifers in its dress of bright red tiles and black and white half-timbering. All the elements of Late Victorian suburbia can be found in Ilkley, placed in a magnificent natural setting twenty-five miles away from the source of the householders' wealth; but at the same time as it was being formed, middle-class housing in a planned environment was under development within four miles of the centre of Leeds.

In 1868 William Nicholson, the last private owner of the Roundhay estate,[100] died; his will directed that the whole should be sold by his executors, and the 1871 sale particulars contain descriptions of the character of 'the most charming suburb of Leeds, [presenting] a magnificent landscape unsullied by the smoke of the town, broken into hill and dale, adorned with rich Plantations and fine Parks, and studded with Gentlemen's Seats and Homesteads, which, meeting the eye at every turn, afford an amount of enjoyment seldom associated with so close a proximity to a great commercial centre like Leeds'.[101] Much of that quality of enjoyment seemed assured of remaining in perpetuity when the Mayor, John Barran, on behalf of the citizens, made an offer at the auction for 774 acres. The price was £139,000, and it included the mansion, lakes and ornamental gardens; but the

100 The park of Roundhay was granted to Thomas, Lord Darcy of Temple Newsam *c.*1512, and passed through various Darcys to Sir John Savile of Copley, to Edward, 9th Duke of Norfolk, and to William, 15th Baron Stourton in 1767; it was sold by Charles Philip, 17th Baron Stourton, in 1803 to Thomas Nicholson and Samuel Elam, who purchased the Manor of Roundhay in 1811, uniting the park and manor after a separation of more than 300 years. It was Thomas Nicholson who landscaped the park between 1803 and 1820; after his death in 1821 the estate passed to his wife Elizabeth, then to his brother Stephen, and finally to his nephew William Nicholson Phillips (who took the name of Nicholson in 1827) in 1858.

101 *Particulars of sale of Roundhay Park estate*, 4 Oct 1871. The sale included 'the excellent villa residence known as "Springwood"', the Park farm, the Braim farm (Cobble Hall), Roundhay Grange, as well as 'the Mansion, its lakes, canal gardens, pleasure gardens, and conservatories'.

88. Ilkley, from Panorama Drive; the Wharfedale town which grew as a result of the railway connections with Leeds and Bradford. Heathcote (E.Lutyens 1906) is partly visible in the centre of this view, which illustrates the spaciousness of the gardens surrounding the villas, and the lush planting. In the background the land rises beyond Middleton to Denton Moor.

89. Ilkley, Westwood Lodge (G.Smith 1875) in the foreground typifies the stone houses of the 70s, austere but decorated with ornamental lintels, barge-boards and an occasional fanciful detail such as the tower of Shandon (1875) with its trefoil dormers and cast-iron crown.

90. Ilkley, Queens Drive, Arden Croft; the 'Old English' style was introduced to Ilkley by R.N.Shaw, who was working in West Yorkshire from the late 1860s. T.C.Hope designed houses of this type in Bradford, and this example in Ilkley (1897).

Corporation's intention was to retain only 150 acres as a public park and to sell the remainder for building. The sale conditions had drawn 'the splendid scenery and the high respectability of the neighbourhood . . . to the attention not only of Gentlemen seeking residences but of Capitalists who may be desirous of profiting by its development'; but the owners of the 'Gentlemen's Seats and Homesteads' in the Manor of Roundhay complained (not without a degree of self-interest and protection) that the Corporation had no right to 'enter into a large building speculation', and presented a petition against the purchase. The issue was seen as one between the citizens and the privileged Roundhay landowners, and the poster which appeared in the Leeds streets suggests that Victoria Square was being cleared for the guillotine:

CITIZENS,
The COMMONS OF LEEDS, assembled in their Town Hall, DECIDE to BUY ROUNDHAY PARK.
The COMMONS OF ENGLAND, assembled in their House, ENDORSE THIS DECISION.
The ARISTOCRATS OF LEEDS petition against this Purchase.
The ARISTOCRATS OF ENGLAND entertain this Petition.
WHICH IS TO WIN THE DAY?
A SCORE of Private Gentlemen in Leeds, and 300 Private Gentlemen in the Hereditary Chamber? Or, a Town with a QUARTER OF A MILLION OF INHABITANTS, and the Elected Representatives of a nation of 30 MILLIONS.

91. Leeds, Old Park Road on the Roundhay estate; developed in the 1880s and 90s as restricted housing along the fringe of the public park.

It was for Parliament to decide the question in discussing the 1872 Leeds Improvement Bill; and it was only after its passage that the future of the larger part of the estate could be considered. 'I have no doubt', the Mayor told a Select Committee of the House of Lords, 'that the remaining portion would be very eligible for first-class villa residences. There is nothing in the neighbourhood equal to that land for that purpose'; and when asked if he was aware that 'in other parts of England where parks have been purchased villas have been built in contiguity and people have been very glad to build them and to reside in them', Barran had answered 'I am'.[102] It would have been sad if indiscriminate development, such as was taking place on the carved-up gardens of many early nineteenth-century villa-mansions, had been allowed in the end; but a competition was held and Corson's plan for the park was accepted in 1873.[103] Sales were held at intervals, and the land was gradually released for housing speculation or for private development, subject to restrictions; minimum costs of houses (depending on their proximity to the main part of the estate and the public park), the screening by plantations of views of the houses from the mansion, the obligatory use of stone in their construction, and the prohibition of any 'noisy or offensive trade' in the township, ensured the quality of the new environment.

Corson's plan made available two large areas for development; one was on the site of Spring Wood and Lady Wood in the south-east corner and along the road to Collingham and Wetherby; the other was a long, shallow belt along the west boundary beyond the old Park Road which was planted as a tree-lined avenue. Neither of these materially affected the views into or out of the early nineteenth-

102 *Minutes of Evidence. Select Committee of the House of Lords on the Leeds Improvement Bill*, 20 June 1872,i,10. William Beckett Denison was an enthusiastic supporter of the proposal to buy the park, and he spoke at great length in giving evidence to the Select Committee. The petition in favour of the purchase was signed by '22 Magistrates 5 Bankers all the large Iron Masters and flax spinners and most of the Merchants, Machinists and Manufacturers in the Borough' as well as a large proportion of the citizens.

103 See *B* (1873),xxxi,739 for a review of the designs submitted, in which the hope was expressed 'that a beautiful estate will not be spoiled by cupidity, resulting in over-building, or in buildings of an inferior type ... The person who begins to spoil a park generally is the landscape-gardener, when he puts his arbours and bridges in it, and the person who completes the work of vulgarisation is the speculating builder. Let both these evils be avoided in Roundhay Park, which is too fine a place to be damaged in this way'.

91

92. Leeds, Roundhay from the air; the early nineteenth-century landscape which became a public park in 1872. A part of the planned development can be seen immediately to the left of the large Waterloo Lake; the Old Park road area (pl.91) is on the extreme left of the playing fields on the left.

century landscape, although the laying out of the new Park Avenue leading from Oakwood and then curving steeply down the hill until it reaches a spur of the Waterloo Lake, and of the shorter West Avenue along the hill overlooking the valley, could have been visually disastrous. In the event, the low density envisaged in the plan, and the extensive planting undertaken publicly and privately had the effect of creating a picturesque approach to the park, past half-hidden villas and surrounding trees, which allows brief glimpses of the long sheet of water down below and the wooded hills and open country beyond. It is an effect that is complementary to Thomas Nicholson's original intention when making the landscape; perhaps it was partly a happy accident, but those are often responsible for the greatest successes.

Development of the large, expensive plots was slow, and was, in fact, never quite completed. Woodland, the largest site and house, was built for Charles Barran in the early 80s, probably to a design by W.H. Thorp; but its plain, Italianate character was not imitated in the other houses, which are half-timbered like Smith and Tweedale's Woodbourne,[104] built for Richard Buckton c.1888, or Parcmont, which Thomas Ambler designed for John Barran II in 1883 with black and white gables and dormers, and a jettied porch which forms a large bay window in the first-floor Drawing-room, from 'which is obtained one of the loveliest views in the neighbourhood of Leeds'. Most of the large villas had been built by 1901, including Hatwood (presumably the work of its owner, George Hatton) which is the most up-to-date design and incorporates fashionable 'Aesthetic' details. As architecture they are not outstanding, but their gables and chimneys, conservatories and lodges, their lawns surrounded by forest trees and

104 Demolished in 1975.

flowering shrubs, grew into the suburban panorama that came to one of its moments of maturity at the end of the nineteenth century.

The new residential areas to the south-east and west were divided into smaller plots arranged along tree-lined avenues or quiet culs-de-sacs, at a density of about three per acre. The plain, commodious villas were built between 1881 and 1901 by different speculators with few overt references to an historical style; decorative barge-boards and repetitive ornamental surrounds to door lintels represent the general limit of embellishment, but Virginia creeper and rampant greenery soon softened the harshness of pitch-faced stone and Welsh slates, which peer out through screens of syringa and lilac or over the top of neatly trimmed privet, or act as a sober background to the spikiness of an *Araucaria araucana* or the conical pyramid of a *Chamaecyparis lawsonia*. In its maturity, Roundhay (which soon grew well beyond its original, clearly defined boundary) can be recognised as the essence of the middle-class suburban ideal, in which buildings and settings merge into a picturesque whole which nevertheless respects each man's individuality and privacy. Edgerton in Huddersfield, and Frizinghall in Bradford, possess a similar quality, but Roundhay is unusual in being a suburb built around the fringe of a Late Georgian landscape which each resident can regard as an extension of his own garden – a combination of Regent's Park and Bedford Park; but it represents the much commoner situation that can be found in every West Yorkshire town in the most successful suburbs, in which the whole is greater than the part, and the architectural quality of the houses matters less than that of the entity. Roundhay also demonstrates the influence time and posterity play in shaping a suburb until, in its maturity, it becomes (in the often quoted description from an official memorandum) 'a cherished local scene' with its own distinctive character; the affection in which such communities of houses and gardens are held can be measured by the countless instances of residents who have formed themselves into groups to defend what they regard as their rights and their heritage. It may be that the best of the middle-class suburbs approach most nearly an ideal environment.

4   Working-class housing and municipal enterprise

It is the 'home' of the working man which, more than any other single circumstance, affects his condition, his health, his morals; and its goodness may almost be taken as a measure of his civilization. Mr Disraeli did not use too strong an expression when he said: 'We all eat quite enough, and some of us drink a great deal too much, but this I will venture to say, that no man can be too well housed'.

James Hole, *The Homes of the Working Classes*, 1866

When Defoe travelled from Lancashire into Yorkshire in weather conditions which make his account of the journey sound at least as hazardous as the Grand Tourists' crossing of the Alps, he negotiated the dangers of the Roman way over Blackstone Edge and, thinking 'we were come into a Christian Country again',[1] he was heartened to see signs of industry in the Calder valley. Springs gushed out from the rocky moorland, providing soft water for washing the wool that was the source of the prosperity of the region. He wrote appreciatively of the hamlets made up of the houses of the manufacturers, around which were 'an infinite Number of Cottages or small Dwellings, in which dwell the Workmen which are employed, the Women and Children of whom, are always busy Carding, Spinning, &c.'. The valleys in the southern Pennines, those of the Colne, the Calder, the Holme and the Aire, were scattered, thickly in places, with hamlets of which the domestic textile industry was the mainstay. It was a rural industry, which tended to create a yeoman class in which almost everyone became in some degree a clothier who cultivated the small holding he was allowed to take from the 'waste' or uncultivated land; as the eighteenth century advanced and the industry grew in prosperity and size, the pattern changed and produced groups of cottages or folds, built with unselfconscious picturesqueness on the Pennine hillsides around narrow streets and courts paved with stone flags or setts, or in the valley bottoms close to small stone mills.

An account of the parish of Mirfield, written in 1755 by the vicar,[2] reveals that in the whole parish, which consisted of some two thousand people in four hundred houses in six hamlets, there were four hundred employed in carding, spinning and preparing wool for the looms, and two hundred in making cloth; for the weaving of broadcloth there were one hundred pairs of looms. In or about Hopton Hall, a hamlet with eighty inhabitants, were 'forty pairs of looms for weaving of white broad cloth'; Lee Green hamlet had three public houses, a workhouse (i.e. where paupers or vagrants were employed in carding and spinning), and a Moravian chapel; and Easthorp hamlet had grown up,

1 Defoe,D., *A tour thro' the whole island of Great Britain*, reprint London 1927, ii,599.

2 Ismay,B., 'Some account of the parish of Mirfield', *Yorkshire Notes and Queries*, (1888),i,201ff.

93. Golcar, West End Road; a fine example of weavers' three-storeyed houses with two floors of workrooms.

94. Honley, Exchange; some door lintels are scalloped in the vernacular tradition dating from the seventeenth century, but the two houses at the end of the row, dated 1751, have homely Classical doorways with friezes and entablatures. To the right is St Mary's church (R.D.Chantrell 1842–3).

3 Crump,W.B. and Ghorbal,G., *History of the Huddersfield woollen industry,* Huddersfield 1935,66.

4 *HG,* 20 Aug 1842.

94 as did so many, around two corn-and-fulling mills. Normally the houses or cottages were plain, two-storeyed structures built of stone and roofed with thick stone slates; a typical example would have two rooms on the ground floor, and an upper storey which was one single workroom reached by a ladder. The inventory of the household possessions of a Honley weaver who died in 1779 shows that of the two ground-floor rooms, one (known as the 'house') was the kitchen and living room, and the other (the 'parlour') contained the best bed, a table and chairs, and a 'large bibell'. The upper 'great chamber' was the carding and spinning room, and in this instance there was also a 'little chamber' which was the loom shop.[3] Outside was the tentercroft with the frame on which the cloth was stretched. This was a common type of weaver's house, but there are three-storey houses at 93 Almondbury, Golcar and elsewhere, with the distinctive long rows of mullioned windows on the upper floors; these seem to date only from about 1740, and were probably introduced as a result of the better light needed to weave the fancy cloths that were coming into fashion.

95 It was in such communities as Heptonstall, Almondbury, Goose Eye, Honley, Lumb, Oldfield, Wilberlee and Ainley Place, many of which still preserve to a great degree the seventeenth and eighteenth-century pattern of vernacular building, that there was a quality the *Halifax Guardian* was to recall nostalgically in 1842; 'There was so much of a home character in their little half farmstead, half clothing-shop; the master and his men and domestic apprentices were so much associated in friendly, almost family intercourse'.[4] It was a communal way of life that came to appear almost Arcadian as the years went by and the large towns grew. It was not only the inhabitants of the southern

95. Goose Eye, nr.Keighley; a Pennine community, with the neighbouring Laycock on the hilltop behind.

Pennine valleys who were occupied with domestic spinning and weaving. Any villagers who lived within reach of one of the market towns were likely to be engaged in the industry; the Leeds clothing district, for example, was reckoned to extend along both banks of the Aire for about ten miles, touching the towns of Bradford and Otley, and comprising most of the towns and villages between the Aire and the Calder, touching Wakefield and including Dewsbury, Heckmondwike and Mirfield. A housewife in Harewood was typical of thousands around the town when she spoke in 1770 of having 'put out worsted to spin for several gentlemen in Leeds for nearly forty years';[5] and Harewood happens to be important in local architectural history as the earliest of the West Yorkshire model villages, undertaken by Edwin Lascelles as an integral part of the estate he was fashioning around his new house. John Carr, Robert Adam and 'Capability' Brown were creating Harewood House and its landscape from the late

5 Ashton, T.S., *Economic fluctuations in England 1700–1800*, Oxford 1959, 159.

1750s, and within a few months of the inauguration of the mansion, Carr produced a design for rebuilding the village at the gates.

'Harewood may be distinguished from almost every other village in the kingdom, by its regularity and neatness . . . [it] has been uniformly and modestly rebuilt, so as to exclude every appearancy of filth or poverty', wrote John Jewell in 1819.[6] 'The whole of the town is built with fine stone, procured from the neighbouring quarries, and even the cottages possess a look of neatness bordering upon elegance'. He was describing the small houses in terraces along the re-aligned turnpike road from Leeds to Harrogate, and on the south side of The Avenue, the road from Collingham Bridge to the entrance to the mansion. These were intended to house many of the labourers who were 'constantly employed by the Earl of Harewood, in either one situation or another, for to this village manufacture is a stranger, and, perhaps, many of its concomitant vices'. Yet, apart from the cottage industry which flourished there, there had been an attempt to found a minor industry in 1755, when a ribbon manufactory was set up in some of Carr's new buildings; according to Jewell, this was discontinued after about eleven years, and the factory was converted into cottages. A school was built in 1768, and there were houses for the agent and the doctor, conceived as detached, pedimented buildings placed among terraces which, while in a West Riding vernacular, can almost be called 'palatial' in their composition of a number of small houses in dignified symmetrical blocks with end pavilions. Blank giant arches add a sense of simple grandeur to the stone façades, and the village is a reflection of the architectural order prevailing in the new mansion, as well as of the social order in which the mutual obligations of landowner and tenant were observed. It was a planned scene of honest industry, a

96

96. Harewood; one of the terraces along The Avenue in the model village (J.Carr 1750s) built by Edwin Lascelles. On the left is the entrance to Harewood House (H.Repton 1801, revised J.Muschamp c.1803).

6 Jewell, J., *The history and antiquities of Harewood*, Leeds 1819, 11ff.

Palladian version of a Pennine hamlet; when the Grand Duke Nicholas of Russia was a guest at Harewood in 1816, he was gratified to find 'every cottager busily engaged in some work of usefulness or improvement on his Lordship's estate', and he concluded it 'was an establishment worthy of an English Baron, worthy every man's imitation'.

The building of the village was a slow business, and it was completed only at about the time when the triumphal arch was erected at the end of the long avenue as the main entrance to the mansion in 1803. Meanwhile, not many miles south of Harewood, business was booming in the towns, where the mill chimneys were beginning to pollute the air. Louis Simond, a French émigré, arrived in Leeds by way of America in 1811 and saw 'from a height, north of the town . . . a multitude of fires issuing, no doubt, from furnaces, and constellations of illuminated windows spread upon the dark plain'.[7] Twenty years later, conditions were worse. 'Never in my life did I see a more smoky place than Bradford. The great, long chimneys are doubled I think in number within these two or three years', wrote Miss Anne Lister after she had returned to Shibden Hall one day in 1831, adding 'The same may be said of Leeds'.[8]

The traditional domestic system, within which the cottage weavers had operated, began to disintegrate as the power looms were set in motion. The men and women 'were taken from their cottages, where they worked at their pleasure, with more or less intensity, and at a time when, in consequence of the demand for labour being greater than the supply, their wages were amply sufficient to maintain them, and placed in mills, where their labour was regulated by the machinery, and where sordid masters dictated what wages they chose, and what hours they chose'.[9] In 1795, James Graham (later a Baronet and MP), who owned mills and property in Kirkstall, had personally tried to sustain the traditional communal life of a group of domestic clothiers by dividing several farms near Leeds into small holdings and building cottages on them. Edmund Lodge, his uncle by marriage, made a similar experiment at Eccleshill, near Bradford;[10] but such philanthropy was Canute-like in the face of the machine. The mills inevitably drew the workers to them and created a demand for housing. Recalling the advantages of the old system, the *Halifax Guardian* asked what one could expect of its destruction but evil,[11] and there was a growing tendency to think nostalgically of the old life in the weaving communities, of how 'the women and children . . . flocked on sunny days, with their spinning wheels, to some favourite pleasant spot';[12] but accounts of life in the large towns, especially in the boom town of Leeds, explain why the old ways seemed so desirable.

The population of Leeds was growing at a rapid rate; 52,302 in 1801, 123,546 in 1831, 207,165 in 1861. Workers were moving in from the country and from Ireland in search of a living, and roofs were needed over their heads. In the sixteenth century the frontage to Briggate, the main street, had been filled with houses and shops built on the medieval burgages or lots which were long and narrow with an average

7 Hibbert,C.(ed), Simond,L., *An American in Regency England. Journal of a tour 1810–11*, London 1968,111.

8 Quoted in Hanson,W.T., *The story of old Halifax*, Halifax 1920,239.

9 Wing,C., *Evils of the factory system*, London 1837,vi.

10 *Report and minutes of evidence on the state of the woollen manufacture in England*, London 1806,444f.

11 *HG*, 20 Aug 1842.

12 James, 221.

frontage of slightly less than fifty feet;[13] behind were open courts or yards, gardens, orchards and tenter grounds. These buildings remained, or were refaced or replaced in the eighteenth century, and behind them artisans' housing began to fill in the spaces as early as the 1720s. There are references in newspaper advertisements to these developments: 'a house with a Shop and several tenements down the Yard',[14] 'an entire Yard of Houses, consisting of Six Tenements, two whereof are new built, three stories high next the Street, with Shops and Cellars',[15] 'thirteen Tenements, well tenanted and in good repair',[16] and so on.

By the year of Waterloo, when an accurate survey of Leeds was made, these courts had been tightly packed with cottages, tenements, warehouses and finishing shops. Old photographs show their appearance which, to a twentieth-century observer, might appear picturesque in the casual grouping of the brick houses with stone slate roofs around irregular, enclosed areas of stone paving. There is even a little of the elegance of the polite world, a reflection of the late eighteenth-century developments west of the town, in the Georgian sliding sash windows and the plain six-panelled doors with simple fanlights over; but accounts of these courts in the 1840s shatter such illusions. For many families a single-room cellar-dwelling had to suffice, and some were found with no drainage, 'one mass of damp and filth . . . the floor in many places absolutely wet; a pig in the corner also'. As for the courts themselves, some were 'airless from the enclosed structure', and 'ashes, garbage, and filth of all kinds are thrown upon the surface'.[17] Those are a few comments from a Royal Commission report of 1845; other sections describe the overcrowding, the lack of drainage and water, and all the horrors of life in what the *Builder* called 'a filthy and ill-contrived town' in an attack on 'the town which calls itself the metropolis of the West Riding'.[18]

At the same time as the available space in the town was being filled, artisans' cottages were being built to the east on low-lying ground subject to flooding. As many dwellings as possible were built on the small plots of land, and the main roads out of the town were being filled in a similarly haphazard fashion. The common method was to build field by field, with an access at right angles to the road, in a form of development which perpetuated the long, narrow courts in the medieval town. It has been argued that the court infill, built on each side of the narrow site so that the back of one house was against the back of another in the next court, was the origin of the back-to-back which was to be the most common form of working-class housing in Leeds and most other West Yorkshire towns.[19]

In most cases these houses were built as a commercial speculation by one developer; in others by a building club formed by groups of tradesmen who co-operated to build their houses by pooling their resources to buy the land and materials, and then using their various trades of brick-laying, carpentry, plastering and so on to erect the group of dwellings. The details of such a scheme in Union Street reveal that fifty-two tradesmen co-operated in that enterprise in 1787.[20] It has been calculated that on average 150 new houses were built in Leeds

13 See Rimmer,W.G., 'Working men's cottages in Leeds 1770–1840', *T S* (1961), xlvi,165ff; Beresford,M., 'The back-to-back house in Leeds, 1787–1937', *The history of working-class housing* (ed.Chapman,S.D.,), Newton Abbot 1971,95ff; Tarn,J.N., *Five per cent philanthropy*, Cambridge 1973.

14 *L M*, 5 Nov 1719.

15 ibid., 12 Mar 1728.

16 ibid., 24 Nov 1730.

17 Royal Commission 1845, quoted in *Labourer's friend*, April 1852,53.

18 *B* (1860),xviii,809.

19 Beresford, op.cit.,104ff.

20 ibid.,102.

in each year between 1774 and 1815,[21] but the annual number rose considerably at times, as in 1786 when 'near 400' were erected.[22] Although more elegant houses were being erected in squares and terraces west of the town, and such plain Late Georgian groups as St Peter's Square 'for the Residence of a Genteel family'[23] were being put up by terminating societies, the majority of these dwellings were working-class cottages, one-up-one-down. Rents were low, and the sharing of three walls in back-to-back houses reduced capital costs to a minimum and afforded economical insulation. Fifteen feet square was the average size. Development was piecemeal, and by 1865 the town was described as 'a maze, without plan, order, or arrangement . . . In Leeds every man who lays out land, or builds, does simply what is right *in his own eyes*; if it suits his neighbour, well; if not, so much the worse for his neighbour, and frequently for himself'.[24]

Leeds was not the only offender, but it was subject to greater pressure than the other West Yorkshire towns. Conditions were bad in Bradford in 'the hundred alleys, thoroughfares and streets branching from [the squalid and dense districts of Broomfield, Mill Bank and Silsbridge Lane];[25] but it is apparent from such surviving terraces as Bavaria Place and Silver Street, built (probably by a co-operative building society) in 1847 as two-storey back-to-back houses with small gardens, that life was not unpleasant for all working-class families. There were also signs of organised assistance; for example, the Bradford Freehold Land Society was founded in 1849 with Titus Salt as its first President, and Henry Forbes and W.E.Forster as vice-Presidents. Its object was to buy plots of land, dividing them into small allotments and selling them to working men; thrift was encouraged, and 'a man in humble circumstances [was enabled] to acquire a piece of land, paying for it by monthly instalments, with the view to the ultimate erection of a dwelling in which to live'.[26] Three sites were purchased in Manningham, where building started on the Girlington Estate in 1850–2; Joseph Smith, the Society's surveyor, laid out about 250 allotments on a thirty-acre site, of which Kensington Street is representative. The stone terraces of back-to-back houses are well built, with plain dressed doorways and small gardens, on each side of a wide street with a view from the lower end over what was open country; the carved stone on the end house, inscribed JW 1853 presumably commemorates the builder.

Halifax was called 'a mass of little, miserable, ill-looking streets, jumbled together in chaotic confusion, as if they had all been in a sack, and emptied out together upon the ground, one rolling this way, another rolling that way, and each standing where chance happened to throw it: there is not one handsome or long street in the town, and the cause of this is the want of previously surveying the ground for the town'.[27] The insistence on long, wide streets was a natural reaction to the conditions in the enclosed courts and the piecemeal development of fields; it was the basis of later nineteenth-century bye-laws which produced the often monotonous rows of uniform housing, but that was not the only attempt to plan an environment. With this as the theme, it is necessary to return to the idea of a model village as it was realised

21 Rimmer, op.cit.,fn8,187.

22 *LI*, 27 Mar 1787.

23 Beresford, op.cit.,fn16,123.

24 Hole,J., *The homes of the working classes with suggestions for their improvement*, London 1866,142ff.

25 Collinson,E., *West Riding worsted directory*, Bradford 1851,192.

26 Cudworth,W., *Manningham, Heaton and Allerton*, Bradford 1896,84.

27 Maslen,T.J., *Suggestions for the improvement of our towns and houses*, London 1843,116.

97

97. Bradford, Bavaria Place; two-storey back-to-back houses, built in 1847 (probably by a co-operative building society) with decorative door-hoods and small gardens.

at Harewood; or as it was projected by John Plaw in 1803 in *Ferme Ornée: or Rural Improvements*. In that volume of elegant aquatints, Plaw (who made designs in Yorkshire for estate buildings at Thornville Royal[28] and for the Assembly Rooms in Harrogate) showed a formal layout around an elliptical grass common on which stood a centrally-planned church with a cupola. The design was made 'for a gentleman in Yorkshire, and was intended to have been built in the vicinity of lead mines in that county ... either for labourers and their families, or for persons of more independent circumstances'.[29] At the time Plaw was writing, the building of such a village was the prerogative of great landowners; Harewood and Ripley in Yorkshire, Nuneham Courtenay, Lowther, Lacock and Blaise Hamlet in other counties, were all examples of the estate looking after its own, and in the late 1830s the Duke of Devonshire was building a notable village in various picturesque styles at Edensor on his Chatsworth estate in Derbyshire. The aristocratic precedent was noted in the praise accorded to the Yorkshire industrial model-village builders. Sir Titus Salt 'showed how the graces of the old feudalism ... could be grafted on and exemplified by the men who brought forth and moulded the better age';[30] and a similar theme was taken up in a song, *The Peerage of Industry*, written in honour of his fiftieth birthday:

... a peerage we have to this moment unsung,
And why should they not have the name?
'Tis the Peerage of Industry! Nobles who hold
Their patent from Nature alone ...
The Peer who inherits an ancient estate,
And cheers many hearts with his pelf,
We know and love: but is that man less great
Who founds his fortune himself?[31]

Again, it was said Edward Akroyd was 'desirous of keeping up the old English notion of a village – the squire and the parson, as the head and centre of all progress and good fellowship; then the tenant-farmers; and lastly, the working population'.[32] It was a traditional hierarchy capable of being translated into an industrial equivalent; and Akroyd was hailed in verse as 'the father of thousands round' who trained his 'people in that better part Where only their true welfare can be found'.

There was a remarkable presage of the building of Copley, Akroydon and Saltaire in two novels by Benjamin Disraeli which cannot have been unnoticed by Edward Akroyd and Titus Salt. *Coningsby: or the New Generation*, published in 1844, contains a description of Mr Millbank's Lancashire factory, 'a vast deep red brick pile, which though formal and monotonous in its general character, is not without a certain beauty of proportion and an artist-like finish in its occasional masonry'; close to the factory is 'a village of not inconsiderable size, and remarkable from the neatness and even picturesque character of its architecture, and the gay gardens that surrounded it'.[33] It is a complete community, possessing a church 'in the best style of Christian architecture', a parsonage, schoolhouse, and an Institute in which are a library, lecture room and reading room; moreover, the atmosphere of 'this somewhat striking settlement was not disturbed and polluted by the dark vapour' of industrial towns, for the owner

28 Thornville Royal was the name given to his estate by Col Thomas Thornton when he bought it from the Duke of York in 1791; he changed the name 'by royal permission' after the Prince of Wales was his guest. It was later known as Allerton Park after being acquired by Charles Philip, 17th Baron Stourton.

29 Plaw, J., *Ferme ornée; or rural improvements*, London 1803. The plates are dated 1795; plate xxxiii shows the layout of the village, and xxxiv a design for cottages 'applicable to the above'. Plaw's model village was to have a pump 'placed in each angle of the square for the use of the inhabitants'. He also noted 'a good idea for building a village ... is, to place the houses, either single or in couples, facing the opening or space allowed for garden ground to those opposite. The views would therefore be preserved, and the air circulates more freely'.

30 Balgarnie, R., *Sir Titus Salt, Baronet; his life and its lessons*, London 1877,

31 ibid.,129.

32 B (1863),xxi,110.

33 Disraeli,B., *Coningsby: or the new generation*, Bradenham ed, London 1927, 169.

98. Copley; to the left is St Stephen's church (W.H.Crossland 1863–5), and in the centre is the school (1849). The mill was increased in size in 1847, when the triumphal arch was erected, and again in 1865.

'took care to consume his own smoke'. In his next novel, *Sybil: or the Two Nations*, published in 1845, Disraeli returned to the idea of an industrial village but crossed the Pennines.[34]

Temple Newsam appears as Marney Abbey, and there is a monastic ruin which might be either Kirkstall or Fountains; Mowbray, the industrial town with 'a building which might vie with many of the cathedrals of our land' is probably based on Wakefield, although the Gothic Mowbray Castle is less easy to identify as a West Yorkshire building.[35] Not far away from the scenes of country-house life is the factory owned by Mr Trafford, who has 'gentle blood in his veins, and old English feelings' which suggest to him 'a correct conception of the relations which should subsist between the employer and the employed . . . there should be other ties than the payment and receipt of wages'. The description of Trafford's factory is clearly based on Marshall's Temple Mill in Leeds, with its top lighting, its roof drainage through cast-iron columns, and its controlled temperature.[36] But where was the model for the village?

When the workpeople of Mr. Trafford left his factory they were not forgotten. Deeply had he pondered on the influence of the employer on the health and content of his workpeople. He knew well that the domestic virtues are dependent on the existence of a home, and one of his first efforts had been to build a village where every family might be well lodged . . . In every street there was a well: behind the factory were the public baths: the schools were under the direction of the perpetual curate of the church which Mr. Trafford . . . had raised and endowed. In the midst of this village, surrounded by beautiful gardens, was the home of Trafford himself, who . . . recognised the baronial principle, reviving in a new form, and adapted to the softer manners and more ingenious circumstances of the time.[37]

34 Disraeli,B., *Sybil: or the two nations*, Bradenham ed, London 1927,210ff.

35 It has also been suggested that Mowbray is Ripon, and the ruin Fountains Abbey; in that case Mowbray Castle was probably based on Swinton Castle.

36 See 289f. for an account of Marshall's Temple Mill.

37 Disraeli, *Sybil*, op.cit.,211f.

The paternalism was probably suggested by John Marshall, who built a church for his employees and a school for their children;[38] but there was nothing in Holbeck or anywhere else in Yorkshire like 'the vast form of the spreading factory, the roofs and arches of the village, the Tudor chimneys of the house of Trafford, the spire of the Gothic church, with the sparkling river and the sylvan background'; nothing, at least, in 1845.

The previous year, the Halifax firm of James Akroyd and Son, the greatest worsted-spinning concern in the country, bought Copley Mill in the Calder valley down below the town.[39] It was an isolated building to which most of the workpeople had to travel considerable distances; the only housing was a row of seven cottages dating from the beginning of the century, and after the erection of a second mill in 1847 the firm commissioned a design 'not merely for the purpose of aggregating a sufficient number of operatives for the supply of labour, but also with an eye to the improvement of their social conditions, by fitting up their houses with every requisite comfort and convenience'.[40] While there was undeniably a strong, sincere element of philanthropy in the concept of the nineteenth-century model villages, there was also the practical requirement to keep a permanent pool of labour near the mills, coupled with the sensible belief that healthy and contented workers are more productive. With these objects in mind, a design was made (probably by George Gilbert Scott and William Henry Crossland)[41] for three terraces and a group of four shops close to the mills. The houses were consciously 'old English' in style, 'approximating to the character of many old dwellings in the

38 Marshall's school building is still standing, but the church designed by Scott, St John the Evangelist, was destroyed long ago. However, as it was not built until 1847, it cannot have been Disraeli's model; nor could St Philip's, built in 1847 by Gott near *his* mill.

39 Bretton,R., 'Colonel Edward Akroyd', *H A S* (1948), 74; Creese,W.L., *The search for environment*, New Haven 1966,22ff.

40 Akroyd,A., *On improved dwellings for the working classes, with a plan for building them in connection with benefit building societies*, London 1862,

41 Crossland was working in Scott's office at the time, and his possible authorship of the design was first suggested by Hitchcock, H.-R., *Early Victorian architecture in Britain*, New Haven 1954,i,462.

98

neighbourhood, and also in harmony with the beautiful site . . . on a bend of the river Calder'.[42] These houses were intended solely for living in, and the hand weaving (which had not been entirely superseded by machines in the 40s) was done in a specially built shed.

Although the style in which the Copley houses were built was a reflection of the Pennine vernacular, the roofs were steeply pitched and the uniform terraces had no precedent in the weavers' hamlets. There were allotment gardens separated by privet hedges, which were neatly trimmed at the firm's expense, and the community was eventually provided with all it needed; schools in 1849, a library in 1850, and a church in 1863–5 which was designed by Crossland in accordance with Edward Akroyd's direction that 'in its beauty and entirety [it] should be worthy of the age'. The result was not unlike Disraeli's description of Mr Trafford's village, although Akroyd himself did not live at Copley. There was much interest in the village, but one major criticism. 'There can be no apology for back-to-back houses . . . though it is one of the common features of the country in this neighbourhood', wrote the *Builder*,[43] even though those at Copley were considered the best examples that could be found in Yorkshire. Akroyd, who had become a leading spokesman on behalf of bettering the conditions of the workers, defended his decision in an essay, *On Improved Dwellings for the Working Classes*,[44] but when the designs were made for the next Akroyd model village in 1859, the houses were of a different form; so was the whole procedure, since the firm found it inconvenient 'to invest any large sum in cottage property beyond that already laid out at Copley'.

In his essay, Akroyd referred to workpeople's homes in the Haley Hill area close to his largest mill as 'of an inferior class, inconvenient and ill ventilated, and for the most part with only a single living room and chamber, however numerous may be the inmates'. Considering how to build 'an improved style of dwellings on a large scale', he came to an arrangement with the Halifax Permanent Benefit Building Society, which provided the capital for a Building Association. Akroyd described his plan 'to purchase a suitable plot of land for a building site; to obtain designs from an able architect for building blocks of dwellings, eight or ten each; and to find parties who were willing to take up each successive block, forming themselves into a building association for that purpose'.[45]

Akroyd bought 62,435 square yards of land on Haley Hill in 1855, and four years later he commissioned Scott 'to furnish plans and designs in the domestic Gothic'. The choice of style was as deliberate as at Copley, and Akroyd gave his reasons: 'This type was adopted not solely for the gratification of my own taste, but because it is the original of the parish of Halifax, over which many old houses are scattered of the date of the Commonwealth, or shortly after, and retaining the best features of the Elizabethan domestic architecture'.[46] Scott was an appropriate architect to have been selected to design in the 'taste of our forefathers [which] pleases the fancy, strengthens house and home attachment, entwines the present with the memory of the past, and promises, in spite of opposition and

42 Akroyd, op.cit.,4f.

43 *B* (1863),xxi,109. The designs for Copley are in Hole, op.cit.,pls.7–9.

44 Akroyd, op.cit.,5.

45 ibid,6; Hobson,O.R., *A hundred years of the Halifax*, London 1953,33ff.

46 Akroyd, op.cit.,8.

99. Copley; the houses were designed in the 'old English' style, and four corner shops were incorporated in the layout.

100. Halifax, Akroydon; in the second Akroyd model village (G.G.Scott 1859) the houses are 'domestic Gothic' in style, and the layout incorporates a common, open space (memorial W.S.Barber). In the background can be seen rows of the common form of back-to-back houses.

47 ibid.,8.

48 ibid.,6. The designs for Akroydon are in Hole, op.cit.,pls.10–14.

49 *BA* (1874),ii,139; in 1872 *A* (vii,92) published a design for semi-detached houses by W.S.Barber, who acted as Akroyd's architect in the 70s. The text refers to the 'character peculiar to this district of the West Riding. Modern requirements, however, will rarely admit of the often-repeated lights in each window ... The detail is rude, but very effective, especially the terminations to the label mouldings, which at times assume a formidable and almost exaggerated size. The terminals to the gables, as well as the nearly straight outer splay to the windows, are peculiar to the neighbourhood. The roofs, as a rule, are of a flat pitch, and the chimney stacks always form an important feature in the building'. The layout of Akroydon incorporated a burial ground, in which Mallinson and Healey built a mortuary chapel in the 1860s. It had a stone vaulted roof, a dado of encaustic tiles, and a dramatic monument erected by Edward and Henry Akroyd in memory of their father Jonathan (1782–1847). The latter was the work of Joseph Gott, and it represented Akroyd in a

100

prejudice, to become the national style of modern, as it was of old England'. To a greater degree than at Copley, there was a conscious attempt at Akroydon to create a community on a traditional pattern; as if to reinforce its connection with the past, even the street names were evocative of Gothic splendour – Beverley, Ripon, Chester, Salisbury and York.

The church of All Souls was being built on Haley Hill to Scott's design from 1856–9, and farther up the road Akroyd's mansion, Bankfield, was enlarged in 1867. Facing the church and mansion, the new village was going up in terraces and pairs of houses around an open green space which was a common substitute for individual gardens. Nevertheless, despite the revived vernacular, the formal layout made a different impression from the closely built, irregular hamlets which were stylistically the precedent for Akroydon; and although gables and dormers were used to create a picturesque skyline (monotonous though it is), they were not acceptable houses to the proud Yorkshire workpeople who thought them too reminiscent of almshouses and tainted with the idea of charity and dependence.[47] Nor did they like the 'old English style' which they considered 'antiquated, inconvenient, wanting in light, and not adapted to modern requirements',[48] although Akroyd claimed their criticism was to some extent mollified by the stone shields carved with their monograms, which were fixed over the doors of the houses. To complete his model town, Akroyd began transforming the nearby Shroggs Wood into a pleasure park in 1874. The layout was the work of Edward Milner, the landscape architect responsible for the Crystal Palace site at Sydenham, and Elizabethan entrance lodges were built to designs by W.S.Barber.[49]

The plan of Akroydon envisaged 350 houses 'of all classes' ranging in cost from £130 to £300 each; the mixture of classes was deliberate 'so that the better paid and better educated might act usefully on the

137

recumbent posture on a coach, illuminated theatrically from the side. All were vandalised and demolished in 1968.

50 The smallest houses contained a living-room, two bedrooms and a scullery or wash-kitchen; others, in which the living-room became the parlour, had a kitchen and three bedrooms. All had water and gas.

51 See 114; there are also two groups of almshouses, both designed by Roger Ives, Joseph Crossley's in Arden Road (1863–70) and Sir Frank Crossley's in Margaret Street (1855); both are in a Tudor style.

52 Creese, op.cit.,48ff; Stokes designed a colonnaded pavilion in the People's Park, in which is a seated figure by Joseph Durham (1814–77) of Sir Frank Crossley (1861).

53 Anon., *Sir Frank Crossley, Bart.*, London 1872,13.

54 Hobson, op.cit.,35; Creese, op.cit.,48ff. The designs for some of the West Hill Park houses are reproduced in Hole, op.cit., pls.15–18. Crossley also influenced the building of colliery villages near Wakefield by Pope and Pearson, colliery owners. John Crossley and Sons were the major shareholders in the Sharlston Colliery Co. which laid out the village of New Sharlston (1865) and Lower Altofts (1864–5). Each included a school and chapel, and these plain red brick groups of buildings were the work of John Gomersall, a Dewsbury surveyor and valuer. The New Altofts village includes Silkstone Row, reputed to be the longest three-storey terrace of working-class housing in Europe.

55 Akroyd, op.cit.,8. 'The purpose of this essay is . . . to encourage in all towns the formation of committees of influential gentlemen and workmen . . . for the purchase of land, and the erection of improved dwellings'.

56 See Dewhirst,R.K., 'Saltaire', *Town Planning Review* (1960–1), xxxi,135ff; Suddards,R.W.(ed), *Titus of Salts*, Bradford 1976.

desires and tastes of others in an inferior social position'.[50] Probably inspired by Akroyd's example, John Crossley initiated a similar socially mixed estate in 1863. This is in a part of Halifax closely associated with the Crossley family, on a hill overlooking their mills. Sir Frank Crossley's house, Belle Vue, bought in 1851 and remodelled by George Henry Stokes in 1856–7,[51] formed the nucleus of the area; and in 1856 the People's Park, the most permanent Crossley gift to Halifax, was laid out according to a design by Sir Joseph Paxton, who made the most of the site by screening the industrial buildings so far as possible, while leaving open views of the surrounding moors.[52] The park was Crossley's return for the success of his business enterprises; he had meditated, 'Lord, what wilt thou have me do?' and been inspired 'so to arrange art and nature that they shall be within the walk of every working-man in Halifax; that he shall go take his stroll there after he has done his hard day's toil, and be able to get home again without being tired'.[53]

The park, with its lake, planting and grand terrace decorated with statues and flower-filled urns, was opened in 1857 with a festive procession of brass bands and singing; 3,000 Crossley workmen, each bearing a banner of Crossley carpet, completed the scene. Six years later John Crossley began to build the West Hill Park Estate close to the park. Laid out by Paull and Ayliffe, it was designed around the new Park Place Congregational church, and was intended for workers ranging from those who could find or borrow £160 to better-paid foremen and clerks who were able to afford £500 for the larger houses.[54] The dwellings were planned as stone terraces in which the long line of roof was broken at intervals by gables; there are Gothic porches to the smaller groups of larger houses prominently on view in Gibbet Street, and the corner of each block of six is designed as a shop with alternate Tudor and Gothic stone arched shop windows divided by thin columns. The spaces between the terraces of smaller houses built at right angles to Gibbet Street, are alternately service lanes and lines of individual gardens separated by a stone-flagged path; the best maintained, such as Cromwell Terrace, have become delightful places of roses, laburnum and lilac, which would have pleased their originator.

There was little profit for the promoters of such schemes as Akroydon and West Hill Park, but Akroyd thought 'a rich reward will accrue . . . in the contemplation of the comfort, happiness and social improvement which they will have helped to provide for the industrious and most deserving portion of the community'.[55] It was a similar sentiment that inspired Titus Salt to put aside thoughts of retiring and embark on the building of the most famous of the West Yorkshire model towns, Saltaire.[56] According to his fulsome biographer, it was in November 1850 that the millowner who had already amassed a fortune out of discovering how to make use of the wool of the alpaca, a native of Peru, called to see Lockwood and Mawson in their Bradford office. He announced his intention to build a mill near Shipley costing £30,000 or £40,000, and outlined other ideas, stressing that the mill must come first as it was the source of the rest.

101. Halifax, Gibbet Street; a part of the West Hill Park estate (Paull and Ayliffe 1863) for Crossley employees. Corner shops were included in the layout.

102. Halifax, Cromwell Terrace; the West Hill Park estate catered for a range of employees in the Crossley mills. Cromwell Terrace is a row of the smaller houses, with gardens and a rear service lane.

57 Balgarnie, op.cit.,117.

58 Salt's achievements were described, e.g. in 'The great Yorkshire llama' in *Household Words*, edited by Charles Dickens; more locally, they were the subject of an article, 'Woolgathering at Saltaire', by James Burnley, which was reprinted in *West Riding sketches*, Bradford 1875,201ff.

59 See, e.g., Balgarnie, op.cit.,124f., for an account of the banquet given to 3,750 guests when the mill was opened in 1853.

60 Balgarnie, op.cit.,115.

The first sketch submitted to him was dismissed as not half large enough, but upon being told that even it would cost £100,000, he unconcernedly replied, 'Oh, very likely'. The story continues, 'From this conversation Mr. Lockwood perceived that expense was not a consideration',[57] and from that understanding between architect and client the growth of Saltaire began.

The story has been told many times,[58] and it has a mid-Victorian expansiveness in the statistics of pounds sterling spent, square yards achieved, and quantities of food eaten at various celebrations;[59] to some extent this image is contradicted by the present reality of the town, surrounded as it is now by a Bradford that has expanded and robbed Saltaire of its sense of detachment in the Airedale landscape. The site was selected because it was close to a source of water (lacking in Bradford itself), but also on account of its separation from the industrial town, and for its beauty; 'Surveying the region from the higher ground at Shipley, the eye takes in an extensive landscape of hill and dale, of wood and water, . . . while beyond the hills there is a healthy moorland, stretching away towards Wharfedale'.[60] In its compactness and uniformity of building materials (supplied from twenty quarries), Saltaire might be regarded as a planned magnification of a traditional Pennine weaving community, even though it contains 895 houses (originally 740) in which lived the workers in the huge mill planned in the shape of the letter 'T'. Like Akroydon, the houses ranged in size from the average cottages for workers to the houses for the overlookers and managers which were grouped together along the western edge of the town; but there was little difference between them in appearance and detailing. 'From the sample the whole bulk may be judged', wrote Salt's biographer, inviting the reader to enter one of the houses to inspect the arrangements.

103

139

It is built of the same stone as the mill, and lined with brickwork. It contains parlour, kitchen, pantry, and three bedrooms. Some of the houses are designed for larger families, and others for boarding-houses. These dwellings are fitted up with all the modern appliances necessary to comfort and health; they are well ventilated, and have each a back garden, walled in, and flagged; the rents are moderate, and the houses are in much request.[61]

104 The general style of the town is Italianate, but it is worth remembering that some of the illustrations included under that usefully imprecise heading in early nineteenth-century books of designs are of plain, geometric buildings with a minimum of ornament; the houses at Saltaire were designed in that manner, starkly modelled and detailed, with a quality that, maybe unintentionally, is more in the Pennine tradition than is the self-conscious 'old English style' adopted in the Akroyd villages. Especially good are the tower-like boarding houses in Caroline Street, and the terraces with square terminal pavilions and

61 ibid.,136; there were 740 dwellings in Saltaire, made up of 21 large houses for managers and overlookers, 114 four-bedroom, 550 three-bedroom, 45 almshouses, and a number of rooms for single persons in lodging houses; see Hole, op.cit., pls.5–6 for representative plans.

103. Saltaire; the axially related mill in the form of a T and the Congregational church are sited between the canal and the railway. South of this commercial–spiritual centre, the rows of houses west of the main street, Victoria Road, comprise the original extent of the accommodation for Salt's employees. To the right of the centre can be seen the Institute and the Schools, and further to the right the almshouses.

104. Saltaire, Albert Terrace; the severe, geometrical blocks of Albert Terrace overlook the leafy Aire valley, and the view at the east end is closed by the 250 feet high chimney which was originally crowned with an Italianate machicolated parapet.

105. Saltaire, George Street; the town was designed to incorporate views beyond the river to the moorland, seen here rising above the Congregational church.

106. Meltham Mills, Bank Buildings; James Brook built this terrace of thirty-four dwellings for his workpeople at the end of a glen which he landscaped and renamed the 'People's Pleasure Grounds'.

105

low-pitched hipped roofs; the plain stone walling and the repeated semicircular-headed arches on the ground floor recall the general charactistics of small West Yorkshire hill villages, but they are also reminiscent of the manner in which John Carr designed the model village at Harewood a century earlier. Despite the grid pattern, the effect of Saltaire is less monotonous than the plan might suggest; the steeply sloping ground produces changes in roof levels as the terraces step down towards the river, and almost all the long views down the streets are closed by distant views of green moorland rising on the opposite side of the valley. Across the river, Salt made a park for his workers, enclosing fourteen acres which were laid out for boating, bathing, cricket, croquet and archery by W.Gay. There are winding walks and flower-beds, and in the middle is a large bandstand in which the brass band of the Volunteers played on the July day in 1871 when the park was formally opened.

Saltaire was conceived as a complete community, but on a vaster scale than Disraeli's notion of Mr Trafford's industrial village. Almost the only man connected with the mill who did not live within walking distance was the owner himself, and he had always intended to build a house on a site set aside for that purpose. The first of the community buildings to be erected was the Congregational church; it faces the grand entrance to the mill, 'like a palace built for God' quotes Salt's pious biographer,[62] and it represents Lockwood and Mawson at their best. Beside this rich but firmly controlled monument the remainder of their public buildings (such as the school and Institute discussed elsewhere in this study) are architecturally less significant; but the whole achievement, famous as it is, stands out against the picture of

62 Balgarnie, op.cit.,141; see 206 for further references to the church. Although Salt was an ardent Congregationalist, he gave sites for churches or meeting houses to the Methodists, the Baptists, the Roman Catholics, and the Swedenborgians. He regarded a religious belief as essential, and equally so was abstention from alcohol; 'Drink and lust are at the bottom of it all', he insisted, and refused to allow any public houses in Saltaire.

workers' housing in the large towns as vividly as the clean, newly built, stone group must have appeared in its moorland setting.

The fame of Copley, Akroydon, West Hill Park and Saltaire has obscured the smaller philanthropic ventures of the 60s and 70s. Yet other millowners also considered the welfare of their workpeople. At Meltham Mills, for example, James Brook built St James's church (J.P.Pritchett 1845) and the attached schools (John Kirk 1868) close to his Greek Revival residence; then he employed Joshua Major to landscape the banks of the stream in the valley where his mills were built, renaming it the 'People's Pleasure Grounds'. 'Here the weary Mechanic and his family may recreate amidst the beauties of nature, and reflect that a principle of Divine love, far higher than nature, has spread this "little Eden".' Overlooking a part of this delightful glen, **106** Brook built Bank Buildings, a long terrace of thirty-four dwellings designed with Tudor details and a central, gabled section ornamented with an oriel window. Brook created a picturesque, idyllic community in his valley, and Joseph Hirst was equally generous to his workpeople at Wilshaw, the neighbouring hamlet on the exposed moorland. Like Brook, he began with a church and employed John Kirk to design St Mary's in 1862; not only is the style unusual in an isolated village (or anywhere, for that matter, so strange is its Romanesque detailing), but the form departs from the normal since it also incorporates a Sunday School and a vicarage under one roof within a symmetrical plan. In 1871, Italianate almshouses designed as three pairs of semi-detached homes were erected for retired Hirst employees; then followed St Mary's school in an Elizabethan style, and finally St Mary's Court, all the work of Kirk and spaciously laid out and planted among trees. The last is a formal group of thirty-six houses, built in three terraces around a large courtyard, the fourth side of which is laid out as gardens and space for hanging washing;[63] beyond are wide views of the softly modelled Pennine landscape.

Apart from such philanthropic ventures, there were the products of co-operative communities; at Clayton Heights, for example, terraces of houses were built in 1865 on each side of a large, ornamental arched **234** entrance leading to an earlier utilitarian mill dated 1851 and 1862. At right angles, behind one of the terraces and facing the mill, is another, plainer, terrace looking on to a stone paved courtyard provided with ornamental cast-iron clothes posts. The whole group, including two larger houses at the end of one of the terraces, forms a complete community on the hilltop road from Great Horton to Queensbury, where John Foster's huge Black Dyke Mill dominates the little village of neat stone-built cottages, managers' houses and stables.

It is bathetic to return from these towns and villages where the traditions of the small, self-contained weaving hamlets had not been entirely lost (and better facilities had been provided by philanthropy or self-help), to the towns – especially to Leeds as it was in the 60s and 70s.

When contemplating the ugly, ill-built town, where every little freeholder asserts his indefeasible right as a Briton to do what he likes with his own; to inflict his own selfishness, ignorance and obstinacy upon his neighbours, and

63 I am grateful to Mr Cyril Pearce, who drew my attention to the housing at Meltham Mills and Wilshaw.

107. Bradford; the view from Lidget Green towards Girlington, a district which was developed from the 1850s. In the distance is Lister's Manningham Mill.

upon posterity for generations to come; and where local *self*-government means merely *mis*-government – we are apt to wish for a little wholesome despotism to curb such vagaries.[64]

That indictment of Leeds, written by a Leodiensian, offers a sharp contrast to the benevolent despotism that had created the planned communities. It was part of James Hole's prize-winning and much quoted essay on the houses of the working classes, written as a result of a conference on that subject organised by the Royal Society of Arts in 1864; the prize was offered by the Mayor of Leeds, a town which had received severe criticism in the *Builder* four years earlier:

We will ask the wealthy manufacturers of Leeds – the men whose riches and luxuries are the product of these dwellers in dens of fever and filth, – whether they approve of such a dreadful state of things. Revelling in the beautiful suburbs of Kirkstall and Headingley, surrounded by every luxury that boundless wealth can procure, it would yet be well if these woollen lords would realise the fact, that upon them devolves a responsibility in this matter . . . You, millionaires of Leeds, have no slight responsibility . . . It is impossible that the working men themselves can remedy the evil condition of their dwelling-places . . . The municipal authorities may do a great deal of good by exercising an undeviating control over the building of dwelling-places for the poor.[65]

There were no dramatic signs of improvement in response to this impassioned outburst for social justice, although the work of the Leeds Model Cottage Society which had taken as its motto: 'As the homes, so the people', must be acknowledged. This was a non profit-making society which normally financed itself through a building society and erected a number of rows of dwellings in the southern part of the town.

It was in the 40s and 50s that most of the building societies were formed; the Leeds Permanent in 1848, the Bradford Equitable in 1851, the Halifax in 1853,[66] and their funds were used by promoters as different as Akroyd at Akroydon, and the Leeds Model Cottage Society. The *Builder* reported in 1861 that 'a committee of gentlemen, well known for their interest in the working classes', had erected a block of ten houses in Leeds. These, built in Beeston Hill, were designed by Thomas Ambler in a plain Elizabethan manner, 'with ornamental gables, slated roofs and slightly decorated window-heads'. Each had a basement pantry, a parlour and kitchen, and three bedrooms; there was an enclosed garden five yards wide, and a separate yard and outbuildings at the back. The cost was £150 for each

64 Hole, op.cit.,46.

65 *B* (1860),xviii,809f.

66 The Leeds Permanent Building Society was founded in 1848 with 1,099 members; by 1865 it had grown to 6,782. It did not build houses, but provided for those who wished to build; those who invested knew their money was safe, while those who borrowed trusted the Society to organise the financial transactions while leaving them to concentrate on building.

house, 'and working-men will be put into possession on paying the amount down, or £25 to £30 and taking shares in a building society for the balance . . . This business-like method of destroying dens of filth and fever, and giving each man an independent property, and a reward for sobriety and perseverance, is a good way to remedy evils we are seeking to expose'.[67] Other efforts were referred to in a letter in the *Leeds Mercury* from 'Aedificator', who recalled it was 'with the idea that they might be built at once to live in and to look on, that we made our first essay at building . . . residences for working men whose wages average 18s per week'. The writer reluctantly admitted the houses were back-to-back, 'but this evil will be remedied, it is thought, by the introduction of ventilating flues'.[68]

Yet such worthy attempts were relatively rare; so was William Beckett Denison's work in Leeds on behalf of the provision of lodging houses for working men. The first, built in 1851, was for seventy;[69] but although the wealthy banker persevered, he seems to have had few imitators in Leeds. Huddersfield, on the other hand, opened its first on Chapel Hill in 1854 for 680 people; within ten years there was similar accommodation for 2,870. For 3½d the lodgers had a reading-room, temperance lectures and religious services; for an extra 1d they lived in a separate part of the building, had their own reading-room, and enjoyed the privilege of white bed-covers.[70] John Crossley built an Italianate lodging house in Smithy Street, Halifax, and in 1851 he converted the old Multure Hall in King Street for a similar purpose;[71] presumably it was at that time the fine plastered ceiling now in Bankfield Museum was covered. Andrews and Pepper built lodging houses in Bradford, first in Captain Street, and then another 'externally in plain character' in 1870 in Sunbridge Road, which had space for 186 beds.[72]

Leeds could show an interesting innovation in 1867 when Adams and Kelly designed a block of dwellings for the Leeds Industrial Dwellings Company in Shannon Street.[73] There were shops on the ground floor, and the three upper floors were dwellings with balcony access; each flat had two or three rooms, but although the experiment was favourably reviewed on the whole, it remained an isolated development as the flats were unpopular. The Company went on to purchase and renovate existing properties, and by the end of the century it owned about 1,000 houses. In 1878, the Leeds Social Improvement Society drew attention again to the insanitary state of the town, and in the following year 500 cellar dwellings were closed. The Guardians of the Poor criticised the lack of philanthropic action in the town, although it was only the work of Denison and his friends, and the various improvement societies, that effected any practical remedies.

Meanwhile, back-to-back houses 'were run up in defiance of the universal condemnation of all persons, without the slightest regard to the health and comfort of the inhabitants'.[74] In Bradford the bye-laws of 1860 outlawed such houses in long rows by prescribing an open space at the side and rear of each dwelling; the result can be seen, for example, in Westbourne Road, built in 1878 in the shadow of Lister's

67 *B* (1861),xix,289. The houses designed by Ambler are illustrated in Hole, op.cit.,pl.19; other designs were made by W.H.Crossland (pl.20) and Elisha Backhouse (pl.21).

68 *LM*, 20 Oct 1862. I am indebted to Prof. Beresford for this reference, and for the identification of the houses as Bridgefield Buildings, which were north-west of the South Accommodation Road bridge over the river.

69 Mayhall,J., *Annals of Yorkshire*, London 1878,i,593; *BA* (1878),ix,283 reported that W.B.Perkin was adapting a building in Millgarth, Leeds as a model lodging house.

70 Hole, op.cit.,161ff,52ff.

71 Taylor,D., 'Halifax streets and buildings', *HAS* (1960),63. The Multure Hall was built in 1631 and demolished after a Compulsory Purchase Order was served in 1935.

72 *A* (1870),iv,378. A model lodging house was built in Piccadilly, Wakefield by William Crutchley (1871–2).

73 *B* (1867),xxv,173; see also Hole, op.cit., pls.2–3.

74 *LM*, 14 Oct 1862.

108
107

109

108. Leeds, Quarry Street, Woodhouse; back-to-back houses were built until after the First World War. Yet these examples (1884–5) illustrate the good standard of building and the decorative details added to the lintels and to the brickwork at the eaves.

109. Bradford, Westbourne Road; houses built as a consequence of the town's 1860 bye-laws which laid down minimum widths of streets and the provision of open spaces at the rear and side.

75 Barry,F.W., and Smith,P.G., *Joint report on back-to-back houses to the Local Government Board*, 1888,2.

76 Beresford, op.cit.,119.

77 *Housing* (Building Centre Committee), London 1936,i,162ff.

78 Gauldie,E., *Cruel habitations*, London 1974, 300.

79 The rehabilitation of these tenements was begun in 1976.

awesome Manningham Mill, although the industrialist had no part in their building. The houses, which have sculleries, are built of stone in blocks of four, each block having a central passage seven feet six inches wide. Another type of development can be illustrated by a group of eight houses and two corner shops in Trevelyan Street, Huddersfield, for which plans were prepared by John Kirk and Sons. This is built with three street frontages, slightly Tudor in their details, surrounding a communal drying ground and privies, and each house consists of a basement kitchen, a single ground-floor living room and two first-floor bedrooms. Yet a Government report of 1888 noted 'In all the large manufacturing towns of Yorkshire back-to-back dwellings have been and are still being built to a considerable extent'.[75] It referred to Halifax, Morley, Stainland, Todmorden and Keighley; but gradually the back-to-back fell or was forced out of favour, except in Leeds where, as an historical fact, the last is believed to have been built in 1937,[76] four years after it had been reported there were still 30,000 built before 1872 in occupation, 28,000 built between 1872 and 1890, and 13,000 that were post-1890.[77] Perhaps it was appropriate that the first public resolution in favour of 'town planning' was passed during the Trades Union Congress in 1904 at Leeds.

There was no 'planning' in either Leeds or Bradford in the 1890s (although there were bye-laws), but the Housing of the Working Classes Act of 1890 began slowly to be effective. In 1901 a scheme was approved in Bradford for clearing an area of slum property and replacing it with 432 tenement flats;[78] this was the Longlands Estate, which was laid out as a number of blocks, each containing thirty tenements divided into three storeys with balcony access from open stairs in glazed-brick wells; each consists of two rooms and a scullery. The buildings are stone-faced with slated roofs, but the standard of construction was poor.[79] One of the blocks was designed as a lodging house. At the same time as the Longlands proposal was approved, Bradford agreed to build 925 cottages on a suburban site; the first of these Corporation-built houses were erected in 1902–04 in Foxfleet

110. Leeds, Woolman Street; flats with balcony access (1901).

Street with frontages of fourteen feet six inches on each side of streets fourteen yards wide. Leeds had begun to demolish in 1870, and there were further acquisitions of slum housing, including Quarry Hill, over the next four decades. Flats with balcony access were privately built on a site sold by the Corporation in Woolman Street in 1901, in groups of twelve and fifteen divided into three floors; there is an open staircase between each group, and the brick-built tenements incorporate decorative lintels in a commercialised Pennine tradition over the doors, and horizontal sliding sashes of a Yorkshire type. The Housing Committee proposed to build similar dwellings on an adjoining site (the Marsh Lane tenements) in 1906, consisting of sixty two-roomed and twelve three-roomed flats for 312 people, at an estimated cost of £11,509. There was opposition in Committee, one alderman protesting that 'tenement flats were an evil, and they were disliked by most people';[80] but two blocks were approved, and erected in brick with cement-rendered gables and sash windows. Like the earlier tenements, each opens off an external balcony.

There was no municipal housing policy in Leeds before 1919, but under the Act of that year several cottage estates were built on the outskirts of the city. Concrete houses were tried as an experiment, 500 on the Crossgates estate and 800 on the Meanwood estate, but in spite of a saving in cost they were not used elsewhere. In 1923 H.M.Butler, M P, speaking at a dinner in Leeds, suggested 'it was quite a feasible proposition to take a large sheet of steel plate, and from it press the front of a house, including the wall, with a door and a window at each side and three windows above, and one face of the roof. The back of the house, and the two ends, could be similarly produced in pressed steel, at a total cost of about £25. The house could then be sprayed with the cheap glue which they were using in Germany, and then sprinkled with sawdust – and, thus, a wooden house! . . . in this way the housing difficulty could be overcome'.[81] The suggestion was received with laughter; the pressed steel house was twenty years away, and the majority of the houses on the new estates were of traditional construction. The layouts were made by the City Engineer, and the houses were designed by twenty-one architects in private practice; under this system, 3,329 were built as a result of the 1919 Act, and 6,169 under the 1923 and 1924 Acts. In the 30s Leeds undertook a huge programme of clearance and replacement, and the city's boundaries were extended to make more land available; 30,000 houses were scheduled to go up in six years. This ambitious scheme proved unrealistic, but new cottage estates were started at Gipton, Halton, Seacroft and the picturesquely named Belle Isle. Yet these estates were on a scale very different from the usual connotation of 'cottages'; usually there were between one and three thousand dwellings, and sometimes the estates were intended to be even larger; 7,000 families were to be rehoused on the Seacroft estate. The large Gipton estate, started in 1934, and planned to include 3,400 dwellings, typifies these estates which included up to thirty different types of 'cottage' with from two to six rooms. They are built of brick, sometimes partly rendered, with tiled roofs, gables, wooden casements with glazing bars,

80 *B A* (1906),lxv,356.

81 *Y P*, 25 Jan 1923.

111. **Leeds, Gipton Approach; the Gipton Estate was first laid out (1935) for 3,400 dwellings, mostly as groups of semi-detached houses. The two multi-storey prefabricated flatted dwellings in the centre are representatives of the 1960s, and in the distance can be seen some of the taller, twelve-storey buildings on the Seacroft Estate (c.1961).**

and simple 'Georgian' doorcases; the average density is about twelve to the acre, but a quite different type of estate resulted in thirty-six dwellings to the acre on the site of the demolished slums on Quarry Hill.

Corbusian visions of living in white towers among green parks in a self-contained community with shared facilities had stimulated the imagination of young architects in the 1930s; and the success of the municipal Karl-Marx-Hof in Vienna, designed by Karl Ehm, had been widely praised in the international architectural press. A group of West Yorkshire architects and housing committee members went to Vienna to see the vast, monumental blocks of apartments with their fortress-like exterior and their shops, laundries and kindergartens. It was an inspiration to the officials from Leeds; 'To see all this under a summer sky in Vienna is to see a very fine example of humanised architecture', was a common reaction. In 1934 the committee also went to France, to visit the Cité de la Muette at Drancy, designed by Eugène Beaudoin and Marcel Lods; the prime interest there was the structural system devised by Eugène Mopin, consisting of a light steel frame and a precast, vibrated concrete cladding which could be erected without scaffolding. As the wall rose, the cavity was filled in stages with poured concrete.

Mopin was invited to design the structure of the Quarry Hill estate for 3,280 people in 938 flats, which combined elevational elements of the Viennese estate with structural elements of the Drancy building. The parabolic arches of the entrances, and the Mendelssohnian contrast of streamlined horizontal bands of glazing and walling, were all part of a determined effort to be 'modern' and international; and

112

82 Ravetz,A., *Model estate*, London 1974, 22. In November 1973, it was announced that the City Council had decided to demolish the estate over the next four to five years on account of the structural deterioration and the expense of conserving the buildings (for the second time), the obsolescence of the Garchey waste disposal, and the expected disruptive effect of the north-east motorway which had been built close to the estate and at a high level. Demolition commenced in 1976.

83 The prefabricated system was evolved by the Yorkshire Development Group, a consortium of three of the county's local authorities.

with a similar determination the vast, formal layout at the east end of the new Headrow was imposed on a sloping site with no relevance to its contours. Nevertheless, even if Quarry Hill seems in retrospect to merit a lesser place in architectural history than was once thought, and in spite of failures in the Mopin system which brought the life of the buildings to an end in 1976,[82] the estate remains a considerable achievement for its time and an important experiment in large-scale community housing.

Post-second World War housing in West Yorkshire cities and towns conformed to the various patterns set by the Ministry of Housing; new estates continued to be laid out on the well-tried principle of semi-detached housing spaced along standard width roads and covering large areas of suburban land, without always providing the necessary humanity or social amenities to make living in them have any meaning or identity. Proprietary constructional methods have been used, and terrace housing has been cautiously revived in towns where the term is synonymous with the image of back-to-backs. Point blocks have been built in standardised commercial versions of the once admired sketches of Corbusier, growing higher and higher until 1972 when the culminating tower at Cottingley, Leeds reached a record height of twenty-five storeys; even before it was built, it was obsolete. In the total renewal and obliteration of everything existing on the site, Quarry Hill set a fashion in the 30s which remained unchallenged for a long time after the war. A large area of Hunslet, Leeds was demolished in the 60s to make way for Hunslet Grange, a vast, frightening environment which perpetuates the least successful social and architectural aspects of Quarry Hill.[83]

149

113. Leeds, Chapel Allerton; a small municipal housing development which consciously returns to a traditional village pattern (E.W.Stanley 1970).

It might have been predicted that there would be a reaction against such forms of housing in the conservationist 70s, and that the most interesting and controversial ideas have been related to such areas as Burley Road, Leeds where the City Council experimented with rehabilitation of terrace houses and corner shops in the 60s, or Barkerend, Bradford where a pioneering General Improvement Area was declared and developed in the early 70s. Social and visual qualities have been discovered in some of the hitherto condemned nineteenth-century housing; and a recent study of Quarry Hill perceived that the streets and buildings cleared away were 'not all irremediable slum. [There was] much variety and contrast . . . narrow lanes, steep inclines, steps, blank walls, tight and secret openings, and accidental and sidelong views . . . Where the slum had been enticing, [the new] was merely bland; where the slum had been dramatic, this was bombastic'.[84] This nostalgic, humanitarian reaction, as predictable and explicable as the nineteenth-century vision of weavers in their Arcadian communities in the Pennine valleys, can be seen as an influence on recently designed layouts which have returned to the idea of smaller scale groups, and to rows of houses which are not unlike (though frequently less commodious and substantial) the once despised back-to-backs and scullery houses. In the most admired new designs, village street patterns and semi-enclosed courtyards are being introduced, so that this review of community housing and the various attempts to answer its needs might suggest that the road to the New Jerusalem, as Defoe wrote of crossing the Pennines, is 'all but that of a plain Way . . . as soon as we were at the top of every Hill, we had it to come down again on the other Side'.

113

84 Ravetz, op.cit.,60,206.

5 Medieval churches and monasteries

If our churches are to be viewed like the ruins of Greece and Rome, only as original monuments from which ancient architecture is to be studied, they would be more valuable in their present condition, however mutilated and decayed, than with any, even the slightest degree of restoration. But taking the more correct view of a church as a building erected for the glory of God and the use of Man . . . I think we are then at liberty to examine our best judgement upon the subject.

George Gilbert Scott, *A Plea for the Faithful Restoration of our Ancient Churches*, 1850.

'You would hardly believe it, but there is really a plan on foot for the conversion of the ruins of Kirkstall Abbey into a modern Anglican church; and no less a person than Sir Gilbert Scott has undertaken to carry this almost incredible proposition into execution.' That was the news given to the Architectural Association in 1873 by Edmund Sharpe, the author of *The Seven Periods of English Architecture* and an authority on the monasteries of the Cistercian Order, of which Kirkstall is one of the most important. 'Most of you have, I dare say, learned, from what I have already published on the subject', continued Sharpe with great confidence, 'what such a church was like, with its simple outlines; its utterly plain appearance, devoid of all colour and ornamentation; its puritanic, even poverty-stricken simplicity, and its unmusical ritual. We all know, on the other hand, what sort of aspect the modern church, that we shall have at the hands of Sir Gilbert Scott, will present, – with its alabaster reredos, its gilt choir-screens, its painted vaultings, its gaudy stained-glass windows, and its brilliant encaustic floor'.[1] The reaction of the Architectural Association to this surprising information is not recorded; the conversion was not undertaken, yet it is not difficult to imagine how the abbey church would have looked if Edward Akroyd and his friends, who had requested 'an opinion as to the practicability and cost of bringing it back to a state fitted for its sacred uses', had succeeded in buying the ruins and executing Scott's plan.

The completeness of the ruins of Kirkstall has made the task of the historian easier than on those sites where much of the monastic fabric was used as a quarry after the Dissolution. Thoresby wrote that although the 'roof has been off the Church ever since the Dissolution of the House . . . the *Dortoir*, or *Dormitory*, and some other Places that have been converted to private Uses, are covered. The Tower also . . . is perfect, the Stone smooth and good'.[2] There was slightly less left when a contributor (probably John Carter) to the *Gentleman's Magazine* in 1806, described with amazement how much of the fabric was standing:

114

1 *B* (1873),xxxi,683. It is an interesting fact, worth recording here, that in 1946–7 there was a proposal that the ruins of Fountains Abbey should be converted for monastic use. The architect was to be Sir Giles Gilbert Scott.

2 Thoresby, 167.

114. Kirkstall Abbey, looking from east to west down the length of the choir and nave through the blank east window inserted in the early sixteenth century; at that time the crossing tower was heightened. The lower walls on the north and south are of three chapels which open off each transept.

Ever let me seize each opportunity to hold up to praise the wonderful skill of my ancient brethren, and ever cry, What was their system of construction, and what were their materials, thus to combine, bidding after-ages look on and marvel ... It is impossible to leave these exalted ruins without lamenting (unavailing passion!) to see them left open to every depredation and defilement. Is the remembrance of finer uses forgotten? Are all the fine feelings for English antiquity absorbed in heedless indifference?[3]

There have been further depredations since 1806, and the once beautiful Aire valley has been turned into a scene of industrial squalor; yet as late as 1959 Sir Nikolaus Pevsner wrote 'It requires little imagination to place roofs on the various parts of the church and the monastic buildings round the cloister, and visualise the grey complex group as it must have appeared at the completion of the main works *c*.1175'.[4]

In the nineteenth century, it was often one short step only from imagination to execution, and the result is that our view of medieval architecture is more often than not seen through the subtly distorting vision of Victorian antiquaries and restoring architects. 'The mellowing hand of time ... rounding angles, breaking lines, and softening down' was blessed for its work by topographical artists, but not by those responsible for medieval churches. The well known consequence was, as William Morris wrote, critically and passionately, that 'of late years a great uprising of ecclesiastical zeal, coinciding with a great increase of study, and consequently of knowledge of medieval architecture, has driven people into spending their money on these buildings, not merely with the purpose of repairing them, of keeping them safe, clean, and wind- and watertight, but also of restoring them to some ideal state of perfection.'[5] Inevitably, this study of West Yorkshire ecclesiastical architecture from the twelfth to the

3 *Gentleman's Magazine* (1806). lxxvi,722.

4 Pevsner,N., *The buildings of England: Yorkshire West Riding*, Harmondsworth 1967,340.

5 Mackail,J.W., *The life of William Morris*, London 1899,344.

seventeenth centuries, from Henry de Lacy's Kirkstall Abbey to John Harrison's St John's church, is as much about nineteenth-century transformations as about the original buildings.

Architectural history can offer few comments on Yorkshire in the days when Eborius, Bishop of York, attended the synod of Arles in 314, or Paulinus baptised large numbers of converts in the water of the Calder at Dewsbury in 627. Remains of Saxon churches are scanty, for as Whitaker commented, 'while the Norman edifices frequently remain entire, these more ancient churches have either been destroyed for their diminutive size, or have decayed from length of time'. The well-known fact that the parish of Dewsbury covered an area of four hundred square miles[6] produces no complementary architectural evidence. There is no record of an important church there, although there were undoubtedly buildings, mostly constructed of timber, associated with the stone crosses of which fragments have survived in various parts of the region.[7] All Saints', Ledsham (although restored in 1871) is the most complete Saxon church,[8] and the tower at least remains of All Hallows, Bardsey. There is more substantial evidence of Norman churches, but with the one outstanding exception of Kirkstall, the West Yorkshire religious houses founded from the end of the eleventh century have completely disappeared.

There was, for instance, a Cluniac house at Pontefract which was founded in 1093 as an Alien Priory dependent on La Charité; in 1393, at a time when there were 22 monks, its status was changed to that of a Priory. But nothing remains of its buildings. Twelve nuns under a prioress occupied another Cluniac house at Arthington in the Wharfe valley; it was founded c.1154–5 by Peers de Ardyngton, but it was demolished within fifty years of its suppression in 1540 to provide the material for the present building known as Arthington Nunnery. The Augustinians founded a priory at Nostell c.1114, which was reorganised in 1122 as a house with 26 canons and a number of lay brethren; but whatever survived was taken down by Sir Rowland Winn during the later stages of the building of the eighteenth-century Nostell Priory. Nor does anything remain of the Dominicans' house at Pontefract, which held 29 to 36 friars shortly after its foundation in 1265, but had dwindled to seven at the time of its suppression. Kirklees Priory was founded in the early twelfth century for Cistercian nuns, and according to Whitaker the nave, transept and choir of the church must have been at least 150 feet long. There was a cloister thirty yards square, and the entrance to the house was through a gateway with corner turrets which survived long enough to be included in an engraving published in William Stukeley's *Itinerarium Curiosum* (1776); but Whitaker could only record the 'very pleasant sensations' excited by 'the noble beeches which overshadow the tombs, the groups of deer that repose beneath, and the deep silence' of the site where, according to tradition, Robin Hood died and was buried. Its place had been taken by John Armytage's Kirklees Hall, built c.1610. Another group of Cistercian nuns was housed at Esholt Priory, founded by Simon de Ward in the mid-twelfth century; but the buildings, which were impoverished in 1445 by floods and general

6 Whitaker, 298. Dewsbury was 'the common parent of the parishes of Thornhill and Burton ... and of those of Almonbury, Kirkheaton, Huddersfield and Bradford ... to which may be added ... those of Halifax and Mirfield'.

7 Collingwood,W.G., 'Anglian and Anglo-Danish sculpture in the West Riding', *Y A S* (1914–5),xxiii,129ff.

8 The restoration was undertaken by Henry Curzon. All Saints' dates substantially from the eighth century, with a Norman tower and fifteenth-century battlements, pinnacles and a spire. A century after the restoration, it is not easy to distinguish how much of the stonework of the remarkable eleventh-century doorway in the tower was reworked or renewed by the nineteenth-century masons, but the flowing scrolls of vine leaves carved on the broad band surrounding the arched doorway cannot have been entirely an invention; Taylor,R.V., *Ecclesiae Leodienses*, London 1875,467; Taylor,H.M. and J., *Anglo Saxon architecture*, Cambridge 1965,i,378ff.

153

decay, were replaced in 1706–07 by a house built for Sir Walter Calverley, incorporating some of the fabric of the religious foundation.

Nevertheless, these were minor buildings inevitably overshadowed by the major religious house in twelfth-century West Yorkshire, the great Cistercian abbey in the Aire valley. The origin of Kirkstall is described in a much-quoted manuscript in the Bodleian Library, probably dating from the early fifteenth century, according to which

> There was in those days [the reign of Stephen] in the province a certain man of great possessions . . . by name Henry de Lacy, and it fell out that he was sick for many days [and] made a vow to the Lord that he would build an abbey of the Cistercian order . . . He recovered, and not unmindful of his vow straightway caused the abbot of Fountains to be summoned to him . . . and assigned to him by donation solemnly made a certain vill, by name Barnoldswick with its appurtenances for the construction of an abbey.

The manuscript continues to describe how Alexander, Prior of Fountains, left his abbey with twelve monks and lay brethren and travelled to Barnoldswick where, 'it may be with some want of consideration', he demolished an existing church. A complaint was lodged, which finally reached Pope Eugenius III, who pronounced it 'a pious thing and worthy of favour, that a church should fall provided an abbey be constructed in its stead' – a decision that might be seen as an infallible excuse for much that was to occur to the fabric of churches in the following centuries.

Yet, having received this judgment, the abbot 'began to turn over in his mind the possibility of a change of site and transference of the monastery elsewhere . . . he passed through a certain valley, then wooded and shady . . . and it seemed to him that the place was fair enough and fit for building an abbey upon it'. Omitting many details, that is the traditional history of Kirkstall's foundation, probably in 1152, in 'a place covered with woods and unproductive of crops, a place well nigh destitute of good things save timber and stone and a pleasant valley with the water of a river which flowed down its centre'.[9] Those particular good things are the main requirements for building, especially when it is also recorded that Henry de Lacy provided money, 'laid with his own hand the foundations of the church, and himself completed the whole fabric at his own cost'. The buildings were constructed 'of stone and wood brought there . . . covered excellently with tiles', and most of them must have been complete by the last quarter of the twelfth century.

Deriving as it did from Fountains, the plan of the church follows the same form of nave and aisles, transepts and a chancel with a square end; three chapels were built on the east side of each transept, and unlike Fountains there is a large tower over the crossing which was raised in height in the early sixteenth century. Apart from this upper stage of the tower, the gigantic east window, and the turrets of the four gables, which are all early sixteenth or late fifteenth-century additions, the church at Kirkstall remains largely as it was completed c.1175. There are some uncertainties, such as whether there was ever a Galilee porch, like that at Fountains, as a prelude to the west front; but so much remains of the abbey that there is relatively little cause for conjecture. Stylistically, the church is Late Norman or Transitional,

9 'The foundation of Kirkstall Abbey', *T S* (1895),iv,169ff.

115. Kirkstall Abbey; T.Smith's view, engraved by F.Vivares (1746/7), illustrates the completeness of the ruin at that time and the picturesquely incursive ivy and saplings.

combining semicircular-headed window and doorway openings with structural arches which are pointed. Before the new east window was inserted, there was a group of three semicircular-headed lancets surmounted by a circular window, as in the east walls of the transept chapels at Fountains. Kirkstall is an austere building, with heavy piers supporting pointed arches in the nave arcades, and a clerestorey above of small semicircular-headed windows; like Fountains, there is no triforium, and although the nave aisles are elaborately vaulted there was evidently no intention to roof the nave with anything but a timber roof.[10] Before the tower was raised, its massive, low, square form must have appeared almost fortress-like, and it was the tall upper stage added during Kirkstall's last years of existence as a centre of monastic life that gave it the memorable character as a ruin that appealed to the picturesque taste of eighteenth-century writers and painters.

115

Thomas Girtin, J.M.W.Turner, Michael Angelo Rooker and countless artists of every degree of accomplishment came to paint the abbey, and it was the subject of many travellers' poetic reflections. 'A LADY' can represent them all in her verses dated 1797 which begin:

Could hallow'd walls or ruin'd Tow'rs inspire,
Or moss-grown cells call forth Parnassian fire,
Thy praise, O KIRKSTALL! should be sweetly sung,
Thy ancient grandeur dwell upon my tongue . . .[11]

What distinguished Kirkstall from the other Yorkshire abbeys was that, unlike St Mary's, York, the buildings were not used to any great extent as a quarry for materials to repair or build other structures; unlike Bolton, the church was not adapted in part for parochial use; unlike Fountains, Rievaulx and Roche, the ruin was not incorporated in an idyllic romantic landscape attached to a country house, although Kirkstall was a property of the Saviles and then the Brudenells for

10 Hope,W.H.St.J., and Bilson,J., *Architectural description of Kirkstall Abbey*, Leeds 1907.

11 Anon., *A history of the town and parish of Leeds*, Leeds 1797,30.

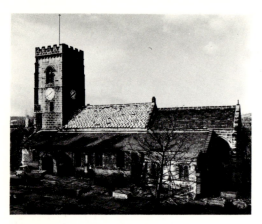

116. Elland, St Mary; the low, widespread body of the church, and the sturdy tower with an embattled parapet supported on a machicolated corbel table, are typical of West Yorkshire.

117. Batley, All Saints; an extreme example of the semi-fortified character of West Yorkshire towers.

most of the time from its dissolution until the late nineteenth century. It was simply left after the roofs had been stripped of their lead and timber. In 1746 the dormitory fell down, and in 1779 a large part of the upper stage of the central tower collapsed, bringing with it a part of the arcade. In 1816 Whitaker could write that because of 'the neglect of two centuries and a half, the unregarded growth of ivy, and the maturity of vast elms and other forest trees, which have been suffered to spring up among the walls, . . . Kirkstall is become, as a single object, the most picturesque and beautiful ruin in the kingdom'.[12] Its still picturesque appearance in 1836 is recorded in W. Nelson's set of six lithographs, and in 1843 in William Richardson's sumptuously coloured plates in *The Monastic Ruins of Yorkshire*; but it was vulnerably located near to Leeds industries. A new turnpike road was built between the church and the gatehouse, and 'an immense woollen manufactory began to pour forth its volumes of smoke, and to emit its din of machinery'.[13]

While the millstone grit walls of Kirkstall were blackening, attention was being given to parish churches, often built to serve small communities but finding themselves in the centre of rapidly growing towns. The frequent neglect of their fabric during the eighteenth century, their 'Georgianising' inside, and the additional galleries and pews which had been inserted to provide additional accommodation, were all under attack independently by A.W.N.Pugin and the Cambridge Camden Society. Nor were these inherited churches always regarded as of sufficient architectural consequence to match their new importance, in spite of their often quaint antiquity. Sir Stephen Glynne, an eminent antiquary whose notes on Yorkshire churches are a valuable record of them in the middle of the century before restoration had become universally popular, slightingly referred to St Mary's, Elland as being in the style of 'the Rough Perpendicular prevalent in these mountainous districts';[14] and he and the Revd.R.V.Taylor (who collected a vast amount of information about churches and published some under the title of *Ecclesiae Leodienses* in 1875) both used the word 'plain' frequently and 'coarse' occasionally when describing these churches.

In the fourteenth century West Yorkshire was still a sparsely populated region uncomfortably close to the Scots who were actively raiding and burning in the first decades of the century, a time when it also suffered from famine and the Black Death. It was a battlefield during the interminable Wars of the Roses, and the centres of the woollen trade which was going to bring prosperity to the region were still Hull, York and Beverley; it is in the East Riding that the great thirteenth–fourteenth-century churches are to be found, but a change was occurring, and by the fifteenth century the rural industry was drawing the woollen trade to West Yorkshire. The change was reflected in the rebuilding or remodelling of the parish churches. With the notable exceptions of Halifax, Wakefield, Pontefract and Leeds, most West Yorkshire churches were plain and functional. Typical are the low, widespread bodies built of millstone grit with stone slated roofs, such as St Mary's, Elland which seems to crouch down on its

12 Whitaker, 120.

13 Parsons, i,408. The gatehouse had been turned into a residence; it is now the Abbey House Museum.

14 Glynne,S., 'Notes on Yorkshire churches', *YAS* (1898),xiv,343.

116

118. Luddenden, St Mary; medieval churches in isolated communities incorporated vernacular elements and insertions until they appeared as picturesque as this example. (Horner, J., *Buildings in the town and parish of Halifax*, 1835)

119. Bardsey, All Hallows; the tenth-century church (of which the tower is intact) was enlarged several times until, in 1851, it appeared as J. Greig recorded it in this watercolour.

15 Whitaker, 403. The church had four aisles 'of which two, with a row of angular columns running up the middle, occupy the ordinary place of the middle aile; on the outside of these are two others, low and sloping to the eaves'. In spite of Whitaker's faith in the tower, the west face fell away in a storm in 1847. The church was dismantled in 1864 when Mallinson and Healey's new building was completed, but the old church remains as a ruin.

16 Horner, J., *Buildings in the town and parish of Halifax*, Halifax 1835.

hilltop site, All Saints', Batley which is similar but with small square-headed clerestorey windows, and the old St Thomas's, Heptonstall which Whitaker called 'low, and on a broad base, to resist the outrageous tempests which often assail it'. He thought the tower, 'if left to itself, is strong enough to defy the fury of the elements for many centuries',[15] drawing attention to the importance of this feature in these sturdy, vernacular buildings. The West Yorkshire towers were built for defence in an emergency, and instances have been quoted of the parishioners resorting to them in times of danger, and of fireplaces being installed in them. It was practical considerations which resulted in the distinctive fortified character of the embattled parapets and the almost machicolated corbel tables found, for example, in St Michael's, Thornhill, St Oswald's, Guiseley, St Peter's, Birstall and All Saints', Batley; less aggressive, but still fortified in character, are the towers of St Wilfred's, Calverley, St Mary's, Whitkirk, St Peter's, Thorner, St Mary's, Swillington, All Saints', Barwick-in-Elmet, and St Mary's, Elland which has a corbel table around the whole body of the church. They were not, on the whole, characteristics likely to appeal greatly to nineteenth-century taste, except to artists like John Horner who could perversely find picturesque qualities in such an uncouth and strange structure as the old church at Luddenden[16] which was rebuilt in a more seemly style by Thomas Taylor in 1817. Clearly there had to be a reconsideration.

Change is a part of the history of a church; the enlargement of chancels and aisles, the raising in height of a tower, the addition of chapels, the installation of monuments, are all commentaries on local life and architectural taste which constitute a continuity of life and call for the respect of later generations. All Hallows', Bardsey, for example, demonstrates in text-book fashion how a small church was extended and rebuilt over the centuries. Probably dating from the tenth century and related to the neighbouring castle, the original consisted of a nave thirty-one feet long and about half as wide with walls two feet thick, a chancel and a west tower; in 1100–25 the north wall was pierced to open up the nave to a new aisle, incorporating cylindrical piers and semicircular-headed arches of Norman type, and adding a small doorway with similar characteristics on the south wall. Fifty years later, or maybe around the time the township of Bardsey was granted by King John to the monks of Kirkstall, an aisle was added on the south, using cylindrical piers but pointed arches, and the earlier doorway was repositioned on the new south wall. The Saxon west tower with its characteristic twin openings was now flanked on each side by an aisle wall, giving the west front an unusual appearance as if the tower were rising out of a gable. In the first half of the thirteenth century, maybe close to the time when the church was appropriated to the chapel of St Mary and the Holy Angels at York, the chancel was enlarged; and in the fifteenth century, square-headed windows were inserted in the aisle walls. Stage by stage the little church had grown, and the whole of its building history was contained within its fabric.[17]

Typical of the development from a small eleventh-century church to one which was almost three times as large by the middle of the sixteenth century is St Helen's, Sandal Magna. The plan of the present church clearly shows how it grew section by section from a plain cruciform with a crossing tower, built *c.*1150; the first extension was an aisle north of the nave *c.*1180, and it was not until *c.*1330 that a rebuilding was undertaken, possibly shortly before it was appropriated to the dean and canons of St Stephen's, Westminster. The chancel was doubled in length, yet retained the same width as the first, and a south nave aisle was built. A new crossing tower was constructed on the foundations of the old, and although the church then had the general

120

17 Kirk,G.E., *All Hallows' church, Bardsey*, Leeds 1937; Taylor, op.cit.,i,139.

120. Wakefield, St Helen, Sandal Magna; largely rebuilt in the early fourteenth century, the west end was enlarged in 1850–60. The south (Waterton) chapel was rebuilt at the beginning of the sixteenth century.

121. Leeds, St John, Adel; dating from c.1140, this is the most complete church of its date in the county. New windows were inserted in the fourteenth or fifteenth century, and the roof was reconstructed in the 1840s; but the memorable south doorway remains unaltered.

appearance of one in the Decorated style, it incorporated a considerable amount of reused material, capitals and mouldings as well as wallstones, from the old building. The last addition was on the south side of the chancel, where a small chantry chapel was built at the end of the fourteenth century and then rebuilt on a larger scale as the Waterton chapel c.1505.[18]

Once again, though on a larger scale than at Bardsey, there was a clear order of growth apparent in the fabric. Yet the *Ecclesiologist*, the influential publication of the Cambridge Camden Society, was recommending in 1842 that 'from existing edifices or from supposition, [we must] recover the original scheme of the edifice as conceived by the first builder, or as begun by him and developed by his immediate successors'.[19] That was considered the ideal treatment, capable though it is of many interpretations. The alternative permitted the retention of 'additions or alterations of subsequent ages, repairing them when needing it, or even carrying out perhaps more fully the idea which dictated them'. The implications of the last possibility are open to boundless speculation; but what happened to West Yorkshire churches during the nineteenth century?

The smallest, simplest and one of the most famous in the region is St John's, Adel. 'The church is undoubtedly one of the most ancient structures in the county, and owes its preservation in a great degree to the retired situation in which it is built', comments the beautifully illustrated *The Churches of Yorkshire* (1844),[20] dating it to c.1140 on the evidence of a mid twelfth-century charter. The simple form of a rectangular nave and a rectangular chancel is decorated externally by a corbel frieze of human and animal faces set immediately below the

18 Walker, 307ff. It would be a pleasure to be able to comment that the churches at Bardsey and Sandal Magna escaped restoration, but the former was altered in 1806 when new roofs were put over the nave and chancel; it was restored in 1909 by Connon and Chorley when 'special care was to be taken of ancient architecture'. Sandal had some alterations in the seventeenth century, again in 1850–60, and finally in 1872 when there was much mutilation of the fabric and destruction of woodwork.

19 *E* (1842),i,65.

20 *The churches of Yorkshire*, Leeds 1844. This was issued in parts, directed by G.A.Poole, and the lithographic plates were made from drawings by R.D.Chantrell, J.W.Hugall, G.T.Andrews, N.Compton, S.Sharp, and C.W.Burleigh. The woodcuts were made by Orlando Jewett. It seems to have been intended to perform some of the functions of the *Ecclesiologist*, in making suggestions for improvements as well as giving brief historical particulars, plans and views.

122. Leeds, St John, Adel; the chancel as restored (G.E.Street 1878). The carvings in the capitals on the left of the chancel arch represent the Baptism of Christ, and on the right his Crucifixion.

eaves of the steeply pitched roofs; the windows combine semicircular-headed lancets and splayed reveals with evident insertions of the fourteenth and fifteenth centuries, but the outstanding decorative element is the large, elaborate south doorway. Similar to that placed at the west end of the church at Kirkstall, it is more richly carved on the receding arches of the four orders set under a sculptured gable. The Lamb stands at the apex over Christ in Majesty, and at each side are two of the four symbols of the evangelists. Inside, an equally elaborate chancel arch is carved with a zig-zag ornament and a series of grotesque faces; the capitals of the three orders represent a centaur and a horseman, fantastic beasts, and illustrations of Christ's baptism and crucifixion.

Adel is the most complete twelfth-century church in West Yorkshire; the genuine Norman work at St Peter's, Hartshead is incorporated in Neo-norman, and the more complete St Mary's, Birkin (which is just over the border in North Yorkshire) has some later additions. In 1844 it was noted that although Adel had been 'more fortunate than many in having had *comparatively* few of the *modern improvements* bestowed upon it . . . yet there is much to offend the eye', including the 'now greatly depressed' pitch of the roofs, concluding it 'might with more ease than most churches be restored to much of its former beauty'.[21] These changes had come about through re-roofing in 1686, and building a gallery across the west end in the early eighteenth century; the latter was enlarged a century or so later at a time when the roof was said to be 'tumbling down'.[22] In 1838 'the old Belfry . . . fell down from decay'[23] and was replaced by a new one designed by Robert Dennis Chantrell in a Neo-norman style which probably gave

21 ibid, no page refs.

22 Draper,W.H., *Adel and its Norman church*, Leeds 1909,143.

23 ibid.,158.

161

123. Harewood, All Saints'; founded in 1116, the present church was built c.1330, altered in 1793, and restored in 1862 (G.G.Scott). The interior is notable for six alabaster medieval monuments, including the two on the south side of the chancel; (left) Sir William Gascoigne of Gawthorp, Lord Chief Justice of England, and Elizabeth his wife, daughter and co-heir of Sir William Mowbray of Kirklington, (right) Sir William Ryther of Ryther, and Sybil his wife, daughter and co-heiress of Sir William Aldburgh.

24 Lewthwaite,G., *Adel: the restoration of its church: and the discovery of a Norman roof*, Leeds 1887,5f.

25 Draper, op.cit.,230f; see also *The churches of Yorkshire* for a section of the roof.

26 ibid.,232.

27 Lewthwaite, op.cit.,5.

28 ibid.,1.

29 MacDonald,A.S., *Ecclesia Batliae*, unpublished thesis, Kesteven College of Education, 1964.

30 Thornton,F.C., *Calverley parish church 1154–1854*,Calverley 1954,20.

123

him the idea of designing St Paul's, Shadwell in that manner in 1841. The vicar took out two windows in the west wall (probably eighteenth-century insertions) and substituted one of a Norman design as well as rebuilding the east gable to what was considered its original height.[24] He then rebuilt the west gable and the chancel roof, employing Chantrell 'to restore it to its original Anglo-Norman form, which I found a difficult task, never having been certain what a Norman roof was'.[25] However, the architect was able later to write a paper describing how he found some of the original timbers which had been reused in the seventeenth-century reconstruction, coming to the conclusion that the roof had been open, 'like the cradle roofs of the thirteenth century ... upon many churches in Yorkshire ... I have restored this roof with partly new oak using the old materials as far as practicable, and the effect is good, harmonizing with the general form of the building, and its ornaments'.[26] There was less satisfaction with this work of the 40s thirty years later. A purist dislike of all but the evidently original Norman windows suggested the rest were 'deformities [which] might easily be rectified'; it was true the church would be dark without them, but 'light could be admitted by means of a new and simple roof' – a curious suggestion that is not easy to understand in view of the insistence upon historical accuracy. In 1869 Richard Norman Shaw made a report, advising that the west wall should be rebuilt as it was a foot out of perpendicular; the vicar thought that solution 'more satisfactory to an architect than to an archaeologist',[27] anticipating the official attitude of the Ministry of Works more than forty years before they took responsibility for historic buildings, and he was happier when George Edmund Street (who was appointed architect in 1878) 'met the occasion by putting long bolts through into the north and south walls'. Street took out some of the offending windows which had been inserted, substituting narrow Norman lancets, and he replaced the old pews and three-decker pulpit with choir and clergy stalls; the nave was re-floored, the stonework was reworked, and almost a century ago visitors were told the church 'now presents itself to view as it came from under the hand of George Edmund Street, RA. It was one of the last works of that eminent architect'[28] – a strange way to describe a church then more than 700 years old.

It is customary to censure Victorian vicars and restoring architects for their work on old churches, but it has to be acknowledged they were often the inheritors of buildings which had been treated harshly. All Saints', Batley, for example, had been 'beautified' in 1740 when the chancel and nave roofs had been underdrawn with plastered ceilings ornamented with Classical decoration, and the clustered columns of the south arcade had been filled in with plaster to match the octagonal columns of the north arcade.[29] In All Saints', Otley, the capitals of the columns had been cut away in 1750 to facilitate the insertion of a gallery; and the majority of churches had been treated like St Wilfred's, Calverley where, in 1773, ceilings were erected in the nave and chancel, the whole building was plastered and whitewashed, and galleries were built in 1836.[30] All Saints', Harewood was improved in

124. Thornhill, St Michael; the north chapel, built by Sir Thomas Savile (1447), enlarged by William Savile (1493), and housing the family monuments; (left) Sir John Savile (d.1481) and his wife, on a tomb chest; Sir George Savile (d.1622) carved by Maximilian Colt and set within an elaborate framework; sarcophagus carved by William Barlow, commemorating George Savile of Rufford (d.1743); (right) Sir George Savile (d.1614) and his wife (sister of 1st Earl of Strafford); the oak tomb of Sir John Savile (d.1504) with his two wives, Alice Vernon and Elizabeth Paston.

1793 when the medieval glass was removed from the windows; 'some was secretly sold; the children of the village played with other portions, and not a vestige was left in the church ... The altar rails of carved oak, with Lord Strafford's initials on them, the six stalls for the officiating priests, the lattices and screens, and the canopies over the tombs of Ryther and Redman on each side of the choir ... were also removed ... the old oak open roof was removed to make way for deal rafters, whose hideousness was concealed by a lath and plaster under-drawing; and a gallery ... was erected, partially hiding several windows, and otherwise deforming the interior'.[31] St John's, Kirkheaton, which was described as 'a shapeless, spoiled building' by Glynne in 1854, originally had 'a nave and chancel, each with north aisle and western tower ... The chancel with its north aisle or chapel are comparatively untouched, as is also the tower, but the nave has been entirely rebuilt in utter disregard of propriety, the arcade destroyed and the walls heightened, so that the tower looks almost buried and not belonging to the body ... The tower is Late Perpendicular and now looks most unhappy, standing against the lofty sprawling roof of the nave ... The interior is exactly like a conventicle'.[32] Fate intervened at Kirkheaton when the church was burnt in 1886 and reopened two years later in a more acceptable style; but otherwise it would probably have been treated in a similar way to St Michael's, Thornhill.

Glynne noted that the west tower of Thornhill was a late Perpendicular design in the characteristic fortified West Yorkshire manner already described, but he also wrote in 1858 that the fifteenth-century nave had been rebuilt in 'a poor style' in 1777.[33] Thornhill is

31 Taylor, op.cit.,350. All Saints' was restored by Scott in 1862. 'Every part shows that a master hand has been employed ... Those who were acquainted with the unsightly appearance of the interior of this fine old church will be surprised at the transformation which has been effected in it by the eminent architect'.

32 Glynne, op.cit.,(1898),xiv,176.

33 ibid.(1917),xxiv,191.

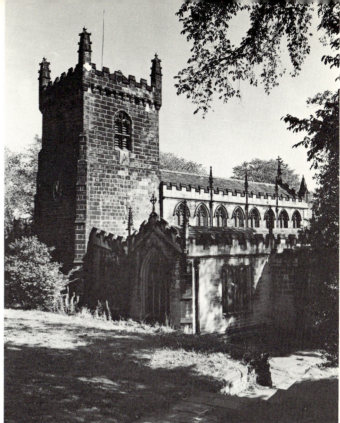

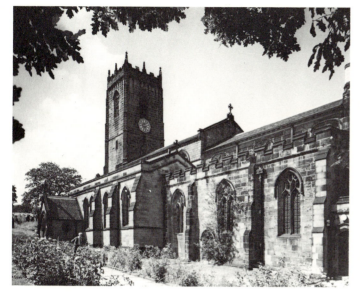

125. Thornhill, St Michael; in this view can be identified the late fifteenth-century tower, the restored chancel and south aisle of the same date, and the nave and aisles (G.E.Street 1877–9).

126. Birstall, St Peter; apart from the medieval tower, the church was rebuilt with an additional nave bay and two additional chapels (W.H.Crossland 1863–70).

124 an important church, containing the Savile Chapel erected by Sir Thomas in 1447 and enlarged by Sir John in 1493, and a Perpendicular chancel completed in 1499 by the Revd. Robert Frost who inscribed on the glass of the Jesse window that he had 'made new Est window, and also clerestoried and archede this choir'. The church had been rebuilt in part several times since its probably Saxon foundation, and there are fragmentary remains of Early English mouldings and capitals among the mainly Perpendicular fabric. In the 1870s Street was called in to remedy the defects, and it is said that as he could find no trace of

125 any Decorated work he decided to rebuild the nave in that style to provide the missing link that ought to have been there to illustrate the successive periods of English Gothic. His clerk of the works described how the clergy vestry had been designed in a Perpendicular style 'in conformity with the architecture of the Chancel, which has not been taken down, but has had all its decayed portions removed, and been thoroughly restored'. This was restoration on a large scale, and he went on to note the south aisle had been rebuilt 'six feet wider than the old one', complacently (or maybe regretfully) adding, 'the appearance of the body of the building is very fine, but the tower is unaltered'.[34]

In the even more comprehensive rebuilding of All Saints, Ilkley, the fifteenth-century tower is almost all that remains unaltered of the old church. Glynne arrived too late to describe it before the work was undertaken in 1860–1, and he had to note that the south wall of the nave and all the chancel 'may be pronounced new';[35] the nave and aisles were extended sixteen feet to the east, and clerestorey windows were inserted in the north wall in 1880. It is said that much of the original material was reused in the extensions and rebuilding, and it is

34 Charlesworth,T., *A guide to the church of St.Michael, Thornhill*, n.d.

35 Glynne, op.cit.,(1898),xiv,345.

true and confusing that 'the new work is so similar to the old that it is not at all easy, at first sight, to tell where one begins and the other leaves off'.[36] The early Perpendicular chancel of St Wilfred's, Calverley, underwent a similar enlargement in 1869–70 when it was rebuilt (for the third time) by T.H. and F.Healey as 'an exact copy of its predecessors, except that it is somewhat broader and of greater elevation';[37] otherwise, it is a good example of a mainly fourteenth-century church which incorporates fabric from a Norman building as well as fifteenth-century insertions.

The Victorians had little love for Stuart and Georgian work. Taylor scathingly wrote of '"Churchwarden's Gothic", or anything else you may please to call those horrid mutilations, which were so fashionable',[38] and he condemned John Carr's rebuilding of parts of All Saints, Dewsbury; it was regrettable, he thought, that a church 'which in its early days must have had some approach to correctness of style, should have been re-edified in utter defiance of all rule and taste. And in its present form it admits of nothing save an entire rebuilding'.[39] It was as a result of such feelings that the eighteenth-century bodies which had been added to the earlier towers of St Michael's, Haworth,[40] St Mary's, Mirfield,[41] and St Peter's, Birstall, were all rebuilt; of the last, Taylor wrote that 'the pious work thus happily consummated has been of no ordinary character ... nothing short of an entire reconstruction of the church seemed possible in order to restore it satisfactorily. The tower only has been preserved. The chancel has been rebuilt about 18 feet further eastward, to allow the addition of a fourth bay to the nave; and the nave has been made 30 feet wider, by the addition of north and south chapels ... The west end of the church is inconveniently below the level of the churchyard. But this is accounted for by the praiseworthy desire of the promoters of the restoration to preserve the old tower ... Prettily situated amongst trees, the church externally has already a venerable appearance'.[42] William Henry Crossland was the architect for the new St Peter's, consecrated in 1870, and Anthony Salvin had designed a similar 'restoration' of St Ricarius, Aberford in 1861.

The little, basically Norman but much altered, church was 'not sufficiently large for the requirements of the parish ... and its internal arrangements were not such as to suit the present improved ideas of church propriety'. Salvin had recently restored the nearby All Saints', Sherburn-in-Elmet (now in North Yorkshire, and a building which still retains much Norman work), but Aberford was a different problem; he designed a new church in which 'nothing of the old ... remains, except the old Norman tower ... and the east end ... as it was rebuilt only thirty years ago'. Yet it would be misleading to suggest there was no regard for old fabric. At Aberford, for example, 'the removal of thick layers of whitewash and plaster disclosed many distinct evidences of the antiquity ... the simple round-headed arches and specimens of massive herring-bone masonry in the lower parts of the walls ... the fine old chancel-arch showed us what a barbarous taste it was which, half a century ago, could cut away and mutilate fine dog-tooth and zig-zag mouldings to fix up a wretched coating of plaster ... unfortunately

36 le Patourel, J., *Ilkley parish church*, Gloucester 1968,7f. In 1633 Reginald Heber 'caused a high pew to be placed and erected at the high end of the south side of the Church of Ilkley towards the Quire adjoining to the north side or ends of Sir Peter Middleton's Quire, which is not uniform to any other of the Stalls ... set about with five ballesters or turned posts and compassed about with a border of wood ingraved with sentences and his name and his wifes, the height whereof from the ground is 2 yeardes and a half'. This supported a tester and 'six persons at least may conveniently sit' in the pew. Within a year an order was given for its removal.

37 Thornton, op.cit.,20.

38 Taylor, op.cit.,456. This reference is to St Oswald's, Leathley, which has a Norman tower and chancel arch.

39 ibid.,285. A part of the church was rebuilt in 1884–5 in the Decorated style by A.E.Street and A.H.Kirk.

40 St Michael's was rebuilt in 1655 and enlarged in 1755 when it had six semicircular-headed windows in the Georgian vernacular style. This was demolished to make way for the present church by T.H. and F.Healey in 1880. The tower is said to be fifteenth-century.

41 When Scott built the new St Mary's in 1871, the tower of the medieval church was left standing but given a picturesque upper part.

42 Taylor, op.cit.,194.

126

the poor old arch had been so mutilated, that it would have been useless to attempt to restore it'.[43]

During restoration, forgotten details were discovered; fragments of old crosses and demolished decoration were found embedded in walls, and in All Saints', Batley, the staircase which once led to the rood-loft was revealed, in an excellent state of preservation, in the pillar on the south side of the chancel.[44] A Roman coffin was found under the nave floor of St Mary's, Kippax, a mainly Norman church restored by Hugh Gough in the 70s,[45] but there were few discoveries of old decoration to be compared with what was seen when the nave roof of St Mary's, Woodkirk, collapsed and brought down part of the walling. This church had been built for a cell of black canons attached to Nostell Priory in the time of Henry II, and its name (Woodchurch) suggests a Saxon foundation. According to Taylor, the nave and chancel appear older than those of Batley (also belonging to Nostell),[46] and there was antiquarian speculation when the collapse occurred in 1831. Norrison Scatcherd, a country gentleman and historian of the parish of Morley, found that under later lath and plaster were substantial remains of decoration.

Judge of my surprise when I perceived a portion only of the ancient interior! It now appears that the *whole* of these walls (or nearly so) have been beautifully *painted* and *gilded*, having on them roses, white and red, tulips, anemonies or poppies, and other flowers; grapes, peaches, and various choice fruits, with leaves and other decorations, the colours of which, even yet, are delightful. What a train of thoughts now broke upon my mind! The spacious chancel *in its pristine state*, rich with fruits and flowers, bespangled with gold, glowing with the rays of the sun through its painted windows, or the candles or torches of the priests from the high altar, – the canons, in their conventical dresses, seated in the rich stalls or 'sellae', which still distinguish this interesting edifice, – their solemn chaunt, the pomp and splendour of their worship and processions, – all these and many other reflections passed in review before me, as the rude innovating hands of the workmen tore from the south wall the painted and gilded plaster unmindful of its beauty.[47]

Scathcherd's imaginative enthusiasm illustrates one aspect of nineteenth-century restoration, its romanticism, and it is sad to record his unsuccessful attempts to persuade the Earl of Cardigan, the patron of St Mary's, Woodkirk, and Chantrell (who was presumably responsible for the repair of the church) to preserve the decoration; he had to content himself with the drawings he made (as well as of 'the ancient porch with "Beatae Mariae" upon it, now pulled down'), reflecting on 'the Goths and Vandals of the nineteenth century' and the way by which 'property comes into the hands of strange men, of men equally devoid of historical knowledge, of reflection, of taste, of concern for the opinions of their contemporaries or the gratification of posterity'.

It would have been instructive to listen to Scatcherd's glowing sentences on the subject of Pontefract Castle, but Defoe must suffice:

here *Henry*, the great Earl of *Lancaster*, who was at the same time Lord of the Castle, and whose Ancestors had beautified and enlarged it exceedingly, and fortified it too, was beheaded, in King *Edward* the IId's time, with three or four more of the *English* Barons. Here *Richard* IId, being deposed and imprisoned, was barbarously murthered, and, if History lies not, in a cruel manner; and here *Anthony*, Earl *Rivers*, and Sir *Richard Gray*, the first Uncle,

43 ibid.,70.

44 ibid.,163. The restoration was undertaken by Sheard and Hanstock in 1872–3. There were new roofs, new windows, new plastering and new pews.

45 Gough also restored St Oswald's, Methley in 1874 when he rebuilt the east wall, and repaired and lengthened the chancel of this important church. Robert Waterton of Methley bequeathed £200 in 1424–5 for a south chapel as long as the chancel, but apparently it took fifty years to execute his wish (cf.Waterton chapel, St Helen's, Sandal Magna). This chapel has been refaced and the details have been renewed (Kirk,G.E., *The churches of St Oswald, Methley and St Margaret, Mickletown*, Leeds 1955).

46 Taylor, op.cit.,119.

47 ibid.,120; *LI*, 2 Feb 1832.

127. Pontefract, All Saints'; principally of fifteenth-century construction, and a picturesque ruin since the Civil War. (Aquatint T.Malton and J.Gandon 1778)

48 Colvin,H., *The history of the King's Works*, London 1963,ii,781ff.

49 In *The ... history of the loyal town of Rippon*, York 1733,8, the eccentric Thomas Gent wrote of 'the several Angles ... ornamented with the Images of the Apostles, as those of the Square were enrich'd with the Effigies of the Four Evangelists'. Gent is hardly a reliable source, but he was writing relatively soon after the destruction of the tower. Recent work has included the addition of a building within the ruined nave.

and the last Brother-in-law to King *Edward* the Fifth, were beheaded by that Tyrant *Richard* III ... [but] the Castle lies in its Ruine.

A famous engraving published by the Society of Antiquaries in 1734, based on a drawing from an Elizabethan survey, showed a romantic, almost theatrical, group of towers, machicolated, embattled, turreted, surrounded by a defensive wall; immediately outside the castle walls and close to the south-east corner of the town fortifications, can be seen the church of All Saints which must have been, as Glynne wrote when looking at the ruins in 1833, 'a noble structure'.

There is virtually nothing authenticated about this splendid relic; some parts suggest a thirteenth-century date, but more is in the Perpendicular style and probably contemporary with the considerable rebuilding and repairing of sections of the castle in the reigns of Henry VI and Edward IV.[48] In its pre-Civil War state, All Saints was obviously a large church, cruciform in plan with a clerestoreyed, aisled nave and a chancel with a large south chapel; the north transept had an east aisle, and there were north and south porches. It seems likely that the square crossing tower with an open battlement and crocketed corner pinnacles was surmounted by a tall octagonal lantern which had battlements and pinnacles, and was decorated with carvings of the Saints and Apostles;[49] possibly it was not unlike the tower and lantern of All Saints, Pavement in York (1475–1501), but this is surmise. The church was severely damaged during the Civil War, and in 1660 the remains of the lantern collapsed. The town was compensated for the loss of its parish church by being allowed the proceeds from the sale of the materials of the slighted castle, but the money was embezzled and the chapel of St Giles was used for services until it became the official parish church in 1789. All Saints' was left as a ruin, but some money was spent on it during the seventeenth century to repair the top of the truncated lantern and to roof the north transept so that it could be used for funeral services. More work was begun in 1831, and two years later Glynne noted the roofed transepts 'form the present church, and the restoration is on the whole neat'. This had been undertaken as an economical design by Chantrell, who contrived a church within the shell by combining the two transepts with new polygonal additions on the east and west sides of the crossing, an ingenious solution which avoided the necessity of costly restoration. An ecclesiastical district was assigned to the church in 1838.

Chantrell's rebuilding of St Peter's, Leeds and the importance of the new church in the revival of Gothic architecture and ritual is discussed elsewhere; but it should be emphasised that, although Walter Farquhar Hook's decision that the old church was inadequate is understandable, and Chantrell's report on its structural defects was professionally sound, the building was not unimpressive. No West Yorkshire church has been as fully described as St Peter's, Leeds; Thoresby devoted twenty-one pages of *Ducatus Leodiensis* to the building and its monuments, and he published the separate *Vicaria Leodiensis* in 1724. His often quoted account is of 'a very spacious and strong Fabrick ... it doth not pretend to the Mode of reformed Architecture, but is strong and useful ... plain, but venerable; the

128. Leeds, St Peter; the crossing tower and nave dated from the mid-fourteenth century, the chancel from the late fifteenth, and the nave aisle from the early sixteenth. (Thoresby, R., *Ducatus Leodiensis*, 1715)

129. Leeds, St Peter; the late fifteenth-century chancel and north aisle, recorded by J. Rhodes (c.1838). The altarpiece and ceiling were painted by Jacques Parmentier.

128

129

50 Thoresby, 39ff.

51 ibid.,248. It is useful to quote Thoresby's account of the early eighteenth-century improvements. As well as Parmentier's paintings, 'the Windows before darkened with fragments of painted Glass . . . are now entirely new glazed with new Squares . . . The high Quire now cieled . . . The Skreen and Seats in the Quire, the Pillars there, and through the Nave of the Church, with the Galleries, are all new painted in a decent manner . . . a new Gallery of right Wainscot hath been erected along the South Side of the Church, and a very fine large *Organ*; the Case whereof is adorned with very curious carved Work'. In 1778 another gallery was erected at the west end; the 16 pews in it were sold by auction for £905 17s (*LI* 10 Nov 1778).

52 Whitaker, 49.

Walls wholly of Free-stone, the Roof entirely cover'd with Lead . . . It is built after the Manner of a Cathedral, with a large cross Aisle, and the Steeple or Tower in the middle of it. The Dimensions of the Church are, length 165 Foot, Breadth 97; Height of the Nave of the Church 51, and of the Steeple 96'.[50] Although there were fragments of Norman work, the nave and tower seem to have dated from the mid fourteenth century, the chancel from the late fifteenth; and a fourth nave aisle had been added in the early sixteenth, producing an unusual plan and a church notable for its spaciousness (with a chancel eighty feet wide and sixty deep) if not for outstanding architectural quality. Most of the internal columns were of the plain octagonal type common in West Yorkshire (although there were earlier clustered columns east of the transept), and the windows in the north aisle were of the square-headed, mullioned, Perpendicular pattern equally common in the region. It was said the windows contained little stained glass, and the west window was removed in 1708; but the chancel ceiling was painted in the early eighteenth century by Jacques Parmentier with a scene of 'Moses giving the Law, the thunder and lightning rending the Clouds . . . expressed . . . in Suitable Terror, but qualified by the lovely aspects of a Choir of Angells & cherubs'.[51] There was also a painted altarpiece by the same artist, in which figures of Moses and Aaron flanked the Commandments and the Lord's Prayer, in gilt on black marble slabs, set in a panelled reredos of Classical design with urns and gilded ornament. Obviously, there were admirable parts in this building, but it might be appropriate to remember the Papal judgment respecting Barnoldswick that it was 'a pious thing and worthy of favour, that a church should fall' provided something superior were erected in its stead.

Whitaker added his own commentary on old St Peter's in 1816, noting its 'solid substantial air of unpretending dignity, not ill suited to an opulent commercial town';[52] but he was not led (as Thoresby

169

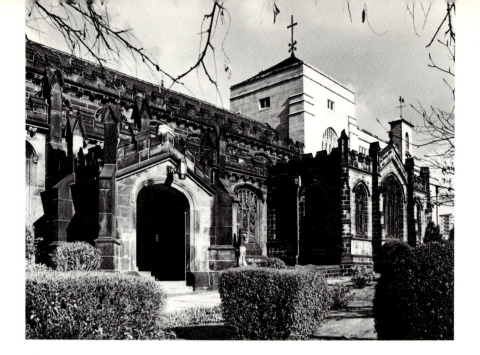

130. Bradford, St Peter (now the Cathedral); basically a mid-fifteenth-century church with an early sixteenth-century tower, it was repaired (J.Clark 1833) and transepts were added (T.H. and F.Healey 1899). Its elevation to cathedral rank in 1919 ultimately resulted in an extension (Sir E.Maufe 1951–65).

certainly was) to overrate its merits, or those of West Yorkshire parish churches generally. He offered no comments on the architecture of St Peter's, Bradford, other than to record it as 'a spacious church, which is known to have been erected in the reign of Hen.VI, and was finished in the 36th of his reign. [1457–8] The tower was of later date, and finished in or about the 23rd of Hen. VII [1507–08]'.[53] It is indeed a large building (the nave is 107 feet long, the chancel 47), erected at a time when, as already noted, there was considerable rebuilding and remodelling of churches in the region as a result of the growth of woollen manufacture and the more settled state of the country. It was apparently an almost complete rebuilding, as nothing remains of the small Norman church which preceded the present, and little of what appears to have been a fourteenth-century rebuilding of the nave arcades.[54] The elevated site on which St Peter's is built is now surrounded by commercial buildings, and great imagination is needed to relate it to its original environment; but it is a church that belongs to the West Yorkshire tradition evolved for exposed sites, where its sturdy tower and low, widespread body of millstone grit, embattled and with Perpendicular windows, would seem more appropriate. Whitaker had probably not forgotten St Peter's when he wrote that 'In travelling northward from Lincolnshire, where every church is beautiful, and many are of surpassing beauty, it is impossible not to be struck by the rapid depravation of taste in ecclesiastical architecture. Wakefield is the last church in this direction which has a spire, without crockets indeed, or other ornaments, but light and graceful. The church of Halifax is very plain and unadorned; but the choir, by some undesigned deviation into grace, has an airy boldness of design, which I have seldom seen exceeded'.[55]

The parish churches of Wakefield and Halifax are in a different class from those already considered; they were built in the two wealthiest wool towns in the region in the fifteenth century, and in both cases

130
187

53 ibid.,354.

54 Since 1951, additions have been made to St Peter's (which was raised to cathedral rank in 1919) by Sir Edward Maufe. The effect is not harmonious.

55 Whitaker, 49.

131. Wakefield, St Mary-on-the-Bridge; the richly ornamented fourteenth-century building was restored in the 1840s (G.G.Scott), when a new west front was built.

there was an obvious intention to match the church to the town's prosperity. Looking ahead 400 years, they are both churches to which Scott was summoned. His earliest restoration in Wakefield was of the **131** famous chantry chapel of St Mary-on-the-Bridge, dating from the 1340s and built, according to Camden, 'by Edward IV in memory of the persons slain there in battle'. There appears to be no evidence at all for this, and according to Archbishop John Kempe, the shrine was 'wholly built of costly stonework by the inhabitants and community of Wakefield'.[56] A single cell, fifty feet by fifteen, it is built with the west front to the medieval bridge, and was erected on a small islet in the Calder. The less easily seen north, south and east fronts are elaborately designed with a deep, arcaded parapet which continues along the east gable where it is crowned at the apex by a statue of the Virgin Mary standing within a canopied niche. At the south-east angle is a small turret, and at the north-east a larger staircase tower which is believed to have been surmounted originally by an open crown. The flowing, **132** Decorated tracery of the three windows of the north and south fronts is ingeniously inventive, and the large east window which fills most of the gable wall is made up of subtly intersecting lights. The west front is a lavishly ornamented composition with three doorways in five ornately traceried arches with ogee cornices, niches, crocketed pinnacles, and the whole repertoire of the richest of the Gothic styles crowded into the small area of walling. The parapet contained five sculptured panels under triple cinquefoil arches, representing the mysteries of the Rosary – the Annunciation, the Nativity, the Resurrection, the Ascension, and the Coronation of the Virgin (which was superseded by the Descent of the Holy Ghost when the panels were renewed).

The chapel has long been famous as the finest remaining example of a not uncommon medieval building type, though few can have matched its elaboration. Inevitably, its use as a chantry was

56 Walker, 228ff.

132. Wakefield, St Mary-on-the-Bridge; the south front of the chantry chapel built on a small islet in the Calder.

57 West Riding Quarter Sessions Rolls, Order Book A,4.

58 Walker, 245.

59 Buckler,J.C. and G., *Remarks upon wayside chapels with observations on the architecture and present state of the chantry on Wakefield bridge*, Oxford 1843,31,34f.

60 *Gentleman's Magazine* (1809), lxxix,126. This account of the chapel, probably written by John Carter, differs from Buckler's in calling it 'a woeful instance of mutilation by these pretenders to architectural knowledge ... But it has been repaired – REPAIRED ? yes, and in a truly Gothic style – the beautiful tracery of the windows, rarely to be equalled, is totally demolished – not a wreck is left behind, and its place is now supplied by cross headed mullions filled up with spruce modern sash squares. What Goths some of these modern architects are! ... The front, that inimitable example of rich tracery and chaste ornament, presented itself to the despoiler, and in order to give a finish, probably as he thought to the dilapidated buttresses, he propped them up with short round pillars – four little short round laughable things, all in a row ... every admirer of our ancient buildings must tremble for their fate when they are to be repaired'.

61 Scott,G.G., *Personal and professional recollections*, London 1879,101f.

discontinued after the break with Rome, and in 1638 there was reference to the 'great ruyne and decay of the stone bridge at Wakefield ... and the Chappell adjoyneing'.[57] After minimal repairs had been made to the fabric, the building was degraded by a variety of uses. Defoe wrote it was 'made use of for Civil Affairs, for we do not now pray for the Souls of those slain in Battle, and so the intent of that Building ceases', perpetuating Camden's account of the foundation, but he was spared the sight of its use by a dealer in old clothes, 'who was in the habit of hanging on the precious traceries, his filthy ware'.[58]

There had probably been a number of repairs before 1797, but there was a minor restoration at that time which John Chessell Buckler and his brother praised as 'creditably performed; as much of the *ancient* masonry as could be found, being collected, and carefully reinstated; no new stone-work of consequence was added, nor anything injurious done to the character of the building'.[59] Other accounts suggest the Bucklers were being over-generous,[60] but their description of the interior of the building as they saw it in 1843 is melancholy. 'Every member and ornament of the architecture which stood in advance of the walls ... has been hacked away to prepare the surface for plaster, paper, woodwork, or whatever best suited the convenience (not to say taste) of the occupant', and they could only call it a 'spectacle of unrestrained mischief and deplorable ravage'.

This was the state of the chapel in 1842 when it was taken over by the Ecclesiastical Commissioners. Subscriptions were raised, and its restoration was the subject of a competition organised by the Yorkshire Architectural Society. 'I devoted myself with the greatest earnestness to the investigation of the relics of its destroyed detail', recollected Scott, 'and by examining the heaps of debris in the river wall, &c., we discovered very nearly everything; and I made, I believe, a very perfect design, illustrated by beautiful drawings ... My report I viewed as a masterpiece. I succeeded, and the work was carried out'.[61] The intention was to repair the richly carved west front, taking out as little stone as possible, and replacing the missing parts according to Scott's conjectural design; but the outcome was extraordinary. The carver persuaded Scott to allow him to accept 'a handsome offer made him for the semi-decayed front, to set up in a park hard by. He then made an offer to execute a new front in Caen stone, in place of the weather-beaten old one; and pressed his suit so determinedly, that, in an evil hour, his offer was accepted'. The front was re-erected by the new owner, the Hon. George Chapple Norton, as a boat house at the end of the lake at Kettlethorpe, and a brand-new replica was erected in its place. It might be argued it was better the medieval stonework should quietly decay away in a green, watery landscape than at the side of a busy road; but there was no attempt to justify the decision. 'I never repented but once', wrote Scott with unaccustomed humility, 'and that is ever since ... I am filled with wonder to think how I ever was induced to consent to it at all'. Then comes the final irony, 'in just retribution, the Caen stone is now more rotten than the old work'; that was written in the 70s, and in 1932 Sir Charles Nicholson confirmed that the old front hidden away in the grounds of Kettlethorpe was

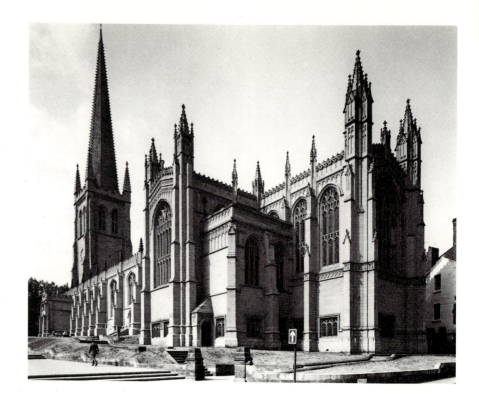

133. Wakefield, All Saints' (now the Cathedral); a long series of rebuildings has produced the present impressive appearance of the early fifteenth-century tower and spire at the west end of a large, spacious parallelogram. It was heavily restored in the 1850s (G.G.Scott), and the new chancel and transept (J.L.Pearson) were added after the church was raised to cathedral rank in 1888.

indeed in a far better condition than Scott's replacement which he, in turn, then had to restore.[62]

Remorse, which is said to have caused Scott to try to raise a subscription to put back the old front, did not prevent his returning to Wakefield to undertake the restoration of All Saints' church in 1858, ten years after the tragi-comedy of the bridge chapel. A Saxon church on the site had been replaced by a Norman, cruciform in plan with a low crossing tower, at the beginning of the twelfth century. This was enlarged by the addition of a north aisle *c.*1150 and a south aisle *c.*1220 (with seven bays in contradiction of the six opposite). Then came an extensive rebuilding after the fall of the crossing tower *c.*1315; the aisles were widened, the chancel was lengthened, the columns of the nave arcades were increased in height, and the new windows were filled with Decorated tracery. When the church was reconsecrated in 1329, it had no tower; and *c.*1400 an assessment was made, based on the rateable value of each house in the parish, of what each parishioner was expected to contribute towards 'the bell-tower of the church [which] is to be built new from its foundation'.[63] Contributions were not always made either quickly or willingly, and in 1409 the Archbishop of York was constrained 'that we may the more effectually incite the minds of the faithful to the construction of the said bell-tower by the alluring gift of indulgences, we grant to all who give or bequeath their goods or in any other way afford help in charity to the construction of the said bell-tower, four days indulgence'.

This promised remission of some of the Purgatorial pains resulted in the erection of an unusually impressive west tower, 105 feet high with buttressed angles, crocketed pinnacles and a battlemented parapet

62 Speak, H. and Forrester, J., *The chantry chapel of St Mary-on-the-Bridge, Wakefield,* Ossett 1972, 19.

63 Walker, 182f.

projected in the typical West Yorkshire manner as a machicolated corbel table. Crowning it was a crocketed spire, 142 feet high, which Camden noted as 'too short for the lofty tower', although the total height of 247 feet gave Wakefield a church unmatched in scale by any other in the region. The tower was built twelve feet from the west front of the church, which was then taken down so that a new bay could be constructed to fill the gap; but the building was still not grand enough to match the town's mid fifteenth-century prosperity. The nave walls were pierced to allow the insertion of square-headed clerestorey windows, and an arcaded parapet with crocketed pinnacles was added to the outer walls; the nave roof was renewed, and the relatively new chancel was entirely reconstructed as a continuation of the nave, including the aisles. The result was a large parallelogram, over 140 feet long and 65 feet wide, lighted by big windows (from which fragments of armorial glass remain), and with plastered walls that were frescoed or ruled to represent stonework. The piers and arch mouldings were painted in imitation of porphyry, in purple with blue veins, and the spandrels of the arcades as well as the wall over the chancel arch were frescoed, the latter probably representing the Last Judgment.[64]

In 1586, following the removal of the altars and hangings, rood loft and images, the walls were all marbled in red and yellow, and a west gallery was constructed. Fifty years later the walls were whitewashed, and in 1635 Francis Gunby, a Leeds craftsman, provided an elaborately carved oak screen to separate the nave from the chancel, fitting it to an existing dado.[65] Contrary to the common story of neglect during the eighteenth century, Wakefield's parish church was evidently well looked after, even if the work did not always meet with the approval of later critics. The new furnishings were of good quality, and there were frequent repairs to the spire. William Lindley and Charles Watson examined it in the 1790s and recommended it should be taken down and rebuilt, and that the tower should be re-cased. John Soane made a report in 1802 and recommended binding the masonry spire with bands of iron, a remedy which probably only caused further damage; and in the 1820s Charles Mountain rebuilt the top fifteen feet.[66] Meanwhile, parts of the exterior had been renewed, especially the south wall which seems to have been redesigned to remove the discrepancies in bay width and fenestration caused by the enlargement of the chancel in the fifteenth century. One of the characteristics of eighteenth-century work on medieval buildings was to rearrange it tidily. Glynne dismissed the south front as 'a modern Gothic fashion ... the details of which will not bear criticism',[67] and Thomas Rickman referred to 'the various barbarisms with which [the church] has been cased and surrounded'.[68] The tracery that can be seen in a view dated 1807 suggests it was very similar to that in John Carr's rebuilding of All Saints', Dewsbury.

In 1855 a new vicar, the Revd.C.J.Camidge, was in charge, and two years later Scott was consulted. His first consideration was the tower, which had 'become so decayed, and had suffered so much from injudicial repairs, as to have lost nearly all its original beauty'. He recommended rebuilding, or restoring, in order of priority, the tower,

64 ibid.,195.

65 Gunby was paid £15 14s 8d, and £2 0s 8d for the wood, in 1635.

66 Walker, 260; Mayhall,J., *The annals of Yorkshire*, London 1878,i,306.

67 Glynne, op.cit.,(1895),xiii,388.

68 Rickman,T., *An attempt to discriminate the styles of English architecture*, London 1819,173. Rickman thought 'the south porch is good Perpendicular, and some of the piers and arches in the nave and chancel are good; the tower seems Early English, but has been much repaired, and a new door and window inserted'.

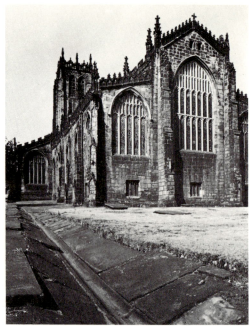

134. Wakefield, All Saints' (now the Cathedral); the restoration of the 1850s included stripping the walls and redressing the stonework, but it spared the screen of 1635. This c.1880 photograph shows the interior before Pearson's addition was built at the east end.

135. Halifax, St John; a more or less complete late fifteenth-century rebuilding, in which the chancel almost equals the nave in size. It was restored in the 1870s, but externally Scott's work was mainly confined to repair.

69 Walker, 267.

70 It must also be recorded that the doors of the screen, 'which had lain for more than half a century in the loft, were brought out, repaired, and re-hung'.

the spire, the chancel and the nave. On the strength of some mouldings discovered in the wall, Scott decided the tower had been built in the fourteenth century and designed a new doorway in an appropriate style; it was only later that J.T.Micklethwaite discovered the tower had been built in the fifteenth century. The south aisle windows were rebuilt following the uncovering of some of the original openings, and filled with tracery based on a seventeenth-century engraving. The plaster was taken off the internal wall surfaces, and all the stonework was redressed 'without much regard to the old mason-marks which existed in abundance'.[69] A new marble and stone pavement was laid in the chancel, and glazed tiles were used in the sacristy, apparently against Scott's advice and confirming that the clergy were often at least as culpable as the architects for excessive restoration. Old furnishings were removed, but the Jacobean screen (characteristically called 'fine . . . but of debased character' by Glynne) was not only suffered to remain but used as a model for an imitation Jacobean reworking or replacement of the fifteenth-century dado below.[70] Glass by Kempe and Hardman was made for the windows, and when all was finished the old parish church was in a fit state to be raised to cathedral status in 1888; it was coldly splendid, but it had lost much of its history.

St John's, Halifax follows a similar development. The first church was built probably c.1120, and aisles were added to it c.1290, but once again it was the increased population and prosperity in the fifteenth century that resulted in a rebuilding, beginning with the nave; all seems to have been new, with the exception of the north aisle wall which contains evidence of the earlier church, of which it could have formed the south wall. 'The workmen seem to have begun at the West end', thought Whitaker, 'with the intention of mounting a tower on the wall of the West front, and on the two next columns Eastward'; but evidently doubts about the capacity of this substructure to bear the weight of the 'very lofty bell tower . . . built by the munificence of the families of the Lacies and the Saviles',[71] caused it to be relocated at the west end of the nave and built on its own foundations. The relatively low nave, without a clerestorey, contrasts dramatically with what Whitaker called 'the bold and lightsome choir' which is as wide as, and almost equal in length to, the nave. The east window was erected in 1480 at the expense of Thomas Wilkinson, the vicar who was responsible for the rebuilding within a relatively short time. In plan, St John's is a parallelogram like All Saints', but with an additional aisle or chapel on the south side of the nave; like the Wakefield church, too, it can be described as wholly Perpendicular with the exception of the earlier fabric found in the north wall, and the choir arcades which possibly incorporate material from a slightly earlier rebuilding. Externally, as Whitaker noted, St John's 'bears every mark of one progressive but consistent plan'. It possesses more of the obviously West Yorkshire characteristics than does Wakefield, such as the low, wide nave, the embattled parapets, and the detached buttresses impaling grotesque gargoyles (cf. All Saints', South Kirkby) on the wall of the south aisle chapel; but the fine tower, 117 feet in height, is outstandingly modelled and greatly superior to others in the region.

135

'Very spacious and handsome . . . very grand and imposing', wrote Glynne after visiting Halifax;[72] at the time he saw it, St John's had been fitted with pews and galleries as usual, which had been 'raised and made even' in 1807–08 when 'the church was perfectly repaired'. In 1817–18 the upper part of the tower, 'including the whole of the pinnacles, parapet, walls, and stone figures, were entirely renewed';[73] then Francis Pigou, who became vicar in 1875, employed Scott to

136

71 Whitaker, 382ff.

72 Glynne, op.cit.,(1895),xiii,387.

73 See Moore,W., *Four interior views of the parish church of Halifax*, Halifax 1840, for a useful record of the pre-restoration church.

136. Halifax, St John; before Scott's restoration, the church incorporated the various alterations made during its history, including the seventeenth-century pews and eighteenth-century screen seen in this lithograph (J.Horner c.1821).

137. Leeds, St John; this important seventeenth-century church was originally ornamented with strapwork decoration over the south porch and at the east end. The tower was remodelled in the early nineteenth century. (Thoresby, R., *Ducatus Leodiensis*, 1715)

138. Leeds, St John; the interior, despite the rearrangement of the pews and other alterations made during the 1860s, remains 'a specimen of church architecture to which no other town ... in England can produce a parallel'.

139. Leeds, St John; R.N.Shaw reported on the condition of the church in 1865, making a watercolour of the interior as then existing, which was subsequently engraved.

advise on the restoration. As usual, the plaster was removed from the walls and much of the stonework was reworked; the seventeenth-century pews were cut down in height, the 1766 organ case was taken away, the early eighteenth-century wooden screen ('of very fine workmanship', according to Parsons)[74] was removed, and new furnishings were introduced. Yet, maybe because of the numerous monuments on the walls, and the old woodwork which was allowed to remain in spite of being altered, Halifax survived the nineteenth-century restoration better than Wakefield; but Scott had died in 1878 and his son, Oldrid, supervised the work.

'Why *I* – who have laid myself out to protest against the havoc which has been made through the length and breadth of the land under the name of Restoration – should be singled out as the special butt of this . . . protest, it is not easy to say',[75] complained Scott in 1877. The answer is obvious; as a result of restoring more cathedrals and churches than any one else in architectural history, he had come to represent the *idea* of restoration which Ruskin and Morris were attacking. There is little doubt Scott's treatment of All Saints', Wakefield and St John's, Halifax was better considered and based on a much greater understanding of medieval work than were the restorations of West Yorkshire churches by local architects such as Perkin and Backhouse or the Healeys. Nor can the clerical opposition to post-medieval additions be overlooked. Scott referred to this, describing how 'I have been circumvented by the prejudices of my clients. I uniformly succeed as regards Jacobean pulpits, and I think altar tables; but am less successful in my attempts in favour of seventeenth-century pewing, unless it be indisputably fine – such as we find at . . . St John's Leeds, or Halifax'.[76]

Scott's reference to Halifax is ironical, since the pews were cut down, but his naming of St John's introduces the final building in this study of medieval churches, although it was consecrated in 1634 after 'taste [had] made a bold step from *Italy* to *England* at once . . . From the most profound ignorance in architecture, the most consummate night of knowledge, *Inigo Jones* started up a prodigy of art'.[77] Maybe; but not in West Yorkshire, where John Harrison 'in Zeale and pious disposition to the honour of God and benefitt of the People . . . built and Erected this Chappell att my onely proper costs and charges with intent that it might be dedicated to the Worship of God'.[78] Harrison was the greatest single benefactor in the history of Leeds; his building of the Free Grammar School and the Market Cross are discussed elsewhere in this study, but his most important architectural gift is the church of St John built, like the school, on his own land slightly to the north of the town. The need for a new church was quite simply expressed in Harrison's petition to the Archbishop of York: 'the said Towne . . . dayly increasing to the number of about nyne thousand Comunicants . . . the ancient Parish Church of this Towne of Leeds is not of Sufficient largeness and capacity to receive and contain a great part of the People which ought to repaire thither for the Service and Worship of Almighty God'.

William Laud had become Bishop of London in 1628, and his

74 Parsons, 318.

75 Scott, op.cit.,398.

76 ibid.,410.

77 Ralph, J., *A critical review of the public buildings, statues and ornaments in, and about London and Westminster*, London 1734,2.

78 Stocks, J.E., 'The consecration service of St John's church, Leeds', *TS* (1919),xxiv, 428.

conviction of the importance of the setting in a revived liturgical form of worship had the support of many churchmen including, one might suppose, Harrison although he was not an especially High Church man. St John's is the most significant foundation at this time in ecclesiastical history, and in its adoption of a rectangular form which has no chancel but a screened east end containing a communion table, it followed the Laudian edict. Nevertheless, as might be expected, the architecture itself is firmly in the West Yorkshire tradition. The plan, a nave and a south aisle of equal width contained within a parallelogram with a tower at the west end, has obvious references to the wide rectangular parish churches in Wakefield and Halifax, and to **137** the four-aisle form of St Peter's, Leeds. Externally, the use of battlements and square-headed Perpendicular windows with mullions and cusps perpetuates the manner in which churches in the region had been built since the fifteenth century or, in the case of the fourth aisle of St Peter's, since the sixteenth.[79] Apparently the tower was also in the local tradition, with a corbel table, battlements and corner pinnacles; and the only part of the exterior which suggested a seventeenth-century date was the south porch, in which a semicircular-headed archway with a keystone was surmounted by a gable decorated with open strapwork cresting, a relatively novel ornamental form which also appeared on the east end at the intersection between the two gables.[80]

Internally, the church is unlike any other. The pointed arches of the central arcade are supported on octagonal columns, some plain and others partly moulded, with capitals carved with acanthus leaves and **138** ball-ornament. The nave and aisle are roofed with open oak trusses[81] decorated with angelic and musical corbels, and openwork drop pendants are fixed in the centre of each tie beam; the ceiling is plastered in panels, each filled with a flowing design of strapwork entwined with roses, oak leaves and acorns, vines and other flowers and plants probably based on plates from a herbal. But it is the woodwork especially that makes St John's so remarkable. Although there is no separate, clearly-defined chancel, the east end of the nave and aisle is divided from the rest of the church by a carved oak screen, designed as a solid panelled dado and an open arcade of tapered balusters with Ionic capitals. The deep entablature is surmounted by a large, open strapwork cresting composed of scrolls, diamonds, circles and obelisk finials surrounding a central panel (originally armorial) within an architectural frame. The frieze and balusters are richly carved with classical ornament freely interpreted by local craftsmen, but deriving directly or indirectly from Serlio's *The Book of Architecture* (first published in an English edition in London in 1611) or the various German and Flemish books of designs which came to this country.[82]

St John's survived the Civil War undamaged, and it was greatly admired by Thoresby at the end of the century. He described it as 'so noble and stately a Structure as is scarce to be parallel'd in England'.[83] Evidently the stonework was decaying when Thoresby was writing in the early eighteenth century, and the more exposed

79 Since the Dissolution, ecclesiastical building had virtually come to a halt, and there was nothing later than the last additions to St Peter's, Leeds to serve as a model.

80 These strapwork decorations were apparently taken away during the work on the exterior in 1791–1801.

81 There is a strange lack of unity (or even good building practice) between the walls, arcades and roof. The bay widths of the building are quite different from those of the roof, and some of the trusses rest on the weakest parts of the structure.

82 There is little doubt that Francis Gunby, who was responsible for the similar screen in All Saints', Wakefield in 1634–5, was the craftsmen at St John's. He was married at St Mary's, Whitkirk in 1633, at the time when Sir Arthur Ingram's rebuilding of Temple Newsam was nearing completion, and there is clearly a link between the great house (where Gunby was employed) and the new church. The resemblance, for example, between the pulpits in St John's and Ingram's chapel points to the use of the same group of craftsmen, and possibly the same sources for the decorative emblems and carvings.

83 Thoresby, 30.

parts of the battlements on the church and on the tower were rendered. Plans of galleries were made by John Moxson in 1765, and John Blayds paid for their erection; these were placed along the west and south walls. The interior was whitewashed, then painted blue in 1720, afterwards apparently reverting to white;[84] the gilding was renewed from time to time, but apart from the refacing or rebuilding of the tower by John Clark (1830–8), there was little change except in a few details. Hatchments added a funereal richness to the picturesque, dark interior filled with oak pews and screens, which remained in use more or less as Harrison left it.

There was a complete lack of understanding of such architecture and decoration in the early nineteenth century. An anonymous author of a description of the churches in the parish of Guiseley, for example, described the chapel at Rawdon as 'not graced by its windows, which are of the kind peculiar to the seventeenth century, when architecture is said to have been at its lowest ebb'.[85] Whitaker thought Rawdon unworthy of notice, and contemptuously described St John's as 'a most unhappy specimen of this taste'. He dismissed the screen as 'clumsy . . . consisting of degraded terms, which have been reverently copied of late by the Wyat school', and concluded the building had 'all the gloom and all the obstructions of an ancient church without one vestige of dignity and grace'.[86] It is quite probable the denunciation of such an eminent antiquary was influential in the suggestion that the church should be demolished and replaced by one more conventionally Gothic or, failing that, by a replica; but if so, there was a long period before anything happened.

Richard Norman Shaw was invited to report in 1865, and his opening paragraph must have displeased the proposers of the scheme: 'I have visited the building, and having examined it carefully am entirely at a loss to understand how any good reason can be assigned for doing anything to it beyond a very moderate amount of restoration'. Shaw criticised the destruction of 'good old work if it can possibly be retained, and were the dilapidations of the church three times greater than they are, I would still say restore it, and restore it only where absolutely necessary – touch nothing you can avoid touching'.[87] Three months later, John Dobson (the Leeds architect who was expecting to design the replacement) sent in an adverse report recommending it should be totally rebuilt. The trustees then turned to Scott, who wrote of being approached by 'a leading Leeds architect as I was starting to inspect it, his last exhortation was, "Paint it black enough"'. Instead, he 'painted it in the most brilliant colours',[88] writing of his astonishment at 'the originality and highly picturesque effect', and his wonderment 'at the idea of such a thought having been for a moment entertained as the destruction of a building so eminently characteristic and so singularly beautiful a church'. He continued in this vein and told the trustees they had 'a specimen of church architecture to which no other town that I know of in England can produce a parallel', ending by complimenting Shaw on his 'timely and efficient protest against demolition'.[89] Evidently taken by surprise, the trustees wrote to the President of the RIBA

84 'St. John's church, Leeds. The Trustees' account book, 1660–1766', *T S* (1919),xxiv, 379ff.

85 Anon, *Churches of the parish of Guiseley*, Leeds 1843, 4. Rawdon chapel was built by Francis Layton, Lord of the Manor of Rawdon, in the early seventeenth century, and it was completed after his death by Henry, his son. The tower survives in the 1864 replacement by A.Crawford.

86 Whitaker, 61, 'Modern eyes are compelled to regard it very differently' from Thoresby's, wrote Whitaker. His reference to 'the Wyat school' is to Jeffry Wyatt's design for a new gallery at Browsholme Hall for Thomas Lister Parker in 1806 (see Linstrum,D., *Sir Jeffry Wyatville; architect to the King*, Oxford 1972,232) and to Lewis Wyatt's work at Lyme Park, Cheshire for Thomas Legh in 1816.

87 These reports are all reproduced in Stocks,J.E., 'The church of St. John the Evangelist', *T S* (1919),xxiv,190ff.

88 Scott, op.cit.,410.

89 Stocks, op.cit.,199.

139

(A.J.B.Beresford Hope), who supported Shaw and Scott, confirming that St John's was 'valued by all intelligent students of our architectural antiquities'.[90] The Bishop of Ripon, who was strongly in favour of replacement, was persuaded to relent only by 'the great respect which I have for Mr. Scott as the highest authority we have on Church Architecture';[91] but there was a complaint from some churchwardens that they were being compelled to 'submit to the use of a church unsuited to the service of Almighty God to gratify the morbid taste of anyone who can admire the debased architecture of the seventeenth century'.[92]

In this classic battle in the history of architectural conservation, Scott and Shaw were the victors, and posterity the benefiters; but sadly, the restoration was not in accordance with Shaw's report, although he was appointed architect. Presumably there was resistance and obstinacy, which has not been recorded, but the plastered walls were stripped and the woodwork suffered; the pulpit was cut down in height and moved to a new position, the sounding board was placed over the entrance doors, the reading desk disappeared; the scroll cresting was removed from the screen, and the two sets of Royal arms were fixed on the west wall; all the pews were rearranged, and most of the doors were lost. Many other details disappeared, for which Shaw's good pastiche south porch was no recompense, and Scott's boast that St John's was saved 'all but its pew doors' was far from true. Fortunately for the church and posterity, St John's was served from 1884–98 by a vicar, John Scott, who slowly and thoroughly collected what could be found of the old woodwork and put right as much as he could of the havoc caused in the 60s. Some of the fittings had disappeared, and the new arrangement of pews remains, but Dean Scott's sensitivity restored St John's uniqueness, in the true meaning of the word.[93]

Meanwhile the ruined abbey at Kirkstall was still untouched. Scott's report of 1873 recommended rebuilding 'the lost pier with the sides of the tower which it sustained . . . [and] the adjoining portions which were destroyed by the fall'. The shell of the church would then be practically complete, and it could be roofed for use. 'Lamentable though it be, one of the great facts of its history is that it has remained nearly three and a half centuries *in ruins*, and the most remarkable fact of all will, I trust, be that, after this lengthened interval of desolation, it has been restored to its sacred uses'.[94] Scott's report was intended to reassure those who feared the abbey would appear a new building; 'it should be clearly seen that it has been *a ruin* and has been rescued . . . Externally, the old bemossed surface would of course remain, as should be the case with any other ancient church'. However well intentioned Scott was (and his *writings* on restoration are often rational and totally convincing) it is almost certain Edmund Sharpe's caution was nearer the truth. 'I need scarcely repeat, that whatever the tool of the modern restorer passes over, loses at once its authentic character, and its historic value; and that Kirkstall Abbey will, from the day that its "restoration" is complete, and that it is delivered over, spick and span, to the bishop of the diocese, for consecration, be to all

90 ibid.,222.

91 ibid.,223.

92 ibid.,224. 'We would ask Mr Scott if he had a church to build in the present day, whether he would take St. John's for a model?'

93 Shaw's drawings for the restoration are in the RIBA Drawings Collection (*Catalogue*, vol. S/49). Canon Scott's work is recorded on a tablet on the south wall near the screen he devotedly restored.

94 Scott,G.G., *Kirkstall Abbey and its restoration*, Leeds 1873,7.

intents and purposes a modern church'.[95]

Scott's report was written at a time when, as Sir John Lubbock told the Commons, 'our ancient national monuments were rapidly disappearing'.[96] He was speaking in the Parliamentary debate in April 1874 which marked the first hesitant steps towards legislation to protect ancient monuments and historic buildings. 'Let it not go forth to the educated world that, notwithstanding the exuberance of their wealth, they were the only people in Europe who were careless of that great inheritance',[97] pleaded Beresford Hope, who had supported Scott and Shaw in their claims for St John's, Leeds; and John Walter spoke of the country's being 'covered from one end to the other with the noblest and most interesting specimens of ecclesiastical architecture . . . which could vie with any in Europe'.[98] Hope also came to the defence of medieval buildings during the second debate in the following year, and there was considerable support for the proposed inclusion in the statutory list of 'abbeys and ruins generally, which were valued by the country quite as much as these monuments of antiquity';[99] but only ancient stones and earthworks were protected by the first legislation. Three years after the first debate, in 1877, William Morris issued his famous manifesto against architectural restoration and founded the Society for the Protection of Ancient Buildings; and in the following year Scott was laid to rest in Westminster Abbey, having done nothing at Kirkstall.

In 1882, the year the first Ancient Monuments Act became law, C. Hodgson Fowler wrote to Edward Birchall agreeing 'It certainly seems most desirable that something should be done to preserve Kirkstall',[100] although the new Act did not apply to ruined abbeys. The Chancellor of the Exchequer had ruled it was unnecessary; 'by far the most efficacious way of preserving most of the monuments would be to trust to private care, stimulated by the watchfulness of those who were interested in them, and by the pressure of public opinion exercised by the welcome visits of the learned societies'.[101] Fowler thought the Yorkshire Archaeological Society, founded in 1863, was the body to undertake the preservation, 'or at least, to inaugurate the movement'. The secretary of the Society for the Protection of Ancient Buildings was consulted; he believed 'nothing short of putting a roof over the vaulting would do any good',[102] and then tried to interest Sir Titus Salt in providing the funds.[103] The Countess of Cardigan, the absentee owner of the estate which included the ruined abbey, was 'quite agreeable to an arrangement . . . for keeping [it] in repair, so that further decay may be prevented';[104] and in 1890 Colonel J. T. North, popularly known as 'the nitrate king', bought the ruins and presented them to the city of Leeds.

W. H. St John Hope took down the invading ivy from the walls and prepared a report on their preservation, recommending rebuilding the fallen pier and arches, using old stone where possible and making up where necessary with new 'roughly hewn . . . so as to make it a modern repair'.[105] The work was undertaken by J. T. Micklethwaite, who had assisted Scott in restoring All Saints', Wakefield; the clerk of the works was J. T. Irvine who had acted in that capacity for Street in the

95 *B* (1873), op. cit.

96 *Parliamentary debates* (1874), ccxviii, 574.

97 ibid., 581.

98 ibid., 584.

99 ibid. (1875), ccxxiii, 895.

100 Leeds Reference Library. Q/L K36(726) 'Edward Birchall's correspondence relating to the restoration of Kirkstall Abbey'. 20 Sept 1882, C. H. Fowler to Birchall.

101 *Parliamentary debates* (1874), ccxviii, 589.

102 'Edward Birchall's correspondence', op. cit., 23 Sept 1882. J. H. Middleton to Birchall.

103 ibid., Jan 1883. Middleton to Birchall.

104 ibid., 12 Oct 1882. B. E. Bennett to Birchall.

105 Hope, W. H. St. J., *Report on the preservation of the ruins of Kirkstall Abbey*, Leeds 1890.

rebuilding of St Michael's, Thornhill. Micklethwaite cheerfully agreed Hope had done well to take away the ivy, however much he was criticised by those who liked the 'parasitic vegetation' and thought a ruin should look neglected, overgrown – and ruinous. In fortunate ignorance of the power station that was to be built down the valley and the skeletons of pylons and festoons of cable that were to be erected on the hills, Micklethwaite commented, 'I fear if Kirkstall is to be saved people will have to be content to lose some of its picturesqueness at least for a time, but with proper care it may in the end become more beautiful than ever'.[106]

106 'Edward Birchall's correspondence', op.cit., 14 May 1890. Micklethwaite to Birchall; 'It was a choice between keeping the ivy and keeping the building, and I vote for the building because you can get ivy elsewhere, and you can not get another Kirkstall Abbey if this one is lost'. But Hope later noted of Micklethwaite's work, 'The visible results . . . can not be said in all cases to be satisfactory or picturesque', and Pevsner comments critically on the filling in of the arches in the south aisle, 'and a special rather clumsy pier [which] had to be built in the nave'.

6 Georgian churches, chapels and meeting houses

What is this Building, so magnificent
With spacious Area, and this grand Ascent;
With Pillars on each Hand? One might suppose
The one was *Jachin*, and the other *Boaz*.
The Door-Steads built with architectal Grace,
Pilasters rising from the solid Base.
Within, what flow'ry Work, of purest Paste,
And all Things finish'd in a superb Taste!
'Tis sure a Pantheon of the present Age,
Or pompous Theatre, to set off the Stage.
Forbear your Taunts, this Structure is design'd
An Habitation for th'eternal Mind.

Revd. Titus Knight, *Hhadash Hamishcan: or, the NEW CHAPEL, at Halifax*, 1772

The relationship between the Established Church and the Nonconformists in West Yorkshire during the eighteenth and nineteenth centuries was not harmonious. When the Revd. Hammond Roberson began to build St James's, Heckmondwike in 1830, he referred proudly and confidently to 'having laid the first stone of a church in the very heart of the West Riding, the seat of Dissent';[1] and when Charlotte Brontë introduced him as a character in *Shirley*, it was as a militant opponent of the 'Dissenting and Methodist schools, the Baptists, Independents, and Wesleyans, joined in unholy alliance'. Yet an impartial architectural historian might comment that there was little difference between the Anglican and Nonconformist places of worship in West Yorkshire by the end of the eighteenth century.

In Sir Christopher Wren's often quoted advice to early eighteenth-century church designers, 'it is enough if [the Romanists] hear the Murmur of the Mass, and see the Elevation of the Host, but [our churches] are to be fitted for Auditories'.[2] It was Wren who popularised the room plan of a church so that all could 'hear distinctly, and see the Preacher', and in the internal arrangement of both Anglican church and Nonconformist chapel, the preaching of the Word was the primary function. 'A moderate Voice may be heard 50 Feet distant from the Preacher, 30 Feet on each side, and 20 behind the Pulpit', he wrote, recommending churches should not be made larger than necessary. He believed their sites should be chosen 'not where vacant Ground may be cheapest purchased in the Extremities of the Suburbs, but among the thicker Inhabitants, for Convenience of the better sort'. Externally, 'where most open in View [they] should be adorned with Porticos . . . which, together with handsome Spires, or Lanterns, rising in good Proportion above the neighbouring houses . . .

1 Peel,F., *Spen valley: past and present*, Heckmondwike 1893,397. In 1830, Roberson wrote to a friend that the first stones were about to be laid of three new churches in his parish, St John's, Cleckheaton, St James's, Heckmondwike, and All Saints', Roberttown.

2 Wren,C., *Parentalia: or, memoirs of the family of the Wrens*, London 1750,318ff.

3 Apart from Wren's own basilican churches, there are the provincial examples of St Philip's, Birmingham, All Saints', Oxford, All Saints', Derby, and St Paul's, Sheffield (a near-contemporary of Holy Trinity).

4 The first proposal was made in 1714, but as a promised subscription of £1,000 was not forthcoming, the scheme lapsed until 1722 when it was revived by Lady Elizabeth Hastings. The foundation stone was laid on 27 August 1722, and the church was completed in 1727 at a cost of £5,463 12s. 5d.

5 Yorkshire Archaeological Society, MS 10; a letter dated 15 May 1723 from William Cookson to Ralph Thoresby, enclosing 'a draught, the south front of our new church; it was drawn by Mr. Etty of York'. There was a payment of £19 19s. to Etty on 1 April 1723 for the wooden model which was still in existence in the early nineteenth century. There are superficial resemblances between Halfpenny's published design (for which he was paid £1 11s. 6d. on 8 May 1723) and that used for the building, although they differ in most details. Halfpenny proposed to crown the tower with a square, open colonnade, surmounted by an obelisk spire.

6 Etty's design, which was reproduced in Thoresby's *Vicaria Leodiensis*, suggests there was no intention to build a spire, but an incongruously homely one was added (see illustration in Whitaker, facing 65). Whitaker thought this 'was unquestionably one instance among many of private interference, by which the better judgment of real architects is often overruled, and for which they are unjustly considered as responsible'.

7 Cookson's letter (see 5 above), notes 'we have got the north side 4 yards high, and are in so good forwardness with the front and ends that we hope to have it all so high by Whitsuntide, tho' we begun but the Wednesday in Easter week to lay the superstructure'. The chief craftsmen employed were: John Pate, Thomas Thackrey and John Prince, stonemasons; Thomas Goodall, Edward Haselgrave and Joshua Turner, joiners; John Bagnall, plasterer; and John de Goulons, carver. Whitaker commented, 'The masonry, carpentry, and joiners' work are all admirable; but there is one material which it would now be difficult to procure for any price, namely the massy and excellent oak with which the whole is constructed. Nor was the roof, strong as it is, trusted to the mechanical tricks like those of modern carpenters for its chance of duration ... Architects had not learned at that time the art of combining real security with apparent danger, and of supporting enormous weights upon slender props of iron ... Between the solidity of construction and the stability of a landed endowment there is a natural and pleasing affinity. Our ancestors endowed as they built – for duration'.

may be of sufficient Ornament to the Town'. On the whole, this was the accepted model for the design of eighteenth-century Anglican churches, but Nonconformists had to wait another hundred years before their places of worship too could be reckoned 'Ornaments to the Town'.

Wren's recommendations suggested a model for a large town church in which the Roman basilica was adopted as a suitable plan.[3] Normally a communion table stood in an apsidal chancel at the east end, and the interior was dominated by a pulpit close to the centre of the chancel, from which the preacher addressed the congregation sitting in their pews and in the galleries facing him and to left and right. This was the form of building chosen in Leeds in the 1720s when the leading merchants joined with the philanthropic Lady Elizabeth Hastings of Ledston Hall to erect Holy Trinity church in Boar Lane.[4] It was built 'among the thicker Inhabitants' in the part of the town where many merchants had their houses; and it was certainly intended for 'the better sort', who purchased the majority of the pews and ensured the social exclusiveness of the congregation. The foundation stone was laid in 1722, but the consecration had to wait five years.

The credit for the design of Holy Trinity has traditionally been given to William Halfpenny, who included a view of a very similar building in *The Art of Sound Building*, first published in 1725, in which it is described as 'of my Invention for Leeds in Yorkshire'. It is, however, quite clear from a letter written by William Cookson to Ralph Thoresby that the design of the church as executed was made by William Etty, who also provided a wooden model 'for our workmen to go by'.[5] Etty's drawing was given to Thoresby, who used it for the engraving published in his *Vicaria Leodiensis* (1724). The symmetrical elevation to Boar Lane, with balancing doors in the east and west end bays, is divided by Doric pilasters supporting an entablature with triglyphs and a solid balustrade crowned by urns. The large, lower windows (placed at this level in reversal of Wren's usual practice) have alternate triangular and segmental pediments, broken into in a Mannerist fashion by huge keystones, and the doors are set in surrounds with blocked architraves and oversized voussoirs and keystones. The whole design suggests that Etty was not unaware of Gibbs's church of St Martin-in-the-Fields, which was then under construction, although the present spire is a Wren–Gibbs pastiche ingeniously added in 1839 by Robert Dennis Chantrell.[6]

Internally, giant Corinthian columns divide the nave into seven bays and support an entablature with an ornamented soffit. These monumental colonnades, terminating in a segmental apse with a Venetian window framed by plaster garlands, possess a quality of Burlingtonian Palladianism reminiscent of the York Assembly Rooms which were to be built a few years later, but the effect is slightly misleading since the bases in the church were lowered by two feet in 1887. Cookson's letter to Thoresby reveals the sense of pride in the ambitious monumentality of this church, which is as great a tribute to the prosperity of the town's merchants as to God.[7] It is essentially a city church, closely modelled on the recent London examples, but

140

140. Leeds, Holy Trinity; the original spire (not a part of W.Etty's design 1723–7) was replaced in 1839 by the present feature (R.D.Chantrell).

141. Sowerby, St Peter; designed on the model of Holy Trinity, Leeds and executed 1763–6.

8 Watson, 449. The nave was tiled and repewed in the nineteenth century, but otherwise few changes have been made since the church was completed.

9 Leeds Archives Dept. Sowerby Parish Records/17. The repair of the old chapel was first considered in 1758, but it was soon decided to rebuild. In 1759 it was resolved that John Wilson was 'a Proper Person' to undertake the mason's work, and he also produced a plan, which was amended several times. James Bradley was the joiner; probably he was related to Thomas (his brother?) who designed Crow Nest House and was formerly credited with the Piece Hall, Halifax.

10 The general plastering was executed by —.Exley, but Cortese was paid £31 11s for 'the Altar piece' in 1766.

thirty years later another church on a very different site was built in obvious imitation of Holy Trinity.

St Peter's, Sowerby is in a hilltop village overlooking the broad green Calder valley, a little community in which 'one of the most elegant chapels in the north of England'[8] stands like a palace. The old chapel had become 'greatly decay'd in the Roof & other parts thereof' by 1758, and it was also so small that 'for want of Room many repair to Conventicles and Dissenting meeting houses that would otherwise attend Divine Worship'. £1,200 was raised by voluntary subscription to remedy this lack of space, and to recapture those who had strayed from the Established Church; John Wilson, a master-mason from Halifax, provided the plans.[9] Externally, as at Leeds, the seven bays are divided by giant Doric attached columns (instead of pilasters), and there are rusticated doorways in each end bay; internally, there are monumental Corinthian colonnades, even repeating the identical fret on the soffits of the entablatures. Unlike Holy Trinity, St Peter's has retained its pewed galleries. The elaboration increases in the chancel and apse, in which the richly decorated Venetian window is flanked on each side by two tabernacles; the outer contain tablets displaying texts, the inner figures in coloured stucco of Moses and Christ. Above spreads a vast rococo Royal Arms, with cartouches on each side, the extreme ones filled with armorial achievements. This theatrical display, dated 1766, is the work of Giuseppe Cortese, who was working at the time for John Carr on the stucco decoration of John Royds's house in Halifax.[10] These are the two largest eighteenth-century churches in West Yorkshire, but several smaller churches and chapels of ease were built at the expense of local landowners.

141

142

187

142. Sowerby, St Peter; the sumptuous plasterwork in the apse (G. Cortese 1766).

143. Tong, St James; a traditional medieval church expressed in Early Georgian language, built (1727) by Sir George Tempest on his estate.

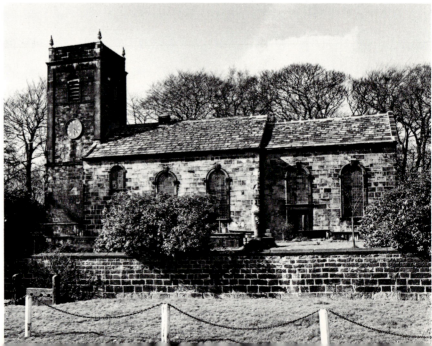

11 There is also a connection between Shelton and St Giles, Pontefract. The tower was rebuilt in 1707 by William Wright, mason at the expense of Sir John Bland of Kippax, and in the following year the Corporation and Vicar were authorised to 'agree with such workmen as shall be convenient for building a Cupelow on the top of St Gyles Steeple pursuant to such a modell thereof as Theophilus Shelton, Esq., shall draw for that purpose'; but there is no evidence a cupola was ever built. (Holmes, R.(ed), *The booke of entries of the Pontefract Corporation 1653–1726*, Pontefract n.d.,283). Alterations were made to the church at various times during the eighteenth century, including the remodelling of the south front with 'Gibbs' surrounds to the windows and doors before 1742 when the church was shown on the fine map of the town made by Paul Jollage. The tower was rebuilt at the end of the eighteenth century, including the present open crown; in 1793 the *Leeds Intelligencer* (28 Jan) invited 'all Persons inclined to contract for enlarging the Parish Church of Pontefract . . . to send in their proposals'.

12 The portrait used to hang in Bretton Hall (see *C L* (1938),lxxxiii,558,pl.11).

13 Parsons, i,436. The building has been demolished, but the cupola survives and is in the churchyard of Chorley and Connon's 1885 replacement.

14 Horsforth chapel was described as 'Italian . . . the only door is at the west end, and the entrance is surmounted by a blank arch intersected by a balustrade. On each side are an Ionic pilaster and a plain half column. The pediment is bold and enriched with modillions . . . Over the west end is a cupola'. The altar stood in an apse 'of pleasing appearance, being gracefully decorated with festoons of plaister work'. (*Churches of the parish of Guiseley*, Leeds 1843,6). The chapel was built at the expense of John Stanhope, for whom Carr was working at Cannon, and it is very likely that he supplied the design.

15 The church was enlarged in 1828 when an addition was built and a Tuscan portico was put up in front of Carr's doorway.

16 Wragg, R.B., 'John Carr: Gothic revivalist', *Studies in architectural history* (ed. Singleton, W.A.), London 1956,18f. There were large-scale alterations in 1884–5 by A.E. Street and A.H. Kirk, including the building of transepts and a chancel. It was probably at that time the south aisle was remodelled in a more conventional Gothic than Carr's.

17 Whitaker, 301.

143 St James's, Tong was erected in 1727 by Sir George Tempest of Tong Hall in a plain manner with semicircular-headed windows in simple dressed surrounds in both nave and chancel. A square tower with a parapet and corner urns completes the design of what is an early eighteenth-century version of a medieval church, in which vernacular Classical elements replace Gothic; inside St James's, the north aisle is separated from the nave by a Tuscan colonnade. Possibly Theophilus Shelton, the designer of Tong Hall, was also responsible for advising on the church.[11] When Sir William Wentworth of Bretton Hall built the chapel on his estate in 1744 he designed it himself and proudly had it painted in the background of one of his portraits.[12] It is a simple little rectangular building, with three windows and flanking doorways on the south front, and pedimented gables supported on Tuscan corner pilasters with outrageously exaggerated entasis. There is a Venetian window in the east end, and a small circular turret with a dome over the west; inside there are box pews and a gallery, and a complete absence of decoration. A Palladian box, such as this, was the basis of many eighteenth-century churches and chapels, Anglican and Nonconformist. Carr developed a more refined version, as in St Michael's, Farnley in 1761, 'one of the most elegant and beautifully simple edifices of the kind which can be found in this part of the country',[13] decorated with an open cupola with an ogee top; and the chapels at, for example, Horsforth (1758),[14] Chapelthorpe (1771), Meltham (1782–6) and Slaithwaite (1789), were built in a similarly unpretentious manner.

144 Carr's design for St John's, North Bierley, built in 1766 by Richard Richardson of Bierley Hall, is an austere Palladian exercise in which the well-detailed ashlar contributes as much as the neat proportions to the effect of the building. There are three large semicircular-headed windows on the south and a Venetian window on the east; the west front shows Carr's conservative fondness for a Gibbs surround to a doorway, and the heavily dentillated pediment terminates in a domed bell turret with a surmounting obelisk.[15] Occasionally Carr moved away from Palladianism and Neo-classicism, and produced a Gothic design. Between 1764 and 1767 he rebuilt the tower and outer walls of **145** All Saints', Dewsbury in a mixture of Classical and Gothic, with pilaster-buttresses and aisle windows in which semicircular heads were more prominent than pointed; there is a suspicion of *chinoiserie* in the doorways, but the effect has an unexpected charm and the replacements were minimal.[16] Whitaker noted that, 'by a judicious forbearance which would not have been exercised now [1816], all the inside of the church which could be preserved was allowed to stand'.[17] In 1776 Carr built the delightful little St Helen's, close to Denton Park; it follows the usual form of a rectangular box with a tower at the west end, but the windows are pointed and quatrefoil, and battlements appear on the tower. The east window is an ingenious Tudor version of a Venetian, with a wide four-centred arch flanked by two narrow pointed ones. But these churches were of little significance compared with the most important late eighteenth-century church in West Yorkshire, Carr's gift to his native town, Horbury.

144. North Bierley, St John; built by Richard Richardson (J.Carr 1766) close to his house, Bierley Hall. It was enlarged in 1828.

145. Dewsbury, All Saints'; the medieval church was partly rebuilt (J.Carr 1764–7) in a rococo Gothic style with a hint of *chinoiserie*.

146. Horbury, St Peter and St Leonard; the finest West Yorkshire Neo-classical church, and Carr's gift to his native town (1791).

146

HANC AEDEM SACRAM: PIETATIS IN DEUM ET AMORIS: IN SOLUM NATALE MONUMENTUM: PROPRIIS SUMPTIBUS EXTRUXIT JOHANNES CARR ARCHITECTUS: GLORIA DEO IN EXCELSIS: ANNO CHRISTI MDCCXCI, runs the proud and prominent inscription on the pediment of St Peter and St Leonard's; and the tall tower of four diminishing stages rises above the town as a landmark in the Calder valley. The church was designed, as Wren had recommended, with a portico to the street (though Horbury is not quite London or Westminster). In this case it is Ionic and attached, but being placed in the centre of the south front it causes an ambivalence by setting up a north–south axis which conflicts with the orthodox east–west. Carr did not completely resolve this problem, but he lavished his accustomed attention on the detailing of the ashlar and the carefully considered scaling of the rising stages of the tower from a smooth ashlar base, through variations in texture and modelling to a colonnaded rotunda and a crowning spire. Internally, the church is in effect a basilica in which are two apses, the western filling the space below the tower, the eastern projecting as a polygonal bay. The chancel is a double square on plan, with Corinthian colonnaded screens dividing the quasi-transepts or porches from the main body of the church, and the whole interior was detailed with a fine sense of space and of balance between form and decoration. 'He who builds a church

190

147. Rastrick, St Matthew; built (1796–8) under the influence of Carr's neat, workmanlike Neo-classicism.

148. Wakefield, St John; built as the central element in a formal residential layout (Watson and Lindley 1791–5), and enlarged in 1904–05 at the east end (J.T.Micklethwaite).

18 ibid.,295ff. Ill-judged recent alterations to the east apse have upset Carr's balanced design.

publishes a work', wrote Whitaker, whose antiquarian prejudice about such niceties as precedents for apses at both ends was on the whole overcome by the effect of the interior, which 'might have been copied from . . . some temple of the time of the Antonines, when Corinthian and Composite ornaments had well nigh supplanted the severer graces of the Doric or even Ionic orders'.[18]

There are several churches which illustrate Carr's influence in the county; the now demolished one at Lightcliffe, for example, which was the work of William Mallinson of Halifax in 1774–5, could have been a Carr design. So could St Matthew's, Rastrick, built in 1796–8; this incorporates many of his characteristic elements – the precisely detailed ashlar, the neat arrangement of three semicircular-headed giant arches enclosing fanlights and lower rectangular windows, the balancing pair of doors surmounted by tablets, and the west tower terminating in four pedimented gables and a domed, colonnaded bell and clock turret. Inside, the gallery around three sides is supported on thin Tuscan columns, and there is a Venetian window in the apsidal chancel. There is no record of the architect, who might have been Peter Atkinson of York, Thomas Johnson of Leeds, or Charles Watson of Wakefield, who all worked in a similar manner. Watson (with his partner, William Lindley) designed St John's, Wakefield as the major building in the newly planned residential area north of the town, and it was built between 1791 and 1795, many years after it was first proposed in 1776. 'The inhabitants . . . are in high spirits upon the happy prospect they at length have of a new Church being shortly to be erected', reported the *Leeds Intelligencer* (27 Feb 1776), but they had to wait a long time. It follows the pattern of a rectangular nave with apsidal east chancel and west tower, and originally the entrance was in

19 The land was bequeathed in 1776, but the Act for the erection of the church was not passed until 1791. The first stone was laid on 3 November 1791 'amidst thousands of surrounding and exulting spectators' (*LI*, 8 Nov 1791). The first architect was John Hope (the designer of Halifax Piece Hall), but Watson and Lindley replaced him, presumably due to the influence of John Lee, the Wakefield solicitor who was the major entrepreneur of the residential development surrounding the church. The tower was demolished in 1880 on the advice of J.T.Micklethwaite, who rebuilt it in 1885–95 to the original design. At the same time he remodelled the interior, and in 1904–05 he added the present chancel in the manner of the original design.

20 St Paul's was built in 1793 (see Whitaker, 69). It was constructed of brick with stone dressings, and both east and west fronts were designed as Ionic temple fronts. The church was demolished in 1905. According to Allen,T., *History of the county of York*, London 1831,ii,510, the architect was W.Johnson, who died in 1795, and has been suggested as the possible designer of the White Cloth Hall and Assembly Room, Leeds (see 284,330).

149. Leeds, St Paul; designed as a part of the Parks estate (W.Johnson 1791), the gable façades were identically treated as Ionic temple fronts, with a tower rising out of the west. The 1878 photograph shows St Paul's House, west of the church, under construction.

150. Meltham, St Bartholomew; dating from 1651, the church was rebuilt (J.Jagger attrib.1782–6). The tower was added in 1835, and the Neo-norman chancel in 1877–8 (J.Kirk).

the centre of the south front. The façade is an elegant composition of coupled Doric pilasters on a rusticated basement, the square tower neatly becoming octagonal in its upper stage before being crowned by a dome. Internally, the galleries around three sides were supported on fluted Doric columns, and in the centre stood a three-decker pulpit surrounded by pews lined with green baize.[19] Thomas Johnson designed the tower of Holy Trinity, Halifax (1795–8) in a similar manner to the Wakefield church, but he used a rectangular plan in which the altar is in the middle of one of the long sides, below a large tripartite window, and with entrance doors to left and right. The galleries around the other three sides are supported on Ionic columns, and their fronts are panelled. Johnson was probably partly responsible for the execution of St Paul's, Leeds to a design by his father William.[20]

149

150

St Paul's, a rectangular design surmounted by a tall tower and domed cupola, is a convenient building in which to pause to illustrate how, by the end of the eighteenth century, the differences between the new town churches of the Anglicans and the larger meeting houses of the Nonconformists were disappearing, though only the former had towers. Holy Trinity, Holmfirth (rebuilt 1777–81) and St Bartholomew, Meltham (rebuilt 1782–6), for example, might easily be mistaken for meeting houses from their façades; and the churches which preceded the present St Mary's, Mirfield and St Michael's, Haworth were plain rectangular stone boxes with a line of windows down each side, all in the West Yorkshire vernacular. The unusual arrangement inside Holy Trinity, Halifax has already been noted, and in St Paul's an organ was placed in the gallery at the east end above the communion table – an arrangement favoured by the Nonconformists in their larger buildings. There was no real difference between the internal planning of the churches at Rastrick and Halifax, and the contemporary meeting houses and chapels. In the places of worship of all denominations (save the Society of Friends), a three-

151. Bramhope chapel, built in 1649 on the estate of Robert Dyneley; a well-known early example of Puritan architecture.

152. Dean House, nr.Holmfirth; the building (c.1789) appears to be two cottages on the street front, but is obviously a meeting house when seen across the valley. The pulpit was in the centre of the long wall, and a gallery was formed around the other three sides.

21 Similarly, later in the eighteenth century, the Catholic Relief Act of 1778 was no guarantee of safety, as the Gordon Riots of 1780 demonstrated; consequently the first post-Reformation Catholic churches were often designed to resemble houses from outside. Carr's unexecuted design of 1772 for the Catholic Gascoigne family's chapel and chaplain's house on their Parlington estate disguised them as a castellated garden building (Leeds Archives Dept., Gascoigne papers, uncatalogued). The possible reason why the design was not executed may be found in the *Leeds Intelligencer* (20 June 1780); it reported 'great rejoicings . . . on account of Sir Thomas Gascoigne's . . . renouncing the errors of the Church of Rome, and embracing the Protestant religion'. There was no difference externally between the Catholic church built in Lady Lane, Leeds in 1793–4 to a design by Thomas Johnson, and a Dissenting meeting-house, although internally it was 'adorned with columns and pilasters of the composite order . . . Over the entrance is placed a small organ . . . The pulpit is peculiarly light and elegant' (Ryley, J., *The Leeds guide*, Leeds 1806,40).

decker pulpit was the most conspicuous object. A description of St Paul's draws attention to the beautiful workmanship of the central group of 'pulpit, reading-desk, and Clerk's pew' which was to be found inside this church which could also have served as a sophisticated Nonconformist chapel; yet the origins of the latter had been very different in the seventeenth century.

On the road from Leeds to Otley can be seen a little rectangular **151** stone chapel with mullioned windows and two entrances, built by Robert Dyneley, 'an ardent and unswerving Puritan', on his estate at Bramhope in 1649; it was buildings of this type that numerous communities struggled to provide after the ejection from their pulpits of those clergy who refused to comply with the 1662 Act of Uniformity. Their unobtrusive external appearance was a result partly of the relative poverty of the ejected clergyman and his followers, partly of prudent precaution. In spite of the Toleration Act of William III in 1689, there were repeated attacks by organised mobs under various banners, and many new buildings were burned down during the eighteenth century;[21] it was wiser not to draw attention to them, but some recognisable types began to emerge towards the end of the seventeenth century. An early example was the work of Oliver Heywood, who was suspended from preaching in his church at Coley, fined and imprisoned until James II's declaration of liberty for conscience permitted him to preach again. In 1688 Heywood built a chapel at Northowram, almost at his own expense, although the stone was given by a quarry owner. His diary records the progress of the building, from laying the foundation stone on 23 April 1688 until 'the work was finished, glasse set in, plaistered, &c., so it was ready for me

and people to make use of, and accordingly I did preach in it July 8, 1688'. The only decoration on the plain rectangular stone building with two rows of windows and a door at each end of the front wall was the builder's carved monogram, an O encircling an H, with 16 above the bar and 88 below.[22]

Many of the early buildings were built in this way by the congregation. At Booth chapel, near Halifax, in 1761, 'those who had no money laboured alternately in digging the foundations, getting stones in the quarry, and serving the masons'.[23] A little chapel for the Baptists was built in Heptonstall in the middle of the eighteenth century single-handed by a collier, Dan Taylor, who quarried the stone on the moors, carried it to the village on his back and walled it. Such buildings were necessarily plain and simple, rectangular in plan and built of coursed Flags with dressed stone surrounds to the windows and doors in the West Yorkshire vernacular manner that made no distinction between houses in which to live and to meet for worship. More or less standard plans were used in some areas; for example, the design of the Baptists' 'plain, commodious building' of 1777 at Hebden Bridge was 'so much approved, that it has been, with some slight variations, the model followed in the numerous meeting houses throughout the neighbourhood'.[24] Two survivors from this era illustrate the internal arrangements and external appearance considered suitable by all denominations, including the Methodists, although John Wesley insisted the houses of his followers were not alternatives to churches, but complementary.

Turning its face to the green valley and Netherthong, and away from the hamlet of Dean House, near Holmfirth, is a building c.1789 which appears to be a pair of single-storey cottages from the street; the opposite front, two storeys high because of the sloping site, is more obviously that of a meeting house, possibly the most delightful in West Yorkshire. Five bays wide, it has alternate clerestorey and full height semicircular-headed windows with Gothic heads, and an entrance in each end bay, again with a Gothic fanlight. Internally, it has been altered, but Wesley Chapel at Greetland (1777) is more complete; a rectangle, 50 feet by 36 with a gallery around three sides and a pulpit against the fourth, it had separate entrances originally for men and women.[25] Externally, it is similar to Dean House but without its charm.

The meeting houses of the Society of Friends were appropriately and predictably modest, and built in the domestic West Yorkshire vernacular. In Leeds the Friends paid £162 for their galleried building in Water Lane in 1699; it accommodated about 250, but it had to be enlarged in 1723, and it was rebuilt in 1787 according to a design prepared by fourteen members of the Society. The new building was divided for men and women, and once again it was galleried. Externally, a three-bay pedimented centre was flanked by two-bay wings.[26] 'This building with its gable ends, Shows the quiet meeting-house of Friends', reads a verse printed under an engraving of the building, which was large compared with the little one at Rawdon dated 1697 on the door lintel, or that at Brighouse which cost

22 Pearson,M., *Northowram: its history and antiquities*, Halifax 1898, 114. The history of Heywood Chapel, altered in 1711, galleried in 1783 and rebuilt in 1836, is typical of the early meeting-houses.

23 Parsons, ii,350.

24 ibid.,ii,355.

25 Dolbey,G.W., *The architectural expression of Methodism*, London 1964,86f.

26 Allot,W., 'Leeds Quaker meeting', *T S* (1965),l,no.111,1ff.

153. Wooldale, the Friends' Meeting House; built in a quiet, plain manner characteristic of the early Quaker buildings.

154. Heptonstall, the Octagon; designed in one of the forms favoured by John Wesley (1764). It was enlarged in 1802, but without affecting the original character.

27 Lindley,K., *Chapels and meeting houses*, London 1969,60f.

28 Perkins,E.B., *Methodist preaching-houses and the law*, London 1952,13.

29 Chapman,E.V., and Turner,G.A., *The Heptonstall octagon*, n.d.; Dolbey, op.cit.,101.

30 In 1802 the Heptonstall octagon was partly rebuilt by lengthening two sides, but preserving an octagonal form. It was probably at that time the gallery was reconstructed with thin Tuscan columns, on top of which blocks decorated with wreaths support the framework of the timber gallery.

153

154

£114 14s 8d when it was built in the 1740s. There is a special quality in these meeting houses such as the touchingly simple one at Gildersome (1756) in a walled garden entered through an archway in a roadside building that offered stabling to the Friends who had travelled long distances, or those near Holmfirth in the Quaker hamlets of High Flatts and Wooldale.[27] The simplicity extends to the interiors, in which there are only plain walls and wooden benches arranged around three sides.

These, and a few others which escaped rebuilding as their congregations grew, illustrate the small, remote meeting houses scattered around West Yorkshire; almost the only exceptions to the rectangular stone buildings were those of the Methodists at Heptonstall and Bradford. The early meetings of Wesley's followers were in the open air, but when the parish churches were closed to Methodist preaching and fellowship their leader was compelled to agree to the erection of their own buildings,[28] even if he was at first unwilling to admit dissent from the Church of England. Most followed the usual pattern, but the best form for an auditory is one in which the preacher is close to the centre and to all his hearers. When Wesley was preaching in Leeds in 1780 he noted 'a considerable part of the people could not hear. Indeed the church is remarkably ill constructed; had it been built with common sense, all that were in it, and even more, might have heard every word'. A central form is an obvious solution, and Wesley said of the octagonal Rotherham building, 'All our houses should be of this shape if the ground allow'. The 'New House at Heptonstall' was built in that form in 1764.[29] It is believed Wesley employed the Rotherham carpenter to make the roof, which was brought on pack horses in sections to the hilltop village overlooking Hebden Bridge by the most hazardous but direct route over the moorland heights. Externally, the Heptonstall Octagon is a plain stone building with dressed quoins and window surrounds; internally, it is furnished with a gallery around all eight sides.[30]

155. Wakefield, Westgate Unitarian Chapel; a sophisticated design (1752) possibly by John Carr, who was the architect for the neighbouring houses for the Milnes family.

Two years later another Octagon was built, in Great Horton Road, Bradford; in 1768 Wesley wrote appreciatively in his journal of this 'preaching-house fifty-four feet square, the largest octagon we have in England; and it is the first of the kind where the roof is built with common sense, rising only a third of its breadth, yet it is as firm as any in England; nor does it at all hurt the walls. Why then does any roof rise higher? Only through want of skill, or want of honesty in the builder'. This Octagon, which cost £977 8s 9d, was built partly by the members, who dug the foundations and helped with the erection.[31] The members of Lady Huntingdon's Connexion in Leeds also built an Octagon, similar in appearance to the others, but crowned by a central dome or cupola; there was a tall, thin Doric column attached to each corner, and a thinly detailed Venetian window flanked by blank circular openings on the entrance front.[32] Its more sophisticated, though less attractive, character introduces the difference between the meeting houses in the remote valleys and moors, and those in the towns.[33]

From the earliest days of Dissent there were architecturally ambitious places of worship. The Unitarians built Mill Hill Chapel, Leeds in 1672 as 'one of the most stately fabrics, supported by a row of pillars and arches'; and in 1690–1 they built another in Call Lane 'with a turret above the leaded roof', pilasters between the two-storeyed bays, and pedimented doorcases.[34] These were on prominent sites close to merchants' houses, and John Cossins's map of Leeds c.1725 suggests that the former was a large building seven bays wide with a projecting central section; presumably, according to Thoresby's description, it had a ground-floor arcade. The Unitarians' building in Bradford was erected in Chapel Lane in 1717 as a plain stone house with mullioned windows and a pair of little gabled porches with columns or pilasters; but its chief interest was that it was furnished with panelling from Howley Hall after the demolition of the great Savile house in 1730, and the members entered through a re-erected gateway.[35] The Unitarian chapel in Westgate, Wakefield, erected in 1752 as a neat brick building with a pedimented gable, a central Venetian window, and two pedimented doors, all with 'Gibbs' surrounds, marks a more sophisticated phase in Nonconformist architecture; perhaps Carr was the designer.

The larger chapels followed an almost identical pattern of a rectangular plan with a capacious tiered gallery supported on thin cast-iron columns. If there was an organ, it occupied the end facing the entrance, and below it was the pulpit. Although the practice of dividing men from women soon lapsed, the custom of providing doors in the two outer bays of the main façade usually continued; in later versions, these led to the gallery staircases, and there was a central door and lobby into the body of the chapel. The erection of a gallery divided the building into two storeys, and the side elevations were usually designed with two rows of regularly spaced windows of equal height. The architectural ornament was concentrated on the main façade, the horizontal division of which resulted in a limited range of treatment.

155

31 *The Bradford Antiquary* (1905),ii,96.

32 The building was taken over by the Established Church in 1794 and consecrated in the name of St James; Parsons, i,430; Whitaker, 70. The church was demolished in 1950.

33 The octagonal form was relatively rare and its use was confined to the early years of Methodism before the final separation from the Church of England, but it was revived in Bradford in 1903 when Eastbrook Hall was designed by W.J.Morley as a large octagon behind an eclectically detailed façade in Leeds Road; this replaced Eastbrook Chapel, designed in 1825 by Joseph Botham of Sheffield with a flat façade and two rows of Gothic-topped sash windows.

34 Thoresby, 4,76.

35 James, 226. The facing illustration is of the gateway from Howley Hall. It had rusticated piers, a panelled frieze, and an open strap-work cresting. There was a similar re-use of material from a demolished house after Lord Houghton's Fryston Hall was dismantled in 1931; the stone, including the portico, was used in the construction of Holy Cross, Airedale.

The most commonly used design for the façades of the larger chapels can be seen as a humble, modest descendant of Lord Burlington's house for General Wade (1723), or Robert Adam's Royal Society of Arts (1772–4), in which a Venetian window, the most popular element in the English Palladian vocabulary, occupied the central bay in the *piano nobile*. In its simplest form, as a façade divided by a string course and displaying a Venetian window in a pedimented central section, the provincial relative of these well-known metropolitan buildings appeared on the Congregationalists' first showpiece in Halifax in 1771–2; Square Chapel, for which Thomas Bradley (who drew the perspective view published in the anonymous *The History of the Town and Parish of Halifax*, 1789) was probably responsible, was built of brick with stone dressings, and on a much larger scale than any previous Nonconformist place of worship. It was an obvious model for emulation by other congregations, but it was not without its critics. To commemorate its opening, a poem was published under the title of *Hhadash Hamishcan: or, the NEW CHAPEL, at Halifax*; its author was anonymous, but it can be assumed the Revd. Titus Knight was responsible for the verses as well as for promoting the erection of the chapel.[36] The long poem, including learned references to Hebrew and Classical authors, is a vindication of the 'vast Expence [of] a House, so elegant, and great'. Square Chapel was a pioneer in Nonconformist splendour, which was to be matched and then excelled during the next fifty years by the Methodists.[37] After John Wesley's death in 1791, the division between his followers and the Established Church which he himself had tried to avoid, soon occurred; the 'Plan of Pacification' adopted by the Methodist Conference in 1795 completed the break.[38]

There is no necessity in this brief account of Nonconformist places of worship to pursue the complications of the Methodist New Connexion and the Primitive Methodists, but each community was building chapels to keep pace with the membership that was increasing at a rate as rapid as that of the populations of West Yorkshire towns. 'Perhaps there is no part of the kingdom in which the Methodists are so numerous, and in which they exert so extensive an influence upon the population', thought Edward Parsons by 1834.[39] Most of the new chapels continued to be built in the plain rectangular box tradition during these years of expansion; Wesley had directed, 'Let every octagon house be built after the model of Yarm; every square house after the model of Bath or Scarborough',[40] but there were exceptions to this rule. Parsons observed that whereas the early members had been 'persons of the humblest circumstances in life . . . now they have among them considerable opulence and high respectability, and many of them are secularly eminent'. This social change was inevitably reflected in the chapels, which became 'truly splendid edifices [transcending] the public buildings of any other denomination whatever'. Wesley Chapel in Meadow Lane, Leeds (1816),[41] in which a central Venetian window was placed over a pedimented porch, represents a common form which could be varied by such additions as the builder of the Wesleyan Methodist Chapel (1824–5) in Horsefair, Pontefract devised; not only was there a Venetian window in the

36 This poem was printed in Halifax by 'E. Jacob, for the Author, 1772', and on its title page is the couplet:
'The Author doubts not, but his Name you'll guess,
As Men are known to Men by Face, and Dress'.

37 When the new Square Church was opened in 1857, the old chapel became a Sunday School. It is still standing (1977) but it has suffered from vandals and its survival is unlikely.

38 Dolbey, op.cit.,117.

39 Parsons, ii,52.

40 Myles,W., *Chronological history of the people called Methodists*, London 1813,426. The Octagon at Yarm, N Yorks was in use in 1764; Bath Chapel was built in 1779, and Scarborough in 1772.

41 As the Methodists grew in number in Leeds, their buildings increased in size and occupied more prestigious sites; from an obscure beginning developed, in ascending order, the Old Chapel (1771); Albion Street Chapel, 'A beautiful structure, completed in 1802, capable of containing a large congregation'; Wesley Chapel, Meadow Lane, 'A handsome building, erected in 1816'. Whitaker, Appendix 30.

156
177

156. Halifax, Square Congregational Chapel; this once-famous building (T.Bradley attrib.1771–2) has become a victim of vandalism and neglect. To the right is the lower part of the tower of the replacement in fourteenth-century style (J.James 1857), which has come to an equally pathetic end.

157. Huddersfield, Queen Street Chapel (1819) illustrates the civic dignity attainable by Nonconformist architecture in the early nineteenth century, equal in importance to the County Court (1825) on the extreme right of the view.

157

42 The builder was William Moxon, and the joiner W. (or T.) Pease, both of Pontefract. The chapel seated 820 and cost £3,706 18s. 8d., but it was too small and in 1849–50 it was enlarged. In 1960 it was demolished.

43 Queen Street Chapel is now an Arts Centre, but its future is uncertain (1977).

44 Jobson,F.J., *Chapel and school architecture*, London 1850,43.

45 Broadbent,G.H., 'The life and work of Pritchett of York', *Studies in architectural history*, op.cit.,ii,110. Ramsden Street Chapel was demolished in 1936.

upper part of the pedimented façade, but below it was a large window based on Robert Adam's design for the Offices of the Paymaster-General in Whitehall.[42] In this case, the chapel must have been the equivalent in scale to St Giles's at the other end of the Market Place, and very little inferior to the Town Hall opposite. It is a characteristic of the early nineteenth-century chapels that they were being built, as Wren had recommended of Anglican churches, 'among the thicker Inhabitants, for Convenience of the better sort'; and many became an 'Ornament to the Town'.

The chapel in Queen Street, Huddersfield (1819) displays this new dignity; set back from the general building line in a courtyard, it is as much a part of the urban quality of the handsome Classical street as is the County Court.[43] Indeed, it assumed the conventional character of contemporary public buildings so that, as an architectural adviser wrote of such designs, 'On looking upon the building (unless an inscription-board was on it) he could not tell whether it was a Concert-Room, a Theatre, a Town-Hall, or a Chapel'.[44] Queen Street Chapel was built with a wide ashlar façade of seven bays, dominated by an enormous overarched Venetian window in the pedimented (but not projecting) central section; the flanking windows are semicircular-headed in the upper storey and square in the lower. When completed, it was said to be the largest of its kind anywhere, with the widest roof span of any ecclesiastical building. It is an impressive, but slightly incoherent assemblage of Neo-classical elements, and its designer is unknown.

Five years after the completion of Queen Street Chapel, Watson and Pritchett's design for the nearby Ramsden Street Congregational Chapel offered a different version of a five-bay façade; it had a rusticated lower half or basement, and Ionic pilasters on the *piano nobile*, the whole crowned by a blind attic and an undersized pediment.[45] It was not entirely successful, and the very similar Queen Street Congregational Chapel in Leeds (1823–5) improved upon it and

158. Leeds, Brunswick Methodist Chapel; a memorable interior (J.Botham 1824–5), greatly enhanced by the erection of a monumental organ in 1827.

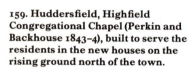

159. Huddersfield, Highfield Congregational Chapel (Perkin and Backhouse 1843–4), built to serve the residents in the new houses on the rising ground north of the town.

added a more sophisticated quality to the arrangement of the few basic elements on the façade;[46] but it was no match for Joseph Botham's[47] Brunswick Methodist Chapel in Leeds (1824–5), proudly dominating the streets of town houses nominally honouring Brunswick and Cobourg, Nile and Trafalgar. This is an exceptionally lavish building, rectangular in plan with a semicircular end, and completely faced in ashlar. The main façade offers yet another version incorporating a large overarched Venetian window, but in this example, the basement is rusticated and the end bays of the *piano nobile* are treated as slightly projecting pavilions with coupled Ionic pilasters.[48]

The interior, a large but comfortable space filled with box pews and an enormous semicircular-ended gallery supported on thin cast-iron columns, was a practical design to accommodate a congregation of around 2,500. The proposal, two years after the opening of what was called 'one of the largest and most magnificent ecclesiastical buildings in the empire', to install an organ which would confirm Brunswick Chapel's pre-eminence, was violently opposed by a number of local preachers; they believed it would be a measure destructive of 'the excellent form of our venerable founder ... at variance with, and subversive of, that spirituality in our congregational worship ... which we believe to be so acceptable in the sight of God'.[49] The instrument was suspected of being an insidious snare 'to please the ear and captivate the passions', and the objectors removed themselves to set up another body, the Protestant Methodists, which has no place in architectural history. The organ was erected in a monumental case, Baroque in spirit and modelled on the magnificent instruments in Dutch reformed churches; at each side of the console, which is screened by an elegant façade of carved mahogany and gilded pipes, there are carved, fretted desks for the leading singers. In the body of the chapel, below this symbol of the West Yorkshire Nonconformist musical tradition,[50] stood a two-decker pulpit raised on fluted Doric columns, surrounded by a gilded, iron balustrade.[51]

As a representative of its kind, Brunswick Chapel was not surpassed by any other in the region, but there were others which were at least the equal of the new Neo-classical courthouses, libraries, exchanges and assembly rooms. There was Sion Chapel, Halifax (1819) with Doric columns *in antis* between pavilions, incised Greek decoration in the fine ashlar, and stained glass illuminating the ceiling; or South Parade Baptist, Leeds (1826) with a convex façade decorated with Ionic pilasters on a *piano nobile* over a rusticated basement, and the similar but plainer Salem Independent, Bradford (1836); or Highfield Congregational, Huddersfield (Perkin and Backhouse 1843–4) with giant attached orders; or Zion Congregational, Wakefield (William Shaw 1843–4), unusually designed with a giant arcaded treatment around the three exposed sides; or East Parade Congregational, Leeds (Hurst and Moffat 1839–41) which was appoached through a hexastyle Doric portico like the one John Clark provided for the Baptists on their Academy at Undercliffe (1831–4), to which a chapel was added in 1839.[52]

46 Queen Street Chapel was closed in 1936 and later demolished.

47 This building has formerly been attributed to James Simpson, I am grateful to Mr Colin Dews (Wesley Historical Society) for giving me the reference to a payment of £300 16s. od. to Botham in the *Brunswick Trustees Minute Book, 1827–1857*, now deposited in Leeds City Archives.

48 Parsons, ii,53. Brunswick Chapel is at present (1977) in a neglected condition, perched unhappily on the brink of a new inner ring road and with a doubtful future.

49 ibid.,ii,61; Scholes,P.A., *The Oxford companion to music*, Oxford 1944,571.

50 Scholes, op.cit.,572, 'On special occasions, as those of the annual missionary services in that chapel whose erection of an organ once cost the society so many members, the singing was ... such as "to lift the roof off".'

51 The two-decker pulpit was remodelled in 1905, incorporating the carved panels and fluted columns in the new design.

52 Clark's work was replaced by Lockwood and Mawson's Gothic design in 1874–7.

158

159

160. Leeds, Friends' Meeting House; the character of Quaker architecture had changed by 1866 when E.Birchall designed the Italianate building which has little in common with the simple eighteenth-century meeting houses.

161. Bradford, Great Horton Methodist Chapel; many buildings were remodelled on a larger scale in the 1860s and 70s, such as this 1814 chapel which was faced with an imposing Palladian temple front in 1862.

162. Saltaire, Congregational Church (Lockwood and Mawson 1858–9). *Quid non Deo juvante* (What not, God helping) was Sir Titus Salt's motto, and in this building, the apotheosis of West Yorkshire Nonconformity, he acknowledged his Divine partner's assistance. The family mausoleum (1860) at the side of the church is an Italian *cinquecento* design with a square dome which is coffered externally.

53 Now the Leeds headquarters of the B.B.C.

54 As an active member of a Congregational community, there was presumably no objection to Pritchett's working for the Established Church.

55 Neale,J.M., and Webb,B.(ed.), Durandus,W., *The symbolism of churches and church ornament . . .*, London 1843,xxii.

56 E (1845),iv,184. A correspondent in the *Ecclesiologist* returned to the attack (ibid.,277ff) with a facetious account of the design and erection of a church, the architect of which, on the day of consecration, 'leaves in the evening in high spirits, in order to meet the committee for erecting a new

160

This Nonconformist expansion and growing grandeur affected even the Friends; their major West Yorkshire building is at Ackworth, where the meeting house fitted in the earlier Foundling Hospital by William Lindley in 1779 was replaced in 1846 by a much larger one in an austere Classical tradition by Pritchett. Then, in 1864, the Leeds Friends, finding their Water Lane building 'so remote from the present dwellings of our members' bought a plot at Carlton Hill in Woodhouse Lane and employed Edward Birchall to design an Italianate meeting house on a civic scale with a dentillated pediment and a Tuscan portico.[53] It cost £14,287, and contained a large galleried room for men and a smaller one for women.

Among West Yorkshire architects, Pritchett designed for the Established Church as well as for the Nonconformists, but that was exceptional;[54] two leading members of the Cambridge Camden Society found it unthinkable 'that any Churchman should allow himself to build a conventicle',[55] and the *Ecclesiologist* reproved Gilbert Scott (who replied at great length) for undertaking a Lutheran church: 'We are sure that the temporal gains of such a contract are a miserable substitute for . . . we must say it, its sin'.[56] In its first volume, that influential publication had firmly declared there was an almost sacred obligation for a church architect to dedicate himself to ecclesiastical work. The alternative was too painful to contemplate: 'Fresh from his Mechanics' Institute, his Railroad Station, his Socialist Hall, [the architect] has the presumption and arrogance to attempt a church. Let it be remembered what a church is – a building set apart for the highest purposes, adapted to the administration of solemn rites, symbolical in every part'.[57] There was no comparable sentiment about commissions for West Yorkshire Nonconformist chapels, which are often closer in architectural character to the Mechanics' Institute and the Railroad Station than to the churches of the Establishment; the sacred Gothic style was used for some important chapels discussed elsewhere in this study, but the exuberant eclecticism that resulted

Baptist chapel, or for building another wing to the hideous Union Workhouse'. The writer concluded by suggesting 'as concerns the education of architects, the best and most correct plan would be to have men educated together upon a conventual or collegiate system, whose education should be not simply architectural, but at the same time, religious'.

57 ibid,(1842),i,70.

58 Holroyd,A., *Saltaire and its founder, Sir Titus Salt, Bart.*, Saltaire 1871.

59 Peel, op.cit.,434 contains an illustration of this astonishing design. A central giant Corinthian colonnade with a heavy, urn-decorated balustrade is flanked by twin towers; the lower stage consists of a Venetian window in a heavily rusticated surround; the intermediate stage is a semicircular-headed window framed by coupled Corinthian half-columns; the upper stage incorporates a pair of semicircular-headed windows with large keystones, a bracketted cornice, dormers, corner pedestals and urns, and a Second Empire slated dome with cast-iron balustrades and finials. This extravaganza was demolished to make way for a modest Health Centre, leaving a void in the town.

60 An enthusiastic, maybe slightly starry-eyed, description of the influence of chapels on society can be found in Kellett,E.E., *As I remember*, London 1936, 'It took, by itself, the place now filled by theatre, concert-hall, cinema, ballroom and circulating library put together. Here were all things required for social intercourse; recitals, songs, lectures with or without the lantern, authorised games and talk. It was a liberal education. Politics were freely discussed, books criticised and lent, music, and that not merely sacred, appraised . . . It may have been a small and narrow society, but it was one which pulsed with life'.

61 Betjeman,J., *First and last loves*, London 1952,103ff. 'They are the public equivalent of the parlour mantelpiece . . . the thresholds of a better world than this, the brick and stone expression of individual conversion and acceptance, not the stilted copying of a religion based on Prayer Books and Missals and idol worship. This was the Liberal vote'.

from the substitution of enthusiasm for dogma and direction produced a richly varied assortment in stone, brick and terracotta throughout the region.

The final major phase of Nonconformist activity began in the 60s, often because of a need for a larger chapel or a feeling that prosperity should be evident. The difference is neatly illustrated at Great Horton where, within a few yards of one another, are two buildings; the Congregational chapel of 1851–2 is still in the traditional square pattern with a central Venetian window, but the Methodist (an 1862 renovation of the 1814 chapel) is a dignified building with a central, pedimented loggia of giant Corinthian columns and flanking wings, deriving directly from a Palladian precedent. Many of the designers of these buildings are anonymous, waiting for a dedicated researcher who will examine and categorise the remaining examples of the 1,100 Sions, Ebenezers, Bethels and Salems that existed in 1891; but the showy, opulent style that might be called 'the Lockwood and Mawson' was a great influence. Following the Italianate taste in civic and commercial architecture, the Bradford firm's chapel designs took on a new grandeur.

Naturally they contributed a number in the Bradford area; the demolished Horton Lane Congregational (built in 1784 as a six-bay wide façade with a pedimented gable), a fashionable place of worship, was rebuilt in 1860–62 with twin towers and cupolas; and Sion Baptist (a plain design of 1823) was rebuilt in 1873 with a heavy Corinthian façade suggesting municipal grandeur rather than worship. They designed Providence Place Congregational, Cleckheaton (1857–9) in a similarly noble style with a Corinthian arcaded façade surmounted by a bracketted entablature and a pediment (a curious combination which exemplifies the increasingly debased Italianate style the firm employed as the century advanced); but their masterpiece is the contemporary Congregational Church in Saltaire facing the gigantic mill in the centre of Salt's empire. At the side is the domed mausoleum of the Salt family and inside are scagliola pilasters supporting a segmental vaulted ceiling; but the most impressive part of the design is the portico, semicircular on plan, and probably suggested by the very similar parish church in Banbury, designed by Samuel Pepys Cockerell (1792–7) and completed by his son in 1822; above the Corinthian columns rises a tower, circular on plan with half-columns, topped by a dome. It is a building designed as the central ornament of Salt's town, and one might speculate how consciously Lockwood was attempting to incorporate what was described as 'the most exquisite example of pure Italian architecture in the kingdom'[58] as part of a Renaissance ideal city translated into mid nineteenth-century industrial reality.

The 'Lockwood and Mawson' style appears in such chapels as Zion Methodist, Batley (1869), the demolished Central Methodist, Cleckheaton (Reuben Castle 1875–9),[59] the now mutilated Roundhay Road Methodist, Leeds (D.Dodgson 1878) and the enormous Upper Independent Congregational, Heckmondwike (Arthur Stott 1890); with their giant orders, porticos, domed and oversized urns, these

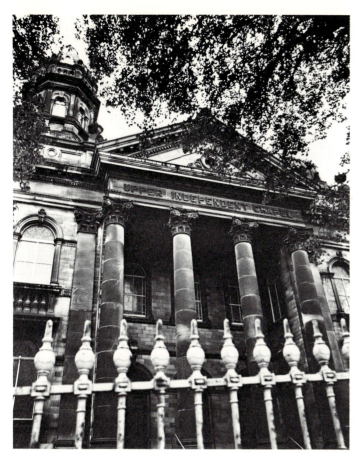

163. Heckmondwike, Upper
Independent Congregational Chapel;
the ambition of congregations in
relatively small towns is well illustrated
by this awesome building (A.Stott 1890).
The graveyard at the side bears witness
to the wealth and solid achievement of
the members who helped to make such
a monument possible.

164. Leeds, Oxford Place Methodist
Chapel; J.Simpson's large but plain
chapel (1835) was refaced (Danby and
Thorp 1896–1903) with a Baroque façade
and a campanile.

164

ornate buildings which appear to be the principal works of their
otherwise obscure designers, flaunt their opposition to the Established
Church with a Baroque rhetoric, even if it does have a Yorkshire
accent. The final burst of this Baroque spirit occurred in Leeds in
1896–1903 when G.F.Danby and W.H.Thorp built a new front to
Oxford Place Methodist Chapel, replacing James Simpson's plain
façade with one in which a pedimented upper storey flanked by domed
cupolas is linked by scroll wings to the lower; there are columns and
broken pediments, and the whole Roman composition is joined by a
quadrant wing to a tall campanile with an open lantern, ornamented
with scrolls and a crowning obelisk.

These architect-designed chapels can be regarded as the basilicas
of West Yorkshire Nonconformity, but like Rome itself every other
prosaic street in Elland, Cleckheaton, Hebden Bridge and all the
towns in the region seems to contain a lesser religious building. They
were the centre of community life,[60] and they shared with the public
houses which were anathema to many members of their congregations
the distinction of being, as Sir John Betjeman wrote in his pioneer
appreciation of Nonconformist chapels, 'the true architecture of the
people'.[61] A basic façade, three bays wide and two storeys high, was
embellished, often with great ingenuity, with an infinite variety of
pediments, giant or superimposed pilasters, brackets, urns, cupolas
and towers. Like the Italian precedents of which these are the humble

207

descendants, all the attention was lavished on the main façade, and the others were regarded as relatively unimportant. Ambitious congregations often attempted more than they could afford and planned for larger numbers than they could reasonably hope to attract except on the important dates in the Nonconformist calendar, Harvest Festival and Sunday School Anniversary; the original builders left a heavy burden for those trustees who are struggling to maintain the ornate fabric and the vast interiors with gigantic organ-cases, pitch-pine pews and spacious pulpits. Of all the building types found in West Yorkshire, the Nonconformist chapel is the least appreciated and the one most likely to disappear; yet it was once the centre of life for a large proportion of the population. Is it because the days of the great autocratic preachers are apparently over? Or because the pleasures of music-making represented by the annual performances of *Messiah* and Stainer's *Crucifixion* have fallen out of fashion? It was for such uses that these auditories 'in which every Person may conveniently hear and see' were built, and although their appearance was probably not in conformity to Wren's ideal, there can be no denial that they became an 'Ornament to the Town'.

How grand the sight! how beautiful to view
The thousands thronging round the churches new;
To see the colours waving on the wind,
The great Archbishop with his flock behind;
To hear the new, the dulcet virgin chime,
Which brings to mind the day of olden time!
John Nicholson, *Lines on the Consecration of St Paul's Church, Shipley*, 1823

The nineteenth-century revival of Church life in Yorkshire is inextricably linked with the revival of interest in medieval architecture. They arrived together to counteract the state of affairs in the Church which Gladstone later recalled as having been 'dishonouring to Christianity, disgraceful to the nation ... our services were probably without a parallel in the world for their debasement',[1] and to correct 'the neglect of the mere fabrics – cathedral, minsters, and parish churches were all falling into decay'.[2] The extensive restorations undertaken in the nineteenth century are evidence of this neglect, but the first signs of a revival that was to be both spiritual and architectural were not encouraging. The First Church-building Act was passed in 1818 in order to ensure 'the education of the poor in the principles of the Established Church', to which the welcome given to Nonconformity in West Yorkshire (where it rapidly gained popularity) represented a threat or a challenge; but the duty of the Church Commissioners, appointed by the King and empowered to draw upon the interest on £1,000,000, was to provide 'a proper accommodation for the largest number of persons at the least expense'. It was not an inspiring injunction. There was to be no 'useless splendour', though Lord Liverpool expected to see 'that decent decoration which would mark the character of the Established Church'.[3]

Early in 1818 the three architects who were officially 'attached' to the Office of Works prepared designs and made their recommendations about appropriate dimensions and materials, and about such important elements as galleries, ceilings and pews; but all those offered were rejected as too expensive.[4] The Bishop of Chester produced a design made by Thomas Rickman,[5] and sent it to Lord Liverpool with the observation that 'churches with the appearance which churches ought to have, and containing 1,500 persons may be built upon an average for £6,000'. But who would define that appearance? Other architects submitted designs, some Gothic and some Classical, but the Commissioners declined to give a firm ruling on the style to be adopted.[6] Grecian for the town and Gothic for the country was

1 Gladstone,W.E., *Gleanings of past years, 1843–78*, London 1879,vi,119.

2 Fletcher,J.S., *The making of modern Yorkshire*, London 1918,215.

3 For a full account of the Commission from 1818 to 1856 see Port,M.H., *Six hundred new churches*, London 1961.

4 Port, op.cit.,38ff. The architects, John Nash, John Soane and Robert Smirke were appointed to the Office of Works pending its reorganisation following the death of James Wyatt in 1813. For an illustrated commentary on the model designs see Liscombe,R., 'Economy, character and durability', *Architectural history* (1970),xiii,43ff, and Carr,G., 'Soane's specimen church designs of 1818; a reconsideration', op.cit.(1973),xvi,37ff.

5 Port, op.cit.,50. Rickman's most notable church in West Yorkshire is St John's, Oulton, built 1827–9 by John Blayds in the grounds of his home, Oulton Hall. The interior is vaulted, and there is a fine west tower with a spire.

6 Nevertheless, they were sometimes tempted to make pedantic observations on designs. For example, Archdeacon Cambridge wrote to the secretary of the Commission of 'a correction that occurred to me in reading over the minute respecting the proposed church at Wakefield – the battlements of which should rather be of the *fourteenth* than the thirteenth century, as the buildings on which they are found are chiefly of the reign of Edward the 3rd'. (Church Commissioners' file 21744,pt.2, 15 July 1819).

7 These extra-territorial churches are St George's, Barnsley (Rickman 1821–2), St George's, Sheffield (Woodhead and Hurst 1821–5), St Mary's, Sheffield (Joseph Potter 1826–9) and St Philip's, Sheffield (Taylor 1822–7, completed by Woodhead and Hurst).

8 See Beckwith,F., *Thomas Taylor, Regency architect*, Leeds 1949 for a full account of the architect's life and work.

9 Trimen,A., *Church and chapel architecture*, London 1849,82f.

10 *LI*, 9 Sept 1811.

11 Revd. Hammond Roberson (who lived at Heald's Hall) was the model for Revd. Matthew Helstone in Charlotte Brontë's *Shirley*. He put down bull-baiting in Dewsbury, defended a local millowner when he was attacked by the Luddites, and delighted in breaking in difficult horses as well as building churches. 'Every farthing of the expense . . . [of Christ Church] was borne, it is believed, by Mr.Roberson alone, the sum total . . . being £7,474 11s. 10¾d. This large sum, too, did not come out of the income of a rich man, but it was the entire savings of his own many years of hard toil'; Peel,F., *Spen Valley: past and present*, Heckmondwike 1893,395. Roberson was also active in the building of St John's, Cleckheaton (Peter Atkinson 1830–2), St James's, Heckmondwike (Atkinson 1830–1), and All Saints, Roberttown (Chantrell and Shaw 1844–6). He is buried in the churchyard at Liversedge, under one of the small, uniform stones that are an unusual feature.

12 Beckwith, op.cit.,25ff.

13 Taylor's letter begins, 'In the church I have had the honour of designing for you, I have, to the utmost of my ability, followed the most simple Gothic style to be met with in Churches and Monastic Buildings in this country; and, I believe, the county of York, can, in this respect, vie with any other district in the United Kingdom. I offer this observation with a degree of confidence and pride, as being the result of visits and numerous architectural drawings, which I have made from these buildings, during the eight years I have been in Yorkshire'.

14 A.P.S.D.,iv,14; see also *B* (1847),v,300.

15 Whitaker, 249.

16 Beckwith, op.cit.,31f; James, 230. Demolished 1878.

17 *LI*,15 July 1816.

18 See biographical information 369ff.

generally accepted as a reasonable compromise, but the Commissioners' churches subsequently built in Yorkshire were, without exception, Gothic. Since the object of the Act was to cater spiritually for the expanding industrial towns, the Yorkshire churches built with the aid of the first Parliamentary grant were inevitably in the West Riding, and out of the sixteen erected between 1821 and 1829 only one in Barnsley and three in Sheffield fall outside the territorial limit of this study.[7] Two architects stand out prominently in this church-building activity of the 20s – Thomas Taylor and Robert Dennis Chantrell. Out of the twelve West Yorkshire churches, seven were the work of Taylor, who was singled out for special praise by Andrew Trimen, an obscure architect who wrote of the 1818 Act's gift of an 'impulse . . . to the study of architectural science, which promises to make this country celebrated as the era when the glorious fanes of the Middle Ages shall be imitated by those whose talents and acquirements have already contributed to the intelligence of the age'.[9] Most of Taylor's churches survive for testing in the light of such an eulogy.

When Taylor advertised his services in the *Leeds Intelligencer* in 1811 he claimed he was able 'to calculate Estimates upon an unerring Principle'.[10] That useful quality, added to his experience with James Wyatt, the restorer of cathedrals, might well have proved an advantage when dealing with Commissioners' churches, but Taylor had already acquitted himself satisfactorily before the Church-building Act. In 1812 the Revd. Hammond Roberson[11] obtained a private Act of Parliament to enable him to build a church at Liversedge.[12] Taylor's opinion was sought about the cost of building in the Gothic style, and his detailed reply reassuringly confirmed 'With respect to the exterior of a Church, much character is to be gained in Gothic, at the same expense, and, in some cases, at *less* expense, than in the other mode'.[13] The Liversedge church, built on a mound surrounded by trees and of a stone which has weathered agreeably, was dedicated to Christ and consecrated in 1816; it was favourably noticed by several writers; one called it 'one of the best formed modern churches of plain character',[14] and another complimented the author on that 'perfect conception of old English models' which enabled him to produce 'beautiful copies instead of monsters'.[15] Christ Church, Bradford (1813–15),[16] for which Taylor provided 300 sittings for £5,000, followed; and in 1816 Taylor advertised his services once again, understandably addressing 'the clergy of Great Britain';[17] ten more commissions followed.[18] Taylor used two basic designs, both favoured by the Commissioners; one was a rectangular body with a tower, and the other a slightly more ambitious transeptal rectangle with a spire (represented only by his churches at Earlsheaton, Huddersfield and Roundhay). The details are a little thin, and the decoration minimal, but the costs were low; they varied from £4 per head to twelve guineas at St Lawrence's, Pudsey (1821–4), which the enthusiastic Trimen thought a model of its kind.

The foundation stone of Taylor's St Mary's, Quarry Hill, which is still a prominent building in its much changed surroundings, was laid

165

165. Liversedge, Christ Church;
T. Taylor's first, consecrated in 1816, was
praised as 'one of the best formed
churches of plain character'.

19 *LI*, 30 Jan 1823.

20 See biographical information 369ff.

on the same January day in 1823 as that of another Commissioners'
church in Leeds, Chantrell's Christ Church, Meadow Lane; side by side
the architects walked in procession from Taylor's Court House,
carrying their plans.[19] Chantrell provided designs for many Yorkshire
churches between 1823 and 1848; Christ Church, a dignified building
with an impressive tower that was a landmark in the town's skyline for
150 years, was followed by almost twenty others.[20] Considering how
many designs he had to supply, working always within a limited
budget, it is a surprising and perhaps unnoticed fact that he was able
to maintain a high standard and a variety of solutions. At times he
used variants; for example, Emmanuel, Lockwood and All Saints',
Netherthong, which were built within a year of one another, are
basically the same rectangular building with side buttresses and a west
front surmounted by a belfry and flanked by battlemented octagonal
corner towers; each has a slightly projecting porch with battlements
and turrets, but the details are all different, and Chantrell changed the

211

silhouettes of the buildings. The west front of Emmanuel is crowned by an ogee, crocketed belfry, while All Saints' terminates in a curiously involved belfry with miniature flying buttresses. Sometimes he used a spire, as at St Stephen's, Kirkstall, and sometimes a tower, as **94** at St Mary's, Honley. Internally, many Chantrell churches incorporate slender cast-iron nave arcades and galleries with traceried or arcaded panels; but different forms of roofing were used. Christ Church, Leeds was covered with lath and plaster vaulting, while timber trusses are **166** exposed in St Mary's, Honley, an elegantly detailed building not far removed in spirit from Georgian rococo Gothick in spite of its relatively late date, 1842–3. St Mary's also demonstrates Chantrell's skilful siting of a church and his ability to use a tower to its best advantage in a 'townscape' sense; in the narrow, picturesque streets and folds of Honley, the tall, thin tower always seem to fit inevitably in the view. His contribution to West Yorkshire architecture has been underrated.

Another architect who had a large ecclesiastical practice in the 20s and 30s was John Oates of Halifax, a Catholic who worked more often for the Established Church than for his fellow-worshippers. Christ Church, Sowerby Bridge (1819), which seems his earliest, is a finely modelled design well above the average; the south front is a graceful essay in the Perpendicular style, and the west tower has a Pennine sturdiness. Like most churches of this time, it was built without a chancel, and with galleries around three sides.[21] Oates's later designs are, on the whole, more conventional than Chantrell's but little inferior in quality.[22]

These churches of the 20s were inevitably governed by the requirement of as many sittings for as little money as possible; yet their architects often endeavoured faithfully to follow the correct models. Peter Atkinson's St Peter's, Stanley (1821–4),[23] for example, introduced polygonal west towers closely modelled on the lantern of All Saints', Pavement in York; and Chantrell wrote to the Commissioners in 1828, 'I have in progress a design in the Early English style . . . partly on the model as far as respects the west front, of Ripon Minster, and the east part a composition from buildings of the same date which abound in this county'.[24] There was a serious attempt at times to follow the local tradition, and both Chantrell and Oates detailed their churches from a closer observation of medieval originals than Taylor. They succeeded in producing a picturesqueness of outline, principally by using richly decorated pinnacles and battlemented parapets, which made their churches positive additions to the skyline of many West Yorkshire towns. Ironically, Chantrell's feeling for an effective silhouette is most strikingly apparent, not in a **140** Gothic design but in the pastiche of a Wren-Gibbs spire he added to Holy Trinity, Leeds in 1839; but St Peter's, his major design, was an important addition to Leeds, and a church which became widely known outside the county. It is also the major West Yorkshire combination of the early nineteenth-century revivals of Church life and medieval architecture.

In 1837 Walter Farquhar Hook was appointed to the living of St Peter's, the parish church of Leeds. It had been described by Thoresby

21 The chancel was added 1873–9.

22 See biographical information 369ff.

23 Largely rebuilt by W.D.Caroe 1911–12 after a fire.

24 Church Building Commission, Minute Book 32.382. In 1846 Chantrell wrote a letter about church design which was published in the *Civil engineer and architect's journal*, April 1846; he added a postscript illustrative of his range of styles, 'I have now some new churches in progress on this principle – 'first pointed' at Halifax; 'second' (decorated), at Huddersfield and at Leeds; 'third' or perpendicular, at Keighley . . . which latter, though perfect as a building must be degraded by galleries, which I cannot acknowledge as in any way belonging to the building'.

in the eighteenth century in Biblical terms as black but comely: 'Unhappily, since his time it has become more black, but certainly not more comely', commented Whitaker, and Hook was not impressed by his new church, which had acquired many additions. Internally, it was a scene of picturesque confusion. There were remains of seventeenth-century paintings on the walls and ceiling, 'a bold oak screen of Italian design, carved and gilded mouldings, and the walls and pillars were covered with mural monuments, escutcheons, etc., and the floors with brasses'.[25] The nave alone was used for services, and it was filled with tightly packed pews surrounding a three-decker pulpit standing in front of the south arcade. The upper part of the nave and aisles was filled with galleries inserted only at the expense of cutting away sections of the fourteenth-century columns, and at the east end the chancel arch had been almost walled up to provide a fixing for an organ gallery. As recently as 1809, the south wall and transept gable had been rebuilt,[26] but within a few months of his arrival Hook was proposing to improve or rebuild his church.

This was not an uncommon situation after the eighteenth-century neglect of the fabric of churches and the attempt to convert them cheaply to accommodate increasing congregations in those parishes which were turning into industrial towns. Leeds was not unique, and the parish churches in Bradford and Huddersfield were both in a dilapidated condition. In 1833 St Peter's, Bradford was repaired by John Clark at a cost of £1,800; he reslated the roof and refaced part of the exterior, using millstone grit walled in such a way that John Ruskin assumed later it must have been the work of railway engineers. Clark also put up a ceiling which covered the oak trusses, an ill-judged addition that remained in position for thirty years.[27] St Peter's, Huddersfield was inspected in 1834 by J.P.Pritchett, who recommended rebuilding the chancel and nave at a cost of £2,000. Work began, but as each part was renewed, a decision was taken to rebuild another, until the whole church had been completely replaced. In rebuilding, Pritchett followed the style of the old church, and when it was finished the Building Committee advised 'those who may be about to engage in building suitable edifices to the praise and glory of God [to consider complete rebuilding] after the best model of church architecture – until their church rises up as Huddersfield has done, excelling in beauty the former Temple'.[28]

After deliberating on alternative proposals for improvements, bearing in mind Hook's belief that a handsome church was 'a kind of standing sermon', the Building Committee in Leeds also decided on complete rebuilding; but what was 'the best model of church architecture' in the 1830s? A few years later, the *Ecclesiologist* (the influential journal of the Cambridge Camden Society which set itself up as a mentor to Anglican church-builders) decided 'It would be difficult to assign any reason why ancient churches should not be exactly copied as models for new ones ... The old churches are everywhere decaying and falling away from time ... They are, in fact, *worn out* ... Yet how well worthy of imitation are the least and humblest of these'.[29] In placing St Peter's in the history of the Gothic

25 Moore,R.W., *A history of the parish church of Leeds*, Leeds 1877,4. Moore was a pupil of Chantrell.

26 A report on the structural condition of the tower was obtained from Charles Watson in 1810. The previous year the south wall had been taken down and was subsequently rebuilt; an account of this appeared in the *Leeds Intelligencer* in 1812. The new work included a window designed by Thomas Taylor, 'a beautiful specimen of Gothic architecture', filled with stained glass by Jacob Wright of Leeds, partly based on a design by Charles Henry Schwanfelder, the Leeds artist who became official Animal Painter to the Prince Regent. It was in 1812 that John Flaxman's fine memorial to Captains Samuel Walker and Richard Beckett, who fell at Talavera, was completed; this was retained in the new church, together with most of the old monuments and some of the glass.

27 James, 207; Scruton,W., *Bradford fifty years ago*, Bradford 1897,15f; Ayers, 28.

28 Broadbent,G.H., 'Life and work of Pritchett of York', *Studies in architectural history* (ed.Singleton,W.A.), London 1956, ii,113ff.

29 *E* (1844),iii,134; see White,J.F., *The Cambridge movement*, Cambridge 1962,95ff.

167. Huddersfield, St Peter; rebuilt (J.P.Pritchett 1834–6) following the style of the old church, and with only one transept.

168. Leeds, St Peter; in R.D.Chantrell's rebuilding (1837–41), the most memorable and individual feature externally is the centrally placed tower on the north front.

169. Leeds, St Peter; W.Richardson's lithograph (1841) shows the chancel, the regularly applied Perpendicular panelled decoration, and the ornate fronts to the galleries which surround the nave.

30 Several of Chantrell's designs and working drawings are in the collection of drawings from the Incorporated Church Building Society in the Society of Antiquaries library. Attached to them are the specifications and tenders for the work of the mason and excavator, carpenter and joiner, plumber and glazier.

31 *E* (1842),i,45. In *A few words to church-builders*, Cambridge 1844,8, it was explicitly stated that unless a church possessed both chancel and nave, 'it is only a preaching-room or meeting-house ... In such a division our ancient architects recognised an emblem of the Holy Catholick Church. As this consists of two parts, the Church Militant and the Church Triumphant, so does the earthly building also consist of two parts, the chancel and the nave; the Church Militant being typified by the latter, the Church Triumphant by the former'.

32 'Church architecture', *Christian Remembrancer* (1842),iii,358f.

33 Jebb,J., *The choral service*, London 1843, 152. Hook found a choral tradition on which to build when he arrived at St Peter's; in 1818 the first surpliced choir in a parish church (six boys and six men) had been introduced. But it was a great advance to establish the professional choir of men and boys, robed and facing each other (Long, K.R., *The music of the English church*, London 1972,326ff.).

34 *Church Intelligencer*, 11 Sept 1841.

Revival, it is important to remember that Hook and Chantrell were deliberately trying to reproduce a complete early fourteenth-century church by rebuilding in a unified style on the foundations of the old, creating a beautiful copy. Most of the fabric of the south and west walls was incorporated in the new structure, although the latter was refaced and new tracery was inserted in the west window; the parapet of the south wall was raised, the mortar being stained with ashes and soot so that it would match the building of 1809, and two new buttresses were added to complete a regular bay design. The east and north walls were rebuilt on their old foundations, and so were the nave and chancel piers. Salvaged stone and slates were re-used in the new fabric, and the old roof trusses were refixed in the nave and, in part, in the aisles.[30] Nevertheless, St Peter's was a new church by the time it was finished, and Hook brought the abandoned chancel back into use to play an important role.

Whether or not to build a chancel became a much disputed question in Church circles. The *Ecclesiologist* thought there should be one, '*at least* one-third of the length of the Nave';[31] yet there was no practical reason for such expense. As the *Christian Remembrancer* reminded its readers, 'our ancestors had monks to fill these seats ... but we have no monks ... First provide your choristers in parish churches, and then we may listen to your injunctions about the miserere seats for the antiphonal chanting of psalms'.[32] But already Hook, a High Church man, had rationalised the use of a medieval building form in the nineteenth century, and of the Catholic plan for the Protestant service. Like his friend John Jebb, Canon of Hereford, he thought the proper place for a choir, instead of being in a gallery at the west end of a church, 'was, and still is, the Chancel';[33] their ideal was a vision of 'white-robed companies of men and boys, stationed at either side of [the] chancel, midway between the porch and the altar, standing daily administering the service of praise and thanksgiving'. To realise this, Hook introduced the 'CHORAL or CATHEDRAL service ... the highest, most perfect, and most ancient mode' at St Peter's, so justifying the expense of a spacious chancel. Despite this important innovation, the rebuilt church retained some of the character it had before work started. One of the reasons for rebuilding was to accommodate more worshippers, something over two thousand, and huge galleries were built around three sides of the nave over the aisles, as well as over the choir stalls in the chancel. The nave aisles were pewed, their occupants facing one another, and as at Huddersfield, the effect of the western half was not unlike a Nonconformist place of worship in spite of the fourteenth-century architecture; yet the *Church Intelligencer* was unstinting in its praise when the building was consecrated in 1841. 'We trust we shall have no more Churches built in the bald and beggarly style of dissenting meeting-houses, unworthy of God and discreditable to those who build them, but of the manner of the magnificent Church at Leeds, which stands a noble monument to the taste, the sterling Christianity, and the old-fashioned piety and spirit of the Churchmen of that town'.[34]

Nevertheless, St Peter's is in some respects an unusual design. The

35 Pugin,A.W.N., *The present state of ecclesiastical architecture in England*, London 1843,19. 'We are glad to perceive that the architect of the new Protestant church at Leeds has ventured to place his tower on the side of the building. This is certainly an advance towards better things'.

36 *E* (1844),iii,3.

37 ibid.(1847),vii,46.

38 In 1861 the interior was renovated by Dobson and Chorley. Some capitals were recarved, some window sills were lowered, and the whole wall surface was treated with 'a patent indurating solution' and then painted. A new window designed by E.M.Barry was inserted, and statues of the four Evangelists were placed in niches flanking the chancel window (*B* (1861), xix,621). Chantrell wrote to the *Builder* (1861),xix,777f., 'Reared in a noble school of architecture, I would not have dared, during nearly half a century of practice, to have thus intruded myself upon the work of any living brother professor. My church at Leeds is but imperfect; but, had I been unlimited, the clerestorey windows would have had pointed arches, and the open roof of oak, enriched with tracery, and coloured wherewith to harmonize the *tout-ensemble*; and the sedilia, with various embellishments, intended, but left undone, would have enabled me to produce a work in 1840 which I could revisit, after twenty years' absence, with satisfaction'. In 1873, a reredos designed by G.E.Street was installed; the cartoons for the panels were designed by Clayton and Bell, and they were executed in mosaic (*A* (1873),ix,29).

39 Stranks,C.J., *Dean Hook*, London 1954, 56.

40 Cook,E., *Life of Florence Nightingale*, London 1913,i,55.

41 Stanton,P.B., *The Gothic Revival and American church architecture*, Baltimore 1968, 32ff. The influence of St Peter's can be seen too in Christ Church, St Lawrence, Sydney, Australia; the building was begun in 1840, but it was taken over by Edmund Thomas Blacket, an architect with Yorkshire family connections, who arrived there in 1843. In his revised design, the seating and choir were arranged on the model of the Leeds church.

42 Pace,G.G., 'Pusey and Leeds', *A R* (1945),xcviii, 179ff.

168 major alteration resulting from the rebuilding is that the tower (originally over the crossing) is placed in the middle of the north front,[35] with balancing chancel and nave to east and west; instead of being at the west end, the entrance doorway is in the central tower, and immediately facing it is a vast Gothic screen in front of the organ, funereally black like the heavy gallery fronts which are a combination of cast iron, plaster and oak. The overpowering importance of the organ was not in strict accord with current thinking, as the instrument was suspected of bringing in 'a showy but hollow secularity without a particle of solemnity or devotion';[36] but Hook had declared he would have a good service 'even if he went to prison for it'. Consequently, the organ (originally intended to be placed over the north doorway) was finally built in the south transept on the cross axis midway between the nave and chancel, and Samuel Sebastian Wesley was engaged to direct the music. The church, which was pronounced 'the first really great undertaking of the present age',[37] was furnished with rich glass, some from the earlier building, some collected from the Continent, and some armorial and commemorating the patrons; and the interior, with **169** sunlight streaming in through the coloured windows and glowing on the heavy dark furnishings, is strangely like an Ackermann aquatint.[38]

'It would be impossible', commented one of Hook's biographers, 'to calculate the vast effect which the new parish church ... and the type of service which Hook instituted in it, had upon the rest of the Church of England'.[39] Hook was in favour of the reintroduction of some forms of ritual, although he prudently refrained from placing statues in the niches flanking the great east window, and there were many interested spectators at the service of consecration in 1841. Florence Nightingale was there, and she observed 'it was quite a gathering for Puseyites from all parts of England. Papa heard them debating whether they should have lighted candles before the Altar but they decided no, because the Bishop of Ripon would not like it – however, they had them in the evening and the next morning when he was gone'.[40] She was interested to see 'Dr. Hook has the regular Catholic jerk in making the genuflexion every time he approaches the altar'. Another important observer was the Rt.Revd. George Washington Doane, Bishop of New Jersey, who preached the sermon. While in England, he made an extensive tour of cathedrals, churches and universities, but St Peter's represented for him a model new church to suit the present thinking about forms of service and ecclesiastical architecture; memories of it helped to influence the design of churches in the United States after his return.[41]

The building of St Peter's was only a part of Hook's energetic work on behalf of the Church in Leeds. 'He found it a stronghold of Dissent', wrote his biographer; 'he left it a stronghold of the Church'. During his twenty-one years as Vicar he succeeded in building twenty-one churches, twenty-seven schools and twenty-three vicarages; but only one of these churches achieved anything like the national importance of St Peter's. That was the church in the 'Bank' district, of which Hook himself laid the foundation stone on Holy Cross Day in 1842.[42]

Three years earlier, Edward Bouverie Pusey, Regius Professor of Hebrew and Canon of Christ Church, Oxford, had written to Hook about an unnamed person 'who wishes in such degree as he may, if he lives, to make up a broken vow, in amount if not in act. It would amount to about £1,500' which would have to be raised out of income. 'Supposing it was ever raised', asked Pusey, 'would it build you an Oratorium, such as you wish?'.[43] It was generally believed the unnamed man was Pusey himself.

A curious suggestion was made that a redundant church in Portugal might be bought and rebuilt in the notoriously squalid and immoral district of Leeds within a stone's throw of St Peter's. Pusey wrote that he could buy one for £3,000, and Hook considered the practicality of floating the material down the Aire for re-use, but the idea died and Pusey decided 'if he cannot get anything from abroad, to begin on a plan which might admit of embellishment subsequently; if he lives long enough he would gladly spend £6,000 on it'. The two clergymen

43 Liddon,H.P., *Life of Edward Bouverie Pusey*, London 1897,ii,468.

170. Leeds, St Anne; the most important item of furnishing was the reredos (A.W.N.Pugin) which was moved to the south chancel chapel in the later cathedral.

218

171. Leeds, St Saviour (J.M.Derick 1842–5); an austere interior enriched by the glass, much of it designed by A.W.N.Pugin. The Pusey Chapel was added in 1890 (G.F.Bodley) and the reredos in 1921 (T.L.Moore).

44 John Macduff Derick (*c.*1806–61) was a native of Ireland. Among the churches he designed are St John the Evangelist, Marchwood, Hants (1843), St James, Birch-in-Rusholme, Manchester (1845–6), St Mary, Eisey, Wilts, and others in Ireland and USA, where he died (*B* (1861),xix,743,753).

45 Liddon, op.cit.,ii,474. The lithograph showing the intended spire is reproduced in Linstrum, 42.

46 The design is in the RIBA Drawings Collection, London.

47 The reredos was installed in the south chancel chapel in the new cathedral built 1902–4. It was given by Miss Grace Humble of Birtley and Leeds, and cost around £600. According to Phoebe Stanton, *Pugin*, London 1971,201, this reredos is 'one of Pugin's finest of its kind'.

corresponded about the design of the church. Pusey, who had already been accused of too close an association with Rome, wanted no galleries and a chancel closed from the nave by a heavy screen. The Ritual Revival which was growing in strength and beginning to cause some uneasiness to men like Hook who followed the old High Church tradition, was inevitably influencing architectural design. John Macduff Derick, a relatively unimportant architect who had built a Catholic church in Banbury in 1835–8,[44] was chosen to execute Pusey's ideas in the new church which was to be dedicated to the Holy Cross; the plan returned to the medieval form of nave, aisles, transepts and chancel. Over the crossing was to be a central tower and spire, although Pusey wrote to Hook that the donor, who was still officially anonymous, 'probably will never be able to build tower and spire . . . handsome embellishments such as a tower and spire ought to be, should be done in a noble way'.[45]

Nevertheless, although these 'handsome embellishments' never were built, and much of the projected decoration was not executed, the building occupies an important place in the Gothic Revival, as it predates the model Ecclesiologist's church. It was one for which there was no real precedent except by reference to the medieval buildings themselves, and Pusey had to work out for himself many of the details of architecture and furnishing. There is little doubt Pugin was a powerful influence on the design of the church, and his 1839 proposal for St George's, Southwark may well have provided a model.[46] In 1842 Pugin made a design for a reredos and screen in the new St Anne's, Leeds[47] and in the following year Pusey was corresponding with another friend about the reredos for his new church; this was to be 'of

170

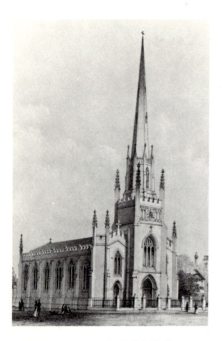

172. Leeds, St Anne (J.Child 1837), a confident expression of freedom to celebrate the Roman Mass, incorporated a western tower and spire.

171

some richness . . . the three richest canopies encompassing the altar'.[48] Pugin himself made his own contribution to what was still known as the church of the Holy Cross; the great west window and those in the south and north transepts dedicated to the Martyrs and the Passion were made by Michael O'Connor to Pugin's design, and in the first he incorporated a representation of the 'Holy Face' of Our Lord.[49]

Finally came the time for consecration in October 1845. The Bishop of Ripon, the see formed in 1836 to take in the rapidly growing industrial towns, refused to perform the ceremony unless the suspiciously Roman 'Holy Cross' was changed to the less objectionable 'St Saviour'. Nor did he like the inscription over the west door exhorting all who entered to 'pray for the Sinner who built it'; but as that had been a condition of Pusey's anonymous gift the Bishop conceded the point. The 'Holy Face' was removed from the west window, and finally the consecration took place in the incense-laden aftermath of Dr Henry Newman's defection to the Catholic Church only two weeks before the ceremony; all the preachers at the services were friends of the future Cardinal.

It is difficult to reconcile the calm interior of the church with all the anti-Puseyite turmoil of the 1840s and 50s, but Anthony Trollope's unpleasant Obadiah Slope represents many clergymen of that time when his 'soul trembles in agony at the iniquity of the Puseyites . . . His gall rises at a new church with high pitched roof; a full-breasted black silk waistcoat is with him a symbol of Satan; and a profane jest-book would not, in his view, more foully desecrate the church seat of a Christian, than a book of prayer printed with red letters, and ornamented with a cross on the back'. On St Saviour's, the cross was raised to the apex of the high-pitched roof, and the result might have been foreseen. In 1851, the year after the restoration of the Catholic Hierarchy in England, Disraeli wrote to Lady Londonderry about the conversion to the Catholic faith of Archdeacon Manning, and he went on to observe that 'the whole of the clergy in one of the principal churches in Leeds have gone over in a body, and part of their congregation. The people of this country are really very agitated'.

The architectural outcome of this mass conversion (slightly exaggerated in Disraeli's letter) was the church of Mount St Mary, an ambitious design on the same hill as St Saviour's and a triumphant gesture from the newly augmented Catholic community. Although the Catholic Relief Act of 1791 had permitted the building of churches provided they were certified by Justices of the Peace and their doors remained unlocked, there had been little change at first in the customary neat, unobtrusive buildings distinguishable from Dissenters' meeting-houses only by a cross on the gable and an altar inside. A steeple or bell was forbidden by the Act, and it was only gradually that a Gothic exterior proclaimed the place where the Roman Mass was celebrated.[50] St Mary's, Bradford was the first attempt, in 1825, at a Gothic church, and then came St Patrick's, Huddersfield, designed and built in 1832 by Joseph Kaye in a thinly detailed style. St Patrick's, Leeds was opened in the same year, and John Child provided a design with lancet windows and turrets. The

48 Liddon, op.cit.,ii,477.

49 ibid.ii,478. Although he had liked Pugin's design, Pusey thought 'the only thing about which one can have doubts is the introduction of the "Holy Face"'.

50 I am indebted to Dr D.M.Chappell for the loan of his unpublished Ph.D. thesis, *Catholic churches – Diocese of Leeds 1793–1916*, University of Sheffield 1972.

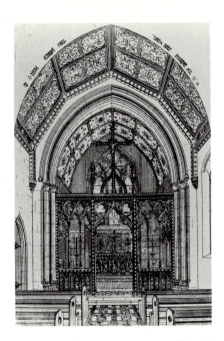

173. Ackworth Grange, the Jesus Chapel;
Pugin's 1841 addition to Mrs Elizabeth
Tempest's house, 'a very faithful
revival' of the time of Edward III.
(Pugin,A.W.N., *The present state of
ecclesiastical architecture in England*,
1843)

51 Waugh,N., *A short history of St.Anne's
Cathedral and the Leeds Mission*, London
1904.

52 Pugin, op.cit.,58 contains Pugin's
thoughts on chancels, including that at
Keighley, 'built precisely after the ancient
models'. The church, which was considerably
altered in 1907 by Edward Simpson, is
illustrated on pl.ix.

53 ibid,96f.pls9,10. The chapel was
demolished in 1966. The altar is now in the
church at Campsall, statues of Christ in
Majesty and the Annunciation are in St
Leonard and St Jude, Doncaster, and the
stained glass has been taken to Durham
Cathedral.

54 See 369ff. for biographical information.

55 Lane Fox,H., *Chronicles of a Wharfedale
parish*, Fort Augustus 1909,52f.

56 See 369ff. for biographical information.

internal gallery had 'richly ornamented panels' and the windows were enriched with borders of coloured glass. Five years later, Child's design for St Anne's, Leeds was chosen in preference to one by Ignatius Bonomi; it was a progressive one for 1837, with a six-bay nave and galleried aisles, a shallow chancel with sacristies and, such was the confidence of the Catholics in their freedom, it had a western tower and spire 148 feet high. Pugin, who provided the design for the reredos, is said to have thought it 'good, for an early attempt'.[51]

In the year St Anne's was completed, the prophet of the revived Christian architecture himself designed a church in Keighley, dedicated to the same saint; a plain little building with a nave, a chancel with a lower roof, no aisles and little decoration.[52] Pugin drew attention to the revival of the belfry as part of a small church 'of exceedingly simple design', and also to the 'small metal tabernacle in the form of a tower' which was a return to the old tradition. He followed a similar model, with the addition of a chantry chapel, in the Jesus Chapel attached to Ackworth Grange near Pontefract, begun in 1841 by Mrs Elizabeth Tempest and intended for the use of her family and local Catholics. It has been demolished, but Pugin left a description of the architecture 'of the decorated period, and to the smallest details . . . carefully and faithfully revived from original authorities'.[53] The interior was richly coloured, 'pricked out in gold and colour; the field [of the ceiling] is painted azure, powdered with stars and suns'. The windows were filled with stained glass, and there were the traditional sedilia, sacrarium, rood screen and sanctuary lamp; 'in all respects', wrote Pugin, 'this chapel presents a very faithful revival of a small religious edifice of the fine period of Edward the Third'.

It was a very different type of church that the Catholics intended to realise in Leeds in 1853 when the foundation stone of Mount St Mary's was laid on ground higher than the site of St Saviour's. The architect was Joseph Hansom,[54] who had already built the monumental St Edward, King and Confessor, at Clifford. In that case he provided the working drawings only for a design made by a young artist called Ramsay who had been discovered in Scotland by Henry Constable-Maxwell of Stockeld Park, on a shooting expedition. Ramsay had made designs for an 'ideal church' in the French Romanesque style during his Continental travels; Constable-Maxwell bought them and handed them to Hansom, and nothing more was heard of the young man.[55] The money for the building of the church was collected by an itinerant priest who was rewarded by such eminent contributors as the Pope and Queen Marie-Amélie of France, as well as many wealthy Yorkshire Catholics. St Edward's was built in 1845–8, entirely of stone with massive columns and semicircular-headed windows and arcades, and it was completed by George Goldie,[56] who added a finely modelled tower based on that of Angoulême Cathedral in 1859–67. The result, especially in its use of Continental Gothic forms and details, was a development in the Revival considerably in advance of its time. For Mount St Mary's, Leeds, Hansom made an ambitious design with nave and aisles, north and south transepts, a chancel, a Lady Chapel, and

221

174. Clifford, St Edward, King and Confessor; J.Hansom prepared the working drawings for this 'ideal church' designed by an unknown young man called Ramsay. Built in 1845–8, it was extended when the west tower was added (G.Goldie 1859–67).

175. Leeds, Mount St Mary; the first architect was J.Hansom (1852), but by 1857 W.Wardell had taken over. The carving of the capitals and corbels in the choir (E.W.Pugin 1866) is still unfinished.

175

57 *B* (1853),xi,,358;(1857),xv,452.

58 *LM*, 30 July 1857; Wardell was the architect of the building from the west end to the transept, the first part of the Community House, a presbytery occupied by the Oblates M.I., and the first part of the Convent of the Holy Family. His designs are in the Mitchell Library, University of New South Wales, Australia (D 381). William Wilkinson Wardell (1823–99) designed at least thirty Catholic churches in England between his conversion in 1843 and his emigration to Australia in 1858; he sold his practice to Hadfield and Goldie. In Melbourne, he became Inspector General of Public Works and Buildings to the government of Victoria (1860–78) with right of private practice. From 1879 until his death, he continued in practice in Sydney and Melbourne. Wardell is best known for his ecclesiastical buildings in Australia, which include many parish churches in Victoria (mainly in thirteenth or fourteenth-century Gothic style) as well as two Catholic cathedrals, St Patrick's, Melbourne (begun 1860) and St Mary's, Sydney (begun 1866). Other works include St John's College, University of Sydney (begun 1859), the English, Scottish and Australian Bank in Melbourne (Venetian Gothic), and Government House, Melbourne (1872–6) modelled on Osborne House as designed by Prince Albert and Thomas Cubitt.

59 *E* (1866), xxiv,359.

60 Edward Welby Pugin (1834–75) was the son of A.W.N.Pugin and took over his work in 1852. After the break up of his partnership with Hansom in 1863, Pugin continued to work independently, designing in a very personal manner.

61 *BN* (1866),xiii,617f.

five other altars; at the west end he incorporated a narthex rather than a porch, thus distinguishing it from an Anglican church.'[57] At the north-west corner he proposed to build a tower with a spire three hundred feet high, which would have been the most prominent architectural landmark in Leeds and considerably superior to that designed for St Saviour's; but neither the Roman nor the Anglican spired tower was built.

At the opening of Mount St Mary's in 1857, only the nave and aisles were completed, and for some unknown reason Hansom had been superseded by William Wardell.[58] The *Ecclesiologist* pronounced the nave 'long, high and broad, and in its way impressive', and looked forward to 'the addition of a good choir, to make up a telling church'.[59] The final section, including the choir, was the work of Edward Welby Pugin,[60] who provided a dramatic, colourful climax to the large body, which has a length of 188 feet, a width of 60 and a height of 83.[61] Glass by John Hardman Powell (a pupil of the elder

176. Leeds, Mill Hill Unitarian Chapel;
an early use (Bowman and Crowther
1847) of the Gothic style by a
Nonconformist community, and also a
very scholarly design.

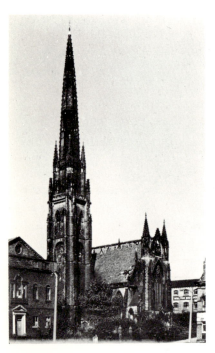

177. Halifax, Square Church; a
fourteenth-century design (J.James
1857) incorporating a tower and spire
235 feet high. Regarded as the model
Congregational church when it was
built, it has been shamefully treated
during the last decade. On the left is the
first Square Chapel (1771-2).

Pugin) fills the tall lancets which reach up into a vaulted ceiling, and the reredos is lavishly faced with marble, alabaster and enamels. Pugin's eccentricities are less obvious in Mount St Mary's than in a church such as Our Lady and St Paulinus, Dewsbury, designed in 1867 as an exaggeratedly tall building raised high above the road on an awkwardly shaped site,[62] and in a personal style of flamboyant Gothic that probably provided a source of inspiration for Edward Simpson, a later designer of Catholic churches (such as St Joseph's, Wetherby, 1880–1). Simpson's eclecticism within a Gothic framework became almost grotesque at times, but it placed his churches in a fascinating category of their own.

There was a certain architectural ambivalence within the Catholic Church. Cardinal Newman admitted, 'however my reason may go with Gothic, my heart has ever gone with Grecian ... We do not want a cloister or a Chapter-Room, but an Oratory';[63] and Cardinal Wiseman's preference for an Italian style was well known. The publication in 1857 of an English translation of St Charles Borromeo's *Instructions on Ecclesiastical Buildings* probably caused deep chancels to be abandoned in favour of Jesuit-inspired shallow preaching chancels, and there were a few attempts to reconcile an Italian plan with a Gothic elevation; but by the late 40s the Gothic forms were being adapted by most denominations for their own purposes. 'They are beginning to love the gothic', commented the *Christian Remembrancer* in 1840 of the 'ambitious gentry' who built Dissenters' meeting houses; 'they are bedizening [them] with all sorts of borrowed honours. Just as in the West Indies a delicately tinted French bonnet and a blonde veil is sometimes seen to hide a sable physiognomy, so do these people throw a screen of buttresses and pinnacles before their sad

62 ibid.,(1867),xiv,313; *Dewsbury Reporter*, 3 June 1871.

63 Davies,H., *Worship and theology in England – from Newman to Martineau 1850–1900*, Princeton 1962,38f.

64 *Christian remembrancer*, (1840),i,478.

65 *E* (1849),ix,144. It is worth comparing this pious reaction to the use of the Gothic style at Mill Hill Chapel with the same journal's comment in 1859 (xx,74): 'Mr. W[illiam] M[itford] Teulon has designed a by no means unsuccessful Butcher's Shop, for Rossington, in Yorkshire ... We are glad to see Pointed features impressed on buildings for every-day use'. Were they serious?

66 *E* (1847),vii,171ff.

67 Henry Bowman (1814–83) and Joseph Stretch Crowther (d.1893) were in practice in Manchester. Among their works are Hyde Unitarian Church (1846–8) which is similar in design to Mill Hill, St Paul's, Stockport (1849–51), St Philip's, Alderley Edge (1851–2), Bank St. Unitarian, Bury (1852), St Matthew's, Stockport (1855–8), St George's, Poynton (1858–9). In addition to the publication referred to in the text, Bowman alone published *Specimens of ecclesiastical architecture of Great Britain from the Conquest to the Reformation*, London 1846.

68 Joseph James was a London architect. He also designed St Matthew's, Smethwick, Worcs (1855) and Spring Hill Congregational College, Moseley, Warwick (1855–6). There is a long description of Square Church in *B* (1857),xv,482. The building was badly damaged by fire in 1970, but the tower and spire are still standing (1977).

69 *B* (1857),xv,482.

and gloomy brow'.[64] Eight years later the *Ecclesiologist* sadly reported, 'The Unitarians of Leeds, *horribile dictu*, are building a meeting-house in florid Middle-Pointed. We hear that they intend to establish in it a kind of choral service, with vestments for their ministers'.[65] Probably a direct result of the work of the Cambridge Camden Society, this exemplified a new direction in the design of Dissenters' churches, which the *Ecclesiologist* interpreted as an indication that their leaders might even be 'good men and good Christians'.[66]

Henry Bowman and Joseph Stretch Crowther[67] (serious Gothicists who published two volumes of measured drawings, *Churches of the Middle Ages*, in 1845–53) designed Mill Hill Chapel, the Unitarians' Leeds meeting-house, as a symmetrical building with a central entrance in a short transept. This gives equal importance to the nave and chancel, in obvious imitation of Chantrell's St Peter's; but there was by no means a general Nonconformist move towards the Gothic style, which was usually adopted only by the wealthier congregations and patrons. In 1857 the eighteenth-century Square Congregational Church in Halifax became a Sunday School when it was superseded as a place of worship by the magnificent building alongside, designed by Joseph James[68] in a fourteenth-century style which combined 'Gothic architecture with usefulness'. It owed its origin, like so many buildings in Halifax, to the Crossley family, to the three sons of John and Martha who had resolved that if the Lord prospered their business they would gratefully tithe their profits. It is well known that the Crossleys prospered, and as a consequence so did the fortunes of Square Church. The new 'miniature cathedral', which cost £15,000 (excluding the tower and spire which were a Crossley gift), was regarded as a model Congregational church. In plan it consisted of a nave with a cloister at each side, north and south transepts, and a tower and bowed spire 235 feet high, described at the time as 'a most conspicuous object to travellers by the railway [which] will always be looked upon as one of the greatest ornaments of the town'.[69] James made use of the design of the east window of Selby Abbey for the 'west front' of Square Church, and he put rose windows in the transepts. Internally, musical angels formed the corbels of the roof, and at the 'east end' an octagonal Caen stone pulpit decorated with the emblems of the Passion stood in front of a large organ case; Gothic tracery panels were incorporated in the pews. Such impressive designs were as much monuments to civic and commercial success as were the contemporary town halls, and they symbolised a direct challenge to the Established Church.

Another Gothic ornament added to Halifax by the Crossleys is Park Place Congregational Church, designed by Roger Ives in 1869 as an essential element in the West Hill Park Estate; like Square Church, it has a large tower and spire at the side of the 'west front'. This became a model form for Nonconformity when there was sufficient money, and examples can be found in most West Yorkshire towns. Outstanding are Brodrick's Headingley Hill Congregational, Leeds (1864–6) with a finely detailed spire; Chapel Lane Unitarian, Bradford (1867–8) by

178. Leeds, St John the Evangelist, Little Holbeck (G.G.Scott 1847–50), based on the Temple Church, London. J.Greig's watercolour shows the interior in 1851, the year after consecration.

179. Leeds, St Thomas (W.Butterfield 1849–52) brought the architect's distinctive constructional polychromy to the town. The buttresses were almost as stark and bare as they appear in this watercolour (J.Greig 1851).

70 Demolished to make way for the new Law Courts.

71 Now used by the Ukrainian Orthodox Church.

72 Sir George Gilbert Scott (1811–78): St Andrew, Cavendish St., Leeds (1843–4), dem: St Andrew, Peterson Rd., Wakefield (1846); St John the Evangelist, Leeds (1847–50), dem; All Souls, Haley Hill, Halifax (1856–9); St Thomas, Manchester Rd., Huddersfield (1858–9); St Mary, Mirfield (1871); All Souls, Blackman Lane, Leeds (1876–80).

73 George Frederick Bodley (1827–1907), born in Hull: St Mary, Horbury (1892–3); St Aidan, Skelmanthorpe (1894–5), St Matthew, Chapel Allerton, Leeds (1897–8); St Edward, Holbeck, Leeds (1902–04). Bodley also extended St Mary, Whitkirk (1900–01).

74 John Thomas Micklethwaite (1843–1906): St Anne, Wrenthorpe (1873–4); St Hilda, Cross Green, Leeds (1876–81); St John, Horbury (1884); St Luke, Sharlston (1866).

Andrews and Pepper in a thirteenth-century style;[70] J.P.Pritchett's Congregational churches at Pudsey (1865–6) and Ilkley (1868); John Gibson's Unitarian, Todmorden (1865–9) endowed as a monument to John Fielden by his sons and planned with nave, aisles and chancel; St John's Methodist, Bradford (1879) by C.O.Ellison, in which the thirteenth-century style was complemented by liturgical services and a choir of men and boys dressed in surplices;[71] and Otley Congregational by T.F. and F.Healey (1899). Sometimes an elaborate 'west front' effect without a tower was used, as in Ebenezer Congregational Church, Dewsbury (1884) by Walter Hanstock, in which a heavily decorated gabled porch and a pair of Flamboyant windows are flanked by octagonal turrets and aisles, or Brearley Baptist Church, nr. Halifax by Horsfall, Wardle and Patchett (1875). Yet even these exceptional examples of Nonconformist Gothic must yield in quality and interest to the churches of the Establishment which were being built from the 1840s.

A region in which Sir Gilbert Scott built seven churches,[72] George Frederick Bodley[73] and John Micklethwaite[74] four each, John Loughborough Pearson three,[75] and William Butterfield,[76] George Edmund Street,[77] Richard Norman Shaw[78] and Temple Lushington Moore[79] two each, is obviously rich in Victorian ecclesiastical architecture; but in addition to these distinguished outsiders there were the West Yorkshire architects themselves. Mallinson and Healey built around twenty-five churches,[80] Perkin and Backhouse eleven,[81] W.H.Crossland ten,[82] and the list of practices which contributed a mere handful is too long to bear repetition. A vision of an endless panorama of towers and spires seems to appear on the horizon, and nothing more than a selective group can be discussed here to illustrate the progress of the pointed arch in the Established church.

The lancets of the Early English style, which were so popular in the Commissioners' churches, were going out of favour in the 40s, but

226

75 John Loughborough Pearson (1817–97): St Helen, Hemsworth (1867); St Margaret, Horsforth (1877–83); St Michael, Headingley, Leeds (1884–5). Pearson also designed the eastern extension of Wakefield Cathedral (see 174).

76 William Butterfield (1814–1900): St Thomas, North St., Leeds (1849–51); St John, Huddersfield (1851–3).

77 George Edmund Street (1824–81): All Saints, Thorp Arch (1871–2); St Michael, Thornhill, nave and aisles (1877); Street also restored St John's, Adel. His son, Arthur Edmund Street, rebuilt a part of Dewsbury parish church.

78 Richard Norman Shaw (1831–1912): Holy Trinity, Bingley (1866–8) dem 1974; St Margaret, Ilkley (1875–9); Shaw also restored St John's, Briggate, Leeds.

79 Temple Lushington Moore (1856–1920): St Wilfrid, Lidget Green, Bradford (1905); St Margaret, Cardigan Rd., Leeds (1908–9). Moore also designed the Priory of St Wilfrid (Hostel of the Ressurection), Leeds (1902).

80 See 369ff. for biographical information.

81 See 369ff. for biographical information.

82 See 369ff. for biographical information.

83 Scott,G.G., *Personal and professional recollections*, London 1879,203; Taylor,R.V., *Ecclesiae Leodienses*, London 1875,381ff.

84 Thompson,P., *William Butterfield*, London 1971,50; Hitchcock,H.-R., *Early Victorian architecture in Britain*, London 1954, i,594ff.

85 Thompson, op.cit.,165f,239;pl.73. Butterfield's drawings are in the RIBA Drawings Collection; see *Catalogue*, vol. B/151.1–4.

86 *E* (1851),xii,69. The black bricks were described as 'a novelty, being unlike the old glazed bricks, as they are black throughout and not glazed'. The floor was paved with red and black tiles. The font is now in the Church of the Epiphany, Leeds. St Thomas's was commissioned from Butterfield by a Leeds merchant, M.J.Rhodes, who had bought several paintings from Friedrich Overbeck (1789–1869), one of the *Lukasbrüderschaft*, or Nazarenes, as they were more popularly called. Rhodes ordered an altar-piece from Overbeck for his new church, and the painter took *The incredulity of St Thomas* as his subject. He worked on it for four years after receiving the commission in 1847, but when the painting arrived in England Rhodes could not afford to pay for it because of the increased costs of the building itself. Butterfield arranged for its sale to A.J.Beresford Hope. It was exhibited at the RA in 1853, and in the Manchester Art

Scott used them in his first Leeds church, St Andrew's, Cavendish Street (1843–4) and again in the unusual church of St John the Evangelist, Little Holbeck (1847–50). 'I well recollect', he wrote, 'when I was, at Holbeck, obliged to build in Early English or "First Pointed", the sort of holy and only half-repressed indignation and pity to which it gave rise'.[83] St John's, the gift of James and Henry Marshall, was based on the Temple Church in London, and its beauties were mainly internal as it was surrounded by factories. It was vaulted with stone, supported on shafts of stone and Derbyshire marble, and richly decorated with foliated carvings in the capitals; Scott contrived to introduce the 'sacred phase' of Decorated or Middle Pointed in at least one side chapel. Butterfield conformed to current taste in St John's, Huddersfield, inaugurated in 1851 when Sir John William Ramsden laid the foundation stone in memory of his father. It was a great social occasion, but Butterfield's design is disappointingly conventional in its fourteenth-century style with a steeply pitched raftered roof and a tall tower.[84] His unfinished, now demolished, St Thomas's, Leeds, begun in 1849, was a far more characteristic example of his individual way of designing.[85] The use of red and black bricks in geometric patterns in the walling was thought to have brought 'an Italian hue and refinement to the coarse and disheartening vicinity of coal-smoke and mill chimneys';[86] but there were no serious imitators of Butterfield's constructional polychromy in West Yorkshire.

There was no absence of size and richness, however. Such impressive churches as Mallinson and Healey's St Paul's, Bradford and St Mary's, Wyke, both built in the 40s, and the later All Saints, Little Horton Green (1861–4), provided opportunities for the introduction of stained glass, metalwork and carved stone; but it was Scott who was fortunate in obtaining the commission to build the outstanding High Victorian church in West Yorkshire in 1856. Edward Akroyd was the patron, and the church of All Souls', Halifax was intended to dominate the town. It was, thought Scott, 'on the whole, my best church',[87] and it also suggests that French Gothic was beginning to influence English designs. The important international competition for the design of Lille Cathedral in 1855 (in which the first prize was won by Henry Clutton and William Burges and a silver medal by Brodrick) had only helped to focus professional attention on French architecture.[88] Scott himself had worked on the Continent, and as usual he took the credit for introducing this wider interest, writing 'I believe my own journeys into Germany: and subsequently into France gave the first impetus in the direction of foreign architecture'.[89] The French influence was at its height in the 60s, as can be seen in such different designs as St Barnabas's, Heaton (1864) with its broach spire and semicircular apse, Crossland's St Stephen's, Copley (1863–5), and George Corson's St Clement's, Leeds (1868).[90]

The signs are there in All Souls', although the design is predominantly in the English manner of the fourteenth century. The commanding site overlooking the town and its Congregational rival in the valley below, combined with the graceful pinnacled tower 236 feet high, make it a memorable church. The west front is faced with

180. Leeds, St Clement; G.Corson's finest church was influenced by French models and by W.Burges, as the detailing in this demolished building of 1868 clearly showed.

181. Halifax, All Souls' (G.G.Scott 1856–9), a proud church commissioned by Edward Akroyd to stand close to his home, Bankfield, and facing the model town of Akroydon. Birnie Philip's statue (1875) of the founder shows him holding a plan of the town.

Treasures Exhibition in 1857; in 1960 it was sold at Christie's, and it is now in the Durrand-Matthiesen Collection in Geneva (Andrews,K., *The Nazarenes, a brotherhood of German painters in Rome*, Oxford 1964,69f.).

87 Scott, op.cit.,176; however, Scott thought 'it labours under this disadvantage, that it was never meant to be so fine a work as it is, and consequently was not commenced on a sufficiently bold and comprehensive plan'.

88 Germann,G., *Gothic Revival in Europe and Britain: sources, influences and ideas*, London 1972,100ff.

89 Scott, op.cit.,202.

90 The church was partly destroyed by fire in 1975 and was demolished in the following year.

91 *B* (1859),xvii,727f. contains a detailed description of the building and its decorations.

92 Scott,G.G., *An essay on the history of English church architecture*, London 1881,1f.

93 His most notable Yorkshire churches are those designed for the Cholmleys at Howsham (1859–60) and for Sir Tatton

182

diapered patterned stone and canopied saints and prophets (for which Scott unwisely selected a limestone which has rapidly decayed), but the colour was reserved for the interior, originally painted by Clayton and Bell. The ceiling was geometrically patterned in pale and dark blues, white, black and gold, and the chancel walls were decorated with painted medallions. Although some of this painted decoration has faded, and some has gone, the stone carvings by Birnie Philip are there to remind the visitor of Ruskin's recommendation to study and imitate natural forms in decoration. The leaves in the capitals are not exotics, but the common varieties of the Halifax district, the ivy and hawthorn, columbine and marsh mallow. The best artists and craftsmen were employed; Francis Skidmore made the wrought-iron screen and gates, and there are polished granites, marbles and mosaics in the chancel and on the monumental pulpit. Clayton and Bell, William Wailes and John Hardman worked on the glass, and Hardman's west window, in which the design of the Last Judgment swirls in a sumptuously coloured movement around the central white figure of Christ in Majesty while the trumpets blow, is a Blake-like vision of great beauty and drama.[91]

Magnificent though All Souls' is, it raises a question of whether one can easily recognise a Scott church. For that matter, extending the question to Scott's West Yorkshire contemporaries, can one easily identify a church by Mallinson and Healey, Perkin and Backhouse, or Crossland, as one can the work of Burges and Butterfield? The answer must be in the negative, even while remembering Scott's cold, noble piles of St Mary's, Mirfield (1871) and All Souls', Blackman Lane, Leeds (1876–80) which is believed to be the final church in the seemingly endless line for which he was responsible, or while thinking not ungratefully of innumerable examples by local West Yorkshire architects, and of St Chad's, Far Headingley, built by Lord Grimthorpe (with assistance from Crossland) in 1868 on the Beckett's estate. Maybe this lack of individuality can be explained by recalling two previous quotations, the obscure Andrew Trimen's belief that the 1818 Act was the beginning of an 'era when the glorious fanes of the Middle Ages shall be imitated', and the *Ecclesiologist*'s thought that 'ancient churches [might] be exactly copied as models for new ones'. Scott himself wrote that nothing was 'more striking at the present day than the absence of true creative power in architectural art . . . Everywhere we meet with reproductions of ancient styles, attempted revivals of lost traditions, nowhere with any genuine power of creating new forms of beauty united to new requirements . . . We must look for this among the unknown possibilities of the future'.[92] Yet, although medieval originals provided the sources, Butterfield and Burges evolved their individual interpretations of Gothic; so did Street, Pearson and Bodley.

Street built nothing of importance in West Yorkshire, although some of his finest early work can be found in North Yorkshire;[93] but until recently Bingley possessed what was called 'one of the best Street-like churches not by Street that exist'.[94] When the young Norman Shaw left Street's office in 1862 and set up practice, one of his

182. Halifax, All Souls'; the wrought ironwork (F.Skidmore), the carved capitals and corbels (B.Philip), the glass (J.Hardman), and the polished granites and mosaics, all combine to create an overwhelming impression of High Victorian richness in the chancel.

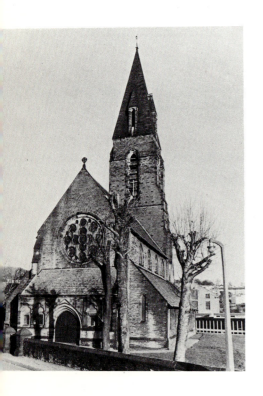

183. Bingley, Holy Trinity (R.N.Shaw 1864) was an austere design in which the lean-to-roofs over the aisles and western narthex seemed like buttresses against the main body, to support the massive tower (1882).

184. Leeds, St Michael, Headingley (J.L.Pearson 1884–6); the cool interior is given a monumental appearance by the stone arches crossing the nave, and by the sharply-cut clerestorey windows. Pearson's alabaster pulpit (1886) and iron screen (1891–2) were complemented by the reredos over the high altar in 1905 (T.L.Moore).

Sykes who built twelve on his Sledmere estates and restored another eight; see Clarke,B.F.L. and Piper,J., 'Street's Yorkshire churches and contemporary criticism', *Concerning architecture* (ed.Summerson,J.), London 1968, 209ff.

94 Goodhart-Rendel,H.S., *English architecture since the Regency*, London 1954, 154.

95 Saint,A., *Richard Norman Shaw*, New Haven 1976,61ff. The church was demolished in 1974.

96 *BN* (1884),xlvii,563;(1886),li,114f. C.R.Chorley was associated with Pearson in the erection of the church, as he was in the restoration of Chantrell's St Peter's, Leeds in 1883.

183 earliest commissions was Holy Trinity, Bingley, for which he took his master's Oxford church of St Philip and St James as a model. Externally, Holy Trinity was a dour stone building, although the west front's narthex and rose window held out a promise confirmed by the quality of the interior and the judicious use of rich materials and Burne-Jones glass. The plan conventionally incorporated the traditional nave, aisles and chancel, and Shaw reverted to the lancet style of which Scott had been ashamed in his Holbeck church; but it was the central tower, massively rising and then tapering until it completely dominated the church and surrounding houses, that made Holy Trinity outstandingly impressive.[95] Owing more maybe to Butterfield than to Street, the tower had been redesigned in 1869 and was a great improvement on Shaw's first proposal. His later West Yorkshire church, St Margaret's, Ilkley (1875–9) is less memorable, although unusual in its wide nave, low pitched roof and feeling of space and light; the Perpendicular style he used in the east and west windows is a relative rarity in Victorian churches.

Pearson's St Margaret's, Horsforth (1877–83) replaced an eighteenth-century chapel with a conventional design distinguished principally by a tall tower and broach spire (built after Pearson's death by J.B.Fraser in 1902) which makes the church a prominent landmark on its hilltop in the Aire valley; the interior is disappointing, but his other replacement in the northern part of Leeds deserves more attention. The old village of Headingley had been chosen as the favourite residential suburb of manufacturers and professional gentlemen, and 'the neighbourhood all around [was] studded with spacious mansions and elegant villas'. The sixteenth-century chapel was replaced by a new church designed by Chantrell in 1837, which was altered and improved by Charles Fowler in 1870; even so, it was too small for the prosperous suburb, and in 1884 the foundation stone was laid of Pearson's new church dedicated, like the previous one, to St Michael. This design was made towards the end of his life and when he had perfected the bold, noble version of thirteenth-century Gothic that appears in its most complete form in Truro Cathedral (1878–1910). The Leeds church, a picturesquely grouped composition like all Pearson's best works, has much in common with the Cornish cathedral; the single west tower closely resembles the twins of the latter in the original design, and in both buildings Pearson achieved a strongly exaggerated verticality by making use of tall, thin buttresses and incorporating in his transeptal façades a pair of high, narrow pointed windows divided by a slender, elongated buttress. Internally, **184** St Michael's is a cool, stone space lit by a high clerestorey and roofed with stone arches and a timber ceiling.[96]

The Pearsonian delight in vertical emphasis appeared for the last time in West Yorkshire in Wakefield. The parish church of All Saints was raised to cathedral status in 1888, and Pearson was commissioned **133** to design a new chancel and transept. In the new work (for which Pearson's son, Frederick Loughborough, was responsible after his father's death in 1897), attenuated slender shafts move gracefully upwards to support an elaborate stone vault designed in the manner of

231

97 Bodley,G.F., 'On some principles and characteristics of ancient architecture', *RIBA Journal* (1899–1900),viii,132ff.

98 Bodley's church replaced a Carr-like mid eighteenth-century building, enlarged and improved in 1840, 1854 and 1866 (the last time by William Perkin and Son).

185. Leeds, St Matthew, Chapel Allerton; a deceptively simple design (G.F.Bodley 1897–8) in which refinement has been carried almost to breaking point.

which the elder Pearson had become a master. The extension was begun in 1904, the year in which Bodley completed his little church of St Edward King and Martyr in Holbeck, Leeds.

'What is the history of architectural art', asked Bodley, 'but the history of refinement in the art . . . What was the one principle that led on from century to century, from style to style, but that of a true artistic feeling, the desire for refinement?'[97] It was in following this principle that he designed St Matthew's, Chapel Allerton in 1897[98] in a fastidious, simplified Gothic manner in which the mouldings are almost eliminated and the elegant window tracery takes on a linear, Beardsleyesque quality. A tall, almost detached south tower rises uninterrupted by any horizontal lines until it terminates in an austere battlemented parapet; extremely narrow corner buttresses add to the effect of height, which is further exaggerated by a central staircase turret ending in a conical roof on which the belfry window appears to

be delicately balanced. 'True refinement . . . denotes restrained power', wrote Bodley; and in St Matthew's gentle, subtly coloured interior he achieved something approaching that ideal in a middle-class suburb.

In his final church design in West Yorkshire, Bodley succeeded in eliminating even more of the traditional Gothic detailing. St Edward's, Holbeck was yet another result of the Anglo-Catholic enthusiasm of the Hon. Mrs Meynell Ingram of Temple Newsam, who was said to have that 'quality of improving, transforming and perfecting a building till it reached the climax of her ideal'.[99] As a memorial to her husband, Bodley had built the church of the Holy Angels, Hoar Cross in 1872–6, and in 1877 he was commissioned to convert the eighteenth-century library at Temple Newsam into a private chapel.[100] The result delighted Mrs Meynell Ingram, especially the Renaissance reredos which in its small way can be related to the large design Bodley made for St Paul's Cathedral; certainly she wrote to her brother of the possible visit of the Dean and that 'St. Pauls may follow at a respectable distance in our wake'.[101] She also delighted in the characteristic blue Bodley used in decorating the chapel, and in the colour of the choirboys' gowns; 'Bodley calls them *red*. All Leeds and all London were hunted for the right shade in vain, but at last a bale was discovered of (what most people would call) a dirty brown, of which Bodley was pleased to approve . . . The masons worked all night and day and the tailors worked night and day, and my Composer worked all day and dreamt of the music all night and the Chapel was finished at last'.[102] Mrs Meynell Ingram continued to support church building and improvements in the Leeds area; Adams and Kelly were employed to design St Mary's, Altofts (1873–90), and Bodley was brought back to extend the chancel of St Mary's, Whitkirk in 1900–01. Finally she commissioned Bodley to design a small church dedicated to St Edward King and Martyr, built in 1902–04 at a cost of £30,000.

There could be no greater contrast than between the great sandstone church at Hoar Cross rising out of the Staffordshire countryside in monumental magnificence, and the plain brick tabernacle in the working-class area of Holbeck. Yet inside St Edward's Bodley created an outstanding example of the calm, serene close of the Gothic Revival which, to use his own words, was 'designed, in an honest spirit, to meet the requirements of the times [and] tries to catch the spirit of old work'. Twelve columns represent the Apostles, yet they are designed not as piers with carved capitals but as integral elements in the graceful, flowing arcading separating the nave from the aisles. Five doorways into the church represent the five wounds of Christ, but such symbolism is not intrusive in this interior which is a product of that simplicity and refinement which come of long experience.[103]

The influence of the Arts and Crafts Movement, which ambitiously 'set itself to undermining the work of the nineteenth century [and] sought to bring back again the quality of prayer, to find out what the new fabric of the world was to be',[104] can be seen in some of Bodley's later work as well as in Temple Moore's designs for churches in Bradford and Leeds; but the most successful and complete fusion in West Yorkshire of the waning Gothic Revival and the new decorative

186. Leeds, St Anne's R.C.Cathedral (J.H.Eastwood 1902–04) is an imaginative building, unconventional in plan and with fastidious detailing of Arts and Crafts Gothic decoration.

99 Meynell, Lady M., *Sunshine and shadows over a long life*, London 1933,143.

100 Gilbert,C.G., 'The Victorian chapel at Temple Newsam', *L A C* (1968),no.62,5ff. Bodley's work was partly removed in 1944, and the Library was restored to its original eighteenth-century appearance in 1975. The reredos is now in the recreated chapel in the basement at Temple Newsam.

101 Garrowby muniments A2/115/2.

102 ibid.

103 St Edward's is now a redundant church and its future is uncertain.

104 Ashbee,C.R., *Where the great city stands*, London 1917,12f.

187. Bradford, Cathedral; the flimsiness of the new work (Sir E.Maufe 1951–65) is emphasised by the rugged, black form of the late fifteenth-century tower in the background.

188. Leeds, St Wilfrid, Halton (R.Wells 1937–9); the pointed arch makes its last, weak gesture in the awkward fenestration of what is nevertheless a strongly individual design rising above the banality of the semi-detached houses surrounding it.

105 There have been assertions that S.K.Greenslade was in fact the designer of St Anne's, deriving from Pevsner, N., 'Goodhart-Rendel's roll-call', *A R* (1965),cxxxviii,262, in which Goodhart-Rendel was recorded as saying 'Greenslade we all admired as a magnificent draughtsman. He did the Leeds Catholic Cathedral'. Dr D.M.Chappell has investigated this, and published the facts about the number of drawings contributed by each architect (*Yorkshire Architect* (1975), issue 45,26f). There seems no doubt that Eastwood was the designer.

106 St Aidan's was intended to have a campanile 200 feet high, ending in a Germanic form of broach spire similar to that at Jerichow, near Stendal. The use of a basilican plan was suggested by the *Ecclesiologist* in 1862 on the commonsensical principle that the most important requirement was that the congregation should be able to see and hear rather than worship in a building of symbolic design but less than perfect practicality. The basilican form of St Aidan's was proposed by Dr Jayne, Vicar of Leeds in the 80s. The furnishings incorporate Mexican onyx, red jasper, Irish green and Belgian blue marbles, pink alabaster and gold mosaic; although such colours and materials have a long tradition of liturgical use, it was apparent the opulent Edwardian decade was not far away when the church was dedicated in 1894. The interior was completed in 1916 when Frank Brangwyn's mosaic decorations in the apse were unveiled.

186 ideas can be seen in the Roman Catholic Cathedral of St Anne, Leeds, built in 1902–04 to a design by John Henry Eastwood.[105] Child's church of 1837–8 had been raised to cathedral status in 1878, but it was compulsorily acquired by the City Council in 1899–1901 for road improvements. Accommodating itself to the site offered in exchange, Eastwood's plan is broad in proportion to its length and departs from a conventional form though divided into nave, aisles and chancel; the effect is more like a centrally planned church, a form which never lost favour with the Catholics. Externally there are tall clerestorey windows with Flamboyant tracery set within large outer blind arches without capitals, and the buttresses and turrets on the west front terminate in free, knuckle-like detailing. The tall sheer tower that owes something to the designs of John Dando Sedding (whose only West Yorkshire church is the small but original St Andrew's, Netherton, 1881), rises from a stark base to an elaborately modelled upper stage and dominates this imaginatively conceived and detailed design.

After St Anne's the pointed arch (flattened though it was in Eastwood's work) declined rapidly. The church-building impetus itself declined, and there were few of the quality of Temple Moore's St Wilfred's, Lidget Green (1905) and the unfinished St Anne's, Cardigan Road, Leeds (1908–09); although W.Carby Hall's St Edmund's, Roundhay (1900) and Walsh and Nicholas's St Matthew's, Northowram (1913) are representative of the good work in an Arts and Crafts Gothic that was being done by local architects. Forms other than Gothic were tried, such as the Romanesque basilica which was the model for the noble, spacious St Aidan's, Leeds (R.J.Johnson and A.Crawford-Hick 1891–4)[106] and St Chad's, Bradford (1912–13);

Sir Walter Tapper used a Norman style for the large church of the College of the Order of the Resurrection, Mirfield (1911–37) which stands dramatically on its hill overlooking the Calder valley as if it were one of the Austrian Baroque monasteries along the Danube. In the 1930s there were experiments; the Church of the First Martyrs, Bradford (J.H.Langtry-Langton 1936) returned to a central plan form well in advance of changes in the Roman Catholic liturgy,[107] and in the Church of the Epiphany, Leeds, N.F.Cachemaille-Day (1938) successfully and apparently effortlessly retained the basic form of a medieval church without making use of any Gothic details. By comparison with the last, quite the most distinguished 'modern' church in West Yorkshire, most of the post-1945 designs already seem dated, although the only important one in which the pointed arch was **130** revived in a conventional manner is St Peter's, Bradford (raised to **187** cathedral status in 1919) which was enlarged in the 50s by Sir Edward Maufe; there was, however, a more individual use of the pointed arch in 1937–9 in Randall Wells's church of St Wilfrid in a Leeds suburb.

188 St Wilfrid's, Halton uneasily overlooks from its elevated site the rooftops of an apparently infinite area of Local Authority and speculative semi-detached housing. The flat stone walls of the geometric form are punctuated by a repeated group of lancets into which a large horizontal window has been awkwardly interpolated, and above the crossing rises a wooden spire emerging from a twelve-gabled base. The result is memorable, though disturbing. It is questionable if St Wilfrid's should be described as Gothic, in spite of the lancets and although it has a nave, chancel and transepts. It is possible to point to its indebtedness to the cubic form used by Lutyens in the 30s, to German Expressionism in the interior, and to a touch of the ubiquitous Scandinavian taste that was so admired;[108] but Wells, who died in 1942, was in a sense the end of a tradition. He had worked for Lethaby,[109] from whom a direct line stretches back through Philip Webb and Street to Scott and the High Victorian supremacy of the revived pointed arch. It was an architectural revival that played an important part in the spiritual and social life of West Yorkshire; its towers and spires were prominent in the skylines of the region's towns and cities until they were gradually obliterated by the commercial and residential blocks of the last two decades. Today, congregations have dwindled and some of the churches referred to in this study have been closed or declared redundant. Some have been demolished, and some have found new uses. In others, the foliated capitals are encrusted with soot, the masonry is disfigured with aerosol graffiti, the windows are broken by vandals, and the doors are shut. Paradoxically, there is a revival of interest in nineteenth-century churches, rivalling at times the enthusiasm of 150 years ago for their relatively few medieval predecessors; but it lacks as yet a complementary spiritual revival to add meaning and life to the vaulted empty spaces, and to counteract the rising damp and decay.

107 'I hope all goes well and that the arrangement of the new Church is winning general approval', wrote Eric Gill to Mgr. John O'Connor; 'I see no hope whatever of any liturgical revival until the Mass is brought away from the mystery mongering of obscure sanctuaries separated from the people by rows of clergy and stuff . . . I don't believe a single atom of good will be done by teaching people the Chant or talking about vestments or Church images until what you have done at the Church of the Holy Martyrs is done elsewhere'. Shewing,W.,(ed), *Letters of Eric Gill*, London 1947,384. Gill made a figure for the church.

108 Pevsner,N., and Radcliffe,E., 'Randall Wells', *A R* (1964),cxxxvi,366ff.

109 Wells was resident clerk of the works at Lethaby's All Saints, Brockhampton-by-Ross, Hereford (1901–2).

8 Building for education

If we look at the benefitting of Church and Commonwealth; wherein can we better imploy our time and study, than in training up of children to become serviceable instruments of much good in both? Nay, should a man but barely respect himself, he may finde it very profitable to augment his learning, and not a little advantagious to the increase of his yearely Revenues.

Charles Hoole, *A new Discovery of the old Art of Teaching Schoole*, 1660

The University of Leeds was established by royal charter in 1904, and four years later Edward VII opened the first new University buildings alongside the earlier, turreted, red brick Yorkshire College buildings which, as Prince of Wales, he had opened in 1885. The architecture of Alfred and Paul Waterhouse called for little comment at the time; the former had done better at Manchester and Liverpool, but these two official ceremonies served to mark the successful efforts of generations of West Yorkshiremen to establish the highest form of education in the region, especially in the sciences and arts related to the major local industries. John Marshall, a pioneer in providing education for working-class children and adults, had proposed the foundation of such a university in 1826, adding to his words a wider concern that there could be no institution 'of more value to society at large, than such as promotes the improvement of the rising generation'.[1] It was a similar concern, arising from the reorganisation of education after the Reformation, that had resulted in the building of free grammar schools in the late Tudor and early Stuart reigns.

Education had traditionally been the responsibility of the Church. In Pontefract, for example, there had been a school connected with an ancient collegiate church of secular canons, and there is a reference in 1267 to the weekly distribution 'to the scholars of Pontefract School [of] 40 loaves'.[2] Such schools continued throughout the Middle Ages; but Henry VIII's closing of chantries also deprived communities of the services of the priests who had acted as schoolmasters, often making use of the chantry as a school in which Latin grammar (and sometimes the rudiments of learning in the native tongue) had been taught. There were established schools in buildings as different as the parish church in Wakefield and the small, isolated Coley chapel. The link between education and the Church continued after the break with Rome, and the foundation of a grammar school was often the work of a churchman, as when Robert Halgate (or Holgate), Archbishop of York and Lord President of the Council in the North, benevolently remembered his native Hemsworth in 1546.[3] Sometimes the foundation was stimulated by a bequest, as in 1552 when Sir William

1 *LM*, 14 Jan 1826.

2 *YAS record series* (1903),xxxiii,ix.

3 Carlisle,N., *A concise description of the endowed grammar schools in England and Wales*, London 1818,817.

237

4 Whitaker, 71.

5 *Y A S record series*, op.cit.,48. In 1564 there was a complaint that 'the schoolmaster which now serveth . . . doth not his endeavour and diligence in the due education and bringing up of children there', and the appointment was given to the Mayor and chief burgesses; hence the 1583 decree. The 'Queen Elizabeth's School in Pontefract' was built in Northgate, but in the latter part of the eighteenth century the school (with an endowment of only £20 per year) fell into decay and was vacant by 1785. A new charter was granted in 1792, and it was resuscitated as the King's School.

6 Cobley,F., *Chronicles of the Free Grammar School at Otley*, Otley 1923,74; Parsons, ii,96; Seaborne,M., *The English school*, London 1971,36f.

7 Salmon,N., *Ilkley Grammar School 1607–1957*, Ilkley [1957],14.

8 Hoole,C., *A new discovery of the old art of teaching schoole*, London 1660,29. Charles Hoole was born at Wakefield in 1610 and was a pupil at the Grammar School. He went to Lincoln College, Oxford, took orders in 1632, became master at Rotherham Grammar School, and later held various livings. He died 1666.

9 Parsons, ii,96.

10 ibid., ii,94f.

11 ibid.,ii,373. This school was added to in the eighteenth century, when a two-storey wing containing repeated Venetian windows in its façade was built backing on to the original.

12 ibid.,ii,374f.

13 ibid.,ii,92f.

14 Hall,I. and E., *Heath, an architectural description*, Heath 1975,33.

15 Parsons, ii,81ff. The school was first housed in an old building known as the 'New Chapel'. The land Harrison gave to the school was part of the estate he bought with his house, Rockley Hall. See Parsons, ii,168ff for an account of Harrison and his benefactions.

16 ibid.,ii,98f; Walker, 367ff.

17 Hanson,T.W., 'Halifax builders in Oxford', *H A S* (1929),256f.

Sheafield (also a priest) endowed 'a Schoole Maister to teach and instruct freely for ever all such yonge Scholars youths and children as shall come and resort to him from Time to Time to be taught, instructed and informed in such a School House as shall be founded, erected and built by the Paryshioners of the said town and parish of Leedes',[4] Inevitably, after the Reformation the parishioners themselves frequently had to take responsibility for building; by a decree of 1583 the inhabitants of Pontefract agreed 'to make and furnishe a fayer schoolehouse',[5] and in 1614 twenty freeholders of Otley petitioned the Archbishop of York, Lord of the Manor, for a plot of land on which 'all we of the jury and the rest of the freeholders in Otley are agreed and very willing that a house for a free grammar school shall be there builded'.[6] Similarly, at Ilkley in 1636, fourteen parishioners undertook 'to pay our proportion towards the erection of a school house'.[7]

Charles Hoole, an ex-scholar of Wakefield Grammar School, wrote in 1660, 'if any one be desireous to contribute towards . . . an eminent work of charity, my advice is, that he erect a Schoole and dwelling house together, about the middle of a Market-Town, or some populous Country-Village . . . and that he endowe it with a salary of (at least) twenty pounds *per annum*'.[8] Most foundations of the sixteenth and seventeenth centuries owed much to private benefactors, to churchmen, local gentry and merchants. Thomas Cave, a merchant of Otley, bequeathed £250 in 1604 on condition the parishioners raised a matching sum,[9] and in 1613 William Lee, a Batley-born cleric, founded a school in that town and endowed it with thirty acres of land.[10] Charles Greenwood, rector of Thornhill and once tutor to Thomas Wentworth, Earl of Strafford, bequeathed a building and land in Heptonstall in 1642,[11] and Matthew Broadley left £40 in his will of 1647, together with other bequests, for the school in Hipperholme.[12] James Margerison, Archbishop of Armagh, built a school in his native Drighlington in 1666, which he endowed in his will,[13] and Lady Bolles of Heath, near Wakefield, endowed the school there in 1660 with £25 12s. 6d. a year for a school master and usher.[14] On a larger scale of benefaction, in 1624 John Harrison 'of my own charge and upon my own land, erected and built one new house, now used as a grammar school' in Leeds;[15] but of all the West Yorkshire gentry, the Saviles were most active in furthering education. In 1593 George Savile gave a close of land in Wakefield, and stone from an adjoining quarry; William Savile 'procured twenty trees to build the schole, the seats and flores thereof', and in 1598 it was confirmed it was 'very fayre builded at the proper costes and charges of Mr. George Savile deceased and two of his sonnes'. The latter were Sir George and Sir John, and all three were commemorated in the inscription carved on the building and embellished with the family arms.[16] In the same closing years of the century, Edward Savile and Sir George Savile joined with Gilbert, 7th Earl of Shrewsbury, to give six acres of land at Heath, Halifax and build on it a school for which Sir John Savile of Methley took responsibility as chairman of the governors.[17]

In his valuable advice to teachers, Hoole described his ideal school as 'a large and stately building placed by it selfe about the middle of

189

18 Hoole, op.cit.,222f. He also recommended the school 'should have a large piece of ground adjoyning to it, which should be divided into a paved Court to go round about the Schoole, a faire Orchard and Garden, with Walks and Arbors, and a spacious green close for Scholars recreations; and to shelter the Scholars against rainy weather, and that they may not injure the Schoole in times of play, it were good if some part of the Court were shedded, or cloystered over'.

19 There are useful accounts of the building of a seventeenth-century school included in Dodd,E.E., *A history of the Bingley Grammar School 1529–1929*, Bradford 1930,31ff.

20 The 1609 building is still part of the school, which was extended in 1848 by Richard Armitage (who said he acted as 'both architect and surveyor'), and again in 1879–83 by W.S.Barber. In 1921 it was handed over to Huddersfield Corporation, and the Borough Architect enlarged it in the following year. Hinchcliffe,G., *A history of King James's Grammar School in Almondbury*, Huddersfield 1963.

21 Parsons, ii,96.

22 James, 199.

the outside of a Town, as near as may be to the Church, and not far from the fields'. His model was more ambitious than any attempted in West Yorkshire; he recommended it 'should be built three stories high … with folding doors made betwixt every Form, as that upon occasion it may be all laid open unto one roome, or parted into six'. Ideally, there should be 'a faire pleasant Gallery wherein to hang Maps, and set Globes, … There should likewise be a place provided for a Schoole-Library [and] the whole Fabrick should be so continued, that there may be sufficient lights and chimneys to every Form and roome'.[18] Those built in West Yorkshire were small and unpretentious, as Hoole must have known. Normally they consisted only of one large schoolroom, and were constructed of stone in the regional vernacular style. They were the work of the builders of the local church and houses, and almost always they were equally anonymous.[19] Almondbury's was a single room with mullioned windows and a stone flagged floor,[20] and Prince Henry's at Otley, built about 1611, consisted of 'a large schoolroom, with a chamber above, and a small room adjoining';[21] the latter is still standing, but it was enlarged in 1790. Bradford's, rebuilt in 1663 on the west side of the churchyard, was described as 'open from the ground floor to its oak roof'; it was lighted by 'a very large ancient window with numerous stone mullions', and there was an 'upper room [which] the head master occupied with his class'.[22] Ilkley's, built *c*.1637 and scarcely altered, is a little stone building with stone slates, and a central door flanked on each side by a four-light mullioned window; Heath's, near Wakefield, built in 1660, is similar but has a curiously deep and massive lintel over the door. Leeds's, dating from 1624 after its removal by Harrison

239

190. Leeds, the old Grammar School; the first building (1624) is on the right, and the 1692 addition, which incorporated a library, is in the left foreground of W.Braithwaite's watercolour.

23 There was painted glass by Henry Gyles in one of the windows, incorporating 'the Founder's Arms, and *Ars Grammatica*', but this was removed in 1784 'and sold . . . to an Antiquary of the Town'. (Thoresby, 83). Photographs taken of the old school after it had been vacated for the new building in 1859 have been used in writing this description, but it is not clear how much work was done (probably by Joseph Cusworth) between 1815 and 1823 when the school was improved at a cost of £1,000. An engraving dated 1822 refers to this work as 'REFECERUNT: AMPLIFICARUNT: ORNARUNT'. Mr A.G. Jackson has kindly shown me a drawing of the 'improved' elevation of the school by Cusworth dated 1822 in his collection.

24 Hanson, op.cit.,256f; Cox,T., *A popular history of the Grammar School of Queen Elizabeth at Heath, near Halifax*, Halifax 1879.

25 Walker, 367ff. The school was reopened in 1896 as the Cathedral Boys' School; it is still standing, but it has been threatened with demolition for about forty years.

26 Priestley,J.H., 'Schools in the Ryburn valley', *HAS* (1951),1ff.

27 Wentworth,G.E., 'History of the Wentworths of Woolley', *YAS* (1893),xii,183. This might have been a refoundation, as there are references to a school at Woolley, at least as early as 1564, and to a bequest of 1710 for endowing free tuition for six children of the poorer inhabitants to be taught English and writing. The eighteenth-century school with six-light mullioned windows, is now a private house, and the present school dates from 1842.

28 Parsons, ii,101f. Another eighteenth-century school, that at Tong built by Sir George Tempest in 1736, is now the post office.

from a converted building, was a single room with arched braced roof trusses; there was a row of three-light mullioned windows down each side and a five-light at each end, all very similar in detail to the nearby St John's church built by Harrison eight years later; probably the same masons were employed. A two-storeyed wing was added at right angles in 1692, the lower room containing a luxury absent from the first schoolroom, 'a Conveniency for a Fire for the Scholars in Winter'; the upper room (which had an oriel window filled with glass by Henry Gyles) was used as a library.[23]

More is known about the building of Queen Elizabeth's at Heath, Halifax. John Akroyd and his brother Abraham were the masons responsible, and the latter drew a plan sent by Dr Favour, the vicar of Halifax, to Sir John Savile in 1597; this was 'not only of the school but of the lodgings for the Mr. and usher, hoping that it will be not only commodious but beautiful'. The timber was given, and the stone and slate were retrieved from a demolished house on the site. The school, which was opened in 1600, was described as 'fair, fine and large, all of Free-stone, with a good School-house', and at the west end it incorporated one of the wheel windows (of the pattern known as 'Apple and Pear') characteristic of the Halifax area and of the Akroyds.[24] Queen Elizabeth's, Wakefield is an unusually large room, seventy-six feet by twenty-three and a half, with five five-light, mullioned and transomed windows down each side. The master resided in a room furnished with 'one faire long joyned table with a forme, one bedstead of waynscott carved and wrought, one writing desk of waynscott'. This room was demolished to make way for a single-storey library in 1717, and although that, in its turn, was taken down when extensions were built in 1896,[25] the old Wakefield school is the most important survivor of the buildings erected in the Elizabethan and Jacobean golden age 'for the teaching, instructing, and better bringing up of children and youth in grammar and other good learning and literature'.

The new schools were not confined to the foundations in which the Classical languages were taught; others were endowed, like that at Barkisland, for 'a competent number of poor children' who had lessons in English from a master whose salary was paid from an invested bequest of £200; a small cottage school was built there by the executors, which was quite overshadowed by a double-fronted house erected for the master in 1787.[26] Eighteenth-century schools were often founded and built at the expense of the local landowner. William Wentworth's endowment at Woolley (1718),[27] Lord Bingley's at Bardsey (1726), Lady Elizabeth Hastings's at Collingham (c.1738), Sir Edward Gascoigne's at Garforth (1757), Lord Mexborough's at Methley,[28] Edwin Lascelles's at Harewood (1768), are typical of those schools where, as at Bardsey, 'the children of the inhabitants . . . might be carefully instructed in reading, writing and the casting of accounts'. Architecturally, there was no difference between those in which Latin and Greek were obligatory, and those where the native tongue was allowed; both were vernacular in form and construction, almost indistinguishable from a Dissenters' meeting house. Nor was

191. Hipperholme Grammar School; built in 1783–4, probably the work of J. Jagger.

29 Houseman, J. W., *Hipperholme Grammar School; tercentenary of endowment 1648–1948*, 1948. An advertisement appeared on 29 March 1783 for 'Carpenters, Joiners, Glaziers & Plasterers' to apply to Mr W. Walker of Crow Nest for a sight of the plan. According to *H A S* (1970),49, Joseph Jagger was the architect, although Pevsner, N., *Buildings of England: Yorkshire, the West Riding*, Harmondsworth 1967,632 refers to a man called Longbottom. A charming coloured aquatint of the school was made by John Horner.

there any real difference between those of the seventeenth and eighteenth centuries, except that the mullioned windows were gradually superseded by sashes, and the carved door lintels by Classical architraves. Hipperholme's, for example, built in 1783–4, is a neat rectangular stone building with a central, projecting gabled porch and bell turret; on each side are three sash windows.[29] Often, as at Wike (another endowment by Lady Elizabeth Hastings 1734), a cottage for the teacher was attached, and exceptionally, as at Harewood, an architect made the design. Carr's building (partly rebuilt 1845), placed next to the inn in the new village, is a single-storey schoolroom with a two-storeyed, pyramidal-roofed pavilion at each side. In its adaptation of the West Riding vernacular to a Palladian taste, it is in harmony with the other buildings in Edwin Lascelles's model village.

241

Two other West Yorkshire villages were built around schools, the weavers' hamlet of Fulneck and the socially superior village of Ackworth which contains the best groups of eighteenth-century houses in the region; in both cases, the educational buildings are of prime importance in the communities. During the eighteenth century, a number of Nonconformist societies established boarding schools in order that children could be brought up according to their families' religious beliefs, untainted by the teaching of the Established Church. The Moravian brotherhood – the Unitas Fratrum – is an international society which, in the eighteenth century, did not believe in close family ties and considered boarding-school education in a community and under constant staff supervision was the best system. Parents who could afford paid fees; otherwise education was free. The brotherhood had made converts in West Yorkshire among the weavers, and in 1744 they began to build a settlement on a steep hillside called Lamb's Hill near Pudsey (to which they gave the name of Fulneck in Moravia), taking over for use two existing houses, one as a dwelling and the other as a meeting house.

In 1746 they began to build a church, a large room with four tall semicircular-headed windows, a gallery and a richly decorated cornice; externally, the ashlar façade overlooking the valley is a handsome design with a central tabernacle in the row of windows, and side wings framed in rusticated giant pilasters over a basement. The design is said to have been made by Edward Graves and his brother from Newark,[30] but their proposal to build flanking three-storey pavilions linked to the chapel by lower wings was not followed when the separate houses for the brethren and sisters were begun in 1748; instead, they were built some distance away on each side as large, pedimented buildings with Venetian windows in the pediments and in the gable walls. Strangely, in spite of being built in a stone area, they are constructed of brick. John Wesley visited Fulneck during the construction of the first building and wrote, 'It is on the side of a hill, commanding all the vale beneath, and the opposite hill. The front is exceedingly grand, being faced with fine white smooth stone'. Experienced in building and knowledgeable about its expense, Wesley tartly added, 'The Germans suppose it will cost by the time it is finished about three thousand pounds. It is well if it is not nearer ten. They are told (and patently believe) that "All the money will come from beyond the sea"!' Certainly, the Norwegian brethren sent timber as a gift to the community in Fulneck for the new buildings,[31] which were finished in 1752.

The long terrace in front of the buildings, overlooking the valley and the newly laid-out gardens, was completed in 1753, the year when it was decided to move the boys from a Moravian school opened in 1748 in Smith House, Wyke[32] to the new settlement in Fulneck; seven years later the girls' school in Chelsea was also moved to the West Yorkshire community, and new buildings were erected for the scholars in 1784–5 and later.[33] They were built in the spaces between the church and the brick houses of the brethren and sisters, and in style they are in the stone vernacular rather than following the more

193

30 Cudworth, W., *Fulneck and Tong, historical account and description*, Leeds nd, 6. Two drawings, at present on loan to the museum at Fulneck, show differing designs, but neither is signed or dated. Edward Graves cannot be traced, but interestingly a letter from B.H. Latrobe dated 3 April 1814 refers to a number of British architects, 'Shaffer, Harris, Wyatt, Soane, Grave, Harrison, Cockerell etc' (Hamlin, T., *Benjamin Henry Latrobe*, New York 1955, 383).

31 Cudworth, op.cit., 6. Maybe a gift of bricks explains why the houses of the brethren and sisters were not built of stone.

32 Waugh, W.T., *A history of Fulneck School*, Leeds 1909, 11.

33 Hutton, R.B.M., *Through two centuries; an account of the origin and growth of Fulneck School*, Fulneck 1953, 14.

34 Hamlin, op.cit.,3ff. The architect's
father, Benjamin, was head of the school at
Fulneck until 1765 when he was moved to
London and placed in charge of all the
Moravian establishments in Britain.
Benjamin Henry Latrobe (1764–1820)
studied in Germany from 1776 to 1784, when
he returned to London to work with John
Smeaton, the Leeds-born engineer, and
Samuel Pepys Cockerell. He went to America
in 1795, and was Surveyor of Public
Buildings of the United States 1803–17.
Among his executed designs are the First
Bank of Pennsylvania (1799–1801), the
Philadelphia waterworks (1799), the Roman
Catholic cathedral, Baltimore (1808–21), and
the Exchange, Baltimore (1816–20).

35 Vipont,E., *Ackworth School*, London
1959; Thompson,H., *A history of Ackworth
School*, Ackworth 1879; anon, *The history of
Ackworth School*, Ackworth 1853.

36 See Nicolson,B., *The treasures of the
Foundling Hospital*, Oxford 1972,11ff.

37 Vipont, op.cit.,19. There is a plan insc:
Ground Plan of Ackworth School Yorks, nd, in
the Yorkshire Archaeological Society (MS
20H). The east wing with cupola was built
1758, the central wing 1759–62, the west
wing 1763, and the colonnades 1765. The
water supply was planned by John Smeaton.

sophisticated model of the first buildings; instead of setting them back
to allow the church and houses to dominate, as in a formal
composition, the façades of the school buildings are on the same
building line, resulting in a long, flat terrace of mixed scale, styles and
materials; but in spite of its architectural shortcomings, Fulneck is
even today a remarkable place of peace and gardens in a panoramic
green valley in the heart of the West Yorkshire conurbation. The
Fulneck school has an unusual connection with architectural history,
as it was in the schoolmaster's house that Benjamin Henry Latrobe
was born on 1 May 1764; his father occupied the pulpit in the church,
and the boy who was to be America's leading architect in the first two
decades of the nineteenth century grew up and was educated in the
Aire valley, visiting and sketching Kirkstall Abbey and other
buildings, until he left the school when he was twelve.[34]

The other important Nonconformist boarding-school in West
Yorkshire was the property of the Society of Friends, although the
building at Ackworth had been erected by the governors of the London
Foundling Hospital in 1758–65,[35] sixteen years after they had started
work on their parent building near Southampton Row.[36] The latter
was designed by Theodore Jacobsen, but the architect of the Yorkshire
hospital was John Watson,[37] who was evidently familiar with the
London building as well as with the type of Palladian country-house
plan in which a central block is linked by quadrant colonnades to side

193. Fulneck, Moravian School; this view of the terrace front shows, on the left, the house built for the Brethren (1748–52) and later used as the boys' school. On the extreme right is the church (1746–8), and between them the additional school buildings (1784 onwards).

194. Shelf, the school built by the British and Foreign School Society (1816).

38 Thompson, op.cit.,22f.

39 Lindley's meeting-house, which was built by Bernard Hartley I of Pontefract (Thompson, op.cit.,31), was replaced in 1846–7 by a new building costing £2,905 13s 8d, designed by J.P.Pritchett, who also planned the Flounders' Institute at the same time. The latter had no official connection with the school, but it was erected for the purpose of training young men as teachers among Friends.

40 There were also notoriously bad schools in Yorkshire, such as Dickens used as a model for Dotheboys Hall; and there were good boarding schools, such as that at Rishworth, near Halifax, built in 1725 as a rectangular stone building with mullioned windows. In 1827 John Oates designed a new school as a central, pedimented block seven bays wide, three storeys high, joined by four-bay wings to dormitories three bays wide and four storeys high. Priestley,J.H., *The history of Rishworth School*, Halifax nd,27f,53ff.

41 Rimmer,W.G., *Marshall's of Leeds, flax-spinners 1788–1886*,Cambridge 1960,105ff.

42 Loudon,J.C., *An encyclopaedia of cottage, farm and villa architecture*, London 1839, 726ff; Seaborne, op.cit.,136ff. Samuel Wilderspin lived in Westgate, Wakefield, where he died in 1866; but 'his efforts were restricted to no portion of the kingdom, but extended to all parts of England, Scotland and Ireland'. His pioneering work in founding schools for the poor was recognised by Sir Robert Peel's government, which granted him an annuity supplemented by public subscriptions.

192 wings. The Ackworth building followed this pattern, in which the main section is thirteen bays wide, with a pedimented three-bay centrepiece, and the side wings are slightly shorter versions of the same composition; all are two storeys high, constructed of stone and, where columns are used, of the Tuscan order. These buildings, described as 'so strong and well constructed that they might be converted into a palace for a nabob or a barrack for a regiment', were bought by the Friends in 1778 and opened in the following year as a school for poor children from Quaker families. In 1780 there were 190 boys and 119 girls, who were given an elementary education which fitted them to be apprenticed to Quaker tradesmen or merchants, or taken into service in their households.[38] The central building was occupied mainly by a hall, forty feet long by twenty-six wide, and boys' and girls' dining-rooms; the west wing was where the girls were taught and slept, and the east was for the boys. The courtyard behind the latter was remodelled and surrounded by a colonnade to form an entrance from the road; probably it was designed by William Lindley, who was responsible for the conversion of part of the east wing to form a meeting-house c.1779.[39]

The schools at Fulneck and Ackworth were isolated worlds, far removed from life in the growing industrial towns,[40] although the Friends had been actively promoting education in Leeds since Joseph Tatham set up a school in the meeting-house in 1757; the schoolroom was enlarged in 1765, again in 1784, and a house was built in 1785 in which pupils could be boarded, but otherwise in 1806 the only education available in the town was at the small Free Grammar School which still occupied Harrison's seventeenth-century building, and at the same benefactor's Charity School where 'a number of poor boys are . . . instructed in reading, writing and arithmetic; the girls, besides being taught to read and write, are instructed in the necessary arts of knitting, sewing, spinning, &c.' Apart from these, there were only Sunday Schools and a School of Industry where fifty poor girls were taught sufficient to prepare them for domestic service. A few years later, John Marshall referred to children who roamed the streets, contracting 'habits of idleness and vice' while their parents were at work, a danger which made a 'moral education' a necessity if the next generation was not to be equally helpless and miserable.[41] It was a situation demanding radically new methods, which affected the size and layout of schoolrooms.

'It is only in modern times that the discovery has been made of the art of teaching children in masses', wrote John Claudius Loudon, who discussed the requirements of the systems practised by Joseph Lancaster, Samuel Wilderspin and Andrew Bell.[42] According to the last two authorities, a rectangular schoolroom fifty feet long by twenty-five feet wide could 'contain as many infants as the most laborious master and mistress can conveniently manage'; and as Wilderspin allowed each child twelve inches of sitting room, such a space could contain from 125 to 150 infants. Bell thought the 'chief and great expense consists in a roof to cover them. The rest . . . is quite inconsiderable'. Schools for mutual instruction were either on the Bell

245

or Lancaster system; the former recommended teaching children in classes forming squares, 'every class . . . saying their lessons at the same time', and each containing twenty-four scholars and a monitor. Lancaster placed the children in rows to teach them in one mass, or at times divided them into smaller groups arranged in semicircles around the room. There were other possible variations of subdivision, but the principle was that one large room should be provided which might take as many as 500 children.

The supporters of Lancaster formed the Royal Lancasterian Association in 1810, which then became known as the British and Foreign School Society in 1814. It was an educational movement closely associated with Nonconformity, and the National Society for Promoting the Education of the Poor in the Principles of the Established Church was set up in opposition in 1811; the Bell or Madras system was adopted as the basis of their teaching method. Joseph Lancaster lectured in Leeds in 1809, and as a result a Lancasterian School was started in the old Assembly Room in 1811; girls continued to be taught there, but a new school for 500 boys was built in Alfred Street in 1812–13 at a cost of £2,100. Thomas Taylor 'gratuitously furnished the plan . . ., superintended its erection, measured off the work, and settled all accounts with the workmen'. Following his example, and in confirmation of a working-class desire for education, the workmen 'in their zeal for the cause, undertook, and completed, their work at less than the current prices'.[43] There were Lancasterian Schools in other West Yorkshire towns; 220 boys were taught in a single-storey building erected in 1812 in Margaret Street, Wakefield close to the fashionable St John's Square.[44] The street elevation of the single large room had a Venetian window in a central, broken-pedimented section, and its architectural character was similar to that of the surrounding brick-built houses. Another was opened in Shelf in 1816; once again it was a single room, built of local stone and having a row of semicircular-headed windows with dressed stone surrounds, and there was a two-storeyed house attached.[45] Yet another was opened in 1818, in Great Albion Street, Halifax, and the Lancasterian system was adopted in a school begun in Bradford in 1816 by the Friends and rehoused in a 'large and handsome structure' in Chapel Lane in 1831; 200 boys, 140 girls, and 130 infants were taught there, and the school was 'free to children of all denominations without distinction'.[46]

The National Society was opposed to this non-sectarian principle and set up schools for the poor which were under the control of the Established Church. One was built in Leeds in 1813, on a site in Kirkgate. Taylor was the architect, but it is not known if he waived his fees once again on behalf of the school described as 'neat and convenient' and costing £1,200.[47] In the same year, the churchmen of Wakefield built the Bell School for boys, and shortly afterwards another for girls in Almshouse Lane.[48] 'A plain brick building', the first National School in Halifax, was built in 1815 behind Holy Trinity church, and in 1831 £1,000 was spent on one in Westgate, Bradford, in which ninety boys and sixty girls were charged 2d per week, and 3d if

194

43 Beckwith, F., *Thomas Taylor, Regency architect*, Leeds 1949,23. The quotation is from the first Report of the Lancasterian School (1814). The building survived in a much altered form until 1975.

44 Walker, 376; Seaborne, op.cit.,148. The building was demolished in the 1950s.

45 Seaborne, op.cit.,148.

46 James, 260.

47 Beckwith, op.cit.,23f.

48 Walker, 376f.

195. Leeds, Roundhay, the school,
almshouses and parsonage built on
Stephen Nicholson's estate in front of St
John's church (T.Taylor 1824).

they wished to be taught to write; and another connected with St
James's church could take forty boys, thirty girls and sixty infants.[49]
A National School was often a large addition to a small town, as at
Honley where the long street front of the 1846 building with five gables
includes such Pennine vernacular details as three-light mullioned
windows with stepped heads. The connection between National
Schools and the Church helped to create a collegiate-ecclesiastical
character for these buildings, which were often located as close to the
church as possible, as Charles Hoole had recommended in 1660; nor
had anyone improved on his practical advice about the use of sliding
partitions to achieve a flexible plan.

The Tudor-Gothic style was becoming regarded as one imparting an
appropriate architectural character to all types of schools by the
1840s. Pugin's all-pervasive influence caused such enthusiasts as
Henry Kendall to plead for 'a return to a better and purer style' in his
1847 publication of designs for schools, and to express his belief that
'the styles of the Middle Ages . . . are best suited for school houses . . .
because the buildings themselves (like the pious and charitable
institutions of olden times) partake, or ought to partake, of a semi-
religious and semi-ecclesiastical character'.[50] He displayed his creed
with conviction, illustrating his folio volume with lithographed views
of little schools with stepped gables, belfries and traceried windows,
each set within a rustic, ivy-entwined frame. Thomas Taylor had
returned to 'a beautiful Gothic style' as early as 1815–17, when he
rebuilt the old Leeds Charity School as the 'New School for Girls' at a
cost of £1,000;[51] and he was probably the designer of the little school
which occupies the central section of the row of almshouses built for
Stephen Nicholson on his Roundhay estate. Humphry Repton
thought, 'if the Gothic character be introduced in any small building,
there is none more appropriate than the schools, which, of late, have
been erected . . . by individuals, as ornamental appendages to their
parks';[52] and it is in that spirit that the long, low building facing the
Leeds–Wetherby road was designed. The ornamental barge boards,

49 James, 260.

50 Kendall,H., *Designs for schools and school
houses, parochial and national*, London 1847.

51 A charity school had been founded in
Leeds in 1705, which was removed to a
chapel in St John's Yard in 1726. In 1815 it
was discontinued, and the endowments were
allotted to the education and clothing of
poor girls to train them for domestic service.
Whitaker, Appendix 27.

52 Loudon,J.C.(ed.), *The landscape
gardening . . . of the late Humphry Repton*,
London 1840,600. As an example, Repton
referred his readers to one of his designs for
Longnor, 'distinguished by massive square-
headed windows, with pinnacles, moulding,
gables, escutcheons, and the lofty enriched
chimneys of former days'.

195

247

lattice windows and tall decorative chimneys add to the charm of the houses and school in their leafy setting close to Taylor's spired church and within sound of the water cascading over jagged rocks from Waterloo Lake to the stream in the valley (which has more recently been replaced by a swimming pool). This is a design in the Picturesque manner of Papworth and Plaw, Lugar and Hunt, which was the basis of many early nineteenth-century schools.

On a larger, urban scale, the Tudor-Gothic style appeared in Wakefield in 1833–4 when the West Riding Proprietary School was built to a design by Richard Lane of Manchester. A Proprietary School was one intended for middle-class children, in which a wider range of subjects was available than those taught in grammar schools, and in which there were no religious restrictions. They were built by shareholders, and the Wakefield school offered three hundred Proprietary Shares of £25 each. The central hall, sixty feet by thirty, in the symmetrical plan was complemented by four classrooms, forty feet by eighteen, on each floor, and eight smaller rooms, twenty feet by sixteen. The school was built on arches, which provided a covered playground and workshops. Externally, the stone-faced building has a central 'King's College Chapel' front, and side wings terminating in pavilions with flat gabled parapets; all the details, including the vaulted corridor, the fireplaces and the iron railings and gates, are in 'the perpendicular pointed mode of Architecture', which Loudon recommended to his readers on account of its *exclusively English* character.[53] The school was offered for sale to Queen Elizabeth Grammar School in 1854, since when it has continued in use as the old foundation's main building.[54]

Leeds Grammar School was still housed in Harrison's small seventeenth-century building (described as 'a veritable old barn, dark, dingy, dusty and decaying') in the 1850s, although the number of boys had greatly increased and a warehouse had been brought into use as an additional schoolroom. The Revd. Alfred Barry (a son of Sir Charles) was appointed headmaster in 1854, and within a short time he had persuaded the governors to build a new school on a site facing the healthy open green space of Woodhouse Moor. The architect was his brother, Edward Middleton Barry, who had worked for Thomas Henry Wyatt before entering his father's office. The first design was for a long, central wing occupied by the lower and upper schoolrooms on two floors; at each end was a cross wing, the west containing a chapel and the east a library which was next to the headmaster's house and dormitories for boarders (although like most grammar schools in large towns, Leeds was always principally a day school). The west wing, and the entrance tower which was intended to be crowned by an octagonal turret and spire, were not built; nor was the proposed arcade along the south front, a modest precursor of the one Barry was to add in 1864 to the west front of his father's Houses of Parliament, but he was able to build a detached chapel in a starved Middle Pointed style in 1862–3.[55] Apart from these omissions, the design was executed as planned in a strongly ecclesiastical character; the lower windows are in the style of the fifteenth century, and the upper of the fourteenth, and there is a

53 Loudon, *An encyclopaedia of . . . architecture*, op.cit.,926.

54 Walker, 372. The schoolhouse in Horbury, built at his own expense by Daniel Gaskell of Lupset Hall in 1842, incorporated a miniature version of the pavilion façade of the Proprietary School in the design.

55 Price,A.C., *A history of the Leeds Grammar School*, Leeds 1919; Barry's original design is in the RIBA Drawings Collection (*Catalogue*, vol.B/57). It is reproduced in Linstrum, 65. The school was altered and considerably extended in 1904–05 by Austin and Paley, and again in 1965 and later by G.A.Burnett and Partners.

196

197

196. Wakefield, the West Riding
Proprietary School (R.Lane 1833–4),
since 1854 a part of Queen Elizabeth
Grammar School.

197. Leeds Grammar School (E.M.Barry
1858–9) was designed in an
ecclesiastical manner reflecting the
ideal education of a Christian
gentleman.

198. Bradford, the old Grammar School; the second building (Andrews and Pepper 1872–4) erected on the site of the first, and in use until the present school was opened in 1948.

199. Halifax Mechanics' Hall (now Marlborough Hall), designed (Lockwood and Mawson 1857) as part of the rebuilding of the Northgate area by John Crossley. The building on the left is the old office of the Halifax Permanent Building Society (S.Jackson 1871–3).

56 Cox, op.cit.,111.

57 Salmon, op.cit.,34.

58 Pickles,W., *History of the Wheelwright Grammar School*, Dewsbury 1973. Extensions were built in 1938.

59 Calderdale Archives Dept., MS diary of Anne Lister, SH:7/ML/E,1834.

60 Busby,A.E., *History of Bradford Grammar School*, Bradford 1969,66.

very positive, almost aggressive, skyline of repeated gables, turrets, pinnacles and a weak spirelet over the 'crossing' of what had turned out to be a cruciform plan because of the excision of the chapel from the first design.

In plan, Barry's school was a novel, impressive arrangement of a few elements, but it was designed for the old system of education; there was only one classroom, and almost all the teaching was done in the two large schoolrooms (each ninety-five feet by twenty-eight) in the traditional manner. When John and Joseph Leeming rebuilt the Queen Elizabeth Grammar School at Heath in 1877–9, they adopted an E-shaped plan, with classrooms placed in balancing wings on each side of a central hall, fifty feet by thirty, which has an open queen post roof. The new building was given an Elizabethan character, 'a feeling having been expressed by some of the Governors for the style of Architecture prevalent in the district at the time the old Building was erected'; and a replica of the wheel window in the first school was incorporated in the gable of the hall.[56] Ilkley Grammar School was rebuilt in 1890 as a similar symmetrical design (C.H.Hargreaves) with a central hall and tower, flanked by plain gabled wings containing classrooms for groups of twenty boys, and accommodation for boarders in houses.[57] A more institutional Gothic design, Wheelwright Grammar School, Dewsbury (J. Lane Fox 1893) has upper and lower halls (sixty-five feet by twenty-seven), but most of the teaching was done in the five or six classrooms opening directly off each hall; dining was in the basement, and there was a lecture room, chemistry laboratory, gymnasium and workshops. Externally, the school has a symmetrical elevation, with gabled central and end bays.[58]

Bradford Grammar School had been rehoused in 1820 in a new building in Manor Row, a single large schoolroom with an elevation made up of curiously assembled Classical details including a Greek doorway tightly crammed in a projecting porch with corner columns. It was designed by William Bradley, whom Miss Anne Lister of Shibden Hall had heard was *'not a man to be depended on – very idle . . . not fit to be an architect'*;[59] that was the experience of the governors of the school, who complained he 'neglected to attend to the building of the new School according to his agreement'.[60] He was paid off with twenty guineas and replaced by Atkinson and Sharp of York. In 1872 this odd building, which did not reflect credit on any of the architects involved, was demolished to make way for a Gothic school designed by Andrews and Pepper on the same steeply sloping site. The first building, reopened two years later, consisted of two large superimposed schoolrooms, of which the upper has exposed timber roof trusses, and coloured glass in the plate tracery windows. The details of the staircase are bizarre, suggesting that the columns and beams are separated by square bellows (made of timber). A tall tower is equally strangely designed as an entrance and two floors of small classrooms; externally it has a corner turret, gargoyles and a gable. The group was completed by a headmaster's house. A poor design, later described as an 'ancient, wandering and dismal-looking pile', it was not improved visually by utilitarian additions of 1874 and 1878

198

250

which provided laboratories, an art room and a gymnasium on the cramped site where the school remained until 1948.[61]

The new Bradford Grammar School was opened by William Edward Forster, Yorkshire millowner, MP for the town, and Vice-President of the Council in Gladstone's 1868–74 Government.[62] In 1870 he had been able to carry his historic Elementary Education Act through Parliament; but although the State's first acceptance of responsibility for education had to wait until this happened, there had been no lack of initiative and self-improvement among the West Yorkshire working classes from the 1820s onwards.[63] Libraries and book clubs were established in connection with a mill, a Sunday School, or a public house, although these benefitted only a relatively small number; but there was little doubt that 'in any of the large manufacturing towns of . . . Yorkshire, a person duly qualified to teach the principles of mechanics and chemistry, and their application to the arts, would find it easy to collect a large class, willing and able to remunerate him for his trouble'.[64] In that belief, Henry (later Lord) Brougham declared in 1825 that 'this is the moment beyond all doubt, best fitted for the attempt when wages are good, and the aspect of things peaceful', to encourage the establishment of societies for the instruction of working men; and it was around 1825 that Mechanics' Institutions were founded in quick succession. In that year they existed in Bingley, Bradford, Dewsbury, Halifax, Huddersfield, Keighley, Kirkheaton, Leeds and Wakefield; and most were very newly founded. Some were established with encouragement from local landowners; in Huddersfield there were donations from Sir John Ramsden and his son. Others were helped materially and morally by millowners and merchants; the Leeds Institute was founded by John Marshall, Benjamin Gott and Edward Baines, father and son, of the *Leeds Mercury*;[65] and Huddersfield's prospered when Frederic Schwann began to take an interest and offer financial help.[66] In contrast to such philanthropic patronage, some were founded by workers themselves; Keighley's Institution was promoted in 1825 by a reed-maker, a painter, a tailor and a joiner; and in the same year a meeting of 'operative mechanics desirous of creating a Mechanics' Institute' in Halifax resolved to found a society for the benefit of their friends and themselves.[67] A number of young working men in Leeds set up an evening school 'for mutual improvement' in the mid-40s, and it was to them that Samuel Smiles, secretary of the Leeds and Thirsk Railway, first addressed the lectures which were to become world-famous when published under the title of *Self-help*.

By 1849, it could be said 'Yorkshire possesses more Mechanics' Institutes, and those, generally speaking, of a more active character, than any other district of equal area or population in Great Britain'. It was not entirely a history of success. There was often opposition from the Established Church, probably because Nonconformists were frequently encouraging and offering help; and the members of some societies quickly lost their initial enthusiasm or were dissatisfied with the type or quality of instruction offered. But on the whole the Mechanics' Institute became an influential element in West Yorkshire

61 A competition for a new school design was held in 1927; the winners were Petch and Fermaud of London, whose entry was described as 'of super-excellent quality, the interior planning deserving unqualified praise'. The foundation stone was laid in 1937, and the school was opened in 1948. As an historical fact, it is probably the last school to be built in this country in a Tudor style.

62 William Edward Forster (1818–86) began his association with Bradford in 1842 when he went into partnership with William Fison as worsted manufacturers at the Waterloo Mill. By 1850 their business had grown to such an extent that they built large mills in the village of Burley-in-Wharfedale, where Forster lived for the rest of his life. He was MP for Bradford from 1861–86, and held the offices of Under Secretary for the Colonies (1865), Vice-President of the Council (1870), and Secretary for Ireland (1880).

63 John Marshall was a pioneer in providing education for child workers. His first experiment was to set up a day school in 1822 jointly with other mill owners in Holbeck, at which local boys and girls were taught to read and write; in the evening there were lessons for pupils who worked during the day. Three years later he also tried sending children from his mills to a day school, but he continued developing his own factory school, adding an infants' schoolroom in 1832 and a juniors' ten years later; John Hives of Leeds, John Wood of Bradford, and a few other industrialists introduced a similar educational system in their factories, which helped remedy the widespread illiteracy.

64 Brougham, H., *Practical observations upon the education of the people, addressed to the working classes and their employers*, London 1825, 27; see also Hole, J., *Light, more Light! on the present state of education amongst the working classes of Leeds*, London 1860.

65 Tylecote, M., *The Mechanics' Institutes of Lancashire and Yorkshire before 1851*, Manchester 1957, 57.

66 ibid., 192

67 ibid., 225.

life as well as an ornament to the towns. The architectural evolution of the Institute closely paralleled that of the Nonconformist chapel. The Bradford Institute, reformed in 1832 after an earlier false start in 1825, moved quickly from hired rooms in Piccadilly to Albion Court, then to Kirkgate, until 1839–40 when Perkin and Backhouse designed a new building at the junction of Leeds Road and Well Street. It was a modest one, with Doric pilasters on the elevation, behind which were a lecture-room, a reading-room and a library containing 10,000 books; yet it taxed the resources of the Institute, and the secretary was more than once threatened with arrest for unpaid accounts. The Keighley Institution, founded in 1825, at first used a room in the Grammar School; but in 1835 a small stone building was erected with three cottages and two shops in a semi-basement to provide an income to sustain the lecture-room, reading-room and library above. The cost was over £1,000, and the building, the work of John Bradley (a local house and sign painter), was a plain one with two doors and an inscribed tablet flanked by scrolls on the blocking course.

The Institute in Halifax was founded in 1825 in the Woolshops, where it was said 'to have exerted a highly beneficial influence upon the town, and is patronized by the most respectable inhabitants of the vicinity'; and the Leeds Institute, also founded in 1825, made use of 'a large lecture room and a tolerably good room for a library . . . in an exceedingly confined and remote situation, at the back of Park Row'.[68] None of the West Yorkshire Institutes possessed a building of any architectural distinction until the 1850s, when a new Mechanics'
199 Hall (opened in 1857) was included in John Crossley's rebuilding of the Northgate area in Halifax. Lockwood and Mawson provided a design for what must have been the first Institute to be built on a civic scale and on a prominent central site. Externally, it is in the firm's *palazzo* style, with engaged Corinthian columns *in antis* and semicircular-headed windows with enriched tympana on the *piano nobile*; internally, the principal room is a large hall with Corinthian pilasters and a coffered, segmental ceiling.[69]

Two years later, in 1859, Huddersfield acquired an impressive three-
200 bayed Mechanics' Institution in Northumberland Street. Once again, it was Italianate in style, designed by Travis and Mangnell of Manchester. It is an extraordinary comment on the change in the status of working-class education that such Institutes should have been opened around thirty years after the first penurious movements towards self-improvement.

In 1860, the *Builder* was writing about the designs submitted in competition for a new Institute in Leeds on an important site close to the newly completed Town Hall. 'We have been accustomed to regard mechanics' institutions as standing illustrations of the utter sacrifice of feeling to apparent use; of beauty and elegance to commodious utility. This is necessarily the case in the management of these institutions; and unnecessarily, though almost invariably, evident in the architectural features of the buildings erected for, or adapted to, mechanics' institutions'.[70] The controversial correspondence which appeared in the *Builder* after Cuthbert

68 Parsons, ii,104. In 1834 there was optimism that 'this excellent institution is likely to have a building corresponding with its claims upon the public liberality, and with the wealth, intelligence and importance of the town . . . We understand that a very eligible site can be procured in Park-Row, . . . and we are certain that the munificence of its inhabitants will soon place its Mechanics' Institution, both in external appearance and internal convenience, on a par with any other edifice reared for a similar purpose in the kingdom'; but it was another thirty years before this ambition was realised.

69 The building is now known as Marlborough Hall.

70 *B* (1860),xviii,831.

200. Huddersfield Mechanics'
Institution (Travis and Mangnell 1859).

201. Leeds Mechanics' Institute
(C.Brodrick 1860–5), a palatial
monument to self-help in education
(now the Civic Theatre).

202. Saltaire, the Institute (Lockwood
and Mawson 1872) was 'intended to
supply the advantages of a public house
without its evils . . . provision is made for
intelligent recreation'.

71 The Institute is now used as the Civic
Theatre.

72 See Linstrum,D., 'Cuthbert Broderick;
an interpretation of a Victorian architect',
Journal of the Royal Society of Arts (1971),
cxix,85, for a discussion of the Manchester
Town Hall design in relation to Brodrick's
other work.

73 The Institute has been demolished; see
Ayers, 23.

74 Smiles,S., *The diffusion of political
knowledge among the working classes*, Leeds
1842,18. The Keighley Institute was
described as 'one of the most pleasing and
striking buildings of the kind in the country'.
It incorporated a lecture room for 700,
reading room, library, news room and
conversation area, and it was linked to the
School of Art on the upper floor.

Brodrick's design had been selected is referred to elsewhere in this
study, but it is more relevant here to quote the journal's opinion that
the 'internal arrangements . . . appear, except in some slight
particulars, all that could be desired', while its external appearance
was of a 'grand and well-designed structure', except for the upper part
of the building which, after its inevitable blackening by smoke, would
be 'like a huge leaden coffin, sepulchral, heavy, and excessively ugly'.
Only Brodrick could have taken a utilitarian design consisting of a
lecture room, gallery, art-studios and classrooms, and made of it a
magnificent palace; it was essential that he should achieve a great

201 height in order to incorporate the awesomely grand entrance with
giant order pilasters and a richly sculptured tympanum allegorically
commemorating those trades and industries to which the building was
to be consecrated. The illusion of height is further increased by setting
the main rooms over a rusticated, battered basement which provides a
gigantic podium for the arcaded wall which was probably suggested by
Labrouste's Bibliothèque Sainte-Geneviève in Paris; but in spite of
some echoes of contemporary Second-Empire architecture, the
Institute is yet another example of Brodrick's command of the mass of
a building and of his idiosyncratic interpretation of the grammar of
Classical architecture. [71]

The Leeds Institute was not built until 1865, by which time
Brodrick was occupied with the erection of the Grand Hotel,
Scarborough and entering on the last years of his professional life
which were marked by ever grander, always rejected, competitive
designs culminating in the stupendously megalomaniacal proposal for
Manchester Town Hall at the end of 1866. [72] No other West Yorkshire
architects could match his confidence, but some attempted. The new
Bradford Institute, designed by Andrews and Pepper in 1870 for an
island site in the centre of the town, used a composition of elements
not unlike Brodrick's; there was a large, exaggeratedly tall central
feature (in fact, an elongated Venetian window rising out of a
balconied doorway), flanked by a series of semicircular-headed
windows which were contained within heavily accented pilastered
corners. But the effect, although conventionally impressive, was dull
and ponderous. [73] Such buildings, including Brodrick's in Leeds,
Waterhouse's in Bingley (1864), and the aggressively Gothic
Institution in Keighley as rebuilt in 1868 to a design by Lockwood and
Mawson might explain why it was claimed that working men
sometimes hesitated to cross the thresholds of the buildings erected for
them; well-meaning but excessive patronage, which was responsible
for these monumental Institutes, was not likely to encourage 'the
intelligent portion of the working-classes [who] hate patronage of any
kind. They are in love with self-government and self-governing
institutions; and they are not likely to become general supporters of
societies in the conduct and management of which they have so little
interest'. [74]

Saltaire in 1872 neatly epitomises the best of elementary and adult
education at an historic time. The centre of the model town (rivalling
the nucleus formed by the mill and the Congregational church) consists

75 Balgarnie,R., *Sir Titus Salt, Baronet; his life and lessons*, London 1877, 136f,228. 'When the Education Act of 1870 came into force, Board schools were erected for the district in the neighbourhood of Saltaire; Mr. Salt therefore resolved to give up his elementary schools, and turn the buildings into middle-class schools ... together with the Club and Institute ... for the promotion and encouragement of education in its advanced branches. These premises have been left in the hands of a board of governors, chosen by the ratepayers of Shipley, and henceforth will be known as "The Salt Schools, Shipley".'

of two symmetrical buildings guarded by Thomas Milnes's lions representing Vigilance and Determination, War and Peace, which face one another across lawns, flower beds and lines of trees; the school of 1868 and the Institute of 1872, both designed by Lockwood and Mawson. The school was planned to accommodate seven hundred and fifty children in the two principal schoolrooms (each eighty feet by twenty) for boys and girls, and the central smaller room for infants. Externally, it is composed of three pedimented pavilions incorporating Venetian windows, tympana decorated with foliage and an entwined T S, and a large bell turret on which are figures of a boy and a girl. The Institute is a much richer design, three storeys high, with a central tower; Milnes's figures of Art and Science over the door prepared the working man to make the best use of the reading-room, library, and the Victoria Hall which could seat eight hundred. There was a smaller lecture room, two art rooms, a laboratory and a gymnasium, in what was intended to be a place where the employees in the Salt empire could 'resort for conversation, business, recreation, and refreshment, as well as for education – elementary, technical, and scientific'.[75]

By the time the Institute was opened in 1872, there had been a significant change in the official attitude towards education. In 1870, Salt's successor as M P for Bradford, W.E.Forster, introduced the Elementary Education Act which established School Boards throughout the country and resulted in an unprecedented educational

202

building programme. 'School-houses are henceforth to take rank as public buildings', wrote Edward Robert Robson, architect to the School Board for London, 'and should be planned and built in a manner befitting their new dignity'.[76] His practical treatise on school design advocates 'compactness of internal arrangement . . . because it bears directly on the question of cost', and the recommended models are flexible plans in which classrooms (divided by sliding partitions) are grouped around a large schoolroom; apparently it was difficult to improve on Charles Hoole's advice of 1660. Architectural style is not discussed, although the London Board Schools for which Robson and J.J.Stevenson were responsible are in the red brick style of the 'Queen Anne' revival which marked a reaction against Gothic. In West Yorkshire, however, the first Board Schools continued to be built with pointed windows, gables and turrets in the same tradition as the National Schools.

Yet many were on a scale inconceivable in the pre-1870 days. Queen's Road Schools, Halifax, were designed by Horsfall, Wardle and Patchett, who had already built a new school for boys in West Parade which attracted attention in the professional press;[77] but their design for Queen's Road was on a far larger scale with a frontage of 196 feet and depth of over 83. The stone façades are decorated with carved panels, and the windows are ornately Gothic; there is a central tower, and the different entrances are through ornamental porches. Sir Henry Cole is said to have made 'special mention of these schools'; he had 'never met with one equal or so conveniently finished for the purpose'.[78] The Bradford School Board acquired a reputation for building progressive, but expensive, schools, of which the first group of eight was allocated to various architects;[79] the design by Milnes and France for Bowling Back Lane (opened 1874) can be taken as typical. There is a central schoolroom or hall, with separate ones for boys and girls at each side; externally there are windows with plate tracery, and a profusion of spires and gables.[80] The cost of these early Bradford schools led to criticism that interior efficiency had been sacrificed to external effect, but the Board refused to lower its standards of space and finish. The most extravagant of the first group is Lilycroft School, built by Hope and Jardine opposite the gigantic Manningham Mill. Similar in plan to Bowling Back Lane School, it has long, narrow rooms for the boys and girls (sixty-seven feet by twenty), supplemented by two smaller classrooms attached to each. Once again, it is Gothic in character with traceried windows and an asymmetrically placed tower to one side of the central gable; inside, carved angels bearing shields support the hammer-beam roof. In its elaboration and its almost obsessional adherence to an ecclesiastical Gothic style, Lilycroft School is probably unique among Board Schools, but Bradford set an example which 'the neighbouring school boards have so far followed [in 1877] that the board school is a pleasing addition to many a Yorkshire landscape'.[81]

The Education Department, a government department set up in 1839, advocated narrow rooms eighteen to twenty feet wide (as in the Bradford example quoted), but the Leeds Board preferred a width of

203

204

76 Robson,E.R., *School architecture*, London 1877,2. 'The importance of education is only beginning to be understood by the average Englishman; that of judicious arrangement of school-buildings lies some distance in the wake . . . The subject may be dry and uninviting to many, but its study has become a necessity'.

77 *BA* (1874),ii,90f. These schools are described as in the style of the 'early Pointed period, carried out with the strictest regard to modern requirements and economy'. In plan, there were 'a spacious school-room, class and cloak rooms on the first floor to accommodate 150 scholars, the ground-floor being devoted . . . as a covered playground . . . The roof of the school is supported by covered roof principals. The walls are lined with red, black, and white facing-bricks, set to pattern . . . The whole of the exterior walls are faced with outside delf-dressed local stone walled in courses relieved with cleansed and moulded ashlar work'.

78 ibid.,90.

79 ibid.,ii,123. Bowling Back Lane (Milnes and France), Lilycroft (Hope and Jardine), Dudley Hill (Knowles and Wilcox), Barkerend (Andrews and Pepper), Horton Bank (E.Simpson), Ryan Street (Jackson and Longley), Whetley Lane (T.H. and F.Healey).

80 ibid.,i,25.

81 Committee of Council on Education, *Report 1876–7*,406; for a description of Lilycroft School, see *BA* (1873),i,233.

thirty feet[82] and had its way in the new schools in their first group
designed by different architects. Typical are those by George Corson
(Bewerley Street 1873, and Green Lane 1874) and Elisha Backhouse
(South Accommodation Road 1874). In the first, Corson planned a
symmetrical E-shaped group with a central infants' schoolroom and
boys' and girls' schoolrooms to left and right, separated by groups of
classrooms; he used a stark Romanesque style, with decorative
corbelled chimneys on the gables, coloured brickwork beneath them,
and a minimum of dressed stone around the semicircular-headed
openings. In the second design, he incorporated elaborately traceried
pointed windows under three central steeply pointed gables, flanked
by wings terminating in gabled pavilions. Backhouse's school was
described as being Byzantine in style, which is not very different from
Corson's Romanesque, and equally stark and undecorated.

The Leeds schools acquired a distinctive appearance after the
appointment of Richard Adams as architect to the Board in 1873. His
first designs were for a group including the identical Burley Lawn and
Hunslet Carr Schools (1874–6),[83] for 700 children in three
departments. The central infants' schoolroom is fifty feet by thirty
with an open timbered roof (eighteen feet high to the wallplate and
over twenty-eight to the ceiling); the boys' and girls' rooms at each
side are identical, but with three attached classrooms to each.
Externally, Adams's schools are built of brick with a minimum of
dressed stone; stylistically, they must be categorised as Gothic, but
their quality derives more from carefully detailed brickwork and the
use of herring-bone and basket-weave patterning than from
elaborately carved Gothic stonework as used on the Bradford and

82 *A* (1873),ix,103.

83 *BA* (1874),ii,43.

259

206. Bradford, Belle Vue Higher Grade School (C.H.Hargreaves 1895) was designed in the 'English Renaissance' style currently fashionable for school buildings.

84 Not all the School Boards were willing to spend large sums. Lockwood and Mawson firmly told the Drighlington School Board that it was 'impossible to build any other than a literally plain brick building for £5,000'. (ibid.,106).

85 *LM*, 14 April 1878.

86 Landless also designed Isles Lane (1891) and Queens Road (1892). Braithwaite was responsible for Gipton (1897), Kepler (1898), Brudenell (1899), Armley Park (1900), Bramley Broad Lane (1900), and Lovell Road (1901). See D.Williams, *Leeds School Board and its architecture 1870–1903*, unpublished thesis (1975), Leeds Polytechnic.

87 Fenn,G.W., 'The development of education in an industrial town', *Researches and studies* (1952), University of Leeds Institute of Education, no.6,19f.

205   Halifax schools. Adams's building in Meanwood Road (1883), surrounded by boldly modelled cast-iron railings and gates, illustrates his style at its best; yet, relatively unornamented as they are, his schools came under attack by the Leeds Ratepayers Protection Society which accused the Board of purchasing costly sites and building magnificent schools.[84] However, the *Leeds Mercury* gave the Board credit for not treating 'the children of the working classes as paupers and criminals for whom the barest and most tasteless sustenance would suffice. On the contrary it has sought to equip them fully for the battle of life'.[85] Adams was succeeded by William Landless (nephew and pupil of John Burnet of Glasgow) in 1889, and the schools built during his short term as architect to the Board are obviously influenced by Robson's work in London; such designs as that at Harehills (1890) incorporate scroll gables, broken rooflines and tall windows in the 'Queen Anne' style, as well as adopting a central hall plan for the first time in Leeds.[86] The next and last architect to the Board, W.S.Braithwaite (1895–1903), made a subtle change by using gables that are more Elizabethan than Dutch, but there was not a great difference between his style and Landless's.

  The Higher Grade Schools (first established in Bradford, where Forster 'took great pride in opening the Feversham Street High School for Boys in 1876') were intended to provide 'a higher and better education for the children of the better-to-do working classes and the lower middle classes'. In 1879 Forster returned to Bradford to open the

206   Belle Vue Schools for 1,206 pupils in four departments,[87] which was added to in 1895 when C.H.Hargreaves designed a richly decorated multi-storey Higher Grade School in a Mixed Renaissance style with gables and turrets. Two years later another of Hargreaves's designs,

260

the Hanson Higher Board School, was built 'in the English Renaissance style, which has now generally taken the place of Gothic for school purposes and lends itself excellently to ample lighting'. The ground floor was set aside for girls, the first floor for boys, 'and the top floor, which is to be used by both, but not simultaneously, is reached by separate staircases for boys and girls'. The most extraordinary of the Higher Grade Schools was opened in Great George Street, Leeds in 1889; its erection had been supervised by Landless, but the design had been made by John Kelly (Adams's partner) and Edward Birchall. This was the Central Higher Grade School for 2,500 children, planned as a solid, forbidding rectangle four storeys high with a central corridor and classrooms on each side.[88] It was functional and grim. The original elevations were designed as brick and glass façades divided by giant pilasters of a bastard order in dressed stone, and crowned by three pediments. Criticism of the lack of playground space caused an alteration, in which the pediments were eliminated, and the roof was constructed as a large open-air playground for boys on the east side of the main industrial part of the town. The girls had the use of the street level playground in a marginally less polluted atmosphere until they moved into the adjacent building designed by Braithwaite as the Pupil Teachers' Centre but subsequently known as Thoresby High School. In this almost equally penitential building, Braithwaite incorporated ventilated staircase towers with copper-covered ogee domes, details which he used again on Armley Park School (1900) combined with Elizabethan gables and tall, Hardwick Hall-like windows to the first-floor Assembly Hall.

The Technical Schools of the later nineteenth century moved into the class of public buildings, either Gothic like Edward Hughes's in

88 Now City of Leeds School.

208. Bradford Technical School (Hope and Jardine 1880–2); a more elaborate version of the Saltaire Institute, richly detailed externally and in the main hall.

207 Huddersfield (1881–4)[89] or Jackson and Fox's in Halifax (1895),[90] or awesomely Italianate like Bradford's, designed by Hope and Jardine, and opened by the Prince of Wales in 1882. The slope of Great Horton Road was no deterrent to the architects, who imposed a heavy

208 composition of giant Corinthian orders, six bays on each side of an ornate central section, on the main façade. The central entrance rises upwards through a Venetian window and a segmental pediment to a square tower which changes into an octagonal cupola with more Corinthian columns and elongated urns, to a masonry dome and tall crowning lantern. The planning is less orderly than the symmetrical façade suggests, but the accommodation includes a large hall with an internal cast-iron frame; the lower columns support a gallery with a lavishly ornamented fibrous plaster front, and the upper columns form part of a semicircular-headed arcade rising to the deeply panelled ceiling.[91] At the same time as these monumental colleges were being built, the Yorkshire College was developing in Leeds.

Founded in 1874 with twenty-four students, the Yorkshire College became a part of the Victoria University in 1887 as a partner of the colleges in Manchester and Liverpool. It was intended 'to supply an urgent and recognised want, viz. instruction in those sciences which are applicable to the Industrial Arts, . . . designed for the use of persons who will afterwards be engaged in those trades as foremen, managers or employers; and also for the training of teachers of technical science'.[92] Nevertheless, there was clearly a feeling that this was only the beginning, and the *Bradford Observer* hoped in 1875 that 'no one will be finally content until literacy is added to scientific culture – until the College of Science has grown into a great Yorkshire University'.[93] Alfred Waterhouse was appointed as architect, largely on the strength of his design for Owens College, Manchester, and inevitably the textile industry was the first consideration in the new college. The foundation stone of the Cloth-workers' Building was laid in 1877; this incorporated a lecture room for ninety students, weaving sheds and a museum, and it was designed as a brick Gothic façade with stone dressings. 'The style of the front buildings is perhaps best described as the Collegiate Gothic . . . A moderate use was made – in those places where there would be no undue interference with light – of arched window-heads,

209 of cusps, of transoms, and even, as in the case of the large Hall, of tracery; but in the main the windows, though mullioned, present large glass surfaces, and though an effect of vertical dignity is gained by the main tower, the turrets of the Hall, and the high-pitched roofs of the frontal range of buildings, all these features were subordinated to the practical needs of the College. All these buildings were faced externally with red pressed bricks, and had dressings of Bolton Wood stone'.[94]

That was how a brochure of 1908 set out the progress already made in building what had become, by a charter of 1904, the University of Leeds; architecturally, it was described (not in the brochure) as 'a piece of Oxford, transplanted and scaled down for the less fortunate North'. In 1909 Paul Waterhouse (son of Alfred and his successor on many projects, including this), told the Senate 'It will be an ambition with me to show that I can produce a building which shall be

89 Now part of Huddersfield Polytechnic. Hughes's building was extended in 1937; Sir Frederick Gibberd's new College of Technology, started in 1957, became the Polytechnic in 1970.

90 Extended in 1954–6 by R.H.Pickles; now the Percival Whitley College of Further Education.

91 An additional Technical College, designed by the City Architect's Department, was completed in 1966, the year the College became the University of Bradford. Building Design Partnership were appointed architects; for their first buildings see *A J* (1971),cliii,1236f. More recently, they have completed a Communal Building linked to the J.B.Priestley Library.

92 *University of Leeds: Report*, 1872,i; quoted in Gosden,P.H.J.H., and Taylor,A.J., *Studies in the history of a university*, Leeds 1974,2.

93 *BO*, 7 Oct 1875.

94 Brochure, 1908, quoted in Gosden and Taylor, op.cit.,151.

209. Leeds University; A.Waterhouse's buildings for the Yorkshire College, which became the University in 1904. The Great Hall (1891–4) is on the left, and in the foreground is the Baines Wing (1882–4).

210. Leeds University; the Burmantofts faience facing to the columns and dado of the staircase to the Great Hall (1891–4).

210

95 ibid.,155.

96 The decorative faience incorporates Latin mottoes, 'Heal the sick', 'Cleanse the lepers', 'Freely ye have received, freely shall ye give'. This was the second School of Medicine, which replaced the still existing building in Park Lane, designed by George Corson in 1865.

97 *University of Leeds : Report*, 1923–4.

artistically worthy and at the same time harmonises with the work that my predecessor did'.[95] By that time, the textiles department (including the pleasant, green Clothworkers' Court), the Great Hall (a first-floor room approached up a staircase faced with Burmantofts faience), the basement Library, and the Baines Wing for physics, chemistry, geology, engineering and the arts, had been completed to Waterhouse designs. The School of Medicine, an attractive Arts and Crafts Tudor building by W.H.Thorp which includes a richly decorated entrance hall in Burmantofts faience unusually cool in tone, had been completed in 1894.[96] Paul Waterhouse's first buildings were for mining, fuel and metallurgy, and they were unmemorably conceived 'with the minimum superfluity of material or ornament'. There was a regretful note in Sir Michael Sadler's last report as Vice-Chancellor in 1924 when he wrote, 'We do not aspire to magnificence in our buildings or even to a standard of beauty which the importance of University work would justify. We know the value of the aesthetic in education; we even cherish the ideal that in time to come Leeds, like some other Universities, may possess buildings so fine in design and execution that they may be held symbolic of the dignity of knowledge and truth'.[97]

It was generally admitted the University had not even approached this reasonable ideal. There were a few interesting innovations inside the Waterhouse buildings, such as the honest exposure of structural beams in the textile industries lecture room, the laminated timber trusses (similar to those used in Bradford warehouses) in the engineering drawing office, and the quite impressive inorganic chemistry laboratory which has an open timber roof and arcade of Gothic columns, as well as walls of decorative coloured brickwork;[98] but these were not likely to impress an ambitious university which had to face the facts of 'struggling makeshifts' ever since its inception, and classrooms which 'would in some cases disgrace an elementary school'.[99] Indeed, the new secondary schools were more impressive than the University buildings. West Leeds School, designed by Fred Broadbent and built in 1907, is twenty-six bays wide, four storeys high in the centre, and three in the wings; pediments, keystones and columns are applied curiously ungrammatically, but the classrooms are light, spacious and airy. The same architect designed the schools at Roundhay (1926) and Lawnswood (1932) in a similar 'Jaggard and Drury'[100] style, using a symmetrical plan with a central hall flanked on each side by an open courtyard surrounded by classrooms and specialist teaching rooms. Even grander is G.W.Atkinson's City of Leeds Training College, built in 1912 in the grounds of New Grange as a formal layout of brick 'Wrenaissance' buildings.[101]

In 1921 there was talk of holding a competition 'to pick the brains of the best Architects in the Country'[102] in an attempt to provide architecture worthy of the University's growing prestige; and in 1927 the assessor's report informed the Senate, 'You have got a very competent man indeed, and you may rest assured that the completed building will not fall short of his fine design'.[103] The architects selected were Lanchester and Lodge, who had submitted a design for a monumental Beaux-Arts composition which would completely obscure from the outside world all the existing, regrettable Waterhouse buildings with grand red brick and Portland stone,[104] including a triumphal arched entrance from Woodhouse Lane and a tall tower 'that will dominate the neighbourhood and be seen from all directions, and symbolise the University'. The grandiose architecture of the 20s and 30s has not yet been reinstated in critical or popular favour, and the work of Lanchester and Lodge is not generally admired; yet the new buildings did provide a more prestigious image needed by the University, and the Brotherton Library is a worthy (though unadventurous) follower in a great tradition of domed spaces dedicated to reading and research. It was unfortunate that the accepted design was continued in a pared-down, sterile version in the Arts Building (1957–64) after the war, and that the new designs for the Houldsworth School of Applied Science (1955–8) and the Engineering Building (1957–63) were so banal. In 1956 a change of architect was considered.

During the years between 1946 and 1956 there had been great developments in the design of educational buildings, foreseen in Oliver Hill's immediately pre-war infants' school at Whitwood Mere, in which the classrooms (which have sliding, folding glazed screens opening on to a covered terrace) are contained in a single curved wing leading to a hall.[105] The 1944 Education Act was conceived at a time of idealism

98 See *The record of technical and secondary education* (1895), October, 8.

99 Appeal brochure, 1925.

100 In 1916 W.R.Jaggard and F.E.Drury published the first of three volumes of *Architectural building construction*; in their introduction, the authors 'disclaim any idea of presenting great architecture, [but] they do claim that the buildings designed fully express their purpose, and enable them in a more or less pleasing manner to assemble the different units of the building'. They provided a complete set of constructional details in the red-brick 'Wrenaissance' tradition, which was the general style for schools, libraries, and government buildings between the two wars; and their books were standard texts for architectural students for thirty years.

101 The College, now a part of the Leeds Polytechnic, was extended by G.A.Burnett and Partners.

102 Sir Ernest Bain, quoted in Gosden and Taylor, op.cit.,162.

103 ibid.,163; see *A & BN* (1934),cxxxvii, 155ff. and *B* (1934),cxlvi,207ff.

104 Finally, the entire facing of the new buildings was executed in Portland stone.

105 *West Riding education: ten years of change*, Wakefield 1953,114; 'built at a cost of £53 16s od per pupil [the school] was considered by some an extravagance'. See *A J* (1941),xciv,398ff.

211

212

213

265

211. Leeds, Roundhay School; built in 1926 (F.Broadbent) and typical in plan and style of the secondary schools designed between the two World Wars.

212. Leeds University; the Parkinson Building, completed in 1950 as the ceremonial centrepiece of Lanchester and Lodge's additions.

106 ibid., 'When the schools of the Riding were measured against these new regulations [of the Ministry of Education] not one single school survived the test'.

107 The realities of the situation compelled Education authorities to adopt various means of fulfilling their programmes. The West Riding County Council became a founder member of CLASP (Consortium of Local Authorities' Special Programme) which developed a standardised building system for use especially on mining subsidence sites, and the same authority produced a portable timber classroom in 1952 for use as additional accommodation. The possibilities of rehabilitation were also discovered; 'There is no doubt that many of the schools which were improved in this way have proved to be superior to what would have been provided had an entirely new school been built. Frequently ... the schools occupy sites which are ideally situated for access by the community they are intended to serve. Secondly, a number of the buildings have architectural features of some merit and convey a sense of well-established tradition. It has been the task of the architects to preserve what is best – indeed, often to enhance it – while adding enormously to its educational effectiveness and amenity. Generally the buildings are robust and almost always afford a greater spaciousness than would be possible in new schools built to the Ministry's cost

and enthusiasm, and 'development plans were prepared showing how all bad old schools were going to be abandoned and replaced by new ones and all passable schools brought up to a specified standard'.[106] Such an ambitious programme inevitably fell short of its initial intention; but the new schools are among the finest achievements of the post-war years. They offered worthwhile opportunities for ingenuity and imagination to a generation of young architects at a time when there was optimism about a brave new world, and they proved that nationally applied standards of cost and planning did not necessarily produce standard solutions.[107] It will be the task of a future historian to assess the lasting qualities of the vast number of educational buildings erected after the early 50s, ranging from the little primary school at Bardsey (1954) to Batley High School spread out on its hilltop site (1960) and the large Boston Spa Comprehensive School (1971); from the urban compactness of Keighley Technical College (1952–6) to the pattern of buildings and spaces surrounding Bretton Hall to give it continued life as a teachers' training college (1948–63);[108] from the unobtrusive, sophisticated infants' school at Ilkley (1953) to the dramatic Shipley Salt School built against the green hillside over the river from Salt's model town (1960–5).[109]

It was Chamberlin, Powell and Bon, the architects of the Shipley school, who were appointed to succeed Lanchester and Lodge at Leeds University in 1958; two years later they produced their report and recommendations for its future development.[110] Unlike the new post-war universities which, for various reasons, chose to build outside town centres, Leeds elected to remain in the city and to develop the sloping hillside south of the existing buildings as far down as Scott's General Infirmary, which is intended to be rebuilt as a new teaching hospital. As the *Architectural Review* commented, 'Cynics will point out that this was due, not to superior wisdom, but to the fact that Leeds had too big an investment in old buildings to contemplate a flit. She was pinned down to her piece of city centre earth by Lanchester and

214

215

213. Castleford, Whitwood Mere Infants'
School (O.Hill 1939) was designed with
completely glazed, south-facing walls to
the classrooms. The curved plan
represents the reaction of the late 30s
against symmetry as 'an acceptance of a
given order of things'.

214. Boston Spa Comprehensive School
(K.C.Evans 1971); built in the CLASP
system devised for subsidence sites, and
designed for 1,230 pupils.

215. Bretton Hall College of Education;
the home of the Wentworths and
Beaumonts was bought by the West
Riding County Council in 1947 for use as
a teachers' training college. Minor
additions, including the College Hall on
the right, were built in 1948–53 (Sir
H.Bennett), and a large expansion
programme was undertaken in 1960–3
(A.W.Glover). The Library on the left
and the Gymnasium in the centre were
part of the latter phase.

Lodge's great tower'.[111] Yet this decision has undoubtedly benefitted
Leeds, and the university as well. It has enabled the architects to
design a flexible arrangement of linked buildings of various sizes and
with different requirements, put together in a manner based on a
practical administrative system of levels of indoor 'streets', with the
avowed intention that it should take no more than ten minutes to walk
from any one point to any other. Another intention was that the
university should develop in such a way that there would be a sense of
completeness from the earliest stage. In contrast to the 1927

requirements'. (*Education 1954–64*,
Wakefield 1964,149).

108 Linstrum,D., 'Bretton Hall: history and
expansion', *Journal of the West Yorkshire
Society of Architects* (1963),xxiii,no.2,4ff.

109 See *A J* (1965),cxliii,747ff.

110 The proposals were published in 1960,
and were well received in the professional
press; see *A J* (1960),cxxxi,787ff, in which it
was thought 'one of the world's finest
universities, not excepting American ones, is
now within [the city's] reach'.

111 *A R* (1974),clv,3.

imposition of a closed university of civic buildings with formal spaces and ceremonial entrances, the present plan offers a different, inherently more picturesque and human, interpretation of urban design in which the city and the university theoretically become integrated.

The incorporation of the old Woodhouse Cemetery (including John Clark's Greek revival gatehouse and chapel) as an open green space,[112] and the later decision to retain the red brick and sandstone of the former Cavendish Road Presbyterian church (J.B.Fraser 1878–9), are characteristic of the design's aims; so is the revaluation of the unassuming, even apparently friendly, Waterhouse buildings which were once despised. The picturesque and topographical quality of the design is even more in evidence in the panoramas of the city framed by soaring concrete propylaea and viewed from the summits of dramatically descending Piranesian flights of stairs. The humanity so evidently intended and, at times, achieved is contradicted by the impersonal uniform design of the faculty buildings, differentiated only by their names on the concrete wall cladding, and by the extrovert monumentality of the huge lecture theatre block which projects into the vast, impressive Chancellor's Court built on a plateau in the approximate centre of the whole layout. Yet the overall impression is that this university is an experience, a convincing statement about urban design as it was ideally conceived in the 60s and 70s. Exceptionally, it succeeds in being a part of its environment, a university belonging in and to West Yorkshire, as its original promoters intended. There is only a difference of language between the hope expressed in 1867 that 'the tastes of the inhabitants of a town [are] much improved by being surrounded with beautiful objects',[113] and that of 1974 that 'human life in the city centre of the future could well be something like this'.[114] The mutual influence of education and the quality of the environment is implicit in both.

216

112 Clark designed these buildings in 1835. The cemetery was landscaped, and many of the monuments were taken away, in 1965–6.

113 Quoted in Gosden and Taylor, op.cit.,145, from a report written by G.H. and A.Nussey to accompany their plans for a technical institute for Leeds in 1867.

114 *A R*, op.cit.,3.

216. Leeds University; a part of the Chancellor's Court, the central space in Chamberlin, Powell and Bon's design for the enlarged university.

9 Theatres and music halls

It is astonishing how good acting refines the mind of an audience.
Mrs Jordan in Leeds, 1810.

It is credibly reported that when the Prince Consort attended the opening of Leeds Town Hall in 1858 he 'had some conversation with local gentlemen respecting the amount of progress and culture to be found in the capital of the West Riding'. When he was told there was not a good theatre he replied 'then you should have one; for nothing is more calculated to promote the culture and raise the tone of a people'.[1] There was no good theatre in West Yorkshire in the 1850s, but the region was not entirely lacking in a theatrical tradition. Strolling players had performed in Leeds in the yards of the *Talbot* and the *Rose and Crown*, and in Bradford in a large room in the *King's Arms* yard or a nearby barn. There was a theatre of some description in Leeds in 1722, in the Kirkgate–Vicar Lane area, and there were two in Wakefield in the yards of the *Bull* and the *George*; but it was not until the 1770s that there were purpose-built, though modest, theatres.

One was built in Leeds across the river in 'a very inconvenient situation . . . being far removed from the centre of the town';[2] in the *Leeds Intelligencer* of 9 July 1771, Tate Wilkinson, the 'Proprietor and Patentee of the Theatres-Royal at York and Hull' announced with a flourish that 'the New Theatre . . . which is now finishing at immense expence, will be opened the week after York Assizes'. Although it was described with a theatrical exaggeration in the newspaper as 'expansive, commodious and elegant', it was more truthfully called elsewhere a 'plain brick building'[3] with 'not the remotest pretence to exterior elegance'.[4] It was built to a design made by an obscure man, John Battley,[5] and according to Mrs Jordan, who made her first stage appearance in Leeds and remained one of the town's favourite actresses, it was 'about the size of Richmond'.[6] That famous eighteenth-century theatre in North Yorkshire is about 60 feet by 28 overall, including the stage;[7] it has a pit, stage level boxes and a gallery, and it is estimated that four hundred spectators were crowded in on the sort of night Mrs Jordan wrote of in Leeds: 'We had great Houses . . . If the theatre had been as large as *Covent Garden* it would have been full'.[8] Certainly there was no comparison between the two, but the Leeds auditorium, described as 'neat, for a provincial establishment, though rather small',[9] was in fact larger than Richmond and probably seated about six or seven hundred; like Richmond, it had 'one circle of boxes, with good galleries and pit', and the better seats were covered. Wilkinson, whose circuit included also

1 *B* (1859),xvii,210; *YP*, 20 Nov 1876.

2 Parsons, i,135.

3 Ryley,J., *The Leeds guide*, Leeds 1806, 59. 'The Leeds Stage can boast of being a nursery for that of London; since the erection of this Theatre the Leeds audience have fostered the opening genius of many performers who have since become the ornament and pride of the British metropolis'.

4 Heaton,J., *Walks through Leeds*, Leeds 1835,99.

5 Redgrave,S., *Dictionary of artists of the English school*, London 1878,32. Battley is referred to as 'of some local eminence in Leeds, where he erected the theatre and several considerable buildings in the town and neighbourhood'.

6 Aspinall,A., *Mrs. Jordan and her family*, London 1951, 130.

7 Southern,R., *The Georgian playhouse*, London 1948, 46ff; Southern,R., and Brown,I., *The Georgian theatre, Richmond*, Richmond 1973, 7ff. The 1850 Leeds O.S. map suggests that Mrs Jordan was not correct in her comparison, and that the Leeds theatre was larger than Richmond's.

8 Aspinall, op.cit.,132.

9 Heaton, op.cit.,99.

the theatres at York, Hull, Wakefield, Doncaster and Pontefract, discontentedly called them all (with the exception of York) 'intolerably confined in length, breadth, and indeed in every part';[10] but nevertheless, in a more sanguine mood, he thought his Leeds building 'very splendid, comparatively speaking to the very mean places, such as the barns, warehouses &c. to which[his actors] had been accustomed'.[11]

The Wakefield theatre was built in Westgate among the merchants' large houses in 1775–6 on a site owned by James Banks, a member of a woolstapling family.[12] Wilkinson referred to the encouragement he was given 'to have a new theatre built there, at great expence'.[13] It is said to have seated 1,000, and the auditorium was evidently divided in the usual way into a level pit and two tiers of galleries supported on oak columns; the gallery fronts were open oak balustrades. Externally, it was similar in character to the surrounding brick houses; it was five bays wide with a slightly projecting central section of three bays, in the middle of which was a characteristic Wakefield detail of a window set in a recessed, semicircular-headed arch. The central doorway was pedimented. There is evidence that it was well patronised, and Wilkinson wrote 'a stranger, even from London, would be astonished at beholding the number of Gentlemen's elegant carriages attending that theatre';[14] Mrs Jordan noted 'The Boxes are great and filled with people of fassion' including the Countess of Mexborough from Methley Hall, who took 'Boxes for every night'.[15] Further evidence of the interest taken in the Wakefield theatre by the county families appears in Michael Kelly's note that the company in which he was playing gave an extra performance by the express desire of the Earl of Scarbrough from Sandbeck Park.[16] However, Mrs Jordan also left a description of back-stage conditions, reporting to the Duke of Clarence that 'The dressing room at Wakefield is dreadful',[17] and 'at Leeds I was obliged to stand on my *great coat* to keep my feet from *wet*'.[18] In 1810 she remarked that the Leeds theatre was 'miserable and cold, half the upper part of it admitting the wind and rain. The receipts are in general so bad that the manager does not think it worth while to repair it'.[19] Presumably that explains why, in 1816, Whitaker was able to note with some satisfaction that Leeds 'had for the space of four years by gradual dereliction and neglect suffered its theatre to be shut up.[20] Eighteen years later Edward Parsons was equally gratified by the failure of the theatre to establish regular support 'although the most spectacular "stars" have been brought to emit their beams within its walls'.[21]

Wilkinson went to Halifax in 1776 where 'our theatre was a dreadful place, being over the stables at the White Lion',[22] and there was another in the yard of the *Old Cock*. A new one was built in Ward's End in 1789–90 at the expense of twelve local men; it cost £1,300 and had the usual pit and two tiers of galleries. It had nothing 'in its exterior appearance to recommend it, . . . its frontage being occupied by the Shakspeare Tavern', but its interior was described as 'small, but very elegant and convenient'[23] in 1834, and it was subsequently improved; in 1841 there were extensive alterations, and in 1853 upper galleries

10 Wilkinson,T., *The wandering patentee*, York 1795,iv,119.

11 ibid.,iv,101.

12 Senior,W., *The old Wakefield theatre*, Wakefield 1894.

13 Wilkinson, op.cit.,i,223.

14 ibid.

15 Aspinall, op.cit.,201.

16 Ellis,S.M., *The life of Michael Kelly*, London 1930,156.

17 Aspinall, op.cit.,201.

18 ibid.,132.

19 ibid.,130.

20 Whitaker, 86.

21 Parsons, i,135.

22 Wilkinson, op.cit.,i,229.

23 Parsons, i,135; see also Crabtree, 346.

24 Porritt,A., 'The old Halifax theatre', *HAS* (1956),17ff.

25 Wilkinson, op.cit.,ii,65.

26 ibid.,iv,37; a photograph taken before demolition is included in the brochure published in 1970 to commemorate Pontefract's 500th Mayoral year.

27 Wilkinson, op.cit.,iv,38.

28 James C, 252.

29 Scruton,W., *Bradford fifty years ago*, Bradford 1897,97.

30 Wilkinson,T., *Memoirs of his own life*, York 1790,iii,11.

31 Wilkinson,T., *The wandering patentee*, op.cit.,ii,40.

32 Aspinall, op.cit.,53.

33 ibid.,120.

34 Cummins died on the stage of the Leeds theatre on 20 June 1817, and there were commentators who used this to attack playgoing as 'not only foolish, but sinful', and 'a warning to those who frequent the theatre'. However, the curate of St Paul's, Leeds reminded his readers that, in 1787, 'BURY PLAY-HOUSE fell down and buried three hundred people under its ruins – five were killed. The floor of a METHODIST MEETING HOUSE gave way at Leeds, in the year 1796 and killed SIXTEEN WOMEN, a MAN and a CHILD – What conclusions will they presume to draw from these few instances, where we find churches, hospitals, and theatres equally liable to the same awful visitations?' There was no rational answer.

35 *YP*, 20 Nov 1876.

36 ibid.

37 James C, 252, 'The building was erected at the cost of a Joint Stock Company (limited), who leased it to the celebrated dramatist and actor, Mr. [John Baldwin] Buckstone, of the Haymarket Theatre, and his partner, Mr. Wilde, who opened it with an effective company on Monday night, December 26th, 1864. On that occasion, amidst the brilliant light, the elegant proportions of the Theatre, and the beauty of its decorations, were exhibited with grand effect, and excited the admiration of the crowded audience. The boxes and gallery (three tiers) are decorated in an exceedingly effective style'.

were constructed.[24] At that time it was probably the best theatre in West Yorkshire, and unlike the other eighteenth-century ones it had a long life and remained in active use until its demolition and replacement in 1904.

In 1779 Wilkinson took his company to Pontefract where they found 'a little building, called by the inhabitants *a Playhouse*. The success they met with, and the genteel neighbouring families who honoured their stage endeavours ... gave rise to my ruminating at some time to have a regular theatre built and established on that little pleasant Montpellier of Yorkshire'.[25] Three years later it was opened in Gillygate, where it occupied a seven-bay wide building with a gabled central section containing a giant recessed arch similar to that on the earlier house attributed to James Paine in the nearby Market Place.[26] The Pontefract theatre appears to have been about the size of Wakefield, but Wilkinson evidently regarded it as more modest than his others, calling it 'too small to afford a meal to London performers with their appetite for gold'.[27] Bradford's first theatre was built in 1820 in Market Street, but it was small and soon 'put to other uses';[28] and in 1841 a Mr Morley put up a wooden building in Duke Street which was refaced *c*.1844 with a Classical temple front approached between a pair of gate piers removed from the old manor house in Kirkgate.[29]

These were the modest theatres West Yorkshire could show when the Prince Consort made his inquiry in 1858; but a new phase of building was about to start as a result of a changing attitude to the acceptance of the theatre as a source of culture. John Wesley had been 'told that you have a wicked playhouse in Leeds, but I do not say you will be damned for going to see a play if you think there is no harm in so doing';[30] but some of his followers were less tolerant. 'Leeds ... has too much methodism to be pleased with the passions of a Shylock or a Richard though in imitation only', thought Charles Macklin,[31] and Mrs Jordan had been begged by a Methodist 'not to come ... to draw the multitude *astray*, ... requesting me to quit the stage and "turn to God"'.[32] Another correspondent wrote to her during one of her stays in Leeds 'that God *had allowed* me to make use of magic for a certain time, and that he was only *watching* for a good *opportunity* to send me to the gulph of h-ll'.[33] The death on stage of Alexander Cummins in 1817 was attributed to 'divine displeasure',[34] and as late as the 1860s 'few people in Leeds who could boast of high respectability cared to enter a theatre ... The stage was believed to be bad, and its professors were looked down upon'.[35]

The endeavours of managers such as John Coleman in Leeds, 'an earnest student of the drama, [who] possessed good taste and skill in stage management ... greatly elevated the tone of the drama'.[36] The theatre began to be respectable, and new ones were built on central sites; in 1864 Andrews and Pepper designed the Royal Alexandra Theatre in Manningham Lane, Bradford which offered accommodation for 1,800 in what was described as 'the most commodious and beautiful theatre in the provinces' in spite of a plain exterior.[37] In 1863 Coleman took over the old Leeds theatre and redecorated it 'in green and gold, adorned profusely with bas-reliefs and other ornaments';[38] and in 1867 he rebuilt it completely with an exterior 'in the Italian style of architecture'. The auditorium, which seated 2,500, was described as 'very handsome . . . The fronts of both boxes and gallery were enriched by scroll work and elaborately ornamented in gold and colours'. On the opening night, 'when the footlights threw up their brightest glare and the superb lustres suspended from the ceiling suddenly blazed out in full effulgence, the scene burst upon [the audience] as by a stroke of magic, and seemed almost to overpower them by its splendour'.[39] But the theatre was burnt down in 1875. The same fate overtook another Leeds theatre, built in 1849 by Joseph Hobson as the Royal Casino in King Charles's Croft; it changed its name in 1856 to the New Alhambra, and two years later to the Amphitheatre. In 1864, after being 'entirely remodelled from designs by an eminent architect', it reopened as 'the largest Theatre in the provinces', with 'a Tier of Dress Boxes, capable of accommodating 500 . . . a new and enlarged pit . . . adapted to hold an audience of 2,000 . . . extensive promenade having accommodation for 1,500' at the Circle level, and a gallery 'capable of holding 1,500';[40] a total of 5,500 which is probably a theatrical exaggeration. It was burnt down in March 1876, but Hobson rebuilt it as the New Theatre Royal and Opera House within seven months. The design was made by Thomas Moore and Sons, who produced as unattractive an exterior as could be conceived, but inside, as the *Yorkshire Post* wrote, it 'could scarcely be improved upon . . . It will probably hold 4,000 persons; the gallery, which runs up to a truly Olympian height, is estimated to accommodate from 1,200 to 1,500 . . . The cellars are so deep, and the height of the building is so great, that a scene of full height can be completely raised or lowered out of view of the audience'.[41] The auditorium was delicately decorated with *carton-pierre* mouldings in a deep cove over the proscenium, and in the centre Hobson placed the Leeds civic arms.[42] A new theatre, the Prince's, opened in Bradford in Manchester Road in the same year as the Leeds Royal; seating 2,680, it survived until the 1960s, after being partly rebuilt in 1878–9 following a fire.

But Leeds was not satisfied that it had answered the Prince Consort's implied criticism of the town's promotion of culture. His words were 'remembered by those to whom they were addressed' and there was an abortive scheme in 1859 'for the erection of a magnificent temple of the drama for the West Riding'. Plans were prepared but then abandoned, yet 'many leading men . . . believing firmly in the ennobling and refining influence of the drama, still cherished the idea of building a theatre worthy of the town'.[43] A limited company was formed, and George Corson was commissioned to make a design on a site in New Briggate. Unusually, it was decided to combine on one site a theatre, an assembly room large enough to seat 1,200, a supper room that could be used in connection with either public space, and six shops with frontages to New Briggate.

The design was undertaken principally by James Robinson Watson, Corson's chief assistant, who was evidently 'familiar with all the great theatres of the European capitals, and with all the modern

38 *LI*, 29 Oct 1864.

39 *YP*, 2 Oct 1867, *LM* 29 May 1875.

40 *LI*, 23 July 1864.

41 *YP*, 30 September 1876.

42 The Theatre Royal was demolished in 1957.

43 *B* (1859), xvii, 275; *YP*, 20 Nov 1876.

217. Leeds, Grand Theatre (G.Corson 1876–8); conceived as an entrance to 'a noble temple of the drama', but some of the proposed decoration shown in this engraving from the *Builder* (1878) remains uncarved.

improvements which have been introduced'.[44] A knowledge of theatre architecture was unusual in an English architect's experience in the 1870s; in his finely illustrated study, *Modern Opera Houses and Theatres* (1896), Edwin Sachs was lukewarm about recently constructed examples in this country, where they were 'governed in [their] requirements by investors, or ambitious actors, who cater for the pleasure of sensation-seekers; among a people practically devoid of any feeling for architecture ... From these contrasting spirits it is easy to see how the building of English theatres has been put into the hands of architects who are merely good planners, good constructors and business men, with the qualification of being able to provide for a maximum audience at a minimum outlay'.[45] Sachs contrasted this attitude with that of the Continental theatre architect, who was called upon to undertake 'the most difficult task' calling for 'a man endowed with the pure and true spirit of the architectural vocation' who could answer the 'numerous, complex and essentially technical demands' while ensuring 'the highest standard of taste'.[46] To illustrate his subject, Sachs drew on Vienna, Budapest, Bayreuth, Paris and most of the European capitals for examples. He included some of the recently constructed London theatres and a selected few in the provinces, of which the earliest was the Leeds Grand, 'by no means the least important of its class to be found in the United Kingdom ... for a provincial town, the breadth of its conception is noteworthy [and] in its architectural rendering ... it stands above the average of buildings of its class'.[47]

There was a pardonable atmosphere of pride in the theatre when it was opened on 18 November 1878. It was claimed to be superior in many respects to Drury Lane, Covent Garden and Her Majesty's in London, and it was reported there was 'no such building in New York, or ... the American continent'. For comfort it was considered as taking precedence of all the Paris theatres with the allowable exception of Garnier's recently completed Opéra, but it was conceded that some of the German municipal theatres, such as Frankfurt, might excel Leeds;[48] yet it was rightly pointed out, as Sachs emphasised in his book, that there were great subsidies in Germany, denied to English theatres which had to be commercial propositions capable of bringing in a profit for their owners. This defect was the theme of Sir Henry Irving's last public speech almost forty years after the opening of the Leeds Grand. Two days before his death in the Midland Hotel, Bradford in 1905 he was entertained to luncheon in the Town Hall by the Lord Mayor; Irving's speech of thanks concluded with the thought, 'It may be that in years to come our countrymen will scarcely understand how in our times so potent an instrument for good or ill as the stage was left entirely outside the sphere of public administration'. Under the circumstances, the praise accorded to the Leeds Grand was not excessive.

The elevation to New Briggate is solemnly romantic in character, maybe to allay the fears of those who were apprehensive of the immoral influence of theatre-going and to emphasise that behind the Romanesque arches, the rose window and the tourelles was 'a noble

44 *YP*, 20 Nov 1876.

45 Sachs,O., and Woodrow,E.A., *Modern opera houses and theatres*, London 1896,i,4.

46 ibid.,i,5.

47 ibid.,ii,44.

48 *YP*, 20 Nov 1876.

217

218. Leeds, Grand Theatre; the gorgeous bravura of the *carton-pierre* decoration of the auditorium has remained almost unaltered.

temple of the drama' in which it could be demonstrated that 'the English stage . . . has attained to a dignity, grandeur, and purity which in our national history has never been surpassed'.[49] Yet the 'noble temple' is surely more related architecturally to the revival of German nationalism in art, to Wagner's *Lohengrin* and to Ludwig II's building of Neuschwanstein in the 70s than to anything in English theatre history; on the other hand, the New Briggate elevation, in which the Romanesque entrance to the theatre was balanced originally by another giant archway leading to a first-floor assembly room (now a cinema), may have been distantly derived from Street's façade to the London Law Courts. Internally, the horse-shoe shaped auditorium is **218** planned with the pit and stalls at ground level; above rise three tiers of dress-circle, upper-circle, and amphitheatre-circle continuing as a steeply raked gallery. It was designed to seat two thousand six hundred people with standing room for two hundred more,[50] and as well as being acoustically satisfactory, it was rightly claimed that 'from the front view of the orchestra stalls to the back row of the gallery there is not a seat from which a good view of the stage cannot be obtained';[51] the relatively shallow depth of the tiers of circles results in a sense of intimacy unusual in such a large theatre.

The auditorium is richly decorated with encrusted ornament, mainly moulded *carton pierre*, which combined such Gothic motifs as

49 ibid.

50 For greater comfort and safety, the theatre now seats 1,552 with 100 standing; Glasstone, V., *Victorian and Edwardian theatres*, London 1975, 62ff.

51 *YP*, 20 Nov 1878.

274

fan-vaults and clustered piers with Italianate scrolls, brackets and paterae in the manner of the great opera houses of Vienna and Paris; apart from the removal of two pairs of free-standing goddesses which originally flanked the stage boxes, the gorgeous bravura of the auditorium has survived virtually unaltered,[52] although the original drop scene on which was painted a view of Kirkstall Abbey (filling the thirty feet wide by forty feet high proscenium opening), has disappeared long ago. Perhaps that too was intended to mollify the Nonconformist conscience; on the evening before the theatre opened, the morality of play-going was discussed in the sermon at Mill Hill Chapel, and after asking 'Does a man commit a sin, even a little sin, by going to the theatre?', the preacher concluded 'it was God who gave us Shakespeare', and asked his congregation to see what they could make of God's gift.[53] Evidently the 'wicked play-house' was a thing of the past, although the music-hall had not yet been redeemed in 1878. Twenty years later, the *Yorkshire Post* commented that 'time was – indeed still is – when paterfamilias would as soon think of bathing in the River Aire at Leeds Bridge as of taking his daughters to a "music-hall"; [yet] if it is competent for decent people to witness a modern pantomime or musical comedy, there would seem to be no reason for antipathy in the case of a well-conducted theatre of varieties'.

The origin of music halls in West Yorkshire is not well documented, but certainly by the time the Grand Theatre was opened, Charles Thornton's White Swan Varieties (an extension of the *White Swan* in Upperheadrow dating from 1865) had closed and reopened again as Stansfield's Varieties, the name it retained until changing again to the City Palace of Varieties. Although the auditorium has received several decorative additions since it was first opened, the general form of the

52 One improvement was made in 1974 when a sunken orchestra pit was constructed in anticipation of the decision that the theatre should become the provincial headquarters of the English National Opera Company in 1978.

53 *YP*, 20 Nov 1876.

219

219. Leeds, City Varieties; some decoration has been added, but the main structure and the boxes of Charles Thornton's music hall (G.Smith(?) 1865) are probably all original.

rectangular room with rows of side-boxes separated by cast-iron columns at the first tier level, and a gallery above, is relatively unchanged. Thornton, the licensee of the *White Swan* (who also built the nearby Thornton's Arcade in 1877–8 with a cast-iron Gothic roof), was evidently planning for entertainments on a different scale from those in Pullan's Music Hall in Brunswick Place, Bradford (1869) which could hold four thousand people.

It was only in the 80s that the music hall began to gain a measure of respectability and was treated more seriously architecturally. Two specialist theatre architects, C. J. Phipps (1835–97) and Frank Matcham (1854–1928) dominated the country from their London offices, but the latter was better known in the provinces. It is said that Matcham had the unique distinction of having designed or remodelled some two hundred theatres and music halls following the success of his first, the London Elephant and Castle, in 1878;[54] he patented his own system of curvilinear cantilevers for balconies, slung between parallel walls, and his own method of manufacturing fibrous plaster decorations to create an illusion of extravagance in what were carefully considered auditoria. 'In the work of Frank Matcham', wrote Sachs, 'his reputation for the successful construction of playhouses is based entirely on his economic planning . . . his plans have a certain individuality [and] he has done a large amount of theatre work, principally in the provinces, which is marked by good seating accommodation, economy in space and cost, and rapidity in execution'.[55] Sachs had his reservations, believing Matcham's work was not 'distinguished for worthy composition, much less for careful architectural rendering, either within or without'; if he was meaning that Matcham had no respect for the accepted rules of Classical architectural grammar, his criticism is a mild understatement. Matcham evolved his own interpretation of Mannerist and Baroque decoration, usually taking as his first source the wilder and more debased historical examples from Germany, the Low Countries and Jacobean England, but adding to them details from Second Empire Paris or any other country and style; 'eclecticism' acquired a wider meaning in his exuberant, opulent Late Victorian and Edwardian theatres and music halls. Yet at his best, Matcham executed his designs with the technical virtuosity of a minor master, whether they are on the grand operatic scale of the Coliseum, London and the King's, Glasgow (both 1904), the Kursaal, Harrogate (Royal Hall), or the 'court theatre' style of the Opera House, Buxton (both 1903).

Matcham made his first appearance in West Yorkshire at Wakefield. The old theatre built for Tate Wilkinson in 1775–6 was still in use over a century later; in 1883 some alterations were made and it was reopened as the Royal Opera House, but it failed to live up to its great name and was refused a licence in 1892 on account of its 'many defects'. Matcham, whose Empire Palace in Edinburgh had recently opened and brought him fame in the theatre world, was employed to design a new theatre on the old site in Westgate. It opened in 1894 as the Opera House. The sober brick façade is ornamented between the five semicircular-headed windows with busts of authors and

54 Glasstone, op.cit.,30.

55 Sachs, op.cit.,iii,30.

composers, and the keystones of the arches continue upwards as thin strip pilasters which cut across a pedimented gable and conclude as spherical finials. A vestibule leads directly into the stalls and pit, above which rise a cantilevered tier of dress and upper circles with two private boxes, and finally a gallery; Matcham claimed that 'every person will have a full view of the stage'. The interior is domed, and the walls were originally covered with 'raised leather paper'.[56]

The 90s was a period of great theatrical building activity. The Queen's, Leeds was built in Holbeck in 1898, behind a façade which incorporated a widely spaced Venetian window above a loggia on the corner entrance front; the design was made by W.Hope and J.C.Maxwell of Newcastle, who planned an auditorium for 4,000.[57] The Empire Palace of Varieties, Bradford opened at the beginning of 1899, with an entrance through the Alexandra Hotel, inside which the staircase windows were decorated with painted glass representing Shakespeare's characters; externally, it was designed by W.G.R.Sprague with a tower, one hundred feet high and capped by a dome and cupola, at each corner of the façade.[58] The Albert Theatre and Opera House, Brighouse (Sharp and Waller) was opened in 1899,[59] illustrating how indispensable a theatre had become in even the smaller towns; and in the same year Matcham had received two commissions, the Grand, Huddersfield[60] and the Queens, Keighley.[61]

Huddersfield had become accustomed to adaptations for its entertainment. The Riding School in Ramsden Street (1848) was used as a theatre until 1863, and in the following year the Philosophical Hall, also in Ramsden Street, served a similar purpose. In 1866 this building underwent alterations and became the Theatre Royal, but it was burnt in 1880; in the following year it was replaced by the new Theatre Royal, designed by B.E.Entwistle of Southport to seat 1,250. A panorama of Shakespearean tragedies and comedies stretched over the proscenium, and the ceiling was filled with representations of Drama and Music. Then came the invitation to Matcham to design the Grand Theatre; it was to accommodate 1,934 and to cost £15,000, but the designs submitted were estimated to cost £28,000 and the promoters withdrew, accusing their architect of attempting to turn a profit-making theatre into a civic building. There were no recriminations at Keighley, where his design was successfully executed with a pit below street level, a dress circle and amphitheatre, and a gallery; once again Matcham provided an uninterrupted view of the stage 'for every person in the house'. The proscenium arch was flanked by figures in aedicules under bulbous canopies, and along the top was a frieze of *putti* holding garlands; strapwork and cartouches decorated the fronts of the circle and gallery, and the whole was illuminated by electric lights hanging from a deeply moulded, panelled ceiling.

Such relatively small theatres were taken in Matcham's stride along with all his other work, but at the same time as he was working at Keighley he was occupied with an unusual design in Leeds, where the old Shambles between Vicar Lane and Briggate was moved away to a new building north of the markets, designed by W.Hanstock and Son (1899)[62] in a florid reminiscence of Hendryck de Keyser's Meat Market

220

221

56 Wakefield Opera House still exists, but it is no longer used as a theatre; see Taylor,K., *Wakefield District heritage*, Wakefield 1976, 98f.

57 *B* (1898),lxxv,296. The theatre was demolished in 1968 after many years of use as a cinema.

58 ibid.(1899),lxxvii,151.

59 ibid.,378.

60 See Chadwick,S., *Theatre Royal, the romance of the Huddersfield stage*, Huddersfield 1941.

61 *B* (1899),lxxvii,474. It was demolished in 1961. Matcham also remodelled the now demolished Theatre Royal, Castleford.

62 Demolished in 1969.

220. Wakefield, Opera House; the auditorium of F.Matcham's first theatre in West Yorkshire, opened in 1894 but no longer used for its original purpose.

221. Keighley, Queen's Theatre; Matcham appears to have had an almost endless supply of ornamental details for use in his interiors, even in relatively small theatres such as this demolished example (1899).

63 Quoted from a programme dated 1903, reproduced in Glasstone, op.cit.,pl.119; see also *YP*, 18 Aug 1898.

in Haarlem; but it was reticent and modest by comparison with Matcham's swaggering replacement of the old Shambles and the surrounding buildings and courtyards, which is discussed in another part of this study. In this design, Matcham left his accustomed world of make-believe and artificial light for one of the largest comprehensive developments in the provinces, in which the Empire Palace was one of the major elements. In January 1897, it was announced that the theatre's site had 'just been marked out and labelled, and . . . a start has been made with the work of demolishing the property'.

The theatre (or music hall as it was from the beginning) was one of the chain which were incorporated as Moss's Empires in 1899. Its frontage was in Briggate, and the entrance foyer was designed on a lavish scale with 'Walls, Columns, and Staircases of Italian Marble, Balconies, and enriched Dome Ceilings [which] give some idea of the magnificence beyond'.[63] The auditorium, which seated two thousand five hundred and offered standing room to another thousand, was rectangular in plan, as usual in Matcham's theatres, but the dress circle was planned as a serpentine horse-shoe terminating in stage boxes leading into a proscenium flanked by aedicules and statues. Widespread arched openings formed the sides of the auditorium, following the model of the Paris Opéra, and the ceiling rose in a deep cove to break upwards as a higher central section. The decoration was

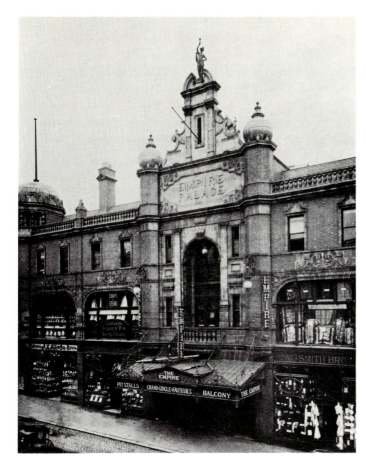

222. Leeds, Empire Palace; the Briggate façade (now demolished) of the major building (1903) in Matcham's comprehensive redevelopment of a large area was an admirable advertisement for the moulded faience manufactured locally at Burmantofts. (*Burmantofts faience catalogue*, 1902)

223. Bradford, Alhambra Theatre; opened in 1914 as the last of the traditional theatres in West Yorkshire (Chadwick and Watson).

222

64 The Empire was closed in 1961 and subsequently demolished, but all the rest of Matcham's development of shops and arcades remains intact externally.

lavishly applied, and over the proscenium was a vast rococo relief of festoons and flying figures. The prevailing tones were cream and gold, heightened by copper bronze over the moulded sections of the ceiling and the fronts of the boxes and circles; the draperies and carpets were 'crushed pink', and there were painted scenes of carnival in the ceiling panels. It was claimed that the 'Eminent Theatrical Architect, Mr. FRANK MATCHAM, of London' had not only luxuriously furnished and upholstered the theatre, but he had, with his customary skill, arranged it so that 'everyone obtains a clear and uninterrupted view of the stage'.[64]

Externally, the Empire appeared in Briggate as the tall central façade of one block in Matcham's layout; octagonal towers crowned by oriental domes rose at the side of a central section filled by a gigantic balconied window set between pilasters and topped by a huge keystone. Higher, above the decorative panel containing the theatre's name, stood a tall, broken-pedimented gable with pilasters and side scrolls, leading up to a life-size figure and an arc light; and this set the note for the whole group of buildings, one vast, colourful, vulgar, music-hall scene. It belongs to no stylistic category, although there are frequent references to squat, tapered, Jacobean pilasters with Ionic capitals, and to curious caricatures of strapwork ornament; bulbous balusters are magnified and metamorphosed into colonnades

279

surrounding domed cupolas decorated with scrolls; Saracenic arched windows are inserted inside segmental openings, and a central decoration on one of the Vicar Lane façades consists of a pair of boldly projecting bay windows surmounted by a balcony with a heavy open strapwork balustrade spanning the space between. There are cupolas with hemispherical or octagonal pointed roofs at each corner, and a high, pedimented frontispiece in the centre of each street façade – the whole executed in hard, glowing red brick and bright orange Burmantofts faience.

The County Arcade, which was built to connect Briggate and Vicar Lane, is equally theatrical;[65] and coloured mosaics representing wine, fish and game add an extra richness to the gorgeously overloaded façade of the King Edward Restaurant. Inside was 'a strikingly handsome grill-room with mosaic floor, polished marble walls and columns . . . From the grill-room a handsome marble staircase, flanked by columns of Mexican onyx with a balustrade of the same stone on the left, and walls panelled the full height in mahogany on the right, leads to what is known as the Grand Hall, also panelled with mahogany'.[66]

This is the apotheosis of the music hall, forsaking the normal restraints of the auditorium walls and spreading out over two acres of the town. After it came two theatres in Halifax, the Palace in 1903[67] and the Royal in 1905;[68] then the Empire in Dewsbury in 1909,[69] and the Alhambra in Bradford in 1914;[70] but they seem only an epilogue in the shadow of Matcham's exuberant display, a shadow that was darkened by the *Builder*'s brief notice in 1910 that Richard Horsfall and Sons were the architects for 'a new electric theatre [which] has been erected near Ward's End, Halifax'.[71]

223

65 See 325 for a discussion of the County Arcade.

66 *LM*, 20 June 1904. 'Throughout the whole of the public rooms an elaborate scheme of decoration has been tastefully carried out, while the beauty of the structural decorations is enhanced by a costly collection of works of art by well-known Academy exhibitors, including works from the brushes of De Heem, the Dutch still-life painter, Atkinson Grimshaw, Liddendale, and others. In the Grand Hall, too, are statues of the Venus de Medici and the Venus de Milo'.

67 Designed by Ernest Runtz and Ford, but Richard Horsfall and Son acted as supervising architects. It was built of brick with faience dressings, concentrating the decoration of Ionic columns, corner turrets and cupolas on the splayed corner entrance. It was demolished in 1959.

68 *HG*, 6 Aug 1904; designed by Richard Horsfall and Son, with an imposing façade to Southgate. The auditorium was planned to hold 2,000, and the upper tiers are carried on steel cantilevers which enabled the views of the stage to be uninterrupted by columns. The building still exists, but it is no longer used as a theatre.

69 *B* (1909), xcvi,69; *Dewsbury Reporter*, 9 Jan, 7 Aug 1909. Designed by Chadwick and Watson with a white faience façade, it was demolished in 1960 after being closed for five years.

70 Designed by Chadwick and Watson on a triangular site, with the main entrance on the corner under a tall domed pavilion with coupled Corinthian columns around the perimeter; behind this rises a higher block, topped by another pair of domes. The auditorium, seating 1,800, is decorated in a more genteel manner than the extrovert style fashionable in the 90s. The architects curiously described the whole as being in the style of the 'English renaissance of the Georgian period'.

71 *B* (1910), xcix,137; see Mellor,G.J., *Picture pioneers*, Newcastle upon Tyne 1971, 48.

10 The clothing trade . . . in all its glory: cloth halls, mills, warehouses and exchanges

A public house the only piece-hall was,
And one small table held the merchants' store.
Behold, how chang'd! so many now her goods,
That she can form a zone to gird the world;
With rich moreens, can deck the Russian court;
In lighter goods adorn the Japanese;
Can far outshine the tint of Persian dyes,
And clothe the world from Zembla's coldest shores,
To hottest tracts of Afric's sultry plains.

John Nicholson, *Commerce of Bradford*, 1820

'The parish of Halifax . . . being planted in the great waste and moores . . . the . . . inhabitants altogether doe live by cloth making';[1] so did those in Leeds and Bradford, and Lord Clarendon wrote of them in the seventeenth century as 'three very populous and rich towns, depending wholly on clothiers'. The West Yorkshire valleys had made their contribution to the country's economic and industrial life since the Middle Ages; there were fulling mills owned by the Lords of the Manor on the Aire and the Calder in the thirteenth century, and such weekly markets as those at Almondbury, Pontefract and Bradford, but there is no clear evidence that the cloth produced was for anything but local consumption. The industry gradually grew in importance, taking over from York and Beverley in the sixteenth century, until during the eighteenth West Yorkshire was responsible for at least three-fifths of the total output of the country's woollen manufacture. This was the product of the domestic industry, which operated in the hamlets within walking or pack-horse riding distance of the markets. Jefferys's 1771 map of Yorkshire shows the hill country south of the Calder, from Halifax and Heptonstall to Holmfirth and Saddleworth, thickly sprinkled with the names of clusters of cottages in which the wool was spun and woven, scoured and washed in the water-operated fulling mills in the valleys, until it was ready to be taken to market.

Yet the sale of cloth often took place in strange surroundings. In Huddersfield the churchyard and the tombstones were used to display the goods, and in Halifax 'great quantities of coloured cloth were sold in the butchers' shambles'. Defoe's description of the cloth market in Leeds in the early eighteenth century is famous but bears partial repetition. It was, he thought, 'a Prodigy of its Kind, and . . . not to be equalled in the World', and it so impressed him that he wrote about its appearance and customs in great detail.[3] It was held in the open in Briggate, the road into the town from the bridge on which the market was first started by the clothiers hanging their goods on the parapets.

1 Watson, 67ff. Extracted from an Act in favour of Halifax, passed in 1555. It gave the town special permission to purchase wool through middlemen, a concession forbidden elsewhere in the country.

2 *Baines's account of the woollen manufacture of England*, (reprint) Newton Abbott 1970, with an introduction by Ponting, K.G., 17.

3 Defoe, D., *A tour thro' the whole island of Great Britain*, (first pub 1724–7) London 1927, ii, 611f. See also 600ff. for a description of the clothiers' houses outside Halifax and the textile trade processes at the time.

As trade increased, the market spread further into the town, and by Defoe's time the whole street was filled with rows of trestles. The clothiers brought their work early in the morning, and as soon as the bell rang 'the whole Market is fill'd; all the Boards upon the Tressels are covered with Cloth, close to one another as the Pieces can lie long ways by one another, and behind every Piece of Cloth, the Clothier standing to sell it'. That was the traditional way of selling, 'all managed with the most profound Silence . . . by the Persons buying and selling'; but greater prosperity brought with it a natural demand for something more dignified than a street in which to sell to London merchants who exported cloth to 'the *English* Colonies in *America . . .* to *Petersburgh, Riga, Dantzic, Narva,* and to *Sweden* and *Pomerania*'.

There had been Cloth Halls since the sixteenth century. A single-storey building was erected in Heptonstall in 1545–58 by the Waterhouse family, Lords of the Joint Manor of Halifax-cum-Heptonstall,[4] who proudly called their little hall Blackwell in imitation of London's cloth market where Yorkshire kerseys were sold in the 'Northern Hall'. Halifax superseded Heptonstall as the market for the Calder valley, just as Almondbury lost its importance to Huddersfield in the Colne valley, and it too had a Blackwell Hall at Hall End which 'conteyne[s] in length by estimation ffower score and ten ffoote and in breadth thirty and six foote'.[5] The date of its erection is not known for certain, but it was probably early in Elizabeth's reign. It was referred to in 1629 as a 'Linnen Hall', and again in 1708 (when it was probably rebuilt or enlarged) also as a 'Woollen Hall'.[6] Wakefield had a Hall in 1710, and in August of that year Ralph Thoresby noted he had ridden 'with the Mayor and others to my Lord Irwin, about erecting of a Hall for white cloths [in Leeds] . . . , to prevent the damage to this town . . . of one lately erected at Wakefield, with design to engross the woollen trade'.[7] Within nine months Leeds had a Cloth Hall in Briggate, 'built upon pillars and arches in the form of an exchange, with a quadrangular court within . . . and a bell in a beautiful cupola painted and gilt';[8] but it was too small, and another was built in Meadow Lane, south of the river, in 1755. Three years later the Coloured or Mixed Cloth Hall was opened at the west end of the town. The largest building in Leeds at the time, it was designed by

4 The Hall had been converted as two cottages by the early eighteenth century, and a second storey was added later.

5 Roth,H.L., *The Yorkshire coiners 1767–1783,* Halifax 1906,207. This refers to a deed of sale of 1629 of two houses described as being near the Linnen Hall, which was located between Cheapside and Crown Street.

6 ibid., In 1708 Lord Irwin, Lord of the Manor of Halifax, let to John Fourness, gentleman, and others the Woollen Hall and the Linnen Hall; Watson, 68.

7 Atkinson,D.H., *Ralph Thoresby, the topographer; his town and times,* Leeds 1885,ii,31.

8 Thoresby, 248.

224

A South East Perspective View of the Mix'd Cloth Hall at Leeds in the County of York.

224. Leeds Coloured or Mixed Cloth Hall (J.Moxson 1758); described as exceeding 'any Building of its kind in Europe'.

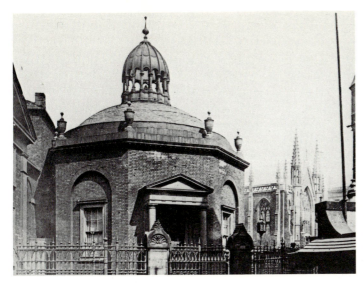

225. Leeds Coloured or Mixed Cloth Hall; the Exchange, built c.1780 at the entrance. In the background is the south end of Mill Hill Unitarian Chapel. From a photograph c.1880.

226. Leeds, White Cloth Hall; the remaining fragment of the 1774–5 building.

9 An undated bird's-eye view of the Coloured Cloth Hall is inscribed 'Design'd, Delineated, and Superintended by John Moxson'. It was engraved by J.Woolfe of York. John Moxson (1700–82) was Surveyor of the Highways in Leeds.

10 Ryley, J., *The Leeds guide*, Leeds 1806, 57.

11 The domestic clothier usually attended to the fulling himself. If he supplied cloth to the Coloured Cloth Hall he also did the dyeing. In the White Cloth Hall the cloth was fulled by the clothiers, then finished by the merchants.

12 'A visit to Chapel Allerton & Harwood in 1767', *T S* (1945), 333ff.

John Moxson and described as exceeding 'any Building of it's kind in Europe';[9] in form it consisted of a large rectangular courtyard surrounded on three sides by single-storey brick buildings and measuring one hundred and twenty yards and a half by sixty-six. There was an entrance in the middle of the fourth side, and at the opposite end of the courtyard the five-bay, pedimented central section was surmounted by a bell cupola. All the façades were plain, consisting only of regularly spaced large windows with segmental heads, although a gable or pediment broke the monotony in each of the long sides. The finest architectural feature of the group was probably built about twenty-five years later than the Hall itself. It stood to the right of a new pedimented entrance, as a detached octagon covered by a shallow dome and an arcaded cupola that was curiously Byzantine in form; this building, entered through a projecting porch, was the Exchange, built 'for the convenience of the Merchants, and for transacting business respecting the Cloth Hall by the Trustees'.[10] The domed interior was neatly decorated in a plain Neo-classical taste, and over the fireplace hung a portrait of Edward III, who was popularly believed to have introduced the woollen manufacture into England in the fourteenth century.

225

The three wings of the Hall were divided into 'six long streets or aisles', each containing two rows of stands two feet wide, where the clothiers stood to display and sell their cloths in rough state to the merchants and finishers.[11] It was said that 3,000 clothiers might be seen in one day in this Hall, which was 'capable of holding Cloth so as to be expos'd to Sale, to the Value of 109200£ at a moderate Computation'. The Hall 'was built in such a position as entirely prevents the rays of ye sun or a blaze of light entering ye Apartments, either in ye Winter or Summer Season till after ye Time appointed for ye Cloth's being exposed to sale. They could not show the Cloth in a true Light if the sun was suffered to shine upon it'.[12]

Soon Leeds added yet another White Cloth Hall, close to where

283

13 In 1786 the old White Cloth Hall was sold for £300, and £14 19s 3d was paid to Mr Johnson 'for valuing the Old White Cloth Hall, taking down the cupola and clock and removing them to the new White Cloth Hall'. (Heaton,H., 'The Leeds White Cloth Hall', *TS* (1915),xxii,137.) This was almost certainly William Johnson of Temple Newsam.

14 Bray,W., *Sketch of a tour into Derbyshire and Yorkshire*, London 1783,261f.

15 Crump,W.B., and Ghorbal,G., *History of the Huddersfield woollen industry*, Huddersfield 1935,100ff. The Hall was demolished in 1930, but photographs of it are reproduced on pls.22,24 and 25. Some fragments, including the cupola, have been re-erected in Ravensknowle Park.

several merchants lived in Kirkgate. It was proposed in September 1774 and completed in October 1775 when it was opened 'for the sale of broad-white cloths, duffils and coatings', to the accompaniment of a 'compleat peal of Grandsire Tripples . . . in three hours and six minutes'. Its completion caused a dispute between 'the Merchants of Leeds and the White Clothiers', but the *Leeds Mercury* (22 June) was able to report this as settled in 1779. 'After being eloquently entertained at the Star and Garter, they went in procession to the Hall, preceded by a band of music playing *God save the King*, when the Clothiers took possession; they then returned to the Inn, where after many local and patriotic toasts were drunk, they parted in the greatest harmony'. Built around a courtyard, the White Cloth Hall was 300 feet by 210; it was divided into five streets and contained 1,213 stalls.

226   Its main frontage still exists – a plain brick façade with a central pedimented section crowned by a cupola containing a bell (both removed from the earlier White Cloth Hall) which rang to signal the opening and closing of the market. The façade which faced on to the Calls had a pedimented section of three bays, seven blank arcaded bays at each side and terminating pavilions with Venetian windows. Possibly the designer was William Johnson, who was employed as agent at Temple Newsam by Lord Irwin.[13] In the two Leeds Cloth Halls, according to one visitor in 1777, 'the clothing trade . . . which is a more genuine source of wealth than the mines of Peru, is seen in all its glory'.[14]

Huddersfield's Cloth Hall, built in 1766 on the instructions of the Lord of the Manor, Sir John Ramsden, was similar in character to those in Leeds, but less conventional in form.[15] Elliptical in plan, 240 feet by 208, it had a main hall across its shorter axis, entered through

228. Halifax, the Piece Hall (J. Hope 1774–9) consists of two storeys of separate rooms opening off colonnaded galleries. An additional lower storey on the east side accommodated the clothiers' pack horses.

16 Internal wings on the long axis were added in 1864. See Hordern, I., *Notes relating to the Ramsden estate and Huddersfield*, Yorkshire Archaeological Society MS 491.

17 James, 271.

18 It should also be recorded that there was a Blanket Hall in Heckmondwike in the eighteenth century, which was replaced in 1840 by a five-bay building with a pediment supported by giant pilasters and crowned by the customary bell cupola (Peel, F., *Spen valley, past and present*, Heckmondwike 1893, 334). It was designed by Perkin and Backhouse. There was also a White Cloth Hall at Gomersal, of which the foundation stone was laid on 23 March 1775 (*LM*, 28 March 1775).

19 Roth, op.cit., 207ff.

20 *LM*, 5 April 1774.

227 the east façade; built of brick, the latter was three bays wide, two storeys high and pedimented, with stone quoins and dressings, a clock tower and bell cupola. Around the circumference of the ellipse was a range of small rooms with windows looking into the courtyard, its inner face consisting of a blank arcade of semicircular-headed arches containing windows with concentric heads. The main hall was divided by a central row of stone Tuscan columns, and the area was laid out with lines of booths or stalls, 148 in all at first, but increased when the building was added to in 1780.[16] The Cloth Hall was a considerable building for eighteenth-century Huddersfield, and as it was built on high ground it towered over the town and closed the view up King Street when approaching from the west. Other West Yorkshire towns were not slow to follow; Wakefield built another hall, seventy yards by ten, in 1778, called the Tammy Hall because of the thin worsteds (tammies) which were a speciality of the town. In 1773 'the gentlemen, merchants, woolstaplers, manufacturers, and others in the town and neighbourhood' of Bradford built a Hall 144 feet by 36, two storeys high; on both floors there was a central wall along the length of the hall, against which were fixed closed stalls where cloth could be kept from one market day to another. Except that it had a cupola for the obligatory bell, little is known about its appearance.[17] Undoubtedly these buildings were the scene of great commercial activity,[18] but architecturally they were overshadowed by Halifax's initiative in 1774.[19]

At a meeting of Halifax manufacturers in April of that year 'it was the Opinion of all present, that a Hall, erected in some convenient Place in the Town and Neighbourhood would be of great public Utility'.[20] The proposal caught the local imagination, and support was

285

strong. 'Let us not quarrel in regard to Situation', wrote A MANUFACTURER in the *Leeds Mercury* in May, 'the bee will find its cell, tho' in the desert: so the Merchants and Manufacturers, tho' detached from the accustomed seat of Business'.[21] The site was selected by ballot, but the advice freely offered to the voters stressed a confidence in the new building's powers of attraction: 'Let no man impose upon you in this Matter ... See you have a large and open situation ... Be not concerned about this or that end of the town – Where you fix your Hall, there will be the head.'[22]

A site on Talbot's Close was chosen, and tenders for the erection of the building, by then referred to as the Piece Hall, were invited.[23] From another published letter written by A MANUFACTURER it appears there were at least two designs, one for a circular building, probably suggested by the Hall in Huddersfield, and made by 'a Native of this town'.[24] This letter has hitherto been interpreted as meaning that Thomas Bradley of Halifax supplied the design executed, but it is now clear that the circular proposal was his and that the credit for the Piece Hall must be given to John Hope of Liverpool.[25] The original broadsheet published in 1779 when the building was opened includes the verse:

Now our Desires are crown'd by HOPE,
We'll be no longer seen
Dispers'd around in ev'ry Street,
As heretofore we've been;
But to a HALL whose Beauty vies
With Palaces of old,
Our Handy-work shall now be brought,
And straight be turn'd to Gold.[26]

The significance of HOPE was recognised only by reference to an original copy of the broadsheet, a rare item, on which an asterisk against the word referred to a footnote stating simply 'The Architect'. A later reprint omitted the footnote and denied Hope the credit for this great commercial monument.

Like Huddersfield's Hall, the outer walls are blank, creating an air of secrecy about the business operations taking place inside, as well as guarding against theft. The main entrance from the west is through a pedimented archway surmounted by a cupola, and this opens into a vast courtyard, 273 feet by 330, surrounded by two tiers of rooms opening off an open gallery; the slope of the ground permitted the building of an additional storey on the east side which provided space for stabling the pack-horses on which the clothiers travelled to Halifax with their goods. The top storey is a Tuscan colonnade, supported on square rusticated piers through the one or two storeys of the substructure, and the total accommodation was for 315 clothiers to display their cloths or pieces in separate rooms, each with a doorway and window. The lowest storey was known as 'The Rustic', the next as 'The Arcade', and the top as 'The Colonnade'; and each manufacturer used his address in the Hall, as well as the inn where he habitually stayed the night, on his invoices and letters'[27] The construction was entirely of stone, and Whitaker noted its great merit was 'that of being proof alike against fire and thieves. With respect to the first, nothing

228

229

21 ibid., 10 May 1774.

22 ibid., 24 May 1774. This letter includes the valuation of 'the most valuable land in Halifax' at 8d per yd.

23 ibid., 3 August 1774. Detailed costs may be found in *H A S* (1904–05), 187ff., including references to the *Estimate of the Manufacturers' Hall at Halifax by Saml, and John Hope, 1775* in the Society's M S collection.

24 *L M*, 20 Dec 1774.

25 John Hope's work was mainly in Liverpool, where he designed a vaulted room in the Exchange in 1766 and was employed on other buildings in the town. His design for St John's church, Wakefield was set aside in favour of Charles Watson's in 1790. (Colvin, 297).

26 'A Song, Sung at the Opening of the Manufacturers Hall, in Halifax'; a copy of the original broadsheet is in the collection of Mr J.S.Roberts, to whom I am indebted for realising that the footnote had been omitted from the song when it was reprinted in Roth, op.cit.,217.

27 Roth, op.cit.,218 quotes e.g. John Murgatroyd of Warley occupied No.18 room in 'The Rustic' and put up at the Old Cock.

28 Whitaker, 390. 'Why is not this idea adopted in the construction of colleges, hospitals, inns, and other public buildings, nay, even in that of private houses. Why are not the partitions uniformly of stone or brick? Why are not the smaller apartments at least arched, and the floors of tarras? Since carpets are become universal, boarded floors are of no use, especially when of pine. Lath and plaster partitions ought also to be proscribed for the same reason, and for another, namely, that they form no partition to the ear. The prevalence of this plan would also reduce, in no inconsiderable degree, the price of foreign timber. Where, then, can the objection lie to a plan which unites the advantages of economy, security, durability, and comfort? What, but the interests of woodmongers and carpenters, aided by the inveterate force of habit?'

29 ibid., 390.

30 The plan of the *palestra* is pl.xxi in the Third Book of *I quattro libri dell'architettura*.

31 Roth, op.cit., quoting *HC* 1887.

32 ibid., 217.

33 The Coloured Cloth Hall lasted until 1889, but by that time it was an anachronism.

34 The main difference between worsteds and woollens is that most woollens are prepared from short-staple carded wools, whereas worsteds are manufactured from long-staple wools which are combed to separate the shorter filaments (noils) from the longer fibres (tops). The noils form an auxiliary source of supply to the woollen industry. Cloths made from woollens are fulled, those from worsteds are not.

35 The textile industry has a language almost meaningless to anyone outside. Alpaca and mohair, tops and noils, mungo and shoddy, serges and baizes, are probably reasonably well known and understood terms; but it is easy to become lost in the poetic images of shalloons, tammies, duroys and everlastings, calimancoes, moreens, kerseymeres and shags, prunelles, wildbores, bombazines, taborines and dobbies. 'How can a man write poetically of serges and druggets?', asked Dr Johnson of John Dyer's poem, *The fleece*.

36 The stalls which disfigured the great courtyard have been cleared away and the Piece Hall appears to have a secure future as an industrial museum and crafts centre. It was reopened after an extensive restoration on 3 July 1976.

about this building can be consumed but the [wooden] roof'.[28] It was a well thought out, practical arrangement, but it was conceived on a monumental scale and with an architectural quality greater than required by pure utility.

Whitaker patronisingly and mistakenly thought the building 'though perhaps the design of common masons only, by a regular boldness of perception, actually produce[s] an effect, of which tame and regular skill frequently fell short'.[29] Its derivation from the idea of a Roman forum, or probably more likely from Palladio's reconstruction of Vitruvius's description of the Greek *palestra*,[30] is fairly obvious; but there seems also to have been an underlying feeling that it was connected with those Neo-classical qualities of Independence and Liberty which were referred to more than once in the discussions about the building. The committee 'saw in it a mighty and noble work, which distinguished their native parish from every other in the kingdom'.[31] It was an early manifestation in West Yorkshire of that identification of architecture with civic pride which found its finest symbol in the nineteenth-century town hall, and the Piece Hall's completion was celebrated by a great procession through the streets. In the evening, Signor Pietro presented a fireworks display which ended with 'A beautiful Egyptian Pyramid, illuminated with spiral wheels, globes, and vertical wheels, to be set on fire by a pigeon', which is surely the Italian pyrotechnician's memory of the traditional *Lo Scoppio del Carro* in the piazza in front of the Duomo in Florence on Easter Sunday morning. If the bird sets fire instantly to the fireworks it is an omen for a good harvest, and the people of Halifax too hoped their new Piece Hall would bring its reward; '. . . may our Industry be blest, And Riches be the Crown'.[32]

The industry did prosper in West Yorkshire, and the Cloth Halls were its centre until well into the nineteenth century; but gradually the methods and organisation changed. The displacement of the hand-loom weavers and the domestic system by the power loom and the mills caused a decline in the use of the Halls until they became relics of the early years of a great industry. Huddersfield's was enlarged as late as 1864, yet soon after 1870 it was almost empty and during the last sixty years of life it was used as an exchange and reading-room. Bradford's ceased to be used by the leading manufacturers, and in 1853 it was converted into shops before being demolished twenty years later. The major part of the White Cloth Hall in Leeds fell a victim to the North Eastern Railway in the 1860s, and was replaced by a conventional Italianate commercial design in King Street which survived until 1895 but was never fully used.[33] The Halifax Piece Hall remained the town's commercial centre until the 1840s when trade began to dwindle. Halifax, slower than the other towns to adopt the factory system, allowed Bradford by degrees to become the chief seat of the worsted trade,[34] and then to develop the manufacture of alpaca and mohair.[35] Yet, although the Piece Hall became a municipal wholesale vegetable and fish market in 1871,[36] it and the other Cloth Halls had established the areas in which they were built as the commercial centres, where the banks and warehouses were to be erected as the towns prospered in their different ways.

Leeds was undoubtedly the first among the West Yorkshire textile towns at the end of the eighteenth century, not only in woollen manufacture but also in flax-spinning. The names of John Marshall and Benjamin Gott are still honoured, and their buildings occupy an important place in industrial architectural history. Marshall began his flax-spinning firm in 1788 at 'a New Erected Water Mill called Scotland Mill' in what was then a rural valley five miles from the town. Within a year he was taking advantage of the ideas of a young metal smith, Matthew Murray, and experimenting with mechanical innovations. Three years later he moved to Water Lane, Hunslet, a site close to the river and canal system on which Leeds was strategically placed, where he built a steam-powered, four-storey mill; the second mill in Water Lane, started in 1794 after Marshall had taken Thomas and Benjamin Benyon into partnership, was five storeys high and fire-proof in construction, but the saving in cost made by using timber floors led to its burning in 1796. It was quickly rebuilt, probably incorporating recommendations made by James Watt after the dramatic conflagration at Samuel Wyatt's Albion Mill, Blackfriars in 1791; it lasted until its demolition in 1853, and it was subsequently joined by other iron-framed buildings added by Marshall, in the street which took his name, in 1808, 1817, 1826 and 1830. The Benyons terminated their partnership with him in 1804,[38] by which time they had completed building on their own account a new flax mill (1802–03) designed by Charles Bage, whom Marshall thought 'possessed of talent, and has a cultivated understanding'; he was also a pioneer in structural engineering and evolved for the Benyons what has been described as 'the first building in which cast-iron beams were designed in a rational manner'.[39] He used a tension flange, and the beams were simply supported by a flexible joint at the columns. Reported to be 'completely fireproof, *no timber whatever being used in the building*',[40] it was probably the first mill with a cast-iron roof, but there are no known contemporary references to its doubtless functional appearance beyond calling it 'very large and elegant'.

Marshall's finest and largest mill, started in 1838 and unique in the relatively rare revival of Egyptian architecture, could not be dismissed so non-committally. Unlike other West Yorkshire mills, including Marshall's earlier ones, this was built on a new principle as a single-storey building with advantages 'for arrangement of work, overseeing, etc.' The idea was proposed by David Roberts, an engineer, and taken up enthusiastically by John Marshall II who employed James Combe as engineer and Joseph Bonomi as architect to build Temple Mill in a style which must have been intended as an allusion to the connection between cotton and Egypt. Bonomi, who advised on the design of the Egyptian Court in the Crystal Palace in 1853 and became the curator of Sir John Soane's Museum in 1861, had spent ten years measuring and drawing temples in Egypt from 1824–34, and then returned to England where he passed part of the next two years in Yorkshire executing sculptured decoration and making use of his unrivalled knowledge of Karnak, Edfu and Philae in providing Marshall with a

37 Scotland Mill, a 'New Erected Water Mill', was a small two-storey building with a water-wheel, probably not unlike the still partly existing Sands Mill, Dewsbury (1751) and Shaw Carr Wood Mill, Slaithwaite (1787); Marshall first introduced looms in Scotland Mill in 1788. See Rimmer,W.G., *Marshall's of Leeds, flax-spinners 1788–1866*, Cambridge 1960, 26ff; Skempton,A.W., and Johnson,H.R., 'The first iron frames', *A R* (1962),cxxxi,178.

38 In 1796 the Benyons, Bage and Marshall built a mill at Shrewsbury; see Bannister,T., 'The first iron-framed buildings', *A R* (1950), clvii,238ff.

39 Skempton and Johnson, op.cit.,185.

40 Ryley, op.cit.,103. This guide book lists the other mills in Leeds at that time. Benyon and Bage's mill in Meadow Lane survived in part until 1940 and was recorded; see Hamilton,S.B., 'The use of cast-iron in buildings', *Transactions Newcomen Society* (1940–1),xxi,141 and Bannister, op.cit.,243. For a list of Yorkshire mills 1774–1835, see Jenkins,D.T., *The West Riding wool textile industry 1770–1835*, Edington 1975,206ff.

230

41 The *Penny Magazine* (1843),499, gives the credit for the design to James Combe, who was probably responsible for everything except the façades, which the writer described as 'enriched by details partly furnished by Mr. Bonomi an architect, who has visited Egypt'. Previously this has been assumed to mean Ignatius Bonomi, but Joseph's responsibility is confirmed by published correspondence in the professional press in 1861, at the time he was recommended for appointment to the curatorship of Sir John Soane's Museum. According to the terms of the bequest, the post has to be held by an architect, and there were complaints that Bonomi did not fulfil this requirement. In the *Building News* (1861),vii,211, he attempted to justify his eligibility, not only because he was the son and brother of architects, but also because he had 'designed and furnished the drawings for a large building with an Egyptian façade at Holbeck, near Leeds'. The *Builder* (1861),xix,165, joined in the dispute mildly by publishing a letter from *ARCHITECTUS* which referred to an example of 'Egyptian architecture, which some enterprising cotton-spinner in the north wished to transplant to his city'; and the *Building News* took up the argument in the editorial of its next issue (p. 217), noting that 'Holbeck is a long way off', and asking, 'Does this mean that it is a cotton mill – *an Egyptian cotton mill*, or only *an Egyptian cotton warehouse*, or is it, perhaps, both? Good heavens!' The writer continued to make heavily humorous remarks about the use of the Egyptian style, but Bonomi's appointment was confirmed, and he remained as curator of Sir John Soane's Museum until 1878. See *Transactions of the Society of Biblical Archaeology* (1878),vi,563 for an account of Bonomi's career.

42 See e.g., Henderson,W.O., *Industrial Britain under the Regency*, London 1968, 109ff., and *J.C.Fischer and his diary of industrial England 1814–51*, London 1972,58ff.

43 Aspinall,A.,(ed.), *Mrs. Jordan and her family*, London 1951,130ff. The Duke of Clarence and Lord Dundas had visited Gott's factory in 1806 when the Prince of Wales and his brother were staying at Ledston Hall as the guests of Michael Angelo Taylor. It was on that occasion that the future George IV 'declared that he would wear with pride the beautiful specimens of cloth manufactured at Bean Ing that he had accepted from the firm'.

44 *Baines's account* . . . op.cit.,52; Crump,W.B., 'The history of Gott's mills', *TS* (1929),xxxii,254ff.

45 As an illustration of the difference between a mill and a factory, Joshua Robinson of Smithy Place, Honley, complained to the Children's Employment Commission that his mill had been classed as a factory in 1833 because 'I am engaged in scribbling, carding and fulling – it is no

design for his mill. An office wing in the same style with papyrus capitals, and a chimney in the form of Cleopatra's Needle (which cracked and was replaced in 1852 by a more conventional design), were quickly added, and even the furniture was in the Egyptian taste; but the design of the mill itself was extremely functional.[41] The working area, almost two acres in extent, is roofed by brick arches supported on cast-iron columns (which also act as rainwater pipes) fourteen inches in diameter, tied together by pairs of iron rods which could be adjusted if there were a serious change of temperature or humidity in the mill. Over the brick vaults was a layer of rough plaster, another of coal-tar, and then a topping of soil as insulation; this pioneer essay in environmental control included a forced warm-air system and channels in the floor which could be filled with water to maintain the humidity necessary in the flax-spinning process. The mill is evenly illuminated by means of sixty-five glass domes, and according to a long and often repeated tradition, the practice of grazing sheep on the grass-covered roof came to an end only after one fell through a dome.

The new mill was praised for 'the convenience of supervision, facility of access to the machines, the power of sustaining uniformity of temperature and moisture, the absence of air currents which are so objectionable in other mills, its simplicity of the driving gear, the excellent ventilation which is so desirable for the health of the workpeople', 2,600 of whom were employed in Marshall's mills and took part in a Temperance Tea in June 1840 to celebrate the opening of Temple Mill. Marshall's friend Benjamin Gott built up another large labour force (1,120 in 1830) in the Leeds building which became renowned throughout Europe and the United States. It was regarded as a *sine qua non* for a visitor to the North of England, and there are many references to it in early nineteenth-century diaries and letters.[42] 'I go on Saturday to your friend Mr. Gott's *manufactory*', wrote Mrs Jordan to her royal lover the Duke of Clarence in 1810 when she was playing at the Leeds theatre; and she reported that the Gotts were in the audience each night.[43] Gott had begun business as a merchant, in partnership with an old-established firm, Wormald and Fountaine; he had bought in the traditional manner in the cloth halls from the domestic clothiers until the coming of machinery persuaded him there was 'a good opportunity for the go-ahead merchant of the eighteenth century to become the great mill owner of the nineteenth'.[44] He came to terms with the innovations and changes which brought disaster to some of the more conservative eighteenth-century merchants and at the beginning of the new century he was one of the largest employers of labour in the country in Bean Ing Mill.

It was the earliest factory in Leeds, that is, a single group of buildings which incorporated steam-driven mills and controlled the whole textile process from wool to the finished cloth. Some owners of fulling mills had begun to introduce scribbling (or carding) machinery in the late eighteenth century, but they had not become cloth manufacturers; the slubbings (ropes of carded wool) still went to the cottages to be spun and woven.[45] Gott employed John Sutcliffe, a Halifax millwright, to plan the building in 1791, and there was

230. Leeds, Temple Mill (J.Bonomi 1838–40); John Marshall's mill on the extreme left was built first, followed by the more ornate office wing on the right.

factory – neither am I a manufacturer but work the mill for the country domestic manufacturers – there is no spinning or weaving carried on in the mill'. (Quoted in Jenkins, op.cit.,12).

46 Tann,J., *The development of the factory*, London 1970,99ff.

correspondence between them about such elements as windows, which Sutcliffe recommended should have an opening height of four feet.[46] He resigned in 1792 after his claim for fees had been disputed, but Gott erected the first section of his building in 1792–3 on a sixteen-acre site with a long river frontage, employing John Moxson as surveyor. This consisted of a scribbling and fulling mill, an engine house and dye house, and it was a timber-framed structure which caught fire in 1799 but was quickly rebuilt on a larger scale in 1801–2. The first section had been added to in 1793–4 by a building with a long frontage to what was to be Wellington Street; this was a part of the familiar view of Bean Ing Mill, a brick façade 300 feet long and four storeys high, which was extended in 1824 when a cast-iron framed wing containing a large entrance archway and a bell cupola was built to a design for which Sir William Fairbairn was engineer.

291

231. Leeds, Temple Mill; the interior, as shown in the *Penny Magazine* (1843), was designed as a pioneer essay in environmental control.

232

The complete mill by then covered a large working area surrounding a vast yard, and there was also a brick-built gas-holder, forty feet in diameter, surmounted by an iron dome and octagonal cupola; sixteen T-shaped iron ribs springing from a stone cornice carried the plates which formed the iron roof. Although Sutcliffe had made the first drawings for this historic group of buildings, and Fairbairn had designed the cast-iron for the later sections, Gott himself was probably largely responsible for the design, maybe with advice from Boulton and Watt of Soho, who supplied engines for Bean Ing. There are several points of similarity between the two famous industrial buildings in Birmingham and Leeds,[47] and Gott numbered among his many friends Matthew Boulton, James Watt and James Murdoch; another engineer friend, John Rennie, designed Wellington Bridge next to the mill in 1819 at the instigation of Gott, who placed busts of Rennie and Watt in the mansion at Armley from which he could look down on the Aire valley and his groups of mills immediately below or to the south-east where Bean Ing stood among the multiplying chimneys. Humphry Repton thought the former could 'never fail to be an interesting object by day light, and at night presents a most splendid illumination of gas light'. He complimented Gott on his 'good taste ... on the unaffected simplicity of this large building, which looks like what it is – a Mill and Manufactory, and is not disguised by Gothic windows, or other architectural pretensions, too often misapplied by way of ornament'.[48] The same could be said of all Gott's buildings which were helping to give Leeds that character awesomely described by Prince Pückler-Muskau in the 1820s after his first sight of the town by twilight. 'A transparent cloud of smoke was diffused over the whole space which it occupies, on and between several hills; a hundred red

47 Albion Mill, Blackfriars, designed and built in 1783 by Samuel Wyatt in collaboration with Boulton and Watt, must also be mentioned in connection with Soho and Bean Ing for the use of a plain, brick version of late eighteenth-century Palladianism; see Skempton,A.W., 'Samuel Wyatt and the Albion Mill', *Architectural History* (1971),xiv,53ff.

48 Repton's *Red Book* for Armley House is in the collection of Mr and Mrs Paul Mellon; see Harris,J., *A catalogue of British drawings ... in American collections*, New Jersey 1971, 172f.

fires shot upwards into the sky, and as many towering chimneys poured forth columns of black smoke. The huge manufactories, five storeys high, in which every window was illuminated, had a grand and striking effect. Here the toiling artisan labours far into the night.'[49]

Although Gott's was the largest of the West Yorkshire mills at that time, it was representative of many built between 1790 and 1830. John Foster in Queensbury, James Akroyd and John Crossley in Halifax, Isaac Holden and Samuel Cunliffe Lister in Bradford, and others were to build larger mills than Bean Ing, but they were not structurally innovatory. The development of cast iron as a structural material was largely due to Boulton and Watt, and to Fairbairn; the latter's designs for Gott and for John Wood of Bradford included beams spanning eighteen feet which were regarded with some mistrust until they had been thoroughly and satisfactorily tested. Wood's mills covered a total of seven acres and were made up of buildings of various dates; the most interesting was the 1833 addition, four storeys high with a central projection consisting of a spiral staircase around a nine-feet diameter chimney, in accordance with Fairbairn's theory that a mill chimney should not be detached, but integrated with the building. Yet it can have been whimsy alone, and not utility, that caused Fairbairn to build matching projections at the angles of the mill.[50] There are similar staircase towers at Black Dyke Mills and Copley Mills, but they do not include chimneys. Apart from such idiosyncracies, most mills followed a standard method of construction linked with an equally standard appearance of plain stone or brick walls pierced by rows of segmental arched lintels over regularly spaced cast-iron window frames. Any decoration was normally confined to the single entrance gateway which might be embellished with stone dressings, keystones, pediments or whatever architectural details caught the fancy of the owner, and often these were added to the first utilitarian buildings to testify to the firm's success. At Copley, the Akroyd mills were **233** approached through a triumphal archway erected in 1847,[51] and Lister's Great Horton Mill is fronted by a pair of monumental gateways. A short distance away from the latter, the modest Highgate **234** Mills at Clayton Heights dated 1851 and 1862 are entered through a

49 Pückler-Muskau, Prince, *Tour in England, Ireland and France by a German Prince in 1828 and 1829*, London 1833,207f.

50 Tann, op.cit.,40f.

51 This impressive building (see pl.98), which was the reason for the creation of the model village, has been demolished.

232. Leeds, Bean Ing Mill; this detail from C.Fowler's 1832 panorama of Leeds shows the extent of Benjamin Gott's group of buildings (begun 1792–3). In the foreground is Wellington Bridge (J.Rennie 1817–19), and beyond to the right is Gott's domed gas-holder.

233. Copley Mill, extended by Akroyd's when the triumphal arch was erected in 1847; one of the staircase towers can be seen immediately to the right of the entrance.

234. Clayton Heights, Highgate Mills; the utilitarian buildings (1851 and 1862) for multiple use were fronted in 1865 by the ornamental entrance arch flanked by rows of cottages.

52 *The Building Chronicle*, Edinburgh, May 1857; Clark's obituary, 197.

huge rusticated archway dated 1865 and decorated with a giant head on the keystone.

Fairbairn described how he had successfully persuaded a millowner in 1827 to add decoration to a utilitarian building, and he encouraged others to agree to pay the extra cost of cornices and pilasters. If architects had been more widely employed, they would probably have been more insistent on the use of decorative trimmings, but it is difficult to trace the names of any who provided designs for mills before the 50s. It is known that John Clark made plans for two in Leeds, a flax mill (Bank Mills) near the river for Hives and Atkinson *c.* 1833, and a cotton mill in Balm Road for John Wilkinson in 1842;[52] and the Crossley mills at Dean Clough were designed by Roger Ives, and later added to by F.M.Petty. But many mills were planned by the owners, who were not especially interested in architectural refinement. The Dean Clough Mills were proudly described as 'plain substantial structures . . . designed with a view to utility, rather than ornament [with] little or no attempt at embellishment about them'. As there were approximately 600 woollen and worsted mills in West Yorkshire by 1835, and 2,000 by 1870, there can be only a generalisation about their architecture; but just as some of the early ones were influenced by the model of Bean Ing, so the world-famous mill at Saltaire can be seen as the apotheosis of the hundreds of rectangular stone and glass buildings which fill the Pennine valleys and dominate the towns that grew to serve them. Standardised forms of fireproof construction combined with a maximum area of glazing, north-lights on the upper storey, and the use of local stone as the building material, resulted in a functional anonymous West Yorkshire tradition that changed surprisingly little throughout the nineteenth century. A chimney, and a tower to support a water tank, are normally the only appendages; and the sparsely applied decoration is almost invariably Italianate in the manner of Sir Titus Salt's mammoth model. 'Saltaire is the creation of a manufacturer who had attained success and reconstructed his works as a whole in the height of his success', commented the author of a (perhaps slightly apologetic) account of Crossley's Dean Clough Mills in 1885, 'and was thus able to pay attention to detail, to architectural embellishment, and to adapt every portion of his gigantic work to the special uses for which it was intended'.

First conceived in 1850 as the nucleus of a complete working community, the Salt mill was the wonder of the Age when it was completed in 1853.[53] It was on a scale that impressed even a public accustomed to the splendours of commerce in the Crystal Palace, where the Bradford manufacturers 'stood pre-eminent among the exhibitors of worsted textiles' and exhibited an infinite variety of cloths in contrast to the Leeds manufacturers who offered the traditional broadcloths which were already unfashionable. When the Great Exhibition closed Salt considered buying part of Paxton's building for re-erection as a weaving shed, but rejected the idea on the advice of his architects, who designed a structure two acres in area to contain 1,200 looms. The official statistics state that the south front of the Salt mill is 545 feet in length ('exactly that of St Paul's'), and the warehouse 330 feet; that 2,400 tons of solid stone were used in constructing the bases for the beam engines; that there are two tanks, one containing 500,000 gallons of rainwater and another 70,000 gallons from the Aire for fire-fighting; and that the total length of cloth produced in one year would stretch from Saltaire to Peru, the home of the alpacas whose hair was the foundation of Salt's success. The bust by Thomas Milnes which was presented to Salt by his grateful workpeople rests on a shaft supported by an alpaca and an Angora goat; 'at their feet lies a fleece enwrapping a cornucopia, from which is pouring forth a profusion of rich and luscious fruit, and falling as it were on the works and dwellings of Saltaire'.[54]

The design of the building was the joint responsibility of Fairbairn, who advised on the iron structure and the machinery, and of Lockwood and Mawson, who made the plans in the shape of a vast 'T'. The frame of the six-storey mill was enclosed by walls built of local stone and crowned by an ashlar cornice. The Italianate decoration was concentrated on the central section of the long wall of the mill, and on the offices – a symmetrical two-storey building with projecting end bays and a monumental entrance surmounted by an enormous pedimented frontispiece pierced by an open arch. The other monumental element is the chimney, 250 feet high; Salt decreed it should be 'an ornament to the place' and his architects designed it as an Italian campanile. However, another Bradford manufacturer improved on that detail in 1871–3 when Andrews and Pepper designed Manningham Mill for Samuel Cunliffe Lister (later 1st Lord Masham); the decoration is more ornately Italianate in this gigantic building with sixteen acres of floor area and a frontage to Heaton Road of 1,050 feet. The campanile chimney, 249 feet high and described as 'perhaps the handsomest and most majestic erection of its kind in England', is panelled vertically in the manner of the supreme Venetian model in Piazza San Marco.[55]

53 See Hitchcock,H.-R., *Early Victorian architecture in Britain*, London 1954,i,460f; Balgarnie,R., *Sir Titus Salt, Baronet; his life and times*, London 1877,131ff.

54 Balgarnie, op.cit.,163f.

55 Other notable Bradford mills are: Alston Works (Milnes and France) 1862–66; Bank Top Mills, Queensbury (Milnes and France) 1866; Midland Mills (Andrews and Pepper) 1871; Buttershaw Mills 1852; Whetley Mills (Milnes and France) 1865; Legrams Mills (Lockwood and Mawson) 1873; Lumb Lane Mills (Lockwood and Mawson) 1858. The last three incorporate notable chimneys with decorative elements.

235. Saltaire Mill; the south front of the building (Lockwood and Mawson and Sir W.Fairbairn) which was opened in 1853 with great festivities.

236. Bradford, Manningham Mill (Andrews and Pepper 1871–3), built for Samuel Cunliffe Lister with a main frontage almost twice as long as that of Saltaire Mill.

The architectural splendour of Manningham Mill, built on a commanding site west of Bradford, was calculated to impress buyers; but most mills were not so conspicuously on view. *The Century's Progress*, published in 1893, illustrates innumerable West Yorkshire textile buildings, ranging from vast groups like Illingworth's Whetley Mills (Milnes and France 1865) and Ambler's Midland Mills (Andrews and Pepper 1871), both in Bradford, to smaller ones in Keighley, Cleckheaton and all the textile towns; but almost without exception they are in that category described by Fairbairn as having 'no pretension to architectural design', however much they might impress by their severe, geometric monumentality in their manmade settings of canals and railway viaducts. There was no need to indulge in expensive ornament unless it was going to be profitable, and so it was the warehouses in the towns which became the architectural showpieces.

Changes in the methods by which cloth was sold and distributed were responsible for the growth in importance of the warehouse. Within thirty or forty years of the building of the Cloth Halls merchants were finding it an advantage to show their cloths to customers in private warehouses. This was especially true in what was called 'the fancy trade where novelty and design counted for much and privacy was essential'.[56] In 1822 there were 102 manufacturers of fancy goods attending the market in Huddersfield who used as warehouses small, rented rooms in yards; and by 1830 woollen manufacturers were also showing their goods in this way. The use of the Cloth Hall was on the wane, and ultimately an area north of the old town centre, a part of the Ramsden Estate around the new square in front of the railway station, was developed for warehouses. New streets, laid out in a rectangular grid pattern were lined by these buildings which have more or less uniform, ashlar-faced Neo-classical or Italianate street frontages. William Tite was retained as a consultant to approve the designs of the warehouses on the Ramsden Estate, and he himself provided some of the best. These warehouses are not unlike town houses, each having an entrance hall and staircase leading to the offices in the street front of the building and to the warehouses built out at the rear. These latter are large, rectangular rooms with cross-lighting through windows opening to the intermediate courtyards (as well as being top-lit on the upper floor), and they have service access by hoists from narrow streets at the rear. Many still survive in John William Street, and in the area south of the station where Britannia Buildings (built as warehouses for George Crossland to a design by William Tite),[57] in its adapted form as the headquarters of the Huddersfield and Bradford Building Society, handsomely balances the George Hotel on the other side of St George's Square.

237

It was a characteristic in all the towns to build warehouses as near as possible to railway stations; not only in Leeds, Bradford, Halifax and Huddersfield. There are fine Italianate warehouses immediately opposite Dewsbury's little Tudor station, and the road down the hill from Batley's station is lined with Venetian Gothic and Italianate warehouses, some designed by Sheard and Hanstock c. 1873. But it was in Bradford that the 'home-trade' warehouse, in which was stocked a wide range of textiles to display to buyers, was raised to a level of architectural magnificence which caused them to be described justifiably as 'palatial structures . . . the most splendid of their kind in the kingdom'.[58] By the middle of the century Bradford had become the acknowledged centre of the trade, and the number of visiting merchants from Leeds, Manchester and abroad (especially Germany, from whence many emigrated to become residents in the town) soared to great heights. The first warehouses were built in Piccadilly to Greek Revival designs by James Richardby in 1830–4, and these were quickly followed by others built on an area of meadow, ten acres in extent, on which Thomas Dixon laid out a number of streets, all uniformly thirty feet wide. Those built in the 1830s were relatively utilitarian warehouses, but in the 40s and 50s the increased trade, swollen by the coming of the railway and the demand for stuff

56 Crump and Ghorbal, op.cit.,108.

57 It is not easy to ascertain which of the Huddersfield warehouses were the work of Tite himself, but it is believed those surrounding St George's Square and in Railway Street were built from his designs.

58 James, 244.

237. Huddersfield, Britannia Buildings; representative of the Italianate warehouses built on the Ramsden Estate by or under the control of W. Tite, this detail is of a bay of Crossland's warehouse (now the Huddersfield and Bradford Building Society) dating from 1856.

238. Bradford, Hall Ings; Milligan and Forbes' warehouse (Andrews and Delaunay 1852–3), an example of the Italian *palazzo* style which was almost universally adopted by Bradford merchants (now *Bradford Telegraph and Argus*).

59 I have been greatly helped in writing this section by being allowed to make use of an unpublished M.Sc. thesis by Roberts, J.S., *The Bradford textile warehouse 1770–1914*, University of Bradford 1976.

warehouses, called for a more splendid image of prosperity.[59] Jonathan Dixon provided austere designs in 1849 for buildings in Leeds Road for John Haigh and Frederic Schwann; but St George's Hall, completed in 1853, introduced an architectural illusion of Italy, and two of the Bradford palace-warehouses finished at the same time were equally allusive. There is a tenuous analogy between the late fourteenth-century Florentine wool-merchant's residence and place of business and its nineteenth-century counterpart, which did not escape notice at the time although the Bradford merchants did not live above the shop. The point need not be laboured, but it is noticeable the Yorkshire town was quick to identify itself with the city on the Arno whenever there was an opportunity, even to the extent of recreating the tower of the Palazzo Vecchio in its Town Hall.

238   The two designs of 1852–3 which raised the warehouse to a new level of architectural quality were those made by Andrews and Delaunay in Hall Ings for Milligan and Forbes, and by Lockwood and Mawson in Leeds Road for Titus Salt. The first, built next to St George's Hall, was a free adaptation of an Italian *palazzo*, in which the presumed *piano nobile* moved up one storey; the second was a vast building on a corner site, ten bays long in each direction from a single-bay canted corner. The ground floor of Salt's building was rusticated, and there were three upper floors, the topmost designed as a Corinthian arcade crowned by

a huge bracketed cornice; both designs were nobly Roman. Leeds Road, and the sloping ground between the new Peel Square and the parish church, became the palace-warehouse area in which tall, richly detailed façades facing across narrow streets, created an unforgettable effect, especially after they had changed to jet-black canyons. Almost without exception, their plans followed the pattern of large, normally irregular, rectangles with two street frontages and an entrance on a quadrant or canted corner, leading directly into a circular or octagonal staircase-hall which was usually handsomely decorated with ornamental plasterwork and a cast-iron staircase balustrade. [60] Externally, most corners were canted, slightly inset and decoratively detailed, but a design by Andrews and Delaunay in Currer Street (1860) more gracefully incorporates a quadrant corner which curves into a long concave front following the line of the street.

The great period of Bradford warehouse building was 1860–73, when Continental markets opened up. Prosperity was at its height, and Lockwood and Mawson headed the architectural profession in the town. They made the design for the Law Russell warehouse in Vicar Lane (1873), concentrating the decoration on the splayed corner which was visible from the bottom of the steeply sloping street. It was treated as a pavilion, with coupled Corinthian columns framing each of the five superimposed stages, as in the New Louvre; the first and second have windows with shallow pediments on brackets, and the third and fourth are Venetian; the whole is crowned with a small Second Empire dome. Lockwood and Mawson's most satisfying elevation is that of the American and Chinese Export warehouse, also in Vicar Lane, and built in 1871. The ground floor recalls the rusticated, vermiculated treatment of St George's Hall, and above is a richly detailed *piano nobile* of closely spaced, pedimented windows. Such a lavish substructure is strong enough visually to support the three upper floors and heavy, bracketed cornice without any strain.[61]

Above all, however, it was the firm of Milnes and France that was principally associated with the Bradford palace-warehouses; Eli Milnes alone claimed to have built more than thirty in the Leeds Road area between 1852 and 1860. They evolved a dignified, austere form of building, such as Foster's in Well Street (1858, improved 1863), Briggs Priestley's in Vicar Lane (1866–7), Leo Schuster's in Leeds Road (1869–73), Delius's in Peckover Street (1873), Behrens's in East Parade (1873), and the two Well Street warehouses (1864–7).[62] Their detailing, like Brodrick's in Leeds, was generally of a monumental simplicity with bold mouldings entirely suited to the nature of the stone, and splayed plinths in scale with the tall façades; but Milnes's best known building was the group of three warehouses in Peel Square which shared a long, convex frontage of fifteen bays of richly carved ashlar. The arcaded ground floor was embellished with panels of arabesque ornament on the piers and spandrels, and the elaborately detailed arches to the windows and doors contained keystones which rose to support the sills of the first-floor windows; these in turn had heavy brackets and segmental pediments linked with the second-floor windows, which were set in projecting surrounds and had their own

240

241

242

60 Several of these staircase-halls have been spoilt by the insertion of lifts, but their elaborate decoration often survives.

61 These are two of the Bradford warehouses which have been restored and adapted as offices; see Linstrum,D., 'Tough grandeur', *Architectural conservation in Europe* (ed.Cantacuzino), London 1975,11f.

62 *B* (1862),xx,281.

240. Bradford, Vicar Lane; on the left is Lockwood and Mawson's warehouse for Law Russell (1873–4), and on the right their American and Chinese Export warehouse (1871). In the distance is Briggs Priestley's warehouse (Milnes and France 1866–7).

63 ibid.,750. 'The basement floor of each [warehouse] consists of piece-rooms and blanket-stores; on the ground floors are the counting-houses, grey rooms and packing shops. The three intermediate floors are occupied as goods, stock, and sale rooms; and the top floor as making-up rooms. Hoists worked by steam power communicate with each story; . . . Speaking pipes communicate from the counting-houses to the different sale rooms, and to the making-up and packing shops'. The carving, symbolic of local trade and commerce, was executed by Mawer and Ingle of Leeds; J.S.Roberts points out (op.cit.120) that stonecarvers were scarce in Bradford but plentiful in Leeds. Consequently, many Bradford buildings were constructed in stone from the Leeds area, to which the craftsmen were accustomed. Even the stone for St George's Hall came from the Earl of Cardigan's quarries near Leeds.

keystones and dentillated cornices; above these were masks in the middle of floriated decoration rising to connect with the top storey, in which panelled lintels became the base of the bracketed cornice.[63] The cumulative effect was magnificently overdone, with the prodigality of expense characteristic of these Bradford palace-warehouses, but more overtly displayed than usual. The tradition changed little; woollen warehouses became more elaborate after the pattern had been set by the stuff warehouses, as in Rhodes Calvert's austere building in Manor Row (1883) and the neighbouring Manor House by Fairbank and Wall (1892). The tradition was so well established that it was followed in such buildings as those in Canal Road dating from immediately before the First World War.

The development of warehouses in Leeds was less consistent, and less impressive in the total architectural effect, but in the 1860s they began to fill the area at the east end of Wellington Street, close to the two railway stations and the latest of the Cloth Halls in King Street. An interesting early example is the warehouse for William Lupton and

243

302

241. Bradford, Vicar Lane; many warehouses in the area traditionally known as 'Little Germany' incorporate bold, large-scale masonry detailing, as in the monumental gateway to the yard in Briggs Priestley's warehouse (Milnes and France 1866–7).

242. Bradford, Peel Square; a group of three, now demolished, warehouses (E.Milnes 1862). (*Builder* (1872))

Co., designed by William Reid Corson; the brick façade with ashlar rusticated dressings to the lower windows is conventional, but the detailing of the doorway is an original amalgam of a number of widely assorted stylistic motifs. Whilst superfically Italianate, it incorporates Greek ornament in the capitals, and Gothic in the semicircular fanlight within the rusticated arched opening. The *Building News* complimented Corson on the skill with which 'the seemingly discordant elements blend most harmoniously together' in this 'design [which] sprung from nature and intimate study by one who is evidently capable of analysing and comprehending the merits of the old examples'.[64] When a proposal to build on the neighbouring site was made by D. and J.Cooper, Lupton's offered to hand them plans and details of the cost of their building provided Corson were employed as architect.[65] The result was the impressive line of frontages in this section of Wellington Street, consistent in scale and bold detailing. William Reid Corson left Leeds in 1860, handing over his practice to his younger brother, George, who continued to design warehouses in a neat Gothic style in King Street and York Place. Edward Birchall built a lavish, wildly ornamented Gothic warehouse in Wellington Street in 1868 for Walter Stead,[66] and next to it Henry Walker built an equally impressive Gothic façade with a projecting tower and fine wrought iron entrance gates in 1874 for William Smith;[67] but Cuthbert Brodrick had set Leeds an example in another style and materials in the early 60s. The *Builder* commented in 1862;

Mr. Brodrick has done good service by introducing the use of this moulded brickwork into his King-street warehouses. Thus, with red, blue and black brick, moulded brick string-courses and mouldings, encaustic tiles and terracotta, we have a stock of materials which no climate will touch or destroy; and with them a field for design, both in form and colour, that will give our architects opportunities for exercising every artistic faculty they possess.[68]

This design for three warehouses was in the same idiom as Brodrick used for the enormous Scarborough hotel which was started in 1862 as the Cliff and completed five years later as the Grand;[69] the warehouses consisted of a central section of seven bays with the wider end bays slightly projected, and two flanking sections of five bays each set back from the central and having a lower eaves level. It was a dignified design which owed much of its effect to the contrasted colours of the orange-red brickwork, the moulded red brick and terracotta surrounds to the windows, and the buff stone doorways and dressings to the lower window arches which were detailed with the boldness and imagination that make Brodrick's designs so individual.[70] There is a resemblance in this building to Leo von Klenze's War Office in Munich (1824–6),[71] and it is very likely the warm coloured materials Brodrick was using in the 60s in these warehouses, the Scarborough hotel, and the Oriental Baths in Leeds (1866)[72] were suggested by the Bavarian government buildings by Gärtner and Klenze which Brodrick would have seen when he visited Munich. A few yards away a smaller warehouse, 1-2 York Place, by Stephen Smith, is in a similar manner to Brodrick's, and executed with great sophistication and attention to detail.

64 *BN* (1860),xviii,552.

65 Wilson,T.B., *Two Leeds architects*, Leeds 1937,48.

66 *BA* (1874),ii,262. This warehouse was gutted by fire, but is still standing (1977).

67 ibid.,i,152.

68 *B* (1862),xx,623.

69 See Linstrum,D., 'Cuthbert Brodrick; an interpretation of a Victorian architect', *Journal of the Royal Society of Arts* (1971), cxix,83f. for an account of the Grand Hotel.

70 The warehouses were demolished in 1967. A photograph of one of the windows is in Linstrum, 62.

71 See Hitchcock,H.-R., *Architecture: nineteenth and twentieth centuries*, Harmondsworth 1958,26,fig.4. Brodrick's sketchbook confirms he had visited Munich.

72 The design for the Oriental Baths is in the RIBA Drawings Collection (see *Catalogue*, vol. B/109), and is reproduced in Linstrum, 62. The building was remodelled in 1882 and demolished in 1969.

244

243. Bradford, Manor Row; on the right are two late nineteenth-century warehouses (R.Calvert 1883, Fairbank and Wall 1892), and on the left the Poor Law Guardians office (Andrews and Pepper 1876), now the Registry Office.

244. Leeds, King Street; a group of three, now demolished, warehouses (C.Brodrick c.1862) in his personal brick and terracotta Italianate style.

The use of coloured brickwork and terracotta continued in the work of Thomas Ambler, who provided several designs for Sir John Barran, who pioneered the wholesale clothing manufacture which was later to become Leeds's principal connection with the textile trade. His first design for Barran was for a large building (originally a Temperance Hotel but later Trevelyan Chambers), at the corner of Lower Briggate and the widened Boar Lane; this is a relatively conventional Italianate-Second Empire affair in brick and stone which forms a dignified introduction to the fine curving Boar Lane in which

305

Ambler supplied many of the designs in the 70s.[73] He is best remembered, however, for the second building he provided for Barran in 1878 on a site which occupies one half of the south side of the eighteenth-century Park Square (which it shared at first with the classical St Paul's church in what must have been a strange relationship). The style of this enormous factory-warehouse, St Paul's House, is Hispano-Moorish.

Four storeys high, the façades consist of a repeated bay design in which the ground and mezzanine windows are united within a large segmental arch framed in decorative terracotta. The first and second floor windows are similarly linked, with the additional elaboration of a transom at the intermediate floor level and Moorish colonnettes as mullions; the top floor is treated as triple Moorish arches. Above this, a brick and terracotta parapet pierced with cinquefoil openings approximates to Moorish battlements although it has a Venetian flavour; and at each of the five corners a slender octagonal tower rises above the parapet until it flowers as a terracotta minaret. The entrance doorway is a finely detailed composition in terracotta and brilliantly glazed tiles, and the Moorish arch is closed by magnificent wrought-iron gates made by Francis Skidmore. The Hispano-Moorish style was probably a joint whim of the clothier and his architect (as must have been the decision to build the chimney-shaft of Harding's Tower Works, Leeds as a copy of the campanile of the Duomo in Florence); but St Paul's House is one of the relatively few executed buildings influenced by the publication of Owen Jones's measured drawings of the Alhambra in the 1840s, and it was on a far greater scale than Jones himself ever attempted.[74] Ambler designed other warehouses in Leeds, notably 30 Park Place, and one at the corner of Basinghall Street and Boar Lane which had an iron, timber and glass façade in Tudor-Gothic (c.1873).[75] On the whole, the groups of warehouses in Leeds lacked the unity of material and scale of those in Bradford, but there was not the same emulative incentive. The town had developed other industries, and was no longer dependent on textiles alone for its prosperity; for that reason, this account of the architecture of the cloth trade must conclude in Bradford in 1863.

'So great of late years had been the growth of the trade of the town, and the influx of spinners, manufacturers, and merchants to its markets'[76] that a new Wool Exchange had become a necessity. John Ruskin had been invited to address an audience about the design and style of the proposed building, and it was hoped the oracle would speak and settle the matter. But instead 'my good Yorkshire friends' were surprised to be told the great man did not care about this Exchange of theirs.

You are going to spend £30,000, which to you, collectively, is nothing ... But you think you may as well have the right thing for your money. You know there are a great many odd styles of architecture about; you don't want to do anything ridiculous; you hear of me, among others, as a respectable architectural man-milliner; and you send for me, that I may tell you the leading fashion; and what is, in our shops, for the moment, the newest and sweetest thing in pinnacles.[77]

The audience was asked to understand they could not have good

73 The whole south side of Boar Lane was condemned to demolition in 1976.

74 See *BN* (1879),xxxvi,62 for an account and illustration of St Paul's House. One other building in this style must be mentioned – the Royal Panopticon of Science and Art in Leicester Fields (Square), London; it was built in 1852 to a design by Finden and Hayter Lewis (*Art Journal* (1852),220f) and subsequently became the Alhambra Theatre. It was reconstructed by John Perry and F.H.Reed after a fire in 1882. Sir John Barran's firm continued to expand after building St Paul's House; in 1888 they built 'another huge structure, which is said to be one of the largest clothing factories in the world [with] a ground area of one thousand five hundred square yards'. In 1891–2 they built yet another factory and warehouse next to St Paul's House but lacking its architectural distinction (see *BO* 28 Feb 1891). St Paul's House was the subject of a public inquiry in 1970, as a result of which it has been restored and adapted as offices.

75 *BA* (1875),iv,49; Linstrum, 77. Demolished 1974.

76 James, 136.

77 Ruskin's lecture in Bradford was reprinted in *The crown of wild olive* (1866) under the title of 'Traffic'.

245. Leeds, Park Square, St Paul's House (T.Ambler 1878), Sir John Barran's Hispano-Moorish factory-warehouse. The plate-glass windows and the canopy in the foreground were added during alterations and restorations (1976).

246. Leeds, Globe Road, Tower Works; the chimney-shaft based on Giotto's campanile in Florence was designed (W.Bakewell 1899) to form part of a dust-extraction plant.

architecture merely by asking people's advice on occasions. 'All good architecture is the expression of national life and character; and it is produced by a prevalent and eager national taste, or desire for beauty'. If any of them thought of disagreeing they were told 'taste is not only a part and an index of morality; – it is the ONLY morality'. His denunciation of the modern worship of the 'Goddess of Getting-on' probably only confused his hearers, who were there because they had 'got on'; and then they were advised they would know how to build if they could 'determine some honest and simple order of existence, following those trodden ways of wisdom, which are pleasantness, and seeking her quiet and withdrawn paths, which are peace'.

Perhaps the audience was slightly bewildered; they had asked only for a simple word of advice about architectural style, and could Mr Ruskin have been serious when he suggested decorating the frieze of their new building with pendant purses, and putting in the centre, not Minerva (as Halifax had on its Town Hall), but a statue of Britannia of the Market holding a weaver's beam instead of a spear, and having on her shield a semi-fleeced boar and the legend 'In the best market', and wearing a leather corselet in the shape of a purse with thirty slits in it, for a piece of money to go in at, on each day of the month? Could he have been serious? However, he told them finally what they wanted to know:

307

247. Bradford, the Wool Exchange (Lockwood and Mawson 1864–7) was a symbolic climax to the progress of the textile trade, although the Mayor of Leeds, speaking at the opening, 'sincerely wished ... if he lived ... for twenty years longer he might ... be present at the inauguration of another hall three times as large'.

247

78 This advice was not included in the published version of the lecture, probably because Ruskin did not want to be thought responsible in any way for the executed design. His disappointment that the Oxford Museum had 'failed signally of being what he hoped' was the beginning of a disillusionment and a sense that his enthusiastic writing about the glories of Venetian Gothic architecture had been sadly misinterpreted; by 1872 he was horrified to find 'I have had direct influence on nearly every cheap villa-builder between [Denmark Hill] and Bromley; and there is scarcely a public-house near the Crystal Palace but sells its gin and bitters under pseudo-Venetian capitals ... And one of my principal notions for leaving my present home is that it is surrounded everywhere by the cursed Frankenstein monsters of, *in*directly, my own making'. But at the time he was lecturing in Bradford, Ruskin still had high hopes. In the previous December he had visited Manchester and written a letter full of praise of the Assize Courts to his father. It was not only the architecture that made his visit enjoyable. 'The workmen were pleased to see me; the clerk of the works, when he was a youth, copied out the whole three volumes of the *Stones of Venice*, and traced every illustration'. (The works of Ruskin (1905),xviii,p.lxxv).

79 James, 136.

If you want a model for your Exchange, I cannot tell you of a better than the new Assize Courts in Manchester, a very beautiful and noble building indeed, as lovely as it can be in general effect, containing a hall of exquisite proportions, beautifully lighted, the roof full of playful fancy, and the corridors and staircases thoroughly attractive and charming.[78]

Lockwood and Mawson, who provided the design selected after the Committee had held a doubtful competition, looked quite closely at Alfred Waterhouse's Courts in Manchester and gave the Exchange a 'Venetian Gothic ... character, freely treated, and admitting of great picturesqueness of effect, and beauty of detail, without entailing heavy cost'.[79] Yet the general effect of the long façade to Market Street and the monumental tower placed on the short end of the wedge-shaped site is more Flemish than Venetian. The main façade suffers from a too mechanical repetition of the bay design of one traceried window on the ground floor, a double pointed on the first, and a triple on the second, all more or less identical in their detailing. Nevertheless, the combination of the red and yellow stone, the open arcaded balustrade, and the corner turrets and pinnacles is rich and picturesque; and the large hall, 625 yards in area, is an impressive setting for the ritual of commerce when light is pouring in through the clerestorey windows and the dormers in the open timber roof, although it hovers uncertainly in form between Renaissance and medieval. Around the exterior of the building a number of carved portrait medallions were inserted between the ground floor windows, commemorating the great names of Cobden, Gladstone, Palmerston and Salt.

None less than the Prime Minister would suffice to lay the foundation stone, and Lord Palmerston arrived to perform the ceremony on 9 August 1864. It was 'one of the most auspicious days which had dawned upon Bradford', wrote its contemporary historian;[80] and at the same time their distinguished visitor was received at Saltaire where Salt conducted him over his empire. It was a symbolic climax to the progress of the industry, and the Mayor of Bradford who spoke at the opening of Saltaire Mill in 1853 deserves to close this survey of its architecture,

Instead of manual labour, they had availed themselves of the wonderful resources of mechanical science; instead of a master manufacturer carrying a week's production on his back, he harnessed the iron horse to the railway train, and daily conveyed away his goods by the ton; instead of being content with old English wool only, they now ransacked the globe for materials to work up ... And in doing all that, they had built palaces of industry almost equal to the palaces of the Caesars![81]

80 ibid.,139.

81 Balgarnie, op.cit.,127.

11 Markets and market halls

The interior is so strikingly like a caravanserai, that I could almost have fancied myself back in India the first time I saw it.

T.J.Maslen on Leeds Market, *Suggestions for the Improvement of our Towns and Houses*, 1843.

'Here is a cross of some antiquity, though not curious', wrote James Watson of the old market place in Halifax;[1] at least as early as 1331, there was a cross in Wakefield market place on the west side of the parish church;[2] and the old Oswald's Cross, which commemorated the Christian king of Northumbria and was probably the meeting-place of the Wapentake of the district, was at the centre of buying and selling in the market at Pontefract.[3] A cross in a churchyard is the earliest form of structure associated with the origin of a market; it is an obvious place in the centre of a community, where the whole population would inevitably meet. John James wrote about the Sunday market in fourteenth-century Bradford that the people, 'being compelled to resort once a week to the parish church on spiritual affairs, . . . contrived to make the journey one also of secular business, and purchased the articles they required at home'.[4] By the early eighteenth century, compulsory attendance at church had long ago been forgotten, and it was a combination of dealing in cloth and purchasing food that made the West Yorkshire markets scenes of activity such as Defoe experienced at Halifax, 'by reason of the Multitude of People who throng thither, as well to sell their Manufactures, as to buy Provisions'.

In the earliest Royal charters, provision for a market is an important consideration and privilege. In 1251 Henry III granted Edmund de Lacy 'that he and his heirs for ever, shall have one market every week, on *Thursday*, at his manor of BRAFFORD . . . unless this market should be to the injury of the neighbouring markets'; and forty years later Edward I confirmed the privilege to Henry de Lacy, Earl of Lincoln, as well as granting a five days long fair in August in celebration of the Feast of St Peter ad Vincula.[5] The same Earl's charter of 1278 'confined to . . . men of Pontefract, all the sheds (or stalls) which they shall be, or their ancestors have been able to erect in the market'.[6] Almondbury was granted a market in 1294, but it lost its importance as a trading centre to Huddersfield, where John Ramsden of Byram Park was granted one by Charles II in 1672.[7]

The second charter to the borough of Leeds in 1661 referred to the first of 1626 by virtue of which 'a common market was holden . . . on

1 Watson, 203. Halifax 'never had a charter for the holding of a market', noted Watson, but 'this may be held by prescription, and length of time will make this as good a title as any charter can give'.

2 Walker, 126.

3 Boothroyd,B., *The history of the ancient Borough of Pontefract*, Pontefract 1807,33.

4 James, 66.

5 ibid.,48,55.

6 Boothroyd, op.cit.,20.

7 See McCutcheon,K.L., 'Yorkshire fairs and markets', *TS* (1940),xxxix.

311

248. Pontefract, Market Cross (1734). To the left is the tower of St Giles's church, rebuilt 1707, and again at the end of the eighteenth century when the open crown was constructed.

8 Whitaker, Appendix 57.

9 Thoresby, 178.

10 ibid.,19. The Cross was taken down when the Corn Exchange was built in 1826; some columns from the demolished building were built into an unidentified wall between the Shambles and Kirkgate, which was demolished at the end of the nineteenth century (Leeds Reference Library, Leeds Scrapbook, 30 Oct 1897).

11 Boothroyd, op.cit.,442.

12 Fox,G., *The history of Pontefract*, Pontefract 1827,355. This refers to a 'dome' which preceded the present roof, but it is difficult to see what was meant. Paul Jollage's map of Pontefract, dated 1742, shows the Cross as it was originally built.

13 Boothroyd, op.cit.,442.

tuesday in every week', and confirmed the grant.[8] Thoresby left a lively account of the Leeds street market as he knew it at the beginning of the eighteenth century. There were 'the Country Linnen-Drapers, Shoo-makers, Hard-ware-men, and the Sellers of Wood-vessels, Wicker-Baskets, Wanded-Chairs, Flakes, &c. Fruit of all Sorts . . . five hundred Loads of Apples only, upon one Day'. Then there were the 'Milk-Cows', and the Fish Market learnedly referred to as the *Ichthyopolium*; and around the Moot Hall was the 'best-furnished *Flesh-Shambles* in the North of *England*'. The butchers cared little for the newly refaced civic building which was reported to be 'in great decay' in 1723 because of their habit of whetting 'their knives . . . upon both the Moothall stairs and likewise upon the Pillars and Walls of ye said Hall'. Moving further north up Briggate, there was 'the *Cross*, which is well stock'd with Poultry', and afterwards the Corn Market and the Horse Fair. The Cross Thoresby knew was one erected by John Harrison near his church of St John, 'for the Conveniency and Ornament of the Market';[9] Cossins's plan of 1725 shows a small colonnaded structure with a pointed roof and ornamental weather-vane, but there is no indication of its size or whether it was square or circular on plan. It was replaced in 1776 by one 'about fifteen yards long by nine yards wide . . . the roof supported by eight pillars, four square ones at the ends, and four round ones at the sides . . . in the centre above the roof was a square pedestal surrounded by palisades, from the centre of which rose an ornamental rod supporting the four cardinal points and surmounted by a fleece'.[10] There is a glimpse of this Cross beyond the Moot Hall in Thomas Taylor's well-known view of Briggate, but more is known about other West Yorkshire market crosses.

Outside the south front of St Giles's in Pontefract, where the market has been held since the twelfth century, there was a cross erected to St Oswald. Gough regretted its removal in 1734, 'as if Pontefract was to shew no evidence of its former splendour' by substituting 'an unmeaning market-house'; but a later historian believed 'the inhabitants of the town and country are of a very different opinion . . . They enjoy essential benefit from the latter, while the former, if it had been suffered to remain, would be wholly useless'.[11] The Pontefract Cross is an open rectangular building of rusticated masonry with three giant arches on each long side; each of the ends is in a triumphal arch form, with one giant arch flanked by two smaller ones surmounted by blind openings. Originally it had a flat roof and a stone balustrade, but these were replaced in 1763 by the present pitched roof.[12] Mrs Elizabeth Dupier erected the building 'in a cheerful and generous compliance with his benevolent intention' after her husband's death in 1734,[13] but its designer's name is not recorded. It forms an impressive centrepiece in the western part of the market place where it widens in front of the church, and it is prominently in the foreground of Thomas Malton's beautifully detailed view of the town in 1777.

Wakefield had begun to build a Market Cross in Cross Square in 1707, to be paid for by voluntary subscriptions; but it was completed only after John Smyth of Heath gave £100. The design was

266

248

313

presumably made by Theophilus Shelton of Heath, who gave Sir Charles Hotham and Sir Michael Warton the design for the Beverley Market Cross in 1714; there are obvious similarities. The Wakefield

249

Cross was square and consisted of eight Doric columns and a modillioned entablature, supporting a lead-covered dome and a square, four-pedimented tower with its own dome and lantern; each side of the tower contained a large sash window, as it housed the Commissioner of Streets, the Constables and the Overseers of the town, who reached their room by an open spiral staircase inside the Cross.[14] It was an elegant building, demolished in 1866 in spite of considerable public protest. Dewsbury, where an ancient market was revived c.1740 by the Duke of Leeds and the Lord of the Manor of Wakefield, had an early nineteenth-century Cross built by the thirty-two shareholders of the Dewsbury Market Cross Company in 1826; it was a rectangular podium containing permanent stalls, and above it was a covered shelter supported on six Doric columns, but it was short-lived and disappeared in 1853.

As the West Yorkshire towns grew in size in the nineteenth century, their street markets became a source of great congestion. The timber-framed Market Cross in Halifax, 'three stories high, with an ugly Cross and stone steps'[15] was pulled down in the late eighteenth century, and there seems to have been no alternative covered space. An Act of 1810 was obtained by the market company to forbid stalls anywhere except in their market place in Southgate. Brick buildings were erected there for the sale of fish, fruit and vegetables, and there was a colonnade 'used by the country people for the sale of poultry, butter, etc'. In the middle stood an 'ornamented iron pillar serving as a pump and lamp post';[16] this was probably a standard catalogue item like that in Soho which Pugin sadly compared in *Contrasts* with the fifteenth-century West Cheap Conduit.[17] The market in Huddersfield expanded into the Shambles, and in 1857 there was a dispute between the Lord of the Manor and the stallholders. Bradford's market had a curious history of disagreements and litigation between private citizens and the Lord of the Manor; after its early beginnings around the parish church, it was moved to a triangular island site in Westgate. A market building was erected in Bower's Croft in 1782 by a group of private gentlemen, but legal proceedings were threatened if it were used in defiance of Manorial rights. In 1801 this building was increased in size by the Lord of the Manor, who added on to it one which was said to have been built from a design specially obtained in Italy; it is difficult to believe this from the illustrations which survive of an odd structure with a cantilevered arcaded canopy. In 1823, another market house was erected privately from a design made by James Richardby; the Lord of the Manor took the owner to court and won his case.[18] Finally, the market was moved to a site surrounding the old Manor House, which had been abandoned as a residence; and there it stayed, becoming more of a nuisance until it was as impossible as the congested streets in Leeds. Clearly, strong measures were needed.

During a meeting in the vestry of Leeds parish church in 1823, it was resolved to buy the Vicarage House and an attached site of 9,768

14 Walker, 475f. The bell in the turret of the Cross had evidently hung in an earlier building; it was inscribed with the name of Henry Radcliffe and dated 1655. Radcliffe was a woollen draper in Wakefield, and the uncle of Dr John Radcliffe, to whose bequests English architecture is indebted for the Radcliffe Library and Radcliffe Observatory in Oxford (and the present author for his appointment in the University of York 1971–.).

15 *HAS* (1955), 62. This quotation is extracted from a MS account of Halifax by Thomas Sutcliffe of Ovenden Hall.

16 Crabtree, 356f.

17 Pugin,A.W.N., *Contrasts: or, a parallel between . . . the middle ages, and . . . the present day*, London 1841 (2nd edn).

18 James C, 91,98; Scruton,W., *Bradford fifty years ago*, Bradford 1897,75ff.

249. Wakefield, Market Cross; begun in 1707 and attributed to T.Shelton. The spire of All Saints' church (now the Cathedral) in the background can be compared with the slightly enriched version of G.G.Scott (pl.133). (Kilby,T., *Views in Wakefield*, 1853)

square yards on which to reposition the market stalls. It was an arrangement that suited the parishioners, who 'bought an excellent mansion in Park Square to be the future residence of the vicars, who were thus removed from the midst of smoke, filth, and noise, to one of the best, one of the most respectable, and one of the most salubrious situations in the town'. Everyone gained by the move; 'the property in the neighbourhood of the market rapidly rose in value, and the alteration in every sense has proved conducive to health, to comfort, to trade, and to universal convenience. The projectors of the Free Market deserve the gratitude of Leeds'.[19] At the same time, a company of shareholders built a meat and fish market and slaughter house on a site between Briggate and Vicar Lane, considered then 'one of the most useful [projects] ever formed in the town'.[20] The initiative was taken by two brothers, Joseph and Frederick Rinder, butchers and cattle dealers, who bought up property between 1814 and 1823, built utilitarian structures in Cheapside and Fleet Street for use as shambles with a first-floor 'bazaar', in Fish Street where there were covered stalls and an open octagon for the sale of fish and vegetables, and in Leadenhall Street where a slaughterhouse and wholesale meat market were erected. The largest of these buildings, which was opened in 1826, had an arched entrance flanked by attached Tuscan columns, and above it was a large couchant lion modelled under the superintendence of Joseph Rhodes, the Leeds painter. This project ended in bankruptcy for Frederick Rinder in 1831, after the death of his brother.

From all these changes in the 1820s there emerged only two buildings of architectural interest, both designed for retail rather than

19 Parsons, i,145.

20 ibid.,i,140ff.

GROUND PLAN and ELEVATION of the CENTRAL MARKET, LEEDS.

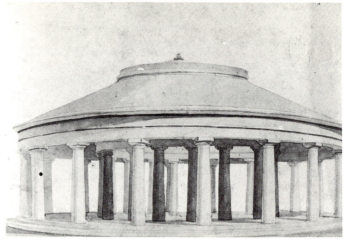

250. Leeds, the Central Market (F.Goodwin 1824–7) was regarded as 'one of the principal ornaments of the town', and it marked the emergence in the region of a market as a public building.

251. Leeds, the South Market (R.D.Chantrell 1823) was an enclosure surrounded by a double row of retail shops. In the centre was a Cross, of which this is the original design; it was built with the addition of a domed cupola.

250

251

21 The Central Market remained in use until 1893, when it was partly burnt down and subsequently demolished.

22 Chantell's design for the Cross is in the Leeds Reference Library; his aerial view of the market is in the collection of the Thoresby Society. Although not originally built for that purpose, the South Market acquired some prosperity as the site of a quarterly Leather Market (Hargrove,E., *History of Knaresborough*, Knaresborough 1828,173).

23 Parsons,i,146f.

24 Maslen,T.J., *Suggestions for the improvement of our towns and houses*, London 1843,107.

wholesale trade. The Central Market was built in Duncan Street in 1824–7 at a cost of £35,000, from a design by Francis Goodwin. He provided a large hall divided into three walks by rows of stalls where fruit, vegetables and dairy produce were sold, 56 in all; there was a gallery around three sides, used as a bazaar for the sale of fancy goods, and the perimeter of the building was occupied by 67 shops, intended for butchers and fishmongers. It was designed in the Greek style, with a central three-bay section of a giant fluted Ionic order and entablature topped by a pedimented blocking course and acroteria; there were similarly decorated doorways between small-paned shop windows under segmental arches.[21] Another undertaking, which resulted in a building similarly Greek in style, had been proposed in Leeds in 1823, the year before the Central Market was started; this was the South Market, on the road to Halifax and Huddersfield. Robert Dennis Chantrell made a design in which a double row of 26 shops was built around the perimeter of a semi-circular open market in the middle of which stood a large circular Cross in which butter, eggs and poultry were sold. Chantrell's first design of a double colonnade of baseless Doric columns was amended in execution when a lead dome and cupola were added above the central open space. Another of Chantrell's drawings suggests building fountains in the open space to add dignity to the 23 butchers' shops and stalls, the slaughter house and 18 dwellings which were incorporated in the design;[22] but the choice of site was ill-judged, and in 1834 Parsons reported that despite Chantrell's design and execution of the layout and buildings, all of which were 'honourable to his taste and skill', the £22,000 speculation had been 'a decided failure'.[23] The lesson had been learnt, and the next project was in the traditional market area of the town.

'Is Leeds so poor a place that the inhabitants cannot form a company to build three or four covered market-places for meat, fish, fowl, vegetables, fruit, and fire-wood?', demanded T.J.Maslen in 1843 after inspecting the conditions under which these goods were sold.[24] His view was different from the self-congratulations of twenty years earlier, but it was not until 1857 that the *Builder* was

252. Leeds, Kirkgate Market (C.Tilney with amendments from Sir J.Paxton 1857); the cast-iron structure remained in use until 1902, when this photograph was taken.

253. Bradford, Kirkgate Market (Lockwood and Mawson 1871–8); the opulent cast-iron frame of this now demolished building was painted 'green and gold bronze, relieved by bronze', and rose to form two domes, each sixty feet high. (*Architect* (1872))

25 *B* (1857),xv,136.

26 ibid.,235. There is no reference to this in Chadwick,G.F., *The works of Sir Joseph Paxton*, London 1961; but Paxton was engaged on three Yorkshire schemes in 1855–8, the People's Park, Halifax; Belle Vue, Halifax; and the Spa Saloon, Scarborough.

able to report 'the new covered market is now being rapidly proceeded with'.[25] The site chosen had a main frontage 330 feet long to Vicar Lane, and a width of 130 to where it abutted against the Free Market. The design was made by Charles Tilney, the Borough Surveyor, and completed by his successor, Edward Filliter: however, there was an additional interest in the building, since its design had been 'improved by Sir Joseph Paxton'.[26] It was an iron and glass structure, 'somewhat after the manner of the Crystal Palace', thirty-five feet high and

252

covered with three longitudinal roofs. A double row of shops surrounding the perimeter occupied the ground level, and above was a glazed screen. 'So far as an architectural character is admissible in such a structure', reported the *Builder*, the design 'is of the Tudor style'; and that style was consistent throughout. Externally, the façade was divided into standard bays by structural columns with moulded capitals and bases, and each bay consisted of a shop window with four four-centred arches (or, at every third bay, an entrance, of which there were seventeen), a solid bracing plate, a glazed panel terminating in a delicately moulded four-centred arch with pierced spandrels, and a lattice beam across the top. The effect was light and elegant, and the design was repeated internally by using the same columns and arches to form two arcaded intermediate frames. It is easy to believe a writer was not exaggerating when he described the nocturnal effect of 'this beautiful crystal hall . . . well illuminated by 200 gas lights, arranged around handsome stone pillars'.[27]

Six years after the new Leeds market was opened, Bradford Corporation came to terms with the Lord of the Manor and leased the land surrounding the Manor House for 999 years, including the manorial rights and privileges, in order to build a covered market. Lockwood and Mawson, virtually the town's official practice, was the inevitable choice. The site was an irregular rectangle on a slope, but the *Architect* truthfully wrote the 'design has been so arranged as to combine architectural unity and a perfect concealment of the defects of the ground'. In the centre of the building was the main hall with an area of 5,520 square yards, and enclosing it were shops adapted in size on plan to the different widths between the hall's perimeter and the street frontages. The entrances at each end of the rectangle led into octangular pavilions opening on to avenues of stalls constructed with canted corners; it was intended to maintain a uniformity in the latter,

254. Bradford, Kirkgate Market set a new standard for this type of building in West Yorkshire, and provided a model for other towns.

255. Huddersfield, the Market Hall (E.Hughes 1878–80) was unusually designed on two floors; it has been demolished. (*The century's progress*, 1893)

253

318

**256. Huddersfield, Brook Street Market
(R.S.Dugdale 1887–8) represents the
handsome utility attainable by the use
of more or less standard cast-iron
components.**

27 The market remained in use until 1902,
when it was demolished and the materials
were sold. It is said that part of the structure
was incorporated in the Halifax Market Hall,
but this is not confirmed. There was an
extension to the Kirkgate Market in 1875,
when part of the open market at the rear was
covered with an iron and glass structure
designed by Alfred William Morant, the
Borough Engineer; this was burnt down in
1975.

28 *A* (1872),viii,218.

even to the numbering and lettering on the cast-iron fascia plates. The
iron structure was modelled from full-size details made by the
architects, and the high-level arched windows around the external
walls were designed as huge geometric fanlights. It was said that 'the
lighting . . . has received the most careful attention . . ., the lights being
so arranged as to hinder the penetration of the direct rays of the sun –
a plan which has not been adopted before except in the construction of
the new Smithfield Market'.[28] Externally, this magnificent structure
was surrounded by a masonry building elaborately detailed in an
Italianate–Second Empire manner. William Day Keyworth was
employed as the sculptor of the huge figures of Pomona and Flora in
the spandrels over the arched entrance in Kirkgate, and the Coalbrook
Dale Company provided the sliding gates and grilles which filled the
gigantic openings. Kirkgate Market set a pattern and scale for the
other West Yorkshire towns, which they followed in time.

Huddersfield Corporation bought the market rights and tolls from
the Ramsden Estate in 1876, and chose to build on the site of the
Shambles. Edward Hughes was the architect. Unlike Bradford's,

319

257. Halifax, Borough Market; the new scale and sense of civic grandeur which the Town Hall and the rebuilding of the Northgate area had given the town were complemented by the new market in Southgate (Leeming and Leeming 1891–8).

258. Halifax, Borough Market; the arrangement of architectural elements within the cast-iron structure is slightly incoherent, but the effect is spacious, light and rich.

29 *BA* (1878),ix,182.

256

258

which was designed for retailing only, Huddersfield's was intended to combine wholesale and retail trade. Consequently, it was designed on two floors as a central space 166 feet by 71, with a wide outer lining of shops; it was a practical design, although the wholesale market moved out in 1888 to a fine cast-iron building with glazed curtain walls in Brook Street. Externally, the Classical tradition that Pritchett and Tite had given Huddersfield was abandoned in favour of a vaguely romantic Gothic style; the main three-storey front to King Street had corner turrets and conical roofs, and the central section incorporated a Perpendicular entrance, a Decorated window in the gable, more corner turrets, and a tower in which a tall pointed roof rose above gablets into which were fitted clock faces.[29]

Halifax was the next town to follow Bradford's example, when its new hall was opened in 1898 on the old open market site in Southgate, thirty-five years after the Corporation had bought the market and its rights from the company that had owned them since 1810. The Piece Hall had become a wholesale fruit and vegetable market in 1871, and the new building was intended to complement it for retail trade. The local architects, John and Joseph Leeming (who also had an office in London), produced a design in competition in 1891, based on Lockwood and Mawson's building in Bradford; once again there is a main hall, 200 feet by 170, with a central octagon supported on eight cast-iron columns rising to semicircular arched trusses which carry an

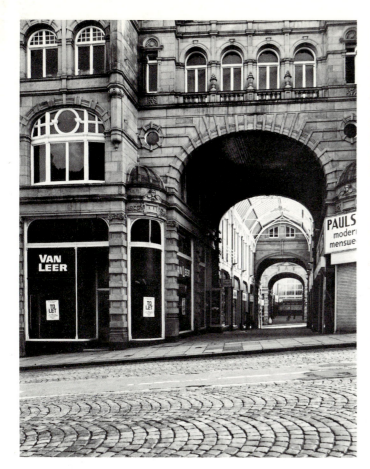

259. Halifax, Russell Arcade (Leeming and Leeming 1898); the new market was designed so that the layout of avenues between the stalls continued as an arcade, forming a continuous pattern of pedestrian shopping under cover.

259

260. Leeds, Thornton's Arcade (G. Smith 1877–8), the first of a series of shopping arcades which have now been incorporated in the large traffic-free area in the centre of Leeds.

257

30 *HG*, 18 July 1896. 'In designing the building the architects have endeavoured to combine gracefulness with strength and utility'.

31 ibid.; the designs for the Market are in the RIBA Drawings Collection (*Catalogue*, vol. L-N/19).

octagonal frame sixty feet above the floor level. In the centre is an enormous clock and lamp standard, richly decorated like the rest of the ironwork. Four avenues of stalls radiate from the octagon, one continuing beyond the building as Russell Arcade, linking the market with an existing arcade across Russell Street. The plan included for forty-three butchers, twenty small shops and thirty-three stalls; the perimeter was designed as shops with twenty-one flats on the upper floors, and the surrounding masonry building containing them is ornamented with gables and carved decoration in a Flemish-French Early Renaissance style, mild and restrained by comparison with the spectacular architectural display the same architects were to give Leeds a few years later.[30] The cost was nearer £120,000 than the estimated £34,000; but as the *Halifax Guardian* commented, 'there is a good deal of detail in the façade, and the turrets, carved gable, and pedimental heads which adorn the windows make the building one of the most imposing the town possesses'.[31]

Leeds was contemplating great improvements in 1896, including the widening of Vicar Lane, although that would necessitate the demolition of the 1857–60 market. In his report, the City Engineer recommended rebuilding it 'in such a manner that its modern architecture would lead to the creation in the neighbouring streets of a higher rate property than would otherwise be the case'. Clearly, he had in mind the removal of the old Shambles and the development of its

261. Bradford, Royal Arcade (1897); built as an arcade entered through the large central arch and flanked by groups of shops, this building was later altered to form a department store. A speculative venture, it was designed by the engineer-developer, Destin Asman.

262. Huddersfield, Byram Arcade (W.H.Crossland 1880–1); the centre of the town was developed by the Ramsden Estate Company, including Byram Buildings, Westgate, which incorporates this arcade entered beneath the Ramsden arms.

32 *YP*, 30 April 1896.

33 ibid., 20 Jan 1897.

34 *LM*, 15 March 1898.

35 In London, e.g., there were Royal Opera Arcade (1816–8), Burlington Arcade (1818–9), Lowther Arcade (1829–31), Exeter Arcade (1842–3), etc. In Newcastle, there was Royal Arcade (1831–2); but it was not until the 1870s that the vogue for arcades reached the major industrial towns. For a full history of arcades, see Geist, J.F., *Passagen, ein Bautyp des 19. Jahrhunderts*, Munich 1969.

36 Howard,E., *To-morrow: a peaceful path to real reform*, London 1898,14.

valuable site, described as 'one of the most important freehold properties offered in Leeds'. It was suggested that 'the estate was specially worth the attention of a syndicate or company desirous of acquiring a large property suitable to form a fine central site for a combination of theatre and shops',[32] and ultimately the Leeds Estates Company was formed and continued to buy up sites. At the beginning of 1897 it was announced that almost £200,000 had been spent already, and the company intended to lay out another £100,000;[33] their purchases were completed early in 1898, when they were able to announce the proposed 'making of two streets . . . also the construction of a handsome arcade [and] over two hundred new shops'.[34]

Arcades were not new; there were early nineteenth-century examples in London and Newcastle, but they grew in scale and popularity in the last quarter of the century,[35] until Ebenezer Howard inevitably included one in his visionary City of Tomorrow in 1898. He described his imaginary 'wide glass arcade' as being 'in wet weather one of the favourite resorts of the people [where] manufactured goods are exposed for sale, and . . . most of that class of shopping which requires the joy of deliberation and selection is done'.[36] The form of a covered street lined with shops, an idea closely associated with that of a covered market with rows of stalls, had become popular in West Yorkshire by the end of the nineteenth century, especially in Leeds, where eight had been built by 1900. Most are, in effect, roofed streets

322

built over some of the yards and courts which were traditional elements in the medieval town; and many were associated with places of entertainment.

Charles Thornton, the owner of the *White Swan* public house and the builder of the White Swan Varieties, was responsible for the first Leeds arcade, which was built in 1877–8 from a design by George Smith, and it still bears Thornton's name. The Gothic street frontages to Briggate and Lands Lane are crude, but the tall, narrow arcade with a series of Gothic roof trusses and a clock with mechanical figures over the main entrance possesses considerable style. There are giant pointed arches at 'triforium' level above the shop fronts, and a row of smaller 'clerestorey' windows below the cornice from which the glazed vault springs. Market Street Arcade was built about the same time, and then, in 1889, Queen's Arcade was built parallel to Thornton's and leading to the theatres in King Charles's Croft;[37] plainer in style than its predecessor, it has a continuous, stepped gallery with cast-iron balustrades at first-floor level. These two began to form a pattern of covered links between the main shopping streets, to which Thomas Ambler added Victoria Arcade in 1897 in celebration of the Diamond Jubilee.[38] Farther to the north, the Grand Arcade was built in 1896–7 along the side of the Grand Theatre as a part of a group of shops and the Tower Picture House, designed by Smith and Tweedale. The arcade itself is a utilitarian design, enriched by a mechanical clock which reminds the passer-by that *Time and Tide wait for no man*, and *Come what may, time and the hour runs through the roughest day*. The street façades to New Briggate and Vicar Lane are faced with polychromatic Burmantofts faience.[39]

Other West Yorkshire towns had built arcades. Milnes and France designed Swan Arcade, Bradford (1877–81) as a monumental building with frontages to Market Street, Brook Street, and Charles Street. This was an unusual layout, which incorporated 44 shops, 46 offices and 65 stock-rooms, and there were in effect five arcades within the whole building; it was designed in the Italianate style, with finely detailed cast-iron gates and roof trusses, and there were six entrances, some framed by gigantic semicircular-headed arches.[40] Another Bradford arcade, this time in the Gothic style, was incorporated in the Royal Arcade, Manningham Lane when it was first built in 1897; but this was later enclosed when the building became a department store.[41] Huddersfield has the Byram Arcade, built from W.H.Crossland's design in 1880–1 as a part of one of the commercial developments undertaken by the Ramsden Estate in the centre of the town; once again it is Gothic, with carved decoration over the entrance from Westgate, emphasising its importance in the plain, Hanseatic warehouse style of the façade of Byram Buildings. Russell Arcade, Halifax, was incorporated by Leeming and Leeming in their design for the town's new market; the internal glazed façades are elegant cast-iron frames with decorative spandrels, and the masonry of the external walls matches the style of the market itself.

The most successful of these West Yorkshire arcades were the ones which formed links between established shopping streets or extended

37 *B N* (1889),lvi,87.

38 ibid.(1900),lxxvii,510. The Victoria Arcade was demolished in 1959.

39 ibid.(1897),lxxiii,904.

40 Swan Arcade was built for Angus Holden, at a cost of £150,000. It was demolished in 1962 when the centre of Bradford was destroyed to make way for a commercial comprehensive redevelopment.

41 Now Debenham's, the building was converted for Busby's as a department store. Although built in 1897 by Destin Asman, who acted as designer and developer, the completion of the symmetrical Gothic façade was delayed until 1937 because the site of the north end of the building was occupied by a castellated villa which had been the home of the Behrens family until 1896, and was then used as the Girls' Grammar School for the next forty years.

**263. Leeds, County Arcade;
F.Matcham's design for 'two streets . . . a
handsome arcade [and] over two
hundred new shops' included an
opulent arcade (1900) executed in
Burmantofts faience, marbles, mosaics,
cast iron and wrought iron.**

263

42 Geist, op.cit.,196; 'Die Säulenreihen, die
Galerien tragen, die schmiedeeisernen,
barock geschwungen Gitter, die Reihen der
steinernen Kugeln, die auf den
Brüstungspfeilern sitzen, der Dreier-
Rhythmus der Rundfenster, die von kleinen
Giebelfragmenten belasteten Pilaster, hinter
denen sich die Auflager der schweren
gusseisernen Bögen verstecken, geben dem
Passageraum etwas wild Bewegtes, eine
Atmosphäre, die nach Menschenmassen
geradezu verlangt und im verlassenen
Zustand grotesk wirkt'. (The rows of columns
supporting the galleries, the wrought-iron
railings with their Baroque curves, the rows
of stone balls which cap the piers of the
balustrades, the triple-rhythm of the round-
headed windows, the pilasters crowned with
little pediments, behind which are hidden the
supports of the heavy cast-iron arches, all
give the arcade a somewhat frantic sense of
movement, an atmosphere which cries out
for crowds of people, and seems almost
grotesque when it is deserted.)

43 *Y P*, 30 May 1904.

the aisles of the covered markets into the neighbouring shops and
streets. The County Arcade (and the associated Cross Arcade) which
formed an essential part of the development in Leeds undertaken by
the Leeds Estates Company, proved to be the finest and most
successful of all. Frank Matcham, an architect with a great reputation
as a designer of theatres and music halls, was given the responsibility
for the whole group of buildings behind the richly decorated,
flamboyant façades of bright red brick and glowing orange
Burmantofts faience. The County Arcade was designed in a palatial
manner complementary to Matcham's Empire Theatre; pink marble
columns with white Ionic capitals and dark red bases separate the
shopfronts and support a cast-iron balustraded gallery. Above are
Jacobean tapered pilasters and strapwork panels, crowned by a frieze
designed as a flowing pattern of fruit and foliage, all of Burmantofts
faience. Spanning the entire arcade is an elaborate cast-iron and glass
vault, interrupted by three galleried domes rising from mosaic-faced
pendentives on which are represented selected arts and industries as
mildly *art-nouveau* figures.[42]

The County Arcade forms the monumental covered way between
Briggate and the new City Markets, in which the Leeming brothers
provided a grand climax. In 1904, the *Yorkshire Post* commented, 'One
has only to think of the state of things that existed a few years ago,
and glance at the stately building now practically finished, to realise
the vastness of the improvement that has been effected. Ten years ago
we had abattoirs in the very heart of the city, a roofless market in
Kirkgate left buyers and sellers to the mercy of wind and rain and
snow, while on the very site on which the new hall has been raised
stood stalls and shops sadly out of date'.[43] The Leeming brothers' new

**264. Leeds, City Markets (Leeming and
Leeming 1903–04); the stalls (originally
uniform in design) are planned around a
central octagon where (as this 1904
photograph shows) a cast-iron clock
tower was originally located under the
dome at the point where all the avenues
crossed.**

City Markets, claimed at the time as 'the finest building of its kind in the country', and one attracting 'a great deal of attention from architects as well as from other municipal authorities', is in direct succession from those in Bradford and Halifax.

The structural form is a combination of cast-iron and steel, the former being exposed to view in the central octagon and the two arcades along the length of the hall, while the latter is mostly concealed inside the masonry building. Twenty-four tall clusters of Corinthian columns support a glazed clerestorey and the upper part of the octagon, and the structurally necessary horizontal ties and beams are incorporated in the decoratively modelled panels and spandrels which include tripartite blank windows framed in scrolls and pediments, and the Leeds civic arms repeated eighty times. A mezzanine balcony around the hall is supported on dragons projecting

264

265. Leeds, City Markets; the culmination of the redevelopment of the traditional market district, it followed the models of Bradford and Halifax, although the exterior is more richly modelled and carved than either.

326

from the glazed brick walls, and Burmantofts faience is used to emphasise the giant arched openings at the main entrances to the rectangular hall, 243 feet by 102, in the middle of which stood a tall, domed cast-iron clock tower.[44] A double row of shops forms the perimeter of the three street frontages, with entrances from the street or from the hall, and the uniformly designed stalls are laid out in the form of a cross overlaid by a diagonal cross.[45]

The new market added an extravagantly romantic skyline to the city. The four-storeyed façades are faced with stone in a predominantly Flemish style, but one in which the architects had no scruples about including scaled-down versions of the Venetian dome of S.Maria della Salute for the corner pavilions, or *art-nouveau* flowing forms in the spandrels of the entrances. Between the shopfronts, granite-faced piers are surmounted by *putti* (obviously related to John Thomas's on the main entrance to the Town Hall) playfully draping themselves with lengths of West Yorkshire cloth; as the *Yorkshire Post* thought, 'there is sufficient ornamentation to save the edifice from dulness'.[46] The roofline rises and falls in pediments, domed pavilions, stepped gables and spirelets arranged around a central cupola 180 feet above the ground. The President of the Leeds and Yorkshire Architectural Society considered 'the general richness of effect' could have been maintained if there had been 'a judicious use of the pruning knife among the lead ornamental mansards, turrets, pinnacles, domes, etc',[47] but it was said Leeds was 'proud of it, despite its cost, which cannot be short of £110,000 or £120,000, while the original estimate was between £87,000 and £90,000'.[48]

The Leeds Markets completed the West Yorkshire group,[49] which all remained in use until 1972, when the Huddersfield building was superseded by a new market conceived as a part of a relocated town centre. In 1973, Bradford's was demolished in spite of considerable public opposition to the loss of the building which had become as much a part of the city's life as the Wool Exchange and the Town Hall.[50] Leeming and Leeming have been more fortunate, and their halls in Halifax and Leeds have been cleaned to reveal the quality of these remarkably confident examples of Late Victorian and Edwardian corporate patronage which raised the humble process of buying and selling the necessities of life to the level of a pilgrimage to the temple of those goddesses, Pomona and Flora, who once presided over Bradford's market.

44 The clock now stands at Oakwood, close to the south boundary of Roundhay Park.

45 Apparently the Kirkgate frontage was intended to include 'an hotel, containing a spacious restaurant, a billiard room, a coffee room, and a club and tea room'. Special consideration was given to the mechanical services, e.g., 'By a novel system of ventilation fresh air is drawn from apertures on the roofs to the shops below, and around the building is a subway, more than six feet in height, by means of which the least stoppage of pipes may be instantly remedied'. (*YP*, op.cit).

46 ibid.

47 *BA* (1904),lxii,385.

48 *YP*, op.cit.

49 Reference should also be made to Pontefract Market Hall (James Wilson 1859–60), of which the main façade survives.

50 Huddersfield Market was designed by the J.Seymour Harris Partnership, and that in Bradford by John Brunton and Partners.

12 Municipal grandeur

We don't now live in the days of Barons, thank God. We live in the days of Leeds, of Bradford, of Halifax and of Huddersfield.
Henry Brougham MP, 1830.

In what is now a leafy Leeds suburb, there stood what Thoresby called 'a remarkable Oak, to which the inhabitants repair'd upon publick Occasions'[1] and where justice was dispensed. This was the centre of the Wapentake of Skire-ake or Skyrac, and it might be said that the monumental public buildings which symbolise corporate life and government had their origin in such places. A less romantic view might look back no further than the moot halls in which courts were held, but there must be some conjecture about these buildings, as none survives intact in West Yorkshire and few were adequately described. There are references to some, such as the one near Sandal church in the fourteenth century; it was known as *le Wodehole*, but there is no record of its appearance although the material from which it was constructed is obvious.[2] Until recently, there was a late thirteenth-century building with an undercroft and upper hall next to Dewsbury parish church;[3] this was the court house of the rectory manor, and probably there were similar buildings in which manorial courts were held.

Several halls were rebuilt in the sixteenth century. The Moot Hall in Wakefield, built during the reign of Henry VIII on the south side of the churchyard, was a large timber-framed structure surrounding three sides of a courtyard, and had a stable attached.[4] The Halifax Moot Hall was an Elizabethan rebuilding on the site of a thirteenth-century court house. It was timber-framed, with an open roof, and two-thirds of the small floor area was inclined; the rest was level for the bailiff, jurors, witnesses and prisoners.[5] Bradford's courthouse, or Hall of Pleas, was a first-floor room (probably built in the sixteenth century) over a toll booth with an entrance from Ivegate; it was replaced in 1678 by a building in Westgate 'fitted up in the form of a court of justice', but it was very modest in size and appearance.[6] Pontefract's Hall was said to be in a dilapidated condition in 1656, and it was rebuilt as 'a single oblong room . . . entered at the centre of its west side by a pair of stairs which projected eight feet into the street . . . it had a window on each side of the doorway, and a triangular portico front, surmounted by a bell turret'.[7] The Leeds Moot Hall, which had been built in the centre of Briggate before 1619 with money and stocks appropriated to the relief of the poor, was a large first-floor room raised above shops; the profit from letting these was then

1 Thoresby, 148.

2 Walker, 75.

3 Chadwick, S. J., 'The Dewsbury Moot Hall', *YAS* (1911), xxi, 345ff. The building has been demolished.

4 Walker, 87.

5 Crabtree, 358; Bretton, R., 'Halifax courts of justice', *HAS* (1951), 57f. Later faced with stone, this little building survived until 1956.

6 Scruton, W., *Old Bradford*, Bradford 1891, 109; James, 298f; James C, 248, 250. In 1866 the old Hall of Pleas was still standing in Ivegate; James noted the slates were 'pegged or fastened to the laths of the roof with sheep shanks'.

7 Holmes, R., *The booke of entries of the Pontefract corporation 1653–1726*, Pontefract nd, 24.

8 Leeds Archives Dept., Minute Book, Leeds Pious Uses Committee 1664–1788, Part 1, 151ff.

9 Thoresby, 18,248f. A painting by Joseph Rhodes in the Leeds City Art Gallery shows the Moot Hall as it was in the early nineteenth century. The building was demolished in 1825. The statue was made by Andrew Carpenter (c.1677–1737). See Friedman,T.F., 'A noble magnificent statue', *LAC* (1973),no.72,5ff. In his diary, Thoresby refers to visiting on 20 May 1712 'Mr. Carpenter's, in Piccadilly, to see the Queen's statue, in Marble, in her Parliament robes, with crown, globe and sceptre', and on 27 May 1713 he recorded 'the setting up of the noble statue of the Queen'. When the Moot Hall was demolished, the statue was moved to the recently built Court House, then in 1828 to the new Corn Exchange, in 1868 to the new Town Hall, and finally to the City Art Gallery where it can be seen today.

10 Wittkower,R., 'Burlington and his work in York', *Studies in architectural history* (Singleton,W.A.ed), London 1954,i,47ff.

11 Walker, 400. This Assembly Room was adjoining the White Hart Hotel.

12 This building is still standing, but it was partly mutilated in the last century when the railway cut through the White Cloth Hall. Since then, most of the interior has been destroyed.

13 The older building remained in existence under the name of the Old Assembly Room or Mr Brown's Long Room; but it was quickly converted to other uses, such as an additional Cloth Hall, a Baptist meeting house, and a school. The new Room was opened on 16 June 1777 'by the most brilliant appearance of genteel company, that were ever before assembled together upon any occasion ... The company in general were very agreeably surprised at the neatness and elegance of the different apartments, which are allowed on all hands, to be as complete and highly finished as any set of rooms of that kind in the whole Kingdom' (*LI* 17 June 1777).

14 The Infirmary was built in 1770–71 at a cost of £2,500. Carr's fee was £90 5s 0d. Built of brick, it was eleven bays wide, the central three surmounted by a pediment, and the end two having attics. The first-floor windows were set in recessed arches, and the first, sixth and eleventh were Venetian. The Infirmary was enlarged in 1782, again in 1822, and demolished in 1893. An engraving dated 1771 shows it in its original form (see Linstrum, 21).

15 Thomas Malton's view of the Market Place in 1777 shows the relatively small scale of the old Town Hall.

16 Holmes, op.cit.,24.

devoted to charitable purposes. The upper room was where the Council met after the granting of a charter to the borough in 1626. It was probably a plain building, but in 1710 the Leeds Pious Uses Committee agreed to adopt a design for repairs and improvements made by William Etty.[8] Instructions were given to him and to Richard Wakefield to execute the work, which consisted principally of rebuilding the south front 'of fine wrought Stone upon Columns and Arches, with rustic Coins and Tabling'. A pair of giant Corinthian pilasters framed the new façade, in which a portico of two open arches was surmounted by a cartouche containing the town's arms between crossed maces. In the centre of the upper wall a niche within a pedimented frame was filled in 1713 by a statue of Queen Anne, described by Thoresby with typical Yorkshire forthrightness as 'the best that ever was made, not excepting the most celebrated one in *St. Paul's* Church-yard'.[9] In the transformation of this building can be seen the beginning of the growth of civic pride which was to produce the municipal monuments of nineteenth-century provincial architecture, but their genesis was complicated.

The building of Lord Burlington's masterpiece, the Assembly Rooms in York, in 1731–2 for 'all public diversions, such as assemblies, concerts of music, etc' added another type of public building to the Yorkshire social scene.[10] It is true no other town attracted the nobility and gentry as did York, the social centre of the North; but each had its own local gentry and prosperous merchants who might be satisfied with a moot hall for courts and council meetings but not for such diversions as York had introduced to the county. Wakefield had an Assembly Room as early as 1727;[11] then Leeds built one in Kirkgate, which was soon superseded by a larger building forming the north wing of the new White Cloth Hall. It is a dignified design, seventeen bays long with a series of giant recessed arches over an arcaded ground floor, and a large central Venetian window rising to an open pediment.[12] The shell remains of the 'spacious and handsomely decorated' ballroom which had Ionic pilasters and a vaulted, coved ceiling,[13] but there is no sign now of the handsome decorations or the 'Card Rooms and other appendages'. The architect is unrecorded, but William Johnson is the probable designer of this building which seems to have been modelled on John Carr's recently built Infirmary.[14] Carr's influence can also be seen in the rebuilding and enlargement of Pontefract Town Hall in 1785 to make a more impressive termination to the long view down the market place from St Giles's church and the arcaded market cross;[15] it was rebuilt as a large first-floor room over a rusticated, arcaded basement. The design, reminiscent of Carr's sweeping Crescent in Buxton (1779–84), was made by Bernard Hartley I, Surveyor of Bridges to the West Riding.[16] The many uses of such a building are well illustrated in the 1822 Directory which refers to the holding of quarterly Borough Sessions, the weekly meeting of the magistrates in the Rotation Office, the weekly attendance of officers of the Savings Bank to receive deposits and make accounts – and finally its use as an Assembly Room for Pontefract and district.[17]

The eighteenth century also saw the introduction of another type of

266. Leeds, Moot Hall; remodelled (W.Etty 1710) and embellished by Andrew Carpenter's statue of Queen Anne (1713). This engraving (probably from the painting T.Taylor exhibited in 1811) shows the Cross faintly in the background to the left, and it illustrates the mixture of jettied, timber-framed houses and Georgian façades which lined Briggate.

267. Pontefract, Town Hall (B.Hartley I 1785) incorporated the Borough Gaol on the ground floor and a large, multi-purpose hall on the first; like the Leeds Hall, it is closely related to the Market Place, forming the termination at the east end.

17 Baines, i,240. The Town Hall was enlarged in 1881 when Perkin and Bulmer's design for a new Assembly Room at the rear of the building was accepted (B (1881),xl,168). The most striking feature inside the main room on the first floor is a full-size plaster cast of John Edward Carew's bronze relief of 'The death of Nelson' from the column in Trafalgar Square.

18 Drake,F., *Eboracum*, London 1736,330.

19 Doncaster Mansion House, designed by James Paine, was built 1745–8, but only the central section was built; the upper part was altered by William Lindley in 1801. See Paine,J., *Plans, elevations, sections and other ornaments of the Mansion House at Doncaster*, London 1751.

20 Ripon Town Hall was designed by James Wyatt and built in 1799. It was the gift of Mrs Allanson, the owner of Studley Royal.

public building intended to reflect civic prosperity and importance. In 1725–6 the Mansion House was built in York to a design doubtfully attributed to Lord Burlington and more likely the work of William Etty. It is said the original intention was to build a store for the city's records, and that the idea grew until it became a building of unprecedented splendour, in which the Lord Mayor could live and hold civic entertainments during his term of office. In tracing the evolution of West Yorkshire public buildings, York Mansion House is important. Francis Drake, the York historian, was quick to note 'it had the honour to be a precedent for the city of London to copy',[18] and it does predate George Dance's Mansion House in London by fourteen years. The idea of building an official residence for the chief citizen was not taken up in any of the towns within this present study, although both Doncaster[19] and Ripon[20] were to follow York's lead; but the suite of entertaining-rooms became one more element to be incorporated in the ideal nineteenth-century town hall.

As the arts flourished, another need arose. In 1794 a Music Hall was opened in Albion Street, Leeds, described as 'exceedingly commodious, and finished with great elegance; qualities which it is said to possess equal to any other room, merely as a Concert Room, in the county'.[21] It had an orchestra and gallery, and 'a lofty coved ceiling from which several handsome glass chandeliers are suspended'.[22] It was in this building that the Northern Society held art exhibitions from 1809 onwards.[23] 'Annual exhibitions are ... with respect to the advancement of a just taste for the fine arts, as important instruments as public libraries with respect to polite letters and general science',[24] wrote a correspondent to the *Leeds Mercury*, and as a taste for the fine arts burgeoned, more buildings were needed to house them.

In that respect Wakefield, where a second Assembly Room had been built in Crown Court in 1801,[25] was considered deficient. 'That [it] should be totally unprovided with any Building adapted to the purpose of Public Amusements, of Lectures or Exhibitions, has long

21 Ryley, J., *The Leeds guide*, Leeds 1806, 61f. It is typical of the town's devotion to trade that the ground floor was 'a Hall for Woollen Manufacturers, which will accommodate such as are excluded from the Cloth halls, and afford great convenience to the manufacturers of blankets &c. in the sale of their goods' (*LI* 9 July 1792).

22 Mayhall, J., *Annals of Yorkshire*, London 1878, i, 177.

23 See Fawcett, T., *The rise of English provincial art*, Oxford 1974 for an account of the work and exhibitions of the Northern Society. The Music Room was extended for the convenience of the Society in 1823 (*LM* 24 May 1823, 28 May 1825) when a sixty feet long gallery was added.

24 *LM*, 17 July 1830.

25 Walker, 418, 481. The Assembly Room in Crown Court became the Town Hall until 1880.

26 *YAS* collection, MS1142. Appeal dated 1 July 1820.

27 The architects' names are given in ibid. This building has been known variously as the Public Rooms, the Mechanics' Institution and the Music Saloon. It is now used as the City Museum.

28 Parsons, i, 148f.

29 Beckwith, F., *Thomas Taylor, Regency architect*, Leeds 1949, 68ff.; Mayhall, op. cit., i, 325f. A watercolour of the Concert Room, probably by Clark, is in the collection of the Thoresby Society. The building was demolished in 1871 and replaced by the Royal Exchange built in 1872–5 to a design by T.H. and F. Healey. That, in turn, was demolished in 1964. The engraving by John Lucas of Clark's design is reproduced in Linstrum, 35.

30 Scruton, op. cit., 120. The building still survives in a much altered state as Post Office Chambers.

31 Crabtree, 347f. Demolished.

caused a feeling of regret . . . Nor is this the only want of which Wakefield has to complain; there is not another town in the Riding, perhaps in the County, whose Library and News-Room are so inadequate'. Thus began an appeal for a public subscription, which sought to use emulation of Leeds as an inducement. 'The town of Leeds, originally of no greater extent or importance than Wakefield, has . . . become entitled to rank as the first town in the county, whether it be considered for its extent and population, or for its wealth and public spirit'. The appeal then enumerated all the recent innovations in Leeds, concluding, 'These observations upon the prosperity of a neighbouring town have not been called forth by envy or jealousy, but rather with a view to hold it up as an example worthy to be followed, and as a proof of what may be accomplished by a *little exertion and public spirit*'.[26] Designs were invited for a Library and News-room, and the premium of twenty guineas was awarded to Watson and Pritchett, whose neat, Neo-classical building in the Ionic order was opened in Wood Street in 1822.[27] But Wakefield had not succeeded in matching the exertion and public spirit of Leeds, where an ambitious project estimated to cost nearly £30,000 was proposed in 1825. This was the Commercial Buildings, for which the committee examined designs by Francis Goodwin, Robert Dennis Chantrell, Thomas Taylor, Anthony Salvin, Charles Barry and John Clark. The last named was finally chosen as architect, and the building was completed in 1829 when it was described as 'a lasting monument of past successful enterprise, and as likely in the future to promote the trade and prosperity of the borough'.[28] It combined commercial uses with a concert room and news room behind an impressive Ionic façade which brought to Leeds an Athenian architectural quality from Edinburgh, Clark's native city. Built on a corner site, the curved screen on the angle was crowned by a circular drum ornamented with a cornice and a honeysuckle scroll taken from the Choragic Monument of Lysicrates.[29] The Commercial Buildings were greatly admired, and in 1825 the *Bradford Courier* advised the committee concerned with the town's new public rooms (to be known as the Exchange), that it too should 'hold fast to the models which have been handed down to us from the days of Greek excellence'; Francis Goodwin's accepted design of 1828 was in the same style.[30] In the same year the New Rooms in Halifax were built to John Oates's severe Neo-classical design of a central two-storeyed section with a single bay wing at each side. Behind this façade were a news room and a billiard-room, and on the first floor were 'a splendid Ball room, Card room, and Supper room, forming, when needed, a noble suite of Assembly rooms'. Everything was of the best; 'the cornices are richly and tastefully moulded; the ceiling is arched and supported by eight fluted Corinthian pillars . . . The rooms are elegantly and tastefully furnished with crimson damask curtains, sofas and ottomans, *en suite*: tasteful cut-glass chandeliers are suspended from the ceiling'.[31]

Justice had not been forgotten in this provision for the social and cultural ambitions of the expanding towns. Charles Watson's design for a noble Greek Doric courthouse was built in Wood Street,

268. Wakefield, Music Saloon (or Mechanics' Institution); designed as a Library and News-room (Watson and Pritchett 1820–2), it was built as a result of an appeal to the town's civic pride.

269. Leeds, Commercial Buildings (J.Clark 1826–9), consisting of public rooms and commercial offices, reflected the growing prosperity and architectural ambition of the town.

Wakefield in 1806, and in the following year his Ionic design for Pontefract courthouse was started.[32] In Leeds, Thomas Taylor built a courthouse and prison in Park Row which, when opened in 1813, was considered 'worthy to be ranked among the first of the public buildings of the town'. The courtroom could accommodate 800 and the cells 13, and the main façade had a tetrastyle Corinthian portico.[33] Twenty years later James Richardby built a courthouse in Bradford, in which he used the Ionic order with sober dignity.[34]

The early 1820s was a time of national and local prosperity, which was reflected in the extraordinary number of building enterprises. 'Scarcely a week elapses that we have not the pleasure to announce some project for improving and adorning the town', wrote the *Leeds Intelligencer* on 2 December 1824; and the prosperity was shared by the other West Yorkshire towns, each of which had its group of restrained, Neo-classical public buildings, small though they were, and reticent in comparison with what was to follow.[35] 'Why . . . should not Leeds . . . have all the advantages experienced in the other large Manufacturing Towns?' demanded the *Intelligencer* on 27 May 1824; but those advantages were not to be confined to Leeds. 'We don't now live in the days of Barons, thank God. We live in the days of Leeds, of Bradford, of Halifax and of Huddersfield', cried out Henry Brougham[36] in 1830, and it was in that spirit of proud independence, which at the same time maybe masked a parvenu feeling of inadequacy in their architectural heritage, that the West Yorkshire towns considered their public buildings in Victoria's reign.

In the first of those sixty-five glorious years, 1837, the scale began to change when Wakefield, the greatest corn market in the North, replaced its earlier Exchange with a rich Greek design by William Moffat. The attached colonnade of coupled Doric orders in the basement supported a high superstructure with end bays emphasised by giant Corinthian pilasters; the inspiration was clearly nothing less than John Nash's Buckingham Palace, and the Saloon was very little short in size of the Banqueting House in Whitehall.[37] This building, used for concerts and public meetings as well as for commercial purposes, was an impressive monument to prosperity which was incorporated in the town's seal; but it was soon eclipsed by Bradford's new hall.

Within ten years of its completion the 1834 Exchange in Piccadilly proved too small for the concerts and gatherings in Bradford, the town which was increasing at a rate of around 25,000 each decade. In 1849 a company of shareholders was formed to build a new hall, and a capital of £16,000 was subscribed in £10 shares.[38] In 1851, that memorable year for trade, art and international peace, the foundation stone was laid of St George's Hall. This was not a town hall in which any municipal business was conducted; nor was it a courthouse. It was simply a large hall, 'bigger than Birmingham's,' boasted the Mayor when he opened the building in 1853 and inaugurated a musical festival which 'at once gave Bradford an important position in the eyes of the musical world'. The paternalistic philanthropy of the Victorian masters of trade and commerce shines through the Mayor's belief that

32 Watson's designs for the Wakefield and Pontefract Court Houses are kept in the Wakefield Metropolitan District Council's office, Wakefield.

33 Beckwith, op.cit., 18ff.

34 Demolished in the 1950s.

35 Chantrell also designed the Leeds Philosophical and Literary Institution's building in Park Row and the Public Baths in Wellington Road (both 1819–20) as neat Neo-classical buildings.

36 Henry Brougham (later 1st Lord Brougham and Vaux) was returned as MP for Yorkshire in 1830. It was at a meeting in the Coloured Cloth Hall yard in Leeds on 27 July that he made his declaration about the extension of voting 'to the great towns of England . . . We live in the days when men are industrious and desire to be free'.

37 Walker, 444. Woodhead and Hurst of Doncaster were awarded second prize, and William Billinton of Wakefield third. The outstanding quality of the Corn Exchange and the lack of a public hall in the city make even more inexcusable the demolition of the Exchange in the 1960s.

38 James, 123f.

270. Halifax, New Rooms (or Assembly and Concert Rooms), a plain Neo-classical building (J.Oates 1828) incorporating 'a noble suite of Assembly Rooms'.

39 See Briggs,A., *Victorian cities*, London 1963,153.

40 See Hitchcock,H.-R., *Early Victorian architecture in Britain*, London 1954,i,114.

41 The chapel was largely destroyed by fire in 1907.

42 Even the stalls were 'ornamented with foliated scroll work, executed in *Carton Pierre*' (James, 124). The hall was painted originally in light shades 'which very soon became obliterated by smoke and dirt', and in 1873 it was 'repainted and gilded from floor to ceiling' according to a design made by Lockwood and Mawson (*B* (1873),xxxi, 451f.). The colours were 'based upon the Pompeian style', red, maroon, black, blue-grey, pale green, bronze and gold. The Pompeian red walls were divided into courses with fawn-colour lines, and in the centre of each panel was a wreath, 'enclosing a blue ground, on which will be inscribed in letters of gold the names of the great composers'.

275

after attending concerts there the workmen would return home 'elevated and refreshed, rising in the morning to their daily task without headache and without a regret';[39] but the Established Church felt the promoters of St George's Hall were trespassing on ecclesiastical ground in claiming any responsibility for the moral life of the citizens. The design was made by Lockwood and Mawson, who were to be the town's leading architects for the next thirty years. Henry Francis Lockwood, the designer in the partnership, had completed the Great Thornton Street Chapel in Hull in 1843,[40] and in that Corinthian temple he had contrived a vast building with a façade one hundred and sixty feet long and an auditorium which could seat 1,800, for only £7,000.[41] He had been trained as a Neo-classicist, and his early work in Hull is notable for the assured way in which he handled the grammar of Classical architecture whilst adding a richness to the details.

The interior of the Bradford hall owes much to Lockwood's two large chapels in Hull, Great Thornton Street and Albion Congregational. Like theirs, the ceiling is flat in spite of its large area, and the walls and ceiling panels are richly ornamented with 'foliage, flowers, fruit, musical instruments, emblems, and figures displayed in most harmonious colours and happy taste' in the manner Lockwood had used more modestly in Trinity House Chapel in Hull. In order to accommodate an audience of 3,328 or more, Lockwood built galleries supported on cast-iron columns around three sides of the hall, which increase the similarity between it and the monumental Nonconformist chapels. In St George's Hall can be seen the Victorian love of ornament and elaboration[42] overlaying the Neo-classical framework, and the exterior illustrates the same tendency. Obviously deriving from Elmes's noble St George's Hall in Liverpool, the great model for early nineteenth-century public buildings, the Corinthian temple stands on a high rusticated basement in which the arches have vermiculated voussoirs and giant carved heads in the keystones; the mezzanine windows are framed by huge garlanded brackets, and this rich

271. Wakefield, the Court House
(C. Watson 1806), the first of the civic
group in Wood Street.

272. Leeds, the Court House (T. Taylor
1811–13), of which this is the original
design. It was enlarged (R.D. Chantrell
1834–5), and demolished in 1901 after
forty years of use as the General Post
Office.

273. Bradford, St George's Hall
(Lockwood and Mawson 1851–3) brought
to West Yorkshire the monumental
civic grandeur already established in
London, Birmingham and Liverpool. It
had a profound influence on Bradford's
commercial architecture, such as the
adjacent warehouse to the left (pl.238).

274. Wakefield, the Corn Exchange
(W.Moffat 1836–7) incorporated a large
Saloon or public hall. (Camidge,C.E., *A
history of Wakefield and its industrial
and fine art exhibition*, 1866)

275. Bradford, St George's Hall; the galleried interior is overlaid with applied decoration that is not completely integrated with the architectural form, though pretty in itself.

276. Huddersfield, the Railway Station (J.P.Pritchett 1846–50) was a joint building for two promoters, the Lancashire and Yorkshire Company, and the Huddersfield and Manchester Railway and Canal Company. Each occupied one of the end pavilions (decorated with its arms), but they shared the platforms, refreshment rooms etc.

338

substructure is almost too grand for the temple itself which is more traditional in its use of a giant order, and slightly flat in its effect.

St George's Hall was a monumental addition to Bradford which stimulated other towns into emulation. The completion in 1850 of J.P.Pritchett's long Corinthian façade to Huddersfield railway station marked the first stage in a new architectural group around St George's Square, the town's new piazza. At the same time, the George Hotel was being built to an Italianate design by William Wallen and Charles Child, and on the facing side Sir John William Ramsden (the owner of the estate on which the new area of the town was being built) proposed to erect a Town Hall.[43] In 1853 a deputation met the Improvement Commissioners to urge the necessity for such a building, and a design was made by Pritchett to complement the Classical dignity of his station and to use again a Corinthian giant order; but nothing came of this, nor of a design made by William Tite in 1856.[44] The scheme was abandoned and the Town Hall that was built on another site almost thirty years[45] later was a disappointing substitute – 'a most expensive and ill contrived building', thought a loyal supporter of Ramsden's plan. But the other bid to emulate Bradford had a very different outcome.

The idea of building a public hall in Leeds had been first proposed in 1850, as jealous eyes were watching Bradford's taking shape; but there was a lack of response from the citizens to the attempted formation of a company to promote it.[46] The suggestion was then amended, and it was agreed that if a Town Hall were built it could incorporate a public hall paid for from the rates; out of this apparent expedient came a building which combined in one monumental design the various requirements of a courthouse, a council chamber, a public hall, a suite of ceremonial entertaining-rooms, and municipal offices. It became the model nineteenth-century Town Hall with a scattered progeny in the English-speaking world.[47]

'It may seem a small matter to those who have not studied these questions of local politics, whether a Town Hall in a provincial city shall be of one style of architecture or another; whether it shall be large or small, handsome or the reverse',[48] wrote the biographer of Dr Heaton, the most persistent advocate of a new public building in Leeds; and in another place can be found the belief, 'It is not in London that we find the best specimens of our old English architecture'. This represents a direct challenge to the metropolis, and the writer went on to affirm his faith in contemporary provincial architecture – 'The time may come when the archaeologist of a future age will look for the best specimens of the buildings of the present reign, not to the Law Courts or the Houses of Parliament, but to some provincial towns'.[49] It was a grand gesture of provincial pride. Dr Heaton spoke rapturously after his foreign travels of 'those famous old cities whose Town Halls are the permanent glory of the inhabitants and the standing wonder and delight of visitors from a distance'. He talked of 'a noble municipal palace' and of the town's 'duty . . . to the rest of the community and to prosperity'.[50] Here, side by side, were two different aspects of civic pride. One was the inevitable competition

43 Kirklees Library and Museum Service, DD/RAL/p/13.

44 However, Tite's design for an Italianate warehouse (subsequently altered for the Huddersfield Building Society) forms an impressive south side to St George's Square. It was built in 1856 and may have been derived from his design for a Town Hall (which has not been found).

45 It was designed by John Henry Abbey and built in 1878–81 (*BA* (1878),x,11).

46 See Briggs, op.cit.,137ff for an account of the events leading to the building of Leeds Town Hall.

47 It was said that many Americans travelled to Leeds especially to see the Town Hall, which some esteemed at least as highly as the great medieval cathedrals. The composition of a building with end pavilions and a dominating central tower was adopted in other cities, e.g. Philadelphia City Hall (John McArthur Jr. 1871–1901) which seems the ultimate expansion of Brodrick's idea of a domed tower, crowned with a colossal statue of William Penn. It is also interesting that Fuller and Laver's first design for the New York State Capitol featured a single colossal order, like Brodrick's, and there is a close resemblance between the domed towers of the two buildings (see *B* (1870),xxviii, 426f). The Colonial design closest to Leeds Town Hall is Parliament House, Melbourne (Kerr and Knight 1856); the first design incorporated a tower similar to Brodrick's early version (see fn.54 infra), but this was later revised as a domed structure which was not built (see *Historic public buildings of Australia*, Melbourne 1971,ii,152ff). Other Australian and South African buildings were based, but less closely, on the Leeds model or William Hill's derivatives at Bolton (1866–73) and Portsmouth (1886–90), although some incorporate French Second Empire elements; e.g. Parliament House, Adelaide (Wright and Tayler 1880s), Durban Town Hall (P.Dudgeon 1883–5), Cape Town City Hall (Reid and Green 1893).

48 Reid,T.W., *A memoir of John Deakin Heaton,MD*, London 1883,121.

49 ibid.

50 Heaton discussed his experience of Continental Town Halls and the need for Leeds to build an impressive 'outward symbol' of public government at a meeting of the Philosophical and Literary Society in January 1854.

277. Leeds Town Hall (C.Brodrick 1853–8) attracted international notice. The tower, crowned with a Baroque dome and cupola, symbolised a newly awakened provincial civic pride; and the combination of this mighty vertical element with a long, colonnaded façade became a much-copied model of civic architecture, abroad as well as in Britain.

51 See Linstrum,D., 'Cuthbert Brodrick: an interpretation of a Victorian architect', *Journal of the Royal Society of Arts* (1971), cxix,72ff.

52 ibid. Brodrick's watercolour perspective of the Royal Institution, now in the Ferens Art Gallery, Hull is reproduced on p. 74. The building was demolished after being partly destroyed during the Second World War. See Sheahan,J.J., *General and concise history . . . of Kingston-upon-Hull*, Hull 1864,495f.

53 The perspective of the original design has not been found, but it is reproduced in Wilson,T.B., *Two Leeds architects*, Leeds 1937,opp.18.

54 Brodrick's first idea, which was engraved, was for a Wren-like spire crowning a colonnaded tower, but this was revised and three alternative domed cupolas were designed for consideration. A drawing in the RIBA Drawings Collection (see *Catalogue*, vol.B/109) appears to have been made so that a model could be constructed. Sir Charles Barry had been the assessor of the competition, and the committee sat for eight hours listening to 'an elaborate discourse from [him] upon the productions of the various architects which had been submitted . . . It was in consequence of the strong terms of commendation in which he had spoken of the genius envinced in the design and plan . . . that they awarded the first prize to Mr. Brodrick'. Asked if they could entrust the work to so young a man, Barry said 'after what he had seen of the drawings, he felt sure that there was sufficient talent and genius in the architect who had prepared them to carry out anything which an architect could be required to do' (*LI*, 11 Sept 1858).

55 Ruskin,J., *Lectures on architecture and painting*, London 1854,vi. Ruskin continued to criticise the tower whenever possible; in 1863 he was invited to lecture in Leeds, when he commented 'he should like and intended to come . . . when he would do his best to crucify the snobs or charlatans in architecture who could put such an abortion as that tower upon a town hall of fair Roman composite architecture' (*The works of John Ruskin*, London 1908,xxxiv,725). The unexpected part of that comment is the implied approval of the building itself.

of the *nouveau-riche* provincial with the established metropolitan; the other was the idealism of the patron (in this case a corporate one) who believed it was his duty to bequeath a work of art of enduring quality to posterity; and it was the building of a Town Hall that could satisfy both.

When the foundation stone of Leeds Town Hall was laid in 1853, two weeks before the opening of Bradford's hall, it was to the accompaniment of great cheers from the crowds assembled in the streets and on the neighbouring rooftops. Afterwards the Madrigal and Motet Society burst into a song of praise to the building as a symbol of freedom, peace and trade, justice and mercy, wise government, and the soothing effect of music on the citizens. The architect was Cuthbert Brodrick,[51] a young man from Hull, whose design had been accepted in open competition in 1853. Articled to Lockwood in 1837, and in practice for himself in Hull from 1845, his first important building was the Royal Institution in his native town, designed in 1852.[52] This was conceived as a monumental screen of two pedimented pavilions joined by a colonnade of coupled Corinthian columns, a composition deriving from such well-known French Classical façades as Perrault's east front of the Louvre or Gabriel's palaces in the Place de la Concorde, or possibly from Henry Holland's screen in front of the Prince Regent's Carlton House, itself derived from designs by Ledoux for entrances to Parisian *hôtels*. Brodrick's European tour in 1844–5 left him with a marked preference for France, which ultimately became his home, and for its Classical and contemporary architecture.

In spite of the difference in scale there are, not unnaturally, close resemblances between Brodrick's buildings in Hull and Leeds. The original design for the Town Hall was amended several times, but basically the first proposal was of a giant colonnade surrounding the building, broken by projections and standing on a heavily rusticated basement.[53] Nearly square, and unpedimented, it was reminiscent of Brongniart's Paris Bourse, designed as long ago as 1808 but completed only in 1835. The plan was a simple arrangement of four corner pavilions joined by loggias, and in the middle was a basilican main hall with a semi-circular vaulted ceiling. The first intention was to repeat the apsidal north end on the south at a higher level; this was to be the council chamber, capable of being opened to the main hall and making it possible to find room for 3,470 people sitting or 9,278 standing. It was an ingenious answer to the committee's request for a hall to accommodate so many, a condition which drew down scornful comments from the architectural press, since the town proposed to spend only £35,000. Did they imagine such a sum would pay for the Baths of Caracalla or Westminster Hall?

Nor would it pay for Giotto's campanile, but the growing pride in the new Town Hall as it grew behind the scaffolding caused Sir Charles Barry's recommendation of a crowning tower[54] to be taken seriously. John Ruskin applauded such civic munificence and recalled the Florentine fourteenth-century precedent, whilst contemptuously trusting 'the tower [in Leeds] may not be built on the design there proposed'.[55] The final form was discussed in 1856, and in the following

278. Leeds, Town Hall; the vaulted form of the central Victoria Hall derived from Roman *thermae* but probably more directly from St George's Hall, Liverpool.

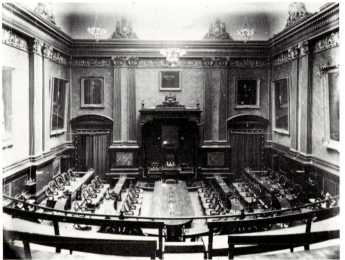

279. Leeds, Town Hall; the now remodelled ex-Council Chamber, for which Brodrick designed the furniture and the typically vigorous Classical treatment of the walls.

56 Elmes's design is in the RIBA Drawings Collection (*Catalogue*, vol C-F/105,69).

277

year Brodrick was given instructions to build the monumental composition which changed the appearance of the building to such an extent that, from some viewpoints, it now seems little more than a massive colonnaded base for the mighty domed superstructure. It was a megalomaniacal decision to add such a tower to an already grandiose design; Elmes had suggested a similar combination in 1839–40 in his unexecuted design for the Assize Courts in Liverpool,[56] but Brodrick accomplished it with an assured effrontery.

Leeds Town Hall symbolised nineteenth-century provincial pride as did no previous building, and the town had good cause to feel proud on the day of its opening in 1858 when the Queen walked through the

57 The sculptor was John Thomas (1813–62), who superintended the stone-carving on the Houses of Parliament; he also worked for Barry at Harewood House (1848–50), and at Halifax (see n.71 infra). The four lions which flank the main entrance were additions to the design, set in position in 1867. They were the work of William Day Keyworth Jr. of Hull and London, and were Brodrick's final touches to the Town Hall; his travel sketches show how sculptured lions attracted him, and during his first visit to Italy he had recorded the noble animals by Francesco Biggi in the Palazzo dell'Università, Genoa, by Carlo Rubatto outside the cathedral of S.Lorenzo, Genoa, and by Canova on the monument to Clement XIII in St Peter's, Rome.

58 There was a limited competition for the decorations, which cost £1,600, and were executed by John Crace, who had built up a great reputation largely on the strength of his work inside the Houses of Parliament. The columns were marbled *rosso antico* with gilt bronze capitals and bases, and the podiums were 'inlaid with precious and rare specimens of marbles, executed in the most finished style of painting. The inter-columns . . . are of a pale green colour, bordered with a fret ornamental margin'. The semicircular clerestorey windows were filled with coloured glass by R.B.Edmundson and Son of Manchester, and the decorative keystones and figures above are the work of John Thomas. Ten cut-glass chandeliers (one of which survives in the Leeds Civic Hall) were designed by Brodrick and made by Osler of Birmingham. The apse behind the organ was 'deep azure, powdered with stars', and the organ case was partly gilded. There have been many changes in the Victoria Hall, which was redecorated in 1878 when new lighting fittings were introduced (*B A* (1878), x,137). A gallery was added by 'a practical engineer' in 1874 (*B A* (1874),ii,124), and then replaced in 1890 by the present design by W.H.Thorp. J.D.Crace made a design for redecorating in 1894 (V. and A., E. 1850–1912), which he reproduced in his book, *The art of colour decoration*, London 1912, fig.2, using it as an example for a detailed analysis of the distribution of colour values. The orchestra was remodelled in 1904 by J.B.Fraser (*B* (1904),lxxxvii,256). The present lighting fittings date from the 1930s, and the inappropriate decoration from the late 1940s.

doorway in the south colonnade, beneath the great sculptured allegory of Leeds as a patron of the arts encouraging the sciences and industries.[57] Immediately she was in the domed vestibule that might be taken as the representation of the Empire; in the centre was Matthew Noble's statue of the Queen herself, and each of the pendentives above was decorated as a tribute to one of the continents which contained large sections of the Empire on which the sun never set. Local commentators joyfully claimed that on that day, as the head of the Empire was in Leeds, the town was her temporary capital. In the Victoria Hall (obviously derived from Liverpool's, but proudly noted as far bigger than Bradford's), the symbolic tributes were to the town of Leeds.[58] Just as Lockwood had invented Classical capitals and decoration incorporating anchors in Hull and musical instruments and other emblems in Bradford, so did Brodrick invent in Leeds. In the capitals of the columns were the Savile owl of the civic arms and the Golden Fleece on which the town's prosperity was originally founded, and around the walls were painted mottoes; 'Weave Truth with Trust', 'Honesty is the Best Policy' and 'Good Will towards Men' – typical Yorkshire comments. There were also such reminders of freedom and justice as 'Trial by Jury' and 'Magna Carta', and the progressive injunction 'Forward'. Leeds was so sure it had triumphed over Bradford that it painted up its neighbour's civic motto 'Labor Omnia Vincit'; and finally the apse at the end of the hall was filled with a monumental organ case surmounted by the civic arms of Leeds flanked by two angels blowing trumpets. There is no doubt whose they were. Like Bradford, Leeds inaugurated its new hall with a musical festival, ending it with a reminder that the building was intended for the ordinary citizen in spite of the splendour of its Royal opening. 'A cheap concert was given on the last day which passed off with great éclat. The number of persons present at this last concert was about 4000'.

There is no record of any discussion about the style in which this great building was to be designed, and although there were occasional references to town halls in Flanders as examples of civic architecture, there was no suggestion that the design should be anything but Classical in style. Nor is there any reason why there should have been. There were no other precedents but Liverpool and Birmingham, both of which had been visited by the Building Committee in the early days of the planning. But there was one passionate voice which had drawn attention to another, earlier precedent. In 1836 Pugin had first published his satirical comment on modern architecture, *Contrasts or a Parallel between the Architecture of the 15th and 19th centuries*, and in this book Pugin had shown side by side recent examples of buildings contrasted with what he believed were their glorious, infinitely superior, medieval equivalents. One of these pairs was of town halls. He chose to deride George Dance's façade to the London Guildhall, a highly individual essay in an Indian-Gothic style which had little bearing on later designs; but he chose to praise the Hôtel de Ville at Ypres and hold it up as a shining example. And in 1857 George Gilbert Scott wrote that town halls are continually being erected in our provincial towns in styles as thoroughly unsuitable as can be conceived, and at a cost which would, in good hands and in a right style, have enabled them to vie with the glories of Brussels, Louvain or Ypres. Conceive for one moment what a glorious structure might have been erected at Leeds.[59]

When Scott wrote that attack on Brodrick and the Classicists he was already engaged in the Whitehall Battle of the Styles,[60] but his reference to provincial town halls had very likely been provoked by the reception given to his design for one at Halifax, a proposal which had been under discussion since 1847. During John Crossley's Mayoralty in 1850–1, he 'conceived the noble project of removing a considerable portion of the old town . . . and rebuilding . . . it upon a costly and magnificent scale'. He purchased the old properties in the Northgate area and spent more than £100,000 on new buildings, leaving the central site vacant for a Town Hall. Lockwood and Mawson were his architects, and they provided him with designs for the Mechanics' Hall, the Halifax Joint-Stock Bank, the White Swan Hotel (which might have been called Palazzo Crossley on account of the Roman style and incorporation of the newly granted family arms in the decoration), and a number of noble warehouses and commercial buildings ornamented with vermiculated quoins and heavily carved keystones; all were erected at Crossley's expense, with the exception of the Mechanics' Hall.[61] 'Perhaps no town of its size has added to the number of its important buildings so rapidly as the good old town of Halifax', thought the *Builder* in 1859, the year in which the Town Hall was begun; but the history of its design is complicated.

Three years before the foundation stone was laid, Crossley had offered to help the Council financially if they would resolve to build a Town Hall and complete his civic layout. Along with this offer he sent a design made by Lockwood and Mawson, Italianate in style and crowned by a dome. The Crossley proposal and design were followed within three months by Edward Akroyd's counter-design which he had obtained from Scott, who was at the time his architect for the church of All Souls on the hill overlooking the town. It was for a building with a steeply sloping roof and a central tower, Gothic in style, and something like the Town Hall in Ypres which Pugin had illustrated in *Contrasts* and Scott was to hold up as an example to be followed. Ruskin wished 'the good people of Halifax joy of their Town-hall, that is to be, I hope, pleading only with Mr. Scott for a little interference of some sort with the lines of quatrefoils in the roof';[62] but his congratulations were premature. Scott was as complacent as usual about his design, looking back on it twenty years later; 'as good a thing of its kind, and of its small size, as had been made at the time; nor do I think I could now do better. It was the first-fruits of my studies for the Government offices; and, in my opinion, was better than any subsequent design for these buildings'.[63] The arguments were long, and complicated by the contribution of the Borough Engineer and another design of which Crossley himself was the suspected author. Finally, in 1859 Sir Charles Barry was invited to comment, and then to submit a design.

59 Scott,G.G., *Remarks on secular and domestic architecture*, London 1857,201. Ruskin's private, cynical comments on architectural style appear in a letter he wrote in 1860 to Ellen Heaton, the sister of the Leeds doctor who spoke frequently and zealously on behalf of the Town Hall and the Infirmary; 'It does not in the least matter what people build at Leeds nor anywhere else at present. The Gothic they build is essentially worse than the Greek. It will be fifty years before we can build *anything*: meantime, people may as well spend their money in caricatures of Greek as of Gothic, for anything I care. There's a beautiful steam engine at Vauxhall bridge – with Doric pillars for cylinders. I don't want to change them into niches and boil my saints'. (Quoted in Surtees,V., *Sublime and instructive*, London 1972,224).

60 Brodrick was also involved in the battle over the style for the new Government buildings in Whitehall. His design for the War Office had been placed fifth in the 1857 competition, and when William Tite led a deputation of about twenty Italophile architects to assure Lord Palmerston that his decision not to allow a Gothic design had their support, Brodrick was among them (*B* (1859),xvii,562).

61 *B* (1858),xvi,319; (1860),xviii,39.

62 *The works of John Ruskin*, London 1904,xiv,118.

63 Scott,G.G., *Personal and professional recollections*, London 1879,179.

64 Reprinted in Hall,R. de Z., *Halifax Town Hall*, Halifax 1963,42f.

65 Palladio,A., *The four books of architecture*, London 1738,81.

66 Edmund Beckett Denison (later Lord Grimthorpe) demanded to know 'how it happened that . . . the Gothic models of the continent had been wilfully rejected' by the builders of town halls, and then answered his own question by expressing the belief 'that the pomposity of the Italian style was in accordance with the modern spirit of the age and of the municipal bodies' which acted as patrons. (*B* (1860),xviii,119).

67 Reid, op.cit.,143.

68 Heaton hoped visitors would come to Leeds to see the Town Hall just as he had been to Ghent for that purpose.

69 Barry died in 1860 and the Town Hall was completed by his son, Edward Middleton Barry (1830–80), who added the mansard roofs to the original design and so gave the building more of a French character than Barry had originally intended. Nevertheless, there was always a quality that derives from the New Louvre and an almost indefinable infiltration of the Second Empire in the whole design.

70 By a curious chance, recent demolition and road construction have opened up views of this building which were never possible before.

71 Once again, John Thomas was the sculptor; his contribution was the allegorical groups of the four continents, lions and colossal angels on the tower. Thomas died suddenly in 1862, leaving the model of Asia untouched. 'The dying artist, it seems, asked his friend, Mr. Maclise, the painter, to superintend the modelling of it' (*B* (1862), xx,336). Daniel Maclise (1806–70) was working at the time on a painting for the staircase wall.

For the benefit of the Council, Barry wrote his definition of the ideal Town Hall, which should be 'the most dominant and important of the Municipal Buildings of the City, . . . [it] should occupy a central and elevated position and be isolated from all surrounding Buildings. It should be a lofty structure, with a tower of commanding importance'.[64] That could be a description of Leeds Town Hall, but it echoes august advice in its obvious derivation from a well-known architectural treatise:

Choose those sites . . . that shall be in the most noble, and celebrated parts of the city . . . on beautiful and ornamented piazzas, in which many streets finish, whereby every part may be seen with its dignity, and afford . . . admiration to whomsoever sees and beholds it. And if in the city there be hills, the highest part of them is to be chosen; but in case there be no elevated places, the floor . . . is to be raised, as much as is convenient, above the rest of the city.[65]

That quotation from Palladio's *I Quattro Libri dell' Architettura* is a restatement of what Alberti wrote in his *De re Aedificatori,* and Barry was in effect repeating what the two great sources for a Renaissance architect had written about the ideal city, with one significant difference. The Italians had both been referring to the siting of the temple, as the church was classically called. Can it be said that in the nineteenth-century ideal city the town hall had replaced the temple? In Birmingham and Liverpool, the Classical civic buildings had been sited in positions which could be likened, in Birmingham to a Roman forum, and in Liverpool to the Acropolis in Periclean Athens. There is also an analogy between the civic or imperial pride that was responsible for the building of Classical temples and the spirit in which Victorian civic buildings were promoted.[66]

It has already been pointed out that there was a strong undertone of morality in the urging of the building of St George's Hall in Bradford for 'the intellectual, moral and spiritual parts of our nature', and in Leeds it was believed the Town Hall 'would become a practical admonition to the populace of the value of beauty and art, and in course of time men would learn to live up to it'.[67] This was a high ideal for a building, but as well as its moral admonition the Town Hall was intended to symbolise 'public spirit, and generous pride in the possession of . . . municipal privileges'. And it was confidently believed the building would be famous and, 'like the noble halls of France, of Belgium, and of Italy . . . attract to our town the visits of strangers, dilettanti, tourists, and the lovers of art from distant places'.[68] Nor were these empty words, for on the list of buildings to be seen by serious American visitors to England, Leeds Town Hall stood high.

How far was Barry able to realise his ideal in Halifax?[69] The site was not open on all four sides, but he designed the building as if it were.[70] The richly decorated repetitive bay treatment of the exterior[71] recalls Palladio's Basilica in Vicenza and Sansovino's Library of St Mark's in Venice, each of which, in a sense, incorporates a tower. But Barry subordinated his building to the gigantic tower, planning it so that this monumental pile (more French than Italian) would look down Princess Street with, as he had advocated,

280

280. Halifax Town Hall (Sir C. Barry 1859–63) dominates the north end of the town, terminating in a tall feature which combines the characteristics of a Gothic spire and a Classical obelisk. The White Swan Hotel on the left is part of Lockwood and Mawson's rebuilding in the Italianate style of the Northgate area in the 1850s.

281. Halifax, Town Hall; the central Hall derives from Barry's London club-houses, reflecting his liking for polychromy in the coloured glass and the marble, stone and encaustic tiles used in the paving.

281

72 Barry thought, 'in considering the ... modern attempts which have been made ... in the splendid structures recently erected ... in the populous & thriving towns in the North of England, it appears to me that a serious error has been committed in partly devoting those buildings to the recreations, rather than exclusively to the serious business of life, whereby a needlessly lavish expenditure has been incurred, & the usefulness & characteristic features of a Town Hall have been impaired'.

73 Parsons, i,148. 'At the back of the exchange is a court with a piazza ... and at the left hand side of the entrance is an excellent and commodious hotel'; *L I*, 28 June 1827.

'commanding importance'. The whole composition is a compromise between a Renaissance palace and a medieval cathedral with an attached tower (even in the Hawksmoor-like effect of a Gothic steeple fashioned from Classical elements), but it is carried off with great swagger. The detailing of the interior is in Barry's 'Pall Mall' manner, and the grand central hall inevitably recalls the Reform Club. It is a composite building, containing law courts, a council chamber, a suite of entertaining-rooms and municipal offices, but not a public hall; indeed, Barry evidently disagreed with the inclusion of the last in Leeds Town Hall.[72] It cost slightly more than £50,000, and it was opened by the Prince of Wales in 1863, shortly after Brodrick had completed another Classical building in Leeds.

Samuel Chapman had built a Corn Exchange at the north end of Briggate in 1827–8, a little three-bay, Ionic, pedimented building with a cupola;[73] but by 1860 it was too small for the expanding trade. At a meeting of cornfactors and the Markets Committee in May of that year

347

74 B (1860),xviii,515. The second prizewinner was William Hill, the third Lockwood and Mawson.

75 It cannot be a coincidence that the most likely book which Brodrick would have consulted (see 76) also refers to the choice at Le Mans of a Corn Exchange circular in plan in preference to rectangular, largely because of the irregularity of the site.

76 Bruyère,L., *Etudes rélatives à l'art des constructions*, Paris 1823,i,13. When Les Halles were rebuilt in 1866 the new market pavilions were planned around the eighty-years-old Exchange; it was rebuilt in 1889 as the Bourse du Commerce, retaining the circular shape of its predecessor.

77 B (1861),xix,151.

78 ibid.,648f.

79 It is quite obvious from Brodrick's detailing that the Italian architects he admired were Ammanati, Vignola and Antonio da Sangallo the younger, and the photographs which have survived of pages from his Continental sketchbook include drawings of their buildings. Brodrick might have taken the idea of the diamond-pointed rustication from one of the buildings he knew in Italy, e.g. Palazzo dei Diamanti in Ferrara, Palazzo Santacroce in Rome, the Gesù Nuovo in Naples; but bold overall rustication had been used in the nineteenth century, e.g. Schinkel's Palais Redern in Berlin (1832–3).

80 The dome seems to have been a surprise to a writer in the *Architect* (1870),iv,315, who commented 'No roof that it has been our fortune to see has ever impressed us more than this one, as a work of original genius and thorough practical utility'.

there was some discussion about the type of building needed, and David Cousin's Edinburgh Corn Exchange was considered as a possible model. The chairman assured the meeting that the new Leeds Exchange would be 'in every way a suitable one', and plans were advertised for in June; two months later Brodrick was announced the winner,[74] and in May 1861 the foundation stone was laid of a building unique in England.

The site, next to the White Cloth Hall, was of an irregular shape and it is likely that this constraint led to Brodrick's adoption of an elliptical plan;[75] but it is even more likely that he had in mind the outstanding French example of a corn exchange, the Halle au Blé in Paris,[76] regarded as one of the city's major architectural sights. 'This edifice is remarkable for its circular form, resembling the amphitheatres, &c. of the ancients', is the comment in *Picturesque Views of Public Edifices in Paris* (1814), and the *Builder* commented on Brodrick's design that 'A form has been adopted unusual in this country, – the form of the Roman theatre'.[77] It was an out-of-date model to use in the 1860s when 'the ancients' were no longer as reverently evoked as exemplars as they had been in the seventeenth and eighteenth centuries; yet Brodrick's derivative is a magnificent design, in some ways his finest.

The form is basically a large, domed elliptical hall surrounded by an outer ring of offices on two floors, and with storage in the basement.[78] The ground floor is raised above the street level and there are two semicircular porticoes which are the only projections from the ellipse. It is a practical plan, well suited to an awkward site, but Brodrick succeeded in making out of it a remarkable, monumental building. The exterior is faced with diamond-pointed rustication broken by the regularly repeated arches of the two storeys of windows, and bound together by the severely modelled string course and the garlanded frieze; the two porticoes swell out of the building in boldly contrasting curves. The detailing of the doorways and plinth is derived from massive sixteenth-century Roman models, and the whole design testifies to Brodrick's observation of Italian buildings on his travels.[79] The interior, faced with coloured, moulded brickwork, repeats the pattern of semicircular-headed openings on two floors, each arch representing a corn factor's office; the upper level access is from a projecting gallery with a robustly detailed cast-iron balustrade. And over the whole space rises a dome, 75 feet above floor level at its highest point. This unusual, important design seems not to have received the attention it deserved in the 1860s,[80] although Scott probably had it in mind when he designed Brill's Baths in Brighton in 1866; naturally, he used the pointed arch in the arcades in his domed building.

There is no need to emphasise the influence Scott had on secular architecture, and his design for the Infirmary in Leeds marks a stylistic turning point in West Yorkshire public building. John Carr's ninety-year-old building had been enlarged and altered, but it was no longer adequate in the 1860s; after much discussion and negotiation a new site was purchased, but the choice of architect occupied a great

282. Leeds, Corn Exchange (C.Brodrick 1861–2); a meticulously detailed, ingenious design which created a major architectural monument out of a commercial building.

81 Anning,S.T., *The General Infirmary at Leeds*, London 1963,i,23ff.

82 Brotherton Library, University of Leeds; Gott papers, letter from Scott to Denison, 24 Feb 1862.

83 *B* (1862),xx,859.

deal of committee time.[81] Finally, Scott was selected. He had been asked about the style in 1862 before being appointed, and without hesitation he replied 'I think that some form of Architecture formed on the Mediaeval styles but freely treated would meet the requirements of such a building better than any other'.[82] And so the Infirmary was medieval, in a similar manner to the St Pancras Hotel which Scott was building at the same time. It is less richly detailed than the hotel, but the windows, the *porte-cochère*, the columns, and the decoration in the spandrels are very similar. When it was finished, one commentator wrote that the 'architectural features will probably give the critics a little easy occupation, for styles of the thirteenth, the fourteenth, and the fifteenth century are introduced and mingled with a boldness which must astonish the scrupulous adherents of precedent'.[83]

Since Scott had said he favoured the 'freely treated' medieval style, and he believed Gothic was the only acceptable basis of a nineteenth-

283. Leeds, Corn Exchange; the elliptical form, and the dignified, disciplined effect of the repeated semicircular-headed arches, are combined in a masterly fashion in this memorable interior.

century style, the Infirmary is exactly what might have been expected. His design illuminates in some respects his comments on architecture. His defence of Gothic warehouses, for example, in which he thought 'all which has ever been done that was good for anything in the way of warehouses was either done in the middle ages, or has been derived from traditions of what was then done';[84] there can be seen one aspect of his belief that it was possible to return to medieval architecture, forgetting the decadent Renaissance, and continue to develop it to suit the nineteenth century. It was not necessarily the adoption of a style that he advocated, but a way of designing and constructing. Scott saw merit in some of the functional West Riding warehouses, although he qualified his praise by saying that although they were 'noble structures, a very little more thought in designing them might make them much more so'. He referred to the principle of the medieval builders who made 'everything which is useful and necessary not only beautiful in the abstract, but also beautiful in a degree and in a manner evidently suited to and expressive of its use, and resulting directly from its natural form and mode of construction'.[85] It is quite obvious that the designer of the Albert Memorial, the Foreign Office and St Pancras Hotel had different standards for commercial buildings; but in which category did an infirmary belong? At Leeds Scott seems to have attempted a compromise; the south front is enriched with a little tracery, carved stonework and granite columns, but in the side elevations he expressed what he probably meant by functional architecture in the structural brick pointed arches over the plain windows, and a lack of ornament. The plan of the Infirmary was not medieval; it was based on the latest thinking on hospital planning, and consists of pavilion wards which

284

84 Scott,G.G., *Remarks on secular and domestic architecture*, London 1858,213.

85 ibid.,217.

284. Leeds, the General Infirmary (G.G.Scott 1863–7) helped to establish the Gothic style as an acceptable alternative to Italianate in West Yorkshire. On the extreme right is a later addition (G.Corson 1891–2) which repeats Scott's design.

285. Bradford, Town Hall; despite Lockwood and Mawson's obvious borrowing of elements from Italy, France and other sources, they produced a design that is picturesque in outline, varied in modelling, and full of intricate Gothic detail. It was opened in 1873.

86 There was correspondence with Florence Nightingale about the planning of the Infirmary; see Anning, op.cit.,i,27f. In 1859 she had published *Notes on hospitals*.

87 The glazed roof was added to create an additional covered space when the Infirmary was opened in 1867 by the Prince of Wales with an important exhibition of art. The Winter Garden has been dismantled, and part of Scott's building is likely to be

have cross-lighting and cross-ventilation, with lavatories and sluices in towers at the end.[86] In the centre of the building was a glazed Winter Garden in which convalescents walked among exotic trees, but this appears to have been an afterthought.[87] The building was completed in 1867, but by that time the Gothic style had begun to take root in the West Yorkshire towns.

Bradford had entered late in the Town Hall Stakes. It was ten years after Leeds had achieved its ambition that a competition was announced for a building on a central but restricted site in the centre of Bradford, which was to combine under one roof municipal offices, council chamber, courts and a suite of entertaining-rooms. It was evidently no surprise that Lockwood and Mawson were announced as the successful architects with the entry submitted under the motto 'Let Bradford Flourish';[88] but apart from a feline skirmish in the *Architect*, there was little doubt the most appropriate design had been

286. Todmorden, Town Hall; in designing this large addition to the small Pennine town, J.Gibson (1875) followed the Classical tradition of West Yorkshire public buildings.

demolished in the proposed development of the Infirmary site.

88 *B* (1869),xxvii,840f. is a detailed account of the design. Milnes and France were awarded second place, and Samuel Jackson third.

selected. Nevertheless, the prudent architects sent in alternative Gothic and Classical elevations for their plan, submitting both sets as elaborately coloured drawings and perspectives in glazed, gilded frames; 'richly have all the Bradford architects bedizened their drawings', commented the *Architect*.

The planning of the various elements was convenient, and it was the Gothic version, described as 'Early French' in style 'with a spice of Northern Italy of the same period' that was selected. It is exactly what might have been expected within a short time of the competitions for Manchester Town Hall and the Law Courts in London, and there were many critics ready to point out its indebtedness to the latter. Above the heavy basement, the elevation is arcaded, with coupled and shafted pointed lights on the first floor; then comes a continuous arcade in which regularly spaced niches are filled with statues of the English kings from William I to William IV. Elizabeth and Victoria

285

287. Morley, Town Hall (G.A.Fox 1895); the continuing influence of Leeds Town Hall is nowhere more obvious than in this building, from the tower of which can be seen the original a few miles away.

288. Wakefield, Town Hall (T.E.Collcutt 1877–80); the three oriel windows provide a rich modelling of the main façade, and the asymmetrically placed campanile rises above the town's skyline as a secular equivalent of the tall spire of the Cathedral.

289. Wakefield, County Hall (Gibson and Russell 1893–8) was a distinguished addition to the civic group in Wood Street, in some ways complementing the detailing of the Town Hall, but adding flowing *art-nouveau* cartouches and figures.

89 *B* (1873),xxxi,722f.; *A* (1869),ii,177f, 187ff,249ff;(1872),vii,200.

90 *B* (1873),xxxi,723.

91 *BN* (1873),xxv,252.

were given the places of honour at each side of the entrance. Rising over the high-pitched roof, above the gables, dormers, turrets and finials, is the huge tower based on that of the Palazzo Vecchio; the claim to kinship with Florence through the wool trade was strengthened in the architects' report which drew attention to the similarity of the position of the tower in the valley of Bradford and its fourteenth-century predecessor in the valley of the Arno.[89] The building cost £100,000, and its opening was celebrated by a procession of the town's trades, three miles long. In the section devoted to the building trades there were wagons illustrative of quarryowners and quarrymen, masons and bricklayers in their hundreds, joiners who displayed specimens of their craft in the shape of doors, windows and staircases, slaters who accompanied a model of a roof, plasterers who marched along with a vast Classical pavilion 'tastefully hung round with evergreens', plumbers, glaziers and painters with their symbolic offerings brought as to a temple; but the *Builder* was not impressed and thought 'the want of real art in all that was done was ... very striking'.[90]

Bradford Town Hall is the most picturesque in outline of those in West Yorkshire; its tower 'contributes so much to the architectural character of the town, presenting views from all the main streets';[91] but it was not imitated. The smaller towns preferred to follow the Classical model of Leeds. Todmorden's, built in the 1870s and opened

92 Dewsbury Town Hall was designed by Henry Holtom and George Arthur Fox, and Morley Town Hall by Fox alone.

93 Thirty-five designs were submitted for adjudication by G.E.Street. Another public building in a similar style is Cleckheaton Town Hall, built in 1890–2 to a design by Mawson and Hudson of Bradford. The main component in the plan is a public hall, ninety feet by forty-five, with a vaulted ceiling. Lord Grimthorpe designed the clock in the tower.

94 *B* (1893),lxiv,299f; (1896),lxx,492; (1896),lxxi,470. The first intention was to build the County Hall of brick with stone dressings, but this was amended and stone alone was used.

in 1875, was designed by John Gibson as a temple with an apsidal end, surrounded with a Composite giant order set on a rusticated basement. The ashlar is admirably and richly detailed and executed, and the tympanum of the pediment is filled with figures emblematic of the industries of Lancashire and Yorkshire; the division between the counties originally passed through the middle of the building, and the central figures in the sculptured group represent the two linked in friendship. Dewsbury's Town Hall of 1888–9 and Morley's of 1895[92] looked to Leeds for their inspiration, and the tower of the latter is virtually a copy of Brodrick's a few miles away. The most original design by Yorkshire standards was Thomas Edward Collcutt's for Wakefield (1877–80);[93] his fashionably eclectic style was not affected by any of the local precedents, a tendency that was repeated in 1893 by Gibson and Russell's design for the West Riding County Hall.[94] The two, separated by the earlier Court House and Music Saloon (or

287

290. Wakefield, County Hall; the
Council Chamber presents a complete
image of the taste of the late 1890s.

Mechanics' Institute), form a fine civic group in Wood Street.

'The architect says it is clothed in Renaissance dress', commented the *Building News* of the Town Hall, 'though we think it would be more correct to apply the qualification Jacobean as a prefix . . . the author has more the feelings of a true Gothicist than a classicist; the masses and groupings are thoroughly Gothic in spirit'. The main features of Collcutt's elevation to Wood Street are three large oriels close in design to those on Norman Shaw's New Zealand Chambers in Leadenhall Street, London (1873); in the Wakefield version they are continued above the eaves as dormers. The composition is well conceived, and so is the 194 feet high campanile that might be described as a Flemish version of Venice's San Marco, which dominates the skyline along the hilltop; Gibson and Russell sensibly avoided competition when designing the County Hall and concentrated instead on the modelling of the long elevation to Wood Street. In the whole civic group, their building provides the necessary length and bulk, as well as a regularly varied roofline of gables and chimney-stacks. There is a Shavian flavour again, this time in the gables of the slightly projecting wings flanking the six-bay loggia originally ornamented with W. Birnie Rhind's figures representing West Riding industries.[95] Oriels on the Cliff Parade elevation echo Collcutt's farther down the road, and the domed cupola over the corner entrance complements, without attempting to rival, the Town Hall's vertical assurance.

Inside the Town Hall, Collcutt's Council Chamber is richly decorated with American walnut panelling and plasterwork adapted from 'some fine old leatherwork in the possession of the architect'. Gibson and Russell concentrated their internal effects on the vaulted entrance hall and the suite of rooms on the first floor.[96] The anteroom, decorated with a modelled and coloured plaster frieze by Henry C. Fehr, which incorporates episodes from the Wars of the Roses, leads into the domed Council Chamber in which the white rose of Yorkshire is decoratively triumphant. All these, as well as the committee rooms and the Chairman's room, are still furnished with the original *art-nouveau* lighting fittings, switch plates and door furniture designed by the architects, and they form a remarkably complete illustration of municipal grandeur at the turn of the century.

The continued growth of Leeds and the improvement in municipal services provoked a need for more administrative accommodation as the nineteenth century moved into its last quarter. In 1876 a competition was announced for new public offices on a site facing the east side of the Town Hall. The winner was George Corson, who wisely decided 'the new buildings . . . should be similar in style to the Town Hall, but not identical . . . I think that a certain extent of variation from that building would be to the advantage of the effect of both'. The *Builder* thought there was 'not an original feature or idea in the whole', but conceded Corson had treated 'the stock-in-trade properties of "Italian" design with knowledge and good taste'.[97] The new Municipal Buildings, opened in 1884, is a mannerly but very positive neighbour to Brodrick's great building, demonstrating Corson's advice to the Leeds and Yorkshire Architectural Society's members that

95 These statues were removed in the 1960s.

96 The staircase was decorated by Charles Grange Lowther with lunettes emblematic of the work of the Council, the industries of the West Riding, and the traditional virtues, arts and sciences 'in oil colours and metals, enriched in places with a slight relief in gesso'. Lowther wrote of his 'loving labour [which he hoped would] give more than momentary pleasure; something as far as I am able to make it, to stimulate that interest in art and higher sentiment that is too much overwhelmed by commercialism'.

97 The first design was illustrated in *BN* (1877),xxxii,36; see also *BA* (1884),xxi,40, 54, for a long description and illustrations.

291. Leeds, the Municipal Buildings (G. Corson 1876), framed by the columns and lamps of the east entrance to the Town Hall.

292. Bradford, Town Hall (R.N.Shaw 1902); the façade of the extension incorporates echoes of Lockwood and Mawson at first-floor level, but adds other stylistic reminiscences, crowning the whole with a mighty roof.

293. Bradford, Cartwright Hall (Simpson and Allen 1900–03); the cumulative effect of the theatrical assemblage of architectural elements is swaggeringly decorative.

98 This quotation is from Corson's first Presidential address to the Association, given on 31 October 1877.

99 *BA* (1884),xxi,54.

'some regard should be had to [neighbouring buildings] in designing the one between. They ought to be connected in their horizontal lines . . . and so designed as to group with them'.[98] He followed his own advice when designing the School Board Offices (1878–81) on the site next to the Municipal Buildings, and as a result Calverley Street became the noblest (though short) street in Leeds. Corson designed an ingenious double staircase in the School Board Offices to separate the access for boys and girls to the first-floor examination rooms, and he succeeded in making a dramatic spatial experience out of the staircase (constructed of Devonshire marble, Caen and Hopton Wood stones) in the Municipal Buildings. The *British Architect*'s eye roamed 'over a profusion of graceful arcades and stately pillars, whose effect is very striking, reminding one more of a Venetian palace than a Leeds corporate building',[99] taking in the carved animals, brilliantly coloured geometric tiles, and intricately carved capitals and door surrounds. In 1886 a competition was held for the Art Gallery as an extension of Corson's building, but this time he was placed third in favour of William Henry Thorp's submission, in which the staircase is the best feature.

Bradford also was growing, and in 1902 Norman Shaw, whose entry in the competition for the Exchange thirty-eight years earlier had been rejected in favour of Lockwood and Mawson, was invited to advise on an addition to the Town Hall. Shaw's addition is a brilliantly witty

design, maybe slightly mocking the earnest Gothic style of the 60s in the row of pointed windows at first-floor level and the gargoyled tourelle, while hinting at an extraordinary number of other styles ranging from Romanesque to Queen Anne. 'The whole building must *not* look as if it had had additions made to it entirely regardless of the existing building', wrote Shaw;[100] and the result is a sophisticated, subtle building in its own right, which nevertheless complements the far more ornate original. Bradford's other *fin-de-siècle* civic building is not in the city centre, but in the green Lister Park on the western heights. In 1898 Lord Masham (previously Samuel Cunliffe Lister) suggested replacing his old family home with a new building which would also commemorate Edmund Cartwright, the inventor of the power-loom, and he offered his native town £40,000 and a free hand. After considering a technological museum and rejecting the idea, the Council decided to build a hall 'devoted to the arts and to a museum of art products and natural history',[101] combined with a suite of official entertaining-rooms in which the dining-room balanced the art gallery. A competition was announced, at first open only to Bradford architects, but then widened to include the whole country. The winners were Sir J.W.Simpson[102] and E.J.M.Allen of London, who had already built the Glasgow Art Gallery (1892–1900).

'Now that an age of palace-building has returned to England – democratic palaces this time – the younger architects are naturally turning to French models for suggestions', wrote the *Yorkshire Daily Observer* in neatly categorising the Grand Manner in which Simpson and Allen designed the Cartwright Hall. Symmetrical in plan, a monumental central section is flanked by linked side wings. Inside, there is an extravagant use of colonnaded screens and open arches through which views of other spaces dramatically enlarge the sense of grandeur. Externally, the exaggeratedly rough and heavy rusticated basement forms a solid foundation for the upper walls of fine ashlar ornamented with giant Ionic orders and segmental pediments on the pavilion wings, and with exuberant Baroque sculpture which disguises the absence of windows in the galleries. Commenting on the quality of the stonework, the *Observer* rhetorically inquired, 'If Bradford, in the very heart of the finest building stone that the country can afford, could not produce good work, where would one look for it?' The entrance front is further enhanced by a central *porte-cochère* which continues upwards as an open gallery of embellished Venetian arches, until it narrows and ends as a crowning domed cupola. The uncertainty of scale evident here is better resolved on the corresponding front, in which a large semicircular apse curves out from the body of the building with a grandly sweeping gesture of confidence that was less in evidence in Leeds Civic Hall, the last West Yorkshire public building in the great tradition.

In 1889 the Leeds City Council had passed a resolution (repeated many times since) that new Law Courts were imperative if justice were to be adequately administered; but there was no addition to the city's public buildings until 1930 when opportunity was taken of money available from the Unemployed Grants Committee to promote a Civic

100 See Saint, op.cit.,367; *BN* (1905), lxxxix,165. Shaw was acting as consultant to F.E.P.Edwards, the Bradford City Architect.

101 *Yorkshire Daily Observer*, 13 April 1904; *BN* (1900),lxxviii,750.

102 Sir John William Simpson (1858–1933) was almost entirely responsible for the Cartwright Hall because of the retirement of his partner, Edmund John Milner Allen (1859–1912); he also collaborated with Alfred Drury on the Victoria Memorial, Bradford, and this is an appropriate place to note the quality of the sculpture commissioned for Leeds and Bradford at the beginning of this century. Drury (1858–1944) provided the statue of Joseph Priestley, and the 'Morn' and 'Eve' figures in City Square, Leeds; Henry Charles Fehr (1867–1940) was responsible for John Harrison and James Watt in City Square, and for Edmund Cartwright in the Cartwright Hall; and Frederick Pomeroy (1856–1924) for Dean Hook in City Square. The most notable civic sculptures are Sir Thomas Brock's (1847–1922) equestrian figure of the Black Prince in City Square, and Sir George Frampton's (1860–1928) Victoria Memorial, Leeds. The carvings on Cartwright Hall were undertaken by A.Broadbent, a Bradford-born assistant to Frampton (who had worked with Simpson and Allen on the Glasgow Art Gallery). 'They may all be characterised as excellent examples of the work of the younger generation, miles above the ordinary run of memorial sculpture in vitality and force' (*YP*, 17 Sept 1903).

293

294

294. Leeds, the Civic Hall (V.Harris 1933) abandoned the traditional Yorkshire stone and is built of Portland, a material which responds to its bland, smooth Classicism.

103 *B* (1933),cxlv,301f.

104 *Leeds Civic Hall*, official souvenir book, Leeds 1933.

105 Herman Cawthra was the sculptor of the four groups on the south front, and John Hodge provided the owls on the towers.

Hall in which to house a suite of formal reception rooms and offices of the municipal departments. Vincent Harris, who had recently built Sheffield's City Hall and Manchester's Public Library, was selected as architect.[103] There was a current belief that 'local materials are no longer a first necessity',[104] and the substitution of sophisticated Portland stone for native millstone grit is reflected in the gentility of the chosen 'Wrenaissance' style. The main elevation consists of a Corinthian porticoed central section flanked by twin campanile of diminishing stages topped by obelisks crowned with gilded owls. The effect is not unlike that of the west front of St Paul's without the dome, but a parallel between a civic building and a temple is less convincing than when applied to the great High Victorian examples. Although the design has undoubted merit in the massing of the elements and the sculptural effect of the blind niches at the summit of the pavilion-like blocks at each side of the main façade,[105] it makes no concessions to the traditional character of West Yorkshire.

Inside, Harris used a variety of polished stones, marbles and scagliola in the entrance hall and in the staircase which leads to the

361

reception hall on the first floor and then into the long Assembly Hall which was described as 'an eminently civilized room, in itself an invitation to good manners, and one could easily imagine it the scene of a painting by Orchardson'. The last of a long line, it was opened in 1933 by George V and wickedly described by the young John Betjeman in the *Architectural Review* as 'a symbol of the Civic Pride of the Conservative Party'. Yet he also drew attention to the picturesque quality of the building as 'the sightseer . . . suddenly catches a glimpse of one or other brilliant white steeple, rising above tram lines and turrets, terminating an otherwise dreary street'.[106]

It is difficult in the bleak 70s to imagine a future time when great monuments might be added to West Yorkshire towns. Maybe there are sufficient, and economy and sentiment are against them; but civic pride is not dead. It finds a different expression in the cleaning of a century's grime from the millstone-grit façades, and in an increased affection for the newly revealed architectural symbolism of a past generation's confidence and assertiveness. Nor did the 60s fail to add to the region's stock of civic buildings. In 1970 Castleford, a mining town that retains no indication of its Roman origin, completed the first part of its Civic Centre, the result of a competition held in 1964 and won by three young architects (later the Griffiths Goad Partnership). Like the Halifax Council a century earlier, Castleford's elected representatives had held their meetings for many years in makeshift surroundings, but they persisted with their determination in spite of difficulties and were rewarded with a building which is practical, workmanlike and subtly related to that mixture of hardness and humanity which is the local character.[107] Like the civic buildings of the last century, Castleford's had a Royal opening; and a youthful choir proclaimed that Castleford lasses are bonny and fair, for they washed in the Calder and bathed in the Aire – a remarkable manifestation of local pride.

It is no longer possible to dream of a new 'noble municipal palace' or of 'a lofty structure, with a tower of commanding importance', but architecture can still express those sterling Yorkshire qualities which inspired the promoters of Leeds Town Hall, 'public spirit, and generous pride in the possession of . . . municipal privileges'.

295

106 Betjeman, J., *First and last loves*, London 1952, 37.

107 *A J·*(1970), cli, 1224ff.

295. Castleford, Civic Centre; the first phase, completed in 1970, of a design won in competition by the Griffiths, Goad Partnership.

Epilogue

Yes, Bradford is a rising place,
And quite a rising town –
(I take it as a rising sign
The buildings coming down)
Bradford Review, 17 Jan 1867

Despite the great country houses, the medieval churches, the Pennine vernacular and such an exceptional building as the Halifax Piece Hall, the character of the West Yorkshire conurbation is predominantly Victorian although medieval or eighteenth-century street patterns persist in the central areas of several towns. Few parts of the region are without a reminder at least of the Industrial Revolution which brought an increase in prosperity and population, and there is nothing strange about the nineteenth century to a native; it is a part of his existence, the familiar environment into which he was born, probably in a Victorian hospital. His church or chapel, school, college or university, office, mill or warehouse, were probably built in the nineteenth century; he has enjoyed music in a Victorian town hall, drama in a Victorian theatre, drink in a Victorian public house, according to his leisure interests; he has probably spent at least a part of his life in Victorian houses, and when he dies he will be laid to rest close to the blackened, rhetorical monuments to his Victorian predecessors or maybe cremated in a converted Victorian mortuary chapel. Nineteenth-century architecture is a part of life in West Yorkshire, and the towns of which the conurbation is made up reflect the complexities and contradictions of that age of expansion.

'The violent enterprise of an hour, the single passion that has thrown street on street in a frantic monotony of disorder ... these shapeless improvisations ... represented nothing but the avarice of the jerry-builder catering for the avarice of the capitalist';[1] the vast areas of slate-roofed, red brick back-to-back houses spreading up and along the Leeds hills bear out this indictment, as they recall Ruskin's doubtful compliment, inspired by a view of 'the south-eastern suburb of Bradford ... and the scene from Wakefield Bridge, by the chapel', that he could not but 'more and more reverence the fierce courage and industry, the gloomy endurance, and the infinite mechanical ingenuity of the great centres, as one reverences the fervid labours of a wasp's nest, though the end of it all is only a noxious lump of clay'.[2] Yet, on the other hand, one Victorian thought 'the time may come when the archaeologist of a future age will look for the best specimens of the buildings of the present reign ... to some provincial towns'[3] – with

1 Hammond, J.L. and B., *The town labourer 1760–1832*, London 1917, 39f.

2 Ruskin, J., *Fors clavigera*, Orpington 1875, v, 46.

3 Reid, T.W., *A memoir of John Deakin Heaton, M D*, London 1883, 121.

363

296

296. Leeds, Park Row in 1882 (Atkinson Grimshaw). On the left is the porticoed façade of the Philosophical Hall and Museum (R.D.Chantrell 1819–20), and beyond is the indistinct mass of the Bank of England (P.C.Hardwick 1862–4). At the north end is the silhouette of St Anne's R.C. church (J.Child 1837–8). On the right, from right to left, are Beckett's Bank (G.G.Scott 1863–7), the Royal Insurance Company (A.Waterhouse 1860), music rooms for Archibald Ramsden (G.Corson 1871), Headland (later Sun) Buildings (G.Corson 1877), a fragment of the eighteenth-century domestic buildings which lined the original street, and the Scottish Widows' Fund and Life Assurance Society (G.Corson 1868–9). The last-named and the Bank of England are the sole survivors of this scene of commercial splendour.

West Yorkshire towns in mind; while Gilbert Scott thought the warehouses and factories he saw in the region were, at times, 'noble structures'.[4] We have now arrived at a point in history when we can assess Victorian architecture without prejudice; we can see its failures, understanding the misgivings of many nineteenth-century architects that they had not succeeded in discovering a style of their own, but we can appreciate the qualities of confidence, grandeur and consummate craftsmanship they achieved. We might regret that the great wealth of the industrial towns did not create another Florence or Venice, feeling that the Victorians could have done better; but we are no longer blind to the merits of the public buildings which symbolised civic success, the churches and mechanics' institutes which illustrate different ways of striving for a better life, the mills and factories which display technological virtuosity, and the middle-class suburbs which represent a long step towards an ideal environment. We can look with nostalgia at Atkinson Grimshaw's gas-lit, misty images of busy streets in West Yorkshire, or his memories of quiet suburban lanes in which the villas set among trees promise warm, comfortable interiors and a decanter of port; yet we can also look practically and with an eye to economics at the possible use of Victorian commercial buildings, churches and housing of all types.

Our attitude to a nineteenth-century conurbation, such as West Yorkshire, has begun to mature in the mid-70s. The post-war planners' stigma of 'obsolescence' decreed that the Victorian town centres should be replaced, sparing none but the most prestigious buildings. Bradford suffered most during the 50s, as the result of the determined realisation of a ruthless traffic scheme which necessitated total clearance of a complete area, accompanied by a depressingly banal replacement. Individual losses have been the noble Swan Arcade (Milnes and France 1877–81), several warehouses in the Leeds Road area (including the magnificent examples in Peel Square, by Eli Milnes) and Lockwood and Mawson's Kirkgate Market; but it was the destruction of an entity with a strong individual character that was the greatest loss. Changes in Leeds have been less dramatic, but hardly less complete in the end; Albion Street, Bond Street, South Parade and Park Row (which possessed 'the full flavour of commercial Leeds') have been largely rebuilt, and single buildings of outstanding quality which have been demolished include Brodrick's King Street warehouses, Corson's Sun Buildings (1877), and Scott's Westminster (Beckett's) Bank – the last the saddest destruction of all. Wakefield handed over part of its town centre to a developer and systematically removed almost all the buildings with any character in the vicinity of the Cathedral, as well as the magnificent Corn Exchange. Huddersfield embarked on a bold plan to relocate the town centre which, whatever positive advantages it possesses, put at risk the continued life of the old centre without adding any new buildings of quality around the Town Hall and the Art Gallery. New roads have been built in or around all the towns, with obvious benefits but some visually regrettable effects; the threatened excommunication of Halifax Parish Church (standing now in a waste of demolished streets and buildings)

4 Scott,G.G., *Remarks on secular and domestic architecture*, London 1858,217

from the rest of the centre is deplorable, but on the whole Halifax has survived to demonstrate that traditional character and values are not incompatible with the requirements of the last quarter of the twentieth century.

There is no cause for complacency that the essential character of West Yorkshire architecture and townscape will survive all the large-scale changes in prospect. Pennine villages have been condemned by too rigid application of the Public Health Act without considering the positive merits of the clusters of stone houses and the unselfconsciously picturesque integration of buildings, spaces and landscape which were uniquely and irreplaceably West Yorkshire. The determination to execute the proposed demolition of most of Boar Lane, Leeds, a complete street of the 1870s which picturesquely links City Square and the Corn Exchange, in spite of a reluctant approval expressing grave doubts from the Secretary of State for the Environment, might seem to offer no indication of a change in official attitude towards nineteenth-century buildings in general.[5] Nor can the threat of increased costs of maintenance and repair without any tax relief help the already serious plight of many owners of country houses; when the exhibition, *The Destruction of the Country House*, was on view in 1974 Yorkshire had the doubtful distinction of having lost more than any other county, twenty-three of them in West Yorkshire.[6] The 1977 exhibition, *Change and Decay*, recorded that thirty-one churches and chapels in Leeds alone were demolished during the previous twenty years. There is no reason to suppose the erosion has ceased, or that many of the churches at present under threat of closure will escape demolition. Many textile mills, the most evocative symbols of West Yorkshire prosperity, are abandoned and decaying; or only the ground floors are in use because of the present preference for horizontal working. It is said that during the years between 1967 and 1976 the number of firms declined from 797 to 448, and a number of important textile buildings, including Akroyd's Copley Mill itself, and Rock Mills, near Huddersfield, have been demolished. Yet, on the other hand, the rehabilitation for office use of St Paul's House (now advertised nationally as 'A Victorian extravaganza' in happy contrast to when it was a neglected, decaying warehouse deprived of its minarets) and the old Bank of England (P.C. Hardwick 1862–4), both in Leeds, and a number of warehouses in Bradford's 'Little Germany', illustrates a more mature encouragement of an alternative to unnecessary demolition – preservation by use. A policy of positive conservation linked with an insistence on new buildings designed in a manner which perpetuates the West Yorkshire quality of tough grandeur could ensure that the region's architectural character remains a living tradition, although the outcome of a commendably enterprising competition for a small central area redevelopment in Hebden Bridge in 1971–2 suggests that straightforward preservation of the existing (almost irrespective of its quality) is more popular than the risk of a failure.[7] Fidelity to the familiar is an element in the human character which, as much as economics, explains the current policies of rehabilitation, General Improvement Areas, and Housing Action

5 Linstrum,D., 'Tough grandeur', *Architectural conservation in Europe* (ed. Cantacuzino,S.), London 1975,11f.

6 Strong,R., Binney,M., Harris,J., *The destruction of the country house*, London 1974, 190f.

7 Linstrum,D., 'Hebden Bridge, something old – something new', *RIBA Journal* (1972),lxxix,54ff.

8 See *RIBA Journal* (1976),lxxxiii,324f. The scheme was designed by E.W.Stanley, Director of Architecture and Planning, Leeds City Council.

297. Halifax, the headquarters of the Halifax Building Society (Building Design Partnership 1975) towers over its neighbours in Commercial Street (including the Victoria Hall, W.E.Williams 1900, on the right) with a startling, brutal arrogance.

9 Linstrum,D., 'Civic centre symbol', *A J* (1970),cli,1224ff.

10 Special number of the *Yorkshire Post*, 10 Dec 1970. The building was given a RIBA award in 1971.

11 See *Yorkshire Architect* (1975), September/October, and (1976) January/February, 10ff. The building was given a RIBA award in 1975.

Areas; they help to answer the need for roots and a sense of identity in a shifting, uncertain world. Similarly, it is noticeable that the most successful designs of the 70s have been the small-scale residential groups based on traditional, humane patterns (such as the scheme in Potternewton Gardens, Leeds, which won a RIBA award in 1976.[8]

Despite the many depressing new buildings which have failed to respond to the West Yorkshire *genius loci*, a few stand out as exceptional in various respects; the hard but human Castleford Civic Centre (Griffiths, Goad Partnership 1970),[9] the rough, bulky *Yorkshire Post* building, Leeds (John Madin Design Group 1970),[10] the integrated Kirkgate Market, Bradford (John Brunton and Partners 1975), the smooth, sophisticated Lloyd's Bank, Leeds (Abbey, Hanson, Rowe and Partners 1976), and the controversial, gigantic Halifax Building Society's offices in its home town (Building Design Partnership 1975.).[11] All these buildings are large, but the last,

297

367

standing at one end of the town, towers over its neighbours with a startling, brutal arrogance; it shocks, as the massive new buildings of the nineteenth century must have done, declaring with a symbolic gesture that its owners are a force in the town. It has its critics, who hate its bulk and its lofty, hard outline. It has its defenders, who make an analogy with the Victorian confidence which produced the West Yorkshire mills, warehouses and town halls which give the region its character; but even they are unlikely to deny it is a unique, prestigious example which cannot be taken as a model when designing a new building for a site in a familiar environment.

The conservation policies, legislation and grants of the 70s have had two obvious effects. The once black towns have been cleaned, and the photographs taken for this study of West Yorkshire architecture show the buildings as they have not been seen since the scaffolding was struck after their completion. Doubts about the latent effect of some of the cleaning methods used remains, but many buildings which were once unregarded have received more appreciative attention since their surface qualities have become more obviously visible. At the same time, the procedure for 'listing' buildings, which is based principally on the external quality, has given an increased value to a façade and encouraged rebuilding behind it. The full implications of current legislation and subsequent planning policies must remain for discussion by a future historian, but it is safe to predict that the *intentions* to respect the traditional architectural character of the region will be stronger in the late 70s and early 80s than in the previous decade. Time alone can tell how well they are realised; there is no cause for optimism, but the large number of buildings now statutorily listed as being of 'special architectural or historical interest' places a responsibility on the Local Authorities to treat them carefully and to consider their context when future development is under discussion. The enthusiastic designation of conservation areas, of which such different examples as the unique village of mansions at Heath and the central area of Halifax have been singled out as 'outstanding', is another hopeful indication that the sweeping changes and the consequent loss of urban identity envisaged in the early post-war years have become a part of history; regrettable when they were realised, these attitudes can be cautiously predicted as being superseded now by a more rational, civilised acceptance of the need to maintain and use what is valuable in the familiar streets and buildings which contribute to the regional character. It is in the return of human qualities to such traffic-free districts as Southgate in Halifax, the cathedral precinct in Wakefield, and the linked pattern of Victorian arcades and pedestrian streets in Leeds, that the most obvious signs of an attempt to consolidate the elusive elements of 'the cherished local scene' can be seen; and it is in the proliferation of local groups of citizens dedicated to protecting what *they* believe important in their West Yorkshire streets, suburbs and towns, that a healthy interest in the past and its future can be engendered.

368

A select biographical list of Yorkshire architects (1550–1900) who worked in West Yorkshire

The lists of known or attributed works include only those within the boundaries of West Yorkshire, but reference is made to important works outside the region in the biographical information, especially in those instances when there is little information available elsewhere in dictionaries, etc. In general, works designed later than 1900 are not included, but they have been listed occasionally for the sake of completeness when an architect's career extended only a few years into the twentieth century. The works are arranged chronologically, with the undated buildings collected at the end of each list. In addition to the general abbreviations on p.10, the following have been used:

BCh	Baptist Church or Chapel
BS	Board School
BSAS	Bradford Society of Architects and Surveyors
CCh	Congregational Church
Ch	Church or Chapel
CP	County Primary School
CS	County Secondary School
GS	Grammar School
HGS	Higher Grade School
HS	High School
Inst	Institute or Institution
IS	Infants' School
LYAS	Leeds and Yorkshire Architectural Society
MCh	Methodist Church or Chapel
MFCh	Methodist Free Church
MNCCh	Methodist New Connexion Church or Chapel
MSSch	Methodist Sunday School
PCh	Presbyterian Church
PMCh	Primitive Methodist Church or Chapel
Sch	School
SchCh	School-chapel
SecSch	Secondary School
SSch	Sunday School
UCh	Unitarian Church or Chapel
UMCh	United Methodist Church
UMFCh	United Methodist Free Church
URCh	United Reformed Church
WCh	Wesleyan Church or Chapel
WMCh	Wesleyan Methodist Church or Chapel

Abbey, John Henry (d 1880) practised in Huddersfield, where he held the part-time appointment of Borough Surveyor 1868–79. He designed Lockwood Mechanics' Inst (1864–6) and the Municipal Offices, Huddersfield (1878): but his major building was the Town Hall, Huddersfield (1878–81), which was completed posthumously.

Adams, Richard L. (d 1883) was in partnership with John Kelly (*q.v.*) in Park Row, Leeds *c.*1866–83; he was appointed architect to Leeds School Board in 1873, and after his death Kelly continued the practice with Edward Birchall (*q.v.*) as his partner.
Bibl: Williams, D., *Leeds School Board and its architecture*, unpublished BArch thesis, Leeds Polytechnic 1975.

Leeds: Church Inst, Albion Pl 1866–8; Shannon St, dwellings for Leeds Industrial Dwellings Co 1867; Christ Ch, Upper Armley 1869–72.
Batley: St Mary of the Angels 1869–70, additions by Kelly 1884.
Leeds: Armley Hall Ch 1870; Holy Trinity, New Wortley 1870–2; St Luke, Beeston 1871–2
Gildersome: St Peter 1873.
Altofts: St Mary Magdalene 1873–90.
Leeds: St Mark, Woodhouse, alterations 1873; Jack Lane BS 1874 (now Leeds Athletic Inst); Saville Green BS 1874 dem; Cross Stamford St BS 1875; Sheepscar BS 1875; Burley Lawn BS 1876; Farnley BS 1876 dem; Hunslet Carr BS 1876; Leylands BS 1876 dem; Lower Wortley BS 1876; Upper Wortley BS 1876; Woodhouse BS 1876; Bramley BS 1877; Ellerby Lane BS 1877 dem; Park Lane BS 1877 dem; Rodley BS 1877; St Peter's Sq BS 1877 dem; Shadwell Industrial Sch 1877; York Rd BS 1877; Armley BS 1878; Low Rd BS 1878; Roundhay Rd BS 1878; Sweet St BS 1878 (now Thomas Danby Coll annexe); Blenheim BS 1879; Chapeltown BS 1879 (now Chapel Allerton CP); Beeston Hill BS 1880 (now Hillside Middle); Little Holbeck BS 1880 dem; Old Farnley BS 1880 dem; Emmanuel Ch 1880; Headingley BS 1882; Kirkstall BS 1882 (now Beecroft CP); Stanningley BS 1882; Belle Vue Rd BS 1883 (now Belle Vue Centre); Castleton BS 1883; Dewsbury Rd BS 1883; Meanwood Rd BS 1883; Whitehall Rd BS 1884 (now Thomas Danby Coll annexe); Beckett St BS 1885 (now Lincoln Green CP); St Mary of Bethany, Tong Rd 1885–6; Quarry Mt BS 1885; Whingate Rd BS 1886; All Hallows, Burley 1886; St Patrick 1889–91; Sacred Heart, Burley 1890 (Kelly and Birchall, enlarged Kelly 1893).
Huddersfield: St Joseph 1894.
Leeds: Holy Family 1894–5; St Francis of Assisi 1896.

Akroyd, John (1556–1613) was the eldest son of William Akroyd, a mason of Warley, Halifax. He was a master mason who was responsible for the Grammar School at Heath, Halifax (1598–1601), for which his brother, **Abraham Akroyd**, made a plan, and he was employed extensively by the Savile family. It is very likely Akroyd was responsible for the design and execution of Bradley Hall and Methley Hall for Sir John Savile, and also for Howley Hall, the residence of another Sir John Savile. Sir Henry

Savile took Akroyd to Oxford where he and **John Bentley** (a mason from Elland) were employed to build the Great or Fellows' Quadrangle in Merton Coll in 1608/9 for £570. Thomas Holt, another Yorkshireman, was the carpenter. Akroyd was then employed by Sir Thomas Bodley to build a part of the Bodleian Library (1610–11), and he and Bentley undertook in 1613 to build the Schools Quadrangle. Akroyd died six months later, and Bentley was dead within another three; the work continued under Bentley's brother Michael (d 1618). Another reference to Bentley illustrates the employment of a mason as architect; in 1611 Sir Edward Pytts of Kyre Park, Worcs, 'brought John Bentley ffreemason from Oxford (where he wrought the newe addition to Sir Thomas Bodleigh his famous library) with me as I came from London to Kyer to take instructions from me by veinge the place to draw me a newe platte' (Mrs Baldwyn-Childe, 'The building of the manor-house of Kyre Park', *The Antiquary* (1890), xxii, 25). Mr Howard Colvin (to whom I am grateful for being shown the entry relating to Akroyd before the publication of the revised edition of his *Dictionary*) suggests it is possible to 'see the Merton tower and its successor in the Schools Quadrangle as a Yorkshire idea which Sir Henry Savile imported to Oxford together with his masons, and if so John Akroyd no doubt made the necessary drawings from which they were built.'
Bibl: Hanson, T. W., *Halifax builders in Oxford*, Halifax 1928.

Ambler, Thomas (1838–1920) was the son of Joseph Ambler, a Leeds engineer. He was articled to George Smith (*q.v.*) after a short spell in a builder's office, and in 1860 he set up his own practice as architect, surveyor and valuer at 10 Park Row. In 1867 he was at 9 Park Pl, where he stayed until he retired. From 1891–7, **George Frederick Bowman** (1860–1920), who had been articled to Ambler, was in practice with him. Ambler was associated with the Leeds Permanent Building Soc for most of his life, as Director and President, and he made designs for model dwellings for the Society. He was retained as a valuer by Leeds Corp. He had a varied practice, most of it commercial and unremarkable, but he was given some unusual opportunities by Sir John Barran, for whom he designed Trevelyan Temperance Hotel in Boar Lane, Leeds as the beginning of the rebuilding of the whole street in the 1870s; Ambler was responsible for many of the new buildings, and then he undertook St Paul's House for Barran, as well as a house in Roundhay for John Barran II.
Bibl: *CB*, 361; obit, *YP* 14 Jan 1920.

Leeds: Beeston Hill, working-class housing 1861; 30 Park Pl, warehouse for N. P. Nathan *c.*1863; Boar Lane, Trevelyan Temperance Hotel (later Chambers) *c.*1866–70.
Ilkley: Woodbank, house for T. P. Muff 1871 dem.
Leeds: 46 Basinghall St, warehouse *c.*1873 dem; Burley Rd BCh 1874; New Wortley CCh 1876; York St, St James's Public Hall, Temperance Hotel and Dining Rooms 1878, enlarged 1884;

Park Sq, St Paul's House, factory and warehouse for Sir John Barran 1878; Park Sq, factory for Arthur and Co, *c.* 1882; Parcmont, Roundhay, house for John Barran II 1883; Clowes PMCh, Meanwood Rd 1894; Lands Lane, Victoria Arcade 1897 dem; Greek St, factory for J. Buckley and Sons.

Andrews, William (1804–70) was born at Holme, nr Howden. In 1832 he moved from Hull to Bradford, where he subsequently became a partner of **Frederick William Delaunay** at 5 Leeds Rd, later moving to 2 Aldermanbury. Among their early commissions were the stations along the Bradford–Colne railway, e.g. Keighley. In the 1860s, Delaunay had been succeeded by **Joseph Pepper**, and the firm was then known as Andrews and Pepper. William's son, **Thomas Garlick Andrews** (1838–81), later became a partner.

Bradford: Girlington, Daisy Bank, house for Alfred Illingworth *c.*1845; Leeds Rd, warehouse for Rennie Tetley 1845 dem.
Bingley: Bankfield, house for William Murgatroyd 1848, enlarged for Henry Masson 1871.
Bradford: Manningham, Rose Mount, house for John Douglas 1849–51; Hall Ings, warehouse for Milligan and Forbes 1852–3 (now *Bradford Telegraph and Argus*); Kirkgate, Bradford Banking Co 1858 (now Midland Bank); Currer St, warehouse for Downs Coulters 1860; 40 Chapel St, warehouse 1860; 8 Burnett St, warehouse for Hoffman, Hurter and Co 1862; Manningham Lane, Royal Alexandra Theatre (later Theatre Royal) 1864.
Farsley: West Royd, house for John Butler 1866.
Bradford: Chapel Lane UCh 1867–8 dem; Bank St, Bradford Commercial Bank 1867–8 (now National Westminster); Manningham, Oakwell, house for ? 1868, enlarged 1888; Sunbridge Rd, Model Lodging House 1870; Bridge St, Mechanics' Inst 1870–71; Godwin St/Westgate, store for Illingworth, Son and Co 1871; 38 Chapel St, warehouse 1871; Midland Mills for Jeremiah Ambler 1871 dem; Manningham Mill for Samuel Cunliffe Lister 1871–3; North Parade, Church Inst 1871–3.
Wike: WCh 1871.
Bradford: Manor Row, GS 1872–4, enlarged 1878; Leeds Rd, Penny Oaks Hospital 1872; St Augustine's WCh 1873; Westgate, Dispensary 1873; St James, Bolton 1876–7; Manor Row, Poor Law Guardians' Office 1876 (now Registry Office).
Rawdon: Cragg Wood, Woodlands Convalescent Home 1877.
Bradford: Kirkgate, Talbot Hotel 1878; Great Horton Rd, Alexandra Hotel 1879.

Armfield, Charles Noel was in practice *c.*1861–70 at 23 Park Row, Leeds. He refurnished Armley Ch (1861), Christ Ch, Meadow Lane (1864), and redecorated St Barnabas, Holbeck (1866), all in Leeds.

Atkinson, Peter II (*c.*1776–1843) was the son of **Peter Atkinson I** (1735–1805), who was an assistant and successor to John Carr (*q.v.*) in his York practice. Peter II trained under his father and took over the practice, with **Matthew Phillips** (c.1781–1825) as a partner until 1819 when Richard Hey Sharp (q.v.) became a partner and the firm was known as Atkinson and Sharp. This arrangement came to an end in 1828 when Sharp left, and afterwards Peter II's sons, **John Bownas Atkinson** (d 1875) and **William Atkinson** (retired 1878) became partners. In 1877 **James Demaine** (1842–1911) became a partner, and the style was Atkinson and Demaine. Subsequent partners were **Walter H. Brierley** (1862–1926), **James H. Rutherford** (1874–1946), **John Stuart Syme** (1872–1958); the firm is now under the style of the present partners, Leckenby, Keighley and Groom.

Bradford: Manor Row, Grammar Sch 1820, taken over from W. Bradley (q.v.).
Stanley: St Peter 1821–4, reconstructed W. D. Caroe 1912–3.
Rothwell: Holy Trinity, new N aisle and galleries 1823–6.
Alverthorpe: St Paul 1823–5.
Leeds: St Mark, Woodhouse 1823–5, altered Adams and Kelly (q.v.) 1873.
Linthwaite: Christ Ch 1827–8, chancel added Hodgson Fowler (q.v.) 1895.
Crosland: Holy Trinity 1827–9.
Golcar: St John 1828–9, chancel added later.
New Mill: Christ Ch 1829–30, reconstructed F. Moorhouse 1882.
Birkenshaw: St Paul 1829–30, chancel added 1892.
Wakefield: St James, Thornes 1829–31.
Cleckheaton: St John 1830–1, chancel added 1864.
Heckmondwike: St James 1830–1, chancel added 1916.
Wetherby: St James 1839–41.
Clifford: St Luke 1840–2.
Leeds: Manston Lodge 1840–1.
Wetherby: Town Hall 1845.
Boston Spa: Baths 1847.
Aberford: house for C. P. Eden 1851.
Halifax: Bankfield, extensive additions to house for Edward Akroyd 1867.

Atkinson, Thomas (d 1798) was an architect and statuary in York who made unexecuted designs for Parlington Park in 1774 for Sir Thomas Gascoigne. His major work is the Archbishop of York's palace at Bishopthorpe (1763–9), and he is commemorated by a tablet in St Saviour's, York.
Bibl: Colvin, 46.

Backhouse, Elisha was articled to Benjamin Jackson (q.v.), who took him back into partnership in his Leeds office in 1835. Subsequently, c.1839, Backhouse became a partner of William Perkin (q.v.), and they built up a large practice in Leeds (see under **Perkin** for a list of their works).

Bakewell, William (1839–1925) was articled to H. A. Darbishire. After working for a time in Sir Charles Barry's office, he commenced practice at 12 East Parade, Leeds in the late 60s. In the early 70s he was in partnership with George Mallinson (q.v.) in Dewsbury, Halifax and Leeds; but apparently this arrangement was short-lived.

Bibl: obit B (1925), cxxviii, 229.

Leeds: Masonic Hall, Carlton Hill 1872; Queen Anne's Bldgs, New Briggate c.1874.
Wakefield: Clayton Hospital 1876–9.
Leeds: Oriental Baths, Cookridge St, alterations and additions 1882; Coliseum, Cookridge St 1885; Athenaeum Bldgs, Park Lane c. 1890; London and Midland (now Trustee Savings) Bank, Kirkgate 1892; Tower Works, Globe Rd, extensions for Thomas Walter Harding 1899; Holbeck Public Library 1901; City Sq, layout for T. W. Harding 1902.
Ilkley: Town Hall 1906–8.
Leeds: Pearl Bldgs, East Parade 1911.

Barber, William Swinden was in practice with James Mallinson (q.v.) at 6 George St, Halifax in 1870. He appears to have had an office in the town from c.1866.

Halifax: Akroydon, houses for Edward Akroyd 1872.
Wakefield: West Riding Industrial Home for Discharged Female Prisoners (now St John's House) 1872, enlarged 1877.
Heath, nr Wakefield: BS 1873.
Lightcliffe: St Matthew 1874.
Halifax: Shroggs Park, lodges for Edward Akroyd 1874.
Drighlington: St Paul 1878–80.
Warley: St John 1878.
Almondbury: GS, extensions 1879–83.
East Ardsley: St Michael 1881.
Huddersfield: St Mark 1886.
Cleckheaton: St John, new nave and aisles 1886–7.
Stainland: St Andrew, alterations 1887–8.
Salterhebble: St Jude 1889–90.
Brighouse: Town Hall c. 1898.

Battley, John was described as 'of some local eminence in Leeds, where he erected the theatre and several considerable buildings in the town and neighbourhood . . . about 1770–80' (Redgrave, S., *A dictionary of artists of the English school*, London 1878, 32). The theatre in Leeds was built in 1771.

Bedford, Francis William (1866–1904), the son of J. E. Bedford of Leeds, was a pupil of W. H. Thorp (q.v.) and later of Ernest George and H. A. Peto. He set up practice in Leeds c.1893, and was joined in the late 1890s by **Sydney Decimus Kitson** (1871–1937), the youngest son of James Kitson of Elmete Hall. Kitson was Hon Secretary of the RIBA from 1928 onwards; shortly before his retirement in the mid-1920s, he formed the partnership of Kitson, Parish, Ledgard and Pyman, which is still in practice under the title of Kitson and Partners. During the early years of their partnership, Bedford and Kitson's work was mainly domestic; their houses, of which Red House, Chapel Allerton, Leeds (1902–3) is representative, are neo-Georgian, imaginative and finely detailed. On his own, Bedford designed Arncliffe, Shireoak Rd (1894–5) and Old Gardens, Cardigan Rd, both in Leeds, for his father. Redhill, Shireoak Rd (c. 1900), was illustrated by Hermann Muthesius in *Das englische Haus* (1904–05). Their other works in

Leeds included the Church of the Holy Spirit, Beeston (1902), the School of Art (1903), and the Dispensary, North St (1904).
Bibl: obits *RIBA Jnl* (1905), xii, 139f, (1937), xliv, 859f.

Bedford, John was in practice in Elland, where he designed Huddersfield Rd MCh (1874).

Beevers, William Henry (1855–1933), the son of John Beevers of Leeds, was articled to William Perkin (q.v.), and then became an assistant to T. Clark of Bradford and W. Wheater of Leeds. He commenced practice in Leeds in 1882, and had a variety of work, including Arthington WCh (1895) and the laying out of building estates.
Bibl: *CB*, 362.

Belwood, William (d 1790) was employed as superintendent of the works at Harewood House. In 1775 he advertised in the *Leeds Mercury* (11 July) that he had set up as an architect in Lendal, York. 'He humbly hopes, that having conducted several very capital Buildings under the great Masters in Architect, Robert and James Adams, Esqrs., of the Adelphi, will enable him to give perfect Satisfaction'. Maybe because of the Adam connection, Belwood made the design for the stables at Newby Hall for William Weddell.

Benson, Robert, 1st Lord Bingley (1675–1731) was the son of Robert Benson of Wakefield, who prospered during the Commonwealth after being appointed clerk of assize to the Northern Circuit. He bought an estate at Wrenthorpe, close to his native town, and after the Restoration he came under the patronage of Sir Thomas Osborne, later 1st Duke of Leeds and the builder of Kiveton Park. Robert Benson I died in 1676, and his son was brought up by his widow and her second husband, Sir Henry Belasyse (later of Brancepeth, Northumberland and related to the owner of Newburgh Priory). Robert Benson II travelled to Italy during the last years of the seventeenth century, returning to Yorkshire in time to be chosen as Deputy Lieutenant for the West Riding in 1700. Elected M.P. in 1702, he became a Commissioner of the Treasury in 1710, Chancellor of the Exchequer in 1711, and Ambassador to Madrid in 1713. His knowledge of architecture dated from his stay in Italy, and he soon acquired a reputation as a connoisseur of design and a practical man who could be relied on for sound advice. He was one of the Commissioners appointed under the 1711 Act for building fifty new churches in London, but he was also advising Lord Raby of Stainborough and the Duke of Chandos about their houses. He made a design for Lady Elizabeth Hastings to demonstrate how Ledston Hall might be remodelled, but he also built his own house at Bramham on the estate granted to his father by the Crown. In it he showed what the 2nd Earl of Bute referred to as 'the consummated [architectural] experience of Bingley'.
Bibl: Collick, T. R., 'The patronage of Robert Benson: 1675–1731', *AR* (1965), cxxxviii, 429f.

Billington, John (d 1773), Surveyor of Bridges to the West Riding 1771–3, was employed as a carpenter at Hickleton Hall, S Yorks by Godfrey Wentworth; as James Paine refers to him in a letter to Sir Rowland Winn of Nostell Priory (30 May 1760), it is probable he was also working there. Another **John Billington** (c.1780–1835), probably related to the former, was a joiner in Wakefield who advertised in 1812 that he was starting business as a builder and surveyor; in 1822 he had an office in Southgate, and he was very likely the man who added a portico to the Strafford Arms Hotel, Wakefield (1830). He was possibly the father of **William Billinton** (b 1807), who spelt his name without a 'g'; he was engineer to the Wakefield Waterworks Co and practised as an architect and civil engineer in Bond Tce, Wakefield (a row of houses he built as a speculation). He exhibited designs at the Northern Soc for the Encouragement of the Fine Arts for a savings bank in Wakefield, and Woodhouse Cemetery, Leeds (1834). He also submitted unsuccessful designs for the Proprietary Sch (1833) and the Corn Exchange (1837), both in Wakefield; the latter was awarded third prize. His most ambitious design seems to have been for the layout and buildings of the Leeds Zoological and Botanical Gardens c.1837; assisted by Edward Davies, 'botanist and landscape engineer', he produced plans which were approved and 'proposed to be erected when a sufficient sum has been subscribed'. But the Gardens were not a financial success, and Billinton's grand scheme was never executed; all that remains of it is the castellated Bear Pit in Cardigan Rd.

Birchall, Edward (1838–1903) was a member of an old Quaker family in Leeds. He was articled to William Perkin (q.v.) and then worked for a time in Sir George Gilbert Scott's office until the early 60s, when he set up practice in Leeds. 'Possessed of ample means, he did not push his practice, but carried it on in a somewhat old-fashioned leisurely manner,' wrote W. H. Thorp (q.v.) who worked in Birchall's office. He collaborated occasionally with John Kirk (q.v.), and went into partnership with John Kelly (q.v.) in 1883; but his first major building, the Leeds meeting house for the Society of Friends, was probably his best. Unusually, considering his Gothic background, it was Italianate in style to meet the wishes of his clients. Birchall was President of the LYAS in 1883–5.
Bibl: obits, *B* (1903), lxxxiv, 465; *RIBA Jnl* (1903), x, 336.

Leeds: Friends' Meeting House, Carlton Hill 1866–8 (now BBC); Wellington St, warehouse for Walter Stead 1868.
Thick Hollins: Convalescent Home 1871.
Leeds: Albion St, Blind, Deaf and Dumb Inst 1875–6 dem.
Meltham: The Mount 1878, with John Kirk and Sons.
Leeds: Headingley, house for J. P. Webb 1878; St Agnes, Burmantofts 1886–7 with J. Kelly; Central HGS 1889 with Kelly; Richmond Hill BS 1890 with Kelly; Basinghall St, premises for Marsh, Jones and Cribb Ltd; houses in Leeds, Harrogate and elsewhere.

Booth, Isaac was in practice in George St, Halifax in the 1860s. He is best remembered as the first architect employed by John Edward Wainhouse to design the Wainhouse Tower near Halifax. 253 feet high, and built at a cost of £14,000, this monumental folly was built between 1871 and 1875 as a circular brick chimney connected with Wainhouse's dye works. Its erection displeased Sir Henry Edwards of Pye Nest, the next estate, who also employed Booth and persuaded him to sever connections with Wainhouse, who then engaged **Richard Swarbrick Dugdale** (a former pupil of Booth and later Borough Surveyor of Huddersfield 1879–97) to complete the tower. The practice in Halifax continued as Isaac Booth and Sons until the early 90s.

Botham, Joseph, whose address in 1837 was Portobello, Sheffield, provided the executed designs for Brunswick MCh, Leeds (1824–5), and the neatly Gothic Eastbrook Ch, Leeds Rd, Bradford (1825).

Bottomley, John Mitchell was in practice at 46 Albion St, Leeds in the 1890s, moving later to Harrogate. He designed Darley St BS (1895), the Masonic Hall, Gt George St (c.1900), and the Southern HGS, later known as Cockburn (1902), all in Leeds.

Bradley, John was a house and sign painter in Keighley, who designed the town's first Mechanics' Inst (1835).

Bradley, Thomas, surveyor to the Calder and Hebble Navigation, was probably a son of Thomas Bradley, a Halifax joiner, to whom he was apprenticed in 1758. Crownest House, Lightcliffe (1788), virtually a copy of John Carr's Pye Nest House (c.1775), was built for William Walker from Bradley's drawings (Richardson, G., *New Vitruvius Britannicus*, 1802, i, pls 64–5), and he was probably the author of Square CCh, Halifax (1771–2). He made a design for the Piece Hall, Halifax (1774–9), and the present building has been supposed to be Bradley's; but John Hope was its architect. Another Bradley, James, also a joiner in Halifax, was employed on the construction of St Peter's, Sowerby (1763–6), and in 1784 he was referred to as a surveyor in connection with alterations to the Halifax building known as 'the house at the Maypole'.

Bradley, William, also of Halifax, was probably a son of Thomas. He was trained as a joiner, but made the designs for Coley Ch (1816) and Bradford GS (1820). He subscribed to Richardson's *New Vitruvius Britannicus*, in which he is described as an architect. Miss Anne Lister of Shibden Hall heard he was '*not a man to be depended on – very idle . . . not fit to be an architect*', which probably explains why Atkinson and Sharp (q.v.) took over the Bradford school.

Braithwaite, Walter Samuel (1854–1922) was the son of a Leeds builder, J. E. Braithwaite. He was articled to Thomas Ambler (q.v.), to whose office he returned after working for John Winn and Son, builders. He set up practice in 1880 at 6 South Parade, and in 1895 he was appointed architect to Leeds School Board. In 1896–7 he was Vice-President of the LYAS. Apart from the schools listed below, Braithwaite also undertook such designs as a printing factory for Petty and Sons, Whitehall Rd, and buildings for the Leeds Industrial Co-operative Soc (1891). **Harry F. Jackman** was taken into partnership in 1919, and the practice continues under the title of Braithwaite and Jackman.
Bibl: *CB*, 363.

Leeds: Hunslet Lane BS 1895 dem; Beeston Hill, St Luke's IS 1895; Ventnor St MSSch 1897; Gipton BS 1897 (now Harehills Middle); Hall Lane MNCCh 1897–8; Kepler BS 1898 (now Gledhow Annexe); Blenheim Walk, Blind & Deaf Sch 1899; Brudenell BS 1899 (now Brudenell CS); Pupil Teachers' Centre c. 1900 (later Thoresby HS); Armley Park BS 1900 (now Armley Park CS); Bramley (Broad Lane) BS 1900; Lovell Rd BS 1901 (now Lovell Park Special); Tempest Rd MNCCh 1907–08.
Kirkburton: Storthes Hall Asylum 1907–08.
Castleford SecSch 1909.
Elland SecSch 1911.

Brayshaw, Mark was in practice in Bradford, where he designed Brick Lane PMCh (1874).

Brodrick, Cuthbert (1822–1905) was born at Hull into a family of merchants and shipowners, and in 1837 he was articled to Henry Francis Lockwood (q.v.). After the expiry of his seven years, Brodrick set off on an architectural tour of Europe, returning in 1845 to Hull, where he set up in practice. His first works were minor, an unidentified railway station in the East Riding (1846), an hotel in Whitefriargate, Hull (1848), and lodges and gates to the General Cemetery (1850). In 1847 he sent in a design for a Fish Market and Corn Exchange in Hull, but in 1852 he was more successful with his entry for the Royal Institution, Hull, which was demolished after being partly destroyed during the Second World War. This was an important building, but it was overshadowed by Brodrick's success in winning the competition for Leeds Town Hall shortly afterwards. This gave him a national reputation after its opening by the Queen in 1858, but his career did not follow what must have seemed at the time an apparently predictable pattern. In 1856 he won a silver medal in the competition for Lille Cathedral, and in 1858 he was placed fifth in the contest for the War Office, Whitehall. He unsucccessfully submitted designs for many buildings, Manchester Assize Courts (1859), Preston Town Hall (1861), Bolton Town Hall (1865), Manchester Royal Exchange (1866), the Dock Offices, Hull (1866), and Manchester Town Hall (1867). He was invited to submit a design in a limited competition for extensions to the National Gallery, Trafalgar Sq (1866), but all the designs were rejected. He was commissioned to plan a Custom House in Bombay (1866), but it was not built, and his relatively few executed designs can be found principally in West Yorkshire, where they set a high standard for public architecture. Outside West Yorkshire, his major works were the Grand Hotel, Scarborough (1862–7), and Hull Town Hall (1861), which was

demolished early in this century. He opened a London office in 1863, but in 1869 he gave up practice altogether and went to live in France, settling at Le Vesinet in 1876. He left France c.1891 and went to Jersey, where he died in 1905.
Bibl: obit *B* (1905), lxxxviii, 272; Harbron, D., 'Cuthbert Brodrick or cabbages at Salona', *AR* (1936), lxxix, 36ff; Wilson, T. B., *Two Leeds architects*, Leeds 1937; Linstrum, D., 'Architecture of Cuthbert Brodrick', *CL* (1967), cxli, 1379ff, and 'Cuthbert Brodrick: an interpretation of a Victorian architect', *Jnl of the Royal Society of Arts* (1971), cxix, 72ff.

Leeds: Town Hall 1853–8.
Ilkley: Wells House Hydropathic Establishment 1853–8 (now Ilkley Coll of Education).
Leeds: 7 Alma Rd, Headingley, house for J. H. Smalpage 1859; Moorland Tce, Reservoir St, houses for J. O. March 1859; Corn Exchange 1860–3; Mechanics' Inst 1860–5 (now Civic Theatre); King St, warehouse c. 1862 dem; 49–51 Cookridge St, shops and offices 1864; Headingley Hill CCh 1864–6 (now URC); Cookridge St, Oriental Baths 1866–67, remodelled 1882, dem; 9 Alma Rd, attrib; Ashfield, Grove Rd, attrib.

Buckley, Harry Bagshaw was in practice in Batley, where he designed the Technical Sch and Sch of Art (1893).

Burleigh, Charles Walklett was in practice at 40 Albion St, Leeds in the 40s and 50s, probably working with **Philip Boyce**. There is some confusion between the two, but at least three Leeds churches seem to have been built from their designs: St Matthew, Camp Rd (1850–1 dem), St Jude, Hunslet (1852–3) and St Michael, Buslingthorpe (1852–4). Burleigh also designed the National Schs, New Wortley and New Town, Leeds. Writing of Burleigh's design for St James, Woodside, Salop (1846–7) the *Ecclesiologist* (1846, ii, 82) thought 'upon the whole we are well satisfied, and hope to meet [him] again'.

Calvert, Rhodes (d 1926) was in practice at 9 New Kirkgate, Bradford in 1877, and from c.1891 at 4 Forster Sq. He designed the Temperance Commercial Hotel, Manchester Rd (1878), and warehouses at 12 Manor Row (1883), Sunbridge Rd (1883), and one for Richard Fawcett and Sons in Commercial St (1892 dem).

Carr, John (1723–1807) was the son of **Robert Carr** (1697–1760), a stonemason and quarry owner of Horbury, who was Surveyor of Bridges to the West Riding and was sometimes referred to as an architect, e.g. on his memorial tablet in St Peter and St Leonard, Horbury. The younger Carr was trained as a mason and remained closely associated with practical building long after he had made a reputation as an architect. He was making designs as early as 1748, when he was first employed by Edwin Lascelles at Gawthorp, but he became more widely known to the Yorkshire gentry in 1754 when his design for the grandstand on the Knavesmire at York was preferred to those by James Paine (*q.v.*) and Sir

Thomas Robinson. He built up a large practice, principally in Yorkshire but extending to Lancashire and Westmorland, Cheshire and Nottinghamshire, Lincolnshire and Derbyshire, and even to Portugal. Carr's Palladian style of architecture and rococo decoration was affected by his work at Harewood with Robert Adam, and his later designs were refined Neo-classical compositions, externally and internally. He was Lord Mayor of York in 1770 and 1785, Surveyor of Bridges to the West Riding 1760–73 and to the North Riding 1772–1807. In 1791 he was one of the four architects not resident in London who were invited to become Honorary Members of the London Architects' Club. He died at Askham Richard, leaving a fortune of £150,000 to his nephews and nieces, and a church at Horbury as his architectural monument.
William Carr, John's nephew, was working in his uncle's office in the 1790s, but it was Peter Atkinson I who succeeded to the practice when Carr retired towards the end of his life; Peter Atkinson II (*q.v.*) continued the firm, which has survived under various styles until the present day.
Bibl: *APSD*, ii, 36; Colvin, 122; Davies, R., 'A memoir of John Carr of York', *YAS* (1877), iv, 202ff; Wragg, R. B., 'John Carr of York', *West Yorkshire Society of Architects' Journal* (1957–8), xvii, Dec 8ff, Mar 11ff; York Georgian Society, *The works in architecture of John Carr*, York 1973.

Gawthorp Hall (later Harewood House), stable for Edwin Lascelles 1748, erected 1755.
Wakefield: Westgate, new houses or alterations for Robert Milnes and James Milnes c. 1750, and for Pemberton Milnes 1752–3, almost entirely dem; Westgate UCh 1752, attrib.
Leeds: Boar Lane, house for Jeremiah Dixon, c.1753 dem.
Heath Hall, extensions and remodelling for John Smyth c. 1754–80.
Halifax: The Square, houses for John Caygill, late 1750s dem.
Horsforth, nr Leeds: chapel 1758, attrib. dem.
Harewood House, new house for Edwin Lascelles 1759–71.
Harewood: houses, etc in new village 1759–1803.
Hazlewood Castle, alterations for Sir Walter Vavasour c. 1760.
Farnley, nr Leeds: St Michael 1761 dem.
Sowerby Bridge: White Windows, alterations to house for John Priestley c.1763.
Dewsbury: All Saints, partial rebuilding 1764–7.
Gledhow Hall, house for Jeremiah Dixon c.1764–7 attrib.
Ferrybridge: new bridge, with John Watson (*q.v.*) 1765 dem.
Temple Newsam, unexecuted design for S front, executed internal remodelling for Henry, 7th Viscount Irwin 1765.
Halifax: George St, house and warehouses for John Royds 1766, partly dem.
Wakefield: House of Correction, with John Watson (*q.v.*) 1766.
North Bierley, nr Bradford; St John the Evangelist 1766, enlarged 1828.
Harewood: sch house for Edwin Lascelles 1768, rebuilt 1845.
Leeds: Bridge End, house for Mr Green before

1769; Infirmary 1770–1 dem.
Halifax: Well End House, house for John Waterhouse c.1770 attrib; The Shay, house for John Caygill c.1770.
Parlington Park, unexecuted designs for house, chapel and chaplain's house for Sir Thomas Gascoigne 1772; lodges etc probably built to Carr's designs.
Wetherby Grange, unexecuted design for house for Beilby Thompson 1772; alterations to James Wyatt's design 1783–4, dem except for entrance lodges.
Bramham Park, obelisk for George Fox-Lane, Lord Bingley, before 1773.
Wakefield: Westgate, house for John Milnes 1773, extended 1790s, dem.
Leventhorpe Hall, house for Richard Green 1774.
Pye Nest House, house for John Edwards c.1775 dem.
Methley Hall, remodelling for John, 1st Earl of Mexborough 1778 dem.
Thornes House, house for James Milnes 1779–81 dem.
Byram Park, unspecified work, probably new stables, for Sir John Ramsden c.1770s dem.
Bolling Hall, E wing remodelled for Charles Wood 1779–80.
Meanwood, Leeds: 'King Alfred's Castle', ruin for Jeremiah Dixon 1787 dem.
Horbury: St Peter and St Leonard 1791–3.
Bretton Hall, internal remodelling and garden bldgs for Thomas Richard Beaumont 1793.
Woolley Hall, internal remodelling for Godfrey Wentworth c.1790s attrib.
Ferrybridge: new bridge 1797, built by Bernard Hartley (*q.v.*).
Sowerby: Haugh End, house for the Rawson family.

Castle, Reuben was in practice in Cleckheaton, where he seems to have worked exclusively; he designed Greenside Central MCh (1875–9), Whitcliffe Rd Mixed Sch (1888–9), and the Liberal Club, Northgate (1897). He was joint architect with W. H. Howorth (*q.v.*) for the Public Baths, Tofts Rd (1889).

Chantrell, Robert Dennis (1793–1872) was born in Newington, Southwark and became a pupil in Sir John Soane's office (1807–14). A drawing he made of his master's 'Design for an Opera House in Leicester Square' is in the collection in Sir John Soane's Museum. In 1819 Chantrell set up practice at 25 Park Row, Leeds, remaining there until 1846 when he returned to London to become architect to the Incorporated Church Building Society. Although he made several Neo-classical designs for public buildings, he is best remembered for the many churches in the Gothic style he designed between 1823 and 1846; his son, **John Boham Chantrell**, continued the Leeds practice at 5 East Parade. Chantrell, who was appointed surveyor to York Minster in 1829, was a serious student of Gothic architecture, making use of his knowledge in such designs as the influential St Peter's, Leeds (1837–41), and in such papers as that published in the *Builder* (1847), v, 300–2 and his discussion of Norman roof design read to members of the RIBA in 1847. He exhibited at the Royal Academy in 1812–14, and from 1822

at the exhibitions in Leeds of the Northern Society for the Encouragement of the Fine Arts.
Bibl: Colvin 136.

Halifax: St John, repairs 1818.
Leeds: Park Row, Philosophical Hall 1819–20, enlarged Dobson and Chorley 1861–2, dem; Wellington Rd, Public Baths 1819–20 dem; Bond St, three shops for William Hey 1820 dem; Woodhouse, schoolhouse 1821; Commercial St, Leeds Library, alterations 1821–35; South Market 1823–4 dem; Bramley ch, new organ gallery and parsonage 1823 dem; Christ Ch, Meadow Lane 1823–6 dem; St Mary-the-Virgin, Hunslet, galleries inserted 1826; St Stephen, Kirkstall 1828–9.
Lockwood: Emmanuel Ch 1828–9.
Netherthong: All Saints 1828–9.
Morley: St Peter 1829–30.
Leeds: St Matthew, Holbeck 1829–32, spire and chancel added W. Hill 1860.
Pontefract: All Saints, partial reconstruction of ruin 1832–3.
Leeds: St Bartholomew, Armley, enlarged 1834 dem; Court House, additions to building by T. Taylor 1834–5 dem; St Michael, Headingley 1837–8 dem; St Peter 1837–41; Conservative pavilion (temp) 1838; Holy Trinity, Boar Lane, new steeple 1839; St John, Adel, bellcote 1839, chancel restored 1843.
Pool: St Wilfrid 1839, altered 1880.
Holmbridge: St David 1839–40, chancel added 1887.
Farnley Tyas: St Lucius 1840.
Batley Carr: Holy Trinity 1840–1.
Leeds: St Paul, Shadwell 1841–2.
Honley: St Mary 1842–3.
Denholme Gate: St Paul 1843–6, with Thomas Shaw (q.v.).
Golcar: St John, rebuilding of roof of church by Peter Atkinson (q.v.) 1844.
Roberttown: All Saints 1844–6 with Thomas Shaw.
Halifax: St Paul, King Cross 1845–7 dem except for steeple.
Leeds: St Philip, Wellington St 1845–7 dem.
Middleton: St Mary and parsonage 1846–52.
Keighley: St Andrew 1846–8.
Armitage Bridge: St Paul 1847–8.

Chapman, Samuel (b 1799) was the son of the head gardener at Harewood House; he is listed as an architect in Leeds in the 1817 *Directory*, despite his relative youth. He designed St Mary, Low Harrogate (1822–5 dem), but the only West Yorkshire building for which he is known to have been responsible is the old Leeds Corn Exchange (1827–8), which stood at the north end of Briggate until Brodrick's new building deprived it of use in the 1860s.

Child, Charles was employed as a clerk of the works by John Oates (q.v.), and then set up as an architect, first at Eastwood, nr. Todmorden, next in 1842 at Sowerby Bridge, and then in Halifax; in 1853 he had an office at 56 Kingcross St. He designed a number of churches, including St John, Bradshaw (1838–9) and St Andrew, Stainland, which he altered in 1840 (it was altered again in 1880 by W. S. Barber (q.v.)); and he also designed two buildings in Halifax, the Odd Fellows' Hall (1840), and the

Waterhouse Schs and Almshouses (1855). He assisted William Wallen (q.v.) with the George Hotel, Huddersfield (1849–50) and completed the Apsley Lecture Rm, Huddersfield (1853) after Wallen's death in that year. Possibly **Charles Edwin Child** (1843–1911) was a relative; see Goldie, G.

Child, John (d 1868) was referred to as a draughtsman in 1826, but by 1834 he was in practice as an architect at 36 Boar Lane, Leeds, then in Park Row, and by 1847 at 16 Guildford St. He worked from the last address after taking his son, **Henry Paul Child**, into partnership c.1851. Their known works are exclusively Roman Catholic: St Patrick (1831–2), St Anne (1837–8 dem), and St Joseph (1859–60), all in Leeds. It is likely that several houses in Headingley were designed by Child, including his own, The Priory, Cumberland Rd (c.1841) and Ashwood, Headingley Lane (c.1836) for Joseph Austin. The younger Child carried on the practice at 1 Wormald Row until the mid-60s.

Chorley, Charles R. (d 1914) commenced practice in Leeds in 1854, entering into partnership with John Dobson (q.v.); from 1860–85 he was in practice on his own account, and then with John Wreghitt Connon (q.v.) from 1885–97 under the style of Chorley and Connon. His son, **Harry Sutton Chorley** (1868–1939), entered the firm in 1897. Both were Presidents of the LYAS, in 1886–8 and 1906–8 respectively.
Bibl: obit B (1939), clvii, 429.

Leeds: Park Row, Philosophical Hall, enlarged 1861–2 dem; Vernon Rd Ch Sch 1874; Spring Bank, Headingley, alterations for J. Kitson c. 1880; Holbeck UCh 1881; Ch of the Holy Name, Woodhouse 1881 dem.
Farnley: St Michael 1885.
Leeds: Home for Waifs and Strays, Meanwood 1885; houses at Newton Park, Potternewton c.1885; Whitehall Rd, stables for Monkbridge Iron Co 1886; Newton Park, house for F. M. Lupton c.1886; Albion St, offices for *Yorkshire Post* 1886–7 dem; North Grange Rd, house for M. Lupton 1887; Gledhow Hall, alterations and farm bldgs for J. Kitson 1888; Parish Ch Mission Rm 1888; Gledhow, stables for Hawkhills 1888. Oulton Hall, additions for E. Calverley 1888.
Leeds: Quebec St, Liberal Club 1890; King St, Metropole Hotel 1897–9; Woodbine Pl, Women and Children's Hospital 1897–9 dem; St Edward, Holbeck, vicarage 1908; Ida Convalescent Home.
Bardsey: All Hallows, restoration 1909.

Clark, John (d 1857) was trained in Edinburgh, his native city. The earliest West Yorkshire buildings for which he was responsible seem to be the Commercial Buildings, Leeds and Thomas Nicholson's villa-mansion at Roundhay. Clark's design for the former was selected in competition with entries submitted by R. D. Chantrell (q.v.), C. Barry, T. Taylor (q.v.), A. Salvin and F. Goodwin in 1825; evidently he had been the favoured man from the beginning, according to the *Leeds Intelligencer* (23, 30 June, 7, 17 July 1825). It is possible that the design for Roundhay pre-dates

the competition, but the building is not fully documented. Clark, who gave his address as Edinburgh on the foundation plate of Commercial Buildings, brought a quality of 'New Athenian' architecture to Leeds, which he made use of occasionally outside West Yorkshire (e.g. the Victoria Baths (1832) and the Royal Chalybeate Spa (1835), Harrogate, and the Wilberforce Column, Hull (1834)); he also designed in the Gothic style (e.g. St Catherine's, nr Doncaster, a house for George Banks (1838), Rossington Ch (1843–4), and St George's, Leeds (1836–8)), but he was at his best when using the Greek orders with or without a fashionable Italianate touch.
Bibl: obit, *Building Chronicle*, May 1857, 197: Colvin, 141.

Leeds: Commercial Bldgs 1826–9 dem; Roundhay, house for Thomas Nicholson c. 1826, now the Mansion Hotel.
Bradford: Airedale Coll, Undercliffe 1831–4 dem; St Peter (now Cathedral), rebuilding of S aisle and clerestorey, S porch 1833.
Leeds: Bank Mills, for Hives and Atkinson c.1833 dem; Gledhow Grove, house for John Hives 1830s (now Chapel Allerton Hospital); Bond St, Trustee Savings Bank 1834 dem; Meanwood Hall, alterations for Christopher Beckett c.1834 (now Meanwood Park Hospital); Woodhouse Cemetery ch and lodges 1835; Boar Lane, Yorkshire District Bank 1836 dem; St George 1836–8, apse added 1900–01; St John, repairs and rebuilding tower, comp 1838.
Oulton Hall, stables for John Blayds 1837.
Leeds: Little Woodhouse, extension of house for John Atkinson 1835; Woodhouse, almshouses c.1840; Roundhay Hall, house for John Goodman c.1840 attrib; Woodhouse Sq, two houses for the Atkinson family 1840 (now Waverley House); Woodsley House, Clarendon Rd, house for (Sir) Peter Fairbairn c.1840–1; Balm Rd, mill for John Wilkinson 1842 dem.
Batley Carr: parsonage 1846.
Rawdon: alterations to BCh 1846; house for Robert Milligan 1847.
Apperley Bridge: house for J. Richardson 1848.

Clarkson, John Albert James (b 1861), son of Edward Clarkson of Wyresdale, Lancs was articled to T. C. Hope (q.v.). He set up practice in Bradford with **Thomas Thornton Empsall**, and they were responsible for the Unitarian Sch, Manor House Bldgs, and offices for the Board of Guardians, all in Bradford. Clarkson was architect and surveyor to the Bradford Central Estates, the Wharfedale Estate, Ilkley, Hollin Bank Estate, Esholt, and Clifton Estate, Manningham.
Bibl: *CB*, 364.

Cliff, John was in practice at 65 Basinghall St, Leeds in the 1850s. In 1848 he designed a villa in New Leeds (Buslingthorpe) for G. M. Bingley.

Connon, John Wreghitt (1849–1921) was the son of Revd John Connon of Whitehaven, Cumb. He was in partnership in Dewsbury with Henry Holtom (q.v.) from c. 1875–80, and then with Charles R. Chorley (q.v.) from 1885–97. Connon was the author of *A guide to Kirkstall Abbey* (1886), *The legal registration of architects*

(1888), and *Bardsey-cum-Rigton, the church and village* (1909). He was President of the LYAS in 1885–6. See under **Holtom** and **Chorley** for a list of the works for which Connon was responsible while in partnership with them; in 1883–4 he designed in his own name alone the LICS stores and People's Hall, Albion St, Leeds, and he restored St Mary, Swillington.
Bibl: *CB*, 364; obit *B* (1921), cxxi, 405.

Corson, George (1829–1910) was born in Dumfries, where his father, James, was Provost in 1831–3. He was articled to Walter Newall, an architect in Dumfries, and in 1849 he joined his brother, William Reid Corson (*q.v.*) in Leeds; in 1854 he was occupied with the supervision of a country house near Hawkhurst, Kent, but most of the firm's work was in the Leeds area. W. R. Corson left Leeds *c.* 1860, and George took over the practice, working from 5 South Parade until 1871, when he moved to 13 Cookridge St; five years later he moved to 25 Cookridge St, where he remained until 1901 when he virtually retired, handing over to **W. Evan Jones**. Corson was the first President of the LAS, founded in 1876, and he was re-elected as President of the renamed LYAS in 1897–9.
Bibl: Wilson, T. B., *Two Leeds architects*, Leeds 1937.

Leeds: 52 Wellington St and 1–3 King St, warehouses for William Ledgard 1861; Fox Hill, Weetwood, house for Francis William Tetley 1862; East Parade, offices and sale room for Hepper and Sons 1863; brewery for Joshua Tetley and Son 1864–72 dem; Park St, Sch of Medicine 1865; 28 Gt George St, photographic studio for Edmund and Joseph Wormald 1865; 14 Commercial St, shop for Harvey and Reynolds 1868; Spring Rd/Clarendon Rd, Clareville, house for John Hepper 1868; 12 Clarendon Rd, house for George Herbert Rayner 1868; 21–23 Park Row, Scottish Widows' Fund and Life Assurance Soc 1868–9; St Clement 1868, Parish Rm and SSch 1896 dem; Wood Lane, St Ives, house and sch 1869 dem; St Silas, Hunslet 1869; 54 Wellington St, warehouse for William Ledgard 1870; 34–35, 37, 39, 40, 41, 44 York Pl, warehouses 1870; 51–55 North St, shops and offices for Major Hartley 1870; 14, 16 Swinegate and Blayds Yard, shops and offices for J. D. Heaton 1870.
Bradford: Peckover St, warehouse for John Heugh and Walter Dunlop 1870–1.
Leeds: St Simon's vicarage 1871; Newton Hall Estate, layout for Messrs Lupton 1871; 12 Park Row, music rms for Archibald Ramsden 1871 dem; Wood Lane, Dunearn, house for own occupation 1871 dem; Bewerley St BS 1873; Roundhay Park Estate layout 1873; Green Lane BS 1874 (now Wellington Middle); Saville Green Sch 1875; Otley Rd, Spenfield, house for James Walter Oxley 1875–7, enlarged 1890 (now office of the Yorks Water Authority); Lawnswood Cemetery, layout, mortuary chs, etc 1875; St Edmund, Richmond Hill 1876; Shireoak Rd, layout 1876; Grand Theatre and Opera House 1876–8; Municipal Bldgs 1876–84; 15 Park Row, Headland (later Sun) Bldgs for Messrs Headland 1877 dem; Bennett Rd, Parochial Inst 1877; School Board Offices 1878–81.

Methley: BS 1878.
Leeds: 9–13 Hyde Tce, houses for W. D. Heaton 1879; Shireoak Rd, St Michael's Mount, house for William Wailes 1883; 31 Lyddon Tce, house for William Woodham Best 1883; Shireoak Rd, Ballamona and Ravenstone, houses 1887; General Infirmary, extensions 1891–2; 78 Wellington St, warehouse for Crowe and Co Ltd 1900–01 (with Perkin and Bulmer, *q.v.*).

Corson, William Reid was the second son of James Corson of Dumfries. He was articled to an architect in his home town, but in the late 1840s he was established at 28 North St, Leeds in partnership with **Edward La Trobe Bateman**. Both had worked for a time with Owen Jones, who was brought in to advise on the decoration of Little Woodhouse House for John Atkinson in 1847. Bateman soon left Leeds, but Corson remained until *c.* 1860 when he went to Manchester and became a partner of William Aitkins. Later he left England and went to live in Santa Monica, California. Among his known works in Leeds are Phoenix Inn, Kirkgate (1854), and warehouses for W. Lupton and Co., and D. and J. Cooper in Wellington St (1860).

Crossland, William Henry was a pupil of Sir George Gilbert Scott, with whom he was probably closely associated in some of the work at Copley and Akroydon for Edward Akroyd. He was in practice, first in Huddersfield, then *c.*1860 in Halifax; but in 1864 he was living and working in Leeds. Later, *c.*1870, he moved to London. Crossley became a FRIBA in 1867, but he disappeared from the Institute's records after 1895, and the date and place of his death are not known. His designs seem to have been Gothic, without exception, and in 1860 he submitted an entry in that style for the Leeds Institute, which was favourably noticed. During the 70s he was closely associated with the Ramsden Estate in Huddersfield, and in 1873 he made an unexecuted design for a concert hall in the town.

Birstall: St Peter 1863–70.
Bradley: St Thomas 1863.
Copley: St Stephen 1863–5.
Ossett: Holy Trinity 1865.
Middlesmoor: St Chad 1866.
Staincliffe: Christ Ch 1867.
Leeds: St Chad, Far Headingley 1868, where Crossland was executant architect of ch nominally designed by E. B. Denison (*q.v.*).
Sutton: St Thomas 1869.
Longley Hall, alterations for Sir J. W. Ramsden *c.*1870.
Huddersfield: St Andrew 1870; Ramsden Estate Office, Railway St 1872; Post Office 1874–6; Kirkgate Bldgs, warehouses 1878; Westgate, Byram Bldgs, etc 1880–1.

Crutchley, William was in practice at King St, Wakefield in the 1870s. He designed a Model Lodging House (1871–2), Town Hall Chambers, King St (1877), and The Towers, Bond St (1880).

Cusworth, Joseph was a pupil of Thomas Taylor (*q.v.*); he worked with Atkinson and Phillips (*q.v.*) in York, and in 1817 he advertised his services as an architect in the *Leeds Intelligencer*. In 1822 he was in practice at 5

Albion St, Leeds, and in the same year he made a design for improvements to Leeds GS. In the following year he enlarged Albion St MCh, and in 1828 he designed an organ and gallery for Holy Trinity, Boar Lane, Leeds.

Danby, George Francis (b 1845), the son of Francis Danby, cabinet maker and upholsterer, of Leeds, was articled to William Hill (*q.v.*), with whom he remained for nine years as pupil and assistant. He set up practice in Leeds in 1872, and was later in partnership with W. H. Thorp (*q.v.*). Danby specialised in Methodist chapels and schools, of which he built several in Leeds, as well as in Apperley Bridge, Shipley, Middlesbrough and Pocklington; he also designed villas in Roundhay and Headingley.
Bibl: *CB*, 365.

Leeds: Woodhouse Carr WMCh 1874.
Thorner: WMCh 1877–8.
Leeds: Roscoe Pl MSSch 1882; Crossgates WMCh (now Sch) 1882; Dewsbury Rd WCh 1887–8, Sch 1891; Lincoln Fields WMCh 1889; Eldon WCh 1890; Hanover Pl WSSch 1891; Hunslet Moor End WMCh 1891; Shadwell WCh 1892; Crossgates WMCh 1892–3; Roseville Rd WMCh 1894–5; Trinity MCh, Roundhay Rd *c.*1894; Richmond Hill SSch 1895; Burley WMCh 1897–8; Lady Pit Lane WMCh, Beeston Hill 1898; Trinity CCh, Woodhouse Lane 1898; Park WMCh, Cross Flatts 1906 (with John Simpson *q.v.*).

Denison, Edmund Beckett, 1st Lord Grimthorpe (1816–1905) was the son of Edmund Beckett (later Sir Edmund Beckett Denison, Bart) of Leeds, a member of a wealthy banking family and a 'railway king' in the 1840s. Denison was called to the Bar in Lincoln's Inn in 1841 and he became a well-known figure, delighting to take part in ecclesiastical controversies. From that interest developed his passion for church architecture and the arrogant belief in his own omniscience which led to the restoration of St Alban's Cathedral by Denison according to his own ideas. He was Chancellor of the Diocese of York from 1877, and he was nominally the architect of two churches in Doncaster, St James (1858) and St Mary (1885); in the first he had the assistance of George Gilbert Scott. His major design in West Yorkshire is St Chad, Far Headingley, Leeds (1868), built on one of the family estates; it is generally believed W. H. Crossland (*q.v.*) was largely responsible. Denison was also an authority on horology; he is best known for the design of Big Ben, but he also designed clocks for Leeds Town Hall, Lincoln Cathedral, Worcester Cathedral, St Paul's Cathedral, etc. His younger brother, William, was a philanthropic promoter of better houses for the working classes, and he took a leading part in the appointment of Scott as architect for Leeds General Infirmary.
Bibl: Ferriday, P., *Lord Grimthorpe*, London 1957.

Dixon, Isaiah was in practice at 4 Park Row, Leeds in the 1850s. He designed a school at Buslingthorpe, Leeds (1858–9).

Dixon, Jonathan was working on his own account in Bradford from the late 1830s. He designed warehouses for Leo Schuster in Charles

St (1838 dem), and in Hall Ings for John Haigh and Co, and Frederic Schwann and Co (both 1849). He was in partnership with Eli Milnes (q.v.) during the 1850s.

Dixon, Thomas acted as a surveyor in Bradford from the 1830s; he laid out the Well St/Leeds Rd area in the 30s, and provided the plans for housing in Hallfield Rd which was erected by the Hallfield Building Club in 1848–52.

Dobson, John was in practice in Park Row, Leeds in the 1850s, when he took Charles R. Chorley (q.v.) into partnership. The latter was joined c. 1883 by John Wreghitt Connon (q.v.).

Leeds: Wade Lane, Harrison's almshouses 1850 dem.
Gomersal: St Mary the Virgin 1850–1.
Leeds: St John the Baptist, New Wortley 1852–3; St Stephen, Burmantofts 1853–4, Sch 1859–60; Parish Ch Sch 1858; St Matthew, Camp Rd, Sch 1860.

Dodgshun, Edward J. was in practice in Leeds from the 1870s. He was President of the LYAS 1894–6. His varied work included St Saviour's Schs (1872), houses in Hyde Tce (c. 1877), Peacock's Bldgs (now St Andrew House), Park Row (1894), and the West Riding Union Bank, Park Row (c. 1900), all in Leeds.

Dodgson, Daniel practised in Leeds c.1872–1904. He was the designer of Roundhay Rd MCh (1878), and he made plans of many houses in the Cardigan Rd area 1877–1902.

Ellis, Walter Stead practised in Heckmondwike and Huddersfield in the 1860s, and also in Dewsbury in the 70s. He designed the Market Hall, Batley (c.1874), and St Mark's Schs, Dewsbury (1866).

Etty, John I (1634–1708/9) was the son of James Etty, a York carpenter, and he obtained his freedom of the City in the same trade in 1654. He was employed by the Duke of Buckingham at Helmsley Castle, N Yorks, in 1665, and in 1674 he rebuilt part of the W wing of Temple Newsam for Edward, 2nd Viscount Irwin. In 1676 he was appointed City Husband and put in charge of the public buildings and works in York, and in the same year he was building a house in the Mint Yard. According to Ralph Thoresby's diary (ed J. Hunter 1830, i, 366), Grinling Gibbons worked with Etty in York when he returned to England c.1667. He held, under Sir Christopher Wren, an appointment as Surveyor to H.M.'s Works at York; in 1688 he reported to Wren on the state of the 'pallace' at Berwick-on-Tweed (Wren Soc, xviii, 33). It has been suggested (Booth, J. A., *Country house architecture in Yorkshire*, unpublished MPhil thesis, London University 1972) that Etty might have been associated with several Yorkshire houses, including Marston, Ribston and Nun Monkton, Whixley, Healaugh and Bell. His name occurs in documents relating to Sir Edward Blackett's Newby Hall and Sir Godfrey Copley's Sprotbrough Hall. Etty's monument in All Saints, North St, York records that, 'By the

strength of his own genius and application he had acquired great knowledge of Mathematicks, especially Geometry and Architecture in all its parts far beyond any of his Co-temporares in this City'.

Etty, William (d 1734) was a son of John Etty I (q.v.); he was apprenticed as a carpenter but turned to architecture, probably designing the Cross in the Thursday Market, York (1705). In 1710 the Leeds Pious Uses Committee accepted his design (with many similarities to the York Cross) for rebuilding the Moot Hall, Briggate, employing Etty and Richard Wakefield to execute the work. In 1712 he laid out part of the landscape around Temple Newsam for the 4th Viscount Irwin, and in 1719 he was writing to Arthur Ingram about work at Barrowby Hall as well as describing his designs for 'Mr Tankred [Whixley Hall] and another for Mr Pelham'. In the same year he was employed by Sir John Vanbrugh to supervise the building of Seaton Delaval, and from 1721 he undertook a similar responsibility at Castle Howard. He built Newby Park, Baldersby for Metcalfe Robinson from a design made by Colen Campbell but amended by Etty, and it is quite probable he designed the Mansion House, York, on which he was working in 1724. In the previous year, Etty made a design for Holy Trinity Ch, Leeds, and also provided a wooden model 'for our workmen to go by'. He is the likely designer of Sheepscar Hall (later known as Bischoff House), Leeds for Nathaniel Denison before 1725. Etty died in 1734, when Hawksmoor wrote to Lord Carlisle to recommend his son, **John Etty II** (1705–38) to the landowner's attention, 'for he is sober, carefull, ingenious and industrious, I hope he is honest, and as he was bread up in ye way of Building under his father, he may be of use to you'. John Etty was employed at Castle Howard, and it was presumably he who made a copy in 1735 'of the Plan sent by the Earl of Burlington for the building to be erected adjoining the Assembly Rooms'. Hawksmoor's professional opinion of William Etty's capabilities is apparent from his letter (25 June 1734) in which he asks his clerk of the works at Castle Howard if he has been able to 'pursue the designe I sent or whether you have bin in necessity to alter it, and I woud wish to know in what parts, you have alterd'.
Bibl: Colvin, 200f; Downes, K., *Hawksmoor*, London 1959, 226ff, 267ff; Beard, G., *Georgian craftsmen and their work*, London 1966, 22ff, 176.

Fairbank, Benjamin Dalby (b 1850), son of Henry Fairbank, was in partnership with **John Henry Wall** in Swan Arcade, Bradford in 1884, and later in Bank St. In the early 1900s **Benjamin Browne Fairbank** became a partner, and the style was changed to B. D. Fairbank and Son. Their work included a wool warehouse, 4 Manor Row (1892), and numerous warehouses, clubs, schools and private houses in Bradford. Fairbank was President of the BSAS in 1898–9.
Bibl: *CB*, 366.

Fairbank, John Tertius was in practice at 26 Darley St, Bradford in 1847, and at 22 Queens Gate from c. 1861–75. He designed St Barnabas,

Holbeck, Leeds (1854–5), but most of his work was in Bradford; it included houses in The Park, Rooley Lane (1860s), Heaton Mount, Frizinghall for Robert Kell (1864), and Bowling Park for Abraham Mitchell (c. 1865). Among Bradford warehouses designed by Fairbank are those at 4 Burnett St (for David Julius Heyn 1859), and 5 Burnett St (1860).

Fowler, Alfred Mountain, a son of Charles Fowler (q.v.), was Assistant Borough Surveyor in Leeds, and in practice in the town on his own account at 33 Grafton St. He took the appointment of Borough Surveyor from 1865–72, when he moved to Salford to take up a similar post.

Fowler, Charles was in practice at 17 Commercial St, Leeds in 1822 as a civil engineer, valuer and agent, engineer and surveyor to the trustees of several turnpike roads, and to the Commissioners for the new Leeds waterworks. He published a plan of Leeds in 1819. In 1845 he was described as an architect also, and two years later one of his three sons, **Henry Fowler** (d 1910), an engineering surveyor, was in practice with him for a few years. From 1867 onwards, the firm was in Britannia Bldgs, Oxford Pl (a Gothic building probably designed by Fowler). Another son, **Charles John Fowler** (1807–1907), went to London in 1837 to work with an engineer, Hamilton Fulton, in Westminster; he returned to Leeds in 1886 to take over his father's practice, which was known as Charles and Charles John Fowler. Among the buildings credited to the firm are the improvement of the old church of St Michael, Headingley (1869–70), and Otley Mechanics' Inst (1871).

Fox, George Arthur was in partnership with Henry Holtom (q.v.) from c. 1887 in Dewsbury. Their major building was the Town Hall, Dewsbury (1888–9), but Fox also designed Batley Conservative Club, Branch Rd (1891), and Morley Town Hall (1895). **Charles Edward Fox** had taken over the practice in the 1920s.

Fox, J. Lane practised in Dewsbury from c.1887, first at 3 Bond St, and then at 5 Market Pl. He was the designer of Dewsbury Technical Sch (1888–9), and Wheelwright GS, Dewsbury (1891–3).

France, Charles (1833–1902) was in partnership with Eli Milnes (q.v.) in Bradford from 1863, and his son **Arthur Alderson France** was taken into the firm as a partner in 1888. See under **Milnes** for a list of the works for which the firm was responsible.
Bibl: obit *B* (1902), lxxxiii, 349.

Fraser, James Barlow (1835–1922) was in practice at 4 Park Pl, Leeds in 1866, and he appears to have continued to work almost to the end of his life. In 1867 he acted jointly with his brother, **John Fraser**, civil engineer, in providing the design for Westgate Station, Wakefield. He restored St Oswald, Leathley (1869), and designed St Augustine, Wrangthorne, Leeds (1870–71) and Cavendish Rd PCh, Leeds (1878–9). In 1902 he completed

the spire of Pearson's St Margaret, Horsforth, and in 1904 he remodelled the orchestra of Leeds Town Hall. He was President of the LYAS in 1882–3.
Bibl: obit *B* (1922), cxxiii, 555.

Freson, Lancelot (b *c.*1615) was described as a gentleman of Leeds in 1665 who, 'for the space of these twenty yeares last past' had been 'employed about and undertaken the Building and reparacons of manye houses and structures for divers gentlemen and persons of quality within the County of York'. Unfortunately, these buildings cannot be identified, but Freson's statement suggests a degree of professionalism. (Information from Mr Howard Colvin)

Goldie, George (1828–87), the grandson of Joseph Bonomi, was born in York. Pugin advised him to join the firm of John Gray Weightman and Matthew Ellison Hadfield (*q.v.*) in Sheffield, and in 1850 he became a partner. During this time they designed St Paulinus SchCh, Dewsbury (1849), St Patrick, Bradford (1852–3), and the tower of St Edward, Clifford (1859–67); by the time the last was being built, Weightman had left the practice, and Hadfield and Goldie had bought that of W. W. Wardell (see 223). In 1860 Goldie left to set up his own practice, and in 1867 he took **Charles Edwin Child** (1843–1911), a former pupil, into partnership. St Joseph's Seminary, Leeds (1877) was designed during this phase of the practice, but St Joseph, Castleford (1891) belongs to a later time when **Edward Goldie** had taken over. The practice was extremely prolific, producing four cathedrals, four seminaries, and more than fifty churches for the Roman Catholics.
Bibl: obit *B* (1887), lii, 367.

Gott, Charles (b 1831), son of Charles Gott, a Hull builder, was Borough Surveyor and Water Works Engineer to the Corporation of Bradford 1855–75. After giving up this appointment, he set up practice at 8 Charles St, Bradford; in the early 1900s the firm was headed by **Charles Henry Gott**, the son of the founder.

Hadfield, Matthew Ellison (1812–85) was a pupil of Woodhead and Hurst (*q.v.*) of Doncaster from 1831–4, and then went to London to work in the office of P. F. Robinson. While working in Doncaster, he met **John Gray Weightman** (1801–72), with whom he entered into partnership in Sheffield in 1838, the year after Hadfield had opened an office there. George Goldie (*q.v.*) was taken into partnership in 1850, and he and Hadfield continued the practice after Weightman left in 1858. Two years later, Goldie left, and Hadfield took **Charles Hadfield** (1840–1916) into partnership in 1864. St Marie's Convent and Girls' HS, Richmond Hill, Leeds (1861), and the Great Northern Hotel, Wellington St, Leeds (1869) were the work of Hadfield alone.
Bibl: obit *B* (1885), xlviii, 397, 512.

Hammerton, Lees was an assistant to Thomas Taylor (*q.v.*); he completed Taylor's Holy Trinity, Ripon (1826–7), and designed St

Martin, Brighouse (1830–1) in a similar manner. In 1853 he was in practice at Rodney Yard, Wakefield.

Hansom, Joseph Aloysius (1803–82) was the son of Henry Hansom, a joiner working from 114 Micklegate, York. He was first apprenticed to his father, and then in 1817 to **Matthew Phillips** (*c.*1781–1825), who was in partnership with Peter Atkinson II (*q.v.*) until he set up his own practice in York. Hansom continued to work with Phillips after completing his articles, then in 1825 he went to Halifax to work with John Oates (*q.v.*); it was there that he met **Edward Welch** (1806–68), with whom he went into partnership in 1828. That episode ended in bankruptcy over Birmingham Town Hall, and Hansom then went into partnership with his brother, **Charles Francis Hansom** (1817–88), who designed Our Lady and All Saints, Otley (1850–1) and Mary Immaculate, Sicklinghall, N Yorks (1849–54); this arrangement lasted from 1854 to 1859, and in 1862 Joseph Hansom went into partnership with **Edward Welby Pugin** (1834–75) in Ramsgate. This came to an end in 1863. During these many changes, Hansom was responsible for building St Edward, Clifford (1845–8) to a design made by (?) Ramsay, designing Mount St Mary, Leeds (1853–7), and making alterations and additions to St Austin, Wakefield (1878–9). He also patented the safety cab bearing his name (1836) and founded the *Builder* (1842).
Bibl: obit *B* (1882), xliii, 43f.

Hanstock, Walter (1842–1900) was in partnership with **Michael Sheard** in Batley from the 1860s. **Arthur Walter Hanstock** (b 1874), who was articled to the firm, was made a partner in 1898 and took over the practice in 1900. The firm made a speciality of public baths, and in 1899 they were awarded second prize in the competition for Leeds City Markets.
Bibl: obit *B* (1900), lxxix, 347.

Batley: mortuary ch 1865; St Thomas 1867–8; St Saviour, Brownhill 1870–1; All Saints, restoration 1872–3; St Thomas Sch 1873; Station Rd, warehouse for Abraham Brooke *c.*1873.
Gomersal: Ch Sch 1878.
Hanging Heaton: MCh 1878.
Gildersome: The Woodlands 1880.
Dewsbury: Ebenezer CCh, Long Causeway 1884.
Normanton WMCh, Wakefield Rd 1885.
Batley: Public Baths 1893.
Leeds: Public Baths, Union St 1894–5.
Morley: Albion St BCh 1896.
Leeds: Public Baths, Holbeck Lane 1897, Meanwood Rd 1898; Meat Market 1899 dem.
Batley: Town Hall 1899; Public Library 1907.

Hargreaves, Charles Henry was in practice at 53 Old Market, Bradford in 1870. He entered into partnership with **Wilson Bailey** at 1 Bank St before 1877, and also had an office in Ilkley, where he lived. He designed Ilkley GS (1890), Belle Vue HGS (1895) and the Hanson HGS (1897), both in Bradford. Bailey is best remembered for the additions, including the Winter Gardens, which he made to Cliffe Castle, Keighley.

Harper, John (1809–42) was a Lancastrian, born at Dunkenhalgh House, nr Blackburn. He was trained in the office of Benjamin and Philip Wyatt in London, and then set up a practice in York, where he built the Proprietary Sch, Clifton (1838, now part of St Peter's Sch). He supervised the building of the Chapel of the Virgin and St Everilda, Everingham (1836–9), designed by Agostino Giorgioli, and he built Holy Trinity, Blacktoft (1841). He was employed by Miss Anne Lister of Shibden Hall in 1835 to remodel part of her house, design a new North Lodge ('one after the manner of the *gate at Kirkham pleased me best*', wrote his employer), and convert Northgate House, Halifax into a hotel and assembly room. Harper also worked for the Duke of Devonshire and Lord Londesborough on their Yorkshire estates. He went to Italy in 1842, where he died of malaria.
Bibl: Colvin 266.

Hartley, Bernard I (*c.*1745–1834) was the first of three generations of Pontefract masons and architects with the same name. Mr Howard Colvin suggests that he may have been the son of Hugh Hartley, a.mason who worked in Yorkshire in the reign of George II. In 1797 Hartley was appointed Surveyor of Bridges to the West Riding, an appointment which ceased only with his death in 1834. In 1785 Pontefract Town Hall was built from his design, and in 1797–1804 he was building the bridge at Ferrybridge as designed by John Carr (*q.v.*). Castleford Bridge, built in 1805, was his own design. **Bernard Hartley II** (1779–1855) was recommended to Miss Anne Lister of Shibden Hall as 'one of the most honest men to be had'; he was appointed Surveyor of Bridges jointly with his father, taking over when the latter died. In 1806 he offered a design for the Wakefield Court House, but that of Charles Watson (*q.v.*) was accepted; he also made designs for a new vicarage at Ledsham (1821) and for enlarging that at Kellington. Miss Lister noted in her diary that 'Jesse Hartley of Liverpool, brother to Bernard [was] also an architect'; so was **Bernard Hartley III**, who succeeded to the Surveyorship of Bridges in 1855 and retained the appointment until his retirement in 1882. He designed Otley Court House (1875).

Healey, Thomas I was articled to R. D. Chantrell (*q.v.*), but nothing else is known about him before 1847, when he was in partnership with James Mallinson (*q.v.*) at 64 Tyrrel St, Bradford and 15 Mount St, Halifax. Their practice was mainly ecclesiastical, and their works are listed under **Mallinson, James**.

Healey, Thomas II was the elder son of Thomas Healy I (*q.v.*), and was probably trained in the Mallinson and Healey practice. After the elder Healey died, Mallinson went into partnership with W. S. Barber (*q.v.*), and the younger Healey, together with his brother **Francis Healey** (1835–1910), continued to specialise in ecclesiastical work. Their practice remained active until *c.* 1910.

Cleckheaton: St John, altered 1864.
Bradford: St Peter (now Cathedral), alterations 1868, transepts added 1899.

Calverley: St Wilfred, restored 1869–70.
Bradford: St James, Thornton 1870; Bowling
Ch Sch 1870; St John Evangelist, Little Horton
Lane 1871–3 dem.
Leeds: Royal Exchange, City Sq 1872–5 dem.
Bradford: Whetley Lane BS 1873; St John
Evangelist, Gt Horton Rd 1874.
Lightcliffe: St Matthew 1874.
Bradford: St Augustine, Undercliffe 1877.
Haworth: St Michael 1880.
Bradford: St Luke, Manningham 1880;
Bowland St Synagogue 1880.
Queensbury: Holy Trinity, restored 1885;
Victoria Hall, Inst and Public Baths 1888.
Yeadon: St Andrew 1891; St John, chancel
added 1893.
Otley CCh 1899.
Shipley: St Peter 1909.

Helliwell, Thomas W. worked in Brighouse;
he designed Bailiff Bridge MNCCh (1872), and
the vicarage for St Peter, Hartshead (c.1870).

Hill, William (1828–89) was articled to Perkin
and Backhouse (q.v.). He set up practice in 1851
at 59 Albion St, Leeds. In 1875 he was at 11
Park Sq, when **Salmon L. Swann** was his
partner. In 1889 **William Longfield Hill**
(b 1864), who had been articled to his father, took
over the practice and completed the drawings
for Portsmouth Town Hall (1884) which, like
Bolton Town Hall (1865), had been modelled by
Hill on Brodrick's famous building in Leeds. The
firm is said to have been responsible for upwards
of 100 Nonconformist chapels, as well as public
buildings and private residences.
Bibl: obit B (1889), lvi, 34.

Leeds: Blenheim BCh 1858; Woodhouse Lane,
MNCCh 1858; East Parade, Poor Law Offices
1859–60 dem; Farnley Cemetery Ch 1859; St
Matthew, Holbeck, enlarged 1860; Dewsbury
Rd, MNCCh 1861; Holbeck Workhouse 1864;
Marshall St, CCh, remodelling 1865; Public
Dispensary 1865; Beeston Hill, WCh 1867;
Ventnor St, MNCCh 1872; Aire St, commercial
premises for Watson Bros 1872; Hunslet Union
Sch and Dormitories 1872; Beckett St MCh
1873–5.
Bradford: Gt Horton Rd MNCCh 1877.
Elland: Bethesda MNCCh 1879–80.
Yeadon: Town Hall and Mechanics' Inst
1879–80.
Leeds: Meanwood MCh 1880–1. extended 1886.

Hogg, John practised in Halifax from the 1850s
to late 70s, with an office at 16 Northgate in
1861, and at Swinemarket in 1875. He designed
the Crossley Orphanage (1857–64) and the
Crossley and Porter Sch (1864). He also built a
group of large, semi-detached Italianate villas in
Park Rd (1856), Marsden Mechanics' Inst
(1859), and Sowerby CCh. He completed the now
demolished, forbidding pile of Castle Carr,
started by Thomas Risling in 1859 for Joseph
Priestley Edwards.

Holtom, Henry was in partnership with John
Wreghitt Connon (q.v.) until c. 1880 in
Dewsbury. During that time they were
responsible for Dewsbury MNCCh (1875), St
Philip, Dewsbury (1878), Holmfirth BS (1878),

and four schools for the Soothill School Board
(Earlsheaton, Mill Lane, East Ardsley, and St
Mary's, Savile Town) in 1875. They submitted a
design for the Municipal Bldgs, Leeds (1876–7).
After Connon left the firm to join Charles R.
Chorley (q.v.), Holtom went into partnership
with George A. Fox (q.v.) in Dewsbury, where
they designed the Town Hall (1888–9); they also
built the Public Baths, Morley (1899).

Hope, Thomas Campbell (1834–1916), a son
of John Hope of Bradford, practised in his
native town from c. 1861. **David Jardine**, who
had probably been articled to Hope, joined him
in partnership c. 1875 at 12 Exchange Bldgs,
and then at 2 Cheapside. This arrangement had
ceased by 1887. **George Roberts** became a
partner c.1912. Hope was largely responsible for
the layout of Manningham as a residential
suburb, and he made the designs for several
villas and terraces. He was President of the
BSAS in 1889 and 1910.
Bibl: CB, 368; obit B (1916), cxi, 243.

Ilkley: Ilkley Coll 1868.
Bradford: Tyrrel St, store for George Thorpe
and Co 1871; Lindum Tce, Manningham 1873;
Lilycroft BS 1873; St Paul's Tce, Manningham
1874; Gt Horton Rd, Technical Sch 1880–2;
Tyrrel St, Albert Bldgs 1884; Grange Rd, Gt
Horton HGS 1886; Cousin Rd, Nutter
Orphanage for Boys 1888; Victoria Sq, shops,
offices, etc for William Whitaker and Co c. 1890.
Ilkley: Queens Drive, Arden Croft, house for
George Thorpe 1897.
Bradford: Northgate, Rawson Market 1904.

Horsfall, Charles Frederick Luke
(1846–1923) was articled to his elder brother,
Richard (q.v.), with whom he worked until 1882,
when he set up his own practice in Waterhouse
St, Halifax. Subsequently he moved to Lord St,
taking his son, **William Edward Horsfall**
(d 1940), into the firm. A third generation,
Charles Edward Horsfall, joined the office and
practised until 1962. The name of the founder is
retained in the present firm.

Halifax: St Augustine, Hanson Lane 1875.
Elland: South End BS 1877.
Stainland: Sowood Green BS 1879; Sowood
WCh.
Halifax: Haugh Shaw IS 1879.
Elland: Town Hall 1888.
Luddenden Foot BS 1894.
Warley BS 1894–7.
Sowerby Bridge: Bolton Brow BS 1897; Bolton
Brow WSSch; Bolton Brow, St Mary's SSch;
Bolton Brow, Brunswick Ch and SSch; New Rd
BS 1900; Tuel Lane UMCCh.
Halifax: Battinson Rd BS 1903; Booth Town
UMCh and Sch; Ovenden, Bethel Ch.
Shelf: UMCh (remodelling?).

Horsfall, Richard (1827–1907) was in practice
in Waterhouse St, Halifax in 1853, and was
joined by **Matthias Harris Wardle** in the mid-
60s, by which time the office had been moved to
George St. **Thomas Lister Patchett** became a
partner in the 70s, when the firm was known as
Horsfall, Wardle and Patchett. Subsequently
Richard Edgar Horsfall (1864–1943), the son

of the founder, became a partner. C. F. L.
Horsfall (q.v.), as well as William Horsfall, were
working for Richard in the 1860s and 70s.
Bibl: obits, B (1907), xcii, 729; (1914), cvii, 250;
(1943), clxv, 158.

Halifax: West Parade, Holy Trinity Boys Sch
1870; West Vale, Mechanics' Hall 1872–4;
Queens Rd BS c. 1874.
Sowerby: National Sch additions 1874;
Bairstow's Endowed Sch (Patchett alone) 1875;
Provident New Sch 1875.
Brearley: BCh 1875.
Sowerby: WCh (Patchett alone) 1878.
Halifax: Palace Theatre (supervision of design
by Runtz and Ford) 1903; Theatre Royal
1904–05; Ward's End, Electric Theatre 1910.

Howdill, Thomas (1840–1918) was born at
Tadcaster, and set up practice in Leeds in 1873.
He is said to have built between 200 and 300
chapels for the Primitive Methodists. His son,
Charles Barker Howdill (1863–1941), after
being articled to his father in 1879, became
assistant and then partner (1893) in the firm; in
1889 he was appointed assistant architect to
Leeds School Board. He taught building
construction at Leeds and Dewsbury Technical
Schools (1886–1903), Huddersfield Technical
School (1914–41) and Batley Technical School
(1928–41). He also taught at Leeds School of
Art, and it was said he was 'probably the first in
the country to attempt the illustration of a
lecture of an architectural character by the aid
of colour photography'.
Bibl: CB, 368; obits B (1918), cxv, 294; (1941),
clxi, 150. I am grateful to Mr Colin Dews for his
help in compiling the list of buildings.

Leeds: Ebenezer PMCh and Sch, Kirkstall 1874.
Morley: Brunswick PMCh 1874.
Bradford: Rehoboth PMCh and Sch 1877–8.
Ilkley PMCh 1877–8.
Bradford: Manningham PMCh, Heaton Rd
1879.
Leeds: Salem PMCh and Sch, Holdforth St
1879; Woodhouse Hill PMSchCh 1879, Ch
1901–02.
Bradford: Tennyson Pl PMSchCh 1880.
Leeds: Tabernacle UMFChSch, Meadow Rd
1881–2; Cardigan Rd PMSch 1883, Ch 1894–5;
Lower Wortley PMCh, ext 1884, Sch 1897.
Skelmanthorpe PMSSch, alterations to Ch
1886–7.
Denby Dale PMCh, alterations 1886.
Cumberworth PMCh, alterations 1887.
Leeds: Stourton WMCh 1892; Viaduct Rd,
tannery for William Beckworth 1892; Cardigan
Rd PMCh 1894; Middleton WMCh and house
1896.
Horbury UMFCh 1897.
Leeds: Silver Royd Hill PMCh, Tong Rd
1901–02; Jubilee PMCh and Sch, Woodhouse
1902.
Liversedge: Millbridge WMCh 1903–04.
Leeds: Armley PMCh and Sch, Branch Rd 1905.

Howorth, William Henry practically
monopolised the architectural work in
Cleckheaton during the last quarter of the
century, although Reuben Castle (q.v.), who
collaborated on the Public Baths (1889), was

occasionally successful. Howorth was in practice in Northgate in 1877, and was joined by his son, **William Henry Howorth Jr** (d 1946), c.1898.

Cleckheaton: White Ch, restoration etc 1877–88; Conservative Club, Bradford Rd 1887; WMCh, Whitcliffe Rd 1889; Public Baths, Toft Rd (with R. Castle) 1889; London City and Midland Bank, Bradford Rd 1891; Fire Station, Bradford Rd 1891; Drill Hall, Whitcliffe Rd 1892; Lancashire and Yorkshire Bank, Market St 1898.
Hartshead WCh.

Hughes, Edward (d 1886) practised at 172 Cambridge St, London from 1863–70, and at Lord St, Huddersfield from 1871–84.

Huddersfield: Beaumont St BS 1874.
West Clayton: All Saints 1875.
Cumberworth: St Nicholas 1878.
Huddersfield: Market Hall 1878–80 dem; Albert Hotel, shops, offices and warehouse 1879; Spring Grove Sch 1879; Coll of Technology 1881–4 (now a part of Huddersfield Polytechnic); Cricket and Athletic Club Pavilion 1884–5.

Hurst, William (1787–1844) was born in Doncaster, where he was articled to William Lindley (q.v.). He later joined the firm of Lindley and Woodhead, which changed its style to Woodhead and Hurst. They were awarded second prize in the competition for Wakefield Corn Exchange in 1836, which was won by W. L. Moffat (q.v.), with whom Hurst went into partnership after the death of John Woodhead (q.v.) in c.1838. Most of their work was in S Yorkshire, especially in the Sheffield area.

Wakefield: House of Correction, additions 1819.
Leeds: Call Lane, warehouse for Aire and Calder Navigation 1827–8 dem; East Parade, New Independent Ch 1839–41 dem.
Ardsley: Christ Ch 1841.
Woodsetts: St Mary 1841.

Hutchinson, Edward, of Pontefract, made designs in 1754 for Campsall House, S Yorks; these are in the RIBA Drawings Collection.

Ives, Roger practised in Halifax from c.1837, when he was at 12 Broad St. In 1853 he had moved to 6 North Parade, and c. 1866 he was joined in partnership by his son, **William Ives**. In the 1890s, there was a change when the practice was amalgamated with that of Francis William Petty (q.v.), and the style was changed to Petty and Ives.

Halifax: Crossley's Dean Clough Mills c.1854–8; Margaret St, Crossley Almshouses 1855; Broomfield, house for Joseph Crossley c. 1855; Arden Rd, Joseph Crossley's Almshouses 1863–70; Park CCh 1869; Bermerside, house for Edward Crossley 1872.

Jackson, Benjamin practised in Leeds from c.1814, when he was at 1 Kirkgate, until c.1841, when he was at 19 Guildford St. He is referred to in an 1818 report on the Leeds Library, and he was doing work at Denison Hall c. 1823 for George Rawson.

Jackson, Benjamin Whitehead (b 1830), son of Joseph Jackson of Chester, was articled to Charles Child (q.v.) in 1845, and remained in the office for ten years. He then set up practice in Halifax, taking **Charles James Fox** into partnership before 1875; the firm's office was at 22 George St. Jackson was Surveyor to the Diocese of Wakefield, and he acted as valuer to Halifax Corp from 1861 onwards. He built several Board Schools, in addition to St George, Ovenden (1868), St George, Lee Mount (1877), the remodelling of Halifax Infirmary (1874), the Percival Whitley Coll of Further Education (1895), and the Alexandra Theatre (1902), all in Halifax. The firm continued until recent times.

Jackson, Samuel (1830–1910) was in practice in Leeds Rd, Bradford in 1856, and in Kirkgate five years later. He took **William Longley** into partnership in the 70s, but this had ceased by 1881. His son, **Walter Jackson I** (d 1947) joined the firm c.1898, and his grandson, **Walter Jackson II**, in 1927. Jackson was awarded third prize in the competition for Bradford Town Hall (1869); he was President of the BSAS in 1881, and again in 1902.

Bradford: Grove House, Bolton for Atkinson Jowett 1860.
Glisburn, nr Kildwick: Malsis Hall for James Lund 1862.
Shipley BCh 1865.
Bradford: Blenheim Tce, Manningham 1865.
Cottingley: Town Hall 1865.
Baildon: Moravian Ch 1868.
Halifax: Princess St, Halifax Permanent Building Soc 1871–3.
Bradford: Ryan St BS 1873; Union Warehouses 1876 dem.

Jagger, Joseph worked in the Huddersfield area in the late eighteenth century, probably as a mason who made designs. His name is associated with the rebuilding of Holy Trinity, Holmfirth (1777–87), St Bartholomew, Meltham (1782–6), and an extension to Hipperholme GS (1783–4).

Johnson, Thomas (d 1814) was probably the son of William Johnson (q.v.). He was in practice in Leeds, where he was responsible for the development of Albion St in the early 1790s, and possibly for Blenheim Tce, Woodhouse Lane after 1795, when he was advertising building land for sale. It is probable that he completed the reconstruction of the S wing of Temple Newsam in 1796 after the death of William, and not impossible that he was partly responsible for St Paul, Leeds. After Johnson's death, **L. Ingham** advertised in the *Leeds Intelligencer* that he would complete his plans.
Bibl: Colvin 326.

Leeds: St Mary (R.C.) 1793 dem.
Halifax: Holy Trinity 1795–8, altered 1877–91.
Leeds: Commercial St, Leeds Library 1808.

Johnson, William (d 1795) was described in the *Leeds Intelligencer* (1 June 1795) as 'many years architect at Temple Newsham near this town'. He was employed by Lord Irwin, and was presumably the 'Mr Johnson' who was responsible for designing the reconstructed S

wing of the house; this was completed in 1796, possibly by Thomas Johnson (q.v.). As Lord Irwin was concerned in the construction of the White Cloth Hall, Leeds (1774–5), Johnson is probably the 'Mr Johnson' who was paid for 'valuing the old White Cloth Hall, taking down the cupola and clock and removing them to the new White Cloth Hall'. Possibly he made the plans for the new Hall and the adjacent Assembly Room (1777). 'W. Johnson' is given as the architect of St Paul, Leeds (1791–3) by T. Allen (*History of the County of York*, 1831, ii, 510), although it is not impossible that this is a mistake for Thomas Johnson.

Jones, George Fowler (1818–1905) practised at 8 Lendal, York.
Bibl: obit *B* (1905), lxxxviii, 272.

Aberford: almshouses for the Misses Gascoigne 1844.
Garforth: St Mary 1844–5.
Barwick-in-Elmet: All Saints, restored 1844–5.

Kay, John Peacock was referred to as a clerk of the works in the early 1870s, but he then set up as an architect at Corn Exchange Chambers, Leeds. He designed the Mechanics' Inst, Calverley (1874), Normanton BCh (1878), and Moortown BS, Leeds (1889).

Kaye, Joseph (1780–1858) was the leading builder in Huddersfield for the first half of the nineteenth century. He was operating in 1798, and he was also a stone merchant, quarry owner, lime-burner and dealer, millowner, maltster and brewer; he referred to himself as an architect from the 1830s, and he is said to have designed St Mary, Mirfield (1825–6), which was rebuilt by G. G. Scott (1871), and St Patrick, Huddersfield (1832). He laid out several streets in Huddersfield for the Ramsden Estate, and built many mills, including four at Folly Hall. In 1851 he employed 75 men. Among the buildings he erected in Huddersfield and district are Holy Trinity (1816–9), Queen St Ch (1819), Ramsden St Ch (1824), Holy Trinity, South Crosland (1827–30), Christ Ch, Linthwaite (1827–8), St John, Golcar (1828–30), All Saints, Paddock (1828), St Stephen, Lindley (1829), St Paul (1829), the Infirmary (1831), St Patrick (1832), the Railway Station (1847–8), the George Hotel (1849–50), and St John, Birkby (1852–3).
Bibl: obit *Huddersfield Examiner* 27 Mar 1858.

Kelly, John (1840–1904) was born at Scarborough, where he was articled to John Petch. He then worked in Manchester for James Medland Taylor, and subsequently for three years in the office of George Edmund Street, where he met John Dando Sedding. He went into partnership in Leeds c.1866 with Richard L. Adams (q.v.), and after the latter's death he took Edward Birchall (q.v.) as a partner. See **Adams, R. L.** for a list of their works.
Bibl: obit *B* (1904), lxxxvi, 641.

Kendall, Jowett was in partnership with **Thomas Barker** at Bank Bldgs, Manchester Rd, Bradford in the 1880s. They designed St John Evangelist, Greengates in 1893.

Kirk, John (1828–86) was the son of a Huddersfield builder of the same name; after running the family business for a time, the younger Kirk set up as an architect in 1850 in John William St, Huddersfield. Ten years later, a branch was opened in Dewsbury with **Albert Holmes Kirk** (d 1920) in charge. In 1863 a second son, **James Sheard Kirk** (b 1842) joined the firm, and then **Frederick Kirk** (1860–1914). The two offices separated in 1905 and continued in existence until the 1930s. They had a general practice firmly based in the West Yorkshire textile towns, although there are unconfirmed suggestions of work in Austria and the Middle East. The range of commissions was comprehensive, including domestic, public and residential buildings. They made plans of working-class housing (e.g. Trevelyan St (1869), Whitehead Lane (1869), Elm St/Newsome Rd (1870) and Carr Pit Lane (1871), all in Huddersfield), as well as for large villas in Edgerton; but one of their most interesting groups of buildings is that at Wilshaw, which was designed for the industrialist and philanthropist, Joseph Hirst.
Bibl: obits, *Huddersfield Weekly Examiner*, 13 Mar 1886, 5 June 1920; *Huddersfield Chronicle*, 13 Mar 1886; *Dewsbury Reporter*, 5 June 1920; unpub notes by Mr Cyril Pearce.

Huddersfield: Brunswick St UMCh 1858–9.
Wilshaw: St Mary 1862–3.
Heckmondwike WCh 1865.
Meltham: Memorial Sch 1868.
Huddersfield: Crosland Moor, workhouse (now St Luke's Hospital) 1870.
Wilshaw: almshouses *c.* 1871; St Mary's Sch *c.*1871; St Mary's Court, housing, *c.*1871, all for Joseph Hirst.
Huddersfield: Paddock CCh 1871–2.
Saltaire: PMCh 1872 dem.
Huddersfield: Ebor Mount, New North Rd 1873; Royal Infirmary, new wing 1874; Hillhouse UMFCh 1874.
Leeds: Joseph St PMCh 1874.
Meltham: St Bartholomew, new chancel etc 1877–8.
Dewsbury: Infirmary 1877–83.
Honley BS 1878.
Meltham: The Mount (with E. Birchall) 1878.
Thornhill: UDC Offices 1879.
Huddersfield: All Saints', Paddock, restoration 1879; Poor Law Union Offices 1880; Holy Trinity, restoration 1880–7; St Paul, restoration 1883; Edgerton Rd/Blacker Lane, pair of villas, Mayfield and Grannum Lodge.
Dewsbury: All Saints', new transepts and chancel (with A. E. Street) 1884–5.
Golcar: St John, restoration 1886.
Dewsbury: Long Causeway, Freemasons' Hall.
Holmfirth: Deanhouse almshouses.

Knowles, George (d 1895) was in practice at 9 Leeds Rd, Bradford in 1853, and he took **William Wilcox** into partnership in the late 60s.

Bradford: Swaine St, warehouse for William Murgatroyd 1859 dem.
Horsforth: alterations to St Margaret 1862–3, later replaced by Pearson's design.
Bingley: Lady Lane, Oakwood, house for

Thomas Garnett 1864.
Bradford: Rebecca St Ragged Sch 1865; North Parade, Inst for the Blind 1868; Market St, store for Brown and Muff 1870; Dudley Hill, Lorne St BS 1874; Hustlergate, Parkinsons Bldgs 1877; Sunbridge Rd, Refuge Chambers 1878.

Landless, William (b 1847) trained in the office of his uncle, John Burnet, in Glasgow before setting up practice in that city in 1873. He worked with Henry E. Clifford, and then went to Leeds, where he was employed as clerk of the works for the Central HGS (1887–9). In 1889 he was appointed architect to Leeds School Board, for whom he designed Harehills BS (1890–1), Isles Lane BS (1891, now Thomas Danby Coll annexe), and Queens Rd BS (1892, now Royal Park Middle Sch). He left Leeds in 1892.

Lawrance, William advertised in the *Leeds Mercury* on 17 Jan 1807 that he was offering his services as an architect. In 1814 he had an office in Park Sq, but there are no known buildings for which he was responsible.

Ledingham, James (1840–1926), son of James Ledingham of Aberdeen, was articled to A. and W. Reid of Elgin and Inverness. He worked in Bradford for Andrews and Pepper (*q.v.*), and set up practice on his own account in the 70s at 53 Market St. He was President of the BSAS in 1896.
Bibl: *CB*, 370.

Bradford: Greenfield CCh, Manningham 1876; Salem Ch, Manningham 1888; houses on the Rosse Estate, Heaton 1889; Manor Row, Yorks Penny Bank 1893; Market St, London and Midland Bank 1893 dem; Children's Hospital 1893; Darley St, Royal Hotel 1897; St Catherine's Home, Manningham 1898.

Leeming, John (*c.*1849–1931) and his brother, **Joseph** (*c.*1841–1929), were the sons of Alfred Leeming of Halifax and were articled to C. F. L. Horsfall (*q.v.*). They opened a practice in Halifax in 1872 and built several designs in the area, but they were also well known outside Yorkshire, and subsequently they opened an office in Old Queen St, Westminster. They won the first premium in the Edinburgh Municipal Buildings competition, and the second in that for the Lisbon Post and Telegraph Offices. In 1881 they won a premium in the Glasgow Municipal Offices competition. Two years later they were placed first in the contest for the Admiralty and War Offices, and in 1891 they were commissioned to design the extensions to the Admiralty. Their other works outside Yorkshire include Kinloch Castle for Sir George Bullough on the Isle of Rhum, and Oldham Market Hall.
Bibl: obits *B* (1929), cxxxvii, 659, (1931), cxl, 808.

Halifax: Booth Town Sch 1874; King Cross MNCSSch 1875; Queen Elizabeth GS, Heath 1877–9; Borough Market 1895–8, incl Old Arcade and 5–7 Russell St.
Leeds: City Markets 1903–04.

Lindley, William (*c.*1739–1818) was a draughtsman and assistant in John Carr's office from the early 1750s until 1774, when he advertised his services in the *York Courant*. He was probably related to Joseph Lindley of Heath, nr Wakefield, whose son, also Joseph (1756–1808) was a surveyor and cartographer. He set up practice in Doncaster, where he built the theatre in 1775 and became a freeman in 1783. In the 1790s he was in partnership with Charles Watson (*q.v.*), and then from *c.* 1810 with John Woodhead (*q.v.*). Lindley continued to design in the Neo-classical tradition tempered with sobriety, which he had learned in Carr's office, employing it in country houses and in the houses he built in Wakefield.
Bibl: Colvin 367f.

Kirklees Priory, designs for internal remodelling for Sir George Armytage 1777.
Ackworth Sch, Meeting House *c.*1779.
Wakefield: St John, St John's Sq, etc 1791–5 (with Watson); South Parade, layout and houses, early 1790s; All Saints, surveyed spire with Watson 1796.
Becca Hall, house for William Markham *c.* 1795 attrib.
Bretton Hall, various suggested improvements for Col T. R. Beaumont *c.*1800.
Parlington Park, unexecuted designs for farm bldgs for Sir Thomas Gascoigne 1803.

Lockwood, Henry Francis (1811–78) came from a building background in Doncaster. He was articled in London to Peter Frederick Robinson, and was then given charge of the supervision of the extensions to York Castle, for which Robinson had been appointed architect in 1826. This stimulated Lockwood's serious interest in antiquities, and in 1834 he published, jointly with Adolphus H. Cates, *The history and antiquities of the fortifications to the city of York*. In 1834 he set up in practice in Hull, where he designed a number of Neo-classical buildings, such as Trinity House Ch (1839–43), extensions to the Royal Infirmary (1840), and Gt Thornton St Ch (1843). Lockwood became a partner of William Mawson (*q.v.*) in 1849, and they opened an office in Bradford, where they became one of the leading firms. They submitted designs in many competitions, including the limited contest for the Law Courts in the Strand (1866–7). Lockwood moved to London in 1874, where he was responsible for the City Temple (1873–4) and the Civil Service Stores, Strand (1876–7). He was first President of the BSAS when it was founded in 1874.
Bibl: obit, *B* (1878), xxxvi, 788.

Bradford: Market St, Yorkshire Banking Co 1850; St George's Hall 1851–3.
Saltaire: mill for Titus Salt 1851–3, followed by dwellings and public bldgs.
Bradford: Union Workhouse 1852 (now part of St Luke's Hospital); Leeds Rd, warehouse for Titus Salt 1853 dem; Manningham, villas in Mornington Villas *c.*1853–71.
Calverley: Ferncliffe, house for Briggs Priestley *c.*1855.
Stanningley CCh 1855 (now used for industrial purposes).
Bradford: 47 Well St, warehouse 1855.

Cleckheaton: Providence Pl CCh 1857–9.
Halifax: Crossley St, Princess St etc, various bldgs for John Crossley, incl Mechanics' Hall and White Swan Hotel c.1857–8.
Bradford: Lumb Lane, mills for James Drummond 1858.
Saltaire CCh 1858–9.
Bradford: 4 Currer St, warehouse for N. Reichenheim, Sons and Co 1859; Horton Lane CCh 1860–2; Manningham, villas in Mount Royd 1863–4; Eye and Ear Hospital 1864–5, enlarged 1873; Exchange 1864–7.
Apperley Bridge: Cragg Royd, house for Nathaniel Briggs 1865.
Bingley: Longwood, house for William Marshall Selwyn 1867.
Bradford: Bridge St, Victoria Hotel 1867.
Keighley: Mechanics' Inst 1868, enlarged 1887, dem.
Saltaire: Sch 1868.
Rawdon: Woodleigh Hall, house for Moses Bottomley 1869.
Bradford: Town Hall 1869–73.
Lightcliffe CCh 1870.
Bradford: Vicar Lane, warehouse for American and Chinese Export Co (now De Vere House) 1871; Wigan St, St Thomas's Sch 1871; Kirkgate Market 1871–8.
Saltaire: Inst 1872.
Bradford: Bank St, Yorkshire Banking Co 1872–4 dem; Vicar Lane, warehouse for Law, Russell and Co 1873–4; Feversham St BS 1873; Harris St, Sion BCh 1873; Salt Memorial 1873; Legrams Mill for George Hodgson 1873; Airedale Coll 1874–7.
Drighlington BS 1874.
Bradford: Liberal Club 1877; Kirkgate, Bradford Club 1877.
Wakefield: Westgate, Wakefield and Barnsley Union Bank 1877–8.
Leeds: South Parade, Victoria Chambers dem.

Mallinson, George (1831–1908), a native of Dewsbury, was articled to Barry and Brown, Liverpool. In 1854 he went to New Zealand, where he built what was claimed to be the first stone church in that country at Port Lyttleton. In the early 1870s he was back in England, and in partnership with William Bakewell (q.v.); subsequently, under his own name, he had offices in Leeds, Dewsbury and Ripon. He designed a number of chapels, including Bruntcliffe MNCCh (1875) and Morley WCh (1878).
Bibl: obit B (1908), xcv, 686.

Mallinson, James was possibly related to **William Mallinson**, a Halifax mason, who built (designed?) the old church at Lightcliffe (1774–5), of which the tower is still standing. There are no known details of his career before 1847, when he was in partnership with Thomas Healey I (q.v.) at 64 Tyrrel St, Bradford and 15 Mount St, Halifax. They built up a large ecclesiastical practice, which was continued by Healey's sons, Thomas II and Francis (q.v.). After Healey's death, Mallinson was in practice with William Swinden Barber (q.v.) for a time, at 6 George St, Halifax.

Bradford: St Mary, Wyke 1846; St Paul,

Manningham 1847–8.
Mytholmroyd: St Michael 1847–8, enlarged 1887.
Baildon: St John 1848.
Bradford: St Matthew, Bankfoot 1848–9; Low Moor, parsonage 1848; Wyke, parsonage 1848.
Halifax: King Cross Sch 1848.
Clayton: St John Baptist 1849–50.
Leeds: All Saints, York Rd 1849–50.
Shelf: St Michael and All Angels 1849.
Heptonstall: St Thomas 1850–4, remodelled 1963–4.
South Ossett: Christ Ch 1850–1.
Bradford: St Andrew, North Horton 1851–2, spire added later.
Barkisland: Christ Ch 1852–3.
Bradford: St Andrew, Lister Hills 1853.
Thorner: St Peter 1855.
East Keswick: St Mary Magdalene 1856–7.
Bradford: St Mark, Low Moor 1857.
Thornhill Lees: Holy Innocents 1858.
Clifton: St John the Evangelist 1859.
Bradford: St Philip, Girlington 1860; St Stephen, Bowling 1860.
Halifax: All Souls' cemetery ch 1860 dem.
Bradford: St Mary, Laisterdyke 1861; All Saints, Little Horton Green 1861–4; St Luke 1862.
Dewsbury: St Mark 1862–5.
Arthington: St Peter 1864.
Halifax: Parish Ch Sch 1867.

Man(n), Thomas, of York, was paid £93 4s 2d in 1672 'for rebuilding ye Cross on ye Pavement' (York Ref Lib, City of York Chamberlain's Accounts, vol 26, 38–40); this was presumably the Ionic Market Cross, now destroyed, illustrated in Francis Drake's *Eboracum*, 1735, 293. Mann's craft seems to be established by a signature on a monument to Katherine Constable (d 1677) in All Saints', Rudston, Humberside, 'Tho Man, Eboraci Sculpsit'. He was also employed to execute additions to Londesborough Hall, apparently according to a design made by Robert Hooke for Richard, 1st Earl of Burlington. Hooke's diary refers to 'Man of York' in October 1676, and in the following January he 'met Man, with him to Boyles' (Robinson, H. W., and Adams, W. (ed), *Robert Hooke, Diary*, London 1935, 249, 279). Mann was corresponding in 1680 with Richard Beaumont of Whitley Beaumont, for whom he had fixed a quadrant, although warning that the hours 'are calculated from London Lattitude and therefore will not serve here'; this suggests that Mann had some practical knowledge of science and mathematics and might explain his acquaintance with Hooke. He also sent Beaumont 'ye Model of ye House', enclosing plans of Whitley Beaumont, one of which shows a proposed remodelling of the east wing and a new north wing with an internal arcade (Kirklees Library and Museums Service, WBM/5–6). Mann recommended Beaumont that if he decided to act on the proposed design (which seems to have been used eventually), he should choose his men carefully, because 'those who are unaccustomed to such kinde of work [would] but Botch it'.

Mawson, William (1828–89) was born in Leeds, the son of William Mawson, a paper manufacturer. He became a resident in Bradford when he and Henry Francis Lockwood (q.v.) were successful in obtaining the commission to design St George's Hall (1851), the foundation of the success of their practice. Lockwood went to live in London in 1874, and after his death in 1878 the firm was renamed W. and R. Mawson, with **Richard Mawson** (1834–1904) as the second partner; under that title they enlarged Keighley Technical Sch (now dem) in 1887. Subsequently, the practice was known as Mawson and Hudson, and they were responsible for Cleckheaton Town Hall (1890–2).
Bibl: obit BN (1889), lvii, 639.

Milnes, Eli (1830–99) was the son of Henry Milnes of Tollerhall, Bradford. He was articled to Walker Rawstorne (q.v.), and then became a partner of Jonathan Dixon (q.v.); in 1853 their office was in Swaine St. In 1863 Charles France (q.v.) and Milnes went into partnership, and the firm, Milnes and France, became one of the largest in the town. Subsequently, **Arthur Alderson France** and **Charles E. Milnes** were taken into partnership in 1888.
Bibl: obit B (1899), lxxvii, 613.

Leeds: Holbeck Mechanics' Inst 1858.
Bradford: 30 Well St, warehouse for John Foster 1858–63 dem; Thornton Rd, Oakroyd Dyeworks 1858–61; 53–5 Leeds Rd, warehouses for David Abercrombie and Samuel Tetley 1859–62; 72 Vicar Lane, warehouse c.1860; 8 Currer St, warehouse 1861; 10 Currer St, warehouse 1862; Peel Sq, warehouses for McKean Tetley 1862 dem; Thornton Rd, Alston Works 1862–6; Leeds Rd, warehouse for A. and S. Henry 1863 dem.
Queensbury: Albert Memorial Fountain 1863.
Bradford: Manningham, Thornfield, house for J. R. Armitage c. 1864; 43 Well St, warehouse for E. Lassen 1864; 45 Well St, warehouse 1864; Royal Infirmary, extensions 1864, 1873; Thornton Rd, baths and wash-houses 1865; Manningham, Ladye Royde Hall, house for Henry Illingworth 1865; Thornton Rd, Whetley Mills for Jeremiah Illingworth 1865; Toller Lane, Woodlands, house for Angus Holden 1866 dem; 66 Vicar Lane, warehouse (later owned by Briggs Priestley and Sons) 1866–7; Beacon Rd, Bank Top Mills 1866.
Queensbury: Bank Top Mills 1866.
Bradford: 1 Burnett St, warehouse 1867; 39 Well St, warehouse 1867; 64 Vicar Lane, warehouse for J. P. Kessler 1867–8; 62 George St/Leeds Rd, warehouse for Schuster, Fulda and Co 1869–73; Market St/Lower Cheapside, restaurant etc 1870 dem.
Birkenshaw: St Paul, roof reconstructed 1870.
Bradford: 61 East Parade, warehouse for Julius Delius 1871–3; Market St, Bradford District Bank (now National Westminster) 1872–3; 26 East Parade, warehouse for S. L. Behrens and Co 1873; Peckover St, warehouse for Julius Delius 1873; Well St, warehouse for Hardy Nathan and Sons 1873–4; Bowling Back Lane BS 1873 dem; Dudley Hill BS 1873; Barkerend BS 1873; Kirkgate, Beckett's Bank (now National Westminster) 1874; St Philip's Sch, Girlington 1874.

Airedale: Emm Lane, Independent College 1874.
Calverley: Knottfield House, house for Hermann Averdieck 1874.
Bradford: 25 Bolton Rd, warehouse for Charles Semon and Co 1877–8; Market St, Swan Arcade 1877–81 dem.
Clayton: Oak Mills for J. Benn and Co 1880.
Bradford: Princeville Combing Works 1886.
Cleckheaton: St Andrew, Oakenshaw 1889.
Bradford: Royal Victoria Nurses' Home 1896–8; Chapel St, warehouse for Edelstein, Moser and Co 1902.
Keighley: Victoria Station Hotel.
Leeds: Whitehall Rd, electrical works and generating station.

Moffat, William Lambie won the competition for Wakefield Corn Exchange in 1836, and designed Holy Trinity, Thurgoland (1841–2), now in S Yorkshire. He went into partnership with William Hurst (q.v.) some time after the death of John Woodhead (q.v.), an arrangement which seems to have lasted until c.1850. See **Hurst, William** for a list of their works.

Moore, Richard William was a pupil of R. D. Chantrell (q.v.), 'with whom I was during the whole time of pulling down the old and erection of the new [Leeds Parish Church of St Peter], having had my share in making the working drawings, &c., and also of superintending the erection thereof'. He wrote A history of the Parish Church of Leeds, Leeds 1877. Moore acted as architect and builder in connection with 3–5 Woodhouse Sq, Leeds (1845–6).

Moore, Thomas had offices in Sunderland and Leeds; the latter, at 34A Bond St, was possibly run by **John Hutchinson Moore** and **Thomas Angelo Moore**. They designed the Theatre Royal, Leeds (1876).

Morant, Alfred William Whitehead (1828–81) held the appointments of Surveyor to Great Yarmouth Corporation (1856–64), City Engineer, Norwich (1865–72), before taking up the post of Borough Surveyor in Leeds (1873–81). During the time he was in Leeds, his work included the laying out of new roads and drainage systems, the widening of Wellington Bridge, the building of several police and fire stations, the extension of Kirkgate Market (1875–6), and alterations to the Town Hall in 1877 (including the addition of a gallery and the covering of the corridor walls with decorative tiles). Morant also edited Dodgson's Guide to Leeds (1879).
Bibl: Papworth, W., Memoir of Alfred William Whitehead Morant, reprinted with additions from B (1881), xli, 228f.

Mountain, Charles II was the son of **Charles Mountain I** (c.1743–1805), who was in practice in Hull. The younger Mountain remained there until 1834, when he removed to Malton. He is known to have worked in Wakefield on at least two occasions, when he rebuilt part of the spire of All Saints' Ch (1823), and designed the Savings Bank (1834).

Moxson, John (1700–82) held the appointment of Surveyor of the Highways in Leeds, where the Coloured or Mixed Cloth Hall was built to his design (1756–8). In 1765 he made plans for additional galleries in St John's Ch. It was probably his son, John Moxson, who was employed by Joseph Gott as surveyor or measurer for the erection of Bean Ing Mill, Leeds (1792–3).

Moyser, James (d 1753) was the son of John Moyser (d 1738), MP for Beverley (1705–08), where a traveller in 1724 saw his 'beautifull Gardens . . . contain[ing] great variety of Avenues of Firrs, of Parterre, of Statues; & also of Arbours, Seats & Vases in Trilliage Work; besides two Seats one of Ionic pillasters, the other of Doric pillars painted by Parmentier'. James Moyser, who spent most of his life in the army, was largely responsible for the designs of Bretton Hall for Sir William Wentworth (q.v.), c.1720, and Nostell Priory for Sir Rowland Winn c.1729, in collaboration with their owners.

Muschamp, John (d 1805) was the master mason employed by John Carr to build Harewood House. He rebuilt the tower of All Saints', Kirkby Overblow in 1781. His son, **John Muschamp II**, made designs in 1803 and 1805 for lodges at Harewood, and in 1801 for restoring Ledston Lodge, a turreted hunting lodge in Ledston Park.

Neill, James had an office in 1870 at 11 Cookridge St, Leeds, where he offered his services as a building surveyor and quantity surveyor. His son, **Archibald Neill** (1856–1933) joined the firm and was probably the designer of such buildings as Leatham, Tew and Co's Bank (now Barclays), Wood St, Wakefield (1880), the Dispensary, Pontefract (1880), and Newton Park Union Ch, Leeds (1887). The firm was still in existence in 1914 at 33 Park Row.

Nelson, Charles Sebastian (1844–1924) was in practice in the 1870s with **Alline James Nelson** at 15 Albert Chambers, Leeds, as well as in Derby. They designed Pudsey MNCCh (1872), and Wharfedale Union Workhouse, Otley (1873).

Oates, John (d 1831) practised at 7 Union St, Halifax from c.1819 until his death. **Matthew Oates** and **Thomas Pickersgill** (both of whom practised later in York) completed the outstanding work after his death. Oates's work was mainly ecclesiastical, and outside West Yorkshire he designed St Mary, Birdsall (1824), Christ Ch, Harrogate (1830–1), and St Mark, Shelton (1831–3).
Bibl: Colvin, 422f.

Sowerby Bridge: Christ Ch 1819, chancel added 1873–89.
Wilsden: St Matthew 1823–5.
Shipley: St Paul 1823–5.
Rishworth GS 1827–8.
Lindley: St Stephen 1828–9.
Paddock: All Saints 1828–9.
Idle: Holy Trinity 1828–30.
Halifax: New Rooms 1828.
Huddersfield: St Paul 1828–30; Infirmary 1829–31.
Halifax: St James 1830–1 dem.

Hebden Bridge: St James 1832–3.
Crosstone: St Paul 1833–5 (prob largely Pickersgill's work).
Golcar: St John, repaired 1834.

Paine, James (1717–89) was born in the south of England, and according to his own account he 'began the study of architecture . . . under the tuition of a man of genius (the late Mr Thomas Jersey), and at the age of nineteen was entrusted to conduct a building of consequence in the West Riding of the county of York'. This was Nostell Priory, which had been designed by Col. James Moyser (q.v.) and the owner of the house, Sir Rowland Winn. Paine was probably responsible for the design of the interior of the house, as well as for supervising its erection. He gradually worked up a practice in Yorkshire, greatly helped by the advertisement afforded by Doncaster Mansion House (1745–8). While working in West Yorkshire, he married, and his only son, **James Paine II** (1745–1829), was baptized at St Giles', Pontefract. Paine and Sir Robert Taylor were said by Sir William Chambers to have 'divided the practice of the profession between them till Robert Adam entered the list', and Paine 'distinguished himself by the superiority of his taste in the nicer and more delicate parts of decoration'.
Bibl: Paine, J., Plans, elevations and sections of noblemen and gentlemen's houses . . . executed in the counties of Derby, Durham, Middlesex, Northumberland, Nottingham and York, London 1767, 1783; Colvin, 431ff; Leach, P., The life and work of James Paine, unpublished D.Phil thesis, Oxford 1975.

Nostell Priory, supervision of new house for Sir Rowland Winn c. 1737–50.
Heath House, extensive additions to house for Robert Hopkinson 1744–5.
Pontefract: Neat (or Naut) Market (now Cornmarket), house for Joseph Kitchingman c.1745–50, attrib.
Milnes Bridge House, new house for William Radcliffe c.1750, attrib.
Bramham, The Biggin, alterations to house for – Allison c.1750–6.
Bierley Hall, refacing of S front and internal alterations for Richard Richardson c.1750, attrib.
Kirkstall, New Grange, extensive alterations to house for Walter Wade 1752, attrib.
Whitley Beaumont, belvedere (now in ruined condition) and remodelling of Great Hall for Richard Beaumont c.1752–4, attrib. dem.
St Ives, house for Benjamin Ferrand 1759 dem.
Bramham Park, temple (now chapel) and additional pavilions to Stable (attrib) for George Lane-Fox c.1760.
Pontefract: house in Market Pl (now Barclays Bank), prob for Revd Thomas Heron c.1760, attrib.
Bradford: Town Hill, new house for John Buck c.1764–8, attrib.

Parkinson, Walter Henshaw had an office in 1870 in Albion St, Leeds. He improved St Peter, Gildersome (1872), and partly rebuilt St Mary, Boston Spa (1872–3).

Payton, Frederick Bartram worked in Bradford. He designed Bingley BCh (c.1874).

Perkin, William Belton was probably a son of William Perkin, master mason, who was employed in the 1790s on the building of St John's Ch, Wakefield. In 1830, Perkin was in practice in the Corn Exchange, Wakefield, and he was possibly responsible for the design of St Austin's RC Ch, Wakefield (1828). He exhibited unsuccessful designs in 1834 for the West Riding Proprietary Sch, Wakefield, and Woodhouse Cemetery, Leeds. By that time he was in practice at White Hart Yard, Leeds; and by 1839 he had taken **Elisha Backhouse** into partnership at Commercial Bldgs. Later they were joined by Perkin's son, **Henry Perkin** (1847–1925), who subsequently took **George Bertram Bulmer** (d 1916) into partnership. William Perkin acted as supervising architect for George Gilbert Scott when the latter's design for Beckett's Bank, Leeds was being erected. Henry Perkin was President of the LYAS 1888–90, and Bulmer held the same office 1892–4 and 1904–05.

Heckmondwike: Blanket Hall 1838–40 dem.
Bradford: Leeds Rd, Mechanics' Inst 1839–40 dem.
Guiseley: Parochial Sch 1840.
Leeds: St Luke, North St 1841.
Huddersfield: Highfield CCh 1843–4.
Leeds: Burley National Sch 1845.
Shadwell: Sch and residence 1846.
Leeds: Moral and Industrial Training Sch 1846–8; Killingbeck, house for E. Ward 1847; St James, Manston 1847; Borough Gaol, Armley 1847, enlarged 1857.
Shadwell: parsonage 1848.
Morton: St Luke, restored 1849–50.
Cullingworth: St John Evangelist 1851–3.
Oulton Hall, extensions to house for John Calverley 1851–74.
Bramham: All Saints, altered 1853.
Leeds: St Matthias, Burley 1853–4.
Eastwood: St Mary Virgin 1854–5 dem.
Pudsey: St Paul 1855–6.
Leeds: Workhouse 1858–61; Belgrave St, Synagogue 1860–1; St Mary the Virgin, Hunslet 1862–4.
Allerton Bywater: St Mary the Less 1863–5.
Leeds: St Margaret, Bramley 1863; Queens Hotel 1863 dem; St Stephen, Kirkstall, restored and enlarged 1863–4; Gt George St, (old) Masonic Hall 1865; St Matthew, Chapel Allerton, alterations 1866 dem; St Peter, Hunslet Moor 1866–8; St Jude, Hunslet, altered 1867; St Peter, Hunslet Moor, parsonage 1870; St Matthew, Chapel Allerton, Sch 1872.
Arthington: Sch and house 1872–3.
Leeds: Roundhay WCh c. 1874; Primrose Hill BS 1874 dem; South Accommodation Rd BS 1874; New Wortley MCh 1875–6; Millgarth, adaptation as Model Lodging House 1878.
Pontefract: Town Hall, Assembly Room 1881.
Leeds: Kirkgate, Central Cocoa House 1883; St Cuthbert, Hunslet 1883–4.
Halifax: Yorkshire Penny Bank 1886.
Leeds: Infirmary St, Yorkshire Penny Bank 1886; Park Row, National Provincial Bank 1892 dem; Wellington St, warehouse for Crowe and Co (with Corson and Jones q.v.) 1900–01; Infirmary St, City Chambers c.1907 dem; South Parade/Park Row, Scottish Union and National Insurance Co 1909; East Parade, Atlas Bldgs 1910.

Peterson, Edward Paterson worked at 5 Charles St, Bradford in the 1870s. He designed St Peter, Allerton (1879).

Petty, Francis William designed additional buildings for Crossley's Dean Clough Mills (c.1867–9), although the earliest record of his practice in Halifax is 1877, when he had an office at 12 Waterhouse St. He also designed the New CCh, Halifax (c.1878). In the 90s, there was a partnership between his office, and that of Roger Ives (q.v.); the firm was known as Petty and Ives, and **Charles H. Petty** (d 1935) was in charge.

Pritchett, James Pigott (1789–1868) was born at St Petrox, Pembrokeshire. He was articled to James Medland of Southwark, and then worked for two years in the office of D. A. Alexander. He became a student at the Royal Academy in 1808, and began to practise in London, but by 1813 he was in York, where he was in partnership with Charles Watson (q.v.) until 1831. He was married twice, and by his second wife he had three sons, **James Pigott** (1830–1911), **Charles** and **George**, who all became architects and worked for a time with their father. His finest Classical design is the railway station in Huddersfield, and it is unfortunate his complementary design for a Town Hall on an adjacent site was not built to complete the group. His designs in York include the new façade to Burlington's Assembly Rooms (1828), the Cemetery Chapel (1836–37) and the Savings Bank, St Helen's Sq (1829–30).
Bibl: Broadbent, G. H., 'The life and work of Pritchett of York', *Studies in architectural history* (ed Singleton, W. A.), London 1956, ii, 102ff; Colvin, 477ff.

Woolley Hall, lodge and gateway for Godfrey Wentworth 1814.
Wakefield: West Riding Lunatic Asylum 1816–8; Wood St, Library and News Room (Music Saloon or Mechanics' Inst) 1820–2.
Leeds: layout of Hanover Sq, Little Woodhouse for George Rawson, partly executed, 1823.
Huddersfield: Ramsden St Ch 1824 dem.
Leeds: layout of proposed New Town (Buslingthorpe) c.1828.
Lotherton Hall, decoration of drawing-room for Richard Oliver Gascoigne c.1828.
Nostell Priory, extension to stables 1828–9.
Huddersfield: St Peter, rebuilding 1834–6.
Meltham: St Bartholomew, addition of W tower and N aisle 1835.
Brearton: St John 1836.
Bradford: High St, Airedale Coll Ch 1837–9.
Meltham Mills: St James 1838, rebuilt on larger scale by Pritchett 1845–6.
Huddersfield: New North Rd, Huddersfield Coll 1839–40.
Burley-in-Wharfedale: Independent Ch 1839–40.
Bradford: Westgate Ch, remodelled 1840.
Brotherton: St Edward rebuilt 1842–3.
Huddersfield: Railway Station 1846–50.
Ackworth: Friends' Meeting House 1846–7; Flounders Inst 1847 dem.
Huddersfield: Lion Arcade 1852–4.
Leeds: Sheepscar WCh 1861 dem.
J. P. Pritchett II designed Pudsey CCh 1865–6,

Ilkley CCh 1868, and Armley Mortuary Ch, Leeds 1885.

Rawstorne, Walker (d 1867) was the son of **John Rawstorne**, an architect who had been a pupil of James Wyatt and advertised in the *York Chronicle*, 19 March 1807, to thank 'his friends for the favours already received during his residence at York'. He wished to 'inform them and the public in general that he continues to draw Plans of Buildings, superintend the same and to Measure and Value as usual', and he claimed he had 'had the direction of several very considerable Public as well as Private Buildings, in this and other Counties', concluding with an offer to teach drawing on moderate terms. Subsequently, the elder Rawstorne practised in Birmingham, and then in Doncaster; his son, who was probably articled to him, was in practice at Halifax Rd, Bradford in 1835, and later in Westbrook Pl until c.1853.

Bingley: All Saints, N ch for Walter Ferrand 1834.
Bradford: St James 1836–8 dem; St Paul, Buttershaw 1838; Westgate, Infirmary 1840–3 dem; St Jude, Manningham 1840–3.
Burley-in-Wharfedale: St Mary the Blessed Virgin 1841–3.
Yeadon: St John 1841–4, tower truncated.
Ingrow: St John, Paper Mill Bridge 1841–2.
Bradford: Leeds Rd, warehouse for Russell Douglas and Co 1844 dem; Leeds Rd, warehouse for Oxley and Co 1844 dem; St Luke, Eccleshill 1846–8, tower truncated.

Richardby, James (c.1776–1846) practised in Bradford; in 1822 he was in Hall Ings, and he remained in practice until his death. His known work in Bradford includes alterations to the Market House, Hall Ings (1823), warehouses in Piccadilly (1830–4), the Court House, Hall Ings (1834–5), and Field House, Smith Lane for Mrs Susannah Ward (1835–6); the last is now part of the Royal Infirmary. Richardby also made the design for terrace housing in Eldon Pl, Manningham (1845).

Robinson, Percy (1868–1950), the son of Daniel Robinson of Leeds, commenced practice in his home town in 1881 after being articled to G. W. Atkinson and working for T. Winn (q.v.). Most of his buildings date from the beginning of the present century, including Armley Public Library (1902), a shop for Messrs Rawcliffe's, Boar Lane (1905), Leeds Exchange, Briggate (1907), and Firemen's Flats in Park Lane (1909 dem), all in Leeds, and a commercial bldg in Cross Sq/Bull Ring, Wakefield (1906). **William Alban Jones** (1875–1960) was in partnership for a time with Robinson, who is probably best remembered for his books, *Relics of old Leeds* (1896), and *Leeds: old and new* (1926).
Bibl: obit YP, 12 Jan 1950; CB, 372.

Robinson, —, of Middleton, made designs in 1796 for alterations to Milnes Bridge House, the seat of Joseph Pickford, who inherited in the previous year and took the name of Radcliffe in compliance with the wishes of his uncle, William Radcliffe. The house had been built c.1750 for the latter's father, William Radcliffe, possibly from a design by James Paine (q.v.).

Sharp, Richard Hey (c.1793–1853) was the son of Richard Sharp, of a Gildersome family. After working in the office of Peter Atkinson II (q.v.), he made a long journey of three years on the Continent, where he met and travelled with Joseph Woods, the author of *Letters of an Architect* (1828). After returning to Yorkshire, Sharp became a partner of his former master, Atkinson; the buildings listed under **Atkinson** between the dates of 1819 and 1828 were their joint work, although it is likely many were Sharp's. In 1822 he exhibited under his own name a design for 'the intended Church at Woodhouse, Leeds' in the exhibition of the Northern Society for the Encouragement of the Fine Arts. In 1827–30 Sharp worked with William Wilkins on the final design and erection of the Greek Revival museum (now Yorkshire Museum) in York. In 1828 Sharp set up his own practice at 18 St Saviourgate, York with his brother, **Samuel Sharp** (1808–74) as partner. They designed the circular museum in Scarborough (1828) and made a plan for laying out villas and a crescent in the Valley, part of which was later realised. After Richard Hey Sharp's death in 1853, his brother moved to Leeds, where he died.
Bibl: Colvin 536.

Wakefield: St James, Thornes 1829–31 (Samuel Sharp alone).
Bradford: Holy Trinity, Low Moor 1836–7; St John, Manchester Rd 1838–9 dem; St John, Bowling 1840–2.
Horbury: National Sch 1845.

Shaw, Thomas was associated with the practice of R. D. Chantrell (q.v.) in the early 1840s, when he was architect jointly with Chantrell or his son for two churches, St Paul, Denholme Gate (1843–6) and All Saints, Roberttown (1844–6). He was in practice on his own account at 17 Park Row, Leeds in 1853, moving to 2 Belgrave Sq in 1861. He made alterations to Woodhouse Grove Sch, Rawdon (1847), designed Great George St BCh, Leeds (which was 'pulled down a few years after building') in the 1850s, the first of the Italianate chimneys (based on the Lamberti tower in Verona) for Harding's Tower Works (1864), St Simon, Ventnor St, Leeds (1865), and Stanley WCh (1874).

Shelton, Theophilus (d 1717) was Registrar of Deeds in the West Riding 1704–17. In 1694 he bought an estate at Heath, near Wakefield, on which he built a house for his own occupation, Eshald House; this was subsequently sold to John Smyth and forms the central section of the present Heath Hall. In 1699 Shelton sent Richard Beaumont a design for a garden house to be built at Whitley Beaumont, and in 1702 he designed Tong Hall for Sir George Tempest. Almost certainly he made the plans for Lupset Hall (1716) for his brother-in-law, Richard Witton, and it is possible he designed Alverthorpe Hall for Daniel Maude, and a building (observatory?) at Clubcliff (or Clumpcliffe) Hall, Methley, which was added soon after John Savile purchased the house from Edward Frank of Campsall in 1691. Shelton was requested to provide a design for a cupola for St

Giles, Pontefract in 1710; if this was done, it seems not to have been erected, but his designs for market crosses for Wakefield (1707) and Beverley (1714) were built. The latter survives. In 1715 Shelton '[one of many solicitants], was told of a vacancy for a chaplain at Cannons', the palace built in Middlesex for James Brydges, 1st Duke of Chandos. He was 'engaged for that post though "he need not yet present himself "' (Baker, C. H. C., and M. I., *The life and circumstances of James Brydges First Duke of Chandos*, London 1946, 126). Had Shelton lived, he would have been a member of the household in which Handel was resident composer, and at the time when James Gibbs was continuing the building of the mansion for which William Talman and John James had successively been employed as architects; but he died at Nottingham in 1717, possibly without having taken up the appointment.

Simpson, Edward (1844–1937) was the son of a Hull builder. After being articled to a local architect, he moved to London for a few years, and then to Bradford, where he remained in practice until 1914, when he handed over to his son, **Charles Simpson**; the firm closed only in 1939. Simpson had a large, almost exclusively Roman Catholic, practice, and he built 12 churches, at least 10 chapels and chapel-schools, countless schools, presbyteries and alterations or additions to existing churches in West Yorkshire alone. His designs were often bizarre, sometimes grotesque, but usually deeply felt individual interpretations of the Gothic style.
Bibl: Chappell, D. M., *Catholic churches – Diocese of Leeds 1793–1916*, unpublished PhD thesis, University of Sheffield 1972.

Bradford: St Joseph SchCh 1868; Horton Bank Top BS 1873; St Mary 1874–6.
Bingley: Sacred Heart SchCh 1877.
Ilkley: Sacred Heart of Jesus 1878–9.
Wetherby: St Joseph 1880–1.
Batley Carr: St Joseph SchCh 1881.
Pudsey: St Joseph SchCh 1884.
Bradford: St Joseph 1885–7; St Ann 1890.
Huddersfield: St Joseph 1894.
Halifax: Sacred Heart and St Bernard 1895–7.
Morley: St Francis of Assisi 1904–05.
Keighley: St Anne, enlarged and reorganised 1907.
Rawdon: Our Lady of Good Counsel and St Joseph 1907–09.
Birstall: St Patrick 1908.

Simpson, James (1792–1864) was a native of Aberford. He was a joiner and builder who lived at 41 (later 12) Trafalgar St, Leeds, close to Brunswick MCh (J. Botham 1824–5), for which he contracted as joiner. In the 1839 *Directory*, he is described as an architect, and the entries continue until 1867. Simpson's buildings seem to have consisted entirely of Methodist chapels, in York, Barnsley, Burnley, Warrington and Derby, in addition to the large number in Leeds.

Leeds: St Peter's St Ch 1834; Oxford Pl Ch 1835, remodelled Danby and Thorp 1896–1903; Wesley Ch, Meadow Lane (prob remodelled) 1837; Lady Lane Ch 1840; Brunswick Sch 1846; Hanover Pl Ch 1847; Richmond Hill Ch 1849.

Bradford: Eccleshill WMCh 1855.
Morley: Queen St WMCh 1860–1.

Simpson, John (b 1831) was aprenticed to his father, James Simpson (q.v.); in 1855–6 he assisted Cuthbert Brodrick (q.v.) in preparing the set of drawings (for which Brodrick received a silver medal) submitted in the competition for the completion of Lille Cathedral. Possibly Simpson was working in Brodrick's office until it closed in 1869, as he first appeared in the *Directory* under his own name as an architect in 1870, when he was practising at 41 Cobourg St, Leeds. He designed some chapels, Baptist Tabernacle, Morley (1874), and Whingate WMCh, Leeds (1878–9), and he collaborated with G. F. Danby (q.v.) in 1906 on Park WMCh, Cross Flatts, Leeds. He also provided designs for several houses in the Headingley area, including Bardon Hill (c.1875) for Thomas Simpson, and Weetwood Lodge for Frederick Baines.

Smith, George was in practice at 101 Park Lane, Leeds in 1856; he moved to York Pl, then to Park Pl, where he remained until the mid-1880s. He made unexecuted designs for the south side of Hanover Sq, and for a station in North St for a proposed railway to Roundhay Park (c.1874). Among his buildings in Leeds are Burley Lawn UMFCh (1859), Hunslet Mechanics' Inst (1861), and Thornton's Arcade, Briggate (1877–8). It is possible he was also the designer of Thornton's other speculations, Thornton's Buildings (1873) and the White Swan Varieties (1865, now City Palace of Varieties).

Smith, George was working in 1870 at Popplewell's Bldgs, Market St, Bradford, and he seems to have remained in practice in the town until the late 80s. He designed Westwood Lodge, Ilkley for Leonard Horner (1875), and probably several similar houses in Bradford and Ilkley, but he is best known for Cliffe Castle, Keighley (1875–8), the remarkable house of Henry Isaac Butterfield. Smith's portrait is incorporated in the carved decoration in the Entrance Hall.

Smith, Stephen Ernest (1845–1925), the son of John Wales Smith of Leeds, was articled to William Hill (q.v.). He then studied at the Royal Academy, subsequently working as an improver with G. Somers Clarke. He travelled in France, Italy and Germany before setting up practice in Wellington Chambers, Leeds in 1868. Nine years later he took **John Tweedale** (1853–1905), who had been articled to him, into partnership; but this was dissolved in 1903.
Bibl: *CB*, 373; obit *B* (1905), lxxxviii, 576.

Leeds: 1–2 York Pl, warehouses c.1870; 6 New Briggate c. 1874; Shaw Lane, three houses 1875; Adel Towers, house for J. A. Hirst c.1875 dem; Kirkstall CCh 1880; Meanwood Rd Baptist SSch (now Ch of God) 1881; Bond St, Imperial Fire and Life Assurance Co 1881 dem; North Hill, Headingley, Gothic billiard-room for J. Wilkinson 1881; Grace St, warehouse 1882 dem; South Parade, Leeds and County Conservative Club, remodelled 1885 dem; Woodbourne, Roundhay, house for R. Buckton c.1888 dem; St Matthias' Sch, Burley 1890; Headingley

cricket ground stand 1890 dem; March Inst, Woodhouse 1892; Park Row, City and County Bank 1892; houses at Newton Park, Potternewton c.1894; New Briggate, Grand Arcade 1896–7; Clarendon Rd, parish room etc; St Luke's Day Sch.
Garforth: Manor Farm, buildings for Agricultural College (later part of University of Leeds) 1900.

Sorby, Thomas Charles (1836–1924) was born at Chevet, nr Wakefield. After travelling in France, he went to London to work in the office of Charles Reeves, County Court Surveyor, who designed the Bradford County Court (1859). Sorby submitted a design for St Pancras Hotel, London (1865), which was placed fourth after those by G. G. Scott, G. S. Clarke and E. M. Barry, but he won outright the competition for Bromley Town Hall (1864), and designed St Michael and All Angels, Neepsend, Sheffield (1866–7). He succeeded Reeves as County Court Surveyor in 1867, and was responsible for a large number of County Court buildings, including those in Leeds (c.1869), Halifax (1870) and Barnsley (1871). In 1885 he left England for Canada, where he designed for the Canadian Pacific Railway (Glacier House Hotel, stations at Peterborough and Yorkville, etc), and was also responsible for a number of buildings in British Columbia, including the Bank of British Columbia, Vancouver (1889), the Court House, Vancouver (1889), and the Weiler Block, Victoria (c.1890). (Information from Dr Harold Kalman).

Stead, John worked in Wakefield, where he had an office in the old Corn Exchange in 1822. He designed a Primitive Methodist Ch (1823) and the Westgate End WMCh (1827) in the town. He was surveyor to the Wakefield and Ferrybridge Canal, which failed to materialise, and in 1827 he became bankrupt and left Wakefield; possibly he went to Liverpool, where he exhibited a design in 1830 for a Gothic church 'intended for Askrigg, Yorkshire'. (Information from Mr John Goodchild).

Stott, Arthur Alfred was a Heckmondwike architect who worked in the town c.1877–97. He is best remembered for the monumental Upper Independent Ch (1890).

Strafford, George appears in the 1797 *Directory* as a carpenter in Wakefield, but by 1814 he was referred to as an architect with an office in Kirkgate. He was the designer of Holy Trinity, Ossett (1806), which was replaced in 1865 by W. H. Crossland's impressively silhouetted building.

Sugden, William Hampden practised in Low Street, Keighley with **Arthur Sugden** in the 1890s, moving to Devonshire Bldgs, North St, where the firm was still in existence up to the Second World War. They specialised in houses designed in a Yorkshire manor-house tradition, such as Currerwood, Steeton (1895), and Thornfield, Utley (1901).

Taylor, Thomas (c.1778–1826) worked in London with a builder, 'Mr Andrews', for five years and then in the office of James Wyatt for eight. He exhibited at the Royal Academy from 1792 to 1811, by which time he had arrived in Leeds and obtained his first important commission, the Court House. He made the drawings illustrating T. D. Whitaker's *Loidis and Elmete* (1816) and his edition of Ralph Thoresby's *Ducatus Leodiensis* (1816), and he exhibited occasionally in Leeds at the Northern Society for the Encouragement of the Fine Arts (1809, 1810, 1811, 1822). Taylor made his reputation as an ecclesiastical architect with Christ Church, Liversedge (1812–16), and afterwards the 1818 Church-building Act provided him with commissions in Yorkshire and Lancashire. He died after catching cold in one of his own churches, St Mary's, Leeds, and was buried in the crypt of his first church at Liversedge.
Bibl: Beckwith, F., *Thomas Taylor, Regency architect*, Leeds 1949.

Leeds: Park Row, Court House 1811–3, enlarged R. D. Chantrell 1834–5 dem; Alfred St, Lancasterian Sch 1812–3 dem; Commercial St, Union Bank 1812–3 dem.
Liversedge: Christ Ch 1812–6.
Leeds: Kirkgate, National Sch 1813 dem.
Bradford: Christ Ch 1813–5 dem.
Leeds: New Sch for Girls 1815–7 dem.
Luddenden: St Mary 1816–7, altered 1866.
Southowram: St Anne 1816–7, altered 1869.
Huddersfield: Holy Trinity 1816–9.
Ossett: Holy Trinity, additions 1821 (see Strafford, George).
Pudsey: St Lawrence 1821–4.
Leeds: St Mary, Quarry Hill 1823–6, altered 1862.
Huddersfield: Christ Ch, Woodhouse Hill 1823–4, chancel added 1894.
Dewsbury: St John, Dewsbury Moor 1823–7; St Paul, Hanging Heaton 1823–5, altered 1894, rebuilt 1917.
Leeds: St John, Roundhay 1824–6, altered 1885.
Dewsbury: St Peter, Earlsheaton 1825–7.

Thackray, John William (1862–1913), eldest son of William Thackray, a Leeds builder who, 'purchasing a disused quarry and a considerable tract of land on Woodhouse Ridge, . . . covered it with houses'. He was awarded several prizes during his youth in design classes at Woodhouse Mechanics' Inst, with which his family had been closely associated since its foundation, becoming an assistant building surveyor to Leeds Corporation 1884–92, and then holding a similar appointment in Sheffield 1892–5. He set up practice at 4 Greek St, Leeds in 1895, acted as valuer to several building societies, and provided designs for terraces of houses in Headingley and Potternewton. He worked for the Wesleyan Methodists, for whom he designed Harehills Lane SchCh (1905) and the Sunday Sch, Trinity Ch, Roundhay Rd (1889), both in Leeds.
Bibl: *CB*, 373.

Thompson, John (d 1792) was referred to as 'an eminent Architect' in Wakefield. He provided the uniform frontage design for St John's St (now North), Wakefield c.1791.

Thompson, Joseph worked in George and Dragon Yard, Leeds in 1847, moving later to Central Market Bldgs, and then to 8 Albion St in 1861. He made the design for St John the Evangelist, Moor Allerton (1852–3).

Thornton, Charles Henry worked in Leeds in the 1880–90s at 3 Park Row. He designed St Mary, Bramley (1885–6), and the Upper and Lower Wortley Liberal Club (1882).

Thornton, William (1670–1721) was a notable York craftsman who was employed as a joiner at Castle Howard, Wentworth Castle, and probably at Bramham Park. He executed the restoration to the vertical of the north transept of Beverley Minster (1716–20) in accordance with the proposal made by Nicholas Hawksmoor, and he was probably responsible in some degree for the design of Beningbrough Hall for John Bourchier c.1716. One of his executors was John Bagnall, plasterer, of York and Leeds, who was employed at Temple Newsam, and it is possible the two worked together in West Yorkshire on other buildings. Thornton is known to have been employed by Lady Elizabeth Hastings at Ledston Hall c.1720, probably as architect as well as craftsman, and he is suggested as the designer of a house for Robert Denison, 10 Town End, Leeds. There is little evidence of the extent to which he was employed as an architect, but he certainly made a design for a house 'for J. Stables', probably on the Ledston estate.
Bibl: Colvin, 612f; Beard, G., *Georgian craftsmen and their work*, London 1966, 24f.

Thornton, William practised with his brother (?) **David Thornton** in Oates St, Dewsbury and Wood St, Wakefield from the early 1870s. They designed Earlsheaton Sch, Dewsbury (1872) and the headquarters of the Wakefield ICS, Bank St (1876). William's son, **Harold Thornton** (b 1886), worked with Charles Reilly at Liverpool and commenced practice in Dewsbury in 1911.

Thorp, William Henry (1852–1944), son of John Hall Thorp, was articled to A. M. Fowler (*q.v.*); he then worked for three years for Edward Birchall (*q.v.*), and set up his own practice in Leeds in 1876. In the 1890s he was in partnership with G. F. Danby (*q.v.*), then with his son, **Ralph W. Thorp**, and from 1919–23 with **George Herbert Foggitt**. Thorp was the first Secretary of the LYAS, and President 1890–2.
Bibl: obit *B* (1944), clxvi, 98.

Leeds: Quarrydene, Weetwood, house for John Rawlinson Ford 1886; Art Gallery 1887–8; Friends' Mission Rm, Denison St 1890; Sch of Medicine 1894; Oxford Pl MCh, remodelled and new façade 1896–1903; YMCA, Albion Place 1900; General Infirmary, Nurses' Home c.1901; Chapel Allerton Police Station and Free Library 1904; Wellington St, warehouse for Hotham and Whiting 1906; Meadow Lane Police Station 1907; Cliff Rd, Orphans' Home.
Cleckheaton: Whitcliffe Mount Sec and Tec Sch 1910.

Vickers, Charles practised in Ropergate, Pontefract in the 1840s. He designed a parsonage house at Seacroft, Leeds (1846), and a church at East Knottingley (1847–8).

Walker, Henry (d 1922) was in practice at 11 East Parade, Leeds in 1867, and at 12 South Parade in 1881. He worked with **Joseph Athron** (who acted as executant architect for Lord Grimthorpe (q.v.) in connection with the erection of St Jude, Hexthorpe 1893), on the design and construction of St Bartholomew, Armley, Leeds; but if this was a partnership, it seems to have been short-lived. Walker was President of the LYAS 1880–2.

Leeds: Wellington Baths 1869; St Bartholomew, Armley 1872; Beckett St, Union Hospital 1872–4 (now part of St James's Hospital), enlarged by T. Winn; Wellington St, warehouse for William Smith 1874; Boar Lane, warehouse (?) for George Morrell and Sons c. c.1874; St Stephen, Kirkstall, restoration etc 1874; St Bartholomew, Armley, Sch 1875.

Wallen, William (d 1853) was in practice at 41 West Parade, Huddersfield in 1842. In the year of his death his address was given as New North Rd, and it is quite possible he was the designer of some of the villas which line the road. He was employed by the Ramsden Estate Office on some of their buildings in Huddersfield, and he was working with Charles Child (q.v.) towards the end of his life.
Farsley: St John the Evangelist 1843–5, tower rebuilt 1895.
Milnes Bridge: St Luke 1845.
Oakworth: Christ Ch 1845–6.
Shepley: St Paul 1848.
Longley Hall, estate office for Sir John William Ramsden 1848.
Huddersfield: George Hotel 1849–50, with C. Child; design for Castle Hill Tower 1851, built as Victoria Tower 1897–8; Apsley Lecture Rm 1853, comp C. Child.

Watson, Charles was the son of John Watson II (q.v.). In the 1790s he was in partnership with William Lindley (q.v.) of Doncaster, although this arrangement lasted only until the beginning of the new century. Their work at this time seems to have been mainly in Wakefield, where designs were made for St John's Ch and the surrounding layout (1791–5). Watson made an unexecuted design for West Parade c. 1804, intended as an extension to South Parade, which Lindley had laid out in the early 1790s. Several houses in Westgate, Margaret St, and Wentworth St suggest that either Watson or Lindley designed them, and in 1806 the former alone made the drawings for the Court House, Wakefield; in 1807 he designed the Court House, Pontefract and was working at Woolley Hall for Godfrey Wentworth. Watson moved to York in 1807, probably with an eye to succeeding John Carr; he practised at 26 Blossom St, and in 1813 he entered into partnership with J. P. Pritchett (q.v.), although they continued to work in Wakefield, e.g. West Riding Pauper Lunatic Asylum (1818), and the Public Library and News Room (1820–2). The partnership was dissolved in 1831. See under **Pritchett, J. P.** for

a list of works executed under the style of Watson and Pritchett.

Watson, John II (d 1771) was the son of **John Watson I** (d 1757); both held appointments as Surveyor of Bridges to the West Riding, the elder at the same time as Robert Carr, with whom he signed the survey of bridges dated 1752, which was probably largely the work of John Carr (q.v.), and there were several links between the two families of mason/architects. In 1752 Watson revised a design made by James Paine (q.v.) for Campsall Hall (where John Carr made designs for garden buildings), and Watson made another drawing in the same year for a house 'in the Sailes at Campsall' (RIBA Drawings Coll). Watson worked with Carr at Ferrybridge, where a new bridge was built in 1765, as well as at the House of Correction, Wakefield (1766). He is presumably the 'Mr Watson' who made the design for the Foundling Hospital at Ackworth (1758–65), which was taken over by the Society of Friends in 1778 and altered by William Lindley (q.v.), who became a partner in the 1790s of Charles Watson (q.v.), the son of John.

Watson, William (1840–1901) practised at Bank Bldgs, Westgate, Wakefield in 1867, moving later to addresses in Barstow Sq and King St. Possibly he was related to the family which included John and Charles Watson (q.v.). He designed a glass and iron hall for the 1866 Wakefield Industrial and Fine Art Exhibition, Normanton WMCh (1868), Wakefield and Barnsley Union Bank (now Barclays), Ossett (1870), Normanton MFCh (1872), Woodhouse BS, Normanton (1876), and Canal Rd BS, Lofthouse Gate. In 1908 the firm was known as Watson, Son and Ellison. Watson was President of the LYAS 1896–7.
Bibl: obit B (1901), lxxxi, 322.

Waugh, John, a member of a Bradford family of builders, designed Queen Anne Chambers, Sunbridge Rd, Bradford (1880) with his partner **Herbert Isitt**. They were among the first occupants of the building, moving from 29 Tyrrel St, where they remained until 1877. They also designed a warehouse for Francis Willey and Co in Upper Piccadilly, Bradford (1884).

Wentworth, Sir William, Bart (1686–1763) of Bretton Hall made the Grand Tour in 1709–12, during which time he agreed to be one of the group of gentry who sponsored William Kent's studies in Rome. Wentworth was High Sheriff of the County in 1723, and as one of the landowners responsible for the promotion of the Assembly Rooms in York (intended to be designed by William Wakefield but subsequently undertaken by Lord Burlington) he signed the documents for the purchase of ground in trust for the subscribers. In the 1720s, Wentworth was co-architect with James Moyser (q.v.) for his new house at Bretton, and in 1744 he designed the chapel on the Bretton estate.

Wilson, George worked with **Charles Bailey** in Central Market Bldgs, Leeds in the 1860s. They had moved to 35 Park Sq by 1881, and apparently ceased practice in the 90s. They made a lithographed design for terrace houses in St John's Hill, Leeds (1864), and designed the vicarage for St Barnabas, Holbeck (1866).

Wilson, John was a master mason in Halifax, who was employed to make the drawings for St Peter, Sowerby in 1759. He was also employed as mason for the erection of the church, which is modelled on William Etty's Holy Trinity, Leeds.

Wilson, Thomas Butler (1859–1942) was articled to Charles Bell of London, and then studied at Leeds School of Art, and the AA School. He set up in practice in 1884 in Leeds and London, later taking **Robert P. Oglesby** (d 1939) into partnership. The firm was well known for large houses with comfortable, well-detailed interiors, several of which were published in professional journals (e.g. Wheatfield Lodge and Castle Grove, Headingley, Leeds, and Grove House, Selbourne House, and Godolphin House, all in Harrogate). Wilson was President of the LYAS in 1901–04, and he was a tireless worker on behalf of improved standards of architectural education. He wrote *Modern house interiors* (1897), and in 1904 he published, at his own expense, a *Draft bill for the statutory registration of architects*. In 1937 he published the first studies of Cuthbert Brodrick and George Corson under the title of *Two Leeds architects*.
Bibl: obits, B (1942), clxii, 366; *RIBA Jnl* (1942), xlix, 125.

Winn, Thomas (d 1908) commenced practice in the early 1880s at 5 Park Lane, Leeds, moving later to 84 Albion St, where he remained until his death. He designed many commercial premises in Leeds, in Bishopgate St, East St, North St, Skinner Lane, Hyde Park Corner, Swinegate, Infirmary St and King St. He made alterations to Holy Trinity, Boar Lane, Leeds (1883–6), and built several public houses in Leeds, including the Mitre, Commercial St (c.1894 dem), the Jubilee, Park Lane (1904), the Black Swan, and the Adelphi. In 1906 he remodelled the Hippodrome Theatre, King Charles's Croft, and among his other designs were the Nurses' Home, Burmantofts (1893–4) and extensions to St James's Infirmary (1903).
Bibl: obit B (1908), xcv, 332.

Woodhead, George made two elevations of Woolley Hall in 1814, showing the external alterations made about that time. He lived at Heath, and one drawing signed 'Mason' after his name suggests he might have been both builder and architect. On the other hand, Watson and Pritchett were making designs in 1814 for a new lodge, and they might have been responsible for the alterations to the house.

Woodhead, John (d c.1838) was probably related to George Woodhead (q.v.). He was in partnership with William Lindley (q.v.) in Doncaster, and after the latter's death in 1818 he took William Hurst (q.v.) into the practice under the style of Woodhead and Hurst.

Index

Index of persons

Abbey, John Henry 339, 370
Abbey, Hanson, Rowe & Partners 367
Abercrombie, David 381
Acland, Sir Henry 39
Adam, James 74, 371; Robert 32, 71, 74, 76–9,
  91, 97, 128, 200, 371, 382
Adams, Maurice B. 23; Richard L. 36, 145, 259,
  370, 379
Aglio, Agostino 83–4
Aislabie, John 30
Aitkins, William 375
Akroyd, Abraham 48, 240, 370; Edward 37, 83,
  133, 136–7, 151, 227, 344, 371, 375; Henry
  137; James, & Son 135, 293; John 25, 48, 240,
  370; Jonathan 137; William 370
Albert, Prince 269, 271
Alberti, Leone Battista 30, 345
Alexander, D.A. 383; Prior of Fountains 154
Allanson, Mrs 331
Allen, Edmund John Milner 360
Allison,–. 382
Ambler, Jeremiah 370; Joseph 370; Louis 55,
  117; Thomas 36, 43, 119, 123, 144, 305–6, 323,
  370, 372
American & Chinese Export Co. 381
Ammanati, Bartolomeo 348
Andrews, G.T. 160; Thomas Garlick 370;
  William 36, 110, 115, 145, 226, 250, 255, 257,
  271, 295–6, 299, 300, 370
Archer, Thomas 62
Architects' Club 32, 34
Architectural Association 151
Ardyngton, Peers de 153
Armfield, Charles Noel 370
Armitage, John Faulkner 116; J.R. 381;
  Richard 239; William Henry 118
Armytage, Sir George Bt 380; John 153
Artari, Giovanni 65; Giuseppe 65
Arthur & Co. 370
Arundell, Hon Richard 29
Asman, Destin 323
Athron, Joseph 386
Atkinson, G.W. 265, 383; John 96, 106; John
  Bownas 83, 371; John William 119; Peter I
  370, 373; Peter II 34, 192, 210, 213, 250,
  370–1, 377, 384; Thomas 32, 371; William 83,
  371
Austin, Joseph 108; and Paley 248
Averdieck, Hermann 118, 382

Backhouse, Elisha 35–6, 38, 81, 145, 203, 226,
  228, 253, 259, 285, 371, 378, 383; Henry
  Perkin 383
Bage, Charles 289
Bagnall, John 186, 385

Bailey, Charles 111, 386; Wilson 85, 377
Baines, Edward 252; Frederick 384
Baker, Sir Herbert 118
Bakewell, William 119, 371, 381
Banks, George 374; James 270
Barber, William Swinden 137, 239, 371, 377, 381
Barker, Thomas 379
Barlow, William 164
Barran, Charles 123; Sir John 1st Bt 120, 122,
  305–6, 370; Sir John 2nd Bt 123, 370
Barry, Revd Alfred 248; Sir Charles 74, 84, 248,
  332, 340, 343–5, 347, 371; Edward Middleton
  217, 248, 345, 385
Basevi, George 83
Bateman, Edward la Trobe 106, 375
Batt, John 55
Battley, John 269, 371
Beaconsfield, Benjamin 1st Earl of 125, 133–4,
  220
Beaudoin, Eugène 148
Beaumont, Lady Margaret 88; Richard 27–8,
  60, 71, 381–2, 384; Thomas 83; Col Thomas
  Richard 79, 373, 380; Mrs (Diana Wentworth)
  33, 79, 83
Beckett, Christopher 83, 374; Sir Edmund 4th
  Bt 37, 375; Ernest William, see Grimthorpe;
  Capt Richard 214
Bedford, Francis William 371; John 371; J.E.
  371
Beechey, Sir William 31
Beevers, John 371; William Henry 371
Behrens, S.L. 300, 381
Belasyse, Sir Henry 61, 371
Bell, Andrew 245; Charles 386
Belwood, William 33, 371
Benn, J. & Co 382
Bennett, Sir Hubert 267
Benson, Robert, see Bingley
Bentley, John 25, 370; Michael 25, 370
Benyon, Benjamin 289; Thomas 69, 289
Best, William Woodham 375
Betjeman, Sir John 207, 362
Bevan, Charles 84
Biggi, Francesco 343
Billington, John 372
Billinton, William 35, 334, 372
Bingley, Robert 1st Baron 28–9, 61–2, 64–5,
  240, 371; George 2nd Baron 373; G.M. 374
Birchall, Edward 183, 204, 261, 304, 370, 372,
  385
Blacket, Edmund Thomas 217
Blackett, Sir Edward 376; Sir William 66
Bland, Sir John 71, 189; Sir Thomas 52; Thomas
  Davison 71
Blayds, John 80–1, 83, 181, 209, 374
Blow, Detmar 62, 69
Bodley, George Frederick 39, 71, 219, 226,
  232–3; Sir Thomas 370

Bodt, Jean 65
Bolles, Lady 238
Bonomi, Ignatius 221; Joseph 289–90
Booth, Isaac 372; Nicholas 26
Borromini, Francesco 96
Botham, Joseph 199, 203, 372
Bottomley, John Mitchell 372; Moses 118, 381
Boulter, John 73
Boulton, Matthew 292–3
Bourchier, John 27, 96, 385
Bowman, George Frederick 370; Henry 225
Boyce, Philip 35, 373
Boyle, Richard, see Burlington
Bradford Equitable Building Soc 144
Bradford Soc of Architects & Surveyors 42
Bradley, James 187, 372; John 253, 372;
  Thomas 32, 73, 80, 187, 200, 287, 372;
  William 35, 250, 371–2
Braithwaite, J.E. 372; Walter Samuel 260, 372;
  and Jackman 372
Brangwyn, Frank 234
Brayshaw, Mark 372
Brierley, Walter Henry 88, 371
Bridgeman, Charles 58, 61
Briggs, Nathaniel 381
Brindley, James 67
Broadbent, A. 360; Fred 265
Broadley, Matthew 238
Brock, Sir Thomas 360
Brodrick, Cuthbert 36, 38–9, 44, 113, 119, 225,
  255, 300, 304, 340, 342–4, 364, 372, 384, 386
Brontë, Charlotte 185
Brook, James 143
Brooke, Abraham 377
Brooks, S.H. 113
Brotherton, Charles 1st Baron 82
Brougham & Vaux, Henry 1st Baron 252, 329,
  334
Brown, James 83; Lancelot 'Capability' 32, 54,
  71, 74, 78, 128; and Muff 380
Brunton, John & Partners 367
Bruyn, Theodore de 79
Brydges, James, see Chandos
Buck, John 382; Samuel 103
Buckler, John Chessell 172
Buckley, Harry Bagshaw 373; J. & Sons 370
Buckstone, John Baldwin 271
Buckton, Richard 123, 384
Building Design Partnership 262, 367
Bulmer, George Bertram 331, 383
Burges, William 39, 41, 116, 227–8
Burleigh, Charles Walklett 35, 160, 373
Burlington, Richard 1st Earl of 27, 60, 381;
  Richard 3rd Earl of 29, 30, 65–7, 71–2, 200,
  330–1, 376, 386
Burne-Jones, Sir Edward 115–16, 231
Burnet, John 260, 380
Burnett, G. Alan 248, 265

Bute, James 2nd Earl of 28, 371
Butler,H.M. 147 ; John 115, 370
Butterfield, Henry Isaac 85, 384 ; William 39, 226–8

Cachemaille-Day,N.F. 236
Calverley,E. 374 ; John 383 ; Sir Walter 60, 154
Calvert, Rhodes 302, 373
Cambridge Camden Soc 156, 160, 204, 214, 225
Camden, William 171, 175
Camidge, Revd C.J. 175
Campbell, Colen 30, 62, 65, 67, 74, 376
Canova, Antonio 343
Carew, John Edward 331
Carlisle, Charles 3rd Earl of 29, 376
Caroe,W.D. 371
Carpenter, Andrew 26, 330
Carr, John 31–3, 61, 71–4, 76–7, 79, 80, 83, 91, 96–9, 101, 128, 166, 175, 187, 189, 190, 194, 199, 241, 330, 348, 370, 373, 380, 386 ; Robert 31, 72, 74, 373, 386 ; William 373
Carter, John 151, 172
Cartwright, Dr Edmund 360
Castle, Reuben 206, 373
Cates, Adolphus H. 380
Cave, Thomas 238
Cavendish, William Spencer, see Devonshire
Cawthra, Herman 361
Caygill, John 98, 373
Chadwick & Watson 280
Chamberlin, Powell & Bon 266–7
Chambers, Sir William 32, 61, 74, 382
Chandos, James 1st Duke of 29, 371, 384
Chantrell, John Boham 373 ; Robert Dennis 33–5, 107, 160–2, 167–8, 186, 210–1, 213, 216–7, 231, 316, 332, 336, 373–4, 377, 382, 384–5
Chantrey, Sir Francis 82
Chapman, Samuel 347, 374
Charles II 311
Charnock, William 103
Child, Charles 34, 339, 374, 379, 386 ; Charles Edwin 374, 377 ; Henry Paul 374 ; John 107, 220–1, 234, 374
Chippendale, Thomas 76
Chorley, Charles R. 22, 160, 189, 217, 231, 374, 376 ; Harry Sutton 374
Christian VII of Denmark 99
Clapham, Richard 97
Clark, John 34, 81–3, 105–7, 181, 214, 268, 294, 332, 374 ; T. 371
Clarke,G.Somers 384–5
Clarkson, John Albert James 374
Clayton & Bell 118, 217, 228
Clérisseau, Charles-Louis 32
Cliff, John 374
Clifford, Henry E. 380
Clutton, Henry 227
Cobden, Richard 309
Coccetti, Pietro Paolo 65
Cockerell, Samuel Pepys 81, 244
Coke, Thomas 61 ; Lady 54
Cole, Sir Henry 257
Coleman, Henry 271
Collcutt, Thomas Edward 355–6
Colt, Maximilian 164
Combe, James 289–90
Compton,N. 160
Connon, Revd John 374 ; John Wreghitt 22, 160, 189, 374, 376, 378
Constable, Katherine 381
Constable-Maxwell, Henry 221

Conyngham, Elizabeth Marchioness 37
Cookson, Ald William 27, 96, 186
Cooper,D. & J. 304, 375
Cope, Charles 106
Copley, Sir Godfrey 26, 60, 376
Corson, George 36, 42, 45, 116, 122, 227, 259, 264, 272, 304, 356, 358, 364, 375, 386 ; James 375 ; William Reid 106, 304, 375
Cortese, Giuseppe 96, 99, 187
Cortona, Pietro da 96
Cossins, John 96, 199, 313
Cousin, David 348
Crace, John 343 ; John D. 343
Crawford,A. 181
Crawford-Hick,A. 234
Crossland, George 298 ; William Henry 38, 135–6, 145, 166, 226–8, 323, 375
Crossley, Edward 379 ; Sir Francis (Frank) 1st Bt 114, 138 ; John 115, 138, 225, 253, 293, 344, 381 ; Joseph 379 ; Louis John 116
Crowe & Co 375, 383
Crowther, Joseph Stretch 225
Crutchley, William 145, 375
Cummins, Alexander 271
Curzon, Henry 153
Cusworth, Joseph 34, 240, 375
Cutler, Sir John 73

Danby, Francis 375 ; George Francis 207, 375, 385
Dance, George 331, 343
Darbishire,H.A. 371
Darcy, Lord, of Temple Hurst 52, 120
Darnley, Henry Lord 53, 88
Davies, Edward 372
Dearden, John 55
Defoe, Daniel 15, 125, 150, 167–8, 172, 281, 311
Delaunay, Frederick William 36, 110, 115, 299, 300, 370
Delaval, Admiral 26
Delius, Julius 300, 381
Demaine, James 371
Denison, Edmund Beckett, see Beckett, Sir Edmund and Grimthorpe
Denison, John 97 ; Nathaniel 27, 96, 376 ; Robert 27, 96, 385 ; Thomas 83, 97 ; Sir Thomas 37 ; William 101 ; William Beckett 39, 122, 145, 375
Derick, John Macduff 219
Devonshire, William Spencer 6th Duke of 133
Dickens, Charles 139, 245
Disraeli, Benjamin, see Beaconsfield
Dixon, Isaiah 375 ; Jeremiah 19, 80, 98–9, 373 ; John 99 ; Jonathan 299, 375–6, 381 ; Thomas 109, 298, 376
Doane, Rt Revd George Washington 217
Dobson, John 35, 181, 217, 374, 376
Dodgshun, Edmund J. 376
Dodgson, Daniel 206, 376
Doe, Richard 71
Douglas, John 110, 370
Douglas, Russell & Co 383
Downs, Coulters 370
Drake, Francis 331
Dresser, Christopher 116
Drummond, Charles 381
Drury, Alfred 360
Dudgeon,P. 339
Dugdale, Richard Swarbrick 372
Dundas, Thomas 1st Baron 290
Dunlop, Walter 115, 375
Dupier, Mrs Elizabeth 313

Durham, Joseph 138
Dyneley, Robert 60, 194

Eastwood,D. & J. 111 ; John Henry 234
Eborius, Bishop of York 153
Edelstein, Moser & Co 382
Eden,C.P. 371
Edmundson,R.B. & Son 343
Edward I 311 ; II 167 ; III 283 ; IV 168, 171 ; VII 237, 345, 352
Edwards, Sir Henry 372 ; John 80, 373 ; Joseph Priestley 84, 378
Ehm, Karl 148
Elam, Samuel 105, 120
Elizabeth I 53
Ellis, Walter Stead 376
Ellison,C.O. 226
Elwick, Edward 96
Empsall, Thomas Thornton 374
Entwistle,B.E. 277
Epstein, Sir Jacob 76
Etty, James 376 ; John I 26, 60, 64, 376 ; John II 376 ; William 26–7, 30, 96, 186, 330–1, 376, 386
Eugenius III, Pope 154
Eure [or Evers], Ralph 3rd Lord 51
Evans,K.C. 267
Exley,–. 187

Fairbairn, Sir Peter 106, 374 ; Sir William 291–5
Fairbank, Benjamin Browne 376 ; Benjamin Dalby 302, 376 ; Henry 376 ; John Tertius 114, 376
Favour, Dr 240
Fawcett, Richard & Sons 373
Fawkes, Walter 80
Fehr, Henry Charles 356, 360
Ferrand, Benjamin 69, 382 ; Walter 383
Ferrey, Benjamin 40
Fielden, John 84, 226
Filliter, Edward 317
Finch, Daniel, see Nottingham
Fisher, Richard 71
Fison, William 252
Flaxman, John 214
Flitcroft, Henry 30
Foggitt, George Herbert 385
Forbes, Henry 132
Ford, John Rawlinson 385
Forster, William Edward M.P. 132, 252, 256, 260
Foster, John 143, 293, 300, 381
Fowler, Alfred Mountain 376 ; Charles 231, 376 ; Charles John 376 ; C.Hodgson 183, 371 ; Henry 376
Fox, Charles Edward 376 ; Charles James 262, 379 ; George Arthur 355, 376 ; J.Lane 250, 376
Foxcroft, John 55
Fox-Lane, George, see Bingley
Frampton, Sir George 360
France, Arthur Alderson 376, 381 ; Charles 36, 39, 115, 118, 257, 295–6, 300, 323, 353, 364, 376, 381
Frank, Edward 384
Fraser, James Barlow 231, 268, 343, 376 ; John 376
Freson, Lancelot 27, 377
Frost, Revd Robert 165
Fuller, Thomas 339

Gainsborough, Thomas 101
Galilei, Alessandro 65

Gamston, Philip of 25; Robert 25
Garling, Henry 38
Garnett, Thomas 115, 380
Garrett, Daniel 30, 71–2
Gascoigne, Sir Edward 65, 240; Elizabeth-Oliver 379; Mary-Isabella-Oliver 379; Sir Richard 32; Richard Oliver 383; Sir Thomas 32, 194, 371, 373, 380; Sir William 162
Gaskell, Daniel 99, 248; Elizabeth 17
Gay, W. 142
Gent, Thomas 168
George IV 32, 37, 214, 290; V 362
George & Peto 371
Gibberd, Sir Frederick 262
Gibbons, Grinling 64, 376
Gibbs, James 27, 62, 65, 186, 384
Gibson, John 84, 226, 355–6
Gill, Eric 236
Gillows of Lancaster 118
Gingell, William Bruce 20
Giorgioli, Agostino 377
Girtin, Thomas 81, 155
Gladstone, William Ewart 209, 309
Gledhill, John 56
Glover, A. W. 267
Glynne, Sir Stephen 156, 164–5, 168, 175, 177
Godwin, Edward 41
Goldie, Edward 377; George 221, 377
Gomersall, John 138
Goodall, Thomas 186
Goodman, John 83, 374
Goodwin, Francis 107, 113, 316, 332, 374
Gott, Benjamin 33, 35, 80–1, 104, 135, 252, 289–92; Charles 377; Charles Henry 377; Joseph 82, 137
Gough, Hugh 167
Goulons, John de 98, 186
Graham, Sir James 130
Graves, Edward 243
Gray, Sir Richard 167
Green, James 73; Richard 80, 373
Greenslade, S. K. 234
Greenwood, Revd Charles 238; William 93
Greville, Sir Fulke 54
Griffiths, Goad Partnership 362, 367
Grimshaw, Atkinson 280, 364
Grimthorpe, Edmund 1st Baron 36–7, 39, 228, 345, 355, 375, 386; Ernest William 2nd Baron 45
Gunby, Francis 26, 175, 180
Gyles, Henry 96, 239

Hadfield, Charles 377; Matthew Ellison 377
Haigh, John 299, 376
Halfpenny, William 186
Halgate (Holgate), Robert Archbishop of York 237
Halifax, Charles 2nd Viscount 88
Halifax Permanent Building Soc 136, 144
Hall, W. Carby 234
Hallfield Building Club 109, 376
Hamilton, Sir William 73
Hammerton, Lees 377
Handel, George Frederick 384
Hansom, Charles Francis 377; Henry 377; Joseph Aloysius 43, 221, 377
Hanstock, Arthur Walter 377; Walter 167, 226, 277, 298, 377
Harding, Col Thomas Walter 306
Hardman, John 176, 228, 230
Hardwick, Philip Charles 366
Hare, Augustus 88

Harewood, Edward 1st Earl of 71, 79, 129; Edwin 1st Baron 31–2, 61, 65, 71, 73–4, 76, 128, 240, 373
Hargreave, William 107
Hargreaves, Charles Henry 250, 260, 377
Harper, John 35, 49, 377
Harris, Thomas 85; Vincent 361
Harrison, John 93, 179–81, 238–9, 313
Hartley, Bernard I 32, 245, 330, 373, 377; Bernard II 35, 377; Bernard III 35, 377; Jesse 377; Major 375
Harvey & Reynolds 375
Haselgrave, Edward 186
Hastings, Lady Elizabeth 27–8, 61, 186, 240–1, 371, 385
Hatton, George 123
Hawksmoor, Nicholas 27, 91, 376, 385
Headland, Messrs 375
Healey, Francis 166, 170, 226, 257, 332, 377, 381; Thomas I 34, 110, 137, 226–8, 377, 381; Thomas II 166, 170, 226, 257, 332, 377, 381
Heaton, Ellen 344; John Aldam 115; Dr John Deakin 339, 375
Heber, Reginald 166
Helliwell, Thomas W. 378
Hemingway, Ernest 88
Henderson, James 96
Henry, A. & S. 381
Henry II 167; III 283, 311; VI 168, 170; VII 170; VIII 53, 237
Hepper, John 375; & Sons 375
Heron, Revd Thomas 382
Hertford, Isabella Marchioness of 53
Heugh, J. 375
Hey, William 374
Heyn, David Julius 376
Heywood, Revd Oliver 194
Hill, Oliver 265; William 38, 339, 374–5, 378; William Longfield 378
Hirst, J. A. 384; Joseph 143
Hives, John 83, 252, 374; & Atkinson 294
Hobson, Joseph 272
Hodgson, George 381
Hoffman, Hurter & Co 370
Hogg, John 36, 84, 111, 378
Hole, James 125, 144
Holden, Angus 115, 323, 381; Isaac 293
Holland, Henry 340
Holt, Thomas 25–6, 370
Holtom, Henry 355, 374, 376, 378
Hood, Robin 153
Hook, Revd Walter Farquhar 213–4, 216–9
Hooke, Robert 27, 60, 381
Hoole, Revd Charles 237–8, 247, 257
Hope, A. J. Beresford 39, 182–3, 227; John 193, 287, 372; Thomas Campbell 45, 109–10, 120, 257, 262, 374, 378; W. H. St John 183–4; W. 277
Hopkinson, Robert 69, 382
Hordern, Isaac 35
Horner, John 94, 158, 241
Horseley, Edward 52
Horsfall, Charles Edward 378; Charles Frederick Luke 36, 378, 380; J. G. 110; Richard 36, 226, 280, 378; Richard Edgar 378; William Edward 378
Hotham, Sir Charles 313; & Whiting 385
Houghton, Richard Monckton Milnes, 1st Baron 47, 88
Howard, Charles, see Carlisle; Ebenezer 322; Edward, see Norfolk
Howdill, Charles Barker 378; Thomas 378

Howorth, William Henry 373, 378
Hudson, George 37
Hugall, J. W. 160
Hughes, Edward 261–2, 319, 379
Humble, Grace 219
Hunt, Thomas Frederick 248
Hurst, William 34, 203, 210, 334, 377, 379, 382
Hutchinson, Edward 379

Ibbetson, James 79; Sir James 80
Ikin, Thomas 80
Illingworth, Alfred 370, 381; Jeremiah 381; Son & Co 370
Ingram, Arthur 376; Sir Arthur 26, 51, 53–4, 180; Charles, Edward, Henry, see Irwin
Irvine, J. T. 183
Irving, Sir Henry 273
Irwin, Charles 9th Viscount 78; Edward 2nd Viscount 376; Edward 4th Viscount 26, 282, 376; Henry 7th Viscount 71, 373
Isitt, Herbert 386
Ives, Roger 36, 225, 294, 379, 383; William 379

Jackman, Harry F. 372
Jackson, Benjamin 35, 379; Benjamin Whitehead 262, 379; Joseph 379; Samuel 36, 109, 114, 257, 353, 379; Walter I 379; Walter II 379
Jacobsen, Theodore 244
Jagger, Joseph 193, 241, 379
James I 53
James, Henry 47, 88; John (architect) 384; John (historian) 311; Joseph 225
Jardine, David 257, 262, 378
Jebb, Canon John 216
Jersey, Thomas 382
Jewell, John 129
Jewett, Orlando 160
Johnson, R. J. 234; Thomas 32–4, 102, 192–4, 379; William 32, 71, 193, 284, 330, 379
Jollage, Paul 97, 189, 313
Jones, George Fowler 379; Inigo 54, 69, 71, 80, 179; Owen 106, 306, 375; William Alban 383; W. Evan 375
Jordan, Dorothy 269–71, 290
Jowett, Atkinson 114

Kauffmann, Angelica 76
Kay, John Peacock 379
Kaye, John 51; Joseph 34–5, 105, 220, 379
Kell, Robert 114, 376
Kelly, John 36, 145, 261, 370, 372, 379; Michael 270
Kempe, Charles Eamer 88, 176; John, Archbishop of York 171
Kendall, Henry 247, 379
Kennedy, Thomas Stewart 116
Kent, William 29, 61, 66, 69, 71, 73, 386
Kerr, P. & Knight, J. G. 339
Kessler, J. P. 381
Keyworth, William Day 319, 343
Kingsley, Charles 84
Kirk, Albert Holmes 166, 189, 380; Frederick 380; James Sheard 380; John 36, 112, 143, 146, 193, 372, 380
Kitchingman, Joseph 382
Kitson, James 371, 374; Sydney Decimus 371; & Partners 371
Klenze, Leo von 304
Knatchbull, Wyndham 64
Knight, Revd Titus 185, 200
Knowles, George 115, 257, 380

Labrouste, Henri P.-F. 255
Lacy, Edmund de 311; Henry de 153–4, 311
Lamb, Edward Buckton 39
Lancaster, Henry Earl of 167; Joseph 245–6
Lanchester & Lodge 265
Landless, William 260–1, 380
Lane, Richard 248
Lane-Fox, George 382
Langtry-Langton, J.H. 236
Lascelles, Daniel 71, 74; Edward, see
    Harewood; Edwin, see Harewood; Henry 73
Lassen, E. 381
Latrobe, Benjamin 244; Benjamin Henry 244
Laud, William, Bishop of London 179–80
Laver, Augustus 339
Law, Russell & Co 381
Lawrance, William 33, 380
Lawrence, Sir Thomas 82
Layton, Francis 181
Leach, Thomas 55
Leckenby, Keighley & Groom 371
Ledgard, William 375
Ledingham, James 110, 117, 380
Lee, John 103, 193; T.Stirling 118; Revd
    William 238
Leeds Architectural Association 42
Leeds Model Cottage Soc 144
Leeds Permanent Building Soc 144
Leeds Social Improvement Soc 145
Leeds, Thomas 1st Duke of 60–1, 371
Leeds & Yorks Architectural Soc 42–4
Leeming, Alfred 380; John & Joseph 250, 320,
    323, 325–7, 380
Legh, Thomas 181
Leicester, Thomas 1st Earl of 74
Lennox, Ludovick 1st Duke of 53; Matthew 4th
    Earl of 53
Leoni, Giacomo 62
Leroux,–. 85
Lethaby, William Richard 236
Leverton, Thomas 32, 79
Lewis, Sir John 54–5, 73
Lindley, Joseph 380; William 32, 74, 83, 103,
    175, 192, 204, 245, 331, 379–80, 386
Lister, Anne 25, 35, 88, 130, 250, 372, 377
Lister, Samuel Cunliffe, see Masham
Liverpool, Robert 2nd Earl of 209
Livesey, Thomas 105
Livett, R.A.H. 149
Lloyd, Thomas 102
Lockwood, Henry Francis 35, 42–3, 80, 139, 335,
    343, 372, 380–1; and Mawson 35–6, 38–9, 41,
    96, 109–10, 118, 138, 142, 203, 206, 253,
    255–6, 295, 299, 300, 308, 318, 335, 340, 344,
    352–3, 358, 364
Lodge, Edmund 130
Lods, Marcel 148
Longbottom,–. 241
Longley, William 257, 379
Loudon, John Claudius 83, 105, 245
Lowther, Charles Grange 356; Sir William 98–9
Lubbock, Sir John 183
Lucas, John 332
Lugar, Robert 248
Lumb, John 103
Lumley, George, see Scarbrough
Lupton, F.M. 374; M. 374; William & Co 302,
    304, 375
Lutyens, Sir Edwin 88–9, 91, 118, 236

Macdowell, Patrick 83
Macklin, Charles 271

Maclise, Daniel 345
Madin, John, Partnership 367
Major, Joshua 105, 119, 143
Mallinson, George 371, 381; James 34, 110, 137,
    226–8, 371, 377, 381; William 192, 381
Malton, Thomas 75, 97, 313, 330
Mann, Thomas 27, 58, 60, 381
Manning, Henry Edward, Cardinal 220
Mar, John 6th Earl of 66
March, J.O. 373
Margerison, James, Archbishop of Armagh 238
Marie-Amélie, Queen of France 221
Markham, William 380
Marot, Jean 26, 60
Marsh, Jones [& Crib] 84
Marshall, John I 69, 134–5, 237, 245, 252, 289;
    John II 289
Marvell, Andrew 39
Mary, Queen of Scots 53
Masham, Samuel Cunliffe-Lister, 1st Baron 293,
    295, 360, 370
Maslen, T.J. 316
Masser, J.Fallowfield 111
Masson, Henry 370
Matcham, Frank 276–8, 325
Maude, Daniel 28, 60, 384
Maufe, Sir Edward 170, 236
Mawer & Ingle 302
Mawson, Richard 355, 381; William 35, 355,
    380–1
Maxwell, J.C. 277
McArthur, John Jr 339
Medland, James 383
Metcalfe, Thomas 95
Mexborough, John 1st Earl of 60, 240, 373, 384
Meynell Ingram, Hon Mrs (Emily Charlotte
    Wood) 88, 233
Micklethwaite, John Thomas 176, 183–4, 193,
    226
Middleton, William 69
Millais, Sir John Everett 107
Milligan, Robert 374; and Forbes 299, 370
Milner, Edward 137; William 79
Milnes, Charles E. 381; Eli 36, 39, 115, 118, 257,
    295–6, 300, 323, 353, 364, 376, 381; Henry
    381; James 80, 99, 373; John 99, 373;
    Pemberton 99, 373; Robert 80, 99, 101, 373;
    Thomas 256, 295
Mitchell, Abraham 114, 376; John 57
Moffat, William Lambie 203, 334, 379, 382
Moffatt, William Bonython 36
Monkbridge Iron Co 374
Monkhouse, Cosmo 23
Moore, John Hutchinson 382; Richard William
    106, 214, 382; Temple Lushington 219, 226,
    230; Thomas 382; Thomas Angelo 382
Moorhouse, F. 371
Mopin, Eugène 148
Morant, Alfred William Whitehead 319, 382
Morley, W.J. 199
Mornay, Duc de 87
Morrell, George & Sons 386
Morris, Roger 72; William 115–6, 152, 183
Morrish, John Samuel 106
Mountain, Charles I 382; Charles II 175, 382
Mowbray, Sir William 162
Moxon, William 201
Moxson, John 32, 181, 283, 291, 382
Moyser, James 29, 30, 66–7, 382, 386; John 382
Muff, Thomas Parkinson 119
Murdoch, James 292
Murgatroyd, James 56; William 370, 380

Murray, Matthew 289
Muschamp, John I 382; John II 32, 129, 382
Muthesius, Hermann 371

Napoleon I 87
Nash, John 33, 209, 334
Nathan, Hardy & Son 381
Neill, Archibald 382; James 382
Nelson, Alline James 382; Charles Sebastian
    382; W. 156
Nesfield, William Andrews 81
Nettleton, G. 34
Newall, Walter 375
Newman, Henry, Cardinal 220, 224
Nicholas, Grand Duke of Russia 130
Nicholls, Thomas 85, 116
Nicholson, Sir Charles 172; Stephen 120, 247;
    Thomas 80, 82, 120, 123, 374; William 120
Nightingale, Florence 217, 352
Noble, Matthew 343
Nollekens, Joseph 31, 101
Norfolk, Edward 9th Duke of 120
North, Col J.T. 183
Northern Soc for the Encouragement of the Fine
    Arts 34, 107, 331, 372–3
Norton, Hon George Chapple 172
Nottingham, Daniel 2nd Earl of 62
Nussey, G.H. & A. 268

Oates, John 34, 213, 245, 332, 374, 377, 382;
    Joseph 105; Matthew 382
O'Connor, Mgr John 236; Michael 220
Oglesby, Robert P. 386
Osborne, Thomas, see Leeds
Overbeck, Friedrich 227
Oxley, James Walter 116, 375; and Co 383

Paine, James I 30, 60, 62, 67, 69, 71–2, 78, 91,
    97, 271, 331, 372–3, 382–3, 386; James II 31,
    382
Palladio, Andrea 29, 30, 69, 288, 345
Palmerston, Henry John 3rd Viscount 309, 344
Pape, William 60
Papworth, John Buonarotti 248
Parker, J.H. 39; Thomas Lister 181
Parkinson, William Henshaw 382
Parmentier, Jacques 96, 169, 382
Parnell & Smith 115
Parsons, Edward 200, 270, 316
Patchett, Thomas Lister 226, 378
Pate, John 186
Paulinus, St 153
Paull, H.J. 117; and Ayliffe 138
Paxton, Sir Joseph 138, 295, 317
Payton, Frederick Bartram 382
Pearson, Frederick Loughborough 231; John
    Loughborough 174, 226–7, 231–2
Pease, W. (or T.) 201
Penn, William 339
Pepper, Joseph 145, 226, 250, 255, 257, 271,
    295–6, 370
Perfect, Joseph 67
Perkin, Henry 331, 383; William 383; William
    Belton 35–6, 38, 40, 81, 105, 145, 203, 226,
    228, 232, 253, 285, 371–2, 378, 383
Perritt, Thomas 71, 78
Perry, John 306
Petch, John 379
Petch & Fermaud 252
Peterson, Edward Paterson 383
Petty, Charles H. 383; Francis William 294, 379,
    383; and Sons 372

Pevsner, Sir Nikolaus 152, 184
Philip, Birnie 228, 230
Phillips, Matthew 371, 377
Phipps, Charles John 276
Pickersgill, Thomas 382
Pickles, R.H. 262
Pietro, Signor 288
Pigou, Revd Francis 177
Pilkington, William 32
Piper, John 15
Piranesi, Giovanni Battista 32
Plaw, John 133, 248
Pomeroy, Frederick 360
Poole, G.A. 160
Pope, Alexander 73; Peter 52; and Pearson 138
Potter, Joseph 210
Powell, John Hardman 223; Powell Bros 87
Priestley, Briggs 118, 300, 380–1; John 373
Prince, John 19, 186
Pritchett, Charles 383; George 383; James
    Pigott I 32, 35, 105, 143, 201, 204, 214, 245,
    320, 332, 339, 383, 386; James Pigott II 226,
    383
Pückler-Muskau, Prince 292
Pugin, Auguste Charles 108; Augustus Welby
    Northmore 108, 156, 219–21, 247, 314, 343–4,
    377; Edward Welby 85, 116, 223–4, 377
Pusey, Revd Edward Bouverie 218–20
Pytts, Sir Edward 370

Quadri, Martino 65

Radcliffe, Henry 314; Dr John 314; Joseph 383;
    William 69, 382–3
Radnor, Elizabeth Countess of 73
Ramsay,–. 221, 377
Ramsden, Archibald 375; John 311; Sir John
    4th Bt 79, 252, 284, 373; Sir John William 5th
    Bt 227, 252, 339, 375, 386
Rawdon, George 118
Rawson, George 105, 379, 383; William 96
Rawstorne, John 383; Walker 381, 383
Rayner, George Herbert 375
Reed, F.H. 306
Reeves, Charles 385
Reichenheim, Sons & Co 381
Reid, A. & W. 380; Reid & Green 339
Rennie, John 33, 292
Repton, Humphry 13, 32, 81–3, 129, 247, 292
Reynolds, Sir Joshua 31, 73
Rhind, W. Birnie 356
Rhodes, Abraham 83; Joseph 315, 330; M.J.
    227; Robert 103
Ricardo, Halsey 22
Richard II 167; III 168
Richardby, James 109, 298, 314, 334, 383
Richardson, J. 374; Richard 189, 382; William
    156
Rickman, Thomas 175, 209–10
Rinder, Frederick & Joseph 315
Risling, Thomas 84, 378
Rivers, Anthony, Earl 167
Roberson, Revd Hammond 185, 210
Roberts, David 289; George 378
Robinson, Daniel 383; Joshua 290; Metcalfe
    376; Percy 383; Peter Frederick 377, 380; Sir
    Thomas 29, 30, 373; –. 383
Robson, Edward Robert 257, 260
Rooke, Sir William 55, 99
Rooker, Michael Angelo 155
Rose, Joseph I 71, 73, 78; Joseph II 76, 78
Rossetti, Dante Gabriel 115

Rossi, Domenico de 96
Rossini, Gioacchino 87
Royal Institute of British Architects 25, 36–7,
    42–5
Royds, John 98–9, 373
Rubatto, Carlo 343
Runtz, Ernest 280
Ruskin, John 13, 15, 24, 39, 44, 214, 228, 306–7,
    340, 344, 363
Russell, S.B. 356
Rutherford, James H. 371
Ryther, Sir William 162

Sachs, Edwin 273, 276
Sadler, Sir Michael 264
Salt, Sir Titus 1st Bt 80, 132–3, 138–9, 183, 256,
    294, 309, 380; Titus Jr 84–5
Salvin, Anthony 50, 166, 332, 374
Sanders, J.H. 119
Sangallo, Antonio da 348
Saunders & Co 85
Savile, Edward 238; George of Rufford 164; Sir
    George of Thornhill 238; Sir George 1st Bt of
    Thornhill 164, 238; Sir George 2nd Bt of
    Thornhill 47; Sir Henry of Bradley (and
    Oxford) 370; Sir Henry of Thornhill 48; Sir
    Henry of Methley 51; John, see Mexborough;
    Sir John of Copley 120; Sir John of Howley
    51, 53, 370; Sir John of Lupset 238; Sir John
    of Methley 48, 51, 238, 240, 370; Sir John of
    Thornhill (d 1481) 164; Sir John of Thornhill
    (d 1504) 164; Robert of Shibden 93; Sir
    Thomas of Thornhill 164–5; William 164
Scarbrough, George 5th Earl of 270
Scatcherd, Norrison 167
Schinkel, Karl Friedrich 82
Schuster, Leo 300, 376; Schuster, Fulda & Co
    381
Schwanfelder, Charles Henry 214
Schwann, Frederic 252, 299, 376
Scott, Sir George Gilbert 21, 36–40, 135–6, 151,
    164, 166, 171–2, 174–7, 179, 181–2, 204,
    226–8, 236, 266, 343–4, 348–9, 364, 372, 375,
    383, 385; Sir Giles Gilbert 151; Canon John
    182; Oldrid 179
Sedding, John Dando 234, 379
Selwyn, William Marshall 381
Semon, Charles & Co 382
Serlio, Sebastiano 180
Settrington, John 50, 55, 61
Sharlston Colliery Co 138
Sharp, Richard 384; Richard Hey 250, 371, 384;
    Samuel 160, 384; Thomas 55; and Waller 277
Sharpe, Edmund 151, 182
Shaw, Richard Norman 39, 119, 121, 162, 181–2,
    226–8, 356, 358–9; Thomas (Halifax) 116;
    Thomas (Leeds) 38, 210, 384; William 203,
    374
Sheafield, Sir William 238
Sheard, Michael 167, 298, 377
Shelton, Theophilus 28, 58, 60–1, 189, 313, 384
Shillito, Daniel 77
Shrewsbury, Edward 8th Earl of 26, 52; Gilbert
    7th Earl of 238
Simond, Louis 130
Simpson, Charles 384; Edward 224, 257, 384;
    James 203, 207, 384; John 384; Sir John
    William 360; Thomas 384
Skidmore, Francis 115, 228, 230, 306
Slingsby, Sir Henry 51
Smalpage, J.H. 373
Smeaton, John 244

Smiles, Samuel 252
Smirke, Sir Robert 35, 82, 209; Sydney 81
Smith, George (Bradford) 85, 119, 384; George
    (Leeds) 43, 105, 275, 323, 370, 384; John
    Wales 384; Joseph 132; Stephen Ernest 123,
    304, 323, 384; William 304, 386
Smyth, John 73, 313, 373
Smythson, Huntingdon 55; John 51, 54, 55;
    Robert 26, 48, 51, 52
Soane, Sir John 34, 43, 175, 209, 373
Society of Antiquaries of London 168
Society for the Protection of Ancient Buildings
    183
Sorby, Thomas Charles 385
Sparrow,–. 78
Spencer, John 79
Spencer-Stanhope, Walter 73
Sprague, W.G.R. 277
Stables, J. 61, 385
Stanhope, John 60, 189
Stanley, E.W. 366
Stapleton, Thomas 79
Starkie, Edmund 57
Stead, John 385; Walter 304, 372
Stevenson, John James 257
Stewart, Henry, see Darnley
Stewart, Ludovick, see Lennox
Stewart, Matthew, see Lennox
Stokes, George Henry 114, 138
Stott, Arthur Alfred 206, 385
Stourton, William 15th Baron 120; Charles
    Philip 17th Baron 79, 120, 133
Strafford, George 385; Thomas 1st Earl of 47,
    51, 54–5, 73, 91, 164, 238; Thomas 1st Earl of
    (sec creation) 28, 65, 371; William 2nd Earl of
    65
Street, Arthur Edmund 166, 189, 227; George
    Edmund 39, 40, 161–2, 183, 217, 226–8, 236,
    355, 379
Stukeley, William 153
Sugden, Arthur & William Hampden 117, 385
Sunderland, Abraham 56; Thomas 103
Sutcliffe, John 33, 290–2; Thomas 314
Swann, Salmon L. 378
Switzer, Stephen 67
Sykes, Sir Christopher 2nd Bt 32; James Nield
    118; Sir Tatton 5th Bt 229, 231
Syme, John Stuart 371

Talbot, Edward, see Shrewsbury; Gilbert, see
    Shrewsbury
Talman, William 384
Tapper, Sir Walter 236
Tatham, Joseph 245
Taylor, Dan 196; James Medland 379; John 55;
    Michael Angelo 290; Sir Robert 382; Revd
    R.V. 156, 166–7; Thomas 34, 158, 210, 214,
    246–7, 313, 331–2, 334, 374–5, 377, 385
Tempest, Elizabeth 221; Sir George 28, 60, 189,
    240, 384
Tetley, Francis William 116, 375; Joshua, & Co
    375; McKean 381; Rennie 370; Samuel 381
Teulon, William Mitford 225
Thackray, John William 385; William 385
Thackrey, Thomas 186
Thomas, John 327, 343, 345
Thompson, Beilby 32, 373; John 104, 385;
    Joseph 385; Richard 73; Stephen 30–1
Thoresby, John 93; Ralph 27, 79, 93, 151, 168,
    180, 186, 213, 282, 313, 329–30, 376
Thornhill, Thomas 118

Thornton, Charles 276, 323; Charles Henry 385; David 385; Harold 385; Col Thomas 133; William 27, 61, 96, 385
Thorp, John Hall 385; Ralph W. 385; William Henry 24, 123, 207, 264, 320, 343, 358, 371–2, 385
Thorpe, George 378
Tilney, Charles 317
Tite, Sir William 40, 298, 339, 344
Tobin, Maurice 77
Tower, Walter 88
Travis & Mangnell 253
Trimen, Andrew 210, 228
Trollope, Anthony 220
Trubshaw, Charles 24
Turner, Joseph Mallord William 81, 155; Joshua 186
Tweedale, James Smithers 384; John 123, 323, 384

Unwin, Sir Raymond 45

Vanbrugh, Sir John 11, 27, 61, 65, 91
Vassalli, Francesco 65
Vavasour, Sir Mauger le 51; Sir Walter 373
Vickers, Charles 386
Victoria, Queen 106, 342
Vignola, Jacopo Barozzi 348
Vilett, J. 69

Wade, Benjamin 69; Walter 69, 382
Wailes, William 228, 375
Wainhouse, John Edward 372; Michael 105
Wakefield, Richard 330, 376; William 29, 386
Walker, Henry 304, 386; Capt Samuel 214; William 80, 110, 241, 372
Wall, John Henry 302, 376
Wallen, William 112, 339, 374, 386
Walsh & Nicholas 234
Walter, John 183

Ward, E. 383; James 15; Simon de 153; Susannah 383
Wardell, William Wilkinson 223, 377
Wardle, Matthias Harris 226, 378
Warton, Sir Michael 313
Waterhouse, Alfred 22, 24, 39, 237, 255, 262, 268, 308; John 373; Paul 237, 262, 268
Waterton, Robert 167
Waterworth,–. 79
Watson, Charles 32, 35, 83, 103, 105, 175, 192, 201, 214, 332, 334, 377, 380, 383, 386; James 311; James Robinson 272; Revd John 21; John 96, 244, 373, 386; William 386
Watt, James 289, 292–3
Waugh, John 386
Webb, James 78; J.P. 372; Philip 39, 236
Weddell, William 79, 371
Weeks, Fred 85
Weightman, John Grey 377
Welch, Edward 377
Wells, Randall 236
Wentworth, Godfrey 67, 79, 83, 372–3, 383, 386; Godfrey Wentworth 83; Isabell 48; Michael 47–8; Peter 28; Thomas, see Strafford; Thomas of Elmsall 48; Sir Thomas of West Bretton 48; Sir Thomas 5th Bt of Bretton 67; William of Woolley 240; Sir William 4th Bt of Bretton 29, 65–7, 189, 382, 386
Wesley, Revd John 196–7, 199, 200, 243, 271; Samuel Sebastian 217
West Yorks Soc of Architects 42
Wharncliffe, Lady 53
Wheater, W. 371
Whitaker, Revd Thomas Dunham 94, 105, 117, 153, 156, 158, 169, 176–7, 181, 186, 189, 192, 214, 270, 287–8; William & Co 378
White, Thomas 78
Wilcock & Co 23
Wilcox, William 115, 257, 380
Wilderspin, Samuel 245

Wilkins, William 384
Wilkinson, John 294, 374, 384; Tate 97, 269–71, 276; Revd Thomas 177
Willey, Francis & Co 386
William IV 270, 290
Williams, W.E. 367
Wilson, George 111, 386; James 327; John 30, 187, 386; Richard 99; Thomas Butler 386
Winn, Sir George 67; John, & Sons 372; Sir Rowland 4th Bt 29, 30, 65, 67, 372, 382; Sir Rowland 5th Bt 77, 153; Thomas 383, 386
Wise, Henry 61
Wiseman, Nicholas, Cardinal 224
Witham, William 47
Witton, Richard 28, 60, 384
Wood, Charles 79, 373; Charles, see Halifax; Edgar 118; Frederick George Lindley 88; John 28–9, 252, 293
Woodhead, George 48–9, 83, 386; John 34, 210, 334, 377, 380, 382, 386
Woodrove, Francis 48
Woods, Joseph 384
Woolrich, Thomas 81
Wormald, Edward 375; Joseph 375; and Fountaine 33
Worsley, Thomas 29
Wren, Sir Christopher 27, 185, 190, 376
Wright, Jacob 214; William 189; and Tayler 339
Wyatt, Benjamin Dean 35, 377; James 32–4, 331, 373, 383, 385; Jeffry, see Wyatville; Lewis 181; Samuel 32–3, 289; Thomas Henry 248
Wyatville, Sir Jeffry 33, 66, 83, 181

York, Frederick, Duke of 133
Yorkshire Archaeological Soc 183

Zucchi, Antonio 76–8

Index of places

Aberford 21, 371: Almshouses 379; St Ricarius 166–7

Ackworth 13, 44: Flounders Inst 245, 383; Foundling Hosp 244, 386; Friends' Sch 245, 192; Grange 221, 173; Meeting Ho 204, 380, 383

Adel; see Leeds

Adelaide, S Australia; Parliament Ho 339

Ainley Pl 127

Airedale: Holy Cross 199

Akroydon; see Halifax

Albany, NY, USA; State Capitol 339

Alderley Edge, Ches; St Philip 225

Allerton; see Bradford

Allerton Bywater: St Mary the Less 383

Allerton Park, N Yorks 29, 133

Almondbury 127, 153, 281, 311; GS 239, 371

Almscliff Crag 14

Altofts: St Mary Magdalene 233, 370

Alverthorpe; see Wakefield

Amiens, France: Cath 41

Angoulême, France: Cath 221

Apperley Bridge 20, 118, 374: Cragg Royd 381

Ardsley: Christ Ch 379

Armitage Bridge; see Huddersfield

Armley; see Leeds

Arncliffe Hall, N Yorks 72

Arthington: Cluniac Priory 153; Nunnery 153; St Peter 381; Sch 383; WCh 371

Aske Hall, N Yorks 71

Askham Richard Hall, N Yorks 31

Audley End, Essex 51

Austhorpe; see Leeds

Baildon: Moravian Ch 379; St John 381

Bailiff Bridge: MNCCh 378

Baltimore, Maryland, USA: Exchange 244; RC Cath 244

Bardsey: All Hallows 153, 158–60, 374, 119; CP Sch 266; Sch 240

Barkisland: Christ Ch 381; Hall 56; Sch 240

Barlborough Hall, Derbys 52

Barnoldswick, Lancs 154

Barnsley, S Yorks 11: County Court 385; St George 210

Barwick-in-Elmet: All Saints 65, 158, 379

Bath, Somerset 29, 200

Batley 51: All Saints 158, 162, 167, 377, 117; Conservative Club 376; GS 238; HS 266; Market Hall 376; Mortuary Ch 377; Public Baths 377; Public Library 377; St Mary of the Angels 370; St Saviour, Brownhill 377; St Thomas 377; Station Rd, warehouses 298, 377; Tech Sch 373; Town Hall 377; Zion MCh 206

Batley Carr; see Dewsbury

Bawtry, S Yorks 11, 99

Becca Hall 380

Beningbrough Hall, N Yorks 27, 64, 96, 385

Berlin, Germany: Palais Redern 348

Beverley, Humberside 156: Guildhall 96; Sir Chas Hotham's ho 67; Market Cross 28, 314, 384; Minster 27, 385; John Moyser's ho 96

Bierley; see Bradford

Bingley 15: All Saints 383; Bankfield 370; BCh 382; GS 239; Harden Grange 115; Holy Trinity 227–8, 231, 183; Longwood 381; MechInst 255; Oakwood 115, 380, 84, 85; Sacred Heart SchCh 384; Woodbank 115

Birdsall, N Yorks: St Mary 382

Birkby; see Huddersfield

Birkenshaw: St Paul 371, 381

Birkin, N Yorks: St Mary 161

Birmingham, Warwicks: St Philip (Cath) 186; Town Hall 43, 334, 343, 345, 377

Birstall 51: St Patrick 384; St Peter 158, 166, 375, 126

Bishop Burton, Humberside 29

Bishopthorpe, N Yorks: Palace 371

Blaise Hamlet, Somerset 133

Blackstone Edge 125

Bolsover Castle, Derbys 51, 55

Bolton; see Bradford

Bolton Abbey, N Yorks 11, 15, 155

Bolton, Lancs: Town Hall 339, 378

Bombay, India: Customs Ho 36, 372

Booth: Ch 196

Boston Spa 13, 15, 21, 10: Baths 371; CompSch 266, 214; St Mary 382

Bowling; see Bradford

Bradford 11, 13, 17, 19, 20, 22, 34–5, 42, 44, 95, 128, 130, 132, 153, 281, 363–4

Banks, insurance offices, shops etc: Albert Bldgs, Tyrrel St 378; Beckett's Bank, Kirkgate 381; Bradford Banking Co, Kirkgate 370; Bradford Comm Bank, Bank St 370; Bradford District Bank, Market St 381; Brown Muff's, Market St 380; London & Midland Bank, Market St 380; Manor Ho Bldgs 374; Parkinsons Bldgs, Hustlergate 380; Queen Anne Chambers, Sunbridge Rd 386; Refuge Chambers, Sunbridge Rd 380; Royal Arcade 323, 262; Swan Arcade 323, 364, 382; Yorks Banking Co, Bank St 381, Market St 380; Yorks Penny Bank, Manor Row 380

Churches & chapels: All Saints, Little Horton Green 227, 381; Bowland Rd Synagogue 378; Brick Lane PMCh 372; Chapel Lane UCh 199, 225, 370; Christ Ch 210, 385; Ch of First Martyrs 236; Church Inst, N Parade 370; Eastbrook Ch 199, 372; Eastbrook Hall 199; Eccleshill WMCh 384; Gt Horton CCh 206; Gt Horton MCh 206, 161; Gt Horton Rd MNCCh 378; Greenfield CCh 380; Holy Trinity, Idle 382, Low Moor 384; Horton Lane CCh 206, 381; Manningham PMCh 378; Octagon, Little Horton Rd 199; Rehoboth PMCh 378; St Andrew, Lister Hills 381, N Horton 381; St Anne 384; St Augustine, Undercliffe 378; St Augustine's WCh 377; St Barnabas, Heaton 227; St Chad 234; St James 383, Bolton 370, Thornton 378; St John, Bowling 384, Manchester Rd 384, N Bierley 189, 373, 144; St John Baptist, Clayton 381; St John Evangelist, Gt Horton Rd 378, Greengates 379, Little Horton Green 378; St John's MCh 226; St Joseph 384; St Jude, Manningham 383; St Luke 381, Eccleshill 383, Manningham 378; St Mark, Low Moor 381; St Mary 220, 384, Laisterdyke 381, Wyke 227, 381; St Matthew, Bankfoot 381; St Patrick 377; St Paul, Buttershaw 383, Manningham 110, 227, 381, 76; St Peter (Cath) 170, 214, 236, 374, 377, 130, 187, Allerton 383; St Philip, Girlington 381; St Stephen, Bowling 381; St Wilfrid, Lidget Green 227, 234; Salem IndCh 203, 380; Sion BCh 381; Tennyson Pl PMSchCh 378; Westgate Ch 383

Districts, estates, parks etc: Barkerend 150; Bowling 13; Broomfield 132; Clayton Heights 143; Eccleshill 130; Frizinghall 124; Girlington 132, 107; Idle 20; Laisterdyke 118; Lister Pk 360; Longlands Estate 146; Manningham 108, 114, 132; Mill Bank 132; Oak Estate 110; Peel Pk 96; Rosse Estate 117, 380; Scarlet Heights 13; Thornbury 118

Hotels, public houses & clubs: Alexandra Hotel, Gt Horton Rd 277, 370; Bradford Club 381; Liberal Club 381; Midland Hotel 273; Royal Hotel, Darley St 380; Talbot Hotel, Kirkgate 370; Temperance Comm Hotel, Manchester Rd 373; Victoria Hotel 42, 381

Industrial & warehouses: Alston Wks 295, 381; Bank Top Mills 381; Bolton Rd, warehouses 382; Burnett St, warehouses 370, 376, 381; Buttershaw Mills 295; Canal Rd, warehouses 302; Chapel St, warehouses 370, 382; Charles St, warehouses 376; Commercial St, warehouses 373; Currer St, warehouses 300, 370, 381, 8, 239; East Parade, warehouses 300, 381; Gt Horton Mill 293; Hall Ings, warehouses 299, 370, 376, 238; Highgate Mills, Clayton Heights 293, 234; Leeds Rd, warehouses 299, 300, 364, 370, 380–1, 383; Legrams Mills 295, 381; Lumb Lane Mills 295, 381; Manningham Mill 146, 257, 295–6, 370, 107, 236; Manor Row, warehouses 302, 373, 376, 243; Midland Mills 295–6, 370; Oak Mills, Clayton 382; Oakroyd Dyeworks 381; Peckover St, warehouses 300, 375, 381; Peel Sq, warehouses 300, 302, 381, 242; Piccadilly, warehouses 383, 386; Princeville Combing Wks 382; Sunbridge Rd, warehouses 373; Swaine St, warehouses 380; Union warehouses 379; Vicar Lane, warehouses 300, 381, 240, 241; Waterloo Mill 252; Well St, warehouses 300, 380–1; Whetley Mills 295, 296, 381

Institutions: Board of Guardians 374; Children's Hosp 380; Dispensary, Northgate 370; Eye & Ear Hosp 381; Infirmary, Westgate 383; Inst for Blind 380; Model Lodging Ho, Captain St 145, Sunbridge Rd 145, 370; Nutter Orphanage 378; Penny Oaks Hosp 370; Royal Infirmary 381; Royal Victoria Nurses' Home 382; St Catherine's Home 380; Union Workhouse 380

Mansions & villas: Bierley Hall 382; Bolling Hall 79, 373; Bolton Royd 110; Bowling Pk Ho 114, 376; Daisy Bank 370; Esholt Hall 60; Field Ho, Smith Lane 383; Grove Ho, Bolton 114, 379; Heaton Mt 114, 376, 81, 82; Ladye Royde Hall 381; Manor Ho 96, 314, 319; Oakwell 110, 370; Rose Mt 110, 370; Thornfield, Manningham 381; Town Hill 382; Woodlands, Toller Lane 115, 381

Public buildings: Baths & wash-houses, Thornton Rd 381; Cartwright Mem Hall 45, 360, 293; Cloth Hall 285, 288; County Court 385; Court Ho 334, 383; Exch 332, 334; Hall of Pleas 329; Kirkgate Market 318–20, 327, 364, 367, 381, 253, 254; Market, Bower's Croft 314; Market Ho, Hall Ings 314, 383; Poor Law Guardians, Manor Row 370, 243; Rawson Market 378; St George's Hall 35, 299, 300, 302, 334–5, 339–40, 343, 345, 380, 273, 275; Salt Mem 381; Town Hall 41, 327, 352–4, 358, 379, 381, 285, 292; Victoria Mem 360; Wool Exch 39, 306–9, 327, 381, 247

Schools, colleges, institutes etc: Airedale Coll 374, 381, 383; Board Schools: Barkerend 257, 370;

Belle Vue HGS 260, 377, *206*; Bowling Back Lane 257, 381; Dudley Hill 257, 380–1; Feversham St HGS 260, 381; Gt Horton HGS 378; Hanson HBS 261, 377; Horton Bank 257; Lilycroft 257, 378, *203, 204*; Ryan St 257, 379; Wheatley Lane 257, 378.
Bowling ChSch 378; Coll of Art 44; Friends' Sch, Chapel Lane 246; GS 239, 250, 252, 370–2, *198*; MechInst 253, 255, 270, 383; Moravian Sch, Wyke 243; National Sch, Westgate 246; Rebecca St Ragged Sch 380; St Philip's Sch, Girlington 381; St Thomas's Sch 381; TechSch 262, 378, *208*; Undercliffe Baptist Academy 203; University 262
Streets, terraces etc: Apsley Villas 109; Bavaria Pl 132, *97*; Blenheim Tce 109, 379, *75*; Clifton Villas 110; Eldon Pl 109, 383; Foxfleet St 146–7; Hallfield Rd 109, 376; Hanover Sq 109; Kensington St 132; Leeds Rd 300, 376; Lindum Tce 110, 378; Manningham Lane 108–10; Mornington Villas 109, 380; Mount Royd 110, 381, *77*; Peel Sq 300; Piccadilly 298; Rooley Lane 376; St Paul's Tce 110, 378, *76*; Silsbridge Lane 132; Silver St 132; Tyrrel St 378; Victoria Sq 378; Westbourne Rd 145–6, *109*
Theatres: Alhambra 280, *223*; Duke St 271; Empire Pal of Varieties 277; Market St 271; Music Hall, Brunswick Pl 276; Princes 272; Royal Alexandra 271, 370

Bradley: St Thomas 375
Bradley Hall, nr Stainland 25, 48, 51, 370
Bradshaw: St John 374
Bramham 21: All Saints 383; Biggin 382; Park 28–9, 62, 64, 71, 371, 373, 382, 385, *32, 33, 34*
Bramhope: Castley Hall 60; Ch 194, *151*
Bramley; see Leeds
Brancepeth, Northumb 61, 371
Brearley: BCh 226, 378
Bretton Hall 14, 29, 33, 65–6, 79, 83, 88, 189, 266, 373, 380, 382, 386, *35, 45, 215*
Brighouse 15: Albert Theatre 277; Friends' Meeting Ho 196; St Martin 377; Town Hall 371
Brighton, Sussex: Brill's Baths 348
Brotherton: St Edward 383
Browsholme Hall, Lancs 181
Bruntcliffe: MNCCh 381
Burley; see Leeds
Burley-in-Wharfedale 119, 252: Ind Ch 383; St Mary Blessed Virgin 383
Burley-on-the-Hill, Rutland 62
Burmantofts; see Leeds
Burton Agnes Hall, Humberside 26, 55
Burton Constable Hall, Humberside 96
Bury, Lancs: Bank St UCh 225
Buslingthorpe; see Leeds
Buxton, Derbys: Crescent 330; Opera Ho 276
Byram Park 79, 373
Bywell Abbey, Northumb 79

Calverley 118: Ho 118; Ferncliffe 118, 380; Knottfield Ho 118, 382; Mechanics' Inst 379; St Wilfred 158, 162, 166, 378
Campsall Hall, S Yorks 379, 386
Cannon Hall, S Yorks 73, 79, 189
Cannons, Middlesex 29, 384
Cape Town, S Africa: City Hall 339
Carlton Towers, N Yorks 79
Castle Carr 84, 378, *48*
Castle Howard, N Yorks 27, 29, 64–5, 73, 91, 96, 376, 385

Castleford 15, 22: Bridge 377; Civic Centre 362, 367, *295*; St Joseph 377; SecSch 372; Theatre Royal 277; Whitwood Mere IS 265, *213*
Cawthorne, S Yorks 11
Chapel Allerton; see Leeds
Clayton; see Bradford
Cleckheaton: Conservative Club 379; Drill Hall 379; Fire Station 379; Greenside Central MCh 206, 373; Lancs & Yorks Bank 379; Liberal Club 373; London, City & Midland Bank 379; Providence Pl MCh 206, 381; Public Baths 373, 379; St Andrew, Oakenshaw 382; St John 185, 210, 371, 377; Town Hall 355, 381; Whitcliffe Mt Sec & Tech Sch 385; Whitcliffe Rd Mixed Sch 373; Whitcliffe Rd WMCh 379; White Ch 379
Cliffe Castle 85, 377, 384, *50*
Clifford: St Edward 221, 377, *174*; St Luke 371
Clifton: St John Evangelist 381
Clubcliffe Hall; see Methley
Coley: Ch 372
Collingham: Sch 240
Conisbrough Castle, S Yorks 11
Copley 13, 133, 135–6, 375, *2, 98, 99*: Mill 135, 293, 366, *98, 233*; St Stephen 136, 227, 375
Crosland; see Huddersfield
Crosstone: St Paul 382
Crow Nest House 80–1, 241, 372
Cullingworth: St John Evangelist 383
Cumberworth: PMCh 378; St Nicholas 379

Dean House: Almshouses 390; Ch 196, *152*
Denby Dale: PMCh 378
Denholme Gate: St Paul 374, 384
Denton Park, N Yorks 80, *189*
Derby, Derbys: All Saints 186
Dewsbury 15, 128, 153: All Saints 166, 175, 189, 373, 390, *145*; Earlsheaton BS 378; Earlsheaton Sch 385; Ebenezer CCh 226, 377; Empire Theatre 280; Freemasons' Hall 390; Hanging Heaton MCh 377; Holy Trinity, Batley Carr 374; Infirmary 380; Market Cross 314; MNCCh 378; Moot Hall 329; St John, Dewsbury Moor 385; St Joseph, Batley Carr 384; St Mark 376, 381; St Mary's BS, Savile Town 378; St Paul, Hanging Heaton 385; St Paulinus 224, 377; St Peter, Earlsheaton 385; St Philip 378; Sands Mill 289; TechSch 376; Town Hall 355, 376, 378; Wakefield ICS 385; Wheelwright GS 250, 376
Dobroyd Castle 84, *47*
Doncaster, S Yorks 11: Dispensary 103; Mansion Ho 30, 331, 382; St James 37, 375; St Mary 375; Theatre 380
Drancy, France: Cité de la Muette 148
Drighlington: BS 260, 381; GS 238; Lumb Hall 56; St Paul 371
Dublin, Eire 47: Marino, Casino 74
Durban, S Africa: Town Hall 339

East Ardsley: BS 378; St Michael 371
Easthorpe 125
East Keswick: St Mary Magdalene 381
East Riddlesden Hall 56–7
Eastwood: St Mary Virgin 383
Eccleshill; see Bradford
Edensor, Derbys 133
Edinburgh, Scotland 34: Corn Exch 348; Empire Pal Th 276; Municipal Bldgs 380
Elland 17: Bethesda MNCCh 378; Huddersfield Rd MCh 371; New Hall 51, 55; Old Hall 55; St Mary 156, 158, *116*; SSch 372; South End BS 378; Town Hall 378

Escrick Park, N Yorks 73
Eshald House; see Heath
Esholt; see Bradford
Esholt Priory 153
Everingham, N Yorks: Chapel of Virgin & St Everilda 377

Farfield Hall, N Yorks 65
Farnley; see Leeds
Farnley Hall, N Yorks 79–81
Farnley Tyas: St Lucius 374
Farsley: St John Evangelist 386; West Royd 115, 370
Ferrara, Italy: Pal dei Diamanti 348
Ferrybridge: Bridge 373, 377, 386
Florence, Italy 65: Duomo 288, 306, 340; Pal Vecchio 41, *299*, 354
Fountains Abbey, N Yorks 11, 45, 134, 151, 154–5
Fryston Hall 47, 80, 88, 101, 199
Fulneck: Moravian Sch 243–4, *193*

Garforth: Manor Farm 385; St Mary 379; Sch 240
Gargrave, N Yorks 15
Garrowby Hall, N Yorks 88
Gawthorp Hall 31, 47, 73, 373
Genoa, Italy: Pal dell'Università 343; S Lorenzo 343
Gildersome: Friends' Meeting Ho 197; St Peter 370, 382; The Woodlands 377
Gilling Castle, N Yorks 96
Glasgow, Scotland: Art Gallery 360; King's Theatre 276
Gledhow; see Leeds
Golcar 127, *93*; St John 371, 374, 379–80, 382
Goldsborough Hall, N Yorks 74
Gomersal: ChSch 377; Pollard Hall 55; St Mary Virgin 376; White Cloth Hall 285
Goole, Humberside 11
Goose Eye 127, *95*
Grassington, N Yorks 11
Greengates; see Bradford
Greenland: Claye Ho 7; Wesley Ch 196
Guiseley 119, 181: Par Sch 383; St Oswald 158

Halifax 11, 13, 17, 20, 22, 34–5, 42, 44, 95, 132, 146, 153, 281, 368, *2, 3*
Banks, offices, industrial etc: Dean Clough Mills 294–5, 379, 383; Joint Stock Bank 344; Permanent Bldg Soc 41, 367–8, 379, *199, 297*; Wainhouse Tower 372, *2*; Yorks Penny Bank 383
Churches & chapels: All Souls', Haley Hill 21, 37, 137, 226–7, 344, *181, 182*; CemCh 378, 381; Bethel Ch, Ovenden 378; Booth Town UMCh 378; Holy Trinity 105, 193, 379; King Cross MNCSSch 380; New CCh 383; Park Pl CCh 138, 225, 379; Sacred Heart & St Bernard 384; St Augustine, Hanson Lane 378; St George, Lee Mt 379; Ovenden 379; St James 382; St John (Parish church) 170, 176–7, 179–80, 364, 374, *135, 136*; St Jude, Salterhebble 371; St Paul, King Cross 374; Sion Ch 203; Square Ch 22, 185, 200, 225, 372, *156, 177*
Districts, estates, parks etc: Akroydon 133, 136–9, 371, 375, *100*; People's Pk 111, 138, 317; Shroggs Pk 137, 371; West Hill Pk Estate 138, *101, 102*; Wool-Shops 55
Hotels & theatres: Alexandra Th 379; Electric Th, Ward's End 280, 378; Old Cock 287;

Palace Th 280, 378; Royal Th 280, 378; Shakspeare Tavern 270; White Swan Hotel 344, 381, *280*

Institutions: Crossley Orphanage 378; Infirmary 41, 379; Joseph Crossley Almshouses, Arden Rd 138, 379; Sir Frank Crossley Almshouses, Margaret St 138, 379; Model Lodging Ho, Smithy St 145; Waterhouse Schs & Almshouses 374

Mansions & villas: Allangate 116; Bankfield 83–4, 137, 371; Belle Vue 114, 138, *83*; Bermerside 379; Broomfield 379; Hope Hall 73; 'House at the Maypole' 94, 372; Manor Heath 115; Moorside 117; Northgate Ho 35, 97, 377; Ovenden: Hall 94, Holdsworth Ing 93; Park Rd 111, 378; Royds (or Somerset) Ho 96, 98–9, 187, 373, *61, 62*; Shibden Hall 25, 35, 48, 55, 88, 93, 130, 377, *12*; The Shay 373; The Square 98, 373; Well End Ho 373

Public buildings: Blackwell (Cloth) Hall 282; Borough Market 319–21, 327, 380, *257, 258*; County Court 385; Market Cross 311, 314; Moot Hall 329; Multure Hall 145; New Rooms 332, 382, *270*; Oddfellows' Hall 374; Piece Hall 98, 285, 287–8, 320, *228, 229*; Russell Arcade 321, 323, 380, *259*; Town Hall 37, 307, 344, 378, *280*; Victoria Hall 367, *297*

Schools & colleges: Battinson Rd BS 378; Booth Town Sch 380; Crossley & Porter Schs 378; Haugh End IS 378; Heath GS 25, 51, 240, 250, 370, 380; Holy Trinity Boys' Sch 378; King Cross Sch 381; Lancasterian Sch, Gt Albion St 246; Mechanics' Hall, Crossley St 252–3, 344, 381, *199*; West Vale 378; National Sch 246; Percival Whitley Coll FE 262, 379; Queen's Rd Schs 257, 378; TechSch 262

Hardcastle Crags 14
Hardwick Hall, Derbys 52, 88
Harewood 14, 128–30, 133, 142, 373, *96*: All Saints 162–3, *123*; House 32–3, 61, 73–4, 76, 78–80, 84, 91, 103, 128–9, 343, 371, 373–4, *5, 41, 42*; Sch 240–1, 373
Harrogate, N Yorks 11, 119, 129: Assembly Rms 133; Christ Ch 382; Godolphin Ho 386; Gróve Ho 386; Kursaal (Royal Hall) 276; Royal Chalybeate Spa 374; St Mary 374; Selbourne Ho 386; Victoria Baths 374
Hartshead: St Peter 161, 378; WCh 379
Hatfield House, Herts 48
Haworth 17, *6*: St Michael 166, 193, 378
Hazlewood Castle 21, 79, 373
Headingley; see Leeds
Heath 72, 368: BS 371; Dower Ho 72, *39*; Eshald Ho 28, 60, 73, 384, *28*; GS 238–9; Hall 73, 76, 373, *39, 40*; (Old) Hall 52–3, 73, *17*; Ho 69, 73, 382, *37*
Heaton; see Bradford
Hebden Bridge 13, 42, 366: BCh 196; St James 382
Heckmondwike 128: Blanket Hall 285, 383; St James 185, 210, 371; Upper Ind CCh 206, 385, *163*; WCh 380
Helmsley Castle, N Yorks 376
Hemsworth: GS 237; St Helen 226
Heptonstall 13, 22, 127, 281, *1*: BCh 196; Cloth Hall 238; Octagon 197, *154*; St Thomas 158, 381
Hexthorpe, S Yorks: St Jude 386
Hickleton Hall, S Yorks 372
High Flatts: Friends' Meeting Ho 197
High Sunderland 56–7, *24*

Hillhouse; see Huddersfield
Hipperholme 17, 20: GS 238, 241, 379, *191*
Holbeck; see Leeds
Holmbridge: St David 374
Holmfirth 281: BS 378; Holy Trinity 193, 379
Honley 42, 127, 290, *94*: BS 390; Nat Sch 247; St Mary 213, 374, *94, 166*
Hopton Hall 125
Horbury: Nat Sch 248, 384; St John 226; St Mary 226; St Peter & St Leonard 32, 189–90, 373, *146*; UMFCh 378
Horsforth: Ch 189, 373; Hall 60; St Margaret 226, 231, 377, 380
Horton Hall 55
Houghton Hall, Norfolk 73
Hovingham Hall, N Yorks 29
Howley Hall 25, 51, 199, 370, *16*
Huby Hall, N Yorks 29

Huddersfield 11, 13, 17, 22, 34–5, 42, 44, 153, 281

Banks, offices, shops etc: Albert Hotel etc 379; Britannia Bldgs 298, 339, *237*; Byram Arcade 323, *261*; Byram Bldgs, Westgate 323, 375; George Hotel 298, 339, 374, 379, 386; John William St, warehouses 298; Kirkgate Bldgs 375; Lion Arcade 383; Ramsden Estate Office, Railway St 375

Churches & chapels: All Saints, Paddock 379–80, 382; Brunswick UMCh 380; Christ Ch, Woodhouse Hill 385; Highfield CCh 383, *159*; Hillhouse UMFCh 380; Holy Trinity 113, 379–80, 385, Crosland 371, 379; Paddock CCh 380; Queen St Ch 201, 379, *157*; Ramsden St CCh 201, 379, 383; St Andrew 375; St John 226, Birkby 379; St Joseph 370, 384; St Luke, Milnes Bridge 386; St Mark 371; St Paul 379–80, 382, Armitage Br 374; St Patrick 220, 379; St Peter (Parish ch) 214, 216, 383, *167*; St Thomas, Manchester Rd 37, 226; St Stephen, Lindley 379, 382

Mansions & villas: Banney Royd, Lindley 118, *87*; Birkby Lodge 118; Briarcourt, Lindley 118; Ebor Mount *80*; Milnes Bridge Ho 69, 382–3; New North Rd, villas 113, *79, 80*

Public buildings & institutions: Art Gallery 364; Brook St Market 320, *256*; Chapel Hill, Model Lodging Ho 145; Cloth Hall 284–5, 287–8, *227*; County Court 201, *157*; Crosland Moor Workhouse 380; Grand Th (prop) 277; Infirmary 379–80, 382; Market Hall 319–20, 327, 379, *255*; Municipal Offices, Ramsden St 370; Philosophical Hall, Ramsden St 277; Poor Law Union Offices 390; Post Office 375; Railway Station 339, 379, 383, *276*; Riding Sch, Ramsden St 277; Th Royal 277; Town Hall 339, 364, 370; Victoria Tower, Castle Hill 13, 386, *4*

Schools, colleges etc: Apsley Lecture Rm 374, 386; Beaumont St BS 379; Huddersfield Coll 383; Mechanics' Inst 44, 252–3, *200*; Polytechnic 44, 262; School of Art 44; Spring Gr Sch 379; Tech Sch 262, 379, *207*

Streets, districts etc: Carr Pit Lane 380; Edgerton 113, 124; Edgerton Rd 390; Elm St 380; Greenhead Pk 113; John William St 298; Lindley 118; New North Rd 113, 380, *79, 80*; Newsome Rd 380; Railway St 298; St George's Sq 298, 339; Trevelyan St 146, 380; Trinity Rd 113; Wentworth St 113; Whitehead Lane 380

Hull, Humberside 35–6, 156: Albion Ch 335; Dock Offices 372; Gen Cemetery 372; Gt Thornton St Ch 335, 380; Holy Trinity Ch 96; Royal Infirmary 380; Royal Inst 340, 372; Town Hall 372; Trinity Ho Ch 335, 380; Whitefriargate 372; Wilberforce Col 374
Hunslet; see Leeds
Huthwaite Hall, S Yorks 31, 72
Hyde, Lancs: UCh 225

Idle; see Bradford
Ilkley 15, 42, 119, *88*: All Saints 165–6; Arden Croft 120, 378, *90*; Arden Lea 120; Ben Rhydding Hydro Est 119; Church St 119; CCh 226, 383; Cowpasture Rd 119; Craiglands 119; GS 238–9, 250, 377; Heathcote *88–9, 91*, 118, *52*; Hospital 119; Ilkley Coll 378; IS 266; PMCh 378; Railway Station 119; Sacred Heart of Jesus 384; St Johns 384; St Margaret 227, 231; Shandon 119, *89*; Town Hall 119, 371; Wells Ho 105, 119, 373; Westwood Lodge 119, 384, *89*; Woodbank 119, 370
Ingrow: St John 383

Keighley 17, 44, 146: Mech Inst 253, 255, 372, 381; Queen's Th 277, *221*; Railway Stn 110; St Andrew 374; St Anne 221, 384; Tech Sch 266, 381; Victoria Stn Hotel 382
Kinloch Castle, Isle of Rhum 380
Kippax: Hall 30, 52–3, 71; St Mary 167
Kirby Hall, N Yorks 29, 31, 72
Kirkburton: Storthes Hall Asylum 372
Kirkby Overblow, N Yorks: All Saints 382
Kirkheaton 153: St John 164
Kirklees Priory 153, 380
Kirkstall; see Leeds
Kiveton Pk, S Yorks 60–1, 371
Knowsthorpe (Knostrop) Hall 57
Kyre Pk, Worcs 370

Lacock, Wilts 133
Laycock 95
Leathley: St Oswald 166, 376
Ledsham 21: All Saints 153; Vicarage 377
Ledston Hall 21, 27–8, 47–8, 52–4, 61, 186, 290, 371, 385, *20, 21, 31*; Lodge 382

Leeds 11, 15, 17, 22, 34–5, 42, 95, 130–2, 143–4, 146, 281, 363, 368
Banks, insurance offices, shops etc: Arcades: County 280, 325, *263*, Cross 325, Grand 323, 385, Queens 323, Market St 323, Thornton's 276–3, 384, *260*, Victoria 323, 385; Athenaeum Bldgs, Park Lane 371; Atlas Bldgs, E Parade 383; Bank of Eng, S Parade 366, *296*; Beckett's Bank, Park Row 37, 40, 364, 383, *296*; Boar Lane, shops 383; Bond St, shops 374; Briggate, Exch 383; Britannia Bldgs, Oxford Pl 376; City Chambers 383; City & County Bank, Park Row 385; Commercial Bldgs 34, 107, 332, 374, *269*; Commercial St, shops 375; Cookridge St, shops etc 373; Gt George St, studio 375; Headland (Sun) Bldgs, Park Row 364, 375, *296*; Hepper Ho, E Parade 375; Imp Fire & Life Ass Co, Bond St 384; Leeds & W Yorks Ass Co, Commercial St 20; LICS St & People's Hall 375; Lloyd's Bank, Park Row 367; London & Midland Bank, Kirkgate 371; Nat Prov Bank, Park Row 383; Peacock's Bldgs, Park Row 376; Pearl Bldgs, E Parade 371; Queen Anne's Bldgs 371; Prud Ass Co, Park

Row 22; Royal Exch 332, 378; Royal Ins Co, Park Row 296; Scottish Union Ins Co, S Parade 383; Scottish Widows Ass Co, Park Row 375, 296; Thornton's Bldgs, Headrow 384; Trustee Savings Bank, Bond St 374; Union Bank, Commercial St 385; Victoria Chbrs, S Parade 381; W Riding Union Bank, Park Row 376; William Williams Brown & Co Bank, Park Row 22, 24; Yorks District Bank, Boar Lane 374; Yorks Penny Bank, Infirmary St 383; Yorks Post, Albion St 22, 374, Wellington St 367

Churches & chapels: Albion St MCh 200, 375; All Hallows, Burley 370; All Saints, York Rd 381; All Souls, Blackman Lane 226, 228; Armley Hall Ch 370; Armley Mortuary Ch 383; Armley PMCh, Branch Rd 378; Beckett St MCh 378; Beeston Hill WCh 378; Belgrave St Synagogue 383; Blenheim BCh 383; Brunswick MCh 203, 372, 384, *158*; Burley WMCh 375; Burley Lawn UMFCh 384; Burley Rd BCh 370; Call Lane UCh 199; Cardigan Rd PMCh 378; Cavendish Rd Pres Ch 268, 376; Christ Ch, Meadow Lane 211, 370, 374, Upper Armley 370; Ch of Epiphany 227, 236; Church Inst, Albion Pl 370; Clowes PMCh 370; Crossgates WMCh 375; Dewsbury Rd MNCCh 378, WCh 375; E Parade ICh 203, 379; Ebenezer PMCh, Kirkstall 378; Eldon WCh 375; Emmanuel Ch 370; Farnley Cem Ch 378; Friends' Meeting Ho, Carlton Hill 204, 372, *160*, Water Lane 196; Friends' Mission Rm 385; Gt George St BCh 384; Hall Lane MNCCh 372; Hanover Pl WMCh 375, 384; Harehills Lane MSchCh 385; Headingley Hill CCh 225, 373, *70*; Holbeck UCh 374; Holy Family 370; Holy Name, Woodhouse 374; Holy Spirit, Beeston 371; Holy Trinity, Boar Lane 27, 30, 96, *186–7*, 213, 374–6, 386, *140*, New Wortley 370; Hunslet Moor End WMCh 375; Joseph St PMCh 380; Jubilee PMCh, Woodhouse 378; Kirkstall Abbey 19, 81, 134, 151–6, 159, 182–4, 244, *114, 115*; Kirkstall CCh 384; Lady Huntingdon's Conn, see St James; Lady Lane MCh 384; Lady Lane RCCh 194; Lady Pit Lane WMCh 375; Lincoln Fields WMCh 375; Lower Wortley PMCh 378; Marshall St MNCCh 378; Meanwood MCh 378; Middleton WMCh 378; Mill Hill UCh 199, 225, 275, *176*; Mount St Mary 220–1, 377, *175*; Newton Pk UCh 382; New Wortley CCh 370, MCh 383; Old Ch 200; Oxford Pl MCh 207, 384–5, *164*; Par Ch Mission Rm 374; Park WMCh, Cross Flatts 375, 384; Priory of St Wilfrid 227; Queen St CCh 201; Richmond Hill MCh 375, 384; Roscoe Pl MCh 375; Roseville Rd WMCh 375; Roundhay Rd MCh 206, 376; Roundhay WCh 383; Sacred Heart, Burley 370; St Agnes, Burmantofts 372; St Aidan 234; St Andrew, Cavendish St 36, 226–7; St Anne (RC Cath) 107, 219, 221, 234, 374, *170, 172, 186, 296*; Cardigan Rd 234; St Augustine, Wrangthorne 376; St Barnabas, Holbeck 370, 376, 386; St Bartholomew, Armley 370, 374, 386; St Chad, Far Headingley 228, 375; St Clement, Sheepscar 227, 375, *180*; St Cuthbert, Hunslet 383; St Edmund, Richmond Hill 375, Roundhay 234; St Edward, Holbeck 226, 233, St Francis of Assisi 370; St George 106, 374; St Hilda, Cross Green 226; St James, New York St 199, Manston 383; St John, Adel

160–2, 227, 374, *121, 122,* Briggate 95, 153, 179–82, 227, 240, 374, 382, *137, 138, 139,* Roundhay 248, 385, *195*; St John Baptist, New Wortley 376; St John Evangelist, Little Holbeck 36, 135, 226–7, *178,* Moor Allerton 385; St Joseph 374; St Jude, Hunslet 373, 383; St Luke, Beeston Hill 370, North St 383; St Margaret, Bramley 383, Cardigan Rd 227; St Mark, Woodhouse 370–1; St Mary, Bramley 374, 385, Lady Lane 379, Middleton 374, Quarry Hill 210, 385, Whitkirk 158, 180, 226; St Mary of Bethany, Tong Rd 370; St Mary-the-Virgin, Hunslet 374, 383; St Matthew, Camp Rd 373, 376, Chapel Allerton 226, 232, 383, *185,* Holbeck 374, 378; St Matthias, Burley 383; St Michael, Buslingthorpe 373, Farnley 189, 373–4, Headingley 226, 231, 374, 376, *184*; St Patrick 220, 370, 374; St Paul, Park Sq 104, 193–4, *149,* Shadwell 374, 379; St Peter (Parish ch) 39, 96, 168–9, 180, 213–4, 216–7, 225, 231, 374, 382, *128, 129, 168, 169,* Hunslet Moor 383; St Peter's St MCh 384; St Philip, Wellington St 135, 374; St Saviour 217–20, 223, *171*; St Silas, Hunslet 375; St Simon, Ventnor St 384; St Stephen, Burmantofts 376, Kirkstall 213, 374, 383, 386; St Thomas, North St 226, *179*; St Wilfrid, Halton 236, *188*; Salem PMCh, Holdforth St 378; Shadwell WCh 375; Sheepscar WCh 383; Silver Royd Hill PMCh, Tong Rd 378; South Parade BCh 203; Stourton WCh 378; Tabernacle UMFChSch 378; Tempest Rd MNCCh 372; Trinity CCh, Woodhouse Lane 375, MCh, Roundhay Rd 375, 385; Ventnor St MNCCh 372, 378; Wesley Ch, Meadow Lane 200, 384; Whingate WMCh 384; Woodhouse Carr WMCh 375; Woodhouse Hill PMCh 378; Woodhouse Lane MNCCh 378

Districts, estates, parks etc: Armley 13; Beeston Hill 370; Belle Isle Est 147; Burley 150; Burmantofts 23–4; Buslingthorpe 105; Chapel Allerton *113;* Cottingley Est 149; Crossgates Est 147; Gipton Est 147, *111;* Halton Est 147; Headingley Hill 107, 144; Hunslet Grange 147; Killingbeck 383; Kirkstall 13, 144; Lawnswood Cem 375; Little Woodhouse 105–6; Meanwood 19, 147, 373; Newton Pk 374–5, 385; New Leeds 105, 374, 383; Oakwood 123, 327; Parks Est 101, 104, *63;* Potternewton Gdns 367; Quarry Hill 147–50, *112;* Roundhay Pk 120–4, 327, 375, *91, 92;* Seacroft Est 147, *111;* Woodhouse Cem 105, 268, 374, 383; Zoological & Botanical Gdns 372

Hotels, public houses & clubs: Gt Northern Ho 377; Jubilee Ho, Pk Lane 386; King Edward Rest 280; Leeds & County Con Cl, S Pde 384; Liberal Cl, Quebec St 22, 374; Masonic Hall, Carlton Hill 371, Gt George St 372, 383; Metropole Ho 22, 374; Mitre Ho, Commercial St 386; Phoenix Inn, Kirkgate 375; Queens Ho 24, 383; St James Hall, Temp Ho etc, York St 370; Trevelyan Temp Ho, Boar Lane 305, 370; Upper & Lower Wortley Liberal Cl 385; White Swan Ho 323

Industrial & warehouses: Aire St, warehouses 378; Armley Mill 82; Balm Rd, cotton mill 294, 374; Bank Mills 294, 374; Basinghall St, warehouses 370, 372; Bean Ing Mill 33, 82, 104, 290–2, 382, *232;* Benyon & Bage's mill, Meadow Lane 289; Boar Lane, warehouses

306, 386; Burley Mill 82; Call Lane, warehouses 379; Grace St, warehouses 384; Greek St, factory 370; King St, warehouses 304, 364, 373, 375, *244;* Kirkstall Forge 104; Park Pl, warehouses 306, 370; St Paul's Ho, Park Sq 306, 366, 370, *149, 245;* Scotland Mill 289; Temple Mill 134, 289–90, *230, 231;* Tetley's Brewery 375; Tower Wks, Globe Rd 306, 371, 384, *246;* Viaduct Rd, tannery 378; Water Lane, mills 289; Wellington St, warehouses 302, 304, 372, 375, 383, 385–6; Whitehall Rd, electrical wks 382, printing wks 372, stables 374; York Pl, warehouses 304, 375, 384

Institutions: Blind, Deaf & Dumb Inst, Albion St 372; Borough Gaol, Armley 113, 383; Dispensary, New Briggate 378, North St 371; Gen Infirmary 39, 101, 266, 330, 348–9, 351–2, 373, 375, *284;* Home for Waifs & Strays 374; Ida Con Home 374; Model Lodging Ho, Millgarth 145, 383; Nurses' Home, Gen Inf 385; Orphans' Home, Cliff Rd 385; Park La, Firemen's Flats 383; St James's Inf 386; Union Hosp, Beckett St 386; Wade La, Almshouses 376; Women & Children's Hosp 374; Woodhouse, Almshouses 374; Workhouse, Beckett St 383, Holbeck 378; YMCA, Albion Pl 385

Mansions & villas: Adel Towers 384; Alma Rd (J.H.Smalpage) 113, 373, *78;* Armley Ho 13, 35, 80–1, 292, *44;* Ashwood 108, 374, *73;* Austhorpe Hall 57, 60, *27;* Ballamona 375; Bardon Hill 384; Belle Vue 105; Belmont 105; Bischoff Ho, see Sheepscar Hall; Boar Lane (J.Dixon) 98, 373; Bridge End (-Green) 373; Carr Ho 85, 116; Castle Gr 386; Claremont 105; Denison Hall 97, 105, 379, *60;* Dunearn 116, 375; Fox Hill 116, 375; Gledhow Gr 83, 374; Gledhow Hall 80, 373–4; Harehills Gr 83; Hatwood 123; Hawkhills 374; Headingley Castle 108; Headingley Hill Ho 107, *71;* Kirkgate (W.Denison) 101, (J.Thoresby) 93, *53;* Knowsthorpe (Knostrop) Hall 57, 83, *25;* Manston Lodge 371; Meanwood Hall 83, 97, 374; Meanwood Towers, see Carr Ho; Mill Hill (R.Wilson) 96; Mount Pleasant 105; New Grange 69, 71, 382; North Hill Ho 108, 384, *74;* Old Hall 94–5; Parcmont 123, 370; Park La (J.Blayds) 81, 104; Quarrydene 385; Ravenstone 375; Red Hall 21, 95; Red Ho 371; Rockley Hall 92, 238; Roundhay Hall 82–3, 374; Roundhay Pk 80, 82, 247, 374, *92;* St Ives 116, 375; St Michael's Mt 375; Sheepscar Hall 27, 96, 376, 57, *58;* Spenfield 116, 375, *86;* Temple Newsam Ho 21, 26, 30, 32, 48, 51–4, 71, 78, 88, 134, 180, 233, 284, 373, 376, 379, 385, *19, 38, 51;* The Calls (J.Atkinson) 96; The Priory 107, 374, *72;* Town End (R.Denison) 27, 96, 102, 385, *56;* Vicarage Ho 314; Wade Hall, see Old Hall; Weetwood Lodge 384; Wheatfield Lodge 386; Woodbourne 123, 384; Woodhouse Ho 106, 374, *69;* Woodland 123; Woodsley Ho 106, 374, *68*

Public buildings: Art Gallery 358, 385; Assembly Rm 193, 246, 330, 379; Central Market 316, *250;* City Markets 321, 325–7, 377, 380, 204, 265; Civic Hall 360–2, *294;* Coloured or Mixed Cloth Hall 101, 282–3, 334, 382, *224, 225;* Corn Exch 38, 113, 313, 330, 347–8, 366, 373–4, *282, 283;* County Court 385; Court Ho 210, 330, 334, 374, 385, *272;*

Covered Market 317–8; Kirkgate Market 315, 317, 382, *252*; Leeds Library 374, 379; Market Cross 179, 313, 331; Meat Market 277, 377; Moot Hall 26, 313, 329–30, 376, *266*; Municipal Bldgs 356–7, 375, 378, *291*; Music Hall 331; Philosophical Hall 334, 374, *296*; Police Stn, Chapel Allerton 385, Meadow La 385; Poor Law Offices 378; Public Baths, Cookridge St (Oriental) 304, 371, 373, Holbeck La 377, Meanwood Rd 377, Union St 377, Wellington Rd 334, 374, 386; Public Library, Armley 383, Chapel Allerton 385, Holbeck 371; Sch Board Offices 357, 375; Shambles 277, 315, 321; South Market 316, 374, *251*; Town Hall 36, 104, 269, 327, 330, 339–40, 342–3, 347, 372–3, 375, 377, 382, *9*, *277*, *278*, *279*; Victoria Mem 360; White Cloth Hall 193, 282–4, 288, 330, 348, 379, *226*

Schools, colleges etc: Blind & Deaf Sch 372; Board Schools: Armley 370; Armley Pk 261, 372; Beckett St 370; Beeston Hill 370; Belle Vue Rd 370; Bewerley St 259, 375; Blenheim 370; Bramley 370; Bramley Broad Lane 372; Brudenell 372; Burley Lawn 259, 370; Castleton 370; Central HGS 261, 372, 380; Chapeltown 370; Cross Stamford St 370; Darley St 372; Dewsbury Rd 370; Ellerby La 370; Farnley 370; Gipton 372; Green Lane 259, 375; Harehills 260, 380; Headingley 370; Hunslet Carr 259; Hunslet La 370, 372; Isles La 380; Jack La 370; Kepler 372; Kirkstall 370; Leylands 370; Little Holbeck 370; Lovell Rd 372; Low Rd 370; Lower Wortley 370; Meanwood Rd 260, 370, 205; Moortown 379; Old Farnley 370; Park La 370; Primrose Hill 383; Quarry Mt 370; Queens Rd 380; Richmond Hill 372; Rodley 370; Roundhay Rd 370; St Peter's Sq 370; Saville Green 370, 375; Sheepscar 370; S Accommodation Rd 259, 383; Southern HGS 372; Stanningley 370; Sweet St 370; Thoresby HS 261, 372; Upper Wortley 370; Whingate 370; Whitehall Rd 370; Woodhouse 370; York Rd 370; Buslingthorpe Sch 375; Charity Sch 245; City of Leeds Sch, see Central HGS; City of Leeds Training Coll 265; Cockburn Sch, see Southern HGS; Friends' Sch 245; GS 179, 238–40, 245, 248, 250, 375, *190*, *197*; Hunslet Union Sch 378; Lancasterian Sch, Alfred St 246, 385; Lawnswood HS 265; March Inst 385; Meanwood Rd Baptists' Sch 384; Mech Inst, Cookridge St 38–9, 44, 252–4, 373, 375, *201*, Holbeck 381, Hunslet 384; Moral & Ind Training Sch 382; National Sch, Burley 383, Kirkgate 246, 385, New Town 373, New Wortley 373; New Sch for Girls 247, 385; Polytechnic 44; Roundhay Ch Sch 247, *195*; Roundhay Sch 265, *211*; St Joseph's Seminary 377; St Luke's Sch 372; St Marie's Convent & Sch 377; St Matthias's Sch 384; St Saviour's Schs 372; Sch (Coll) of Art 4–5, 371; Sch of Industry 245; Sch of Medicine (University) 24, 264, 375, 385; Shadwell Ind Sch 370; University 22, 24, 44, 237, 262, 264–8, *209*, *210*, *213*, *216*; Vernon Rd Ch Sch 374; W Leeds Sch 265; Woodhouse, Sch Ho 374; Yorks Coll, see University

Streets, terraces etc: Albion Pl 23, St 102, 364, 379; Beeston Hill 144–5; Blenheim Tce 102, 379; Blundell Pl 106; Boar Lane 95, 305, 366; Bond St 364, 374; Bridge End 373; Bridgefield Bldgs 145; Briggate 93, 130,

281–2, 313; Burley Rd 150; Cardigan Rd 371–2, 376; City Sq 360, 366, 371; Clarendon Rd 106, 375; Cookridge St 373; Duncan St 23; East Parade 101, 103; Grove Rd 113; Hanover Sq 105, 383–4; Harehills Ave 111; Headingley Lane 107; Headingley Tce 107, *70*; Headrow 149; Hyde Tce 106, 375–6; King Edward St 23, *11*; Kirkgate 95; Lyddon Tce 106, 375; Marsh La 147; Millgarth 145; Moorland Tce 113, 373; New Briggate 384; North Grange Rd 374; North St 375, 384; Old Park Rd 122, *91*; Park Ave 123, La 81, 101, 103–5, 383, Pl 101, 103, Row 22, 101–2, 364, 375, *296*, Sq 101, 103, 314, *64*; Potternewton Gdns 367; Preston Pl 106; Quarry St *108*; Queen Victoria St 23; St John's Hill 111, 113, 386; St Peter's Sq 132; Shannon St 145, 370; Shaw Lane 384; Shire Oak Rd 371, 375; Simpson's Fold 33; South Parade 101–3, 364; Springfield Pl 106; Town End 95; Union St 131; West Ave 123; Woodhouse La 102, Sq 105, 374, 382, *67*; Woolman St 147, *110*

Theatres etc: Amphitheatre 272; City Pal of Varieties 275, 323, 384, *219*; Coliseum 371; Empire Pal 278–80, 325, *222*; Grand Th 272–5, 323, 375, *Frontis*, *217*, *218*; Hippodrome 386; New Alhambra 272; Queen's Th 277; Royal Casino Th 272; Th, Hunslet 269, 271–2, 371; Th Royal 272, 382; Tower Pict Ho 323; White Swan Varieties, see City Pal

Lee Green 125
Lees Hall, Thornhill 48
Le Mans, France: Corn Exchange 348
Le Vésinet, France 373
Leventhorpe Hall 80, 373
Lightcliffe 20: CCh 381; St Matthew 192, 371, 378, 381
Lille, France: Cath 227, 372, 384
Lincoln: Cath 227, 375
Lindley; see Huddersfield
Linthwaite: Christ Ch 371, 379; Hall 55
Lisbon, Portugal: Post & Telegraph Offices 380
Liverpool, Lancs: Exch 287; St George's Hall 335, 343, 345
Liversedge: Christ Ch 210, 385, *165*; Millbridge WMCh 378
Lockwood: Emmanuel Ch 210, 374; Mech Inst 370
Lofthouse Gate: Canal Rd BS 386
Londesborough Hall, N Yorks 27, 29, 60, 381
London: Admiralty 380; Albert Mem 351; Albion Mill, Blackfriars 289; Banqueting Ho, Whitehall 54, 69, 334; Berkeley Sq 71; Buckingham Pal 334; Burlington Arcade 322; Carlton Ho 340; City Temple 36, 380; Civil Service St 36, 380; Coliseum 276; Crystal Pal, Sydenham 137, 289; Elephant & Castle Th 276; Exeter Arcade 322; Foreign Off 351; Foundling Hosp 244; Gov Offices, Whitehall (comp) 36, 38, 344, 372; Guildhall 343; Holborn 54; Houses of Parliament 248, 339, 343; Law Courts 41, 274, 339, 353; Lowther Arcade 322; Mansion Ho 331; National Gallery (comp) 36, 40, 372; New Zealand Chambers 356; Reform Club 347; Royal Exch 40; Royal Opera Arcade 322; Royal Panopticon 306; St George, Southwark 219; St Martin in the Fields 186; St Pancras Hotel 349, 351, 385; St Paul's Cath 361, 375; Temple Ch 227; Whitehall Pal 28

Longley Hall 375, 386
Lotherton Hall 383
Lower Altofts 138
Low Moor; see Bradford
Lowther, Westmor 133
Luddenden: Kershaw Ho 56; St Mary 158, 385, *118*
Luddenden Foot: BS 378
Lumb 127
Lupset; see Wakefield
Lyme Pk, Ches 181

Malham, N Yorks 15
Malsis Hall, N Yorks 379
Malton, N Yorks 51
Manchester, Lancs: Assize Courts 308, 372; Owens Coll 262; Public Library 361; Royal Exch 372; Town Hall 255, 353, 372
Manningham; see Bradford
Manston; see Leeds
Marsden: Mech Inst 378
Melbourne Hall, Derbys 61
Melbourne, Victoria, Australia: English, Scottish & Australian Bank 223; Government Ho 223; Parliament Ho 339; St Patrick's Cath 223
Meltham: Memorial Sch 380; St Bartholomew 189, 193, 379–80, 383, *150*; The Mount 372, 390
Meltham Mills: Bank Bldgs 143, *106*; People's Pleasure Grounds 105, 143; St James 143, 383
Menston 119
Methley: BS 375; Clubcliffe (or Clumpcliffe) Hall 60, 384; Hall 25, 51, 71, 79, 80, 370, 373, *15*; Sch 240; St Oswald 167
Middlesmoor, N Yorks; St Chad 375
Middleton; see Leeds
Milner Field 84–5, *49*
Milnes Bridge; see Huddersfield
Mirfield 15, 125, 128, 153: Hostel of the Resurrection 236; St Mary 166, 193, 226, 228, 379
Morley 51, 146: Albion St BCh 377; Bapt Tabernacle 384; Brunswick PMCh 378; Public Baths 378; Queen St MCh 384; St Francis of Assisi 384; St Peter 35, 374; Town Hall 355, 376, *287*; WCh 381
Morton: St Luke 383
Moseley, Warwicks: Spring Hill Cong Coll 225
Munich, Germany: War Office 304
Mytholmroyd: St Michael 381

Naas, Co Kildare 47
Naples, Italy: Gesù Nuovo 348
Netherthong: All Saints 210, 374
Netherton: St Andrew 234
Newburgh Priory, N Yorks 61, 96
Newby Hall, N Yorks 33, 66, 79, 371, 376
Newby (now Baldersby) Pk, N Yorks 376
Newcastle, Northumb: Royal Arcade 322
Newland Hall 72
New Mill: Christ Ch 371
New Sharlston 138
New Wortley; see Leeds
Norland Hall 55
Normanton 22: BCh 379; MFCh 386; WMCh 377; Woodhouse BS 386
North Bierley; see Bradford
Northowram 20: Heywood Ch 194, 196; St Matthew 234
Nostell Priory 29, 30, 65, 67, 69, 71, 77–8, 91, 97, 153, 167, 372, 382–3, *36*, *43*

397

Nun Appleton Ho, N Yorks 39, 79
Nuneham Courtenay, Oxon 133
Nun Monkton, N Yorks 15

Oakwell Hall 55
Oakworth: Christ Ch 386
Oldfield 127
Oldham, Lancs: Market Hall 380
Oporto, Portugal: Hospital of the Misericordia 31
Ossett: Holy Trinity 375, 385; Wakefield & Barnsley Union Bank 386
Ossington Hall, Notts 101
Otley 15, 42, 128: All Saints 162; CCh 226, 378; Court Ho 377; Mech Inst 376; Our Lady & All Saints 377; Prince Henry's GS 238–9; Wharfedale Union Workho 382
Oulton: Hall 80–1, 83, 374, 383; St John 209
Ovenden; see Halifax
Oxford, Oxon: All Saints 186; Bodleian Lib 25, 370; Lincoln Coll 238; Merton Coll 25, 370; Radcliffe Lib 314; Radcliffe Observatory 314; St Philip & St James 231: Schools Quad 25, 370

Paddock; see Huddersfield
Padua, Italy: Università 65
Paris, France: Bilbiothèque Sainte-Geneviève 255; Bourse 340; Bourse du Commerce 348; Halle au Blé 348; Louvre 340, 345; Place de la Concorde 340
Parlington Pk 32, 65, 79, 194, 371, 373, 380
Pateley Br, N Yorks 11
Penistone, S Yorks 11
Philadelphia, Penn, USA: City Hall 339; First Bank 244; Waterworks 244
Plompton, N Yorks 74
Pontefract 25, 34, 97, 281: All Saints 168, 374, 127; Castle 25, 167–8; Cluniac Priory 153; Court Ho 334; Dispensary 382; GS (King's Sch) 237–8; Horsefair WMCh 200–1; Market Cross 313, 330, 248; Market Hall 327; Market Pl 69, 97, 271, 313, 382; Micklegate Ho 96, 59; Neat Market 382; New Hall 26, 52, 18; Oswald's Cross 311, 313; St Giles 28, 31, 168, 189, 201, 313, 330, 382, 384, 248; St John's Priory 52; Theatre 271; Town Hall 201, 329–31, 377, 383, 267
Pool: St Wilfrid 374
Port Lyttleton, New Zealand 381
Portsmouth, Hants: Town Hall 339, 378
Poynton, Ches: St George 225
Preston, Lancs: Town Hall 372
Pudsey: CCh 226, 383; MNCCh 382; St Joseph 384; St Lawrence 210, 385; St Paul 383
Pye Nest Ho 80, 372–3

Queensbury 20, 143: Albert Mem Fountain 381; Bank Top Mills 295, 381; Black Dyke Mill 143, 293; Holy Trinity 378; Inst 378; Public Baths 378; Victoria Hall 378

Rastrick: St Matthew 192, 147
Ravello, Italy: Villa Cimbrone 45
Rawcliffe, Humberside 11
Rawdon 118: BCh 374; Ch 181; Friends' Meeting Ho 196; Hall 118; Our Lady of Good Counsel & St Joseph 384; Woodhouse Gr Sch 384; Woodlands Con Ho 370; Woodleigh Hall 118, 381
Richmond, N Yorks: Theatre 269
Rievaulx Abbey, N Yorks 155

Ripley, N Yorks 133
Ripon, N Yorks 11, 134: Holy Trinity 377; Minster 213; Town Hall 331
Rishworth: GS 245, 382
Roberttown: All Saints 185, 210, 374, 384
Roche Abbey, S Yorks 155
Rokeby Pk, Durham 29
Rome, Italy 65: Pal Santacroce 348; St Peter 343
Rossington, S Yorks 225
Rotherham, S Yorks 11: GS 238; Octagon 197
Rothwell: Holy Trinity 371
Roundhay; see Leeds
Royds Hall 55
Rudston, Humberside: All Saints 381

Saddleworth 281
St Albans, Herts: Cathedral 375
St Catherine's, nr Doncaster, S Yorks 374
St Ives 69, 91, 382
Saltaire 36, 133, 138–40, 142–3, 380, 103, 104, 105; CCh 142, 206, 381, 105, 162; Inst 142, 256, 381, 202; Mill 142, 294–5, 309, 380, 103, 235; PMCh 380; Sch 142, 256, 381; Shipley Salt Sch 266
Salterhebble; see Halifax
Sandal Magna; see Wakefield
Scarborough, N Yorks: Grand Hotel 255, 304, 372; MCh 200; Museum 384; Spa Saloon 317
Scout Hall 57, 26
Seaton Delaval, Northumb 27, 376
Selby, N Yorks 11: Abbey 225
Shadwell; see Leeds
Sharlston: St Luke 226
Sheffield, S Yorks 11: City Hall 361; St George 210; St Mary 210; St Michael & All Angels, Neepsend 385; St Paul 186; St Philip 210
Shelf: British Sch 246, 194; St Michael & All Angels 381; UMCh 378
Shelton, Staffs: St Mark 382
Shepley: St Paul 386
Sherburn-in-Elmet, N Yorks: All Saints 166
Shipley 15, 17, 139: BCh 379; St Paul 382; St Peter & St Paul 378
Sicklinghall, N Yorks: Mary Immaculate 377
Silcoates Ho 103
Silkstone Row, New Altofts 138
Skelmanthorpe: PMCh 378; St Aidan 226
Skipton, N Yorks 11, 15
Slaithwaite: St James 189; Shaw Carr Wood Mill 289
Slaugham Pl, Sussex 88
Sledmere Ho, Humberside 32, 78, 231
Slingsby Castle, N Yorks 51
Smethwick, Worcs: St Matthew 225
Snaith, Humberside 11
South Kirkby: All Saints 177
South Ossett: Christ Ch 381
Southowram 20: St Anne 385
Sowerby 13: Bairstow's Endowed Sch 378; CCh 378; Haugh End 373; Nat Sch 378; Provident New Sch 378; St Peter 30, 96, 187, 372, 386, 141, 142; WCh 378; Wood Lane Hall 51, 55, 14, 23
Sowerby Bridge 13, 15: Bolton Brow BS 378; Brunswick Ch, Bolton Brow 378; Christ Ch 213, 382; New Rd BS 378; St Mary's Sch, Bolton Brow 378; Tuel La MCh 378; White Windows 373
Sprotbrough Hall, S Yorks 26, 376
Stainborough; see Wentworth Castle
Staincliffe: Christ Ch 375

Stainland 146: St Andrew 371, 374; Sowood Green BS 378; Sowood WCh 378
Stanley: St Peter 213, 371; WCh 384
Stanningley: CCh 380
Stapleton Pk, S Yorks 71, 79
Stockeld Pk, N Yorks 69, 71, 91
Stockport, Lancs: St Matthew 225; St Paul 225
Stoodley Pike 1
Studley Royal, N Yorks 30, 96
Sutton-in-Craven, N Yorks: St Thomas 375
Swillington: St Mary 158, 375
Swinton Castle, N Yorks 134
Sydney, NSW, Australia: Christ Ch, St Lawrence 217; St John's Col, University 223; St Mary's Cath 223

Temple Newsam Ho; see Leeds
Theobalds Pk, Herts 51
Thick Hollins Con Ho 372
Thorner: St Peter 158, 381; WMCh 375
Thornes Ho; see Wakefield
Thornhill 153: St Michael 39, 158, 164–5, 184, 227, 124, 125; UDC Offices 390
Thornhill Lees: Hall 48; Holy Innocents 381
Thornton; see Bradford
Thornville Royal; see Allerton Park
Thorp Arch: All Saints 227
Thorpe Bassett, N Yorks 113
Thurgoland, S Yorks: Holy Trinity 382
Tickhill, S Yorks 11
Todmorden 146: Old Hall 95; Town Hall 354–5, 286; UCh 226
Tong: Hall 28, 60, 64, 384, 29; St James 189, 143; Sch 240
Truro, Cornwall: Cath 231

Undercliffe; see Bradford

Vancouver, BC, Canada: Bank of British Columbia 385; Court Ho 385
Venice, Italy: Library of St Mark's 345; S. Maria della Salute 327
Vicenza, Italy: Basilica 345
Victoria, BC, Canada: Weiler Block 385
Vienna, Austria: Karl-Marx-Hof 148

Wakefield 11, 15, 22, 34–5, 42, 44, 51, 95, 128, 363
Banks etc: Leatham, Tew & Co, Wood St 382; Savings Bank 382; Town Hall Chambers, King St 375; Wakefield & Barnsley Union, Westgate 381
Churches & chapels: All Saints (Cath) 37, 174–5, 179–80, 183, 226, 231–2, 380, 382, 133, 134, 249; PMCh 385; St Andrew, Peterson Rd 36, 226; St Austin 377, 383; St Helen, Sandal Magna 159–60, 167, 120; St James, Thornes 371, 384; St John 103, 192–3, 287, 380, 383, 386, 66, 148; St Mary-on-the-Bridge 36, 171–2, 131, 132; St Paul, Alverthorpe 371; Westgate End WMCh 385; Westgate UCh 99, 199, 373, 155; Zion CCh 203
Mansions & villas: Alverthorpe Hall 28, 60, 384; Kettlethorpe Hall 65, 172; Lupset Hall 28, 60, 248, 384; Six Chimneys, Kirkgate 94, 54; The Towers, Bond St 375; Thornes Ho 80, 99, 373
Public buildings & institutions: Assembly Rm 330–2; Clayton Hosp 371; Cloth Hall 282; Corn Exch 334, 364, 372, 379, 382, 274; Court Ho 332, 355, 377, 386, 271; Ho of Correction 373, 379, 386; Library & News Rm (Music

Saloon) 332, 355, 383, 386, *268*; Market Cross 28, 313–4, 384, *249*; Model Lodging Ho 375; Moot Hall 329; Opera Ho 276–7, *220*; Tammy Hall 285; Theatre, Westgate 270; Town Hall 355–6, *288*; Westgate Station 376; W Riding County Hall 355, *289*, *290*; W Riding Ind Ho 371; W Riding Lunatic Asylum 383, 386
Schools: Bell Sch 246; Lancasterian Sch, Margaret St 246; Nat Sch 246; GS 238, 240, 248, 383, *189*; W Riding Prop Sch 248, 372, *196*
Streets, terraces etc: Barstow Sq 103; Bond Tce 372; Crown Court 331; Leeds Rd 104; Margaret St 386; Northgate 94–5, 103; Piccadilly 145; St John's Sq 103–4, 192–3, 380, 386, *66*; St John's St (North) 103–4, 385, *66*; South Parade 103, 380, 386, *65*; Wentworth St 386; Westgate 99, 103, 373, 386; West Parade 386

Wanstead Pk, Essex 74
Warley 370: BS 378; St John 371
Warwick, Warks: St Mary 35

Welbeck Abbey, Notts 55
Wentworth Castle, S Yorks 11, 28, 48, 385
Wentworth Woodhouse, S Yorks 11, 30, 47–8, 54, 67
West Clayton: All Saints 379
West Riddlesden Hall 55
Weston Hall, N Yorks 51
Wetherby 15: Grange 32, 373; St James 371; St Joseph 224, 384; Town Hall 371
Whitkirk; see Leeds
Whitley Beaumont 13, 27–8, 60–1, 64, 71, 79, 381–2, 384, *4*, *30*
Wike: Sch 241; WCh 370
Wilberlee 127
Wilsden: St Matthew 382
Wilshaw: Almshouses 143, 380; St Mary 143, 380; St Mary's Court 143, 380; St Mary's Sch 143, 380
Wood Lane Hall; see Sowerby
Woodhouse; see Leeds
Woodkirk: St Mary 167
Woodsetts, S Yorks: St Mary 379
Woodside, Salop: St James 373
Woodsome Hall 55, *22*

Wooldale: Friends' Meeting Ho 197, *153*
Woolley 13–14: Hall 47–8, 79, 83–4, 373, 383, 386, *13*, *46*; Sch 240
Worcester, Worcs: Cath 375
Wortley; see Leeds
Wrenthorpe 61: St Anne 226
Wyke; see Bradford

Yarm, N Yorks: Octagon 200
Yeadon: St Andrew 378; St John 378, 383; Town Hall & Mech Inst 378
York, N Yorks 11, 25–6, 156: All Saints, North St 26, 376, Pavement 168, 213; Assembly Rms 29, 186, 330, 376, 383, 386; Cem Ch 383; Cross, Pavement 27, 381, Thursday Market 376; King's Manor 47–8, 88; Knavesmire, Grandstand 31, 72, 373; Mansion Ho 331, 376; Micklegate Bar 35; Minster 25; Mint Yard 376; Prop Sch (St Peter's) 377; St Mary's Abbey 155; St Olave 27; St Saviour 371; Savings Bank, St Helen's Sq 383; Skeldergate 31; Yorks Museum 384
Ypres, Belgium: Hôtel de Ville 343–4